T0189274

Lecture Notes in Computer Science

Lecture Notes in Artificial Intelligence   14050

Founding Editor

Jörg Siekmann

Series Editors

Randy Goebel, *University of Alberta, Edmonton, Canada*
Wolfgang Wahlster, *DFKI, Berlin, Germany*
Zhi-Hua Zhou, *Nanjing University, Nanjing, China*

The series Lecture Notes in Artificial Intelligence (LNAI) was established in 1988 as a topical subseries of LNCS devoted to artificial intelligence.

The series publishes state-of-the-art research results at a high level. As with the LNCS mother series, the mission of the series is to serve the international R & D community by providing an invaluable service, mainly focused on the publication of conference and workshop proceedings and postproceedings.

Helmut Degen · Stavroula Ntoa
Editors

Artificial Intelligence in HCI

4th International Conference, AI-HCI 2023
Held as Part of the 25th HCI International Conference, HCII 2023
Copenhagen, Denmark, July 23–28, 2023
Proceedings, Part I

 Springer

Editors
Helmut Degen
Siemens Corporation
Princeton, NJ, USA

Stavroula Ntoa
Foundation for Research
and Technology – Hellas (FORTH)
Heraklion, Crete, Greece

ISSN 0302-9743 ISSN 1611-3349 (electronic)
Lecture Notes in Artificial Intelligence
ISBN 978-3-031-35890-6 ISBN 978-3-031-35891-3 (eBook)
https://doi.org/10.1007/978-3-031-35891-3

LNCS Sublibrary: SL7 – Artificial Intelligence

This Springer imprint is published by the registered company Springer Nature Switzerland AG
The registered company address is: Gewerbestrasse 11, 6330 Cham, Switzerland

Foreword

Human-computer interaction (HCI) is acquiring an ever-increasing scientific and industrial importance, as well as having more impact on people's everyday lives, as an ever-growing number of human activities are progressively moving from the physical to the digital world. This process, which has been ongoing for some time now, was further accelerated during the acute period of the COVID-19 pandemic. The HCI International (HCII) conference series, held annually, aims to respond to the compelling need to advance the exchange of knowledge and research and development efforts on the human aspects of design and use of computing systems.

The 25th International Conference on Human-Computer Interaction, HCI International 2023 (HCII 2023), was held in the emerging post-pandemic era as a 'hybrid' event at the AC Bella Sky Hotel and Bella Center, Copenhagen, Denmark, during July 23–28, 2023. It incorporated the 21 thematic areas and affiliated conferences listed below.

A total of 7472 individuals from academia, research institutes, industry, and government agencies from 85 countries submitted contributions, and 1578 papers and 396 posters were included in the volumes of the proceedings that were published just before the start of the conference, these are listed below. The contributions thoroughly cover the entire field of human-computer interaction, addressing major advances in knowledge and effective use of computers in a variety of application areas. These papers provide academics, researchers, engineers, scientists, practitioners and students with state-of-the-art information on the most recent advances in HCI.

The HCI International (HCII) conference also offers the option of presenting 'Late Breaking Work', and this applies both for papers and posters, with corresponding volumes of proceedings that will be published after the conference. Full papers will be included in the 'HCII 2023 - Late Breaking Work - Papers' volumes of the proceedings to be published in the Springer LNCS series, while 'Poster Extended Abstracts' will be included as short research papers in the 'HCII 2023 - Late Breaking Work - Posters' volumes to be published in the Springer CCIS series.

I would like to thank the Program Board Chairs and the members of the Program Boards of all thematic areas and affiliated conferences for their contribution towards the high scientific quality and overall success of the HCI International 2023 conference. Their manifold support in terms of paper reviewing (single-blind review process, with a minimum of two reviews per submission), session organization and their willingness to act as goodwill ambassadors for the conference is most highly appreciated.

This conference would not have been possible without the continuous and unwavering support and advice of Gavriel Salvendy, founder, General Chair Emeritus, and Scientific Advisor. For his outstanding efforts, I would like to express my sincere appreciation to Abbas Moallem, Communications Chair and Editor of HCI International News.

July 2023   Constantine Stephanidis

HCI International 2023 Thematic Areas and Affiliated Conferences

Thematic Areas

- HCI: Human-Computer Interaction
- HIMI: Human Interface and the Management of Information

Affiliated Conferences

- EPCE: 20th International Conference on Engineering Psychology and Cognitive Ergonomics
- AC: 17th International Conference on Augmented Cognition
- UAHCI: 17th International Conference on Universal Access in Human-Computer Interaction
- CCD: 15th International Conference on Cross-Cultural Design
- SCSM: 15th International Conference on Social Computing and Social Media
- VAMR: 15th International Conference on Virtual, Augmented and Mixed Reality
- DHM: 14th International Conference on Digital Human Modeling and Applications in Health, Safety, Ergonomics and Risk Management
- DUXU: 12th International Conference on Design, User Experience and Usability
- C&C: 11th International Conference on Culture and Computing
- DAPI: 11th International Conference on Distributed, Ambient and Pervasive Interactions
- HCIBGO: 10th International Conference on HCI in Business, Government and Organizations
- LCT: 10th International Conference on Learning and Collaboration Technologies
- ITAP: 9th International Conference on Human Aspects of IT for the Aged Population
- AIS: 5th International Conference on Adaptive Instructional Systems
- HCI-CPT: 5th International Conference on HCI for Cybersecurity, Privacy and Trust
- HCI-Games: 5th International Conference on HCI in Games
- MobiTAS: 5th International Conference on HCI in Mobility, Transport and Automotive Systems
- AI-HCI: 4th International Conference on Artificial Intelligence in HCI
- MOBILE: 4th International Conference on Design, Operation and Evaluation of Mobile Communications

List of Conference Proceedings Volumes Appearing Before the Conference

47. CCIS 1836, HCI International 2023 Posters - Part V, edited by Constantine Stephanidis, Margherita Antona, Stavroula Ntoa and Gavriel Salvendy

https://2023.hci.international/proceedings

Preface

The 4th International Conference on Artificial Intelligence in HCI (AI-HCI 2023), an affiliated conference of the HCI International conference, aimed to bring together academics, practitioners, and students to exchange results from academic and industrial research, as well as industrial experiences, on the use of artificial intelligence (AI) technologies to enhance human-computer interaction (HCI).

Motivated by discussions on topical Human-Centered Artificial Intelligence (HCAI), a considerable number of papers delved into the topic, exploring theoretical approaches, design principles, and case studies of AI-enabled systems and services adopting HCAI. One of the facets of HCAI that was largely explored was explainability and transparency. Through reviews, quantitative comparisons, and case studies, as well as the exploration of cutting-edge techniques, contributions on the topic examined the impact of AI explanations on trust, collaboration, and decision-making, advancing understanding of the current landscape and emerging trends in the field. Another aspect that received particular attention was fairness and ethics, with relevant papers discussing approaches to improve fairness, mitigate bias, and promote ethical decision-making, and exploring the impact of cognitive biases and user perceptions of unfair AI. Furthermore, a comprehensive exploration of how artificial intelligence intersects with user experience and design was conducted, in the context of which contributions explored approaches for graphical user interface design, product design, risk assessment and project management, as well as design processes and guidelines.

Contributions included in the proceedings also addressed specific application domains, reflecting topics that capture academic and public discussions. A subject gaining significant traction is AI for language, text, and speech-related tasks, in the context of which papers addressed the design, development, and evaluation of chatbots, argumentative dialogue systems, large language models, as well as language translation and sentiment analysis approaches. Another emerging topic concerns human-AI collaboration, with discussions revolving around human-agent teaming, human-robot interaction, as well as user satisfaction and beliefs about AI agents in the context of collaborative tasks. Furthermore, the role of AI in decision-support and perception analysis was explored, focusing on the exploration of uncertainty in information, contextual recommendations, human perception analysis, and the design of decision-support systems. Finally, several papers explored the design and development of innovative AI-driven solutions, including neural networks, multimodal models, and machine learning approaches for diverse applications across various contexts.

Two volumes of the HCII 2023 proceedings are dedicated to this year's edition of the AI-HCI conference. The first volume focuses on topics related to Human-Centered Artificial Intelligence, explainability, transparency and trustworthiness, ethics and fairness, as well as AI-supported user experience design. The second volume focuses on topics related to AI for language, text, and speech-related tasks, human-AI collaboration, AI for decision-support and perception analysis, and innovations in AI-enabled systems.

The papers of the AI-HCI 2023 volumes were included for publication after a minimum of two single-blind reviews from the members of the AI-HCI Program Board or, in some cases, from members of the Program Boards of other affiliated conferences. We would like to thank all of them for their invaluable contribution, support, and efforts.

July 2023

Helmut Degen
Stavroula Ntoa

4th International Conference on Artificial Intelligence in HCI (AI-HCI 2023)

The full list with the Program Board Chairs and the members of the Program Boards of all thematic areas and affiliated conferences of HCII2023 is available online at:

http://www.hci.international/board-members-2023.php

HCI International 2024 Conference

The 26th International Conference on Human-Computer Interaction, HCI International 2024, will be held jointly with the affiliated conferences at the Washington Hilton Hotel, Washington, DC, USA, June 29 – July 4, 2024. It will cover a broad spectrum of themes related to Human-Computer Interaction, including theoretical issues, methods, tools, processes, and case studies in HCI design, as well as novel interaction techniques, interfaces, and applications. The proceedings will be published by Springer. More information will be made available on the conference website: http://2024.hci.international/.

General Chair
Prof. Constantine Stephanidis
University of Crete and ICS-FORTH
Heraklion, Crete, Greece
Email: general_chair@hcii2024.org

https://2024.hci.international/

Contents – Part I

Explainability, Transparency, and Trustworthiness

Ethics and Fairness in Artificial Intelligence

AI-Supported User Experience Design

Contents – Part II

Human-AI Collaboration

Artificial Intelligence for Decision-Support and Perception Analysis

Innovations in AI-Enabled Systems

Human-Centered Artificial Intelligence

Emotional Internet of Behaviors: A QoE-QoS Adjustment Mechanism

Mina Alipour[1], Mahyar T. Moghaddam[1]([✉]), Karthik Vaidhyanathan[2],
Tobias Kristensen[1], and Nicolai Krogager Asmussen[1]

[1] University of Southern Denmark, Odense 5230, Denmark
{mial,mtmo}@mmmi.sdu.dk, {tokri19,niasm19}@student.sdu.dk
[2] IIIT Hyderabad, Hyderabad 500032, India
karthik.vaidhyanathan@iiit.ac.in

Abstract. The Internet of Behaviors (IoB) approach supports developing socio-technical systems based on humans' goals, characteristics, behaviors, and emotions. This paper shows how emotions and behaviors could impact the quality of software systems. We propose interactive control loops that supervise application and architecture adaptations toward enhancing the system quality of service (QoS) and human quality of experience (QoE). Under the IoB conceptual model, we first show how historical and real emotions could be the source of the design and adaptation of socio-technical systems. We further use a Reinforcement Learning (RL)-based approach as a self-adaptation supervisor of user interfaces (UIs) to users' emotions. The approach aims to maximize applying the essential adaptations and minimize the unnecessary ones towards users' QoE. If the control system detects a drop in QoS in emotion-based adaptations or other functions, another level of adaptation reconfigures the architecture towards better quality. We used the emotional IoB approach to develop a mobile application as a recommender system in emergency evacuation training. The app takes users' facial emotions and positions as input and adapts its UI to impact users' target emotions and task completion. In addition to UI adaptation, the system supports architecture adaptations to decrease response time if required. The evaluation process confirms the efficiency of the RL in iterations, as well as compared to other possible UI adaptation techniques. The results also show that architecture adaptations positively impact the system performance and users' emotions and performance.

Keywords: Internet of Behaviors · Emotions · Quality of Experience · Quality of Service · Software Architecture · User Interface · Adaptation

1 Introduction

Socio-technical systems need to perceive and act on human behaviors. The *Internet of Behaviors (IoB) links the systems to humans*, their characteristics, goals, interactions, and emotions, and provides a desirable adjustment or trade-off

H. Degen and S. Ntoa (Eds.): HCII 2023, LNAI 14050, pp. 3–22, 2023.
https://doi.org/10.1007/978-3-031-35891-3_1

between humans' quality of experience (QoE) and the system's quality of service (QoS) [10, 24] using self-adaptation [39]. Self-adaptation is typically performed by control elements that interact with the *application* (concerning dynamic environment) and *architecture* (concerning dynamic computation infrastructure) components. This research deals with interactive systems adaptive to users' contexts. Thus, at the application level, the question is: *can interactive systems observe and react to what users tacitly want to see on their screens* [36] *or a manual interaction is needed* [41]? At the architectural level, the question is: *how could computation infrastructure handle degradation in QoS?*

This research focuses on emotions as the primary part of the human essence, leading to specific behaviors under IoB. Emotions could adapt systems and their user interfaces. Such adaptations require a supervisor that could be model-based, optimization-based, rule-based, or data-driven [28]. The main difficulty is that human behavior can hardly be modeled, optimized, or structured within the rules. Humans may show fluctuating, unpredictable and irrational behaviors due to their personal, social, or environmental context. Another issue is that modeling complex behaviors impose system QoS degradation that could, e.g., delay systems' reaction to dynamic behaviors. Lack of consideration for human and system dynamics can lead the interactive systems to failure, low quality, or discomfort for people.

We use a specific class of Reinforcement Learning (RL) technique, namely, Q-learning [21] for UI adaptations to emotions. It facilitates a trial-and-error approach where the agent has to learn by taking actions from states repeatedly, which is known best for dynamic fluctuating human behavior [35]. In our approach, the built-in camera on a device detects and infers Ekman's basic emotions (namely joy, sadness, surprise, fear, disgust, and anger [11] and neutral, that are *one of the state attributes in our RL algorithm*) and sends them to Q-learning based approach. The plan receives the emotional states and assigns reward/punishment values each time. Based on the values, a specific UI adaptation occurs (*an action in Q-learning*) among various UI configurations (*the other state attribute in Q-learning*) to possibly reduce the emotions associated with punishment and improve the emotions associated with reward. Q-Table values correspond to selecting an interface (*action*) from the set of interfaces (*state*). The RL approach supervises application-level adaptations, interacting with another supervisor that monitors system QoS and performs architecture-level adaptations in case of a quality drop.

We apply the approach to a mobile application called *EvacuationApp*, which we developed for *emergency evacuation training*. It captures emotions and location data and teaches people how to safely and quickly reach a safe zone in emergencies. The location information is used to give contextual awareness. The emotion data is used to change the UI to impact users' emotions and mobility behavior to improve QoE. This training app is a suitable IoB case since it pushes people to show intensive emotions in simulated danger [15] while avoiding real risks [3]. The objective is to assess whether application and architecture adaptations positively impact user task completion and target emotions.

The main contributions this paper makes are: *i)* a conceptual model of emotional IoB; *ii)* a framework for separating interactive systems concerns in application and architecture level adaptations and addressing their coordination; *iii)* re-usable emotion-based UI adaptation engines; *iv)* application of the approach to a real case.

The remainder of this paper is organized as follows. Section 2 presents the Background. Section 3 gives an overview of designing emotion-based IoB systems. Section 4 presents the approach. Section 5 discusses the evaluation, and Sect. 6 concludes the paper.

2 Background

IoB provides an extensive definition of human involvement compared with current software engineering, human-computer interactions (HCI), and human-in-the-loop (HITL) descriptions [24]. *Software engineering* deals with developers and clients, and the way their collaboration and interaction improves the software product's quality. For instance, the concept of behavioral software engineering (*BSE*) [20] addresses the cognitive, behavioral, and social aspects of software development toward a company's financial success. *HCI* focuses on the interaction of *users* with computers and with developing interfaces to ease and enhance such interaction [7]. HCI gives a high priority to users, their needs, and limitations [8]. *HITL* is defined as a model that requires human interaction [33] and conforms to human factors impacting the system. The HITL approach combines human intelligence with machine intelligence mainly for learning purposes. In fact, the HITL approach re-frames an automation problem as an HCI design problem.

In the IoB concept, system and human behaviors are drivers of adaptation to improve QoS and QoE (or make a trade-off). IoB is focused on the activities of humans, who are sometimes even unaware that they are part of the system. In IoB, the social environment is interlinked with a software system through intelligent elements. Considering emotions as a primary driver of behaviors, IoB could support establishing systems that adapt based on emotions.

Emotions are reactions to events and are tied up with the physiological, affective, behavioral, and cognitive state of a person [18]. Emotions involve changes in our biological system and can be detected from various measurements of biological changes (e.g., heart rate or muscular electrical changes) as well as by the impacts of these changes on exposed behaviors, for instance, by measuring changes in the face. Facial expression analysis is the most common modality of emotion recognition [19]. There are two main theoretical categories in implying facial emotions: *the categorical models* [12] and *dimensional models*[32]. Categorical theories define emotions using tags from identified collections of emotions. The most prominent approach in this category is Ekman's basic (universal) emotions [11]. It represents six basic emotions of *anger, disgust, fear, joy, sadness* and *surprise*, which cover positive and negative emotions. The dimensional model expresses emotions in a two-dimensional form, i.e., valence and arousal [32].

Users' emotions are significant in designing interactive systems [34]. Characterizing users has specifically been raised in the HCI field and raised the problem of adaptation to users' needs. Emotions could drive changes in the UI and vice versa. Two main techniques for *UI adaptations* are tailor-made, and rule-based adaptations [13]. For instance, researchers [42] proposed a rule-based approach to adapt a user interface to various contexts, such as the user's age, color preferences, and weather status. Another research [22] developed a UI adaptation environment to improve the user's satisfaction while interacting with a system. Apart from these two methods, machine learning methods such as *reinforcement learning (RL)* could be adopted as adaptation supervisors. There exist two main approaches in reinforcement learning: model-based and model-free. Model-based methods rely on planning as their primary component, while model-free methods primarily rely on learning. In the model-based approach, the model is trained to assume that all humans are the same or that their behavior can be predicted. Recent research [37] presents an approach of adaptive UI using model-based reinforcement learning to improve user satisfaction and avoid surprises. However, the Q-learning technique would be more suitable for individual-level adaptation [40], but it is not yet discovered in UI adaptation to the emotion domain.

While emotions have been studied broadly in Human-Computer interaction, there needs to be more study on how stakeholders' emotions can affect software architecture adaptations. Software architecture adaptation refers to adapting the design of the software systems to meet the changing requirements while maintaining the QoS and QoE. Software architecture can specifically be interesting to be adapted to the software system users' emotions. For instance, [9] demonstrated the specific software architecture tailor-made for elderly emotion recognition. Researchers also demonstrated the importance of including emotions in robot architecture design [9]. Furthermore, *QoS* should be satisfied using *architecture adaptation*. The generic architectures of adaptive systems [39] could be adopted based on dynamic situations and requirements. The architectures are specified based on distribution and collaboration characteristics [30]. This means that data analysis software sometimes needs to be deployed on a single node (*centralized model*), several collaborating nodes (*distributed model*), or hybrid nodes (*hierarchical models*). As discussed in our approach, assessing these architectures and their associated QoS at design-time could feed the run-time knowledge-base.

3   Overview

The IoB conceptual model for emotions is shown in Fig. 1. The model is divided into three parts: the left side of Fig. 1 depicts the *human components*; the right side deals with the *system components*; the middle part shows the *interrelation* between system and humans.

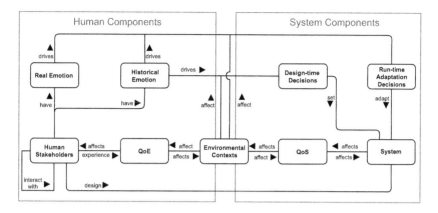

Fig. 1. The emotional IoB approach.

3.1 Human Components

The **stakeholders** are users, developers, clients, managers, citizens, and in general terms, humans. Humans have characteristics, behaviors, goals, and intentions. Stakeholders could have an active or passive role, meaning that they could dynamically impact the system or be impacted by it. As shown in the figure, stakeholders can interact with each other, and this interaction could further impact their state. Therefore, while the interrelation between humans and systems is fundamental, the dynamics among humans impact emotions too.

Historical and Real Emotion. Emotions are an essential part of humans' nature and shape behaviors. Emotion-driven systems are generally built around expected or historical emotions, i.e., what the developers think, or the users show while interacting with the system. Historical emotions could be gathered through observations, surveys, profiling, or learning. Real emotions are observed at run-time and could differ from historical emotions. Observation may not be reliable because irrational behaviors may not be normally shown, or some emotions may not be aroused. Using a survey, humans describe some emotions associated with a specific context, but their descriptions may be prone to biases. Profiling users' behavior is another option, where users' past preferences, interactions, and behaviors are recorded. This method requires a decision-making system if any change needs to be performed at run-time. Using machine learning approaches such as reinforcement learning for such decision-making could be a practical solution. Observing the run-time state of users is crucial since real emotions could be significantly different from historical emotions.

Quality of Experience (QoE) concerns ensuring that users experience proper moods, feelings, and emotions when using a system directly or indirectly [24]. That could be by developing techniques to quantify or qualify people's preferences and choices in different contextual situations. If the designs do not highlight QoE, systems will not be responsive to their users. While the environmental context is the primary driver of QoE, human characteristics also play a crucial role. For instance, while the design of a physical space impacts people's mobility behavior, their speed and vision variations, grouping, and social attachment could have a significant impact similarly. It is worth mentioning that QoE is not always in line with arousing positive emotions (such as happiness) since, in some specific contexts, arousing negative emotions (such as fear) could desirably impact satisfaction and task performance. *Privacy* is a significant challenge in QoE, and it is a priority to protect people's data while still providing behavior-oriented services. IoB is more interested in behaviors than individuals, meaning that to change the system, only the emotional data are continuously captured. Thus, the individuals showing the emotions and their faces, voice, or movements are not captured. Formal solutions also exist to use the authorized data (by law).

3.2   System Components

An intelligent **system** has functional and non-functional goals and requirements [16], which specify the system's functionality and quality under various contextual constraints and guarantee the system's operation. The environment and its contextual variability might also influence the **architecture** of the system. The architecture design [30] is also affected by the desired functional and non-functional requirements. The architecture includes a set of *components* bounded by *connectors* based on specific rules and constraints. Constraints imposed on the system by the operational environment to the architecture should also be considered. Such constraints (that are a part of the context component) may be due to the availability of IoB resources (sensors, network, processors, actuators) and time aspects in real-time systems.

Quality of Service (QoS) considers quality factors that can be measured and used to define, design, and adapt systems. In IoB, the main question is how QoS measurements and control could be related to human perception of a service. It also considers the impact of QoS degradation on QoE. Thus, to choose proper measures to keep human-perceived service quality above an acceptance threshold, the system should translate QoS parameters into user-level QoE perception and vice versa through the context. The main quality requirements IoB should assure are not only performance [4,25], energy efficiency [1,17], resiliency [28], interoperability, and dependability, but also usability, ease of use, and efficiency. In this paper, we study how enhancing QoE is tied with performance enhancement using, e.g., reconfiguration of processing elements.

Design-time Decisions and Run-Time Adaptation Decisions. As Fig. 1 shows, historical emotions drive the architectural design decision [27], and run-time adaptation decisions should get input from both historical and real emotions. Modeling systems similar to IoB is challenging, mainly as systems and contextual dynamics should be supported at run-time. There are various steps to take: *i)* historical emotions and other contextual information should be anticipated; *ii)* the system and physical environment constraints should be understood;

iii) different architectural models that are associated with QoS-QoE adjustment should be designed; *iv)* the emotions, architectures, and system variables should provide input to the knowledge base of run-time systems; *v)* an adaptation decision-maker should be designed; *vi)* the run-time phase should adopt a feedback control loop (such as MAPE-K [39]) for adaptation. Based on monitoring and analyzing contextual and system data, the control mechanism makes decisions based on the knowledge-base content, executing further adaptations if needed.

3.3 Human-System Links

The interrelation among *human* and *system* aspects structures the conceptual idea of IoB [24]. The **environmental context** component that partially falls within both the system and human blocks (but does not belong to them) includes *physical, temporal, social, computational, historical,* and *profile* contexts. Understanding the context is essential for designing the right IoB infrastructure. The lack of a uniform approach for capturing information associated with the context makes it difficult to fully understand the context model needs and design approach based on its main characteristics. The context includes humans' environment: anything happening around humans impacts their intentions and behaviors. This could be the weather, a user interface, or other humans. It is worth mentioning that the impact of context on human behavior requires individual considerations. Regarding **other links**, we emphasize that the *historical emotions* can establish the *design-time* setting to determine the system and its architecture and discover potential adaptation needs. The *run-time setting*, adjusted by *real emotions*, is the source of setting online self-adaptation. As shown, we added an impact feedback loop between the system and humans to reflect the idea that humans can impact software design and adaptation and that the system can impact human behavior within the environment. For instance, in adaptive user interfaces [2], the system could capture humans' emotions and adapt the interface based on their feelings. This adaptation then again impacts humans' emotional behavior.

4   Approach

As shown in Fig. 2, the proposed adaptation approach relies on design-time activities that feed run-time adaptation processes [25, 26, 28]. The **design-time** step includes the activities performed before running the system to guarantee proper functionality and high quality [31]. The design-time layer investigates: *i)* which emotional models should be adopted (here Ekman basic emotions under categorical models [12]); *ii)* what are the time-related aspects of emotions (maximum number of adaptations, values from last few seconds, last interaction results, inference time); *iii)* how the UI should be designed (variables expressing the UI adaptation); *iv)* how we could support our decision-maker with some insights. To this end, a base table is developed which provides a mapping between different possible emotions of the user and the type of UI adaptation the user would

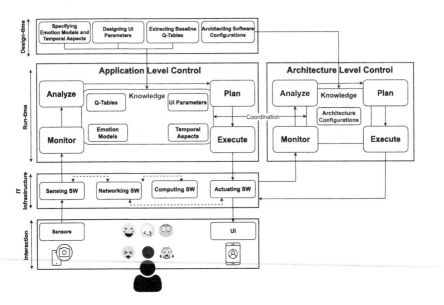

Fig. 2. The emotion-based adaptation approach.

prefer given a particular emotion (creating a first Q-Table with a conducted survey), and *v)* what architectural models provide proper QoS (considering the position of computation).

The ***run-time*** layer handles the adaptations when the software system is running. As Fig. 2 shows, we propose the separation of concerns in controlling the environment (application-level) and infrastructure (architecture-level) events. Both Application Level Control (ALC) and Architectural Level Control (ARLC) are conceptualized using MAPEK loops [39]. At ALC, sensors produce raw data, such as emotions from the user's face. In such a process, the *monitor* step filters raw data into insightful data, watches sensor changes, and infers value changes. Afterward, the *analyze* computes inferred values from raw values. In the *plan* step, the adaptation process performs the decision-making by planning the application of the UI adaptation and getting input from the control loop knowledge-base. The control loop *knowledge*-base contains the historical data and the inputs from design-time step actions (explained above). Following the plan, the *execute* modifies the interface if the adaptation is not stopped.

At ARLC, the *monitor* step watches the required UI adaptations planned by ALC. It *analyze*s the QoS values to be under the specified threshold. The *plan* step performs the decision-making on architecture adaptation and, if needed, chooses an architecture configuration stored in *knowledge*-base. If the adaptation is required, the *execute* modifies the components and connectors of the IT infrastructure. The two levels of control *coordinate* to i) share knowledge on the type of UI adaptation and temporal aspects, ii) adjust to each others' situations and requirements.

As shown in Fig. 2, the **IT infrastructure** layer contains sensing, networking, computing, and actuating components and their connections that form software architectures. The architecture is supported by a continuous reconfiguration imposed by ARLC. The **interaction** layer is a part of the environment and includes *sensors* that are physical components such as cameras and screen surface where the *interface* is rendered. This layer facilitates detecting the users' emotions and showing them stimuli to impact their emotions continuously.

The core of the approach depicted in Fig. 2 is the continuous adaptation performed at run-time based on some initial knowledge obtained through design time execution, studies, surveys, etc. In an IoB ecosystem, there is an active participation of humans, systems, and the interactions between them. Such interactions can significantly impact the QoS of the system and the QoE experienced by the users, as depicted in Fig. 1. Hence, it is essential to consider these different dimensions while performing the adaptation.

To this end, as stated above, our approach builds on top of the traditional MAPE-K loop of self-adaptation. In order to support the adaptation of the system based on human emotion following the IoB conceptual model (refer Sect. 3), we extended the traditional MAPE-K loop with additional responsibilities at ALC and ARLC. In the following subsection, we provide a detailed explanation of the different run-time MAPE activities performed at ALC and ARLC to continuously optimize the overall system QoS and users' QoE.

4.1   Monitor

The monitor activity in the application and architecture level control is responsible for continuously monitoring the QoE and QoS data, respectively. At the application level, the monitor activity is exploited to continuously monitor the QoE of the user. We capture two main types of metrics to measure QoE, namely, i) the present emotion of the user, U_{et}; ii) the user satisfaction factor, U_{st} for a given time interval t. To this end, the monitored data comprises image frames that capture users' facial images. These images are further sent to the Analyze activity in the Application Level control for further processing. On the other hand, the monitor activity in the ARLC is responsible for continuously monitoring the QoS data of the system. These data consist of different metrics information of the system such as response time, throughput, utilization, etc. In this work, we primarily consider one QoS parameter, namely response time, R_{st} for a given time interval t. The monitored data (i.e. R_{st}) is further sent to Analyze in the ARLC.

The process of ingesting the QoE and QoS data into the Analyze activities of different levels keeps continuing throughout the system lifecycle. This means that our approach can be applied to a running system, and this data can be extracted, assuming that the system provides ways to extract the desired QoE and QoS data.

4.2   Knowledge

It acts as central storage for different types of knowledge required by various activities of the MAPE loop of ALC as well as ARLC for performing the adaptations. In the case of ALC, it consists of four types of information: i) Emotion Models consist of different models that will be used to map the user emotion into one of the categories of $\{Joy, Fear, Surprise, Neutral, Sad, Anger, Disgust\}$. These are developed post the model specification activity in design-time (refer Design-time activities in Fig. 2). It defines how the emotion monitored can be mapped into one of the categories; ii) UI parameters defined in design-time and ingested into the Knowledge base is a set U_p where each $U_{pi} \in U_p$ is a pair (a, b) where a denotes the parameter label and b is a vector which consists of different configuration changes that if performed can adapt the UI. For instance, $U_p = \{(FontSize, < large, medium, small >)\}$ denotes that the font size parameter of the UI can be adapted to one among large, medium, and small; iii) Q-Tables consists of the information obtained from the design-time (refer Fig. 2) as well as the information updated during run-time adaptation by the ALC. It is like a lookup table where each row represents the different possible emotions of the user, and columns consist of the various possible UI adaptations as defined by the UI parameters. During design-time, this Q-table is populated with values based on user feedback, surveys, and experiments. At run-time, the Q-table values are updated by the adaptation mechanism employed by the Plan activity (explained in subsequent sections); iv) Temporal aspects stores information related to different context variations that need to be taken into account while performing the adaptation (e.g., at what frequency the image capture needs to happen, what should be the time interval for every adaptation, etc.). These values are determined based on design-time analysis (refer Fig. 2) and are used by Analyze and Plan activities to analyze the real-time monitored emotion and select an adaptation strategy.

On the other hand, Knowledge in ARLC consists of the static information on the configuration of each adaptation pattern, which consists of a set of components involved C, and the set of connectors between the components, $K \subseteq C \times C$. Each set is further encoded with different properties. The MAPE activities of ARLC then use these configurations to perform run-time architectural adaptation. These are first defined at design-time (Architecting software configurations in Fig. 2). The configurations are defined considering various possible run-time uncertainties. In this work, we mainly consider two architectural configurations, one which binds the processing locally and another that enforces some level of processing in the cloud.

4.3   Analyze

The role of Analyze activity in ALC and ARLC is to constantly analyze the emotion of the user as well as the QoS of the system to decide the need for adaptation of application or architecture or even both. To this end, it uses the notion of adaptation goals in the form of QoS and QoE goals (Fig. 1).

– *QoE Goals*, based on the human emotion data gathered through the monitoring process by ALC in the form of images, are defined by the concerned stakeholders through a configuration file. It represents the goals based on the emotion recognized by the application that, if not satisfied, can impact humans' QoE. For example, a QoE goal, $Q_O = (Joy, Joy)$ for a given instant of time t, states that the user should be emotionally joyful during the monitoring as well as post an adaptation.

– *QoS Goals*, for different QoS metrics, are defined by the respective stakeholders through a configuration file. For example, a QoS goal, $Q_S = (response\_time, 1.0, s)$ for a period $t = 10\,min$, states that the average response time offered by the system for 10 min should not exceed a maximum value 1.0 s.

The above goals are used by the Analyze activity in ALC and ARLC to identify the need to trigger the *Plan activity* in the respective layers for planning the adaptation. This is achieved by comparing real-time QoE and QoS values obtained from the monitor activity with the corresponding goals. To achieve this the Analyze activity transforms the data obtained from the monitor activity into a comparable standard format. For instance, in the case of Analyze activity in ALC, the data obtained from Monitor activity is facial images. To this, the Analyze activity applies ML techniques to recognize human emotion from the obtained image. This emotion then forms the real-time emotion, $U_{et} \in U_E$ where U_E represents the set of possible emotions defined by the *Emotion Models* which are created at design-time and added to the Knowledge-base (refer Fig. 2). The same process is repeated to obtain U_{ot}. This is compared with the QoE goals to check for any violation. For example if $U_{et} = \{Sad\}$ and $U_{st} = \{Sad\}$ then it will violate the QoE goal, $Q_{Ot} = (Joy, Joy)$ for a given instance of time, t. This violation further results in the trigger of plan activity at the application level.

As in the case of ALC, the Analyze activity in ARLC uses a similar approach to detect violations. The QoS data obtained is compared with QoS goals to detect violations. For example, if $R_{s10} = (2, s)$ then it will violate the QoS goal, $Q_S = (response\_time, 1.0, s)$ for a given interval of time. This violation further results in the trigger of plan activity at the architecture level.

4.4   Plan

Plan activity is responsible for decision-making on the type of adaptation to be applied. It exploits two different mechanisms at two different levels. At the application level, it uses Model-free Reinforcement Learning (MFRL), particularly Q-learning; at the architecture level, it uses a rule-based approach. Each of these is explained below:

In the ALC, once Analyze activity detects violations, the current emotion of the user captured at run-time along with the current UI Parameters (configurations) is available from the Knowledge-base (refer Fig. 2). This is then used by Plan to adapt the application UI. To this end, it uses RL, particularly Q-learning [38]. The problem of selecting an adaptation strategy to

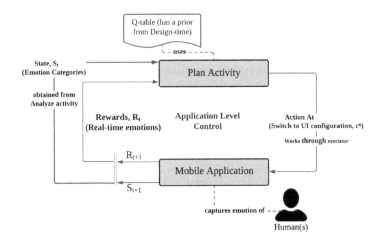

Fig. 3. Q-learning enabled Planning at ALC.

adapt the user application can be considered an infinite Markov Decision Process (MDP). The states, S of the MDP are modeled as a pair, $s = (e^s, c^u)$ where e^s represents the current emotional state of the user which is obtained by mapping the emotion identified by the Analyzer into one of the emotions $\{joy, surprise, fear, disgust, angry, sad, neutral\}$ and c^u represents the current UI configuration which belongs to the set of UI configurations, $C =$ {dark, light, 3dmap}.

The actions, A of this MDP, involve selecting a configuration $c^u \in C$. Therefore the set of possible actions is $(A = C^u = \{c_1^u, c_2^u, \ldots c_m^u\}) where(c_m^u)$ is the action to select the configuration m in C). Figure 3 provides an overview of how Q-learning is used by the Plan activity of ALC.

The states allow Q-learning to identify the current situation, and actions allow Q-learning to select one of the available configurations. To this end, Q-learning uses a lookup table known as a Q-table. It's a $|S|X|A|$ matrix where each (s, a) denotes the relevance of performing an action a from a given state s. Q-learning works by using a combination of exploration and exploitation mechanisms, where exploration refers to the process of exploring different possible actions, and exploitation refers to the process of using knowledge gained to perform selections better. In our case, since humans are involved, too much exploration can result in poor QoE-experienced users, which goes against the overall goal of the system. To this end, the approach uses a pre-populated Q-table generated at design-time (c.f. Figure 2) based on different user studies. This serves as a baseline for run-time plan activity to select more appropriate adaptation actions. Hence, given an emotional state, e^s, which represents the user's current emotional state, the Q-table is used to select the configuration, c_m^u such that $(e^s, c_i^u) = max(e^s, c_m^u) \forall i \in 1..m$. Further, after each selection of a configuration, the Q-table is updated using a bellman equation:

$$Q'(s, a) = (1 - \alpha) * Q(s, a) + \alpha * (r + \gamma * max(Q(s', a)))$$

where $0 < \alpha \leq 1$ denotes the learning rate, which represents the importance given to the learned observation at each step, and $0 < \gamma \leq 1$ denotes the discount factor, which can be considered as the weight given to the next action (selection of an interface configuration). r denotes the reward, which is the mapping of a state to an integer value, $s \longrightarrow Z$.

In this manner, every QoE violation triggered by the Analyze activity selects the optimal interface configuration c^u by selecting the action that maximizes the reward. By assigning negative rewards (penalties) to a selection of interface configuration that leads to an undesirable emotional category (such as anger or fear), the approach ensures that any incorrect selection is penalized in the form of a high negative reward, and this means as the time progresses, the algorithm continuously improves the selection process to ensure that the UI is adapted to maintain an emotional balance of the user by ignoring configurations that can lead to high penalties.

On the other hand, the Plan activity of the ARLC, upon detecting a QoS goal violation by the Analyze activity, uses a rule-based technique to perform architectural adaptation. The adaptation, in this case, primarily involves switching between edge and cloud. The Plan activity consists of two adaptation actions, $A_c = \{cloud, edge\}$ where $cloud$ denotes switching the processing to the cloud, and the $edge$ implies performing the processing at the edge. These actions are defined at design-time (refer Fig. 2) with the help of configuration files, and they are further sent to the knowledge base of the ARLC. The Plan activity then leverages this at run-time to perform architectural adaptation. The adaptation of configuration at the architectural level is immediately communicated to the Knowledge of ALC, which then will be used by the Analyze activity to decide where the processing needs to happen. This process allows the application to intelligently switch between different architectural configurations to perform processing effectively and efficiently. This process is executed continuously throughout the lifecycle of the application. During this process, the Plan activity also ensures that the adaptation performed at the architectural level does not have a negative impact on the QoE perceived by the user. For instance, on some occasions, performing processing at the edge may lead to some delays, which may impact the user's perceived response time, thereby impacting the user's emotions. Further, such emotion may trigger an adaptation at the ALC. To this end, Plan activity coordinates with the ALC to continuously gather the QoE data of the next time interval $t + 1$ for an adaptation performed at time t. This, along with the QoS data of the system, is then used to decide if a configuration reset needs to be performed.

4.5   Execute

The *Execute* activity is responsible for executing the adaptation and thereby re-configuring the application/architecture based on the level of execution. The *Actuating SW* component in the IT infrastructure acts as the effector for applying the adaptation on the system with the support of the Execute activity in ALC and ARLC.

The *Execute* in ALC is responsible for executing the adaptation to update the UI configuration. For every configuration, c^u selected by the Plan activity, the executed activity maps the configuration change to the corresponding change in UI. For instance, $c^u = \{dark\}$ requires the UI to be switched into a dark mode. To this end, the execute maintains a mapping between the configuration selected by the Plan and the configuration that needs to be enabled/disabled at the UI. This is used to trigger *Actuating SW* in the IT infrastructure, which further applies the configuration change in the Mobile UI.

Similar to the operation of *Execute* activity in ALC, the executed activity in ARLC is responsible for executing the configuration to update the architecture of the system dynamically. This is achieved in conjunction with the ALC. For every architectural configuration $a_c \in A_c$, the executor has a mapping of the configuration with the system components, which is used to perform the adaptation. For instance, $a_c = \{cloud\}$ will result in the Execute activity updating the application flow from edge to the cloud. This process is also executed with the help of the *Actuating SW* in the IT infrastructure.

Overall our approach leverages the prior information of the system gathered at design-time to execute the MAPE-K activities of the ALC and ARLC at run-time. This process is continuously performed throughout the execution lifecycle of the system to ensure that the QoE of the users is not compromised and to provide guarantees on the overall QoS of the system.

5   Evaluation

5.1   Implementation

We created the *EvacuationApp* as a *training* mobile application that leads people to safe areas in case of disaster. The routing is shown based on real-time contextual information such as individuals' positions, risk situation, and crowdedness. The routing algorithm is explained in previous work [5,6,23,29]. *EvacuationApp* is developed as a React progressive web application, written in *TypeScript*. The backend is a *NodeJS* application interacting with a *MongoDB* database. The backend is also written in *TypeScript*. Our React application has integrated several pieces, namely *maps, emotion detection software*, and *adaptation engines*. We used the *FaceAPI* library to infer emotions from the user's face every 100ms to be added to the adaptation engines.

In addition to Q-learning, we employed other approaches such as no adaptation, sequential, and rule-based adaptation to compare. Four types of adaptation could take place to train users for safe evacuation: *i) FontSize (Medium-Large), ii)* ColorTheme (Light-Dark), *iii)* Pop-up (Hidden-Visible), *iv)* MapType (SatelliteView-StreetView). We also have one adaptation that is regarding the app functionality: *iv)* MapDestination (DestinationA-DestinationB).

Sequential Engine. The first approach performs predefined random adaptations to the UI every twenty seconds. We chose twenty-second intervals because emotions take, on average, twenty seconds to reach the highest intensity due to external stimuli [14]. The adaptation sequence is chosen randomly among the adaptation mentioned above.

Rule-Based Engine. In rule-based [2], the adaptation occurs based on a set of predefined rules as the logic in an adaptation engine within a control loop. Each rule has a property that demonstrates its priority compared to other rules. The goal is to arouse three target emotions, namely joy, fear, and surprise, necessary for emergency training.

Rule 1. (Priority 1): *If (Surprise < Disgust) or (Surprise < Sad) → Add Pop-up Information*

Rule 2. (Priority 2): *If (Joy < Disgust) or (Joy < Sad) or (Joy < Anger) → Font Size*

Rule 3. (Priority 3): *If (Fear < 0.08) or (Disgust > 0.01) → Satellite View to Street View*

Rule 4. (Priority 4): *If (Sad > Fear) → Background Color*

Model-Free Reinforcement Learning-Based Engine. The Q-learning algorithm sets parameters $\gamma = 0.9, \alpha = 0.5$. These values were fixed based on the sample experiments overall requirements and feedback. The integer reward/penalty [2,35] values are assigned as follows: *Joy:+5, Fear:+4, Surprise:+3, Neutral:0, Sad:-1, Anger:-2, Disgust:-3*. The value assigned is further leveraged to populate the Q-table.

Implementation of Architecture. The options are processing data locally on participants' phones, a server, cloud, or hierarchical way. We created a React context to collect the data from the React application. The results show an average of 66.55 ms system response time, which is too short to be considered an issue. However, we had an issue when the destination had to be adopted due to congestion [5]. The algorithm requires heavy processing when running locally, with an average CPU time of 3.68 s. Therefore, we understood that performing the computation on the users' phones is generally satisfactory, and an architectural adaptation to the cloud occurs when the routing algorithm should be run. In our evaluation, we will test how processing locally (leading to a few seconds delay) vs. the hierarchical architecture would impact the users' state.

5.2   Experiments

Application Level Adaptation Results. This subsection presents the results on how UI adaptations using Q-learning (we represent the Q-learning approach as MFRL in experiments which stands for Model-free reinforcement learning) could lead users to better performance and arouse their target emotions. Fourteen participants (7 female and 7 male) between 19 to 48 were recruited in the experiment. The experiment was divided into seven phases; thus, a total number of 98 experiments on *EvacuationApp* were performed. Each phase showed a route for evacuation and lasted two minutes maximum. Each phase was developed based on a different UI adaptation method, i.e., MFRL1, No adaptation, MFRL2, Sequential, MFRL3, Rule-based, and MFRL4.

UI Parameters and Emotions. To analyze the validity of our defined adaptation with our target emotions, we first computed the average emotion intensity aroused by each type of change in UI parameters. Here the data is assessed independently of the adaptation method. The experiments show that joy intensity was the highest triggered by changes in FontSize to large. Fear was mainly triggered by changes in MapType to StreetView. On average, learners were the most surprised by seeing Pop-up dialogue.

Target Emotions and Adaptation Method. To understand the MFRL effectiveness compared to other approaches in arousing target emotions, we performed a one-way ANOVA test with the target emotions (surprise, joy, fear) as the dependent variable and the type of experiment as the independent variable. Results indicate that type of experiment had a statistically significant effect on all the target emotions with a significance level less than 0.05 (surprise: $F_{(6, 9072)} = 13.930$, $p < 0.01$, Happy: $F_{(6, 9072)} = 71.055$, $p < 0.01.$, Fear $F_{(6, 9072)} = 6.941$, $p < 0.01$). To gain a better insight, we performed a Post-Hoc Tukey HSD. The result indicated the fourth iteration of reinforcement learning was significantly more effective in arousing the target emotions. Moreover, the results indicated that the fourth iteration of the MFRL approach is performing better than the first, second, and third iterations. This result is in line with our expectation that the MFRL approach refines itself in iterations.

Task Completion and Adaptation Method. Our second factor to examine the effectiveness of the MFRL is the completion rate in various types of adaptation approaches. To this end, we performed a one-way ANOVA test, having the completion rate as a dependent variable and the adaptation method as an independent variable. Our result showed that the adaptation method had a statistically significant effect on the task completion rate $F_{(6, 239)} = 1393.84$, $p < 0.01$. In the next step, we were particularly interested to see whether the difference between groups of adaptation methods is significant. To this end, we performed a Post-Hoc test to examine the last MFRL iteration with the other adaptation approaches as well as the previous MFRL iterations. The between-group analysis revealed a significant difference between the fourth MFRL iteration and the other types of adaptations. It showed the fourth iteration of the MFRL approach outperforms the other adaptation methods. Moreover, the results show that the fourth iteration of MFRL also improved compared to the first, second, and third MFRL iterations.

Target Emotions and Task Completion. We also aimed to understand the correlation between target emotions and evacuation task completion rate. The results show a positive correlation (Fear: $r(262) = 0.129$, $p < .005$; Joy: $r(262) = 0.366$, $p < .005$; Surprise: $r(262) = 0.112$, $p < .005$) between the average target emotions and task completion, meaning that arousing joy, surprise, and fear led people to evacuate faster.

Architecture Level Adaptation Results. As discussed, processing locally satisfies performance requirements until the point at which a route change should be calculated. Running the routing algorithm locally (in a centralized way) will increase response time, possibly leading a person to a congested area. Triggering an adaptation to compute the routing algorithm on the cloud under the hierarchical architecture will, however, solves this issue. To study the value of such adaptation, we defined criteria to study the effect of such architectural adaptation on emotions and task completion.

Table 1. ANOVA test results on mean difference between architecture adaptation and *i)* emotions and *ii)* task completion.

		ANOVA				
		Sum of Squares	df	Mean Square	F	Sig.
Negative AVG	Between Groups	0.00001	1	0.000	4.386	0.042
	Within Groups	0.00007	43	0.000		
	Total	0.00008	44			
Completion rate	Between Groups	1941.381	1	1941.381	31.626	0.000
	Within Groups	2639.598	43	61.386		
	Total	4580.980	44			

We first measured the mean task completion rate associated with local vs. hierarchical processing (Table 1). In the case of evacuation route change, the mean completion rate of hierarchical architecture is lower than centralized local architecture. Respectively, the average negative emotion is higher when the centralized local architecture is adopted. Further, our analysis indicates a positive correlation between centralized local architecture and negative emotions ($r(43) = 0.304$, $p < .005$). Finally, a one-way ANOVA revealed a statistically significant difference in average negative emotions between hierarchical and centralized architectures ($F(1) = 4.386$ $p = .042$). The result indicates that adopting centralized local increases the participant's negative emotions compared to running the same service on the hierarchical architecture.

Furthermore, the task completion rate average was significantly higher when the hierarchical architecture was adopted, leading to a reduced system response time. Our correlation analysis reveals a significant negative correlation between the task completion rate and adopting a centralized local architecture ($r(43) = -0.6$, p $<$ .001). Further, a one-way ANOVA was performed to compare the effect of architecture on task completion rate. The result of the ANOVA reveals a significant mean difference between groups ($F(1) = 31.626$ p $<$ 0.01).

6   Conclusion

This paper presented an emotional IoB approach for QoE-QoS adjustment with a separation of concerns in application-level and architecture-level adaptations. The approach is conceptualized based on interactive MAPEK control loops, where adaptations aim at improving users' feelings and task completion. We compared an RL approach with traditional adaptation approaches and proved its better effectiveness. We also demonstrated that adapting to a hierarchical architecture improved the system QoS and users' QoE. Future work will apply the approach in different use cases in the game and social robots domains.

Acknowledgement. This work is supported by the Innovation Fund Denmark for the project DIREC (9142-00001B).

References

1. Abughazala, M.B., Moghaddam, M.T., Muccini, H., Vaidhyanathan, K.: Human behavior-oriented architectural design. In: Biffl, S., Navarro, E., Löwe, W., Sirjani, M., Mirandola, R., Weyns, D. (eds.) ECSA 2021. LNCS, vol. 12857, pp. 134–143. Springer, Cham (2021). https://doi.org/10.1007/978-3-030-86044-8_9
2. Alipour, M., Dupuy-Chessa, S., Céret, E.: An emotion-oriented problem space for ui adaptation: from a literature review to a conceptual framework. In: 2021 9th International Conference on Affective Computing and Intelligent Interaction (ACII), pp. 1–8. IEEE (2021)
3. Alipour, M., Dupuy-Chessa, S., Jongmans, E.: Disaster mitigation using interface adaptation to emotions: a targeted literature review. In: 10th International Conference on the Internet of Things Companion, pp. 1–15 (2020)
4. Arbib, C., Arcelli, D., Dugdale, J., Moghaddam, M.T., Muccini, H.: Real-time emergency response through performant IoT architectures. In: International Conference on Information Systems for Crisis Response and Management (ISCRAM) (2019)
5. Arbib, C., Moghaddam, M.T., Muccini, H.: IoT flows: a network flow model application to building evacuation. In: Dell'Amico, M., Gaudioso, M., Stecca, G. (eds.) A View of Operations Research Applications in Italy, 2018. ASS, vol. 2, pp. 115–131. Springer, Cham (2019). https://doi.org/10.1007/978-3-030-25842-9_9
6. Arbib, C., Muccini, H., Moghaddam, M.T.: Applying a network flow model to quick and safe evacuation of people from a building: a real case. RSFF **18**, 50–61 (2018)
7. Bannon, L.: Reimagining HCI: toward a more human-centered perspective. Interactions **18**(4), 50–57 (2011)
8. Bannon, L.J.: From human factors to human actors: the role of psychology and human-computer interaction studies in system design. In: Readings in Human-Computer Interaction, pp. 205–214. Elsevier (1995)

9. Castillo, J.C., et al.: Software architecture for smart emotion recognition and regulation of the ageing adult. Cogn. Comput. **8**, 357–367 (2016)

10. Dugdale, J., Moghaddam, M.T., Muccini: Human behaviour centered design: developing a software system for cultural heritage. In: Proceedings of the ACM/IEEE 42nd International Conference on Software Engineering: Software Engineering in Society, pp. 85–94 (2020)

11. Ekman, P.: Basic emotions. Handbook of cognition and emotion **98**(45–60), 16 (1999)

12. Ekman, P., et al.: Universals and cultural differences in the judgments of facial expressions of emotion. J. Pers. Soc. Psychol. **53**(4), 712 (1987)

13. Firmenich, S., Garrido, A., Paternò, F., Rossi, G.: User interface adaptation for accessibility. In: Yesilada, Y., Harper, S. (eds.) Web Accessibility. HIS, pp. 547–568. Springer, London (2019). https://doi.org/10.1007/978-1-4471-7440-0_29

14. Hardin, B., McCool, D.: BIM and construction management: proven tools, methods, and workflows. John Wiley & Sons (2015)

15. Hunziker, S., Laschinger, L., Portmann-Schwarz, S., Semmer, N.K., Tschan, F., Marsch, S.: Perceived stress and team performance during a simulated resuscitation. Intensive Care Med. **37**(9), 1473–1479 (2011)

16. ISO/IEC/IEEE: ISO/IEC/IEEE 42010, systems and software engineering - architecture description (2011)

17. Kjærgaard, M.B., Kuhrmann, M.: On architectural qualities and tactics for mobile sensing. In: Proceedings of the 11th International ACM SIGSOFT Conference on Quality of Software Architectures, pp. 63–72. Association for Computing Machinery (2015)

18. Kleinginna, P.R., Kleinginna, A.M.: A categorized list of emotion definitions, with suggestions for a consensual definition. Motiv. Emot. **5**(4), 345–379 (1981)

19. Konar, A., Chakraborty, A.: Emotion recognition: a pattern analysis approach. John Wiley & Sons (2015)

20. Lenberg, P., Feldt, R., Wallgren, L.G.: Behavioral software engineering: a definition and systematic literature review. J. Syst. Softw. **107**, 15–37 (2015)

21. Lin, B., Cecchi, G., Bouneffouf, D., Reinen, J., Rish, I.: A story of two streams: reinforcement learning models from human behavior and neuropsychiatry. arXiv preprint arXiv:1906.11286 (2019)

22. Märtin, C., Rashid, S., Herdin, C.: Designing responsive interactive applications by emotion-tracking and pattern-based dynamic user interface adaptation. In: Kurosu, M. (ed.) HCI 2016. LNCS, vol. 9733, pp. 28–36. Springer, Cham (2016). https://doi.org/10.1007/978-3-319-39513-5_3

23. Moghaddam, M.T., Muccini, H., Dugdale, J.: Intelligent building evacuation: from modeling systems to behaviors. In: Scholl, H.J., Holdeman, E.E., Boersma, F.K. (eds.) Disaster Management and Information Technology. Public Administration and Information Technology, vol. 40, pp. 111–129. Springer, Cham (2022). https://doi.org/10.1007/978-3-031-20939-0_7

24. Moghaddam, M.T., Muccini, H., Dugdale, J., Kjægaard, M.B.: Designing internet of behaviors systems. In: 2022 IEEE 19th International Conference on Software Architecture (ICSA), pp. 124–134. IEEE (2022)

25. Moghaddam, M.T., Rutten, E., Lalanda, P., Giraud, G.: IAS: an IoT architectural self-adaptation framework. In: Jansen, A., Malavolta, I., Muccini, H., Ozkaya, I., Zimmermann, O. (eds.) ECSA 2020. LNCS, vol. 12292, pp. 333–351. Springer, Cham (2020). https://doi.org/10.1007/978-3-030-58923-3_22

26. Moghaddam, M.T., Alipour, M., Baun Kjærgaard, M.: User interface and architecture adaption based on emotions and behaviors. In: 2020 IEEE International Conference on Software Architecture (ICSA), pp. 1–10. IEEE (2023)

27. Moghaddam, M.T., Muccini, H.: Fault-tolerant IoT. In: Calinescu, R., Di Giandomenico, F. (eds.) SERENE 2019. LNCS, vol. 11732, pp. 67–84. Springer, Cham (2019). https://doi.org/10.1007/978-3-030-30856-8_5

28. Moghaddam, M.T., Rutten, E., Giraud, G.: Hierarchical control for self-adaptive iot systems a constraint programming-based adaptation approach. In: HICSS-Hawaii International Conference on System Sciences, pp. 1–10 (2022)

29. Muccini, H., Arbib, C., Davidsson, P., Tourchi Moghaddam, M.: An IoT software architecture for an evacuable building architecture. In: Proceedings of the 52nd Hawaii International Conference on System Sciences (2019)

30. Muccini, H., Moghaddam, M.T.: IoT architectural styles. In: Cuesta, C.E., Garlan, D., Pérez, J. (eds.) ECSA 2018. LNCS, vol. 11048, pp. 68–85. Springer, Cham (2018). https://doi.org/10.1007/978-3-030-00761-4_5

31. Muccini, H., Spalazzese, R., Moghaddam, M.T., Sharaf, M.: Self-adaptive IoT architectures: An emergency handling case study. In: Proceedings of the 12th European Conference on Software Architecture: Companion Proceedings, pp. 1–6 (2018)

32. Posner, J., Russell, J.A., Peterson, B.S.: The circumplex model of affect: An integrative approach to affective neuroscience, cognitive development, and psychopathology. Dev. Psychopathol. **17**(3), 715–734 (2005)

33. Schirner, G., Erdogmus, D., Chowdhury, K., Padir, T.: The future of human-in-the-loop cyber-physical systems. Computer **46**(1), 36–45 (2013)

34. Schrader, C., Brich, J., Frommel, J., Riemer, V., Rogers, K.: Rising to the challenge: an emotion-driven approach toward adaptive serious games. Serious Games Edutain. Appl. **II**, 3–28 (2017)

35. Shteingart, H., Loewenstein, Y.: Reinforcement learning and human behavior. Curr. Opin. Neurobiol. **25**, 93–98 (2014)

36. Sottet, J.-S., et al.: Model-driven adaptation for plastic user interfaces. In: Baranauskas, C., Palanque, P., Abascal, J., Barbosa, S.D.J. (eds.) INTERACT 2007. LNCS, vol. 4662, pp. 397–410. Springer, Heidelberg (2007). https://doi.org/10.1007/978-3-540-74796-3_38

37. Todi, K., Bailly, G., Leiva, L., Oulasvirta, A.: Adapting user interfaces with model-based reinforcement learning. In: Proceedings of the 2021 CHI Conference on Human Factors in Computing Systems, pp. 1–13 (2021)

38. Watkins, C.J., Dayan, P.: Q-learning. Mach. Learni. **8**(3–4), 279–292 (1992)

39. Weyns, D., et al.: On patterns for decentralized control in self-adaptive systems. In: de Lemos, R., Giese, H., Müller, H.A., Shaw, M. (eds.) Software Engineering for Self-Adaptive Systems II. LNCS, vol. 7475, pp. 76–107. Springer, Heidelberg (2013). https://doi.org/10.1007/978-3-642-35813-5_4

40. Yechiam, E., Busemeyer, J.R., Stout, J.C., Bechara, A.: Using cognitive models to map relations between neuropsychological disorders and human decision-making deficits. Psychol. Sci. **16**(12), 973–978 (2005)

41. Yigitbas, E., Hottung, A., Rojas, S.M., Anjorin, A., Sauer, S., Engels, G.: Context- and data-driven satisfaction analysis of user interface adaptations based on instant user feedback. Proceed. ACM Hum.-Comput. Interact. **3**(EICS), 1–20 (2019)

42. Zheng, M., Xu, Q., Fan, H.: Modeling the adaption rule in context-aware systems. arXiv preprint arXiv:1609.01614 (2016)

Examining Simulated Agricultural Tasks Using an Arm-Support Exoskeleton

Byungkyu Choi📍 and Jaehyun Park(✉)📍

Department of Industrial and Management Engineering, Incheon National University (INU),
Incheon, Republic of Korea
jaehpark@inu.ac.kr

Abstract. Agricultural work requires physical labor and often entails repetitive movements of the upper extremities, which can result in musculoskeletal disorders. The purpose of this study was to assess the impact of utilizing an arm-support exoskeleton (ASE) on physical demands and task performance in simulated agricultural conditions. A group of 21 participants used a commercial arm-support exoskeleton to carry out brief simulated agricultural tasks at different height conditions, and the following outcomes were measured: muscle activity (%MVC) of the upper body muscles, task completion time, and ratings of perceived exertion (RPE). The results indicated that while the use of the ASE significantly reduced shoulder muscle activity at the shoulder and overhead work heights, participants spent more time performing the tasks and perceived higher exertion levels. In conclusion, ASE use has the potential as a new intervention for tasks that require arm elevation. Nevertheless, additional research is necessary to fully understand the benefits and limitations of this technology in the agricultural industry.

Keywords: Exoskeleton · Agriculture · Electromyography · Ergonomics

1 Introduction

Musculoskeletal disorders (MSDs) are the most common occupational non-fatal injuries and illnesses among farm workers who engage in labor-intensive practices and are more prevalent in farmers compared to non-farmers [1–4]. Agricultural work is physically demanding and often involves repetitive movements of the upper limbs that can lead to MSDs [2, 5, 6].

An effective intervention for reducing the risk of developing MSDs is the use of exoskeletons. These wearable structures are designed to augment the wearer's strength or agility by providing support or auxiliary torque to the body joints, reducing the influence of inducing factors on the muscles and joints, and enhancing and assisting human movement to decrease physical exertion [7–10].

Over the years, there has been extensive research on the development and effectiveness of exoskeleton technology for augmenting and assisting in areas such as rehabilitation, manufacturing, and the military. However, the use of exoskeletons in agriculture

© The Author(s), under exclusive license to Springer Nature Switzerland AG 2023
H. Degen and S. Ntoa (Eds.): HCII 2023, LNAI 14050, pp. 23–32, 2023.
https://doi.org/10.1007/978-3-031-35891-3_2

has been a relatively recent area of interest. Given the diverse types of work and equipment used in the agricultural industry, there is a need to explore the potential benefits of exoskeletons in this field.

Within the many different types of agriculture, workers in orchard farming, frequently experience shoulder pain, which is primarily brought on by the repetitive nature of arm elevation [11, 12]. To address this issue, arm-support exoskeletons (ASEs) can be implemented as a suitable intervention. The objective of this study was to assess the effectiveness of the ASE in simulated agricultural tasks, which closely resemble the manual work performed in orchard farming and greenhouse cultivation at various heights such as fruit thinning, pruning, and manual harvesting.

2   Methods

2.1   Participants

A total of 24 individuals (12 males and 12 females) completed the study and were recruited from the local university. Before the experiment, the participants were given complete information about the procedures and objectives of the study. In addition, they were made aware that they could terminate the experiment at any point if they desired.

Of the 24 subjects who participated, the data from three female participants were excluded due to their difficulty in performing the maximal voluntary contraction (MVC) measurement and the contamination of the data, which was frequently caused by the electrodes coming into contact with the exoskeleton during the testing process. This resulted in a final sample of 21 participants for analysis. Respective mean (standard deviation) age, stature, and body mass were 23.5 ($\pm$2.8) yrs, 175.8 ($\pm$5.1) cm, and 74.0 ($\pm$10.1) kg for 12 males; and 20.3 ($\pm$1.6) yrs, 162.4 ($\pm$7.6) cm, and 59.0 ($\pm$12.9) kg for 9 females.

2.2   Apparatus

A passive ASE used was VEX (Hyundai-Rotem Co., Republic of Korea). It is worn by the user like a backpack using adjustable shoulder and waist straps. This ASE used a multi-linkage mechanism that stores and dissipates spring-loaded energy according to the user's arm motion, providing assistive torque and support to the shoulder joint to alleviate muscle fatigue [13]. The total weight of the ASE, without testing-related material, is 2.8 kg.

2.3   Experimental Tasks and Procedures

A repetitive pruning task and a manual harvesting task, which are routine activities in agriculture fields like orchard farming and greenhouse cultivation were each simulated at four different work heights and a load lifting/lowering task was also conducted. The four different work heights included two specific heights, knee height (45 cm) and elbow height (100 cm), and two variable heights determined based on the participants' anthropometry, shoulder height and overhead height. The overhead height was set to a relatively low level, with the shoulders and elbows flexed at 90° [14]. For shoulder and overhead height tasks, a height-adjustable workstation (with a maximum height of 200 cm) was used.

For each height level, participants completed two tasks, starting with a simulated pruning task in which they used a 175 g pruning shear to cut 10 pieces of 3 mm wire. Subsequently, they did a simulated harvesting task in which they removed 20 pieces of 40mm spherical Styrofoam balls (Fig. 1).

In the lifting/lowering task, participants lifted and lowered a 10 kg weight from knee height (45 cm) to elbow height (100 cm) five times. The load used in the lifting/lowering task was designed to comply with the lifting equation recommended by the National Institute for Occupational Safety and Health, to ensure participant safety [15]. At the end of each task, participants took a short break and were asked to rate their perceived exertion during the task using the Borg RPE scale, with a range of 6 (no exertion at all) to 20 (maximal exertion) [16].

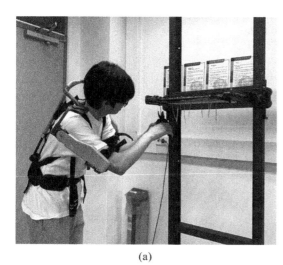 

(a)   (b)

Fig. 1. (a) Pruning task at shoulder height with the ASE (b) Harvesting task at overhead height without the ASE

2.4 Dependent Variables

The dependent variables in the study consisted of three key measures: muscle activity, task completion time, and ratings of perceived exertion (RPE) score. To measure muscle activity, four right-side muscles were focused on: the upper trapezius (UT), anterior deltoid (AD), biceps brachii (BB), and the erector spinae (ES) at the level of the L1 vertebrae. Surface electromyography (EMG) was used to measure muscle activity during work simulations. Pairs of Ag/AgCl electrodes with a 20 mm inter-electrode distance were placed over the muscles following established guidelines for EMG [17, 18]. To normalize EMG signals, maximal voluntary contractions (MVCs) were performed for each muscle before conducting the experimental tasks. The MVC test, as suggested by the Surface Electromyography for the Non-invasive Assessment of Muscles (SENIAM) and kinesiology guidelines, is the most widely employed [19, 20]. Each contraction time lasted for 3 to 5 s [21]. Participants were given rest breaks of a minimum of 5 min after finishing the MVC trials. Raw EMG signals were sampled at 2000 Hz using a telemetered system (Ultium EMG, Noraxon U.S.A. Inc., USA). To process and filter the raw EMG signals (both in each experimental trial and MVCs), the resulting signal was band-pass filtered (10–500 Hz) and subsequently full-wave rectified. To smooth the EMG signals, the root mean square (RMS) envelopes were computed using a moving window of 100 ms. MR 3.18 software (Noraxon U.S.A. Inc., USA) was used to inspect and analyze the data.

Task completion time was recorded as the length of time taken to complete tasks to assess performance and RPE score was rated as a subjective measure of the level of exertion during the tasks. The experiment manipulated two within-subject independent variables: ASE condition (without and with) and simulated tasks in varying height conditions. Both variables were fully crossed, with participants completing all combinations of the ASE condition and simulated tasks.

2.5 Statistical Analysis

Statistical analysis was performed using IBM SPSS Statistics 26 (IBM Corp., Armonk, NY, USA). A repeated measures analysis of variance (ANOVA) was used to compare muscle activity, task completion time, and RPE score, and Student–Newman–Keuls (SNK) method was used for the post hoc test. $p < 0.05$ was considered to be statistically significant.

3 Results

3.1 Muscle Activity

The results of the study indicated that the use of the ASE resulted in a significant reduction in muscle activation levels of the UT and AD muscles. In particular, the UT and AD muscle activation levels showed a decrease of 52.4% and 60.2% during the harvesting task at shoulder height and pruning task at overhead height, respectively.

Additionally, the results indicated that with an increase in working height, the muscle activity of the UT and AD tends to increase, becoming particularly pronounced at overhead height.

The results of the study showed no statistically significant differences between wearing and not wearing the ASE in the BB and ES muscles. However, a higher level of muscle activity was observed during the task of lifting/lowering compared to other tasks. In addition, the use of the ASE resulted in a generally increasing trend in erector spinae muscle activation levels during all simulated tasks, except for the task of lifting/lowering (Fig. 2).

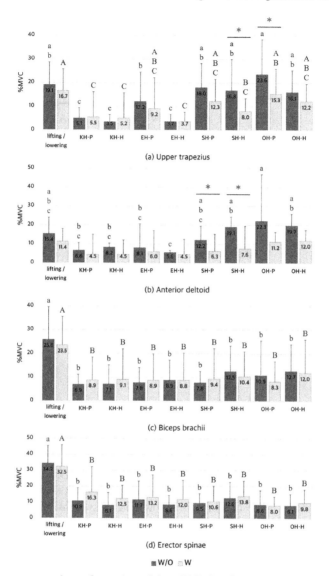

Fig. 2. Average mean values of muscle activity (%MVC) of (a) upper trapezius, (b) anterior deltoid, (c) biceps brachii, and (d) erector spinae during the lifting/lowering task and tasks at various heights including knee height (KH-P, KH-H), elbow height (EH-P, EH-H), shoulder height (SH-P, SH-H), and overhead height (OH-P, OH-H). The labels of the tasks are abbreviated with "P" representing "Pruning" and "H" representing "Harvesting". The tasks were performed both without (W/O) and with (W) the ASE. (* = $p < 0.05$. Different superscript letters indicate statistically significant differences (post hoc test), Error bars refer to standard deviation)

3.2   Task Completion Time

The utilization of the ASE resulted in an overall increase in the time required to complete all tasks, with the most substantial difference observed in the pruning task at shoulder height (Fig. 3).

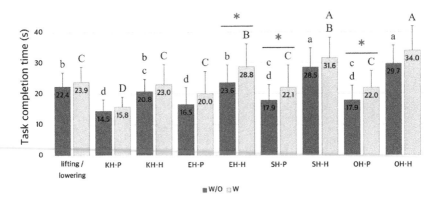

Fig. 3. Task completion time for lifting/lowering task and tasks performed at various heights, including knee height (KH-P, KH-H), elbow height (EH-P, EH-H), shoulder height (SH-P, SH-H), and overhead height (OH-P, OH-H). The labels of the tasks are abbreviated with "P" representing "Pruning" and "H" representing "Harvesting".

3.3   Ratings of Perceived Exertion

The statistical significance of the RPE score in relation to the use of ASE was not observed (Fig. 4). Participants reported higher levels of exertion when using ASE for all tasks, with the exception of tasks performed at overhead height. Differences in perceived exertion levels are most noticeable at knee height. Regardless of the use of ASE, the RPE score was found to be highest during lifting/lowering tasks, consistent with the pattern seen in muscle activity results.

4   Discussion

The reduction in UT and AD muscle activity observed during shoulder and overhead height work can be considered a successful outcome of the design aim of the ASE. A number of studies have provided consistent evidence that using an EXO can reduce upper extremity muscle activity levels [22–26]. The results showed that the ES muscle activity was the highest among all studied muscles, with the exception of tasks performed at the shoulder and overhead height. This finding should be viewed in relation to prior studies that have identified low back pain as the most prevalent MSD in the agriculture industry [27, 28]. Overall, the use of the ASE tended to increase the muscle activity of the ES, except for the lifting/lowering task. This implies that while the load on the specific body part targeted by the exoskeleton design (in this study, the upper extremity)

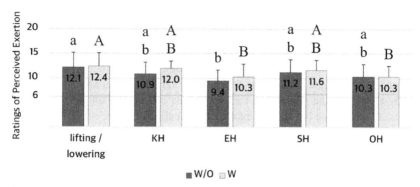

Fig. 4. RPE score for tasks for lifting/lowering task and tasks performed at various heights, including knee height (KH), elbow height (EH), shoulder height (SH), and overhead height (OH)

might decrease, it may lead to an increase in discomfort on other body parts. This is supported by the results of a study by Alabdulkarim and Nussbaum [29], which showed that the use of exoskeleton designs that included mechanical arms resulted in increased loading on the low back.

The use of the ASE resulted in a decrease in upper extremity muscle activity. However, this reduction was accompanied by an increase in both the exertion felt by participants and the time required to complete tasks. There is a conflict and trade-offs between the advantages seen from the biomechanical perspective and the practicality for the user. Task completion time showed a tendency to increase in all tasks and was significant at the elbow, shoulder, and overhead height. This contradicts the decrease in UT and AD muscle activity that was seen during shoulder and overhead height work. This issue, which is closely related to the productivity of agriculture and was highlighted as a challenge in a study exploring farmers' perceptions of the feasibility and practicality of exoskeleton use in agriculture [30], concluded that the successful implementation of exoskeletons on farms will require a harmonious alignment between the exoskeleton design, the user, and the tasks, with practicality issues needing to be addressed. Prior studies have reported that additional weight and restricted movement of some designs can lead to decreased performance and increased perceived task difficulty and postural discomfort [8, 24, 31–35]. The tendency for task completion time and the RPE score to be high when using the ASE may also be due to these factors.

The interpretation of these results should take consider a few limitations. The study participants were mostly youthful and healthy, which does not accurately reflect the entire working population. Furthermore, the experimental tasks were conducted in a controlled lab setting, thus the study only provides a limited perspective on the short-term effects of the ASE.

5 Conclusion

This study investigated the efficacy of an arm-support exoskeleton in simulated agricultural tasks that are typically encountered in real agricultural work. Results showed that the use of the ASE significantly reduced muscle activity for the upper trapezius and anterior deltoid suggesting that it was effective in reducing the risk of developing musculoskeletal disorders in these muscles. However, the completion time for some tasks increased significantly, and there was no clear effect on the biceps brachii and erector spinae. Further research is needed to assess the long-term effects of exoskeleton utilization and to investigate its acceptance among workers in actual agricultural settings. The study highlights the potential for exploring the use of exoskeleton technology in agriculture to reduce the physical demands of manual labor.

Acknowledgments. This work was carried out with the support of "Cooperative Research Program for Agriculture Science and Technology Development (Project No. PJ01709902)" Rural Development Administration, Republic of Korea.

References

1. Fathallah, F.A.: Musculoskeletal disorders in labor-intensive agriculture. Appl. Ergon. **41**, 738–743 (2010). https://doi.org/10.1016/j.apergo.2010.03.003
2. Kirkhorn, S.R., Earle-Richardson, G., Banks, R.: Ergonomic risks and musculoskeletal disorders in production agriculture: recommendations for effective research to practice. J. Agromed. **15**, 281–299 (2010). https://doi.org/10.1080/1059924X.2010.488618
3. Karttunen, J.P., Rautiainen, R.H., Leppälä, J.: Characteristics and costs of disability pensions in finnish agriculture based on 5-year insurance records. J. Agromed. **20**, 282–291 (2015). https://doi.org/10.1080/1059924X.2015.1042179
4. Rostamabadi, A., Jahangiri, M., Naderi Mansourabadi, B., Javid, M., Ghorbani, M., Banaee, S.: Prevalence of chronic diseases and occupational injuries and their influence on the health-related quality of life among farmers working in small-farm enterprises. J. Agromed. **24**, 248–256 (2019). https://doi.org/10.1080/1059924X.2019.1592047
5. Da Costa, B.R., Vieira, E.R.: Risk factors for work-related musculoskeletal disorders: a systematic review of recent longitudinal studies. Am. J. Ind. Med. **53**, 285–323 (2010). https://doi.org/10.1002/ajim.20750
6. Roquelaure, Y., et al.: Epidemiologic surveillance of upper-extremity musculoskeletal disorders in the working population. Arthr. Care Res. Off. J. Am. Coll. Rheumatol. **55**, 765–778 (2006). https://doi.org/10.1002/art.22222
7. Gregorczyk, K.N., Hasselquist, L., Schiffman, J.M., Bensel, C.K., Obusek, J.P., Gu-tekunst, D.J.: Effects of a lower-body exoskeleton device on metabolic cost and gait biomechanics during load carriage. Ergonomics **53**, 1263–1275 (2010). https://doi.org/10.1080/00140139.2010.512982
8. De Looze, M.P., Bosch, T., Krause, F., Stadler, K.S., O'sullivan, L.W.: Exoskeletons for industrial application and their potential effects on physical work load. Ergonomics **59**, 671–681 (2016). https://doi.org/10.1080/00140139.2015.1081988
9. Romero, D., et al.: Towards an operator 4.0 typology: a human-centric perspective on the fourth industrial revolution technologies. In: Proceedings of the International Conference on Computers and Industrial Engineering (CIE46), Tianjin, China, pp. 29–31. (Year)
10. Kim, H.K., Seong, S., Park, J., Kim, J., Park, J., Park, W.: Subjective evaluation of the effect of exoskeleton robots for rehabilitation training. IEEE Access **9**, 130554–130561 (2021). https://doi.org/10.1109/ACCESS.2021.3112263
11. Sakakibara, H., Miyao, M., Kondo, T.-A., Yamada, S.Y.: Overhead work and shoulder-neck pain in orchard farmers harvesting pears and apples. Ergonomics **38**, 700–706 (1995). https://doi.org/10.1080/00140139508925141

12. Kang, M.-Y., et al.: Musculoskeletal disorders and agricultural risk factors among Korean farmers. J. Agromed. **21**, 353–363 (2016). https://doi.org/10.1080/1059924X.2016.1178612
13. Hyun, D.J., Bae, K., Kim, K., Nam, S., Lee, D.-h.: A light-weight passive upper arm assistive exoskeleton based on multi-linkage spring-energy dissipation mechanism for overhead tasks. Robot. Auton. Syst. **122**, 103309 (2019). https://doi.org/10.1016/j.robot.2019.103309
14. Sood, D., Nussbaum, M.A., Hager, K.: Fatigue during prolonged intermittent overhead work: reliability of measures and effects of working height. Ergonomics **50**, 497–513 (2007). https://doi.org/10.1080/00140130601133800
15. Waters, T.R., Putz-Anderson, V., Garg, A.: Applications manual for the revised NIOSH lifting equation (1994)
16. Borg, G.A.: Psychophysical bases of perceived exertion. Med. Sci. Sports Exerc. (1982). https://doi.org/10.1249/00005768-198205000-00012
17. Hermens, H.J., et al.: European recommendations for surface electromyography. Roessingh Res. Dev. **8**, 13–54 (1999)
18. Perotto, A.O.: Anatomical Guide for the Electromyographer: The Limbs and Trunk. Charles C Thomas Publisher (2011)
19. De Luca, C.J.: The use of surface electromyography in biomechanics. J. Appl. Biomech. **13**, 135–163 (1997). https://doi.org/10.1123/jab.13.2.135
20. Burden, A., Trew, M., Baltzopoulos, V.: Normalisation of gait EMGs: a re-examination. J. Electromyogr. Kinesiol. **13**, 519–532 (2003). https://doi.org/10.1016/S1050-6411(03)00082-8
21. Soderberg, G.L., Knutson, L.M.: A guide for use and interpretation of kinesiologic electromyographic data. Phys. Ther. **80**, 485–498 (2000). https://doi.org/10.1093/ptj/80.5.485
22. Yin, P., Yang, L., Qu, S., Wang, C.: Effects of a passive upper extremity exoskeleton for overhead tasks. J. Electromyogr. Kinesiol. **55**, 102478 (2020). https://doi.org/10.1016/j.jelekin.2020.102478
23. De Vries, A., De Looze, M.: The effect of arm support exoskeletons in realistic work activities: a review study. J. Ergon. **9**, 1–9 (2019). https://doi.org/10.35248/2165-7556.19.9.255
24. Rashedi, E., Kim, S., Nussbaum, M.A., Agnew, M.J.: Ergonomic evaluation of a wearable assistive device for overhead work. Ergonomics **57**, 1864–1874 (2014). https://doi.org/10.1080/00140139.2014.952682
25. Huysamen, K., Bosch, T., de Looze, M., Stadler, K.S., Graf, E., O'Sullivan, L.W.: Evaluation of a passive exoskeleton for static upper limb activities. Appl. Ergon. **70**, 148–155 (2018). https://doi.org/10.1016/j.apergo.2018.02.009
26. Kim, S., Nussbaum, M.A., Esfahani, M.I.M., Alemi, M.M., Alabdulkarim, S., Rashedi, E.: Assessing the influence of a passive, upper extremity exoskeletal vest for tasks requiring arm elevation: Part I–"expected" effects on discomfort, shoulder muscle activity, and work task performance. Appl. Ergon. **70**, 315–322 (2018). https://doi.org/10.1016/j.apergo.2018.02.025
27. McMillan, M., Trask, C., Dosman, J., Hagel, L., Pickett, W., Saskatchewan Farm Injury Cohort Study Team: Prevalence of musculoskeletal disorders among Saskatchewan farmers. J. Agromed. **20**, 292–301 (2015). https://doi.org/10.1080/1059924X.2015.1042611
28. Benos, L., Tsaopoulos, D., Bochtis, D.: A review on ergonomics in agriculture. Part I: manual operations. Appl. Sci. **10**, 1905 (2020). https://doi.org/10.3390/app10061905
29. Alabdulkarim, S., Nussbaum, M.A.: Influences of different exoskeleton designs and tool mass on physical demands and performance in a simulated overhead drilling task. Appl. Ergon. **74**, 55–66 (2019). https://doi.org/10.1016/j.apergo.2018.08.004
30. Omoniyi, A., Trask, C., Milosavljevic, S., Thamsuwan, O.: Farmers' perceptions of exoskeleton use on farms: finding the right tool for the work(er). Int. J. Ind. Ergon. **80**, 103036 (2020). https://doi.org/10.1016/j.ergon.2020.103036

31. Kermavnar, T., de Vries, A.W., de Looze, M.P., O'Sullivan, L.W.: Effects of industrial back-support exoskeletons on body loading and user experience: an updated systematic review. Ergonomics **64**, 685–711 (2021). https://doi.org/10.1080/00140139.2020.1870162

32. Kim, S., Madinei, S., Alemi, M.M., Srinivasan, D., Nussbaum, M.A.: Assessing the potential for "undesired" effects of passive back-support exoskeleton use during a simulated manual assembly task: muscle activity, posture, balance, discomfort, and usability. Appl. Ergon. **89**, 103194 (2020). https://doi.org/10.1016/j.apergo.2020.103194

33. Howard, J., Murashov, V.V., Lowe, B.D., Lu, M.L.: Industrial exoskeletons: need for intervention effectiveness research. Am. J. Ind. Med. **63**, 201–208 (2020). https://doi.org/10.1002/ajim.23080

34. Kim, H.K., Hussain, M., Park, J., Lee, J., Lee, J.W.: Analysis of active back-support exoskeleton during manual load-lifting tasks. J. Med. Biol. Eng. **41**(5), 704–714 (2021). https://doi.org/10.1007/s40846-021-00644-w

35. Hussain, M., Park, J., Kim, N., Kim, H.K., Lee, J., Lee, J.: Effects of exoskeleton robot on human posture and lumbar pressure during manual lifting tasks. ICIC Express Lett. Part B Appl. **11**, 439–445 (2020). https://doi.org/10.24507/icicelb.11.05.439

Integrated Solution for Evaluating Emotional Expressions in Learning Management Systems

André Luiz Favareto[1], Luiz A. L. Teixeira Jr[2], Ferrucio de Franco Rosa[1,2] ⓘ,
and Rodrigo Bonacin[1,2(✉)] ⓘ

[1] UNIFACCAMP, Campo Limpo Paulista, SP, Brazil
[2] Center for Information Technology Renato Archer (CTI), Campinas, SP, Brazil
`{luiz.teixeira,ffrosa,rodrigo.bonacin}@cti.gov.br`

Abstract. One of the challenges for distance learning teachers is to be able to assess the emotional expressions of their students in Learning Management Systems (LMS). Modern LMS use formal languages in the assessment process, such as questions and answers, readings, among others, however, they are not able to consider the emotional reactions expressed by the student during the assessment process. In this context, we propose a software architecture and solution that uses SCORM (Sharable Content Object Reference Model) tools in order to integrate LMS with services of emotions expression analysis software. Our solution analyzes images from webcams at the time the remote assessment activity is performed, and it generates reports on Moodle LMS to provide feedback for teachers. We expect the teacher can analyze the students' emotional reactions in assessment activities and adapt its content for higher engagement of students in remote activities. The proposed solution was evaluated by experts, students, and lecturers in a real learning scenario. The evaluation shows predominant emotional expressions, and positive results regarding the feasibility, usefulness, and acceptance of the prototype.

Keywords: Emotions in Learning Assessment · Emotional Expression Recognition · Learning Management Systems · Emotions in Education

1 Introduction

The evolution of artificial intelligence and image processing has brought new perspectives to the use of technologies in education. Through these new technologies, for instance, it has become feasible to consider the emotional expressions in the interaction between students, teachers, and educators in distance learning systems. Indeed, one of the challenges for distance learning teachers is to be able to assess nonformal factors related to their students in Learning Management Systems (LMS), which includes emotional expressions, involvement, motivation, and frustration, among others. This is a natural process of teaching that happens with the teacher in person when interacting with their students. A smile, a sideways look, and a frown are examples of non-formal signs that the teacher can consider during the face-to-face learning process.

© The Author(s), under exclusive license to Springer Nature Switzerland AG 2023
H. Degen and S. Ntoa (Eds.): HCII 2023, LNAI 14050, pp. 33–49, 2023.
https://doi.org/10.1007/978-3-031-35891-3_3

We argue that non-formal reactive languages of facial expressions can be analyzed through facial recognition services, which analyze images from a camera at the moment the student interacts with the LMS. Knowing that modern LMS includes activities with questions and answers, games, readings, among others; the development of new assessment technologies, such as the reactive analysis of facial expressions, can lead to more efficient methods aimed at assessing student development and getting feedback from practices used by teachers. Jayasinghe and Atukorle [1] emphasize that emotion is an important element of summative assessment, where teachers and educators will be able to give constant feedback to their students, readjusting their contents according to this interaction. However, individual monitoring via webcam by teachers is impracticable, especially in larger classes.

Nowadays, there are services of Software for Analysis of Expression of Emotions (SAE) available on the web (e.g., Microsoft Azure Face API - https://azure.micros oft.com/en-us/services/cognitive-services/face/), while the LMSs have evolved to make them more modular and expandable. This includes the adoption of standards, such as the SCORM (Sharable Content Object Reference Model) that address aspects of interoperability in e-learning systems. However, the integration and joint use of SAE and LMS is still a topic to be studied.

In this context, we propose to integrate LMS with software capable of analyzing data on students' emotional reactions, such as the analysis of facial expressions. With these data and appropriate reports, teachers could assess non-formal languages in a synchronous and asynchronous manner and support them to improve teaching practices and content. We propose an architecture and a software solution that integrates LMS with SAE, by means of SCORM tools. In our prototype, we integrate Moodle (a popular LMS) with the Microsoft Face API service from the Azure platform, which is an example of a widely used SAE service. The proposed solution includes reports that aggregate the results of the analysis of emotional expressions of a specific student over time, as well as statistics of expressions of several students while answering a specific question.

Our solution was evaluated in twice. First, a preliminary evaluation was carried out with 6 experts (teachers and instructional designers with experience in Moodle) in order to analyze the software prototype's functioning and feasibility. In the sequence, a more in-depth evaluation was carried out in real situations of use with 17 undergraduate computer science students and 4 lecturers. The results show feelings and the acceptance levels of technology by students and lecturers by using the SAM (The Self-Assessment Manikin [2]) and TAM (Technology Acceptance Model [3]).

This paper contributes by providing the architecture, design, prototype, and practical study of a solution that integrates Moodle with the Microsoft Face API. Our proposal enables teachers to evaluate the students' facial expressions when answering assessment questions through synchronous and asynchronous reports. The evaluation shows predominant emotional expressions, and positive results regarding the feasibility, usefulness, and acceptance of the prototype.

The remaining of this article is structured as follows: Sect. 2 presents the concepts and background of this work; Sect. 3 presents the proposed architecture and integration solution; Sect. 4 details the evaluation of our prototype; and, Sect. 5 presents the conclusions and the next steps in this research.

2   Concepts and Background

We present the main concepts and background used as the basis for this work, including studies related to emotions in education (Subsect. 2.1) and a literature review on solutions to deal with emotions in virtual learning (Subsect. 2.2).

2.1   Emotions in Education

The human being can be understood as an emotion-driven organism, which determines its involuntary understanding of the states of things. Thus, our behavior and our ability to learn are constantly influenced by our emotions, some unfavorable to learning and others favorable [4].

Emotions are linked to processes related to the body and motricity, and they can influence thinking and learning. It impacts students' cognition, by affecting various aspects such as memory, attention, and creativity [5]. Studies have shown that emotions have a significant impact on various aspects of learning, such as achievement, motivation, interest, goals, and meta-cognition [5]. Positive mood induction in children can improve their performance on classic intelligence assessments, such as the block design task, whereas negative emotions (e.g., fear, anger, disgust, boredom, sadness) may be associated with lower performance and abandonment of the activity [5].

From a constructivist view, we assume that meaningful learning is motivating, as it makes the student feel pleasant positive emotions when performing a task or working on certain concepts. This is different from mechanical or memorized learning which may lead to tedious and other negative emotions. Teachers and educators must constantly interact with their students, since this interaction between educational actors, can lead to positive emotional involvement between them [1, 6].

Emotion is a key aspect of summative [1] and formative assessment [7]. The assessment environment may sound threatening and punitive to students, especially when they do not interact with humans but with a machine. Recovering from a mistake can be challenging for students in this case [8]. This reinforces the need to address emotions in LMS assessment activities, as well as support teachers in recognizing and analyzing students' emotions during these activities.

2.2   Emotions in Virtual Learning

A literature review was carried out [9] aiming at investigating solutions connected to emotions in virtual learning, with the following research questions: Q1) "What are the approaches that propose to integrate LMS with emotion analysis software services?"; Q2) "Which and how emotional expressions analysis were aggregated as feedback in activities and assessments?"; Q3) "What are the alternatives to generate reports, so that teachers and content creators can analyze and interact in their activities, making them more attractive?". The following databases were analyzed: IEEE Xplore, ACM DL, Scielo, Elsevier, and Springer Link. As a result of the review, 28 articles were selected, of which 6 articles, identified as having a high degree of contribution to the issues, were summarized in the following paragraphs as related work.

Sathik and Jonathan [10] emphasize that facial expressions indicate the level of interaction and understanding of students during their learning activities. Through quantitative observation, emotional characteristics that can be present in facial expressions were identified, relating them to understanding and the difficulty in the learning process and interaction with content provided by teachers.

Bouhlal et al. [11] present different approaches for the recognition of facial emotions through a synthetic study. The authors point out that the connections between cognition and emotions directly influence the quality of tutoring. They conclude that the concept of connected school, or school 2.0, is useless if it cannot interact emotionally between educational actors.

Jayasinghe and Atukorle [1] propose an online assessment mechanism based on emotion recognition in order to complement the summative assessment. The evaluator can analyze some reactions as he develops his activities, approaching the experience of a teacher who, in person, observes subtle reactions produced involuntarily by the students.

Rekh and Chandy [12] propose an educational model for Academia 4.0 based on the industry 4.0 standard. According to the authors, the advancement of society and industry imposes new conditions on its workers and on education itself. They proposed the use of images and facial recognition algorithms as a useful solution for supporting the assessment of students' interests in the context of Academia 4.0.

Oramas-Bustillos et al. [13] propose an educational resources assessment system, which captures textual opinions about learning objects in an intelligent learning environment. The authors used machine learning classifiers to recognize learning-centered emotions (frustrated, bored, neutral, excited, and engaged) in students' texts about learning objects.

Özek [14] did a study with 103 engineering students with the goal of investigating the effects of merging student emotion recognition with LMS. The article presents an integration solution as well as their results show that the experimental group (using a system that merges emotion recognition with LMS) performed significantly better than the LMS-only group. However, this article differs from ours in not focusing on the integration of LMS with cloud services, as well as not presenting synchronously and asynchronously reports aimed at teachers in assessment activities.

From our literature review, we identified relevant answers for question Q1: (1) facial recognition occurs through computational tools (webcams, sensors, etc.); and (2) most works are aimed to identify the emotional condition to overcome the student's resistance to improve their engagement, empathy, and interest. In relation to Q2, we emphasize that the identification of emotional expression is used to improve learning, through feedback regarding the presented content. Finally, in relation to Q3, we did not find ready-made solutions for creating reports of students' emotions to teachers, nevertheless, several papers analyzed and pointed out the importance of teachers considering emotions in virtual learning.

Several works deal with emotions on virtual learning as well as answer key questions for the design of our solution. However, no works were identified proposing to integrate facial recognition services and LMS aimed at providing feedback through reports to teachers in online assessments. Table 1 presents some related works (selected from our understanding as the closest to this work) categorized according to their solution for emotional expression recognition, type of content or learning environment, integration solution, and type of feedback.

Recent works have explored advanced artificial intelligence techniques to recognize students' emotional expressions in LMSs. For instance, López et al. [15] integrate deep learning techniques (CNN) with Sakai LMS to recognize emotional expressions during video conference sessions, in which the lecturer explains the subject.

Table 1. Related Work

Ref.	Recognition[a]	Environment[b]	Integration[c]	Feedback[d]
[10]	Preclassified face database	Lecture environments	—	Synchronous in the lecture
[11]	Facial recognition algorithms	Learning Environments (not specific)	—	Synchronous (proposed)
[1]	Facial recognition service	Questions	—	Reports to researchers
[12]	Facial recognition algorithms	Show images of topics	—	Interest levels of images categories
[13]	Opinions - textual corpus	Learning objects	—	—
[14]	Local Service (OpenCV)	LMS - Dakos	SCORM Local DB	Reports to researchers
This	*Facial recognition service*	*Questions in LMS*	*SCORM - Json*	*Synchronous and asynchronous reports to teachers*

[a]Solution for emotional expression recognition.
[b]Type of learning environment (or content).
[c]Integration Solution (if any).
[d]Type of feedback for teachers (if any).

3 Emotional Expression Recognition in Learning Management Systems

We propose ERLMS (Emotion Recognition in Learning Management System) as an architecture and integration solution between facial emotion recognition services and LMS. Subsection 3.1 presents details on the design and architecture of a software prototype. In Subsect. 3.2 we present the implementation of this prototype, including its main features.

3.1 Design and Architecture

The design of ERLMS was initially based on the authors' own experiences, studies of the literature, and empirical evaluations, which point out that the teachers' difficulty in recognizing students' emotions expressions in LMS during assessment activities. The research and design method used was composed of four steps: (1) Identification and characterization of the problem, (2) Proposal of an initial set of functionalities and technologies, (3) Iterative development, and (4) Evaluation and analysis of the solution prototype (cf., Sect. 4).

As a result of the first two steps, we summarized the initial design of the solution and described user stories, with which we were able to synthesize the following required features:

- Students must execute assessment activities within the LMS with an activated camera. We expect that these activities will cause some emotional expressions during the execution, to be analyzed together with the responses obtained in the assessment activities.
- Each student has a unique interaction experience, which can be expressed in facial reactions. The solution must capture these expressions in the LMS, which can be captured by a more attentive teacher in face-to-face activities.
- The system must generate reports integrated into the LMS, for synchronous and asynchronous monitoring by teachers. Such reports should highlight the students' expressions during assessment activities so that teachers can analyze them and take some action if necessary.

From these requirements, an integrated solution architecture was designed (Fig. 1). From left to right, there is the LMS (*Moodle* box), in which activities (Activity box) are created. The *SCORM Package* contains *Assessment Questions*. The *Main Program* is executed during the assessment; it captures the student's image, makes format transformations, executes the external service (*Face API*), and, finally, generates reports based on the captured emotions expressions.

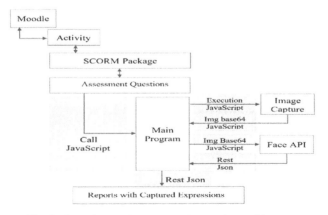

Fig. 1. Overview of the prototype integration architecture.

3.2 Implementation and Functionalities

We developed a prototype of the ERLMS solution integrated with Moodle and using the Microsoft Face API service. Our software was developed in JavaScript language due to the documentation available for the Face API developer platform and its compatibility with Moodle. We have also used a learning object structure, which defines the functionality and communication of objects in the SCORM 1.2 standard[1].

The ERLMS prototype was implemented to be executed on a personal computer with an Internet connection, and with a webcam enabled and correctly positioned to capture facial expressions. Its use on mobile devices is outside the scope of the current version of the prototype.

Figure 2 presents the sequence of activities when a student interacts with the ERLMS prototype. After accessing Moodle (Activity 1), the SCORM package is activated (Activity 2), and the assessment questions are presented to the students (Activity 3). Next, the main JavaScript program is executed (Activity 4), which executes two subroutines: one to access the image in the webcam and transform it into base64 format (Activity 5), and another to access the Face API (Activity 6). The latter activity runs after two seconds in configurable intervals after displaying the question to the student. Activity 6 is composed of four tasks, including sending the image (Sub-activity 6.1), receiving values from the facial expression detection service (Sub-activity 6.2), and displaying the image (Sub-activity 6.3) and its analysis (Sub-activity 6.4) to the teacher in the synchronous interface. After that, the system waits for the student's response (Activity 7) and includes the results in the SCORM package (Activity 8). Finally, asynchronously, the teacher can access a synthetic report of the student's interaction with the LMS (Activity 9) or export this report for external use (Activity 10).

Figure 3 presents a user interacting with the ERLMS prototype (top of the figure), as well as an example of the synchronous (real-time) feedback provided to teachers. The bottom of Fig. 3 presents three images with changes in emotional expressions, from left to right: happiness, neutral, and sadness, i.e., the system presents predominant emotion changes in real-time, according to the aforementioned intervals. It is expected, therefore, to provide immediate feedback to teachers so that they can act in accordance with their teaching strategies. We highlight it is outside the scope of this paper to propose and discuss emotion-based learning methodologies, as ERLMS focuses on providing technical support so that teachers can explore students' emotional expressions in an LMS (Moodle).

3.3 Asynchronous Reports of ERLMS

The ERLMS prototype provides two configurable reports for teachers so that they can asynchronously analyze students' reactions when they respond to evaluative questions. The first report concerns the reactions of each (individual) student to each question. The purpose of this report is to give an overview of the student's emotional expressions over time. In addition to statistical measures per question, the teacher can also visualize a complete list of students' emotional expressions, at each moment, during responses in the Moodle system.

---

[1] https://adlnet.gov/projects/scorm/.

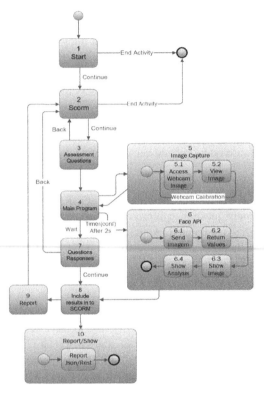

Fig. 2. How the ERLMS prototype works.

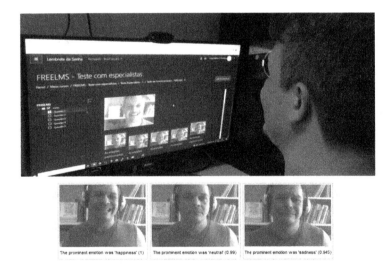

Fig. 3. A user interacting with ERLMS (top) and synchronous feedback for teachers (bottom).

Figure 4 presents an example of a report from a student. This report contains the mode, average, and median measures of the predominant and secondary emotional expression, for each question answered by the student. In addition to these measures, this report also includes ten images for each question, with results of the analysis of predominant and secondary students' emotional expressions. In the case of Fig. 4, we have happiness as the predominant emotional expression of the first question, sadness in the second, and neutral in the third. With this information, the teacher can, for example, identify questions that generated negative expressions in a specific student, identify mood swings or visualize if (s)he has negative expressions as a whole.

Random
Capture

Question	Mode Predominant Emotions	Mode Secondary Emotions
1	happiness (8), neutral (2)	sadness (2)
2	sadness (10)	disgust (10)
3	neutral (10)	sadness (10)

Question	Average Predominant Emotions	Average Secondary Emotions
1	happiness (1.000), neutral (0.927)	sadness (0.072)
2	sadness (0.938)	disgust (0.055)
3	neutral (0.929)	sadness (0.064)

Question	Median Predominant Emotions	Median Secondary Emotions
1	happiness (1.000), neutral (0.927)	sadness (0.072)
2	sadness (0.968)	disgust (0.024)
3	neutral (0.933)	sadness (0.061)

Fig. 4. ERLMS report for an individual student.

The second report concerns statistical measures and charts of a group of students for a given question or group of questions. ERLMS exports the results data in *CSV* format, which is included in predefined Microsoft Excel® templates. Figure 5 presents an example of a chart generated for a specific question for a group of students. According to Fig. 5, 70% of the students had neutral as the predominant emotional expression, *18%* happiness, *9%* surprise, *2%* sadness, and *1%* fear.

Figure 6 presents another example of a chart generated in the ERMLS report. This chart includes the number of emotional expressions captured per question for a given group of users. It includes the predominant and secondary expressions for each question. We aim to provide an interface to facilitate the teacher's graphic and numerical comparison of students' expressions in a set of questions (side by side).

4   Evaluation with Teachers and Students

We carried out a study aimed to analyze the feasibility of ERLMS, its strengths, weaknesses, and its level of acceptance. Subsection 4.1 presents a preliminary evaluation with teachers and instructional designers with experience in Moodle, and Subsect. 4.2 presents an evaluation in real-world situations with undergraduate students and lecturers. Our study was previously approved by the Brazilian research ethical committee.

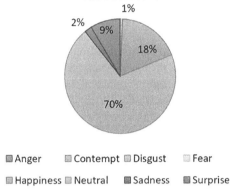

Fig. 5. Example of an ERLMS chart for an individual question.

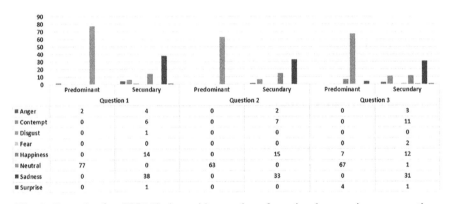

Fig. 6. Example of an ERLMS chart with a number of emotional expressions per question.

4.1 Preliminary Evaluation with Experts

Participants and Evaluation Method. The study was carried out with 6 teachers and instructional designers with experience in using Moodle. Only 1 participant is not from the Information Technology (IT) area, but he has experience in using IT in his industrial automation classes. Two participants are administrators of the Moodle platforms of their institutions.

After the participants read and accept the informed consent form, we executed the study in person, using the researcher's notebook. Initially, each participant answered an assessment question using the student interface, i.e., in the role of a student. Each participant took around 30 s between starting to read the assessment question and answering it.

After interacting with the student' interface, the participants used the teachers' interface, where they could visualize and analyze their own captured images. After that, they answered a questionnaire on the Google Forms platform with multiple choice questions with semantic scales from 1 (most negative) to 5 (most positive). In addition to the questions regarding the users' profile and the functioning of the Face API (outside the scope of this article), the following multiple-choice questions were asked in order to evaluate the ERLMS prototype:

- *Q1.* How do you rate your experience with the ERLMS program in detecting emotion during the application of remote activities? (5. Very Good, 4. Good, 3. Fair, 2. Bad, 1. Very Bad)
- *Q2.* The images (on the ERLMS teacher's interface) represented your real emotional state during the question answering. (5. Strongly Agree, 4. Agree, 3. Neutral, 2. Disagree, 1. Strongly Disagree)
- *Q3.* In view of the experience with ERLMS, how much does it help the teacher to know the student's emotional condition when he performs the remote assessment activity? (5. Totally, 4. A Lot, 3. A Little, 2. Very Little, 1. Not at All)
- *Q4.* What is your level of difficulty in using the ERLMS prototype? (5. Very Easy, 4. Easy, 3. Indifferent, 2. Difficult, 1. Very Difficult)

In addition, they answered open questions about the feasibility and suggestions for improving ERLMS. Finally, the participants and the researcher held a debriefing session about their experience with the prototype.

Results and Discussion. As shown in Fig. 7, most results were positive for all four multiple-choice questions. The only exception was a neutral score to Q2, which may indicate that the image in the report did not fully reflect the person's emotional condition during the assessment (as a student role).

In general, the evaluation results point to positive aspects regarding the usage, as well as a good perception of the design of the ERLMS prototype. However, we emphasize that all the participants had years of previous experience in the use of Moodle as teachers and content writers. Further evaluations are necessary to analyze the receptivity of the prototype for teachers with less experience with LMS.

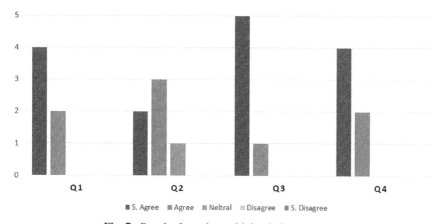

Fig. 7. Results from the multiple-choice questions.

During the activities and debriefing session, the participants did not report difficulties that prevented them from understanding what was proposed. They also pointed out that the features of the ERLMS prototype were well understood. Most participants stated that they are prone to use the system in their teaching activities. They also agreed that the possibility to know if a question causes uncomfortable situations is very useful. According to the participants, this possibility is useful to reformulate assessment questions due to unexpected feelings. We also discussed limitations and suggestions such as making the ERLMS available in the Moodle plugins directory, and the possibility of future research with reports that integrate the emotional expressions with students' personalities [16].

Regarding the answers to the open questions, the participants made observations that pointed out the feasibility of using the proposed software in practice. They also suggested the possibility of developing similar applications for educational games. Two participants also pointed out that they expressed some fear of getting the answers wrong and that this was present in the teachers' reports.

4.2 Evaluation with Students and Lecturers

Participants and Evaluation Method. The study was carried out with 17 undergraduate Computer Science students at a Brazilian university, during an assessment in the Computer Architecture discipline. The students were in the first year of the undergraduate course and were between 18 and 25 years old. All students had experience using the LMS Moodle in distance learning classes. The ERLMS was also evaluated by 4 lecturers that teach in the same institution and course.

After the participants read and accept the informed consent form, the students carried out the assessment activities in the computer lab. Each student answered 3 questions based on the national student performance exam, which is used to evaluate the performance of students in undergraduate courses at the national level. The questions were selected according to the content of the computer architecture classes held prior to this assessment. The students took an average of 5 min to answer each question, ranging from 2 min for the fastest answer to 7 min for the longest one.

Figure 8 shows the students' interface with the first question; the student can browse the questions (left side), view the Webcam image that is transmitted in real-time to the SAS (upper part), and answer the question (bottom).

After carrying out the activity, the students answered forms based on the SAM and TAM techniques. SAM was chosen because it is a qualitative and objective method that allows the subjective feelings of an emotional episode to be evaluated using pictograms. In this evaluation, students answered questions about satisfaction, motivation, and feeling of control over the system using SAM pictograms. We chose to use TAM since it is a method aimed to assess the acceptance of technologies. Students answered a set of 19 questions about the following factors from TAM:

- *Perceived utility*: added value to learning, support to study, study performance, free time, and security.
- *Perceived ease of use*: difficulties with remote learning, discomfort, feeling of lack of human interaction, support to emotional aspects, recognizing how questions affect mood, and changing learning approach due to emotional feedback.

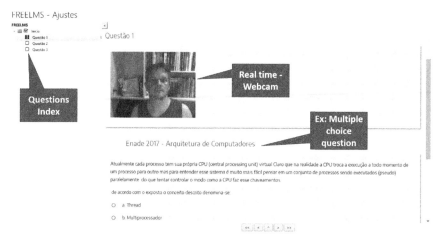

Fig. 8. Student interface with the first question.

- *External variables*: the need for training, prior knowledge of computers, prior knowledge of distance learning, difficulties with distance learning, physical environment, access to computers, and physical limitations issues.

After the activity with the students, 4 lecturers analyzed the features of FreeLMS, the activities carried out with the students, and then answered questionnaires based on SAM and TAM. In addition to questions equivalent (in the teachers' view) to those asked to the students, the lecturers also answered 2 additional questions about the perceived utility of reports, 2 questions additional questions about the perceived ease of use of the reports, and an additional question (external variables) about the possibility of using the ERLMS in their institution. Thus, for the lecturers, there are 3 questions from SAM and 23 questions from TAM.

Results and Discussion. As shown in Fig. 9, most of the students (*76%*) scored the two highest levels of satisfaction with the ERLMS, while *70%* were motivated and *76%* felt in control. This shows that most students had positive reactions to the system, even considering that it constantly evaluates their emotional expressions.

Figure 10 presents a summary of the students' answers to TAM questions grouped by each analyzed factor. As Fig. 10 shows, the students perceived the high utility of having feedback from an SAE inside the ERLMS (*81%* assigned higher scores). In most cases, they also had the perception that the ERLMS is easy to use (*70.6%* assigned higher scores), as well as positive external variables (*73.1%* assigned higher scores). This means good acceptance of the emotional expression recognition technology integrated into the LMS. Detailed data on results for each question can be obtained in [17].

As shown in Fig. 11, all the lecturers scored the two highest levels of satisfaction and motivation with the ERLMS, while *50%* felt in control. This shows that although the lecturers are satisfied and motivated, the system can be improved in terms of control over usage. A hypothesis to be studied is that the automatic analysis of facial expressions

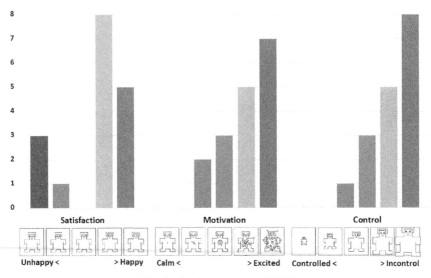

Fig. 9. Student answers to SAM.

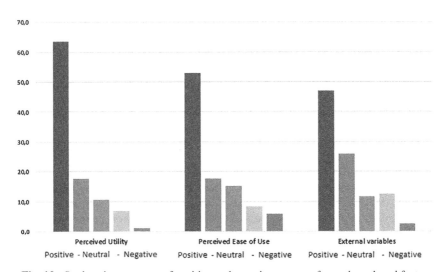

Fig. 10. Students' percentage of positive and negative answers for each analyzed factor.

and automatically produced reports may produce a perception of low control over the system.

Figure 12 presents a summary of the lecturers' answers to TAM questions grouped by each analyzed factor. The lecturers perceived the high utility of having feedback from an SAE inside the ERLMS (*81.3%* assigned higher scores), as well as perceived that the ERLMS is easy to use (*62.5%* assigned higher scores). However, only about half (*53.5%*) of answers to the external variables factor were positive. This was due to

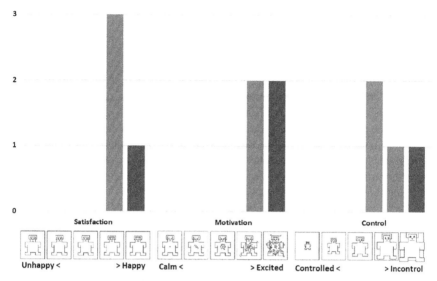

Fig. 11. Lecturers' answers to SAM.

two issues: problems in the remote assessment process and a lack of infrastructure for running the ERLMS. Detailed data on results for each question can be obtained in [17].

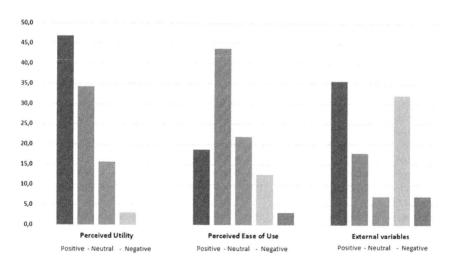

Fig. 12. Lecturers' percentage of positive and negative answers for each analyzed factor.

5 Conclusion

Emotion is a key element of the learning process. In face-to-face assessment activities, teachers are able to observe the emotional expressions of students in the classroom. However, this is limited in distance learning using LMSs, such as Moodle. Recent advances in emotional (face) expression recognition services allow real-time reliable classification, however, these services still lack integration with existing LMSs. We focused on how this integration can occur, as well as the impact on students and teachers. This paper contributes by providing the architecture, design, prototype, and practical study of a solution that integrates Moodle with the Microsoft Face API. Our proposal enables teachers to evaluate the students' facial expressions when answering assessment questions through synchronous and asynchronous reports.

The evaluation with experts (teachers with experience in Moodle), students, and lecturers showed positive results regarding the feasibility, usefulness, and acceptance of the prototype. Further studies and improvements (e.g., to improve the perceived sense of control over the system) of the solution for large-scale use are still needed.

In the next steps of this research, we propose to extend the solution scope to be able to integrate it with other LMS and other types of emotional expression recognition services, as well as to include other means to capture emotional expressions, such as speech signal of a microphone when the students pronounced some sentences. We also plan to include and evaluate the use of facial expression recognition services in other activities (in addition to assessment ones), such as online exercises and hands-on activities. Finally, we expect to carry out a large-scale and long-term evaluation, including a direct comparison between results obtained with and without the support of emotional expressions recognition.

References

1. Jayasinghe, U., Atukorale, A.: Tracking emotions through facial expressions in online education systems based on transient emotion peak. In: Proceedings of The World Conference on Future of Education, Rome, Italy, pp. 7–19. WCFEducation (2019)
2. Bradley, M.M., Lang, P.J.: Measuring emotion: the self-assessment manikin and the semantic differential. J. Behav. Ther. Exp. Psychiatry **25**(1), 49–59 (1994)
3. Davis, F.D.: Perceived usefulness, perceived ease of use, and user acceptance of information technology. MIS Q. **13**(3), 319–340 (1989). http://www.jstor.org/stable/249008. Accessed 23 Jan 2023
4. Pekrun, R., Linnenbrink-Garcia, L.: International Handbook of Emotions in Education, 1st edn. Routledge, Abingdon (2014)
5. Jarvela, S.: Social and Emotional Aspects of Learning. Elsevier, Amsterdam (2011)
6. Ptaszynski, M., Dybala, P., Mazur, M., Rzepka, R., Araki, K., Momouchi, Y.: Towards computational fronesis: verifying contextual appropriateness of emotions. Int. J. Distance Educ. Technol. **11**(2), 16–47 (2013)
7. Kim, C., Balaam, M.: Monitoring affective and motivational aspects of learning experience with the subtle stone. In: IEEE 11th International Conference on Advanced Learning Technologies (ICALT), New York City, pp. 640–641. IEEE (2011)
8. Leite, M., Marczal, D., Pimentel, A., Direne, A.: A conceptual framework to use remediation of errors based on multiple external remediation applied to learning objects. J. Technol. Sci. Educ. **4**(3), 155–166 (2014)

9. Favareto, A.L., Bonacin, R.: Uma revisão da literatura sobre soluções ligadas às expressões emocionais em ambientes virtuais de aprendizagem. In: Anais do XVII Workshop de Computação da UNIFACCAMP, pp. 19–24. Unifaccamp, Campo Limpo Paulista (2021)
10. Sathik, M., Jonathan, S.G.: Effect of facial expressions on student's comprehension recognition in virtual educational environments. Springerplus **2**(1), 1–9 (2013). https://doi.org/10. 1186/2193-1801-2-455
11. Bouhlal, M., Aarika, K., Abdelouahid, R.A., Elfilali, S., Benlahmar, E.: Emotions recognition as innovative tool for improving students' performance and learning approaches. Procedia Comput. Sci. **175**(1), 597–602 (2020)
12. Rekh, S., Chandy, A.: Implementation of academia 4.0 for engineering college education. Procedia Comput. Sci. **172**(1), 673–678 (2020). https://www.sciencedirect.com/science/art icle/pii/S1877050920314174. Accessed 23 Jan 2023
13. Oramas-Bustillos, R., Barron-Estrada, M.L., Zatarain-Cabada, R., Ramírez-Ávila, S.L.: A corpus for sentiment analysis and emotion recognition for a learning environment. In: IEEE 18th International Conference on Advanced Learning Technologies (ICALT), New York City, pp. 431–435. IEEE (2018)
14. Bulut Özek, M.: The effects of merging student emotion recognition with learning management systems on learners' motivation and academic achievements. Comput. Appl. Eng. Educ. **26**(5), 1862–1872 (2018). https://onlineli-brary.wiley.com/doi/abs/10.1002/cae.22000. Accessed 23 Jan 2023
15. López, B., Arcas-Túnez, F., Cantabella, M., Terroso-Sáenz, F., Curado, M., Muñoz, A.: Emo-learning: towards an intelligent tutoring system to assess online students' emotions. In: 2022 18th International Conference on Intelligent Environments (IE), New York City, pp. 1–4. IEEE (2022)
16. Tlili, A., et al.: Automatic modeling learner's personality using learning analytics approach in an intelligent moodle learning platform. Interact. Learn. Environ. **1**(1), 1–15 (2019). https:// doi.org/10.1080/10494820.2019.1636084
17. Favareto, A.L.: Sistema para Avaliação de Expressões Emocionais em Ambientes Virtuais de Aprendizagem. Master's thesis UNIFACCAMP. Unifaccamp, Campo Limpo Paulista (2022)

A Dynamic Fitness Game Content Generation System Based on Machine Learning

Tz-Heng Fu[✉] and Ko-Chiu Wu

National Taipei University of Technology, Taipei City 106344, Taiwan
{thfu,kochiuwu}@mail.ntut.edu.tw

Abstract. The purpose of this study is to explore the applications and design considerations for incorporating machine learning systems into fitness games, and to further examine the feasibility of using artificial intelligence systems to enhance player engagement. In the experimental phase, we used three AI systems to drive the dynamic progress of the game and enrich the changing and challenging elements of the game content. Benefiting from the guidable and generative nature of machine learning AIs, the dynamic progress of the fitness game can be reasonably balanced under the influence of both human player and AI. While the game elements can be generated through the co-creation of human creativity and machine derivation. The experimental results show that artificial intelligence technology can bring a new solution space combined of virtual coach and empowering fitness game systems. Through the advantages of balanced competition and co-created game characters, an AI empowered fitness game can effectively enhance player engagement under reasonable cost.

Keywords: Fitness games · Exergames · Artificial Intelligence · Machine Learning · Player engagement · Virtual coach · Generative AI

1 Introduction

Health is of utmost importance to us. In order to promote the health of all humankind, the WHO recommends that everyone should have at least 30 min of moderate exercise per day. Among them, fitness exercise is a highly purposeful, efficient, and high-value form of exercise. Previous studies have shown that fitness not only promotes personal health [1], but also provides functions such as recreation, socialization [2], stress relief, self-realization [3], help with sleep [4], preventing cancer [5] and avoid obesity [6]. With such a variety of benefits, this activity has become a highly sought-after time investment for busy modern people and has gradually driven the sports trend in various countries, integrating into a massive sports industry chain. Despite the promotion and spread of sports culture over the years, there are still a considerable number of people with low frequency and quality of exercise in the world. How to break through and drive development with new technology is a matter of promoting the well-being of all humankind.

© The Author(s), under exclusive license to Springer Nature Switzerland AG 2023
H. Degen and S. Ntoa (Eds.): HCII 2023, LNAI 14050, pp. 50–62, 2023.
https://doi.org/10.1007/978-3-031-35891-3_4

The fitness game (also known as exergame) discussed in this paper refers to a kind of interactive media that uses electronic software and hardware as the medium and special sensory equipment to meet the fitness needs of users. The key difference between fitness games and general electronic games is that the design of fitness games should effectively meet the fitness needs, and the fun factor is considered as an auxiliary extension of the main fitness function. Therefore, a fitness game system realized by electronic software and hardware should have a core system that meets fitness needs and peripheral modules as supportive game modules, enhancing and consolidating the user's comprehensive experience of the whole system, including the core. The focus of this study is to explore how to enhance user engagement to fitness games through the design of in-game AI subsystems, thereby increasing the frequency of use of the whole fitness game.

2   Evolution of Fitness Games

The development of fitness culture is a part of international and global history. The technologies, tools, and training systems used in fitness gyms around the world today are the results of 20th-century developments and improvements in sports culture [7]. The earliest electronic systems for fitness can be traced back to the late 1960s, when such systems were used as input-output interfaces for fitness equipment and as controllers for fitness programs. During the 1970s, the concept of interval training rose to prominence, and fitness gyms began to focus on bikes and treadmills as their main training methods, with electronic fitness equipment gradually gaining popularity. It was not until the 1980s that fitness and gaming, two previously unrelated concepts, began to intersect. Peripheral devices designed for fitness by video game console developers appeared on the consumer market, bringing the concept of fitness to a wider audience of families with video game consoles.

Since 2000, the fitness industry has been thriving in technological development [8]. Whether it's the large-scale workout equipment in fitness centers or the wearable fitness assistive devices in the retail market, new products and services are constantly emerging [9]. In recent years, in addition to apps and wearable devices, new tech fitness products can even be combined with IOT networks [10], IoT fitness systems designed for sleep apnea patients), using somatosensory cameras to capture user posture, or using commercial AR or VR equipment to run fitness applications (such as applying VR and AI technology to gyms [11], AR applications designed for student fitness activities [12]), diversified technical applications give full play to the advantages of high technology, and bring the user's fitness experience to a whole new level.

Despite the sharp advancement of fitness game in the retail market during COVID-19, the growing and forecast of fitness game has remained stagnant after the epidemic cools down. In order to take advantage of the hard-won market boom, we will go back to analyze and propose a new way to redesign fitness game. This includes examining new technologies such as machine learning and virtual character, redefine design problems, expand the space for solutions, and break down boundaries through comprehensive thinking in order to design a new concept of fitness electronic games with effectively enhanced customer engagement.

3 Categories of Fitness Applications

3.1 Professional Installation

Early fitness systems belonged to the professional installation category, where systems were installed by professional personnel and usage required the accompaniment and supervision of a professional. This type of products view fitness systems as an information application system and they are designed to meet user needs for directly improving their fitness results. These fitness applications often intuitively reported physiological data to players in the form of aggregated data, with common data including heart rate [13], blood oxygen levels [14], calorie consumption [15], etc. Such information application systems can quickly provide direct data statistical feedback to users, or further use augmentative subsystems to perform data inference analysis, in order to achieve the scientific monitoring, feedback and analysis of fitness activities.

3.2 Consumer Product

With the development of micro-electronics technology and the popularity of microcomputer applications, the fitness system as a type of consumer product hits the market. The targeting market moved from professional market to retail market and the functions for entertainment gradually improved along with market demand. In addition to being able to purchase in the retail market, installation and operation are no longer restricted to the accompany of a professional, making the fitness system accessible to everyone. Considering the appeal to people of all ages, the relaxed restrictions, the lower risk of injury during exercise, and the training rigidity of these retail systems were all deliberately adjusted to customer demands.

3.3 Online Service

With the flourishing development of the internet, online services have become a trend, promoting the possibility of the evolution of fitness systems towards online forms. This type of fitness system faces a challenging design obstacle, which is the balance between internet bandwidth, mobility, customer demands, and development and operation costs, making it difficult to find a replicable, balanced, and optimal design. Moreover, though networking mechanism is greatly beneficial for competitive content, but its effectiveness is limited for training content. The first reason for this phenomenon is repetition, as most fitness benefits rely on repetition, training content often requires users to cooperate with fixed frequency repetitive activities, and only when the duration reaches a certain level can they enter an effective exercise cycle [16]. Therefore, when users need to focus most of their attention on the high-repetition cycle activities, the unpredictable information introduced by the inbound network connection may attract their attention and even break the exercise cycle.

3.4 Metaverse Service

The concept of online fitness has gradually emerged during the COVID-19 lockdown period. And thanks to the rapid revolution of AR technology, simple motion capture schemes based on single RGB camera and image recognition give rise to motion capture-based fitness applications and games [17]. As motion capture equipment technology upgrades and costs decrease, metaverse XR interaction platforms emerge gradually. People in the future will be able to participate in integrated virtual and real fitness activities in the metaverse, using virtual trainers, XR fitness games, motion capture, and somatosensory equipment, to immerse themselves in a multi-modal fitness experience. This would be the type of next generation fitness game in the future.

4 Fitness Game Design Methodology

Sinclair found that an exergame follows Csikszentmihalyi's flow construct and proposed a dual flow model which encompasses both attractiveness and effectiveness of player's exercise [18]. Benzing found that although long-term use of fitness games could be difficult, evidence suggests that fitness games can improve health by increasing physical activity levels [19]. By the way, owing to the highly dispersed types of fitness games, we need more researches to investigate potential mechanisms and specific fitness game characteristics in order to grasp their impact on physical activity levels [19]. Skjæret suggests that sports games have the potential to improve physical function, but more research is needed to establish them as an effective exercise and rehabilitation tool [20]. Most research results show that fitness games have the potential to improve health and physical function, but the current fitness games are not completely effective, and the relationship between the two deserves further design and research.

Furthermore, based on the social support theory by House, the four forms of social support include instrumental, informational, emotional, and appraisal [21], where emotional support is an essential element for motivation and persistence [22]. The persistence of an exercise activity is closely related to the encouragement and positive feedback received from the exercise leader and members in all interpersonal relationships [23]. Kwok, after confirming the high impact of fitness coaches on fitness motivation, further investigated the functional completeness of mobile virtual fitness games and found that these games are not as effective as physical fitness coaches in terms of social support and persuasiveness, and need further development and innovation [24].

As a game, fitness electronic games can also be discussed from the perspective of game design. For example, Campbell proposed seven design principles for fitness games, including Core mechanics, Representation, Micro goals, Marginal challenge, Free play, Social play, and Fair play [25]. He emphasized that the engagement of game players and the level of fun in the game are highly related, and meaningful play can stimulate players' enjoyment and affordance. The social interaction has a comprehensive impact on sports games and usability is the key [26].

5 Characteristics of Fitness Games

The characteristics of fitness games can be divided into three categories: functionality, entertainment, and social interaction. Most of the current fitness applications and games on the market are able to implement the main functionalities of supporting the exercise process, and some new fitness games even use more advanced technologies as their selling points and marketing appeals. The implementation cost rises if the game utilizes high-speed network interaction, virtual or augmented reality, gesture recognition, or physiological signal detection. It is not always beneficial to invest a huge money on technology for fitness game. The key to success is the balance between technology innovations and fitness sport theories. One will lose its freshness and fade from the market very soon for badly blending of those two important elements.

The entertainment aspect of fitness games has been represented by many classic examples in recent years, including XBox's Kinect, Nintendo's Switch fitness ring, and Valve's SteamVR, which can fully utilize the advantages of new technology to design amazing gaming experiences. On mobile platforms, there are gesture-based games that use the camera of a phone and LBS games that use GPS. Although fitness games that prioritize entertainment have elements of fitness activities, they do not actually optimize fitness performance, so they are not suitable for analysis from a perspective that primarily focuses on fitness functionality.

The social performance of fitness games can generally be divided into realtime and periodic. Currently, realtime social features include competition and cooperation, messaging, interactive system operations, and live game streamings. Periodic social features include activity boards, message boards, leaderboards, and personal social pages. Realtime social features have higher technical requirements for manufacturers, such as data synchronization, load balancing, and network security issues, which are not within the domain knowledge of most sports industry manufacturers without information system operation experience.

Based on the functional, entertaining, and social characteristics of fitness games, we have made the following three findings.

5.1 Trade-Off Between Repetitiveness and Randomness

Training and competition have always been sports activities with completely different properties. The focus of training is to sculpt physical abilities, while competition emphasizes the interpretation and control of the game. Most of the training effectiveness relies on repetition (especially for strength training [27], so the training routine requires the user to perform repetitive activities around a fixed frequency, and only after a certain duration can they enter an effective workout period. This constant repetition is where most trainers easily feel bored, tired, temporarily stop or even give up. Compared to training routines with high repetition, competition content is full of random changes, sudden events and uncertainties, and participants must maintain high alertness at all times in case of unexpected events. Therefore, training routines with high repetition can easily bring boredom and tiredness, while training routines with high randomness can bring more excitement and focus. Although the randomness of competition can provide better entertainment, the uncertain intensity and frequency of competition can also cause improper posture and sports injuries, so the lack of comprehensive consideration of random competition elements may actually lead to a decline in fitness functionality.

5.2 Hard Limits vs Soft Limits

One of the keys to game design is to properly impose activity restrictions on players. Fitness games can be divided into two categories based on the restrictions imposed on players based on their physical abilities: hard limits and soft limits. Both of these categories have design trade-offs that can easily conflicts with functionality. Hard limits refer to a strong relationship between an individual's physical ability and the progression of the game. When a player's physical ability or skill is insufficient, it will cause difficulties in passing the game, and the player must temporarily or permanently improve their physical ability or skill to have a higher chance of passing. On the other hand, soft limits will allow the player to continue by taking a detour, or having a break, or even temporarily lower down the difficulty. In today's video game market, hardcore-style game restrictions based on ability or skill have become less popular among most video game players. Rigid challenge processes lead to difficulty in selling games. Despite this, restrictions on ability and skill are crucial to the effectiveness of fitness games in terms of functionality. If rigid restrictions are not imposed on player ability or stronger challenges are not provided as player ability increases, players will become bored or discouraged and distance themselves from the state of flow, leading to a decline in immersion and engagement.

5.3 Cross Reality Socializing

The network-based social mechanisms have boosted the development of fitness games, but the design, operation and cost of network security of internet services are not an easy burden to bear. By cross-utilizing virtual and reality integration in socializing, not only can the cost of designing and operating network services be reduced, but also a brand new virtual and reality integration experience can be generated, and the concept of virtual coach was born. The design purpose of the virtual coach is not to replace real coaches, but to use artificial intelligence in a networked or metaverse virtual environment to realize a social element that can catalyze user engagement. After the user leaves the virtual environment, the physical coach takes over to complete the physical experience. Therefore, the design of the virtual coach must not only refer to the duties and functions of the physical coach, but also break away from the stereotype of the physical coach, achieving a seamless virtual and reality integration fitness experience.

In conclusion, if we examine fitness games from a multi-faceted perspective, it has features in terms of functionality, entertainment, and sociality. The first two are trade-offs, while the third is subject to cost constraints. Therefore, when designing a fitness game, we must maximize sociality within a fixed cost while striving for a balance between functionality and entertainment. This is the practical design problem faced by fitness games.

6 System Design

The system design concept diagram of this research is shown in Fig. 1. Firstly, in order to meet the users' social needs within limited costs, we adopt an AI system that requires no internet and uses machine learning, which generates lifelike virtual social avatars through its sophisticated generative dynamics. The avatars generated in this way has high variance comparing to those generated from asset composition through limited samples in the way used in traditional interactive games. Secondly, to balance functionality and entertainment, we introduce an AI assisted empowering game system that allows players to have a responsive and entertaining competition experience even while performing monotonic repetitive fitness exercise. Before the experiment, players will be informed of the basic information about the technology and features of the system, including the randomness and high differential of the virtual coach generation module and the operation of the empowering game system. Detailed explanations of each subsystem are provided below.

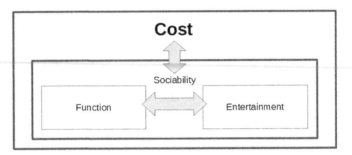

Fig. 1. System design concept diagram.

6.1 Virtual Fitness Coach System

The virtual coach system focuses on enhancing the fitness social experience of users. It can meet social needs through low-cost virtual socializing. The system creates basic information about the virtual fitness coach through real-time human-machine co-creation. Figure 2 is the block diagram of the virtual fitness coach generation system which utilizes a latent diffusion model [28]. First, the user inputs a text description of the fitness coach through a prompt, which is then converted into an embedding vector by a text encoder. The vector serves as the control input and is fed into the UNET module, which estimates the noise. The UNET module performs a limited number of iterations in the latent space under the control of the Noise Scheduler. The Noise Scheduler receives a set of random numbers from the Random Noise Generator and uses them as initial values for reverse diffusion. After each iteration, the UNET estimates a noise value, and the Noise Scheduler subtracts part of the noise from the image and inputs the resulting image back into the UNET module. At the end of the iteration, the VAE on the right converts the latent space image into an output image, giving us a beautiful portrait that matches the user's text description (shown in Fig. 3). The latent diffusion model has high derivative properties, so when inference is performed using different random seed values, the result images will also be different. This brings highly diversified visual avatars (examples shown in Fig. 3) for the virtual fitness coaches which are displayed on the user interface.

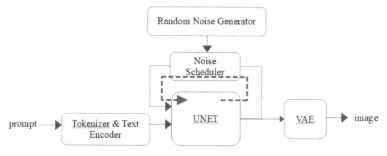

Fig. 2. The stable diffusion model used in virtual coach generation.

Fig. 3. Generated virtual coach avatar samples.

Fig. 4. Virtual coach generation user interface.

Besides avatars, the parameters of the virtual coach are generated using OpenAI's GPT-3 text-davinci-003 model, which requires GPT-3 to generate a single data item separated by semicolons. The game application splits the data into columns based on the separator after receiving the data. Figure 4 shoes the user interface for virtual coach generation. To use it, the user must first input the expected description of the virtual coach in the prompt text window, such as appearance, personality, gender, and expertise, and then click the Generate button. The latent diffusion model will then generate the avatar of the virtual coach based on the prompt. Generating each virtual coach consumes a certain amount of Fitness points, and once all points are consumed, no more generations can be performed. Fitness points can only be obtained by completing fitness games tasks.

6.2 Empowering Game System

The biggest advantage of this empowering game system is that it uses a slow, high repetition, and AI generated random interaction to effectively attract player's attention, thereby replacing the original real-time, low repetition, and overly excited confrontation mechanism. As mentioned earlier, there is a trade-off between entertainment and functionality. The design challenge is usually that designers cannot maintain high repetition while achieving fitness game functionality and entertainment. The empowering game system can solve such design difficulties through the follow features:

Low-Pass Pre-processing: The game hardware and software system does not response to the high-frequency real-time components of the player's input signals. Instead, it performs some combinations of low-pass pre-processing tasks, such as filtering, summation, integration, and activate-threshold on the player's input signals before they are passed to the game core module for further gameplay operation. As a result, players must put their attention on controlling their low-frequency input activities in order to effectively control the game state.

Artificial Intelligence Player Agent: The reason why traditional fitness games may lead to dangerous or ineffective hustle play is highly possible because that players attempt to use their instincts to respond those randomly generated challenge events. If the player's capability do not match well with the intensity of the game challenges, then it will induce excessive strain or force. To solve this problem, we can add a controllable buffer block between the player's controller output and the game input module. This buffer block should be able to output a full-bandwidth control signal subject to the low-frequency part of player's input. However, the high-frequency part of the player's input signal have been filtered out in the pre-processing step, because we do not want the player's high-frequency operation to be passed into the game input module, so how can we remake the missing high-frequency input signal? A reasonable and creative approach is to use artificial intelligence player agent to generate another possible full-bandwidth input based on the player's status and the low-frequency part of the controller output, then use the AI generated full-bandwidth signal for game play.

Somatosensory Dumbbell: The input device used in this research (shown in Fig. 5) is a WiFi somatosensory dumbbell, which is mainly constructed of an ESP8266, an MPU6050, and an 18650 battery. Its function is to count the number of times the user lifts the dumbbell. The weight of the dumbbell is 1.5 kg, which does not cause too much pressure for users in age of 20 s, and it allows repeated lifting for about 1 min.

Figure 6 is the diagram of the empowering fitness game system with a real player using the wireless WiFi haptic bell on the left and a virtual coach on the right. During the game, the player lifts the WiFi dumbbell at a frequency according to their comfort, and the MPU6050 detects the acceleration value of the dumbbell, which is then sent directly to the game core module after subtracting the gravitational force. After the game core module receives the acceleration value, it performs low-pass filtering on the value using arithmetic mean, and further calculates the number of lifts the player has made. To avoid too much uncertain experiment variables, the game core module in this research uses rules from a simple but classic game, Pong, and the first player who scores 11 points

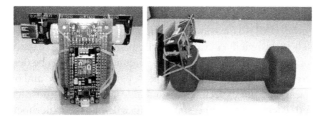

Fig. 5. WiFi somatosensory dumbbell.

wins the game. Notably, the two players who interact in this empowering game system are both actually AI agents. The abilities of a AI agent are saved as numerical data, which are in proportion to how easily an AI agent can influence the game state. Under this design, the player can only change the ability attributes of AI agent through the low-frequency part of his input. And the AI agent will generate more realtime responses for confrontations and competitions based on its ability attributes.

In this research, every 10 lifts the player performs will earn one point which the player can use to boost one of the ability attributes of his AI agent. Our research assistant will help the player to allocated the newly earned points. There are three attributes for the AI agent: Energy, which determines the probability of hitting the ball; Speed, which determines the movement speed; and Control, which determines the additive angle variation of the reflecting ping pong ball. To keep experiment as simple a possible, the AI agent's movement logic is designed with an extremely simple rule-based approach. The input to the AI agent is the difference in the y-axis between the ping pong ball and the character, while the output is the direction of the character's movement in the y-axis.

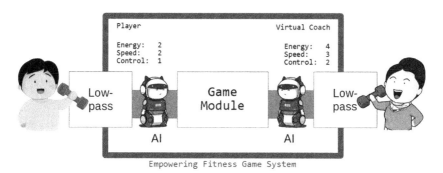

Fig. 6. Diagram of an empowering fitness game system.

7   Measurement Results

The research recruited 30 participants, consisting of 30 males and 10 females, with ages ranging from 20 to 55 years old. Before each time the experiment started, the research assistant would explain the purpose and steps of the whole experiment, and asked the participants to sign a research agreement. The research used the Intrinsic Motivation Inventory (IMI) to measure the participants' level of involvement and intrinsic motivation, which is designed to evaluate participants' subjective experience of target activity in a laboratory environment. Four measurement values can be derived from IMI assessment: interest/enjoyment, value/usefulness, perceived choice and overall intrinsic perception. We designed the experiment as a single-group pre & post test, with paired sample two-tailed T-tests to examine statistically whether the experiment results have significant differences between pre-test and post-test.

Each participant would experience two runs of fitness processes. In the first run the participant performed 30 repetitions of bicep curls in a normal manner, then took the pre-test. After resting for five minutes the second run would start. In the second run the participant used the empowering game system with virtual coach to finish one round of pong, then took post-test.

Table 1. The experiment results of four measurements from IMI

	Interest/Enjoyment	Value/Usefulness	Perceived choice	Overall
t value	5.418	2.287	3.64	3.953
Critical value	2.045	2.045	2.045	2.045

For this experiment, the null hypothesis (H0) is that the mean difference ($\mu A - \mu B$) is equal to 0, while the alternative hypothesis (HA) is that the mean difference is not equal to 0. The significance level was set to $\alpha = 0.05$, and the corresponding critical value for the rejection region was ± 2.045. From the pre-test and post-test data of the experiment, the t-values for all four measurement values were all greater than the critical value of 2.045, indicating a significant improvement in the post-test compared to the pre-test. The results are listed in Table 1 with an improved effect on engagement level brought by the proposed AI assisted fitness game system.

8 Summary

In this research we define our design problem for a fitness game as a balancing task between functionality and entertainment which subjects to a cost limitation. With the help of machine learning artificial intelligence, the need for realtime network is alleviated which dominates game sociability, and an equilibrium between fitness functionality and entertainment is derived from empowering game system with virtual coach module. The measurement result provides a significant positive relationship between the innovative fitness game system and player engagement.

References

1. Penedo, F., Dahn, J.: Exercise and well-being: a review of mental and physical health benefits associated with physical activity. Curr. Opin. Psychiatry **18**, 189–193 (2005)

2. Treiber, F.A., Baranowski, T., Braden, D.S., Strong, W.B., Levy, M., Knox, W.: Social support for exercise: relationship to physical activity in young adults. Prev. Med. **20**, 737–750 (1991)
3. Chatzisarantis, N., Hagger, M.: Intrinsic motivation and self-determination in exercise and sport: reflecting on the past and sketching the future, pp. 281–296. Human Kinetics (2007)
4. Gerber, M., Brand, S., Holsboer-Trachsler, E., Puehse, U.: Fitness and exercise as correlates of sleep complaints. Med. Sci. Sports Exerc. **42**, 893–901 (2009)
5. Shephard, R.J.: The value of physical fitness in preventive medicine. In: Ciba Foundation Symposium, vol. 110, pp. 164–182 (1985)
6. Sinha, G.: Homing in on the fat and cancer connection. J. Natl. Cancer Inst. **104**, 966–967 (2012)
7. Andreasson, J., Johansson, T.: The fitness revolution. Historical transformations in a global gym and fitness culture. Sport Sci. Rev. **23** (2014)
8. Nigg, C.R.: Technology's influence on physical activity and exercise science: the present and the future. Psychol. Sport Exerc. **4**, 57–65 (2003)
9. Passos, J., et al.: Wearables and Internet of Things (IoT) technologies for fitness assessment: a systematic review. Sensors **21**, 5418 (2021)
10. Yong, B., et al.: IoT-based intelligent fitness system. J. Parallel Distrib. Comput. **118**, 14–21 (2018)
11. Zhao, C.: Application of virtual reality and artificial intelligence technology in fitness clubs. Math. Probl. Eng. **2021**, 2446413 (2021)
12. Hsiao, K.-F.: Using augmented reality for students health - case of combining educational learning with standard fitness. Multimedia Tools Appl. **64**, 407–421 (2013)
13. Freedson, P.S., Miller, K.: Objective monitoring of physical activity using motion sensors and heart rate. Res. Q. Exerc. Sport **71**, S21–S29 (2000)
14. Shruthi, P., Resmi, R.: Heart rate monitoring using pulse oximetry and development of fitness application. In: 2019 2nd International Conference on Intelligent Computing, Instrumentation and Control Technologies (ICICICT), vol. 1, pp. 1568–1570 (2019)
15. Carneiro, S., et al.: Accelerometer-based methods for energy expenditure using the smartphone. In: 2015 IEEE International Symposium on Medical Measurements and Applications (MeMeA) Proceedings, pp. 151–156 (2015)
16. Shephard, R.J.: Intensity, duration and frequency of exercise as determinants of the response to a training regime. Internationale Zeitschrift fur angewandte Physiologie, einschliesslich Arbeitsphysiologie **26**, 272–278 (1968)
17. Ganesh, P., Idgahi, R.E., Venkatesh, C.B., Babu, A.R., Kyrarini, M.: Personalized system for human gym activity recognition using an RGB camera. In: Proceedings of the 13th ACM International Conference on PErvasive Technologies Related to Assistive Environments, vol. 21, pp. 1–7 (2020)
18. Sinclair, J., Hingston, P., Masek, M.: Considerations for the design of exergames. In: Proceedings of the 5th International Conference on Computer Graphics and Interactive Techniques in Australia and Southeast Asia, pp. 289–295 (2007)
19. Benzing, V., Schmidt, M.: Exergaming for children and adolescents: strengths, weaknesses, opportunities and threats. J. Clin. Med. **7**(11), 422 (2018)
20. Skjæret, N., Nawaz, A., Morat, T., Schoene, D., Helbostad, J.L., Vereijken, B.: Exercise and rehabilitation delivered through exergames in older adults: an integrative review of technologies, safety and efficacy. Int. J. Med. Inform. **85**(1), 1–16 (2016)
21. House, J.: Work Stress and Social Support. Addison-Wesley Publishing Company (1981)
22. Cutrona, C., Russell, D.: Type of social support and specific stress: toward a theory of optimal matching, social support: an interactional view, pp. 319–366 (1990)
23. Duncan, T.E., McAuley, E.: Social support and efficacy cognitions in exercise adherence: a latent growth curve analysis. J. Behav. Med. **16**, 199–218 (1993)

24. Kwok Chi-Wai, R., et al.: Can mobile virtual fitness apps replace human fitness trainer? In: The 5th International Conference on New Trends in Information Science and Service Science, vol. 1, pp. 56–63 (2011)
25. Campbell, T., Ngo, B., Fogarty, J.: Game design principles in everyday fitness applications. In: Proceedings of the 2008 ACM Conference on Computer Supported Cooperative Work, pp. 249–252 (2008)
26. Wang, Z., Deng, R., Jiang, Q.-L.: Exploration and study of the factors influencing users' adoption of games for fitness behavior. Int. J. Hum. Comput. Interact. 1–12 (2022)
27. Lai, S.-P., et al.: StrengthGaming: enabling dynamic repetition tempo in strength training-based exergame design. In: 22nd International Conference on Human-Computer Interaction with Mobile Devices and Services, vol. 7, pp. 1–8 (2020)
28. Rombach, R., Blattmann, A., Lorenz, D., Esser, P., Ommer, B.: High-resolution image synthesis with latent diffusion models. In: 2022 IEEE/CVF Conference on Computer Vision and Pattern Recognition, pp. 10674–10685 (2021)

"Do we like this, or do we *like* like this?": Reflections on a Human-Centered Machine Learning Approach to Sentiment Analysis

Sourojit Ghosh[(✉)] [ID], Murtaza Ali, Anna Batra, Cheng Guo, Mohit Jain, Joseph Kang, Julia Kharchenko, Varun Suravajhela, Vincent Zhou, and Cecilia Aragon [ID]

University of Washington, Seattle, USA
ghosh100@uw.edu

Abstract. Machine Learning is a powerful tool, but it also has a great potential to cause harm if not approached carefully. Designers must be reflexive and aware of their algorithms' impacts, and one such way of reflection is known as human-centered machine learning. In this paper, we approach a classical problem that has been approached through ML - sentiment analysis - through a Human-Centered Machine Learning lens. Through a case study of trying to differentiate between degrees of positive emotions in reviews of online fanfiction, we offer a set of recommendations for future designers of ML-driven sentiment analysis algorithms.

Keywords: human-centered natural language processing · natural language processing · sentiment analysis · qualitative coding

1 Introduction

Participation in online communities is a common part of our digital lives, and brings about several benefits such as community building [20,62] and informal learning [25,35]. Emotional expression is one of the central features of interactions between members of online communities, and a large amount of effort from community designers goes into building in affordances for varied emotional expression. Consider, for instance, the range of emotions available at a single click on Facebook or LinkedIn. Emotional expression has been seen to be correlated with making connections in online communities [26,37] and finding social support [28,39], among several other benefits, making it an important topic of research in recent years. One vein in this field is concerned with identification of emotions expressed online, known as *sentiment analysis*. While sentiment analysis has commercial benefits, it has been criticized for its potential age bias [18], sexist nature [65], and several other problems (elaborated in Sect. 2.1).

While sentiment analysis can be done by human annotations, the more common approach is to use machine learning (ML) [10,67]. While the ML approach has several benefits, such as being able to handle large quantities of data,

H. Degen and S. Ntoa (Eds.): HCII 2023, LNAI 14050, pp. 63–82, 2023.
https://doi.org/10.1007/978-3-031-35891-3_5

there are also growing concerns about the accuracy of this approach, along with the potential for introduction of bias, error, or contextual understanding. Such issues may involve reusing models trained on some specific dataset on unrelated datasets [46] or the models' failure to consider data in their contexts [6].

In this paper, we advocate for the adoption of a *human-centered machine learning* (HCML) [13] approach to sentiment analysis, as opposed to a standard ML approach. We present a case study of applying HCML to design an ML-classifier to detect and differentiate between degrees of positive emotions in a dataset of fanfiction reviews. We highlight and reflect upon the various stages of the HCML process, and evaluate the various successes and failures of our model. We conclude with recommendations for applying HCML to sentiment analysis.

2   Related Work

2.1   Sentiment Analysis Using ML

Sentiment analysis is a computational technique used to determine the presence of emotions or feelings in pieces of text [52]. There are two broad types of sentiment analysis techniques: a lexical method and an ML approach.

In the lexical method, pieces of texts are typically assigned scores based on the cumulative presence of positive or negative words based on dictionaries of word-score pairs. Though simplistic in their approach, such approaches have been demonstrated to be highly accurate according to some metrics [5]. Such algorithms break down pieces of text through techniques such as stemming (removing prefixes and suffixes e.g. 'playing' is stemmed to 'play'), computing n-grams (breaking down text into phrases instead of individual words) and Parts-of-Speech Tagging (evaluating words/phrases in conjunction with associated parts of speech). Designers of lexical sentiment analysis algorithms can leverage existing word corpora such as WordNet, SenticNet or SentiFul [48,53], though there are some known disadvantages of using them such as their failure to classify emotions into hyponymic relationships [57], low representation of words for nonbinary gender identities [31], and low accuracy outside of English [8].

The other popular approach is to use machine learning models. Such approaches typically begin with manually classifying a small chunk of data with emotions, training a model on this chunk of data (called training data), and then deploying the model on the remaining data. This approach is known as supervised learning, though variations of this exist with partially-labeled training data (semi-supervised learning) [51] or unlabeled training data (unsupervised learning) [33]. The algorithms vectorize the data similarly as their lexical counterparts (through techniques like stemming, POS tagging etc.) and then apply techniques such as Support Vector Machines [1], Naive Bayes [27], Maximum Entropy [36], Random Forest [30], K-nearest neighbors [17], or a combination of those [2,34,54]. The results of such classifications are calculated by observing the output metrics, such as Precision, Accuracy, Recall or f-score.

Both of these types of sentiment analysis methods are usually built to detect three types of emotions: Positive, Negative, or Neutral [47,58]. Other sets of emotions commonly used for sentiment analysis are Ekman's [21] six basic emotions: Anger, Disgust, Fear, Joy, Sadness and Surprise [40, 72].

However, such approaches to sentiment analysis has come under some criticism over the past few years, especially when they are used in conjunction with recommender systems that analyze users' reactions and use that data to determine what type of content to recommend. Users who are subjected to sentiment analysis processes dub them 'invasive and scary', associating them with loss of autonomy [4] as they are boiled down to single data points [38]. A similar criticism is of its potential for bias because of different types of bias baked into the training data, such as overrepresentation of content produced by men over women or gendernonbinary individuals [65] or annotators failing to recognize intentional stylistic choices inherent to specific Englishes [60]. Beyond technical challenges such as failure to recognize textual devices such as sarcasm or irony [44], ML-driven sentiment analysis algorithms should not simply be designed and deployed without careful introspection of their appropriateness, impacts and potential for harm. We believe that such an introspection is supported by a HCML approach, as we explain in the next section.

2.2   Human Centered Machine Learning

Human-centered machine learning (HCML) is defined as 'a set of practices for building, evaluating, deploying, and critiquing ML systems that balances technical innovation with an equivalent focus on human and social concerns.' [13]. It is a rising sub-field that seeks to examine the impacts of ML on individuals and communities, and how designers of such technologies can evaluate their own practices [9]. HCML is a timely area of research, as more and more ML algorithms are abandoning the previously popular publicly available corpora of text data such as WordNet [45] in favor of human-generated data that users might not even be aware is getting used for such purposes [23]. At its core lies the directive of being responsible with the 'silver bullet' that ML is widely considered to be [13] in 'a deliberate, careful, and inclusive way that will set a standard for the future of algorithmic accountability' [50].

Past researchers of HCML have put forward practices of being more human-centered in applications of ML. Such practices include considering whether ML is the right solution for a given question [13, 46], recognizing that ML algorithms contain and reflect the opinions of their annotators [13, 15], and that they might cause harm and perpetuate negative biases [64, 69]. At their core, such practices are rooted in human-centered design and design justice principles of knowing who a design is for and how designs might impact them [14, 16]. In this paper, we adopt such practices as we design a ML model to differentiate between degrees of positive emotions in online fanfiction reviews. We present this as a case study of lessons learned in a HCML approach to sentiment analysis.

3   Case Study: Detecting Degrees of Positive Sentiment in Fanfiction Reviews

Fanfiction is "writing in which fans use media narratives and pop cultural icons as inspiration for creating their own texts." [7] Online fanfiction communities are some of the most active text-based communities, supporting over 2.5 million users daily [42] in 2020, at the last time of counting, with numbers most likely having grown since then. A majority of users on popular online fanfiction communities like Fanfiction.net and Archive of Our Own (AO3) are female or gendernonbinary young adults [42,43] and their active participation has been seen to be impactful in the formation of informal mentorship networks [12], helped them explore gender identities [20] and strengthen language skills [7].

On online fanfiction communities, users can upload stories or add chapters to existing stories, and other users can respond to them by leaving reviews. These reviews are one of the most common methods of communication between users, especially since platforms like Fanfiction.net lack robust direct messaging affordances. Prior research into reviews [12,22] has found the tone of reviews to be overwhelmingly positive, with as few as 2% reviews being negative. However, with the abundance of positive reviews, it becomes important to determine degrees of positivity between them because, while reviews such as 'I like this' and 'I love this so much, this has changed my life!!' are both positive, there are very different degrees of positivity expressed in them. In this case study, we aimed to build an ML classifier to differentiate between different degrees of positive sentiment in fanfiction reviews. We work with a dataset of fanfiction reviews which contains over 176 million reviews scraped from Fanfiction.net [71].

4   Methods

4.1   Considering Appropriateness of ML

Prior to the design of our classifier, we began with considering whether ML was an appropriate approach towards the question we were trying to answer, and how our approach could potentially be harmful. Such a consideration was especially important given that that fanfiction reviews often known contain sensitive content [66], and mostly come from young adults [41].

We recognized that classifying degrees of positive emotions in a dataset of over 176 million pieces of text would not be humanly possible. An ML approach would make our task achievable, but we had to come up with some considerations of mitigating the potential harms we could cause. We decided that we would not report any reviews verbatim, such that they could either be searched in the dataset or on Fanfiction.net. We also decided that for any reviews we consider reporting, even if we are obfuscating them for anonymization, we would first check if the user who published that review still had an active account and if not, then we would not report their review in this paper. These considerations aim to protect the users' choices, since they likely did not author fanfiction reviews knowing that those reviews might one day be analyzed for research purposes [23]. We also determined that our work has a low potential for harm, since we are not producing actionable results with respect to online fanfiction communities, or using our findings to suggest interventions or changes to how such communities currently operate. Based on these considerations, we decided that our HCML approach would be appropriate for the question we aim to answer.

4.2 Positionality

We begin our case study with a consideration of our positionalities. ML models have positionality [11] because of the positions and biases, both conscious and unconscious, of their creators [19,59] and we believe that any representation of ML work is incomplete without including mention of its creators' positionalities.

All the authors of this paper have experience reading or writing fanfiction in online fanfiction communities. Some did not have this experience at the start of the project, but acquired it by immersing themselves into reading, reviewing and, in some cases, writing their own works of fanfiction over the course of this research. The first author has over six years of experience with reading and writing in online fanfiction communities, and two years' experience with studying them. Some of the fandoms to which we are most connected to are Harry Potter, Naruto, Lord of the Rings, the Marvel Comics, Batman, and Twilight, and our connections with these fandoms likely influenced how we analyzed reviews on stories related to them. All of the authors are fluent in English (though not all are native speakers or have English as their first language) but share no other language between them, a fact that prompted us to analyze only English reviews in our study. We can account for some other subconscious biases that likely impacted our manual annotation (discussed in next Section), such as annotators' preferences towards particular fandom characters, but acknowledge that there likely were several other individual or collective subconscious biases that impacted our data annotation.

4.3 Data Collection and Annotation

As mentioned before, in this study we used a dataset of over 176 million fanfiction reviews [71]. We began with a random sample of 15,000 reviews from that dataset, and removed all the non-English reviews from it to arrive at a reduced dataset of 11,292 reviews, hereafter referred to as Dataset 0. We then made two copies of this dataset, hereafter referred to as Datasets I and II.

To determine a slate of positive emotions to analyze our datasets with, we drew inspiration from a slate of review types identified by Evans et al. [22] in their work on reviews in online fanfiction communities. They identified two mutually-exclusive review types expressing different degrees of positivity (Shallow Positive and Targeted Positive) and a third non-mutually exclusive review type to label reviews excitedly asking for updates (Update Encouragement). From Ghosh et al.'s [26]'s slate of emotional expression in online fanfiction communities, we adopt three emotions to mirror the topics: Like, Joy/Happiness and Anticipation/Hope. Like and Joy/Happiness are mutually exclusive positive emotions, with Like being the milder of the two, and Anticipation/Hope is non-mutually exclusive to Like or Joy/Happiness. Due to this partially mutually and non-mutually exclusive nature of the codes, we measure agreement using the Generalized Cohen's kappa [24].

Dataset I was manually annotated entirely by the first author, and Dataset II was annotated by the remaining members of the team. During the process of annotation of Dataset II, the annotators demonstrated over 95% agreement for Anticipation/Hope, but only 52% and 63% agreements respectively for Like and Joy/Happiness. Annotations in Dataset II were consolidated by two-thirds agreement within the team. We discuss comparisons between annotations of Datasets I and II in Sects. 5.1 and 6.2.

Annotation processes involved checking whether a review contained Like or Joy/Happiness, and whether it contained Anticipation/Hope or not. Thus, each review had 6 possible annotations: (Like), (Joy/Happiness), (Anticipation/Hope), (Like, Anticipation/Hope), (Joy/Happiness, Anticipation/Hope), and (None). None was used for all negative reviews (e.g. 'I hate this'), as well as those stating facts (e.g. 'Harry Potter was the son of Lily and James Potter').

During the annotation processes, a debate arose of how annotators could distinguish between Like and Joy/Happiness, since such distinctions could be incredibly subjective. Anticipation/Hope was easier to recognize, with the presence of phrases such as 'I hope...', 'I'm excited for the next update' or 'Please update soon'. Similarly, annotators agreed upon which reviews did not contain any of the three positive emotions.

After annotating the first 1000 reviews, annotators identified seven common aspects of reviews expressing Like or Joy/Happiness, mentioned in Table 1. For each of these, we believed that their presence in a review indicated a higher positive emotion than an absence, because the reviewer made a conscious decision to use such aspects. We annotated another 1000 reviews and, having observed patterns of reviews being labeled as Like or Joy/Happiness, determined that any positive review that contained 4 or more of the aspects mentioned in Table 1 could be strong candidates for Joy/Happiness. However, annotators still used their own interpretations of review contents to determine whether a given review with less than 4 of these aspects could still be considered Joy/Happiness, or whether a review with 4 or more of these could still be annotated with Like. We did so to retain the human element in annotation, rather than designing a rule that could be mechanically applied.

We completed our annotations of Datasets I and II using these rules, and compared differences at the end.

4.4 Model Design and Training

Our ML model is a supervised Naive Bayes classifier. Naive Bayes algorithms are some of the most popular for text classification [29,56], and for our use case, its assumption of independence of features across data points holds true. We also considered Linear Support Vector Classification (SVC) approaches, but Naive

Table 1. Aspects of Positive Reviews, used for Annotation.

Aspect	Sample Usage
Intentional Capitalization	I LOVE this
Emoticons	I <3 this
Exclamation Points	I love this!
Repetition	I love love love this
Intentional Misspelling	I loooooove this
Actions	*dies* I love this
Keyboard Smashing	askhwwifnwwervbu I love this

Bayes performs better over datasets containing short pieces of text over those containing longer pieces of text [68], making it more appropriate for our use. We experimented with the Bernoulli Naive Bayes model and the Multinomial Naive Bayes models, but abandoned those because of their poor performance [55] to deal with unbalanced datasets such as ours where we expect far more reviews to be classified with at least one positive emotion than not. We thus chose a Complement Naive Bayes model, because of its known effectiveness in accurately classifying unbalanced text data [55].

We preprocessed our data by filtering out all non-English reviews, and tokenized them with TF-IDF Vectorizers [61]. Given the gulf in size between our training data (11,292) and test data (over 176 million), we performed Laplace smoothing by setting the alpha hyperparameter to 0.07, a value experimentally determined. Based on our annotation, we identified and built a list of stop words appropriate for our dataset.

We trained two different models, hereafter referred to as Prototype Models I and II, for testing purposes. Prototype Model I was trained on a random sample of 2000 reviews from Dataset I, and used to classify the remaining reviews in Dataset I. Similarly, Prototype Model II was trained on a random sample of 2000 reviews from Dataset II, and used to classify the remaining reviews in Dataset II. In these classifications, Prototype Model II returned an overall f-score of 0.67, far superior to Prototype Model I's score of 0.23. Prototype Model II's better performance was also confirmed by manual examination of the reviews classified by both Prototype Models I and II. We thus adopted Dataset II as our 'ground truth' dataset, both because it led to more accurate classifications and because it represented the opinions of a larger majority within the research team. We discuss this further in Sect. 6.2.

After identifying the ground truth dataset, we continued fine-tuning Prototype Model II. This process consisted of modifying both the algorithm code and re-auditing Dataset II to be more consistent in the annotations. Through this process, we identified a few issues that we could fix, such as a bug in emoticon recognition, and some misclicked annotations in Dataset II. A few iterations through these issues resulted in an increased overall f-score of 0.76. We tested it further by obtaining and classifying a random sample of 1000 reviews from the master dataset, and manual examination of these classified reviews showed over 90% true positives. At this stage, we were satisfied with the model.

We then applied the trained model over full dataset of over 176 million reviews. The algorithm was executed on the Mox supercomputer at the University of Washington, Seattle. Once it returned an output dataset of classified reviews, we randomly selected a sample of 10,000 reviews to manually examine.

5   Results

5.1   Comparing Datasets I and II

Because the performance of supervised ML models are direct results of the data they are trained on, we began our analysis by taking a look at this training data. We compared annotations in Dataset I (annotated entirely by the first author) and Dataset II (annotated by the rest of the researchers) to examine similarities and differences between the two. These results are depicted in Table 2. All numbers are out of 11,292 reviews.

Table 2. Comparison of Annotations of Datasets I (annotated by first author) and II (annotated by other members of research team. All numbers out of 11,292 reviews.

Emotions	Reviews Annotated with Emotion in Dataset I	Reviews Annotated with Emotion in Dataset II
Like	4,537	3,966
Joy/Happiness	3,268	2,912
Anticipation/Hope	851	803
Like, Anticipation/Hope	1,167	1,662
Joy/Happiness, Anticipation/Hope	923	1,631
None	346	318

We also present a set of examples of reviews where annotators of Datasets I and II differed in their applications of Like and Joy/Happiness, along with their rationale for their annotation. These are depicted in Table 3.

Through our observations in Table 2, we find that the first author interpreted more reviews as expressing a single emotion (e.g. Like or Joy/Happiness), while the rest of the researchers identified more reviews with a combination of emotions (e.g. Like, Anticipation/Hope or Joy/Happiness, Anticipation/Hope). We also observe that annotators of both Datasets have high agreement for reviews that either show no positive emotion (i.e. annotated with None) or express Anticipation/Hope, but differ greatly in their interpretations of Like and Joy/Happiness.

Table 3. Examples of Disagreement between Annotations of Like and Joy/Happiness in Datasets I and II.

Review Text	Annotation in Dataset I	Annotation in Dataset II
It's such a great story for your first time. Thank you for sharing your stories with us!	Like	Joy/Happiness
LOVE this story. Very well written!	Joy/Happiness	Like
Absolutely fell in love with this story. Please with a cherry on top continue!	Joy/Happiness, Anticipation/Hope	Like, Anticipation/Hope
Hurray! Congrats for becoming a published author! I am waiting to buy your book! :D	Like, Anticipation/Hope	Joy/Happiness, Anticipation/Hope

5.2 Model Performance

We report the performance of our model in terms of its f-score, given the unbalanced nature of our dataset. Our model returned an overall f-score of 0.694, with individual f-scores of 0.829 for Anticipation/Hope, 0.601 for Joy/Happiness and 0.622 for Like. Based on our manual examination of 10,000 randomly selected reviews, we identified 77.2% reviews where we agreed with the model's classification. The breakdown for this random set is shown in Table 4, and some sample disagreements of annotation are shown in Table 5.

Table 4. Results from manual examination of classified reviews.

Emotions	Number of Annotations	Number of Manually-determined True Positives
Like	4,691	3,462 (74%)
Joy/Happiness	3,378	2,744 (81%)
Anticipation/Hope	699	628 (90%)
Like, Anticipation/Hope	302	117 (39%)
Joy/Happiness, Anticipation/Hope	886	730 (82%)
None	44	42 (95%)

We thus observe that our model is moderately successful at identifying the emotions Like, Joy/Happiness, Anticipation/Hope or some combination of those in online fanfiction reviews. We observe that it does better for Anticipation/Hope than for Like or Joy/Happiness, both in terms of performance metrics and

Table 5. Examples of Disagreement between ML Classifier and Human Annotation

Review Text	Model Classification	Human Annotation
It ends here? But I also love the happy ending. Do a sequel!	Anticipation/Hope	Like, Anticipation/Hope
LOVE THIS! I read it all in one day, it's so amazing!!	Like	Joy/Happiness
this is great	Joy/Happiness	Like
I'm so angry you stopped here	None	Anticipation/Hope
oh my gosh this is SO good!:)) I love this, I hope you update soon! *eager waiting*	Like, Anticipation/Hope	Joy/Happiness, Anticipation/Hope

upon manual observation. The high performance for Anticipation/Hope can be attributed to the high agreement between annotators of Dataset II, which led to high-quality of training data annotated with Anticipation/Hope. This implies the model's success in being able to identify a positive emotion when it does not need to distinguish between two mutually-exclusive ones.

The fact that human annotators (both within Dataset II and across Datasets I and II) could not consistently identify Like and Joy/Happiness explains the model's relatively lower confidence in classifying reviews with either of those emotions. We cannot be sure about the model's confidence in classifying reviews with a combination of Anticipation/Hope and either Like or Joy/Happiness because of the lack of a numerical metric representing the entire dataset, but from the disagreements between human annotators and the possibly moderately-low quality of training data supplied, we believe that such classifications are going to be moderately accurate across the dataset.

6   Reflecting on Our Design Process

6.1   Pre-Design Stage: Consideration of Appropriateness

One of the fundamental principles in human-centered design is to consider the potential harms that can come from designing a piece of technology, and whether it should be designed at all. Chancellor [13] encapsulates this within HCML practices as a directive to 'ensure ML is the right solution and approach to take'. We believe that it is important to have this conversation *before* beginning to approach the solution, since it can reveal potential harms of using ML and therefore inform the approach of mitigating such harms. This practice is rooted in design justice [16] principles of prioritizing the impact of design over the intent of the designers.

In our case, we considered ML to be an appropriate approach because it would be able to handle our large dataset better than manual annotation could and, more importantly, we did not foresee much potential for harm because we are not deploying our algorithm to a real-world setting. Were we to do so, and if our algorithm would interpret fanfiction reviewers' words and determine what content to recommend them next, then we would have had to make very different considerations before we built the algorithm.

However, we do not believe that refusing to pursue an ML approach to sentiment analysis is a viable answer, though such notions of design refusal are present both in Chancellor's work [13] and in design justice principles [16]. ML-driven sentiment analysis processes are fairly well-deployed in several systems used by millions around the world, and refusal to design future systems would not alleviate the issues caused by the existing ones. Instead, we call for present and future designers of such systems to be more human-centered in their approach, reflecting upon the power and potential for harm within their design, and strive for algorithmic fairness [3]. These reflections can occur by asking questions like who participated in the design process and who did not, and who benefits from or is harmed by the design [63].

6.2 Training Stage: Working with Subjective Interpretations of Emotions

That ML models reflect and replicate the biases and opinions embedded within its training data has been repeatedly demonstrated over the past few years. Chancellor [13] calls upon HCML designers to 'acknowledge that ML problem statements take positions' and recommends designers publish position statements along with their work or documentation of the influence of individual perspectives on the algorithm. We take this one step further by directly demonstrating the differences between two models trained on the same dataset but annotated differently.

We prepared Datasets I and II as the same copies of Dataset 0, but with one fundamental difference: they were annotated by different people. Dataset I was annotated by the first author and therefore contained only their interpretation of the three positive emotions and differences between them. Dataset II was annotated by the rest of the research team and consolidated by two-thirds majority, meaning that it reflected a strong majority opinion of the research team. A manual examination of the two (Table 2) shows big differences in Like and Joy/Happiness, and this is confirmed by the gulf in scores between Prototype Models I and II trained on Datasets I and II respectively. Examination of specific reviews where annotators differed (shown in Table 3) give specific insights into why such differences occurred, particularly between Like and Joy/Happiness. For instance, the review in the first row of Table 3 is considered Like by the first author in Dataset I, but the fact that the reviewer acknowledges the greatness of the story given it's the author's writing debut was considered by annotators of Dataset II to warrant a label of Joy/Happiness.

By designing and observing the differences between Datasets I and II, we gain an insight into a core issue with sentiment analysis – if interpretations of human emotions are so subjective and if two groups of human annotators can annotate the same dataset so differently, how can sentiment analysis algorithms claim to have reliable understandings of human emotion? The differences across Datasets I and II remind us to continually be aware that our ML model replicates *our* interpretation of the differences between Like and Joy/Happiness. Such interpretations might not align with those of others and so, a different group of designers working with the same problem statement and dataset might have produced completely different results. In our advocacy for a HCML approach to sentiment analysis, we encourage future designers of ML-driven sentiment analysis algorithms (elaborated in Sect. 7) to consider the inherent ambiguity and human subjectivity of sentiment analysis [15] and thus adopt a sociotechnical approach to sentiment analysis which centers and seeks input from the direct users of the algorithms [4].

This exercise also allows us to imagine how Prototype Models I and II would have behaved very differently were they both applied to the entire dataset of 176 million reviews, based on the differences in their respective training datasets. It demonstrates how subjectivities that are embedded within the training data of ML models are replicated in the application of the models, such that their results are also subjective. We believe that in working with ML, it is important to understand just how closely design is tied to designers, especially when systems designed by the few affect the lives of many. This is especially important when making claims about the accuracy or effectiveness of sentiment analysis algorithms, because a model can only accurately identify emotions that the annotators of its training data would agree with, and to claim any accuracy beyond that is unfair (discussed further in Sect. 7.2).

6.3   Design Stage: Prototyping and Iteration

Another aspect of human-centered design is prototyping and iteration, which we consider important to HCML processes. After we determined the annotated Dataset II to be our ground truth dataset, we performed a few rounds of prototyping and iteration before running it on the full dataset. These were relatively low-cost processes, such as spot-checking the accurate functioning of the emoticon recognition or performing automated searches through the annotated datasets to verify no annotations were mistyped. Though low-cost, these processes greatly benefitted our design, with the final version of Prototype Model II demonstrating better performance than its original one.

We would like to see more importance given to prototyping and iteration within the HCML process. This is especially relevant to ML-driven sentiment analysis algorithms which are deployed in conjunction with recommender systems. In such cases, iteration can involve large user testing or signing up potential users to evaluate and comment on small sections of the system.

6.4 Evaluation Stage: Measuring Performance Through Manual Examination and Anticipating Failure

Finally, we focus on the evaluation of our algorithm, moving beyond quantitative metrics of performance and focusing on manual examination of classified reviews. For sentiment analysis problems, we hold manual verification to be especially important, preferably by involving people who might be eventual users. Since we did not have any future users of our algorithm, we performed the manual verification ourselves.

Our moderately successful classifier performance is underwhelming, especially in light of most ML algorithms reporting high successes [32, 70], because our model is not able to reliably distinguish between degrees of positive emotions. However, the result is not surprising because we can attribute it to the researchers' inability to, between themselves, could not determine a rigid rule for what constituted Like and what elevated it to Joy/Happiness. The closest we came was to determine a set of common aspects of reviews we believed expressed Joy/Happiness (Table 1), but even then we did not feel that it would be accurate to say that for a review to be considered Joy/Happiness, it had to have more than half of those. Such a rule would have taken away from the fact that different people express degrees of positivity in different ways, and their typed-out text might not always encapsulate the exact strengths of their emotions. It would not have been realistic to expect a model trained on data that did not have a clear pattern to be able to infer such nuances, and thus we went in expecting moderate results.

Such algorithmic failure was anticipated given the subjectivity of our annotations and instead of considering it a defeat, we use it as an opportunity to improve our understanding of how HCML should work. In line with Chen et al. [15], we advocate for using manual examination as a means to better understand how and where annotators disagree. For sentiment analysis problems, such manual examination can reveal scenarios where two annotators disagree with the machine classification of sentiment, which can be then pursued to examine how these two annotators' opinions are embedded within the ground truth dataset.

Above all, we imagine a HCML approach to set realistic and human-centered expectations, instead of imagining ML as a magical force with unlimited potential. Designers of ML algorithms must remember at every step of the way that models only amplify their own opinions, and that it can be very easy to think of their results as 'highly accurate' if the results confirm the designers' opinions. Therefore, designers must involve direct users of the algorithms throughout the design process, especially during the training and evaluation stages, to see if the opinions of designers align with those of users. For sentiment analysis, where the opinions are as subjective as the interpretation of human emotions, this might lead to results that score low on quantitative metrics and show large disagreements between annotators and machine classifications. We advocate for such results to be considered valid, instead of designers manipulating the training data to chase higher scores.

7   Recommendations for Applying HCML to Sentiment Analysis

7.1   Consider Alternative Approaches

Given the aforementioned criticisms against both ML in general and specifically sentiment analysis via ML, we recommend that before taking such an approach, designers carefully consider whether other alternative approaches could be appropriate. Some potential alternatives could be manual analysis of affect in text, or directly asking users to elaborate on their own emotions when they author some text. Such considerations are especially important when sentiment analysis is used to predict user behavior, such as in recommender systems.

7.2   Manually Annotate Your Own Data

We believe that it is important for researchers to train their ML models on data that resembles the data to which the model would be eventually applied, instead of relying on existing datasets of words assosciated with emotions. The reasons for this are twofold. Firstly, manual annotation of data which closely resembles the target data will give designers some insights inherently unique to their data. For our case study, one example of such an insight was the emergence of a set of stopwords, prompting us to use them instead of existing libraries. Secondly, such manual annotation inserts the researchers' own positions into the algorithm such that the views of the model represent the views of the designers instead of those of the creators of other datasets. This creates a sense of algorithmic accountability with emotion recognition [4], which is important in cases of breakdown and failure. This should also serve to help designers represent their work in the most honest way. Rather than saying 'my classifier accurately identifies positive emotions', a more accurate representation would be 'my classifier accurately identifies emotions I think are positive'. We believe that such representations of ML work, centering around the designers or data handlers, must become more common, so that consumers of the work can be more informed.

7.3   Manually Examine Classifier Performance and Involve End-Users

While most ML classifiers report quantitative metrics of evaluation such as f-scores, we recommend that designers of ML-driven sentiment analysis algorithms evaluate their work through manual examination of classified reviews. This can begin during the training stage and reveal insights into potential errors in the process, as it did for us when it showed us that some annotators mislabeled a few reviews. Identifying and rectifying these labels led to a more accurate algorithm, something we would not have achieved were it not for manual examination.

However, manual examination must be considered of highest importance during the classification stage, just prior to deployment. At that stage, the model is likely operating on real people's data, and any issues that exist at this stage will later effect real users if not rectified. This is also a good exercise in identifying potentially harmful algorithmic classifications, such as perpetuating racist stereotypes by labeling speech from Black women as 'angry' [49].

Thus, this is an opportune moment to subject the algorithm to user testing, one of the most important pieces of the human-centered design process. Designers at this stage can recruit a panel of potential users and test whether they agree with the machine classifications. Low agreement between the user and the classifier can be identified early, before the algorithm is deployed and assigns incorrect labels to user emotions.

7.4 Accept and Expect Underwhelming Results

Finally, we ask that developers of ML-driven sentiment analysis algorithms prepare for and accept underwhelming performances from their algorithms. Even though today's world is driven by demands of high speed and high accuracy, designers must realize that interpretations of sentiments are inherently subjective and trying to predict just how much positivity or negativity is embedded within a piece of text might not be accurate for a large number of people. Realizing the limits of one's model might result in more conservative application and deployment, and careful consideration of its ability to predict human behavior.

8 Conclusion

In this paper, we performed a case study of a Human-Centered Machine Learning approach to a sentiment analysis problem over a very large text corpus. We attempted to differentiate between different degrees of positive emotions in over 176 million reviews of online fanfiction, defining two mutually-exclusive positive emotions of different degrees (Like and Joy/Happiness), and a third emotion not mutually-exclusive to those (Anticipation/Hope). We began with a consideration of whether ML would be appropriate for this problem and, once we resolved it, continued with trying to identify the various positions we were bringing to the data. We demonstrated the impact of differently encoded data on a model's performance, through the creation of two datasets annotated by different researchers. Our model demonstrates underwhelming results, which points to the inherently subjective nature of differentiating between degrees of positive emotions. We concluded with some recommendations for future designers of ML-driven sentiment analysis algorithms including going through stages of the human-centered design process by manually annotating their own data and examining the classified data through user testing, as we hope that they would consider a HCML approach.

As ML becomes more and more popularly used as a solution to problems in most fields, we believe that it is important for designers to consider the very real possibilities of causing harm. A Human-Centered Machine Learning practice might alleviate some of those possibilities, and do right by the communities that are subject to these algorithms.

References

1. Ahmad, M., Aftab, S., Ali, I.: Sentiment analysis of tweets using svm. Int. J. Comput. Appl. **177**(5), 25–29 (2017)
2. Al Amrani, Y., Lazaar, M., El Kadiri, K.E.: Random forest and support vector machine based hybrid approach to sentiment analysis. Procedia Comput. Sci. **127**, 511–520 (2018)
3. Altman, M., Wood, A., Vayena, E.: A harm-reduction framework for algorithmic fairness. IEEE Secur. Privacy **16**(3), 34–45 (2018)
4. Andalibi, N., Buss, J.: The human in emotion recognition on social media: attitudes, outcomes, risks. In: Proceedings of the 2020 CHI Conference on Human Factors in Computing Systems, pp. 1–16 (2020)
5. Annett, M., Kondrak, G.: A comparison of sentiment analysis techniques: polarizing movie blogs. In: Bergler, S. (ed.) AI 2008. LNCS (LNAI), vol. 5032, pp. 25–35. Springer, Heidelberg (2008). https://doi.org/10.1007/978-3-540-68825-9_3
6. Aragon, C., Guha, S., Kogan, M., Muller, M., Neff, G.: Human-Centered Data Science: An Introduction. MIT Press (2022)
7. Black, R.W.: Language, culture, and identity in online fanfiction. E-learning Digital Media **3**(2), 170–184 (2006)
8. Bond, F., Foster, R.: Linking and extending an open multilingual wordnet. In: Proceedings of the 51st Annual Meeting of the Association for Computational Linguistics (Volume 1: Long Papers), pp. 1352–1362 (2013)
9. Boyd, D., Crawford, K.: Critical questions for big data: provocations for a cultural, technological, and scholarly phenomenon. Inf. Commun. Soc. **15**(5), 662–679 (2012)
10. Burnap, P., Rana, O.F., Avis, N., Williams, M., Housley, W., Edwards, A., Morgan, J., Sloan, L.: Detecting tension in online communities with computational twitter analysis. Technol. Forecast. Soc. Chang. **95**, 96–108 (2015)
11. Cambo, S.A., Gergle, D.: Model positionality and computational reflexivity: promoting reflexivity in data science. In: CHI Conference on Human Factors in Computing Systems, pp. 1–19 (2022)
12. Campbell, J., Aragon, C., Davis, K., Evans, S., Evans, A., Randall, D.: Thousands of positive reviews: distributed mentoring in online fan communities. In: Proceedings of the 19th ACM Conference on Computer-Supported Cooperative Work & Social Computing, pp. 691–704 (2016)
13. Chancellor, S.: Towards practices for human-centered machine learning. arXiv preprint arXiv:2203.00432 (2022)
14. Chancellor, S., Baumer, E.P., De Choudhury, M.: Who is the "human" in human-centered machine learning: the case of predicting mental health from social media. In: Proceedings of the ACM on Human-Computer Interaction 3(CSCW), pp. 1–32 (2019)
15. Chen, N.C., Drouhard, M., Kocielnik, R., Suh, J., Aragon, C.R.: Using machine learning to support qualitative coding in social science: shifting the focus to ambiguity. ACM Trans. Interact. Intell. Syst. (TiiS) **8**(2), 1–20 (2018)
16. Costanza-Chock, S.: Design justice: community-led practices to build the worlds we need. The MIT Press (2020)
17. Daeli, N.O.F., Adiwijaya, A.: Sentiment analysis on movie reviews using information gain and k-nearest neighbor. J. Data Sci. Appl. **3**(1), 1–7 (2020)
18. Díaz, M., Johnson, I., Lazar, A., Piper, A.M., Gergle, D.: Addressing age-related bias in sentiment analysis. In: Proceedings of the 2018 CHI Conference on Human Factors in Computing Systems, pp. 1–14 (2018)

19. Draude, C., Klumbyte, G., Lücking, P., Treusch, P.: Situated algorithms: a sociotechnical systemic approach to bias. Online Information Review (2019)
20. Dym, B., Brubaker, J.R., Fiesler, C., Semaan, B.: "Coming out okay" community narratives for LGBTQ identity recovery work. In: Proceedings of the ACM on Human-Computer Interaction 3(CSCW), pp. 1–28 (2019). https://doi.org/10.1145/3359256. https://dl.acm.org/doi/10.1145/3359256
21. Ekman, P.: All emotions are basic. The nature of emotion: Fundamental questions, pp. 15–19 (1994)
22. Evans, S., Davis, K., Evans, A., Campbell, J.A., Randall, D.P., Yin, K., Aragon, C.: More than peer production: Fanfiction communities as sites of distributed mentoring. In: Proceedings of the 2017 ACM Conference on Computer Supported Cooperative Work and Social Computing, pp. 259–272 (2017)
23. Fiesler, C., Proferes, N.: "Participant" perceptions of twitter research ethics. Social Media+ Society 4(1), 2056305118763366 (2018)
24. Figueroa, A., Ghosh, S., Aragon, C.: Generalized cohen's kappa: a novel inter-rater reliability metric for non-mutually exclusive categories. In: Proceedings of the Human Interface and the Management of Information Thematic Area in the context of the 25th International Conference on Human-Computer Interaction (HCI International). Springer (2023)
25. Ghosh, S., Figueroa, A.: Establishing tiktok as a platform for informal learning: Evidence from mixed-methods analysis of creators and viewers. In: Proceedings of the 56th Hawaii International Conference on System Sciences, pp. 2431–2440 (2023)
26. Ghosh, S., Froelich, N., Aragon, C.: "i love you, my dear friend": analyzing the role of emotions in the building of friendships in online fanfiction communities. In: Proceedings of the 15th International Conference on Social Computing and Social Media in the context of the 25th International Conference on Human-Computer Interaction (HCI International). Springer (2023)
27. Goel, A., Gautam, J., Kumar, S.: Real time sentiment analysis of tweets using naive bayes. In: 2016 2nd International Conference on Next Generation Computing Technologies (NGCT), pp. 257–261. IEEE (2016)
28. Gui, X., Chen, Y., Kou, Y., Pine, K., Chen, Y.: Investigating support seeking from peers for pregnancy in online health communities. In: Proceedings of the ACM on Human-Computer Interaction 1(CSCW), pp. 1–19 (2017)
29. Gupta, A., Lamba, H., Kumaraguru, P., Joshi, A.: Faking sandy: characterizing and identifying fake images on twitter during hurricane sandy. In: Proceedings of the 22nd International Conference on World Wide Web, pp. 729–736 (2013)
30. Hegde, Y., Padma, S.: Sentiment analysis using random forest ensemble for mobile product reviews in kannada. In: 2017 IEEE 7th International Advance Computing Conference (IACC), pp. 777–782. IEEE (2017)
31. Hicks, A., Rutherford, M., Fellbaum, C., Bian, J.: An analysis of wordnet's coverage of gender identity using twitter and the national transgender discrimination survey. In: Proceedings of the 8th Global WordNet Conference (GWC), pp. 123–130 (2016)
32. Hong, L., Doumith, A.S., Davison, B.D.: Co-factorization machines: modeling user interests and predicting individual decisions in twitter. In: Proceedings of the sixth ACM International Conference on Web Search and Data Mining, pp. 557–566 (2013)
33. Hu, X., Tang, J., Gao, H., Liu, H.: Unsupervised sentiment analysis with emotional signals. In: Proceedings of the 22nd International Conference on World Wide Web, pp. 607–618 (2013)

34. Huq, M.R., Ahmad, A., Rahman, A.: Sentiment analysis on twitter data using KNN and svm. Int. J. Adv. Comput. Sci. Appl. **8**(6) (2017)
35. Kassens-Noor, E.: Twitter as a teaching practice to enhance active and informal learning in higher education: the case of sustainable tweets. Act. Learn. High. Educ. **13**(1), 9–21 (2012)
36. Kaya, M., Fidan, G., Toroslu, I.H.: Sentiment analysis of Turkish political news. In: 2012 IEEE/WIC/ACM International Conferences on Web Intelligence and Intelligent Agent Technology, vol. 1, pp. 174–180. IEEE (2012)
37. Kivran-Swaine, F., Brody, S., Diakopoulos, N., Naaman, M.: Of joy and gender: emotional expression in online social networks. In: The ACM Conference on Computer Supported Cooperative Work Companion, pp. 139–142 (2012)
38. Lazer, D., Pentland, A., Adamic, L., Aral, S., Barabási, A.L., Brewer, D., Christakis, N., Contractor, N., Fowler, J., Gutmann, M., et al.: Computational social science. Science **323**(5915), 721–723 (2009)
39. Levonian, Z., Dow, M., Erikson, D., Ghosh, S., Miller Hillberg, H., Narayanan, S., Terveen, L., Yarosh, S.: Patterns of patient and caregiver mutual support connections in an online health community. In: Proceedings of the ACM on Human-Computer Interaction **4**(CSCW3), pp. 1–46 (2021)
40. López-Chau, A., Valle-Cruz, D., Sandoval-Almazán, R.: Sentiment analysis of twitter data through machine learning techniques. In: Ramachandran, M., Mahmood, Z. (eds.) Software Engineering in the Era of Cloud Computing. CCN, pp. 185–209. Springer, Cham (2020). https://doi.org/10.1007/978-3-030-33624-0_8
41. Lulu: The slow dance of the infinite stars (2013)
42. Lulu: Archive of our own: 2020 statistics, November 2020
43. Lulu: Archive of our own: Overall gender and sexuality of ao3 users, November 2020
44. Maynard, D.G., Greenwood, M.A.: Who cares about sarcastic tweets? investigating the impact of sarcasm on sentiment analysis. In: Lrec 2014 proceedings. ELRA (2014)
45. Miller, G.A.: Wordnet: a lexical database for English. Commun. ACM **38**(11), 39–41 (1995)
46. Mohammad, S.M.: Ethics sheet for automatic emotion recognition and sentiment analysis. Comput. Linguist. **48**(2), 239–278 (2022)
47. Nasukawa, T., Yi, J.: Sentiment analysis: capturing favorability using natural language processing. In: Proceedings of the 2nd International Conference on Knowledge Capture, pp. 70–77 (2003)
48. Neviarouskaya, A., Prendinger, H., Ishizuka, M.: Sentiful: a lexicon for sentiment analysis. IEEE Trans. Affect. Comput. **2**(1), 22–36 (2011)
49. Noble, S.U.: Algorithms of oppression. In: Algorithms of Oppression. New York University Press (2018)
50. O'neil, C.: Weapons of math destruction: How big data increases inequality and threatens democracy. Broadway books (2016)
51. Ortigosa-Hernández, J., Rodríguez, J.D., Alzate, L., Lucania, M., Inza, I., Lozano, J.A.: Approaching sentiment analysis by using semi-supervised learning of multi-dimensional classifiers. Neurocomputing **92**, 98–115 (2012)
52. Pang, B., Lee, L., et al.: Opinion mining and sentiment analysis. Found. Trends Inf. Retrieval **2**(1–2), 1–135 (2008)
53. Poria, S., Gelbukh, A., Cambria, E., Yang, P., Hussain, A., Durrani, T.: Merging senticnet and wordnet-affect emotion lists for sentiment analysis. In: 2012 IEEE 11th International Conference on Signal Processing, vol. 2, pp. 1251–1255. IEEE (2012)

54. Rana, S., Singh, A.: Comparative analysis of sentiment orientation using SVM and naive bayes techniques. In: 2016 2nd International Conference on Next Generation Computing Technologies (NGCT), pp. 106–111. IEEE (2016)

55. Rennie, J.D., Shih, L., Teevan, J., Karger, D.R.: Tackling the poor assumptions of naive bayes text classifiers. In: Proceedings of the 20th International Conference on Machine Learning (ICML-03), pp. 616–623 (2003)

56. Roback, A., Hemphill, L.: "i'd have to vote against you" issue campaigning via Twitter. In: Proceedings of the 2013 Conference on Computer Supported Cooperative Work Companion, pp. 259–262 (2013)

57. Rudnicka, E., Bond, F., Grabowski, Ł., Piasecki, M., Piotrowski, T.: Lexical perspective on wordnet to wordnet mapping. In: Proceedings of the 9th Global Wordnet Conference, pp. 209–218 (2018)

58. Saif, H., He, Y., Alani, H.: Semantic Sentiment analysis of Twitter. In: Cudré-Mauroux, P., Heflin, J., Sirin, E., Tudorache, T., Euzenat, J., Hauswirth, M., Parreira, J.X., Hendler, J., Schreiber, G., Bernstein, A., Blomqvist, E. (eds.) ISWC 2012. LNCS, vol. 7649, pp. 508–524. Springer, Heidelberg (2012). https://doi.org/10.1007/978-3-642-35176-1_32

59. Scheuerman, M.K., Wade, K., Lustig, C., Brubaker, J.R.: How we've taught algorithms to see identity: Constructing race and gender in image databases for facial analysis. Proceedings of the ACM on Human-computer Interaction 4(CSCW1), 1–35 (2020)

60. Shen, J.H., Fratamico, L., Rahwan, I., Rush, A.M.: Darling or babygirl? investigating stylistic bias in sentiment analysis. In: Proc. of FATML (2018)

61. Singh, A.K., Shashi, M.: Vectorization of text documents for identifying unifiable news articles. Int. J. Adv. Comput. Sci. Appl. **10**(7) (2019)

62. Stanoevska-Slabeva, K., Schmid, B.F.: A typology of online communities and community supporting platforms. In: Proceedings of the 34th Annual Hawaii International Conference on System Sciences, pp. 10-pp. IEEE (2001)

63. Sterling, S., Marton, H.: Design justice: an exhibit of emerging design practices, vol. 2. The Allied Media Conference (2016)

64. Suresh, H., Guttag, J.: A framework for understanding sources of harm throughout the machine learning life cycle. In: Equity and Access in Algorithms, Mechanisms, and Optimization, pp. 1–9 (2021)

65. Thelwall, M.: Gender bias in sentiment analysis. Online Information Review (2018)

66. Tosenberger, C.: "Oh my god, the fanfiction!": Dumbledore's outing and the online harry potter fandom. Children's Literature Association Quarterly **33**(2), 200–206 (2008)

67. Venigalla, A.S.M., Chimalakonda, S., Vagavolu, D.: Mood of india during covid-19-an interactive web portal based on emotion analysis of twitter data. In: Conference Companion Publication of the 2020 on Computer Supported Cooperative Work and Social Computing, pp. 65–68 (2020)

68. Wang, S.I., Manning, C.D.: Baselines and bigrams: Simple, good sentiment and topic classification. In: Proceedings of the 50th Annual Meeting of the Association for Computational Linguistics (Volume 2: Short Papers), pp. 90–94 (2012)

69. Wiens, J., Saria, S., Sendak, M., Ghassemi, M., Liu, V.X., Doshi-Velez, F., Jung, K., Heller, K., Kale, D., Saeed, M., et al.: Do no harm: a roadmap for responsible machine learning for health care. Nat. Med. **25**(9), 1337–1340 (2019)

70. Yang, X., Steck, H., Liu, Y.: Circle-based recommendation in online social networks. In: Proceedings of the 18th ACM SIGKDD International Conference on Knowledge Discovery and Data Mining, pp. 1267–1275 (2012)

71. Yin, K., Aragon, C., Evans, S., Davis, K.: Where no one has gone before: a meta-dataset of the world's largest fanfiction repository. In: Proceedings of the 2017 CHI Conference on Human Factors in Computing Systems, pp. 6106–6110 (2017)
72. Zadeh, A., Chen, M., Poria, S., Cambria, E., Morency, L.P.: Tensor fusion network for multimodal sentiment analysis. Empirical Methods in Natural Language Processing (2017)

Therapist Perceptions of Automated Deception Detection in Mental Health Applications

Sayde L. King[1(✉)] [ID], Najare Johnson[2] [ID], Kristin Kosyluk[3] [ID], and Tempestt Neal[1] [ID]

[1] Department of Computer Science and Engineering, University of South Florida, Tampa, FL, USA
saydeking@usf.edu
[2] College of Psychology, Nova Southeastern University, Fort Lauderdale, FL, USA
[3] Department of Mental Health Law and Policy, University of South Florida, Tampa, FL, USA

Abstract. This paper discusses the results of a qualitative study which assessed the perceptions of mental health professionals ($N = 15$) on the use of artificial intelligence for deception detection in therapy sessions. Four themes emerged from coding analysis of the interview data, including Functional Components of the Computer Science Implementation, Perceptions of the Computer Science Implementation, Integration of the Computer Science Implementation, and Suggestions. These themes encompass feedback from practicing mental health professionals suggesting a potential use case for automated deception detection in mental health, albeit considerations for confidentiality, client autonomy, data access, and therapist-client trust.

Keywords: qualitative analysis · AI and mental health · deception detection research

1 Introduction

Deception is defined as "intentionally causing an individual to accept false statements as one(s) that are true" [14]. Deception detection began in the 1930s when research efforts emerged to measure the accuracy of human observers or interviewers at detecting deception from another individual [22]. Deception detection has continued to develop, with recent work leveraging artificial intelligence (AI), using modalities such as eye gaze, body gestures, or facial expressions (e.g., [8,19,20,24,25]) as measures of deceiving behaviors. This paper examines the perceptions of utilizing AI by mental health professionals for automated deception detection in mental health settings.

This study is significant given that there are particularly dangerous outcomes associated with deception in mental health, while studies show that mental

Research reported in this publication was supported by the Alfred P. Sloan University Center of Exemplary Mentoring under award number (G-2017-9717).

health professionals do not perform significantly better than chance in detecting deception [11,13]. For example, Simon et al. [28] found that for 39% of suicide attempts and 36% of suicide deaths, these patients responded "not at all" to their questionnaire item "[Have you experienced] thoughts that you would be better off dead or of hurting yourself in some way." Another study found that 60% of patients who died by suicide did not express suicidal ideation in a psychiatric setting [23]. As such, deception in therapeutic settings inhibits the professional's ability to provide care, potentially leading to life-threatening adverse outcomes.

One might argue that perhaps these research findings are not an indication that individuals deny suicidal ideation even though they are having thoughts of suicide, but instead that they were in fact not thinking of suicide at the time they were asked about it. Additional research has further explored the possibility that those experiencing suicidal ideation may deny this experience when asked. This research suggests that many people who are truly suicidal do not disclose [5,7, 18]. One study suggested one in three psychotherapy patients report lying about having suicidal thoughts when asked in a therapy session [7]. Over 70% of these individuals said they lied out of fear of involuntary hospitalization, while others (45%) cited shame and embarrassment (stigma) as a reason for lying. Richards et al. [26] reported about a quarter of individuals who attempt suicide do not disclose thoughts of suicide when asked via the Patient Health Questionnaire-9 tool during a physician encounter prior to the attempt. Therefore, though some who go on to attempt or die by suicide may not have been thinking of suicide at the time when they were asked about it, many have concealed this experience from their clinician.

This work furthers understanding of how mental health professionals currently encounter and handle deception as it occurs in therapy sessions through qualitative one-on-one semi-structured interviews. We also assess perceptions and acceptability to the proposal of an AI-enabled real-time deception detection tool. By doing so, we learn more about how mental health professionals could potentially interact with the proposed tool, providing future considerations for improved human-computer interaction (HCI) with such a resource. To the best of our knowledge, our study is the first investigation of automated deception detection for mental health applications. Key contributions of this work include:

1. providing a first look into the feasibility and acceptability of automated deception detection in mental health domains as informed by practicing mental health clinicians;
2. enumerating potential merits of AI, such as its application in remote settings when many in-person cues are missing, particularly for detecting deception;
3. and identifying challenges concerning acceptability and implementation of AI in mental health domains, thus informing future considerations for HCI at the intersection of these domains.

This paper is outlined as follows: Sect. 2 discusses related work, Sect. 3 details the methodology used in our qualitative analyses, Sect. 4 presents the findings of our analyses, Sect. 5 discusses the results and summarizes the paper.

2   Related Work

Prior research has explored various modalities for automated deception detection. Two of the more popular modalities include video and audio data. Common features extracted from video data for deception detection include facial action units [10,19,24,25,29,30] and gaze and eye movement characteristics [17,29], extracted using the publicly available facial analysis toolkit, OpenFace [4,33]. From audio data, acoustic features like mel-frequency cepstrum coefficients, spectral and statistical features of audio frames, and prosodic information which capture emotion have been used [16,21,30,34]. Other works consider linguistics in addition to other acoustic features [21].

Recently, Speth et al. [29] introduced a novel dataset called the Deception Detection and Physiological Monitoring (DDPM) dataset which supports analyses of AI for deception detection. DDPM is multimodal, including thermal, video, audio, gaze, near and long-wave infrared, pulse, and blood oxygenation, from 70 individuals as they participated in interviews with professional actors. Participants were given a financial incentive to deceive "convincingly" according to the interviewer. According to the authors, this dataset is meant to replicate an interview scenario, particularly scenarios related to travel (i.e., travel screening), experiences, and opinions.

Nonetheless, many prior efforts on automated deception detection consider specific scenarios (e.g., courtroom, customs or border control, and legal scenarios [8,25,29]) that have less applicability to mental health domains, thus limiting their generalizability. It is common for existing work to consider scenarios where there is a power dynamic or legality in play. On the other hand, mental health applications of deception detection present a unique scenario, where attention to privacy, sensitivity, and patient comfortability are heightened. Further, it is more likely that psychiatrists will have limited use for the technologies used in prior work (e.g., thermal and blood oxygenation), as these are not readily available nor appropriate in therapeutic settings. Table 1 outlines prior work on automated deception detection, including the modalities used, application domains or settings, and features. As shown in this table, the mental health domain is under explored.

3   Methodology

Semi-structured qualitative interviews were conducted to elicit the perspectives of mental health professionals on the use of AI-enabled deception detection in a therapeutic setting. This study received Human Subjects approval by the University of South Florida's Institutional Review Board (Study #004165).

We recruited 15 mental health professionals from online platforms (i.e., TherapyDen [1], PsychologyToday [2]), by reaching out to university counseling centers in the U.S., and through contacting students and faculty in mental health counseling related disciplines (i.e., psychology, social work, mental health counseling, and counselor education) via email, phone, and social media (i.e., Instagram and LinkedIn). Inclusion criteria required participants to be adult (18+

Table 1. Summary of Prior Work on Automated Deception Detection

Ref.	Data	In-person or Remote	Domain	Face	Gaze	Hand Gestures	Body Gestures	Voice
[25]	Video, Thermal, Physiological	In-person	Courtrooms	✓	✓	✓		
[17]	Video, Audio, EEG	In-person	Lab setting		✓			✓
[29]	Video, Audio, Thermal, Physiological, Infrared	In-person	Travel	✓	✓			✓
[10]	Video	Remote	Lab setting	✓	✓			✓
[24]	Video	In-person	Travel	✓				
[19]	Video	In-person	Travel	✓	✓			
[6]	Video	In-person	Courtrooms, Crime, Opinion	✓	✓			
[30]	Video	In-person	Biographical	✓	✓			✓
[34]	Audio	In-person	Biographical					✓
[20]	Audio	In-person	Biographical					✓
[8]	Video	In-person	Crime	✓		✓	✓	

years old) counselors in the disciplines of psychology, social work, counselor education, and mental health counseling, actively seeing clients seeking mental health treatment in some capacity in the U.S. To assess these criteria, we used a 25-item questionnaire asking potential participants about their demographics, counseling experience, and client demographics. These data were evaluated to determine which interested individuals satisfied the inclusion criteria, whom were then contacted to schedule the interview. The demographics of the participants are reported in Table 2. Most participants identified as non-student White Cisgender Female between the ages of 25 and 34. The representativeness in the sample resembles the national representation of psychologists in the U.S. As of 2020, 71% of active psychologists in the U.S. identify as female and 84.47% identify as White [3].

Table 2. Participant Demographics

Race	#	Gender	#	Age (years)	#	Clinical Exp. (years)	#	Student Status	#
White, Caucasian	13	Cisgender Male	-	18 – 24	-	< 1 year	-	Student	2
Black, African American	1	Cisgender Female	15	25 – 34	11	1 – 2	7	Non-Student	13
American Indian, Alaska Native	-	Transgender	-	35 – 44	4	3 – 4	2		
Arab, Middle Eastern, Arab American	-	Other	-	45+	-	5+	6		
Asian, Asian-American	-	Did not disclose	-						
Native Hawaiian / Pacific Islander	-								
Other	-								
Did not disclose	1								

We began each interview providing the definition of deception as *making statements or assertions that are believed to be false to another person with the intent of misleading that individual* to participants so that each interviewee could base their responses on this single definition. The interview guide then consisted of the following questions:

1. As a counselor, how often do you encounter patients whom you believe are feeling a need to deceive you?
2. How does patient deception impact quality of care or patient benefits?
3. What do you look for that may hint that a patient is being deceptive, and how do you confirm this?
4. Can you tell me about specific situations or topics where you notice patients tend to deceive?
5. Can you tell me about any certain populations that are more likely to be deceptive regarding treatment-related information than others?
6. How do you currently document your sessions (i.e., audio recordings, video recordings, written notes)?
7. What are your reactions to an AI-enabled deception detection device that can provide you with real-time notifications of when your patient is likely being dishonest?
8. What would you, as a counselor, find important to add or takeaway from the description I've provided of this tool?
9. What kind of impact would such a tool/device have on the care you provide to patients, especially those with a history of being deceptive?
10. How would you imagine your patients would react to such a device?
11. Do any ethical implications come to mind when considering such a tool, and if so, what are they?
12. Ethically speaking, would you be more comfortable with using such a device with patients who have permitted its use as written in their advance directive?
13. If any, what privacy-related concerns do you have with such a tool?
14. What integration or additional functionality may help to ease such concerns?
15. Can you imagine such a tool being well-received by your peers?

Eight interviews were conducted via telephone and seven via the Microsoft Teams video conferencing service. The average interview time was approximately 42 min, with a minimum of 26 min and maximum time of 57 min. All interviews were audio recorded and transcribed using the AI-enabled transcription service, Temi[1]. Participants were compensated with $15 electronic gift cards for their completion of both the pre-screening questionnaire and interview.

4   Findings

The qualitative interview data were analyzed by two independent coders using structured coding methods following a narrative analysis approach [27]. In total, 341 utterances were coded and included in our qualitative analysis. The coding process occurred in three stages. In stage one, each coder independently reviewed ten interviews and developed generic codes from the reoccurring themes

---

[1] https://www.temi.com.

identified and interview questions. Once complete, both coders met to reach a consensus on the major themes, discussed individual codes, and developed definitions for each. In stage three, each coder independently recoded each interview according to the predetermined code list. During this process, we derived overarching themes of interest based on our research's objective (e.g., Perception of the Computer Science Implementation) and minor themes that emerged during the coding process (e.g., positive client reaction, comfortability, negative peer reaction). Interrater reliability (IRR), or the percentage agreement between the two coders calculated using Cohen's κ [9] in the SPSS statistics software, was 0.311. We attribute our fair IRR to our coding scheme which allowed each coder to select up to four codes for a single utterance. Agreement was only counted when there was total agreement for the utterance; a single deviation would result in disagreement for that utterance. For example, coder C_A may have assigned the codes visual body language, visual gaze, and visual incongruencies to the utterance quoted below, while Coder C_B assigns codes visual gaze and visual body language. Without absolutely agreement, this would lead to disagreement between coders.

People outwardly express certain, you know, behavioral mechanisms, right. Fidgeting, eye contact is poor. You can just tell they don't truly feel fine.

Similar interrater agreement was seen in studies [12,15,31,32], where *kappa* values of 0.3 were deemed sufficient. We derived a total of 49 minor themes which were organized into four overarching themes: (1) Functional Components of the Computer Science Implementation, (2) Perception of the Computer Science Implementation, (3) Integration of the Computer Science Implementation, and (4) Suggestions. We note that the phrase "Computer Science Implementation" refers to the AI-derived deception detection tool discussed with the interviewees. The definitions and organization of the minor themes are available in Table 3.

4.1   Theme 1: Functional Components of the Computer Science Implementation

Theme 1 captures participants' insight on how they identify deception in their clients and how they confirm deception has occurred, along with how they document their sessions. These findings could point to mechanisms for recording ground truth as advised by mental health professionals, in addition to motivating the use of certain modalities in an AI-based application. The most frequent minor theme of Theme 1, *discussion confirmation*, appeared 53 times.

When participants were asked how they detect that a client is being dishonest, 80% reported relying on visual cues, including change in eye contact and a shift in body language.

"People outwardly express certain, you know, behavioral mechanisms, right. Fidgeting, eye contact is poor. You can just tell they don't truly feel fine" [Participant 3].

Table 3. Minor themes and their definitions grouped by overarching major themes.

Theme	Minor Theme	Definition
Functional Components of the Computer Science Implementation	visual gaze	avoiding eye contact, looking around the room
	visual body language	fidgeting, closed off body language,
	visual facial expression	smiling, blushing,
	visual incongruencies	body language inconsistent with speech
	visual other	other visual cues
	verbal incongruencies	context based inconsistencies (deviation from normal symptoms, misaligning reports)
	verbal speech pattern	stuttering, speaking faster, increased pauses
	verbal other	other verbal/auditory cues
	using video	currently uses video to document sessions
	never video	would NEVER use video to document sessions
	consider video	would consider using video to document sessions (training)
	using audio	currently uses audio to document sessions
	never audio	would NEVER use audio to document sessions
	consider audio	would consider using audio to document sessions (training)
	using notes	currently uses written or typed notes to document sessions in real time
	never notes	would NEVER use written or typed notes to document sessions in real time
	consider notes	would consider using written or typed notes to document sessions in real time
	assessment confirmation	counselor confirms deception occurring via reviewing previous client assessments, or challenges
	discussion confirmation	counselor confirms deception occurring via motivational interviewing, stating observations to client
	third-party confirmation	counselor confirms deception occurring via third-party (parents, treatment team, Significant Other, providers)
	no confirmation	counselor does not directly address perceived deception
Perceptions of the Computer Science Implementation	positive reaction	positive reaction to AI tool description (willing to use)
	neutral reaction	neutral reaction to AI tool description
	negative reaction	negative reaction to AI tool description (not willing to use)
	other reaction	
	positive client reaction	counselor thinks it would be helpful for clients who understand behaviors for self-aware
	neutral client reaction	
	negative client reaction	counselor thinks clients will feel uncomfortable, not trusted, adapt to AI Tool
	uncomfortable	uncomfortable with AI tool despite advanced directive
	uncomfortable with reservations	uncomfortable with AI tool despite advanced directive with reservations
	neutral	neither comfortable nor uncomfortable with AI tool despite advanced directive
	neutral with reservations	neither comfortable nor uncomfortable with AI tool despite advanced directive with reservations
	comfortable	comfortable with AI tool given advanced directive
	comfortable with reservations	comfortable with AI tool given advanced directive with reservations
	mixed peer reaction	counselor thinks peer reaction is setting-dependent, specialty-dependent, or mixed
	positive peer reaction	counselor thinks peer reaction would be positive
	negative peer reaction	counselor things peer reaction would be negative
	unsure peer reaction	counselor is unsure of how peers would react
	neutral peer reaction	counselor thinks peer reaction would be neutral
Integration of the Computer Science Implementation	data use	ethical implications of data use (other care providers using scores, using scores as evidence, affects clinical judgment)
	HIPAA compliance	ethical implication of tool's compliance with HIPAA and client confidentiality
	client autonomy	ethical implications of tool on client disclosure, right to lie
	fairness in AI	ethical implications of bias in the model consideration (cultural, racial, disorders)
	data storage	privacy concerns of storage (security of cloud-based systems)
	data access	privacy concerns of 3rd party data sharing, unauthorized access, client access, need to know viewing of info
	cybersecurity risks	privacy concerns of hacking, data breach
Suggestions	robustness of AI	ability of tool to handle occlusions, cultural and racial differences, symptomology of disorders, perceive sense of safety, use physiological signals
	explainable AI	documentation and understanding of decision/confidence score process
	notification	notify counselor only, notify counselor + client, notify during vs after session, confidence score vs yes/no, simple UI, toggle on/off

Another sign of deception mentioned by all participants was if a client's report did not match their clinical assessment, hinting to the clinician that something was not quite right.

"I would look for, um, incongruence essentially. So like they're telling me one thing verbally with one kind of message and their body language is countering that in some way" [Participant 5].

All participants also reported that if there is a deviation of some kind from a client's baseline or typical behaviors, symptomology, and more, this was another indication that the client may be deceptive.

"...you pick up on kind of their everyday mannerisms, how they typically are. And so if they start doing something that isn't typical or start speaking in a way that's a little untypical for them" [Participant 6].

When asking participants how they confirm that their patient is being deceptive, we received varied responses. A majority (93%) reported that they discuss misalignments with their clients, while the dissenting opinions pointed toward relying on third-party sources to obtain a more holistic understanding of the client's report.

"...sometimes that might mean kind of like pointing out some incongruence, like, you know, oh, well you said this, but now I'm hearing this. ...or you told me X, Y, Z, but it sounds like mom was seeing it this way" [Participant 8].

We also asked about documentation to determine if any of their current documentation strategies could be leveraged in AI-enabled deception detection. 73% of participants noted using audio-visual recordings during their time as a trainee; despite this, a slight majority (53.3%) reported they would never consider using audio or visual for real-time documentation in the future.

"...so for like continuing education, that's where I would say like almost never because of that reason for video for audio" [Participant 6].

Others felt that audio recording is more appropriate and less invasive to the client and is worth consideration.

"...but I guess I would never consider using videotaping. [Because] I feel like that would put a lot of pressure on my clients..." [Participant 13].

"using like audio?... yeah, I mean, I would be open to it if there was a way to make it work or if it was found to be like more efficient, I'd be open to that. [Participant 4].

4.2   Theme 2: Perception of the Computer Science Implementation

Theme 2 captures reactions from our participants regarding automated deception detection in mental health settings, and how they believe their peers and clients would react to this concept. These perceptions are critical to gauge potential acceptance of stakeholders to the proposed technology in a therapeutic setting. Notably, the most frequent minor theme of Theme 2 was *negative client reaction*. Additionally, it was the most frequent overall minor theme and was coded 70 times.

We presented to participants a description of an AI-enabled deception deception tool as noted in the interview guide. More than a majority of participants (60%) expressed a negative first reaction to this tool.

"My authentic reaction is I don't like that at all. I do, I think it could lead to far more harm than it would do good" [Participant 5].

Others (6 out of 15 participants (40%)) thought it was a "cool" idea and had a more positive reaction to the description.

"...this tool could actually be really helpful in increasing that detection and then being able to process it in real time and being able to talk about it in real time" [Participant 1].

Out of the 9 participants who had adverse reactions to the description, five later mentioned that the tool could be useful.

"No, my immediate reaction is that feels extremely intrusive. A lot of it would depend on what the actual setup is. So, I mean, it seems like on tele-health, it might be a little easier potentially if it was some sort of software so maybe it's not as intrusive" [Participant 9].

When we asked participants how they believe their clients would react, 14 (93%) participants mentioned that their clients would feel as though the clinician does not trust them, and cause harm to the therapeutic relationship.

"Ooh, my knee jerk is no... it's the therapeutic relationship. And I feel like when you've earned the trust to get the truth, then you get the truth" [Participant 11].

Interestingly, just two (13.33%) participants mentioned that deceptive clients may learn how to deceive the deception tool into recognizing deceptive statements as truthful.

"Um, they would just learn how to be good about deceiving your deception device. I mean, at the end of the day, people who wanna get away with stuff, they gonna get away with it" [Participant 12].

When asked if the participants thought the tool would be well-received by their clinical peers, 73% responded that the response would be mixed or split — that there would be much debate and discussion — and even that the responses to the tool would be setting-dependent (i.e., based on the setting where the mental health professional sees clients).

"Like it, see there being a lot of debate I feel like people they're like, like really like it and think it's so cool or people would be like really concerned about it and maybe feel, um, like that it's invasive. I could really see it going either way" [Participant 1].

Over half (9 out of 15 participants (60%)) believed that their peers would not respond positively to the tool.

4.3 Theme 3: Integration of the Computer Science Implementation

Theme 3 captures the thoughts of participants on the ethics and privacy regarding automated deception detection. These responses provide insight concerning sensitivity that we found unique to mental health. The most frequent minor theme of Theme 3 was *data access* which appeared 38 times.

We asked participants about any ethical concerns regarding an AI-enabled deception tool. Six participants (40%) reported that the tool may inhibit the autonomy of the client by removing the choice to disclose on their terms. Client autonomy is a critical component to counseling. Here, the concern was that the tool would essentially force compliance regardless of whether or not the client chose not to disclose information for any reason (i.e., building rapport or discomfort).

"I feel like, kind of takes away the patient's opportunity to like advocate or get that like empowerment of being honest for themselves" [Participant 11].

Eleven out of 15 participants (73%) had concerns regarding how the data would be used. Many mentioned the potential for the deception scores to be used as evidence or used against the client in some manner. Privacy concerns were also mentioned by participants, which included concerns of data breach or loss and the security of the data storage.

"What happens if it gets subpoena like, oh, well you got a history of lying even in therapy. So how can we trust? You know, then, then we're in that space" [Participant 15].

Further, participants urged the importance of the tool being HIPAA compliant and having considerations for the client's confidentiality.

"how would it be uploaded ... easily hackable, who else gets them? Just privacy concerns. So like basic confidentiality" [Participant 7].

A chief concern made by nearly all participants (86%) was regarding data access. Depending on the setting of the clinician, different entities have access to their clinical notes; for example, parents or guardians may have access to the notes of adolescents. Some clinicians even expressed concern regarding the client having access to these data related to their level of deception in sessions, while five participants communicated concerns with cybersecurity risks as well.

"I personally have fears about privacy on their behalf because even with as many things as we do to prevent information you know, in technology [from] being, compromised, it happens" [Participant 5].

Over half (53%) were also concerned about the fairness of the AI model, mentioning the potential of bias to score some populations as deceptive despite the client being truthful in session.

4.4   Theme 4: Suggestions

Theme 4 details suggested improvements to address concerns reported by participants. Some concerns referred to the aforementioned ethics and privacy concerns, while other suggestions included what they feel would improve the described tool. The most frequent minor theme of Theme 4 was *robustness of the AI*, which appeared 35 times.

We asked participants to share anything that they would change concerning the way we initially described the AI-enabled deception detection tool. Eight of 15 participants (53%) expressed that the tool should be able to handle cultural differences in speech and body language.

"So culturally I would be really concerned about kind of how people's different cultural mannerisms would get read by AI" [Participant 10].

Others mentioned suggestions for how they would like to be notified of when their client is likely being deceptive.

"...a little notification would pop up and you could just glance at it and see like maybe a big green check mark for they're telling the truth or a big red X for their lying, something easy where they could just like glance real quick and they wouldn't know" [Participant 6].

Fewer participants (13%) preferred both the participant and client to receive notification of deception for discussing the deception in real-time.

"...if you are able to use it collaboratively, like making it so that the client can also receive notifications...indicating deception...we both can see that something's going on and like we're in this together" [Participant 1].

One participant mentioned that real-time notification of deception may be distracting and take their attention away from the client.

"I would think after the session would be my preference, not by a landslide, but I would probably prefer after the session because that wouldn't taint my clinical judgment as much" [Participant 10].

Another participant mentioned the danger of becoming reliant on the tool and not engaging as much clinically to detect and confront deception during sessions. Two participants commented on explainability for transparency with the client.

5   Discussion and Conclusion

This work details the findings of a qualitative study consisting of 15 semi-structured one-on-one interviews with mental health professionals to gather their perceptions on automated deception detection in mental health applications. We aimed to learn more about the acceptability of automated deception detection in mental health domains by clinicians, their proposed suggestions for such a resource, and the overall need for this resource. These interviews were analyzed by two independent coders, leading to 4 major themes: Functional Components of the Computer Science Implementation, Perceptions of the Computer Science Implementation, Integration of the Computer Science Implementation, and Suggestions. The independent coders arrived at 49 minor themes which uniquely capture the trends seen across the interviews. The most frequent minor themes per theme were: Theme 1 - discussion confirmation, Theme 2 - negative client reaction, Theme 3 - data access, and Theme 4 - robustness of AI.

Participants largely reported that the ground truth they currently use to confirm when clients are deceptive is by discussing their suspicions with the client. This shows that clinicians rely largely on client self-report. We pitched AI as an additional source to verify observed deception. The impressions from the participants were varied, with nine of 15 participants initially responding negatively to the idea of an automated deception detection tool being used in a therapeutic setting. However, later in their interviews, five of these nine reported more positively that such a technology could be useful. Despite this, participants overwhelmingly reported that they imagine their clients would have a negative reaction, leading to discomfort with the recording of private discussions and, thus, creating an invasive environment. This is not a surprising finding since the nature of the therapeutic setting is to provide a safe, private space.

Interesting perspectives expressed by participants included concerns regarding the robustness of the AI model. Specifically, participants were cognizant of the AI needing to generalize across cultures and interpersonal differences. However, we note that behaviors reported by participants as clues to deception were often specific to the individual (i.e., deviation from baseline). Individuality is often a challenge when developing solutions in HCI. This challenge is similar as this may lead to difficulty in the ability to train a model that can generalize across nuanced individual differences while remaining effective and maintaining the user's trust in the system.

The main limitation of this work is the sample size of 15, which is relatively small for a study with the purpose of gauging perceptions of a larger population. However, we note that the independent raters reached a point of saturation, where, generally, no new information can be derived. It is possible that we reached saturation at 15 participants due to the homogeneity of demographics (i.e., all female-identifying clinicians) and backgrounds in the recruited sample. Additionally, we acknowledge that we are surveying the clinician perspective of how their clients may react and not the clients themselves. Thus, derived insights do not directly reflect the opinions of clients; this investigation was deemed out of the scope of this work as we are primarily interested in the use of AI by clinicians themselves.

Finally, our findings, alongside the detailed suggestions given by participants, demonstrate the potential of a tool for mental health professionals to recognize deception in real-time. The findings also detail a road map of what the automated deception detection tool should address to increase acceptability from stakeholders (e.g., maintaining client confidentiality, cybersecurity of data, data access, data use, client autonomy, HIPAA compliance). That is, we find interest in the proposed tool, although with sound concerns in its implementation regarding privacy, ethics, and the therapeutic relationship. These concerns raised by participants may be critical future considerations at the intersection of AI and mental health in HCI research.

References

1. Find a therapist nearby, compassionate in-person and online therapy - therapyden. https://www.therapyden.com/. Accessed 17 Sept 2022
2. Psychology today: health, help, happiness + find a therapist. https://www.psychologytoday.com/us. Accessed 17 Sept 2022
3. American psychological association. Demographics of U.S. psychology workforce [interactive data tool]. https://www.apa.org/workforce/data-tools/demographics (2022). Accessed 30 Oct 2022
4. Baltrušaitis, T., Mahmoud, M., Robinson, P.: Cross-dataset learning and person-specific normalisation for automatic action unit detection. In: 2015 11th IEEE International Conference and Workshops on Automatic Face and Gesture Recognition (FG), vol. 06, pp. 1–6 (2015). https://doi.org/10.1109/FG.2015.7284869
5. Baumann, E.C., Hill, C.E.: Client concealment and disclosure of secrets in outpatient psychotherapy. Couns. Psychol. Q. **29**(1), 53–75 (2016)
6. Belavadi, V., et al.: Multimodal deception detection: accuracy, applicability and generalizability. In: 2020 Second IEEE International Conference on Trust, Privacy and Security in Intelligent Systems and Applications (TPS-ISA), pp. 99–106 (2020). https://doi.org/10.1109/TPS-ISA50397.2020.00023
7. Blanchard, M., Farber, B.A.: Lying in psychotherapy: why and what clients don't tell their therapist about therapy and their relationship. Couns. Psychol. Q. **29**(1), 90–112 (2016)
8. Burgoon, J., et al.: An approach for intent identification by building on deception detection. In: Proceedings of the 38th Annual Hawaii International Conference on System Sciences, p. 21a. IEEE (2005)
9. Cohen, J.: A coefficient of agreement for nominal scales. Educ. Psychol. Measur. **20**(1), 37–46 (1960). https://doi.org/10.1177/001316446002000104
10. De Marsico, M., Dionisi, G.: Your face may say the truth when you lie. In: Proceedings of the 2022 International Conference on Advanced Visual Interfaces. AVI 2022, Association for Computing Machinery, New York, NY, USA (2022). https://doi.org/10.1145/3531073.3534486
11. Doll, S.: Therapists' perceptions of deception in psychotherapy, Ph. D. thesis, The Chicago School of Professional Psychology (2017)
12. Dorsey, E.R., et al.: Increasing access to specialty care: a pilot, randomized controlled trial of telemedicine for Parkinson's disease. Mov. Disord. **25**(11), 1652–1659 (2010)

13. Ekman, P., O'Sullivan, M., Frank, M.G.: A few can catch a liar. Psychol. Sci. **10**(3), 263–266 (1999)
14. Fernandes, S.V., Ullah, M.S.: A comprehensive review on features extraction and features matching techniques for deception detection. IEEE Access **10**, 28233–28246 (2022). https://doi.org/10.1109/ACCESS.2022.3157821
15. Garot, E., Couture-Veschambre, C., Manton, D.J., Bekvalac, J., Rouas, P.: Differential diagnoses of enamel hypomineralisation in an archæological context: a postmedieval skeletal collection reassessment. Int. J. Osteoarchaeol. **29**(5), 747–759 (2019)
16. Graciarena, M., Shriberg, E., Stolcke, A., Enos, F., Hirschberg, J., Kajarekar, S.: Combining prosodic lexical and cepstral systems for deceptive speech detection. In: 2006 IEEE International Conference on Acoustics Speech and Signal Processing Proceedings, vol. 1, p. I (2006). https://doi.org/10.1109/ICASSP.2006.1660200
17. Gupta, V., Agarwal, M., Arora, M., Chakraborty, T., Singh, R., Vatsa, M.: Bag-of-lies: a multimodal dataset for deception detection. In: 2019 IEEE/CVF Conference on Computer Vision and Pattern Recognition Workshops (CVPRW), pp. 83–90 (2019). https://doi.org/10.1109/CVPRW.2019.00016
18. Hom, M.A., Stanley, I.H., Podlogar, M.C., Joiner, T.E.: "Are you having thoughts of suicide?" Examining experiences with disclosing and denying suicidal ideation. J. Clin. Psychol. **73**(10), 1382–1392 (2017)
19. Khan, W., Crockett, K., O'Shea, J., Hussain, A., Khan, B.M.: Deception in the eyes of deceiver: A computer vision and machine learning based automated deception detection. Expert Syst. Appl. **169**, 114341 (2021). https://doi.org/10.1016/j.eswa.2020.114341. https://www.sciencedirect.com/science/article/pii/S0957417420310289
20. Levitan, S.I., An, G., Wang, M., Mendels, G., Hirschberg, J., Levine, M., Rosenberg, A.: Cross-cultural production and detection of deception from speech. In: Proceedings of the 2015 ACM on Workshop on Multimodal Deception Detection, pp. 1–8. WMDD 2015, Association for Computing Machinery, New York, NY, USA (2015). https://doi.org/10.1145/2823465.2823468
21. Levitan, S.I., An, G., Ma, M., Levitan, R., Rosenberg, A., Hirschberg, J.: Combining acoustic-prosodic, lexical, and phonotactic features for automatic deception detection. In: Proceedings Interspeech 2016, pp. 2006–2010 (2016). https://doi.org/10.21437/Interspeech.2016-1519
22. Mager, H.: Deception: a study in forensic psychology. Psychol. Sci. Public Interest **26**(2), 183 (1931)
23. McHugh, C.M., Corderoy, A., Ryan, C.J., Hickie, I.B., Large, M.M.: Association between suicidal ideation and suicide: meta-analyses of odds ratios, sensitivity, specificity and positive predictive value. BJPsych open **5**(2), e18 (2019)
24. Monaro, M., Maldera, S., Scarpazza, C., Sartori, G., Navarin, N.: Detecting deception through facial expressions in a dataset of videotaped interviews: a comparison between human judges and machine learning models. Comput. Hum. Behav. **127**, 107063 (2022). https://doi.org/10.1016/j.chb.2021.107063. https://www.sciencedirect.com/science/article/pii/S0747563221003861
25. Pérez-Rosas, V., Mihalcea, R., Narvaez, A., Burzo, M.: A multimodal dataset for deception detection. In: LREC, pp. 3118–3122 (2014)
26. Richards, J.E., et al.: Understanding why patients may not report suicidal ideation at a health care visit prior to a suicide attempt: a qualitative study. Psychiatr. Serv. **70**(1), 40–45 (2019)
27. Saldaña, J.: The coding manual for qualitative researchers. The Coding Manual for Qualitative Researchers, pp. 1–440 (2021)

28. Simon, G.E., et al.: Risk of suicide attempt and suicide death following completion of the patient health questionnaire depression module in community practice. J. Clin. Psychiatry **77**(2), 20461 (2016)

29. Speth, J., Vance, N., Czajka, A., Bowyer, K.W., Wright, D., Flynn, P.: Deception detection and remote physiological monitoring: a dataset and baseline experimental results. In: 2021 IEEE International Joint Conference on Biometrics (IJCB), pp. 1–8 (2021). https://doi.org/10.1109/IJCB52358.2021.9484409

30. Takabatake, S., Shimada, K., Saitoh, T.: Construction of a liar corpus and detection of lying situations. In: 2018 Joint 10th International Conference on Soft Computing and Intelligent Systems (SCIS) and 19th International Symposium on Advanced Intelligent Systems (ISIS), pp. 971–976 (2018). https://doi.org/10.1109/SCIS-ISIS.2018.00161

31. Tsuang, M.T., et al.: Attenuated psychosis syndrome in DSM-5. Schizophr. Res. **150**(1), 31–35 (2013)

32. Ventura, M., Colais, P., Fusco, D., Agabiti, N., Cesaroni, G., Davoli, M.: Information on educational level from hospital discharge register: an analysis of validity. Epidemiol. Prev. **37**(4–5), 289–296 (2013)

33. Wegrzyn, M., Vogt, M., Kireclioglu, B., Schneider, J., Kissler, J.: Mapping the emotional face. how individual face parts contribute to successful emotion recognition. PLOS One **12**(5), e0177239 (2017)

34. Zhou, Y., Zhao, H., Pan, X., Shang, L.: Deception detecting from speech signal using relevance vector machine and non-linear dynamics features. Neurocomputing **151**, 1042–1052 (2015). https://doi.org/10.1016/j.neucom.2014.04.083. https://www.sciencedirect.com/science/article/pii/S0925231214013435

Aggregating Human Domain Knowledge for Feature Ranking

Jaroslaw Kornowicz$^{(\boxtimes)}$ ⓘ and Kirsten Thommes ⓘ

Paderborn University, Warburger Str. 100, 33098 Paderborn, Germany
{jaroslaw.kornowicz,kirsten.thommes}@upb.de

Abstract. Human integration in machine learning can take place in various forms and stages. The current study examines the process of feature selection, with a specific focus on eliciting and aggregating feature rankings by human subjects. The elicitation is guided by the principles of expert judgment elicitation, a field of study that has investigated the aggregation of multiple opinions for the purpose of mitigating biases and enhancing accuracy. An online experiment was conducted with 234 participants to evaluate the impact of different elicitation and aggregation methods, namely behavioral aggregation, mathematical aggregation, and the Delphi method, compared to individual expert opinions, on feature ranking accuracy. The results indicate that the aggregation method significantly affects the rankings, with behavioral aggregation having a more significant impact than mean and median aggregation. On the other hand, the Delphi method had minimal impact on the rankings compared to individual rankings.

Keywords: Machine Learning · Feature Selection · Human-in-the-loop · Expert Judgement Elicitation

1 Introduction

In machine learning (ML), ensuring the quality of applications often requires careful consideration of data representation, particularly in supervised learning. A crucial step in this process is feature selection, widely recognized as an established element of the development process [48]. In this context, a feature can be understood as a measurable property or characteristic of a procedure or entity that is being observed [38]. These features may also be called predictors, variables, dimensions, or inputs [29].

The selection of features aims to improve the predictive accuracy, reduce the learning speed and costs, and enhance the understanding of the problem [25]. This is especially relevant for high-dimensional data sets, which may contain irrelevant and redundant features that negatively impact the quality of the learned models for stakeholders [35]. As the number of dimensions increases, the number of observations required for a reliable model grows exponentially, a phenomenon which is known as the "curse of dimensionality" which, for example,

H. Degen and S. Ntoa (Eds.): HCII 2023, LNAI 14050, pp. 98–114, 2023.
https://doi.org/10.1007/978-3-031-35891-3_7

contributes to the gap between the advances in artificial intelligence research and the slower progress in medical practice [1].

While most feature selection methods are data-driven, meaning they automatically select or rank features based on a training data set, our research focuses on knowledge-driven feature selection, specifically, the expert judgment approach [13]. Integrating human expert knowledge in feature selection processes may be relevant in many instances: Most frequently, the problem is discussed if humans need to understand the feature ranks for explainability of the model and features ranked to be necessary should not contradict human knowledge [47]. Guyon and Elisseeff [25] recommend incorporating domain knowledge to "construct a better set of ad hoc features". Human integration may also be needed if humans have superior domain knowledge. For instance, Nahar et al. [40] have demonstrated that features based on a literature review significantly improve the accuracy of a heart disease classifier. Finally, human involvement in the feature selection process may be necessary if the trained machine learning model is sensitive to missing values and the likelihood of missing values is not uniform across all features. For instance, if human experts know that a crucial feature is frequently missing in a healthcare setting, excluding it from the training may be advantageous. Missing data may constitute a problem if a model should give advice, especially when the costs of revealing one feature for a case are not equal and time corroborates feature elicitation. Still, some features require more resources for collecting relevant information than others, so the likelihood of missing data is not equal. Knowledge about suitable features can be elicited directly from domain experts. Cheng et al. [13] asked three cardiologists to select a subset of available features, compared their selections individually, aggregated the subsets, and compared the aggregations to data-driven approaches. However, some previous studies only compare a few judgment elicitation methods, while others lack a ground truth for ranking quality.

Integrating human knowledge into the ML pipeline is not a new concept. While research has shown that the incorporation of expert knowledge can improve the performance of ML models and reduce algorithmic aversion [6], the development, comparability, and reproducibility of these approaches are complex and costly [28]. Additionally, there are no standards for querying and integrating this knowledge.

Asking experts to provide their judgment on a specific topic is not easy, and the literature around "expert judgment elicitation" highlights the importance of understanding belief elicitation, probability, and judgment separately and jointly to effectively utilize expert judgments for modeling purposes [41]. While this literature mainly focused on elicitation and aggregation of point estimations, we apply the developed methods to feature ranking. We examine how different aggregation methods affect rankings and their quality for ML models.

Our study contributes to interactive ML by being the first to use different methods, from expert judgment elicitation, specifically behavioral aggregation, and the Delphi method, for feature ranking. Previous studies in this area have primarily relied on mathematical aggregation techniques, but our study utilizes a higher sample size and is the first to do so. This allows for more robust and accurate results, as a larger sample size can better capture the range of opinions and experiences.

2   Related Work

2.1   Feature Ranking and Selection

The selection of an appropriate subset of features for an ML model can significantly impact the performance and interpretability of the model. Studies have demonstrated that by reducing the number of features utilized in a model, the computation time required to learn the model can be decreased, the risk of overfitting can be mitigated, and the model can be more easily understood and applied in practical settings [8]. The field of feature selection has been heavily researched, focusing on developing automated algorithms for selecting a relevant subset of features from a given dataset. Many of these algorithms are ranking methods that assign a score to each feature based on a specific metric, such as the correlation between the feature and the dependent variable or its contribution to the model performance [34]. These rankings can then be used to select the final subset of features for the model. Data-driven feature selection methods can be broadly categorized into three types: filter methods, which rank features based solely on the dataset; wrapper methods, which evaluate features based on the predictive performance of an ML algorithm; and embedded methods, such as the LASSO regression, which have integrated feature selection mechanisms [7].

In addition to data-driven feature selection methods, utilizing human knowledge for feature selection can also be done in various ways. Like the different categories of data-driven methods, features can be filtered by researching relevant literature [15,40,50] or by consulting domain experts [13,39]. Additionally, humans can be actively integrated into the machine-learning pipeline. For example, in Correia et al. [16], experts were presented with a few records from the data set and were asked to highlight essential features, and this feedback was used to weigh features in the learning process. Bianchi et al. [2] developed an algorithm that allows humans to vote for different models, and these elicited preferences were also used for selecting a feature subset.

Another approach to feature selection is to use multiple selection or ranking methods and aggregate them into a single selection [4,18,49]. This can be achieved by combining feature rankings through mathematical operations, such as taking the mean or median, or by creating a feature subset through the union or intersection of individual subsets. This approach has been applied in studies where multiple responses from domain experts are obtained. For instance, Cheng et al. [13] utilized the responses of three cardiologists and computed the union and intersection of their selections. In contrast, Moro et al. [39] employed an averaging approach for the rankings of three domain experts.

2.2   Expert Judgement Elicitation

Integrating one expert in feature selection would be sufficient and most efficient if a single expert was fully knowledgeable. However, individuals can be missing information or evaluate information highly biased, leading to non-rational decisions. Using multiple experts instead of relying on a single expert is justifiable because individuals' judgments can be influenced by heuristics and biases such as anchoring, availability of information, or overconfidence [41]. Much past research shows that groups outperform experts in decision-making because they cancel out biases and individuals can contribute complementary information [32]. Also, utilizing multiple experts and aggregating their opinions for forecasting purposes has been extensively studied within the domain of expert judgment elicitation [42]. As demonstrated by Wittmann et al. [52], experts were utilized to examine the ecological impact of Asian carps on the Great Lakes for policy making, while O'Hagan [41] solicited expert opinions on the demand for health services in the UK in 2035. Additional case studies can be found in a comprehensive review by McAndrew et al. [37].

By utilizing a group of experts, the potential for these biases can be mitigated, thus improving the accuracy of forecasts. As in decision-making and policy creation, a single forecast or a distribution of forecasts is typically required, and the collective opinions of experts must be aggregated. O'Hagan [41] identified two distinct approaches for aggregation: behavioral aggregation and mathematical aggregation. In behavioral aggregation, experts engage in discussion regarding their knowledge and forecasts. In contrast, in mathematical aggregation, there is no interaction between the experts, and their forecasts are pooled together through mathematical formulas. Past research finds ambiguous results in behavioral aggregations: In some instances, a group discussion did not significantly improve decision quality, e.g., [30].

Moreover, decision quality depends on interaction quality, e.g., equal power and dissent [45]. Researchers have developed various protocols to elicit and aggregate expert judgments to ensure forecasting is as scientifically rigorous as possible. The Cooke protocol [14] is an example of mathematical aggregation, in which the experts' knowledge, measured during the elicitation process, is considered for the aggregation. A long-standing debate in expert elicitation method, for instance, also deals with whether incorporating correlations in seemingly independent judgments improves forecast performance [3,51] or whether a simple mean outperforms other measures in most of the times [23]. Another process that can enhance forecasts is the Delphi method, employed in the IDEA protocol [26]. With the Delphi method, experts first work on their forecasts and then receive the forecasts of other experts and can update their initial responses, which also has some weaknesses, among others, no robustness against biases [21].

While there is ample evidence that groups outperform individuals in point estimations, the question remains whether these results are also transferable to feature selection as the question to be asked is even more complex: Instead of asking "How likely is a specific event in the future?" or "What is the most likely event in the future?", the question to be asked is "What information should be used to predict the future?".

2.3   Combining Feature Ranking with Expert Judgement Elicitation

While traditional methods of expert elicitation focus on point estimations and probabilistic distributions, feature selection deals with other data structures, such as sets and rankings. One commonality between these two areas is that the answers are typically aggregated to a single final solution in cases involving multiple experts or algorithms. Mathematical aggregation is an established procedure for data-driven feature ranking, as demonstrated by studies conducted by Wald et al. [49] and Dittmann et al. [18], where both showed that aggregation techniques perform comparably well. However, only a limited number of studies have applied this method to rankings based on human knowledge, as such rankings are often derived from literature or single experts. One notable exception is the study conducted by Moro et al. [39], in which three experts were selected to minimize bias. Their rankings were averaged, similar to the approach adopted by Cheng et al. [13], where the union subset of expert judgments performed better than the whole set of features. Behavioral aggregation plays a relatively minor role in designing ML models. In the study by Seymoens et al., [46], potential decision support system users were interviewed in a manner akin to behavioral aggregation.

As the number of human-in-the-loop approaches in ML increases [12,31], eliciting and aggregating domain knowledge efficiently can be beneficial in creating unbiased, more performant, and more relevant decision models. Our study investigates different elicitation and aggregation methods for feature ranking with a larger sample of human participants in various domains. The results of our research can be particularly valuable for developing human-in-the-loop, interactive ML approaches.

3   Materials and Methods

3.1   Online Experiment

To answer our research question, an incentivized behavioral experiment was conducted in November and December of 2022 on the recruiting platform Prolific[1]. The study, "Ranking Information," was programmed using oTree [10] and deployed online. It was conducted in English and targeted participants in the USA and UK.

In total, 234 participants successfully participated in our study. The average age of the participants was 37.1 ($SD = 13.0$), with 118 (50.4%) identifying as male and 199 identifying their ethnicity as white. Although the study was limited to participants living in the UK and USA, a majority of 214 stated their nationality as UK, only eight as US, and 12 had other nationalities.

---

[1] https://www.prolific.co/.

The instructions for the Prolific study were designed to be as accessible as possible for non-technical individuals. The instructions explained that computers utilize information to generate recommendations for decision-makers and that it is beneficial for computers when features are ranked according to their importance. Participants were asked to rank the five domains' most important to least important features. The corresponding ML problem was succinctly explained for each domain by identifying the decision and the available information used to make it.

The experiment had three treatments: (1) Individual ratings (for comparison and also for the mathematical aggregation methods), (2) behavioral aggregation with a chat function, and (3) group rankings via the Delphi method. Treatments (1) and (2) were conducted in the same web version, where participants individually ranked the features. Afterward, some participants were randomly selected to rank in groups while chatting about the best ranking with two other experimental participants. Participants could modify their rankings using a drag-and-drop function, making the changes visible to all group members. They could proceed if all group members reached a consensus on the rankings. The Delphi method (3) followed a similar structure: Participants first ranked the features individually and then received rankings from two other participants who had participated in the two previous treatments of the experiment. For each subject in this treatment, two random participants were allocated and remained consistent across all domains.

In our experiment, thus a total of 234 participants were recruited. Of these, 114 participants underwent only individual ranking of features, while 90 were subjected to a second treatment, following individual ranking. The second treatment formed 30 groups of three participants, which were utilized for behavioral and mathematical aggregations. The 114 participants from the first treatment were randomly assigned to groups of three for mathematical aggregation to ensure parity in group size with the behavioral aggregation groups. Additionally, 30 participants completed a Delphi version treatment, in which they underwent individual ranking followed by a subsequent ranking, where they could see rankings of two participants from the other treatments.

We used the two simple operations for mathematical aggregation, mean and median, but other functions are possible [18,49]. The average feature ranking inside a group was computed in the mean aggregation. For median aggregation, we computed the median value of the feature rankings within a group. The aggregated rankings were then sorted according to these values. In cases of ties, the features were sorted alphabetically based on their abbreviations used in the dataset. To ensure reproducibility and guard against potential p-hacking, the random seed of Python's random module was set to 42 for all computations. This approach ensures that random variations do not influence the results in allocating participants to groups.

3.2   Incentivation

As compensation for completing the study, participants received a fixed and a bonus payment based on the "quality" of their rankings. Since there is no objective ground truth for feature ranking, a proxy ranking was used for incentivization. This process entailed running simple linear and logistic regressions with all domain features, sorting the regressions' normalized coefficients as rankings and using these rankings as ground truth for comparison with the participants' rankings using Spearman's foot rule [17]. The smaller the distance between the participant's rankings and the regression rankings, the higher the bonus payment received by the participant. For each domain ranking, participants could earn £0.50.

Besides the bonus payment, participants were compensated with a fixed payoff contingent upon the treatment received. The fixed amount was established to ensure that the participants received a payoff following the minimum compensation standards set by Prolific. Participants in the first or second treatment received a fixed payment of £2.50 for their contributions. Participants who completed the ranking task in the group for the behavioral aggregation received an additional fixed payment of £6.50. Participants subjected to the Delphi method received a fixed payment of £5.00. It is worth noting that Prolific members were only permitted to participate in the study once.

3.3   Experimental Task

To ensure the generalizability of our study and minimize the impact of domain-specific knowledge, the aggregation methods were evaluated using five different decision-making problems based on variant datasets. The selection of these datasets was done with utmost care to ensure they were easily comprehensible for the participants of the Prolific study in terms of the decision problem and the features incorporated. The datasets were also chosen to possess an appropriate number of features to enable variation in the ranking task while ensuring that the task was not excessively prolonged or challenging in the group-based component of the study. The rankings for the different domains were completed in the following order: *housing, cardio, football, covid, cars.*

The first decision-making problem, *housing*[2], is a regression problem to predict the prices of houses in USA by utilizing various characteristics of the house. The dataset includes 1460 observations and 80 features, from which 16 were selected for the ranking task. This dataset has been subject to numerous studies, with a notable example being the use of feature importance algorithms in Greenwell et al. [24]. We selected the following features for the study: *Above ground living area size, Basement size, Car capacity in the garage, Central air conditioning available, Condition of the basement, First-floor size, Lot size, Number of bathrooms above ground, Number of bedrooms above ground, Number of fireplaces, Number of kitchens above ground, Pool area, Quality of kitchen, Second-floor size, Total rooms above ground, Year built.*

---

[2] https://www.kaggle.com/c/house-prices-advanced-regression-techniques.

The second decision-making problem, *cardio*[3], is a classification problem to predict cardiovascular disease by utilizing patient characteristics and symptoms. The dataset includes 70,000 observations and 12 features, with all features selected for the ranking task. Various feature selection algorithms on this dataset have been comparatively analyzed in Hsan and Bao [27]. We selected the following features for the study: *Age, Alcohol intake status, Body Mass Index, Cholesterol level, Diastolic blood pressure, Gender, Glucose level, Height, Physical activity, Smoking status, Systolic blood pressure, Weight.*

The third decision-making problem, *football*[4], includes 4070 observations and 114 features and is used for the classification of whether the home team in a football/soccer match wins based on match characteristics. We selected the following 17 features for the study: *Corners away team, Corners home team, Fouls conceded away team, Fouls conceded home team, Offsides away team, Offsides home team, Passes away team, Passes home team, Possession home team, Red cards away team, Red cards home team, Shots away team, Shots home team, Tackles away team, Tackles home team, Yellow cards away team, Yellow cards home team.*

The fourth decision-making problem, *covid.* includes 696 observations and 11 features and is about the classification of Covid-19 disease based on patient symptoms. This dataset is not publicly available. We selected the following features for the study: *Contact with an infected person, Cough, Digestive problems, Fatigue, Fever, Headache, Limb pain, Loss of smell, Respiratory symptoms, Sniffles, Sore throat.*

Lastly, the *cars* decision-making problem includes 1218 observations and eight features. It is about predicting the prices of used German cars. The dataset was obtained by scraping a German car-selling platform. We selected the following features for the study: *Carbon emission, Fuel consumption, Fuel type, Horsepower, Mileage, Number of previous owners, Transmission type, Year of first registration.*

4   Results

The evaluation and ranking of models is a complex task that various goals and objectives can influence. While the primary objective of developing new ML algorithms is to improve model performance, there are instances where other factors, such as interpretability, are also considered. This is particularly relevant when humans are involved in learning or when models are used in human decision-making processes. In such scenarios, the interpretability, practical feasibility of the models, and individual preferences become critical factors in their use and deployment. Consequently, it is not only necessary to evaluate the performance of models based on rankings generated through different aggregation

---

[3] https://www.kaggle.com/datasets/sulianova/cardiovascular-disease-dataset.
[4] https://www.kaggle.com/datasets/pablohfreitas/all-premier-league-matches-20102021.

methods but also to assess the degree to which these rankings vary from individual opinions. To this end, we propose to analyze the rankings generated by ML models in three ways. Firstly, we will evaluate how rankings change through different aggregation methods and compare the resulting aggregated rankings. Secondly, we will analyze the accuracy of the models resulting from the ranking of different groups and aggregation methods. Finally, we will combine these two approaches by using feature importance methods to generate importance rankings and compare them to rankings based on human input.

4.1   Differences Between Rankings

We first examined the influence of aggregation on rankings and the differences in rankings between aggregation methods. To descriptively measure the distances between rankings, we utilized Spearman's foot rule [17]. There are other methods for comparing rankings [20,33] however, we found that Spearman's foot rule provided a clear and concise measure of distance. To make it possible to summarize the distance across domains that had different numbers of features, we normalized the distance between 0 and 1 by dividing the values by the maximum possible distance in the respective domain.

Table 1 shows the computed differences. We observed that both the behavioral and mathematical aggregations impacted the rankings. The average distance from the individual rankings to the behavioral aggregation was 0.32 ($SD = 0.19$), which was nearly the same to the distances for the mean aggregation ($M = 0.30, SD = 0.11$) and median aggregation ($M = 0.28, SD = 0.14$). We used the Mann-Whitney U test to determine if the differences in the ranking change between the aggregation methods are significant. Behavioral aggregation produced a significantly greater change in rankings compared to the mean ($z = 1.76, p = 0.04$) and median aggregations ($z = 4.42, p < 0.01$). Additionally, mean aggregation resulted in a significantly greater change in rankings than median aggregation ($p = 5.31, p < 0.01$). The Delphi process only slightly changed the rankings with an average distance of 0.09 ($SD = 0.14$).

Although the distances between the initial rankings and the aggregated rankings were similar, the direction of the aggregations could still vary, leading to different rankings between the aggregations. We tested the significance of these differences using the Wilcoxon signed-rank test. The average distances between behavioral and mean aggregation ($M = 0.23, SD = 0.11$), behavioral and median aggregation (4) ($M = 0.22, SD = 0.13$), and mean and median aggregation ($M = 0.14, SD = 0.07$) were all statistically greater than zero ($p < 0.01$).

4.2   Performances

The performance of rankings generated by different aggregation methods was evaluated by training ML models and comparing their prediction accuracy. The ML algorithm computations were performed using the scikit-learn library [43]. To account for individual rankings of features, which most supervised learning algorithms do not consider, we trained models on different sizes of feature

Table 1. Mean Distance and Standard Deviation by Aggregation Method and Domain

Groups	Total	Housing	Cardio	Football	Covid	Cars
Behav. Agg.	0.32	0.29	0.37	0.37	0.27	0.31
	(0.19)	(0.16)	(0.19)	(0.12)	(0.15)	(0.18)
Mean Agg.	0.30	0.28	0.34	0.34	0.26	0.29
	(0.11)	(0.09)	(0.12)	(0.11)	(0.10)	(0.13)
Median Agg.	0.28	0.25	0.32	0.31	0.24	0.27
	(0.14)	(0.11)	(0.14)	(0.13)	(0.12)	(0.16)
Delphi	0.09	0.09	0.07	0.13	0.06	0.09
	(0.14)	(0.13)	(0.11)	(0.21)	(0.11)	(0.12)

subsets. For each domain, three different subset sizes were used to represent approximately 25%, 50%, and 75% quantiles of the number of available features [19]. For example, in domain *housing*, which had 16 features, we used subsets of the sizes 4, 8, and 12. Following the method proposed by Hasan and Bao [27], all feature values were first normalized to the range between 0 and 1. Three different classes of algorithms were selected for the learning process: Regressions, Decision Trees [5], and XGBoost [11]. Given the presence of three classifications and two regression problems, the appropriate version of each algorithm was used, such as *LinearRegression* for regression problems and *LogisticRegression* for classification problems. All algorithms used, except *LinearRegression*, have hyperparameters, so tuning was performed using a grid search method with 5-fold cross-validation. Each dataset was split into a training and a test set, with the training set used for hyperparameter tuning and learning and the test set used for evaluating the model performance. For regression problems, the metric root mean squared error was used, and for classification problems, balanced accuracy was employed.

After training the models, the XGBoost algorithms demonstrated the best performance across all domains, leading to the selection of these models for further analysis, thus simplifying the analysis. To validate the training approach, the models of the domain *cardio* were compared to the results of Hasan and Bao [27], who conducted similar research on the same dataset and showed very similar performance. Table 2 presents the average test score and standard deviation for each aggregation method and domain. We employed the Mann-Whitney U-test to test for differences in test scores between the different aggregation methods. The results showed that the differences were only significant in a few cases. In the cardio domain, the accuracy of individual rankings was significantly lower than that of the behavioral ($z = -1.29, p = 0.09$), mean ($z = -2.24, p = 0.01$), and median ($z = -1.40, p = 0.08$) aggregations. Mean aggregation resulted in the highest prediction accuracy ($M = 0.712, SD = 0.043$), but besides the individual rankings, the performance is only significantly better than the Delphi method ($z = 1.31, p = 0.9$). Similarly, in the football domain, individual rankings resulted in a significantly lower balanced accuracy compared to behavioral ($z = -2.01, p = 0.02$), mean ($z = -1.93, p = 0.03$), median aggregations ($z = -2.20, p = 0.01$). Still, there was also no statistical difference between the aggregation methods regarding performance.

Table 2. Mean and Standard Deviation Root Means Squared Error and Balanced Accuracy for XGBoost Models by Aggregation Method and Domain. Numbers in bold indicate best performance in the domain.

Groups	Housing	Cardio	Football	Covid	Cars
All Individuals	41,087	0.702	0.627	0.537	25,388
	(7,459)	(0.05)	(0.027)	(0.044)	(2,621)
Behavioral Aggregation	41,549	0.708	**0.633**	**0.534**	**25,349**
	(7,579)	(0.045)	(0.022)	(0.041)	(2,720)
Mean Aggregation	**40,749**	**0.712**	0.631	0.536	25,734
	(7,129)	(0.043)	(0.025)	(0.043)	(2,433)
Median Aggregation	41,013	0.708	0.631	0.537	25,700
	(7,148)	(0.045)	(0.025)	(0.043)	(2,486)
Delphi Update	41,714	0.706	0.631	0.539	25,475
	(7,649)	(0.046)	(0.025)	(0.043)	(2,658)

4.3 Similarity with Feature Importance Algorithms

Lastly, we compared the similarity between the rankings of the participants and the feature importance rankings of XGBoost models. We utilized three different methods for computing the global feature importance of the models: the inbuilt `feature_importance` function, Permutation Importance [22], and Shapley Additive exPlanations (SHAP) [36]. The computed importances were then normalized, and an average rank was calculated for each feature across the three methods.

The participants' rankings by groups and their aggregation methods and by domain was compared using Spearman's Footrule. Table 3 presents the average distances between the rankings of the participants and the feature importance rankings. Our results indicate that all rankings differ significantly from the feature importance rankings ($p < 0.01$).

We then compared the distances between the groups. Individual rankings were significantly further away from feature importance rankings than behavioral ($z = 2.92, p < 0.01$), mean ($z = 3.96, p < 0.01$), and median aggregations ($z = 3.43, p < 0.01$), the difference was not significant to the Delphi method ($z = 1.14, p = 0.13$). The distances of the aggregations' methods were only weakly significant from each other. Behavioral ($z = -1.32, p = 0.09$) and mean ($z = -1.39, p = 0.08$) aggregations had a significantly smaller distance than the Delphi method.

Table 3. Mean Distance and Standard Deviation between Rankings and Feature Importances by Aggregation Method and Domain

Groups	Total	Housing	Cardio	Football	Covid	Cars
All Individuals	0.55	0.67	0.48	0.52	0.50	0.58
	(0.14)	(0.08)	(0.15)	(0.13)	(0.1)	(0.13)
Behavioral Aggregation	0.51	0.68	0.41	0.46	0.46	0.54
	(0.14)	(0.06)	(0.13)	(0.11)	(0.07)	(0.13)
Mean Aggregation	0.51	0.66	0.41	0.48	0.45	0.57
	(0.13)	(0.06)	(0.12)	(0.1)	(0.08)	(0.12)
Median Aggregation	0.52	0.67	0.42	0.48	0.45	0.58
	(0.14)	(0.06)	(0.13)	(0.11)	(0.08)	(0.13)
Delphi Update	0.54	0.67	0.45	0.50	0.49	0.56
	(0.14)	(0.09)	(0.13)	(0.14)	(0.11)	(0.14)

Examination of the five domains revealed that the results are consistent with the second part of the analysis, where only a limited number of groups showed significant differences. In domain *cardio*, the distance of the feature importance rankings to the individual rankings was significantly greater than to the behavioral ($z = 2.34, p = 0.01$), mean ($z = 3.14, p < 0.01$) and median ($z = 2.78, p < 0.01$) aggregations. We found this pattern also in the domains *football* and *covid*. In *football*, the difference in individual rankings was significantly greater than that of the behavioral ($z = 2.14, p = 0.01$), mean ($z = 2.21, p = 0.01$), and median aggregations ($z = 2.61, p < 0.01$). In domain *covid*, the behavioral ($z = 2.14, p = 0.02$), mean ($z = 4.0, p < 0.01$), and median ($z = 3.70, p < 0.01$) aggregations had a significantly smaller distance than the original individual ranking. Our findings indicate that, in certain instances, aggregating data can enhance individual rankings. Still, we failed to observe a statistically significant difference between the aggregation types, except for comparing the Delphi method and other methods. In the cardio domain, our results showed that the Delphi method had a weakly significant greater distance than the behavioral ($z = 1.35, p = 0.09$) and mean ($z = 1.37, p = 0.09$) aggregation. In the covid domain, the Delphi method had a significantly greater distance than the mean ($z = 2.06, p = 0.02$) and median ($z = 1.78, p = 0.04$) aggregation.

5   Discussion

In this study, we conducted an online experiment to evaluate various aggregation methods to ensemble individual feature rankings generated by human participants. Our methods were based on point estimation techniques from the literature. We investigated the effect of the methods on the rankings, the performance of machine learning models, and the proximity of the rankings to computed feature importance rankings.

First, we analyzed the impact of each aggregation method on the individual rankings of the participants in our study. We found that behavioral aggregation had the most significant impact on the rankings, followed by mean aggregation and median aggregation. Additionally, we discovered that the rankings produced by each method were significantly different from each other in terms of distance. The Delphi method did not lead to a meaningful change in the rankings.

Based on the feature rankings generated by each aggregation method, we trained machine learning models and evaluated their predictive performances. The analysis indicated that aggregation significantly affected performance in two domains, but the magnitude of improvement was modest and not meaningful. There were no discernible differences in performance between the aggregation methods, except for the Delphi method, which performed worse. Our results are consistent with some previous research on data-driven feature selection methods. While Saeys et al. [44] found that ensemble selection techniques' performances were comparable to single selector methods in their experiments, Chen et al. [9] found that combining filter and wrapper techniques with the union method produced higher classification accuracy. Dittmann et al. [18], similarly to our work, discovered that rank aggregation techniques produced similar performance results with little variance.

Thirdly, we computed feature importance rankings using XGBoost models and compared the individual and aggregated rankings with the calculated ranking. We found that aggregation methods significantly decrease the distance to the feature importance rankings and that the effect is not observable in all domains. Although the differences are statistically significant, it is noteworthy to mention that they were minimal.

Our study has a strength in its relatively high number of participants and multiple domains. Despite this strength, the findings of our study are limited by the fact that the participants were not professional individuals within the domains of real estate, automotive sales, or medical services. To mitigate this limitation, we focused on decision problems designed to be accessible to individuals without specialized domain knowledge. In future studies, researchers may consider recruiting professional participants within specific domains. Additionally, conducting the study in a real-world setting rather than online may enhance the elicitation and aggregation of behavioral data and provide a more comprehensive assessment of domain experts' knowledge to consider individual differences within the groups. Researchers focusing more on mathematical aggregation can try alternative operations to mean, and median [18, 49] and vary the group sizes, which should be also possible in behavioral aggregation. Furthermore, we believe that with higher-dimensional decision problems, the results in terms of performance differences between aggregation methods could vary. With an increase in the number of features, the aggregated models may become more diverse, potentially leading to significant differences in results.

6   Conclusion

As the role of human input in machine learning becomes increasingly important, it is crucial to investigate how knowledge can be elicited and aggregated effectively. This study examined three approaches to aggregating feature rankings based on human knowledge: behavioral aggregation, mathematical aggregation, and the Delphi method. These methods have been widely used in the literature on expert judgment elicitation.

Our study produced multiple results. They indicate that aggregation methods have a significant impact on individual rankings. Specifically, we found that behavioral aggregation has the most substantial influence on the rankings, whereas the Delphi method only slightly affects them. Furthermore, our findings reveal that different methods result in various rankings. However, despite these differences, there seems to be little to no improvement in terms of performance. Finally, we found that aggregated rankings were more similar to feature importance rankings than individual rankings, although the differences were minor.

Practitioners in the field should be mindful of these findings and be aware that how human input is aggregated can lead to varying models. Although the impact on model performance may not be significant, aggregated models can deviate significantly from individual preferences. Future studies should explore efficient methods for eliciting and aggregating domain knowledge to improve performance and practicality and reduce biases. Our research suggests that the field of expert judgment elicitation has ample scope for improvement and holds the potential to enhance human-in-the-loop approaches.

Acknowledgements. The preparation of the manuscript was funded by the Deutsche Forschungsgemeinschaft (DFG, German Research Foundation): TRR 318/1 2021-438445824. The authors thank Eyke Hüllermeier and Michael Rapp for valuable discussion and constructive comments.

References

1. Berisha, V., Krantsevich, C., Hahn, P.R., Hahn, S., Dasarathy, G., Turaga, P., Liss, J.: Digital medicine and the curse of dimensionality. npj Digital Med. **4**(1), 1–8 (2021). https://doi.org/10.1038/s41746-021-00521-5
2. Bianchi, F., Piroddi, L., Bemporad, A., Halasz, G., Villani, M., Piga, D.: Active preference-based optimization for human-in-the-loop feature selection. Eur. J. Control. **66**, 100647 (2022). https://doi.org/10.1016/j.ejcon.2022.100647
3. Bolger, F., Rowe, G.: The aggregation of expert judgment: do good things come to those who weight? Risk Anal. **35**(1), 5–11 (2015)
4. Bolón-Canedo, V., Alonso-Betanzos, A.: Ensembles for feature selection: a review and future trends. Inf. Fusion **52**, 1–12 (2019). https://doi.org/10.1016/j.inffus.2018.11.008
5. Breiman, L.: Classification and Regression Trees. Routledge, New York (2017). https://doi.org/10.1201/9781315139470
6. Burton, J.W., Stein, M.K., Jensen, T.B.: A systematic review of algorithm aversion in augmented decision making. J. Behav. Decis. Mak. **33**(2), 220–239 (2020). https://doi.org/10.1002/bdm.2155

7. Cai, J., Luo, J., Wang, S., Yang, S.: Feature selection in machine learning: a new perspective. Neurocomputing **300**, 70–79 (2018). https://doi.org/10.1016/j.neucom.2017.11.077

8. Chandrashekar, G., Sahin, F.: A survey on feature selection methods. Comput. Electr. Eng. **40**(1), 16–28 (2014). https://doi.org/10.1016/j.compeleceng.2013.11.024

9. Chen, C.W., Tsai, Y.H., Chang, F.R., Lin, W.C.: Ensemble feature selection in medical datasets: combining filter, wrapper, and embedded feature selection results. Expert. Syst. **37**(5), e12553 (2020). https://doi.org/10.1111/exsy.12553

10. Chen, D.L., Schonger, M., Wickens, C.: otree-an open-source platform for laboratory, online, and field experiments. J. Behav. Exp. Financ. **9**, 88–97 (2016)

11. Chen, T., Guestrin, C.: Xgboost: a scalable tree boosting system. In: Proceedings of the 22nd ACM SIGKDD International Conference on Knowledge Discovery and Data Mining, pp. 785–794. ACM, San Francisco California USA, August 2016. https://doi.org/10.1145/2939672.2939785

12. Chen, V., Bhatt, U., Heidari, H., Weller, A., Talwalkar, A.: Perspectives on incorporating expert feedback into model updates (arXiv:2205.06905) (July 2022). http://arxiv.org/abs/2205.06905. arXiv:2205.06905 [cs]

13. Cheng, T.H., Wei, C.P., Tseng, V.: Feature selection for medical data mining: comparisons of expert judgment and automatic approaches. In: 19th IEEE Symposium on Computer-Based Medical Systems (CBMS'06), pp. 165–170, June 2006. https://doi.org/10.1109/CBMS.2006.87

14. Cooke, R., Cooke, A.P.o.M., M., I.R.: Experts in Uncertainty: Opinion and Subjective Probability in Science. Oxford University Press (1991). google-Books-ID: 5nDmCwAAQBAJ

15. Corrales, D.C., Lasso, E., Ledezma, A., Corrales, J.C.: Feature selection for classification tasks: Expert knowledge or traditional methods? J. Intell. Fuzzy Syst. **34**(5), 2825–2835 (2018). https://doi.org/10.3233/JIFS-169470

16. Correia, A.H.C., Lecue, F.: Human-in-the-loop feature selection. In: Proceedings of the AAAI Conference on Artificial Intelligence 33(0101), pp. 2438–2445 (2019). https://doi.org/10.1609/aaai.v33i01.33012438

17. Diaconis, P., Graham, R.L.: Spearman's footrule as a measure of disarray. J. Royal Stat. Soc. Series B (Methodological) **39**(2), 262–268 (1977)

18. Dittman, D.J., Khoshgoftaar, T.M., Wald, R., Napolitano, A.: Classification performance of rank aggregation techniques for ensemble gene selection. In: The Twenty-Sixth International FLAIRS Conference (2013)

19. Effrosynidis, D., Arampatzis, A.: An evaluation of feature selection methods for environmental data. Eco. Inform. **61**, 101224 (2021). https://doi.org/10.1016/j.ecoinf.2021.101224

20. Ekstrøm, C.T., Gerds, T.A., Jensen, A.K., Brink-Jensen, K.: Sequential rank agreement methods for comparison of ranked lists arXiv:1508.06803, August 2015

21. Fink-Hafner, D., Dagen, T., Doušak, M., Novak, M., Hafner-Fink, M.: Delphi method: strengths and weaknesses. Adv. Methodol. Stat. **16**(2), 1–19 (2019)

22. Fisher, A., Rudin, C., Dominici, F.: All models are wrong, but many are useful: Learning a variable's importance by studying an entire class of prediction models simultaneously (arXiv:1801.01489), December 2019. [stat]

23. Genre, V., Kenny, G., Meyler, A., Timmermann, A.: Combining expert forecasts: can anything beat the simple average? Int. J. Forecast. **29**(1), 108–121 (2013)

24. Greenwell, B.M., Boehmke, B.C., McCarthy, A.J.: A simple and effective model-based variable importance measure, May 2018. arXiv:1805.04755 [cs, stat]

25. Guyon, I., Elisseeff, A.: An introduction to variable and feature selection. J. Mach. Learn. Res. **3**, 1157–1182 (2003)
26. Hanea, A., McBride, M., Burgman, M., Wintle, B.: Classical meets modern in the idea protocol for structured expert judgement. J. Risk Res. **21**(4), 417–433 (2018). https://doi.org/10.1080/13669877.2016.1215346
27. Hasan, N., Bao, Y.: Comparing different feature selection algorithms for cardiovascular disease prediction. Heal. Technol. **11**(1), 49–62 (2020). https://doi.org/10.1007/s12553-020-00499-2
28. Holzinger, A.: Interactive machine learning for health informatics: when do we need the human-in-the-loop? Brain Inf. **3**(2), 119–131 (2016). https://doi.org/10.1007/s40708-016-0042-6
29. James, G., Witten, D., Hastie, T., Tibshirani, R.: An introduction to statistical learning, vol. 112. Springer (2013)
30. Kee, F., Owen, T., Leathem, R.: Decision making in a multidisciplinary cancer team: does team discussion result in better quality decisions? Med. Decis. Making **24**(6), 602–613 (2004)
31. Kerrigan, D., Hullman, J., Bertini, E.: A survey of domain knowledge elicitation in applied machine learning. Multimodal Technol. Interaction **5**(1212), 73 (2021). https://doi.org/10.3390/mti5120073
32. Kugler, T., Kausel, E.E., Kocher, M.G.: Are groups more rational than individuals? a review of interactive decision making in groups. Wiley Interdisciplinary Rev. Cognitive Sci. **3**(4), 471–482 (2012)
33. Kumar, R., Vassilvitskii, S.: Generalized distances between rankings. In: Proceedings of the 19th International Conference on World Wide Web. WWW 2010, pp. 571–580. Association for Computing Machinery, New York, April 2010. https://doi.org/10.1145/1772690.1772749
34. Li, J., et al.: Feature selection: a data perspective. ACM Comput. Surv. **50**(6), 94:1–94:45 (2017). https://doi.org/10.1145/3136625
35. Liu, H., Motoda, H.: Feature Selection for Knowledge Discovery and Data Mining. Springer Science & Business Media (Dec 2012), google-Books-ID: aaDbBwAAQBAJ
36. Lundberg, S.M., Lee, S.I.: A unified approach to interpreting model predictions. In: Advances in Neural Information Processing Systems, vol. 30. Curran Associates, Inc. (2017). https://proceedings.neurips.cc/paper/2017/hash/8a20a8621978632d76c43dfd28b67767-Abstract.html
37. McAndrew, T., Wattanachit, N., Gibson, G.C., Reich, N.G.: Aggregating predictions from experts: a review of statistical methods, experiments, and applications. WIREs Comput. Stat. **13**(2), e1514 (2021). https://doi.org/10.1002/wics.1514
38. Mera-Gaona, M., López, D.M., Vargas-Canas, R., Neumann, U.: Framework for the ensemble of feature selection methods. Appl. Sci. **11**(1717), 8122 (2021). https://doi.org/10.3390/app11178122
39. Moro, S., Cortez, P., Rita, P.: A divide-and-conquer strategy using feature relevance and expert knowledge for enhancing a data mining approach to bank telemarketing. Expert. Syst. **35**(3), e12253 (2018). https://doi.org/10.1111/exsy.12253
40. Nahar, J., Imam, T., Tickle, K.S., Chen, Y.P.P.: Computational intelligence for heart disease diagnosis: a medical knowledge driven approach. Expert Syst. Appl. **40**(1), 96–104 (2013). https://doi.org/10.1016/j.eswa.2012.07.032
41. O'Hagan, A.: Expert knowledge elicitation: subjective but scientific. Am. Stat. **73**(sup1), 69–81 (2019). https://doi.org/10.1080/00031305.2018.1518265
42. O'Hagan, A., et al.: Uncertain Judgements: Eliciting Experts' Probabilities. John Wiley & Sons, August 2006, google-Books-ID: H9KswqPWIDQC

43. Pedregosa, F., Varoquaux, G., Gramfort, A., Michel, V., Thirion, B., Grisel, O., Blondel, M., Prettenhofer, P., Weiss, R., Dubourg, V., Vanderplas, J., Passos, A., Cournapeau, D., Brucher, M., Perrot, M., Duchesnay, E.: Scikit-learn: machine learning in Python. J. Mach. Learn. Res. **12**, 2825–2830 (2011)
44. Saeys, Y., Abeel, T., Van de Peer, Y.: Robust feature selection using ensemble feature selection techniques. In: Daelemans, W., Goethals, B., Morik, K. (eds.) Machine Learning and Knowledge Discovery in Databases, pp. 313–325. LNCS. Springer, Heidelberg (2008). https://doi.org/10.1007/978-3-540-87481-2-21
45. Schulz-Hardt, S., Brodbeck, F.C., Mojzisch, A., Kerschreiter, R., Frey, D.: Group decision making in hidden profile situations: dissent as a facilitator for decision quality. J. Pers. Soc. Psychol. **91**(6), 1080 (2006)
46. Seymoens, T., Ongenae, F., Jacobs, A., Verstichel, S., Ackaert, A.: A methodology to involve domain experts and machine learning techniques in the design of human-centered algorithms. In: Human Work Interaction Design. Designing Engaging Automation: 5th IFIP WG 13.6 Working Conference, HWID 2018, Espoo, Finland, August 20–21, 2018, Revised Selected Papers 5, pp. 200–214. Springer (2019)
47. Shin, D.: The effects of explainability and causability on perception, trust, and acceptance: implications for explainable ai. Int. J. Hum. Comput. Stud. **146**, 102551 (2021)
48. Studer, S., Bui, T.B., Drescher, C., Hanuschkin, A., Winkler, L., Peters, S., Müller, K.R.: Towards crisp-ml(q): a machine learning process model with quality assurance methodology. Mach. Learn. Knowl. Extraction **3**(22), 392–413 (2021). https://doi.org/10.3390/make3020020
49. Wald, R., Khoshgoftaar, T.M., Dittman, D., Awada, W., Napolitano, A.: An extensive comparison of feature ranking aggregation techniques in bioinformatics. In: 2012 IEEE 13th International Conference on Information Reuse & Integration (IRI), pp. 377–384, August 2012. https://doi.org/10.1109/IRI.2012.6303034
50. Wang, J., Oh, J., Wang, H., Wiens, J.: Learning credible models. In: Proceedings of the 24th ACM SIGKDD International Conference on Knowledge Discovery & Data Mining, KDD 2018, pp. 2417–2426. Association for Computing Machinery, New York, July 2018. https://doi.org/10.1145/3219819.3220070, https://doi.org/10.1145/3219819.3220070
51. Wilson, K.J.: An investigation of dependence in expert judgement studies with multiple experts. Int. J. Forecast. **33**(1), 325–336 (2017)
52. Wittmann, M.E., Cooke, R.M., Rothlisberger, J.D., Lodge, D.M.: Using structured expert judgment to assess invasive species prevention: Asian carp and the mississippi-great lakes hydrologic connection **48**, 2150–2156 (2014). https://doi.org/10.1021/es4043098

Human-Centered AI
for Manufacturing – Design Principles
for Industrial AI-Based Services

Janika Kutz[1,2(✉)], Jens Neuhüttler[1], Bernd Bienzeisler[1], Jan Spilski[2],
and Thomas Lachmann[2,3]

[1] Fraunhofer Institute for Industrial Engineering IAO, 70569 Stuttgart, Germany
janika.kutz@iao.fraunhofer.de
[2] Center for Cognitive Science, University of Kaiserslautern-Landau,
67663 Kaiserslautern, Germany
[3] Centro de Investigación Nebrija en Cognición (CINC), Universidad Nebrija, Madrid, Spain

Abstract. AI-based services are becoming more and more common in manufacturing; however, the development, implementation, and operation of these services are associated with challenges. The design of Human-Centered AI (HCAI) is one approach to address these challenges. Design guidelines and principles are provided to assist AI developers in the design of HCAI. However, these principles are currently defined for AI in general and not for specific application contexts. The aim of this work is to analyze whether existing design principles for HCAI are transferable to IAI-based services in manufacturing and how they can be integrated into the development process. In an explorative-qualitative research design, the design pattern of the People + AI Guidebook by the PAIR from Google were analyzed regarding their applicability in manufacturing environments. The finding show that a transfer of the design principles is generally possible. According to the experts, 15 of the design patterns have a direct influence on the perception of Industrial AI-based services by end-users or management and can thus increase the acceptance of them. Finally, the design patterns were assessed in terms of their application relevance and complexity in manufacturing.

Keywords: Industrial AI · Human-Centered AI · Design Principles

1 Introduction

The field of Human-Centered Artificial Intelligence (HCAI) has recently gained more importance. A number of research papers have addressed the design of HCAI applications. These studies emphasize the significance of a human-centered design approach in the development and operation of AI-based systems, as these systems have a significant impact on people's daily lives well as their working environment [1–3]. The aim of HCAI is to design AI-based systems that empower people, fulfil humans values and needs [3]. "A human-centered approach will reduce the out-of-control technologies, calm fears of robot-led unemployment, and give users the rewarding sense of mastery and accomplishment" [3].

© The Author(s), under exclusive license to Springer Nature Switzerland AG 2023
H. Degen and S. Ntoa (Eds.): HCII 2023, LNAI 14050, pp. 115–130, 2023.
https://doi.org/10.1007/978-3-031-35891-3_8

This also applies to the use of AI-based systems in manufacturing, referred to as Industrial AI (IAI). The use of IAI is diverse, as it can be applied along the entire value chain from logistics to assembly [4]. All these applications have one thing in common: they influence the working environment. As a result, employees at manufacturing organizations will increasingly need to collaborate with AI-based systems in the future. Even though IAI applications are becoming more common, development, implementation and roll-out are associated with numerous challenges. Challenges identified in our previous research are, e.g., "concerns and fear related to AI-Services", "false expectations of the end-user in the AI service" and "lack of technology acceptance by employees". In addition, we identified several success factors in relation to IAI-based services, e.g., "trust in AI", "confidence in operability of the IT-System", "user-centered development" and the "added value of the AI service must be clear" [5]. Designing HCAI-based services for manufacturing is a necessary step to address these challenges and to strengthen the success factors. The aim of these paper is to analyze whether known approaches to design HCAI are transferable to IAI-based services and how these can be integrated into the development process.

2   Theoretical Background

2.1   Human-Centered AI Design

Throughout the entire AI life cycle, HCAI seeks to put people back in the center of AI-based services. The aim of HCAI is not to reduce the degree of automation, but to create AI-based systems "that increase automation, while amplifying, augmenting, enhancing, and empowering people to innovatively apply systems and creatively refine them" [6]. One way to enhance HCAI design is to apply design principles, patterns, and guidelines throughout the development process. Various guidelines and principles have been published lately for the implementation of ethical and human-centered AI-based services. Principles are developed at various abstraction levels. A distinction can be made between high-level guidelines, which are mainly provided by policymakers, and concrete action-oriented principles, which are published by companies, for example [7]. The former are usually general guidelines that can provide initial guidance on HCAI design. For example, the "Ethics Guidelines for Trustworthy AI" of the High-Level Expert Group on Artificial Intelligence of the European Commission (2019) describes four principles and seven requirements for designing trustworthy AI systems [8]. However, these general guidelines contain only a few concrete development recommendations. The action-oriented principles, on the other hand, offer concrete instructions for action and can thus be understood as design principles in a narrower sense [9]. Google and Microsoft have published such specific design principles. Google's People + AI research team [10] has published 23 design patterns for HCAI in their People + AI Guidebook. The patterns are structured along common questions that arise in the development process [10]. Pattern language is used to describe the principles in the People + AI Guidebook. The patterns are "brief expressions of important ideas that suggest solutions to common design problems" [3]. Microsoft published its Guidelines for Human-AI Interaction in 2019 [1]. These can also be viewed in a web application, are described in detail, and include practical recommendations [11]. This paper focuses on design principles/design patterns, that provide specific instructions on how to apply and implement the principles. However, more general design principles and guidelines are also crucial and can offer basic advice on HCAI design. Finally, it should be noted that the various published guidelines have one thing in common: they are generally applicable and not specifically tailored to concrete application contexts, such as manufacturing.

2.2 The Human Factor in Industrial AI-Based Services

Manufacturing companies are increasingly embracing digitalization, and along with it, the use of AI-based services in manufacturing is growing. Industrial AI applications can be used for, e.g., predictive maintenance, quality management respectively fault diagnosis or as decision support systems [12]. Furthermore, they can be understood as services, as they are not limited to technological aspects, but rather represent an immaterial offer that aims to change the state of people, objects, processes, or information [13]. Nevertheless, AI applications are scarce in the industrial environments [4, 14]. This has several reasons, e.g., lack of skills and experience, lack of development and implementation resources and lack of access to the necessary data [4]. Moreover, the development, roll-out, and operation of IAI-based services is related to various challenges at a technical, organizational, and human level. The development of AI systems has been driven primarily by technology [15] and users at the operational level are poorly considered in the development process [16]. Thereby, IAI-based services should "connect people and things through systems…" [14], which indicates that beyond technological factors, human and organizational requirements should also be taken into account. Employees should not be viewed as objects to be persuaded, but as active participants in the transformation process, to increase the technological acceptance of Industry 4.0 solutions and thus AI-based systems [16].

Hoffmann et al. describe in their "Proposal for requirements on industrial AI solutions" a broader understanding of IAI, which includes, beyond technology, topics such as industrial applications, value creation, human-AI interaction, regulatory aspects, and ethics [12]. Along 5 main issues (Adaption, Engineering, Embedding, Safety/Security, Trust), they formulate 16 requirements in relation to IAI solutions, e.g., "Stepwise introduction", "Virtual learning" and "Proof of capabilities". This work gives AI developers in the industrial context a first orientation for the design, which goes beyond technical aspects.

2.3 Purpose of Research

As previously mentioned, there are several publications that discuss the ethical and human-centered design of AI applications and establish principles and guidelines for them. These, however, are of general application or specifically aimed at mainstream AI applications and have not been developed specifically for IAI-based services. Since IAI has some specific characteristics [12, 14], a simple application of the principles in the context of IAI is not possible. However, the need for HCAI in the industrial environment is high to overcome certain challenges. It should be the aim to develop IAI-based services that are accepted and trusted by the employees. Moreover, they should be perceived as safe by the employees. Furthermore, semi-automated IAI-based services that combine machine learning with human experience have proven to be particularly effective. This also necessitates a human-centered design approach, where the IAI-based service assists the employees rather than replacing them [4]. Integrating HCAI applications into the industrial environment is a necessary step to successfully advance and shape digitalization and automation in industry. The purpose of this paper is to introduce the production perspective on HCAI. Moreover, practical guidance for the application of HCAI design principles in industrial environments is provided. Therefore, the following research questions are answered:

- Which design principles for HCAI known from literature are applicable to IAI-based services?
- When should the design principles be considered during the development process of IAI-based services?
- Which design principles are directly perceptible by the management and end-users?
- How relevant is their use in practice?
- How complex is their application in industrial environments?

After screening various design guidelines, principles and patterns for the design of AI-based systems, we selected the design patterns defined in Google PAIR's People + AI Guidebook [10] to answer the research questions. To analyze the applicability in the industrial environment, design patterns with complete descriptions and practical recommendations were selected. Each design pattern is thoroughly described in the Guidebook, along with helpful actionable advice. Additionally, the development of reliable, safe, and trustworthy AI-based applications should be the main objective, with a clear focus on human-centered design. This is also the case with the Guidebook, as it is according to the People + AI Research: "A friendly, practical guide that lays out some best practices for creating useful, responsible AI applications." [10].

3   Method

To answer the research questions, an explorative-qualitative research design was chosen. Online workshops were conducted with two groups, each consisting of 2 experts for Industrial AI-based services. Two 60-min sessions were held with the first group of participants, and one 120-min session was held with the second group. During the workshops, the participants worked interactively in three steps. First, the 23 design patterns from The People + AI Guidebook [10] were examined and their general applicability to the manufacturing environment was discussed. This ensured that all participants had the same level of knowledge and understanding of the design patterns. In the second step, the design patterns were located in a matrix. On the one hand, an assessment was made in which phase of an AI development process a design pattern should be applied. Following the ML-Ops process [17], the development phases selected here are divided into three steps: (1) Design, (2) Development and (3) Roll-out and Operation. Secondly, the design patterns were assessed with regard to their main target group. A distinction was made between two groups, (1) AI Engineers and (2) End-Users and Management. In the third step, the design patterns allocated to the target group of End-Users and

Management were evaluated based on two variables. On the one hand, the relevance of a design pattern regarding the development and operation of HCAI applications in manufacturing should be assessed. On the other hand, the complexity of applying a design pattern in a manufacturing environment. Each pattern was then located on a graph along the two variables. In addition, at the end of each step, it was reflected whether further design patterns need to be added.

After the conclusion of the workshop, the results were consolidated. Design patterns that were evaluated and classified differently by the groups were discussed in an internal session consisting of two scientists from different disciplines (Group 3). In total, the evaluation of the design patterns was carried out by six experts for Industrial AI-based applications from different disciplines (Table 1).

Table 1. Description of the sample.

Expert	Professional background	Group
1	ML-Engineer for Industrial AI applications	Group 1
2	Digital Business Developer	Group 1
3	Expert for trustworthy AI in industrial applications	Group 2
4	Expert for Industrial AI-based systems	Group 2
5	Expert for acceptance of AI-based services	Group 3
6	Expert for development and quality assessment of smart services	Group 3

4   Results

At the beginning of the workshops, the 23 design patterns were explained to create an equal understanding of them among all participants. Following from this, the design principles were discussed in terms of their general applicability in an industrial environment. All experts agreed that applying the design patterns is theoretically achievable and that all patterns are basically relevant. The experts also mentioned the need for HCAI patterns for the industrial context and confirmed that their application would be beneficial. Only one of the 23 design patterns proved to be irrelevant for the industrial context. The experts consented that a use of the pattern "*Adding context from human sources.*" in an industrial setting would not be appropriate. According to the experts, parameters from the technical installations could be integrated as third-party sources. However, this would require a more detailed examination of the extent to which this could be usefully applied as a design pattern. For this reason, this design pattern is no longer considered in the subsequent presentation of results. Furthermore, the experts also noted that there might be differences depending on the IAI use case. Moreover, no major gaps could be identified and in consequence no further design principles are formulated. The design patterns can be considered as a starting point and provide a comprehensive orientation regarding which aspects should be considered when designing HCAI. However, it also became clear that a one-to-one transfer is not possible, instead specific descriptions are required for the industrial application context.

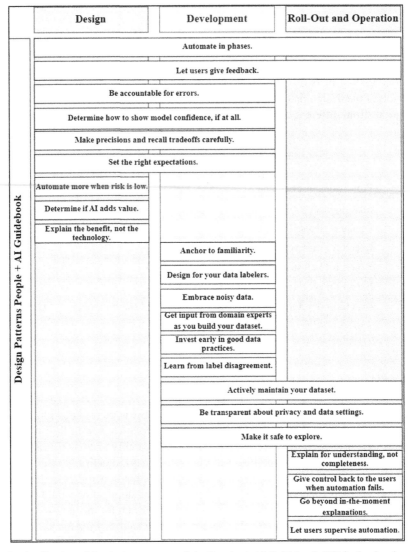

Fig. 1. Application of the design patterns of the People + AI Guidebook [10] in the development process of IAI-based services.

Answering the second research question: "When should the design principles be considered during the development process of IAI-based services?" the design patterns were located along the IAI development process, with each workshop group. A consolidated version of the allocation can be found in Fig. 1.

4.1 End-User Focused Design Patterns

In the second workshop phase, the application of the design patterns in the context of IAI-based services was analyzed in more detail. To answer the following research question "Which design principles are directly perceptible by the management and end-users?" the design patterns were evaluated in relation to their primary target group. The aim was to identify those patterns that end-users perceive directly in their everyday work with IAI-based services. Across the workshops, there was a strong consensus on which design patterns directly address end-users and influence their perception of and interaction with AI-based services. For five design patterns, differentiated opinions on the target group could be identified. For example, depending on the design of the development process, it is quite possible that the end-users will be directly affected by design patterns relating to data in their daily work (e.g., *"Actively maintain your dataset."*, *"Get input from domain experts as you build your dataset."*). Nevertheless, the experts agreed that this pattern is primarily tailored to the AI engineers and only has an indirect effect on the end-users through the increased quality of the AI-based service. Furthermore, it becomes clear that differentiating the pattern of *"Determine if AI adds value."* into a technical and a business level would be beneficial for the application in manufacturing environments.

The findings of the workshops are summarized in the table below, along with a few sample quotes from the workshops. Furthermore, the figures in the appendix illustrate which design principles were classified as end-user-centered in each workshop (Table 2).

The workshop results also indicate that the AI engineers are typically in charge of putting the design patterns into practice. According to the experts, this is not the case for four of the patterns; in these cases, the experts pointed out that the management is responsible. *Automate in phases:* Before the development and introduction of AI-based services, the management should develop an automation strategy for the company and based on this, decide in which automation steps an AI system will be rolled out. *Automate more when risk is low*: According to the experts, management is jointly accountable for analyzing risk and deciding whether to adopt AI projects based on the risk assessment. *Determine if AI adds value*: The experts emphasize that management must decide whether to adopt IAI-based services on the predicted added value. *Make precision and recall tradeoffs carefully*: Is interpreted by the experts as a framework for the actual development, which must also be set by the management.

Based on the results of the second workshop phase, the patterns that were assessed as end-user-centered were further evaluated in the third phase. The experts assessed the patterns according to their application relevance and application complexity in the manufacturing environment. For 7 design principles, the relevance as well as the complexity of the application in the context of IAI-based services was assessed similarly (see Fig. 2).

Table 2. Experts' assessments of the main target group

AI Engineers	Management and End-Users
Actively maintain your dataset	
The experts agree that primarily AI-engineers are targeted Sample quote: "Patterns primarily influence the work of AI engineers, as good data management is important for them to develop and deliver high-quality AI systems." (Group 2)	End-users may also be targeted: "AI developers need support from production to collect data. If the end-users support this process and provide data themselves, they are directly affected by the pattern." (Group 1)
Anchor to familiarity	
/	The experts agree that primarily end-users are targeted Sample quote: "… is relevant for users because they have to work with the system in the end." (Group 2)
Automate in phases	
/	The experts agree that primarily end-users are targeted Sample quote: "Especially relevant for end-users because they can slowly get used to the increasing automation and familiarize themselves with the new technology." (Group 1)
Automate more when risk is low	
/	The experts agree that primarily management and end-users are targeted Sample quote: "… particularly relevant for management, as they are finally in charge." (Group 2)
Be accountable for errors	
The experts agree that primarily AI-engineers are targeted	/
Be transparent about privacy and data settings	
/	The experts agree that primarily management and end-users are targeted
Design for your data labelers	

(continued)

Table 2. (*continued*)

AI Engineers	Management and End-Users
The experts agree that primarily AI-engineers are targeted Sample quote: "… is especially important for AI engineers to ensure that the data quality in the development process is correct." (Group 2)	/
Determine if AI adds value	
"…when it comes to technical feasibility and an assessment of that, the principle primarily addresses AI engineers." (Group 1)	"…relevant for employees, whether their work is facilitated by the use of AI systems." (Group 2) "The management has to decide whether the implementation of an AI adds a value for the organization or not." (Group 2)
Embrace "noisy" data	
The experts agree that primarily AI-engineers are targeted	/
Explain for understanding, not completeness	
/	The experts agree that primarily end-users are targeted
Explain the benefit, not the technology	
/	The experts agree that primarily end-users are targeted
Get input from domain experts as you build your dataset	
The experts agree that primarily AI-engineers are targeted Sample quote: "…das soll man machen, aber Anwender und Management bekommen dies nicht unbedingt direkt mit." (Group 2)	End-users may also be targeted: Werden die Endanwender als Domain Experts einbezogen können diese hier direkt Einfluss nehmen auf die Qualität der Daten. (Group 1 und 3)
Give control back to the user when automation fails	
/	The experts agree that primarily end-users are targeted
Go beyond in-the-moment explanations	
/	The experts agree that primarily end-users are targeted
Invest early in good data practices	

(*continued*)

Table 2. (*continued*)

AI Engineers	Management and End-Users
The experts agree that primarily AI-engineers are targeted	End-users may also be targeted: "If the end-users support the data collection, they are directly affected and can actively influence the development process by providing data according to quality standards." (Group 1)
Learn from label disagreements	
The experts agree that primarily AI-engineers are targeted	/
Let users give feedback	
	The experts agree that primarily end-users are targeted
Let users supervise automation	
/	The experts agree that primarily end-users are targeted
Make it safe to explore	
/	The experts agree that primarily end-users are targeted
Make precision and recall tradeoffs carefully	
/	The experts agree that primarily management and end-users are targeted Sample quote: "Ratio of error rates is especially important for end-users and management." (Group 2)
Set the right expectations	
"In development, it is important to have realistic expectations of an AI system, even within the team of AI engineers responsible for development." (Group 1)	The experts agree that primarily the management and end-users are targeted

Note: The design patterns are the same as in the People + AI guidebook [10].

For example, both groups consider the principle "Let users give feedback" as very relevant, but also as highly complex to implement. Group 2 emphasizes that the complexity increases with the number of people involved in development, and that feedback made by end-users results in a less linear development process. Group 1 mentioned that depending on the AI-based service, it may be difficult to integrate feedback options into the production process accurately. At the same time, it must be guaranteed that the AI engineers take feedback into account and integrate it into the AI-based services. Both groups rated "*Give control back to the users when automation fails*" as one of the most important patterns. According to the experts, this is particularly relevant in the production

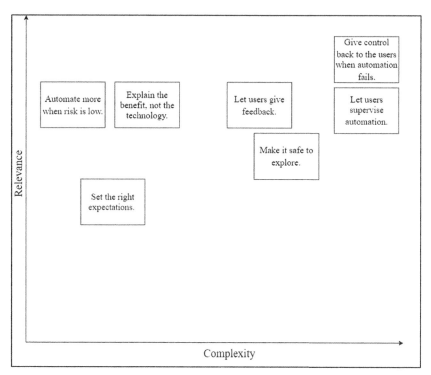

Fig. 2. Consolidated assessment of the relevance and complexity of the application of end-user centered design patterns of the People + AI Guidebook [10].

context because it is usually a prerequisite in manufacturing to have a back-up system. Designing this handover process is a challenge. According to the experts, complexity can change based on the use case, its importance, and its integration into the production process. According to the experts, the design pattern *"Let users supervise automation"* is equally complex to integrate into production processes, as these are currently standardized and offer little freedom for individual adjustments. The design principle *"Explain the benefit, not the technology"* is ranked relatively high on the relevance dimension by both workshop groups. Both groups justify this with the argument that in this way, end-users and management can be convinced to use an AI system. The complexity is rated as rather low by both groups. *"Make it safe to explore"* is classified as a pattern that is very important to build end-user trust in an AI-based service.

In contrast, the assessment of eight design patterns along the dimensions differs between the workshop groups. For example, the pattern *"Be transparent about privacy and data settings"* was assessed differently. Group 1 rated the principle as not very complex, but very relevant, whereas group 2 rated the relevance rather low, but the complexity high. *"Automate in phases"* is rated as rather relevant by both groups, but the complexity is rated differently. Group 1 explains that automation in phases can lead to additional development efforts. Group 2, on the other hand, justifies the low complexity by saying that a step-by-step approach to maximum automation can reduce complexity during development. Group 1 said the pattern "Go beyond in-the-moment explanations" is less relevant, but also less complex in application. Group 2 assesses the application as very complex, since a comprehensible and more in-depth preparation of the contents from the systems would require additional effort. However, this varies depending on the application. Since detailed explanations can build trust, the experts rated the pattern as relevant. *"Explain for understanding, not completeness"* is considered very important by both groups, but the assessment of complexity varies. Group 2 clarified in the workshop that it is in any case more important to provide a simple explanation than the more in-depth explanations. *"Determine how to show model confidence, if at all"* was rated by group 2 as less complex to apply and was placed in the middle of the scale for determining relevance. The first group, on the other hand, rated it as very relevant and placed the complexity in the middle. Both groups pointed out that this can help to increase trust in an AI-based service. The appendix contains a presentation of the assessments per workshop.

5 Discussion and Conclusion

5.1 Discussion, Limitations and Further Need for Research

The use of HCAI is a promising approach for the manufacturing industry to create AI systems that are accepted by employees as they are perceived as safe and trustworthy. Looking at the requirements defined by Hoffmann et al. (2021) for IAI solutions, some requirements can be met by using Designing Patterns. For example, the recommended "stepwise introduction" of IAI solutions is addressed with the design pattern *"Automate in phases"* [12]. However, it can also be seen that the patterns examined go beyond the described requirements and address additional aspects. The design patterns also offer a good opportunity to overcome existing challenges. Among other things, the use of design patterns promotes a user-centered development process, strengthens trust in AI applications, leads to realistic expectation management and can provide orientation in the development process [5].

The results presented here are the result of a qualitative study based on opinions of 6 experts. In order to check the validity of the results, it would be useful to evaluate the results with other experts in further research projects. Also, the design principles should be tested in application, either in experimental settings or in the direct production environment. In this way, deeper insights into the effects of the patterns could be gained and best-practices for application in practice could be elaborated. The experts made it clear that an application is not directly transferable, but that it would make sense to adapt it to the production context. In the current study, the necessary adaptation could not be dealt with in more detail. Furthermore, the assessment of the application relevance and application complexity is only based on the rankings of four experts. Again, further research is needed to validate our findings. It is important to keep in mind when interpreting the findings that the experts may rate relevance and importance differently depending on the particular AI use cases. The ratings given reflect their general view. In further research, the different patterns should be considered separately and detailed elaborations on the application in the manufacturing environment should be conducted. Decision support for AI engineers on which of the principles should be applied in the design of specific AI use cases would also be valuable.

Another potential limitation is that we only analyzed the design patterns of the People + AI Guidebook [10]. Other Design Guidelines, even if they are providing detailed descriptions like the Microsoft Guidelines for Human-AI Interaction [11] were not considered. There might be further design guidelines, principles, and patterns that are also applicable in the manufacturing environment and offer added value, as well as going beyond the patterns contained in the Guidebook. However, it would have been beyond the scope of this research to examine further guidelines. Furthermore, it could not be considered within the scope of this study which specific types of human intelligence are supported by AI and whether different principles can be derived from this for the design of industrial AI based service applications [18].

Nevertheless, the design patterns considered are very focused on the IAI system itself, but the IAI-based service consists of further components. In particular, the processes before and after the AI application should also be considered in the design in an industrial context, since contextualizing factors form the framework for quality perception of AI-based services [19]. Last but not least, the use of design patterns should be aligned with common validation procedures and transferred into a holistic and harmonized approach for design and testing activities during development [20]. In the near future, the regulatory framework should also be taken into account when designing design patterns. Discussions about the safeguarding and certification of AI-based services have gained relevance. The extent to which the design patterns already address these requirements should be examined in the future. The focus of this study was on industrial AI-based services, but the design of HCAI is also relevant in other disciplines. The extent to which design principles can be applied in other disciplines and whether these, e.g., lawyers or medical professionals, have different requirements for the design of AI-based services than production employees should be investigated in future studies.

5.2 Conclusion and Practical Implications

The aim of the paper is to initially address an HCAI design for the manufacturing environment. The experts agreed that the need for human-centered IAI-based services is high and generally consider the application of the design patterns is beneficial. By allocating the design patterns along the AI development process, AI engineers are provided with a practical guide for the future design of IAI-based services. During the development and implementation of IAI-based services, it is particularly important to involve the end-users in the process [21]. In addition, management support must also be ensured to successfully shape the digital transformation [5]. The use of design patterns can help developers to address these requirements. Across the workshops, the experts identified 15 of the relevant 22 design patterns as having a direct impact on end-users' or management's perception of IAI-based services:

1. Anchor to familiarity
2. Automate in phases
3. Automate more when risk is low
4. Be transparent about privacy and data settings
5. Determine how to show model confidence, if at all
6. Determine if AI adds value

7. Explain for understanding, not completeness
8. Explain the benefit, not the technology
9. Give control back to the user when automation fails
10. Go beyond in-the-moment explanations
11. Let users give feedback
12. Let users supervise automation
13. Make it safe to explore
14. Make precision and recall tradeoffs carefully
15. Set the right expectations

The application of the design patterns is considered very relevant in most cases, whereas the complexity of the application varies between the patterns. The remaining 7 design patterns address the AI engineers themselves in particular. To design reliable, safe, and trustworthy AI systems, these principles should also be taken into account, but they are not directly perceptible to the end-user after implementation.

Appendix

The experts assessed the patterns according to their application relevance and application complexity in the manufacturing environment (Figs. 3 and 4).

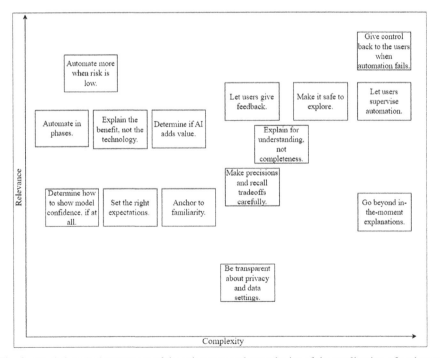

Fig. 3. Workshop 1: Assessment of the relevance and complexity of the application of end-user-centered design patterns of the People + AI Guidebook [10].

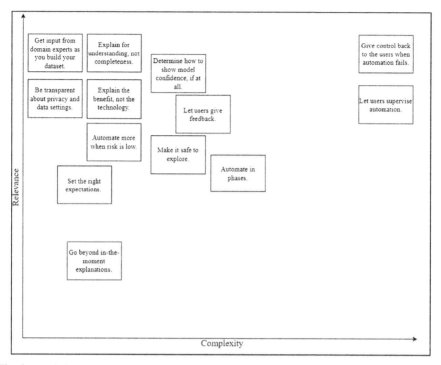

Fig. 4. Workshop 2: Assessment of the relevance and complexity of the application of end-user-centered design patterns of the People + AI Guidebook [10].

References

1. Amershi, S., et al.: Guidelines for human-AI interaction. In: Brewster, S., Fitzpatrick, G., Cox, A., Kostakos, V. (eds.) Proceedings of the 2019 CHI Conference on Human Factors in Computing Systems. CHI 2019: CHI Conference on Human Factors in Computing Systems, Glasgow, Scotland, UK, 04 May 2019–09 May 2019, pp. 1–13. ACM, New York (2019). https://doi.org/10.1145/3290605.3300233
2. Xu, W., Dainoff, M.J., Ge, L., Gao, Z.: Transitioning to human interaction with AI systems: new challenges and opportunities for HCI professionals to enable human-centered AI. Int. J. Hum. Comput. Interact. (2022). https://doi.org/10.1080/10447318.2022.2041900
3. Shneiderman, B.: Human-Centered AI. Oxford University Press, Oxford (2022)
4. Pokorni, B., Braun, M., Knecht, C.: Human-centred AI applications in production. Practical experience and guidelines for operational implementation strategies. Fraunhofer IAO (2021). (in German). http://publica.fraunhofer.de/dokumente/N-6249564.html.
5. Kutz, J., Neuhüttler, J., Spilski, J., Lachmann, T.: Implementation of AI technologies in manufacturing - success factors and challenges. In: The Human Side of Service Engineering. 13th International Conference on Applied Human Factors and Ergonomics (AHFE 2022), 24–28 July 2022. AHFE International (2022). https://doi.org/10.54941/ahfe1002565
6. Shneiderman, B.: Human-centered artificial intelligence: reliable, safe & trustworthy. Int. J. Hum. Comput. Interact. (2020). https://doi.org/10.1080/10447318.2020.1741118

7. Lütge, C., et al.: Automotive. AI4People-ethical guidelines for the automotive sector: fundamental requirements & practical recommendations for industry and policymakers. In: Floridini, L. (ed.) AI4People's 7 AI Global Frameworks

8. High-Level Expert Group on Artificial Intelligence: Ethics Guidelines for Trustworthy AI, Brussels (2019). file:///C:/Users/kutz/Downloads/ai_hleg_ethics_guidelines_for_trustworthy_ai-en_87F84A41-A6E8-F38C-BFF661481B40077B_60419.pdf

9. Smit, K., Zoet, M., van Meerten, J.: A review of AI principles in practice. In: Pacific Asia Conference on Information Systems (2020)

10. Google PAIR: People + AI Guidebook. Designing human-centered AI products (2019). https://pair.withgoogle.com/guidebook/. Accessed 04 Nov 22

11. Microsoft: Guidelines for Human-AI Interaction. Microsoft HAX Toolkit (2022). https://www.microsoft.com/en-us/haxtoolkit/ai-guidelines/. Accessed 8 Feb 2023

12. Hoffmann, M.W., Drath, R., Ganz, C.: Proposal for requirements on industrial AI solutions. In: Beyerer, J., Niggemann, O., Maier, A. (eds.) Machine Learning for Cyber Physical Systems, pp. 63–72. Springer, Berlin Heidelberg (2021)

13. Kutz, J., Neuhüttler, J., Schaefer, K., Spilski, J., Lachmann, T.: Generic role model for the systematic development of internal AI-based services in manufacturing. In: Bui, T.X. (ed.) Proceedings of the 56th Annual Hawaii International Conference on System Sciences, Honolulu, HI, 3–6 January 2023, pp. 909–917 (2023)

14. Lee, J., Singh, J., Azamfar, M.: Industrial artificial intelligence (2019). http://arxiv.org/pdf/1908.02150v3

15. Wang, B., Xue, Y., Yan, J., Yang, X., Zhou, Y.: Human-centered intelligent manufacturing: overview and perspectives. Chin. J. Eng. Sci. (2020). https://doi.org/10.15302/J-SSCAE-2020.04.020

16. Abel, J., Hirsch-Kreinsen, H., Wienzek, T.: Acceptance of industry 4.0. Final report on an explorative empirical study of German industry. acatech – National Academy of Science and Engineering, Munic (2019). (in German)

17. Visengeriyeva, L., Kammer, A., Bär, I., Kniesz, A., Plöd, M.: Machine learning operations (2022). https://ml-ops.org/content/mlops-principles. Accessed 10 Feb 2023

18. Huang, M.-H., Rust, R.T.: Artificial intelligence in service. J. Serv. Res. (2018). https://doi.org/10.1177/1094670517752459

19. Neuhüttler, J., Fischer, R., Ganz, W., Urmetzer, F.: Perceived quality of artificial intelligence in smart service systems: a structured approach. In: Shepperd, M., Brito e Abreu, F., Rodrigues da Silva, A., Pérez-Castillo, R. (eds.) QUATIC 2020. CCIS, vol. 1266, pp. 3–16. Springer, Cham (2020). https://doi.org/10.1007/978-3-030-58793-2_1

20. Neuhüttler, J., Hermann, S., Ganz, W., Spath, D., Mark, R.: Quality based testing of AI-based smart services: the example of Stuttgart airport. In: 2022 Portland International Conference on Management of Engineering and Technology (PICMET). 2022 Portland International Conference on Management of Engineering and Technology (PICMET), Portland, OR, USA, 07 August 2022–11 August 2022, pp. 1–10. IEEE (2022). https://doi.org/10.23919/PICMET53225.2022.9882594

21. Lundborg, M., Gull, I.: Artificial intelligence in SMEs. In this way, AI becomes a game changer for small and medium-sized enterprises. A survey by Mittelstand-Digital Begleitforschung on behalf oft the Federal Ministry of Economic Affairs and Climate Action. wik consult, Bad Honnef (2021). (in German). https://www.mittelstand-digital.de/MD/Redaktion/DE/Publikationen/ki-Studie-2021.pdf?__blob=publicationFile&v=5. Accessed 24 Jan 2022

The Role of Response Time for Algorithm Aversion in Fast and Slow Thinking Tasks

Anastasia Lebedeva[(✉)] , Jaroslaw Kornowicz , Olesja Lammert ,
and Jörg Papenkordt

Paderborn University, Warburgerstr. 100, 33098 Paderborn, Germany
lebedeva@mail.uni-paderborn.de,
{jaroslaw.kornowicz,olesja.lammert,joerg.papenkordt}@uni-paderborn.de

Abstract. Artificial intelligence (AI) outperforms humans in plentiful domains. Despite security and ethical concerns, AI is expected to provide crucial improvements on both personal and societal levels. However, algorithm aversion is known to reduce the effectiveness of human-AI interaction and diminish the potential benefits of AI. In this paper, we built upon the Dual System Theory and investigate the effect of the AI response time on algorithm aversion for slow-thinking and fast-thinking tasks. To answer our research question, we conducted a 2 × 2 incentivized laboratory experiment with 116 students in an advice-taking setting. We manipulated the length of the AI response time (short vs. long) and the task type (fast-thinking vs. slow-thinking). Additional to these treatments, we varied the domain of the task. Our results demonstrate that long response times are associated with lower algorithm aversion, both when subjects think fast and slow. Moreover, when subjects were thinking fast, we found significant differences in algorithm aversion between the task domains.

Keywords: Artificial Intelligence · Algorithm Aversion · Response Time · Dual Process Theory

1 Introduction

AI is designed to provide crucial improvements to healthcare, mobility, policy-making, manufacturing, and countless other domains [26]. A growing number of political as well as private decisions are being made based on algorithm recommendations [2,30]. However, prejudice and biased behavior toward AI often mitigate its potential as extensive research demonstrates [22,25]. The study of biased human behavior towards algorithms is dominated by two streams of research—algorithm aversion and algorithm appreciation [21]. Algorithm aversion describes a general rejection of algorithm advice in favor of human advice [25]. For instance, even though AI algorithms have been repeatedly proven to be more accurate in their predictions than human experts [12,22], humans still exhibit irrational aversion towards AI [7,36]. When the behavioral bias leans in the opposite direction, researchers speak of algorithm appreciation, which is the logical counterpart to algorithm aversion [22]. For instance, it has been demonstrated that people prefer AI recommendation over human advice in multifaceted situations, such as estimating weights, predicting music charts, or national security concerns [21,24]. Based on the inverse definitions of the two phenomena, we consider them to represent "two sides of the same medal" [22]. Therefore, in this paper, we use only one of the two terms—algorithm aversion—to describe the entire range of human reactions to AI recommendations. Our study aims to contribute to a deeper understanding of the influential factors that may trigger algorithm aversion or appreciation. So, we build on the theoretical considerations of Bonnefon et al. [5] and are the first to experimentally investigate whether the Dual Process Theory can serve as a tool and as a perspective to study human behavior toward AI.

The remainder of this study is structured as follows: First, we describe the theoretical approach to adopting the Dual Process Theory in the context of human-AI interaction. Subsequently, we present our methodology and then outline the results of the data analysis. In particular, we examine the effects of AI response time on the advice-taking index for fast- and slow-thinking tasks in three different domains. Lastly, we discuss our main findings in light of previous literature, point out possible limitations of our study, and state our contribution to existing research.

2   Theoretical Framework

The search for influential factors behind human behavior toward AI has yielded a considerable number of studies and insights [14,18]. In their systematic literature review, Mahmud et al. [25] distinguish between individual, algorithm, task, and high-level factors. For example, individual characteristics, like personality traits [27,34], and characteristics of the AI agent, such as its performance [12] or the explainability of the AI recommendation [1,28,33,35], have been found to affect algorithm aversion. Also, contextual factors like task type or domain have been identified as factors influencing the rate of acceptance or rejection of an AI recommendation [11,15,19]. However, Mahmud et al. [25] emphasize that a unified theoretical framework that would comprehensively explain the nature of algorithm aversion is still lacking. One interesting approach to shed light on fundamental principles behind algorithm aversion is provided by the well-known work "Machine Behavior" by Rahwan et al. [31]. They suggest that concepts, methods, and frameworks from social and behavioral sciences may be adapted to study machines and human-machine interactions. The idea of humans transferring human cognition to machines is not entirely new. In the field of explainable AI, for example, a large number of researchers argue that explanations for AI recommendations should be formulated verbally in a human-like manner, enabling users to construct a correct mental model of the system [10,28]. Following Rahwan et al. [31], Bonnefon et al. [5] propose to adopt the widely known Dual Process Theory [9] and its concepts of fast and slow thinking (or System 1 and System 2, respectively) as a framework and a tool to study human-AI interaction. According to Kahneman [9], mental life can be characterized as a dynamic between two agents, System 1 and System 2, which produce fast and slow thinking, respectively. System 1 operates automatically and quickly, with little or no effort, relying on impressions, intuitions, intentions, and feelings. System 2, on the other hand, directs attention to effortful mental activities that require rules and explicit thinking, e.g., complex calculations [9]. Besides the scientific Dual Process Theory, there exists a popular "folk theory" concerning fast and slow thinking, reflecting people's beliefs about their own and others' thinking processes [5]. Humans seem to consciously or unconsciously apply such "folk theory" of fast and slow thinking to explain human behavior in everyday life. Some researchers argue that, in human-AI interactions, people might adhere to similar mechanisms to understand the behavior of an AI agent [5,6,32]. In other words, humans are likely to project their beliefs about fast and slow thinking onto intelligent machines and try to interpret their actions accordingly. Bonnefon et al. [5] propose that humans make inferences about AI if it "thinks" fast or slowly and use these inferences to assess whether AI "thinking" fits the task at hand. Alternatively stated, if people perceive an AI agent to "think" slowly, they would rather trust it with tasks that—from a human perspective—require slow thinking (e.g., logic) than with tasks that require fast thinking (e.g., intuition) [5].

This proposition is supported by several empirical studies regarding the effects of task type or task domain on human-AI interaction. However, prior to Bonnefon et al. [5], such results have not been explicitly linked to the Dual Process Theory. For instance, Lee [23] states that algorithmic and human decisions are perceived as equally trustworthy for tasks requiring "mechanical skill" (e.g., work scheduling), whereas algorithms are perceived as less trustworthy than humans for tasks requiring "human skill" (e.g., hiring). The study by Castelo et al. [7] provides similar results. The authors focus on the perceived objectivity of a task, describing an objective task as one based on measurable characteristics and requiring analytical skills (e.g., weather forecasting), and a subjective task as one that required intuition or a "gut feeling" (e.g., predicting the wittiness of jokes). Their results demonstrate once again that people prefer algorithms for objective tasks and reject them for subjective ones [7]. Generally, it seems that humans are more likely to reject an AI recommendation in tasks that, in their perception, require intuition and "human skill" even though research has revealed that even in supposedly more subjective tasks (e.g., suggesting jokes), an algorithm performs better than humans [36]. The link between these findings and the Dual Process Theory made by Bonnefon et al. [5] offers a new perspective on the question of how people perceive AI in different situations, i.e., for different tasks at hand. This perspective might offer a further understanding of how algorithm aversion can be mitigated, especially in the case of tasks perceived to require intuition. In our study, we adopt the proposition of Bonnefon et al. [5] to define different types of tasks. Specifically, we define fast-thinking and slow-thinking tasks through the approach people selected to solve the task— fast- or slow-thinking, respectively. While our definition is related to those of Castelo et al. and Lee [7,23], it exists independently from task domain and task objectivity. For example, in the recruiting domain, if a subject makes her decision based on explicit, rule-based thinking, we define this as a slow-thinking task. In the same domain, if a subject decides to rely primarily on her intuition, we define it as a fast-thinking task. Additionally, we deem it irrelevant for our definition whether an objectively correct answer to the task (e.g., a calculation result) exists or whether the answer is entirely subjective (e.g., a job candidate should be declined). In our definition, solely the approach chosen to solve the task determines if it is a fast-thinking or a slow-thinking task.

Furthermore, Bonnefon et al. [5] postulate that it is not only relevant to determine how people themselves approach a task but also how they perceive the algorithm—whether they judge it to be "thinking" fast or slowly. While algorithms "think" neither fast nor slowly like humans do [5,6], they might transmit signals that enable people to make conscious or unconscious inferences about the algorithm type of "thinking." The length of the algorithm response time is one possible signal. Consequently, its manipulation might influence human perception of an algorithm by suggesting fast or slow "thinking" [5,29]. Efendić et al. [13] demonstrate that, for analytical tasks, people are more averse to algorithms when response times are longer. This result is contrary to inter-human interactions, where longer response times are usually associated with higher trust— answers following a longer response time are considered well thought through. The authors attribute this contrasting effect to the fact that people perceive analytical tasks to be easy for algorithms and therefore interpret longer response times as a malfunction [13]. The study by Park et al. [29] examines the impact of response time on the acceptance of algorithm recommendations, additionally distinguishing between high- and low-accuracy algorithms. They find that, in the case of a high-accuracy algorithm, participants are more likely to follow its recommendations when response times are long. For a low-accuracy algorithm, participants are slightly more likely to follow recommendations when response times are short [29]. An apparent inconclusiveness between the results of Park et al. [29] and of Efendic et al. [13] could be explained by the fact that Park et al. [29] use a different task type than Efendić et al. [13]. While the former applies a setting we define as a fast-thinking task, the latter selects a task, requiring analytical skills (a slow-thinking task in our definition). Considering the results of Castelo et al. [7] and Lee [23] on the influence of task type on algorithm aversion, one might suggest that the effect of the AI response time varies for different types of tasks. Particularly, the result of Efendić et al. [13] might hold for analytical tasks (in our definition, for slow-thinking tasks, respectively), while the result of Park et al. [29] might be valid for fast-thinking tasks. Therefore, studying the influence of AI response time on algorithm aversion for fast- and slow-thinking tasks might yield a more differentiated view of how algorithm aversion can be reduced, especially for tasks requiring intuition. In our work, we relate existing results on task types and response times to Dual Process Theory, as proposed by Bonnefon et al. [5], and design a behavioral experiment to empirically validate possible implications.

2.1 Research Question and Primary Hypotheses

So far, we have discussed two factors of interest for our investigation—the task type (fast-thinking vs. slow-thinking) and the AI response time (short vs. long). From the perspective of a software designer, the former is rather difficult to influence, whereas the response time is relatively simple to control. Therefore, we construct our research question and hypotheses with a primary focus on the AI response time, taking the task type as a secondary contextual factor. We ground our hypotheses in the Dual Process Theory and previous work on algorithm aversion.

We hypothesize that for tasks that are approached with logic—slow-thinking tasks—people expect the AI advisor to have short response times because such tasks are perceived to be easy for algorithms. Consequently, for slow-thinking tasks, we expect the algorithm aversion to be higher for long response times. This result would be in accordance with Efendić et al. [13]. Castelo et al. [7] and Lee [23] showed that people perceive algorithms as being unable or less capable of solving tasks that require human intuition. Consequently, we hypothesize that people would perceive fast-thinking tasks to be difficult for the AI advisor and to require additional "thinking" on the AI side. Therefore, we propose that, for fast-thinking tasks, longer response times will be associated with lower algorithm aversion. This result would be in accordance with Park et al. [29].

Explicitly, we pose the following research question: Which effect does the AI response time have on algorithm aversion for slow-thinking and fast-thinking tasks? Our research question results in two main hypotheses:

H1: For slow-thinking tasks, the algorithm aversion is higher for a longer response time.

H2: For fast-thinking tasks, the algorithm aversion is lower for a longer response time.

2.2 Contribution

Our study contributes to the research field of algorithm aversion in multiple ways. Firstly, we add to the existing empirical results on the influence of AI response time on algorithm aversion by studying its effects on two different types of tasks. Secondly, we propose and apply an experimental design to empirically test the application of the Dual Process Theory to the study of algorithm aversion. Concerning possible practical applications, the results of our paper shall aid practitioners in gaining a more profound understanding of the nature of algorithm aversion in the context of different task types. Moreover, it shall offer additional empirical results on how algorithm aversion may be reduced by manipulating AI response times.

3 Experimental Design

To answer our research question, we conducted a randomized controlled experiment, utilizing a 2 × 2 between-subjects design with student participants at the

Business and Economic Research Laboratory at Paderborn University. Experimental sessions took place in attendance and in a strictly controlled environment to ensure adherence to the ceteris paribus condition. The experimental design was implemented as a software program using oTree [8]. The software was administered via a browser on personal computers. Each participant was seated individually on a computer and visually shielded from other participants to ensure decision privacy. Between-subject communication was prohibited.

Seven experimental sessions took place between October and November 2022. A total of 119 subjects participated in the study. Two subjects were dropped from the data set because they answered 50% or more of comprehension questions incorrectly. Another subject was deleted because the participant was not a student. One task observation was eliminated due to a typing mistake, and another observation was canceled because the first estimation was equal to the advice, following the suggestion of Gino and Moore [17]. Consequently, our final data set comprised a total of 116 participants and 1042 observations. The gender composition is slightly skewed toward female students (58.62%) compared to males (41.4%). The average age of the subjects is 23.3 years ($SD = 3.6$).

The subjects were randomly assigned to one of the four treatment conditions: (1) Thinking Slow & AI Long, (2) Thinking Slow & AI Short, (3) Thinking Fast & AI Long, and (4) Thinking Fast & AI Short. Distribution was even across the four treatment groups. The experimental setting was based on the Judge-Advisor-System (JAS) [4] framework and included 9 rounds. In each round, the participants had to solve an estimation task, designed to encourage either fast or slow thinking. During the task, they were advised by an AI with either a short or long response time. Thus, to ensure equal and controllable AI performance at all tasks, the AI advisor was simulated by a simple algorithm, with the AI advice being randomly set at either 90 % or 110 % of the true value. Subjects were unaware of the AI accuracy and its simulated nature to prevent anchoring effects.

Before the experiment started, subjects received instructions that explained the rules and the setting of the experiment. Instructions were tailored to the treatments, and subjects' comprehension was tested with follow-up questions. During the experiment, at the beginning of each of the nine rounds, subjects were asked to provide their initial estimate of the solution for the given task. After submitting the initial estimate, subjects received a recommendation from the AI. Subjects then provided their second estimation. Both estimations were rewarded monetarily. Subjects were not informed about the accuracy of their estimates until the end of the experiment to avoid learning effects. The order of tasks was randomized to minimize any possible sequence effects. At the end of the experiment, subjects were asked to participate in a survey that included demographic factors, such as age and gender, and other variables, such as confidence in their estimates and perceived recommendation quality [16].

Within the fast-thinking group, participants were provided with a picture of an object and asked to estimate some numeric quality of the object shown. Our object selection ensured that all participants were familiar with them. In the absence of any additional information, we, therefore, expected subjects to apply their intuition rather than analytical skills to solve the task. Within the slow-thinking group, subjects received additional quantitative information about the object in a textual form. We intended this manipulation to facilitate slow thinking on the subjects' side. Being given quantitative hints, we expected subjects to apply analytical skills and logic rather than intuition to solve the task. It is also worth mentioning that, even with the additional information, the answer to the task could not be estimated with absolute accuracy and remained ambiguous.

The AI response time (the time frame between the submission of the subjects' initial estimate and the display of the AI advice) was set to two seconds in the "AI Short" treatments and ten seconds in the "AI Long" treatments. During this time frame, the task information was not visible to subjects, and a loading bar displayed the simulated progress of the AI (see Fig. 1). After the response time had elapsed, the task became visible once again. Additionally, the AI advice and subjects' own initial estimate were displayed. Subjects were then asked to submit their second estimate (see Fig. 2).

Additionally, the objects, whose numeric qualities subjects were asked to estimate, originated from three different domains. We chose to not introduce new domains but use settings that have been previously applied in other studies. In the "Lentils" domain, subjects were asked to estimate the number of chocolate lentils in a glass based on a photograph, following Park et al. [29]. In the slow-thinking version of the task, the glass size and the number of lentils in a reference glass were additionally displayed. In the "Football" domain, subjects estimated the weight of football players based on a photograph. Additional textual information in the slow-thinking group included weight references for other comparable players. A similar design was used by Gino and Moore [17]. In the "Route" domain, subjects estimated the length of a car route between lesser-known German cities based on a map. In the slow-thinking group, reference distances were displayed additionally to the map. This last domain was designed in accordance with Hofheinz et al. [20]. Estimation tasks were equally distributed between all three domains.

Subjects received a fixed amount of €3 for participating in the experiment. Additionally, they were able to earn a payoff for the accuracy of their estimates. Subjects had to make a total of 18 estimations during the experiment (2 estimations per round across 9 experimental rounds). For each estimation, earnings between €0.00 and €0.50 were possible, resulting in a total maximum reward of €9.00 across all estimations. The closer the subjects' estimates were to the true value, the more they earned. In order to reward the timely completion of tasks, we implemented a time pressure condition. The payoff per estimation started to gradually decrease after 45 s until it reached zero if participants required more than 5 min and 45 s for an estimation. Upon completion of the 9 experimental rounds, subjects were informed about their total payoff. In addition to the fixed payment of €3, subjects earned an average additional payoff of €7.39 ($SD = 0.62$) based on the accuracy of their estimations.

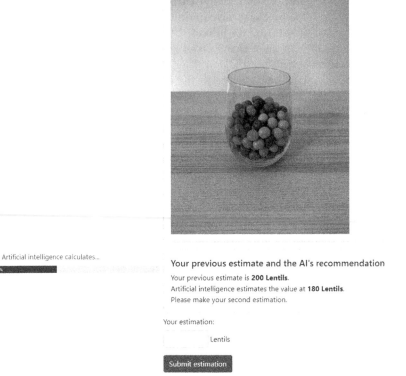

Fig. 1. AI loading bar   **Fig. 2.** AI advice view

3.1 Measurement of Algorithm Aversion

To assess algorithm aversion, we measured the degree to which subjects followed the advice of the AI. Specifically, we used the advice-taking index [20] as the dependent variable in our experiment. The index was calculated as follows:

$$\text{Advice-taking index} = \frac{\text{Second Estimation} - \text{First Estimation}}{\text{Advice} - \text{First Estimation}}$$

The index equals zero when the subject's first and second estimation are identical. The more subjects lean toward the AI advice, the closer the index is to 1. Consequently, at a value of 0.50, the subjects weigh the advice and their first estimation equally. This index is similar to the commonly used measurement "Weight of Advice" in the advice-taking literature [3]. However, the main difference is that the values can be negative. This can occur when a subject decreases the second estimation even though the advice recommends increasing it. Additionally, the index can be above 1 if the subject overshoots the advice, i.e., if the first estimation is 100, the advice is 200, and the second estimation is 300. To ensure accurate results, we follow the procedure of Logg et al. [24]

and winsorize the values below 0 and above 1 to 0 and 1, respectively. A higher advice-taking index indicates lower algorithm aversion.

4   Results

All statistical analyses were conducted using Stata 17.0. The Mann-Whitney U test was applied to determine statistical significance. Table 1 displays detailed descriptive statistics for the four treatment groups. Between the gender groups ($z = -0.61, p = 0.54$), no significant difference in advice-taking index was detected. However, there was a significant difference ($z = -15.08, p < 0.01$) in the time needed for the first estimation between the Fast-Thinking ($M = 17.40$ sec., $SD = 8.05$) and the Slow-Thinking ($M = 27.60$ s, $SD = 12.42$) treatment groups. We can possibly attribute this to the slow thinking induced by the treatment, as well as to the amount of information that needed to be processed by subjects. The time difference disappeared in the second estimation. The Fast- and Slow-Thinking groups also significantly differed in the accuracy of the first estimate ($z = -9.60, p < 0.01$), with subjects in the Fast-Thinking group underestimating the true value by 18.7 % ($SD = 27.3$), while those in the Slow-Thinking group underestimated by only 3.7 % ($SD = 26.1$) on average. A higher average estimation time and accuracy for the first estimation within the Slow-Thinking groups compared to the Fast-Thinking groups are identified as objective indicators, which can reasonably suggest that participants in the Slow-Thinking treatment actually were thinking slowly, whereas subjects in the Fast-Thinking treatment were thinking fast.

Additionally, we control for domain-specific differences in estimation accuracy. In general, the participants seem to struggle particularly with the estimation of the number of lentils regardless of the treatment, whereas the deviations from the true value are lowest for the domain "Football".

After the descriptive analysis, we now focus on the main part of our analysis. As described before, we employ the advice-taking index as a proxy for algorithm aversion. Here, a higher advice-taking index indicates lower algorithm aversion.

We start by calculating the average advice-taking index per treatment. On average, the advice-taking index was found to be higher in the groups with long AI response times than in the groups with short AI response times. The highest average advice-taking index was observed in the treatment group Slow-Thinking & AI-Long ($M = 0.54, SD = 0.31$). The lowest average advice-taking index was achieved in the Fast-Thinking & AI-Short treatment group ($M = 0.45, SD = 0.32$).

Figure 3 presents the graphical comparison within the groups with fast-thinking and slow-thinking tasks regarding the response time of the AI. To test our hypotheses, we conducted non-parametric treatment group comparisons using the Mann-Whitney U test. Since the participants did not receive feedback on their performance after a task and the task sequence was randomized, in our further analysis, we assume that the 9 estimates of each participant are independent of each other. Thus, to investigate whether, for slow-thinking tasks, the algorithm aversion was higher for the longer response time,

Table 1. Summary Statistics for the N=116 observations

Variable	Mean	SD.	Min	Max
Fast-Thinking AI-Long (N=29)				
Avg. time (in sec.)				
1st estimation	16.68	6.87	5.18	36.07
2nd estimation	13.75	7.44	4.97	44.19
Average accuracy				
1st estimation	-0.18	0.28	-0.77	0.70
2nd estimation	-0.11	0.18	-0.73	0.37
Fast-Thinking AI-Short (N=31)				
Avg. time (in sec.)				
1st estimation	18.07	8.97	4.76	52.14
2nd estimation	11.59	6.46	4.26	36.33
Average accuracy				
1st estimation	-0.19	0.28	-0.82	0.73
2nd estimation	-0.13	0.20	-0.75	0.38
Slow-Thinking AI-Long (N=29)				
Avg. time (in sec.)				
1st estimation	28.41	10.09	5.23	58.77
2nd estimation	14.57	7.93	4.57	41.18
Average accuracy				
1st estimation	-0.01	0.29	-0.73	1.50
2nd estimation	-0.01	0.15	-0.69	1.07
Slow-Thinking AI-Short (N=27)				
Avg. time (in sec.)				
1st estimation	26.73	14.47	5.49	166.58
2nd estimation	11.45	6.94	3.36	40.06
Average accuracy				
1st estimation	-0.07	0.23	-0.80	0.50
2nd estimation	-0.04	0.16	-0.70	0.33
Total (N=116)				
Avg. time (in sec.)				
1st estimation	22.31	11.57	4.76	166.58
2nd estimation	12.84	7.32	3.36	44.19
Average accuracy				
1st estimation	-0.11	0.28	-0.82	1.50
2nd estimation	-0.07	0.18	-0.75	1.07

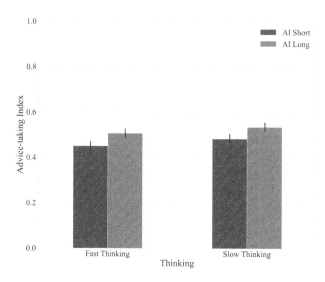

Fig. 3. Average Advice-taking index by treatment. Error bars represent standard errors.

we compared the advice-taking index of the groups Slow-Thinking & AI-Long and Slow-Thinking & AI-Short. The Mann-Whitney U test indicated that the two groups differed significantly from each other. Contrary to our H1 hypothesis, a longer response time in slow-thinking tasks led to a significantly higher advice-taking index ($z = 1.79, p = 0.07$), i.e., to lower algorithm aversion. Similarly, to examine our second hypothesis, we compared the groups Fast-Thinking & AI-Long and Fast-Thinking & AI-Short. We found out that a longer response time led to a significantly higher advice-taking index in the fast-thinking tasks ($z = 2.16, p = 0.03$). Therefore, the H2 hypothesis could be confirmed.

To test for consistency in our results, we investigated whether our results concerning the two hypotheses (H1 and H2) hold within single domains. For this purpose, we compared the group Slow-Thinking & AI-Long with the group Slow-Thinking & AI-Short and the group Fast-Thinking & AI-Long with the group Fast-Thinking & AI-Short within each domain separately (see Table 2).

Table 2 presents the results of the Mann-Whitney U test of the different treatment comparisons within the different domains. The tests revealed significant differences only in the domain "Lentils". Here, the results of the cross-domain analysis were confirmed. Again, longer response times led to a significantly higher advice-taking index, both for Fast- and Slow-Thinking treatment groups.

Subsequently, we investigated the differences in the advice-taking index between the domains within each treatment group. The graphic vividly illustrates that the differences are larger among the domains in both Fast-Thinking groups than in the two Slow-Thinking groups (see Fig. 4). The Mann-Whitney U tests between the domains within the Fast-Thinking & AI-Long treatment

Table 2. Group comparisons of the advice-taking index per treatment separately for each domain

Domain	Treatment		Advice-taking index		p-value
	Thinking	Response time	Mean	SD	
Football	Fast	Long	0.41	0.28	0.63
		Short	0.40	0.30	
	Slow	Long	0.51	0.30	0.57
		Short	0.48	0.33	
Lentils	Fast	Long	0.50	0.32	0.02**
		Short	0.38	0.29	
	Slow	Long	0.56	0.32	0.04**
		Short	0.45	0.33	
Route	Fast	Long	0.62	0.29	0.45
		Short	0.58	0.31	
	Slow	Long	0.54	0.32	0.71
		Short	0.52	0.33	

$^{***}p < 0.01$, $^{**}p < 0.05$, $^{*}p < 0.1$

group confirm that the advice-taking index within the treatment differs significantly between all three domains. The same applies to the treatment group Fast-Thinking & AI-Short, except for the fact that the advice-taking index does not differ significantly between the domains "Football" and "Lentils". In contrast, there are no significant domain-specific differences in the average advice-taking index within the two Slow-Thinking treatment groups. Thus, we conclude that the domain-specific effects only matter in fast-thinking tasks.

To gain more insight into the underlining mechanisms behind the main treatments, we followed Gino et al. [16] and asked participants to rate the perceived quality of the AI advice and their self-confidence in their estimation. We intended to analyze those data to determine if subjectively perceived confidence in the first estimate and the perceived quality of the AI recommendation impacted the actual adaptation of the advice. Group comparisons with the dependent variables *perceived quality of AI advice* and *perceived confidence in their own estimation* per treatment separately for each domain reveal that these two dependent variables do not differ significantly between the compared treatments. Only the perceived quality of AI advice differs significantly between the Fast-Thinking & AI-Long and Fast-Thinking & AI-Short groups within the domain "Football". Moreover, the quality of the AI advice in the groups with short response time is perceived to be tendentially higher, independent of the Thinking-Treatment and the domains. Furthermore, it can be observed that the Fast-Thinking groups feel more confident in their estimation than the Slow-Thinking groups, independent of the time treatment and the domains. However, none of these effects becomes significant.

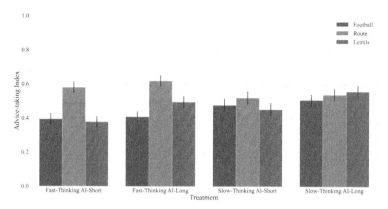

Fig. 4. Average advice-taking-index within a treatment across domains. Error bars represent standard errors.

We further investigated whether a difference in the confidence in their own estimation (see Fig. 5) and the perceived quality of AI advice (see Fig. 6) between the domains within each treatment group existed. While in the Slow-Thinking & AI-Short treatment, only the "Route" domain differs significantly from the other two domains in terms of perceived confidence of own estimation, in the other three treatment groups, the domain "Lentils" significantly deviates from the other two. Consequently, within all treatments, the domains "Lentils" and "Route" always differ significantly from each other. Thus, the perceived confidence in their own estimation is lowest in each treatment within the domain "Lentils".

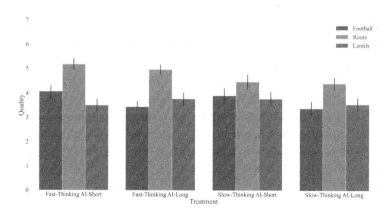

Fig. 5. Average perceived quality of AI-advice within a treatment across domains

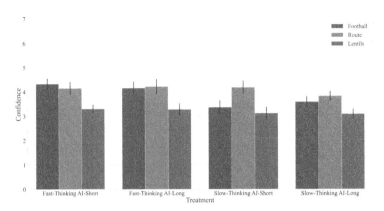

Fig. 6. Average perceived self-confidence in own estimation within a treatment across domains

If we consider the perceived quality of the AI advice using the Mann-Whitney U-test, it becomes apparent that, within the treatments, the domain "Route" always differs significantly from the other two and the quality assessed is highest in this domain (see Fig. 6). Only in the group Slow-Thinking & AI-Short the domain "Route" is not significantly different from the domain "Football". If we relate this to our previous results, we observe that the advice-taking index for this domain is also significantly highest within the two Fast-Thinking treatment groups (see Fig. 4). This tendency regarding the advice-taking index can also be observed in the Slow-Thinking treatments. We can attribute the fact that the comparisons of the perceived quality of AI and the comparisons of self-confidence in their own estimation between the treatments within a domain do not become significant to the fact that the domains within the treatments have very similar effects.

5   Discussion

As proposed by Bonnefon et al. [5], we apply an experimental design to empirically test the application of the Dual Process Theory as a framework to study algorithm aversion. In the course, we relate existing results on task types and response times to Dual Process Theory, derive our hypotheses and test them empirically. Our results suggest that the application of the Dual Process Theory may indeed deepen the understanding of algorithm aversion.

According to our results, in slow-thinking tasks, algorithm aversion is lower for longer AI response time—an effect opposite to our first hypothesis (H1). Moreover, our results for fast-thinking tasks show that algorithm aversion is lower for longer response times, as we suggest in our second hypothesis (H2). The former result regarding H1 may also be seen as contradicting Efendić et al. [13], who find that, in analytical tasks, long response time is associated with higher algorithm aversion. The finding concerning H2 is in line with Park et al. [29], who find that algorithm aversion is lower for longer response times in a task design that corresponds to a fast-thinking task in our definition.

In our experiment, for both task types, the longer response time is associated with lower algorithm aversion, although the difference in the advice-taking index is stronger for fast-thinking tasks. People associate long response times with stronger effort, both in the case of humans and algorithms [13]. Therefore, longer response times might suggest to human agents that AI is exercising a stronger effort for the task, enhancing its task capability. Interestingly, in our experiment, this effect seems to hold for both types of tasks, although previous research demonstrated that people perceive algorithms to be more capable of tasks that require analytical skill (slow-thinking) and less capable of tasks that require intuition (fast-thinking) [7,23,25]. One might attribute this result to the fact that additional quantitative information is insufficient to encourage slow thinking on the participants' side (i.e., participants apply fast thinking independently of task type), especially considering that the type of thinking applied is difficult to measure directly. However, we deem the fact that participants in the slow-thinking group spent significantly more time on the tasks and performed significantly better an objective indicator of actual slow-thinking in the slow-thinking group. Further research may investigate other ways to apply the framework of the Dual Process Theory to task design in the context of algorithm aversion.

The inconclusiveness between our result concerning slow-thinking tasks and the findings of Efendić et al. [13] might be attributed to the fact that Efendić et al. [13] use verbal constructs to describe the length of algorithm response time (e.g., "after a long pause" or "after an extended period of time"). In our experiment, we apply real response times (1 s vs 10 s). Thus, a time range could exist within which longer response times reduce algorithm aversion, as is observed in our study and by Park et al. [29]. Therefore, we advocate for more empirical research on the role of different response time ranges on algorithm aversion.

We consider the domain to be essential for the external validity of our results. Research demonstrates that people react differently to algorithmic recommendations in different domains [7,12,24]. We test our hypotheses in three different domains to achieve a more differentiated view of the effects of task type and AI response time on algorithm aversion. We select domains that are similar concerning complexity, moral impact, and subjectivity since these factors are proven to affect algorithm aversion [7,12,25]. We investigate whether significant differences arise between domains within each of the main treatments. Results suggest that algorithm aversion varies significantly between the domains within each of the two fast-thinking treatments. Within the slow-thinking groups, the domains seem to not affect algorithm aversion. Notably, within each of the fast-thinking groups, the highest advice-taking index is observed for the domain "Route". In every treatment group, participants rate the AI advice quality in this domain higher than in the domains "Lentils" and "Football". Only in the group Slow-Thinking & AI-Short, the AI advice quality in the domain "Route" is not significantly different from the domain "Football". That the AI advice quality in the domain "Route" is perceived as higher could be due to the fact that people are largely familiar with algorithm recommendations in similar tasks, such as determining an optimal route by using a navigation system. In general, the fact that we find significant differences between task domains for fast-thinking groups is in line with the findings of previous research [7,12,24].

Interestingly, these effects seem to disappear in the advice-taking index for slow-thinking tasks. We propose the following interpretation for this finding. As long as participants have only a picture as a single source of information, the depicted object majorly influences participants' behavior. On the contrary, as soon as additional quantitative information is available to participants, the tasks become more comparable to each other (a number has to be estimated based on other numbers), and the origin of the object does not play a significant role anymore. These results are crucial when researchers want to describe different types of tasks. Our findings demonstrate clearly that the domain of a task and the way people approach it are not the same and have different effects on algorithm aversion. Additionally, the fact that we detected said difference only for fast-thinking tasks but not for slow-thinking tasks indicates that both groups were indeed thinking differently.

A noteworthy limitation of our results is that our observations are limited to the three domains "Lentils", "Football", and "Route", which do not differ in terms of complexity, moral impact, and subjectivity. Further research might investigate whether the same result holds in other domains. Additionally, our results concerning the negative effect of long response time on algorithm aversion (i.e., its positive effect on the advice-taking index) are especially strong in the "Lentils" domain. Interestingly, in all treatment groups, participants' confidence in their own estimation is lowest for the "Lentils" domain, suggesting that low confidence enhances the effect of longer response time on algorithm aversion. Mahmud et al. [25] name self-evaluation factors, like self-efficacy, among those influencing algorithm aversion. Logg et al. [24] demonstrate that higher self-efficacy and self-confidence are associated with higher algorithm aversion, supporting our suggestion that low self-confidence could facilitate the effect of response time on algorithm aversion.

6   Conclusion

Our study yielded several insights that might prove valuable for further research and for software developers. Firstly, we demonstrated that longer AI response times, in particular a response time of 10 s, are associated with lower algorithm aversion. This effect is even stronger for tasks designed to facilitate a fast-thinking, intuitive approach. Secondly, among all domains, long response time had the strongest positive effect on the advice-taking index in the domain "Lentils", in which participants displayed the lowest confidence in their own estimations. Thirdly, within the fast-thinking groups, the task domain heavily impacted the advice-taking index, whereas domain differences were not significant within both slow-thinking groups.

On the one hand, our results contribute to the research about the influence of response time on algorithm aversion and suggest that, at least to a certain extent, longer response times may be used to reduce algorithm aversion. On the other hand, our results indicate that advice-taking varies depending on people's approach to the tasks and on the domain of the task. To the best of our knowledge, empirical results testing these differences between the way of thinking and the task domain broach an entirely new subject within the research of algorithm aversion. With our study, we proposed a design and delivered empirical insights following the proposal of Bonnefon et al. [5] to apply Dual Process Theory to studies of human-machine interaction. Therefore, our study can aid other researchers in better understanding the nature of algorithm aversion by considering the thinking used while solving the task and not just the perceived task context.

Acknowledgements. This research is funded by the German Federal Ministry of Education and Research (BMBF) within the "The Future of Value Creation - Research on Production, Services and Work" program (02L19C115). Olesja Lammert and Jaroslaw Kornowicz acknowledge funding by the Deutsche Forschungsgemeinschaft (TRR 318/1 2021 - 438445824). The authors are responsible for the content of this publication. The authors thank Kirsten Thommes and René Fahr for valuable discussion and constructive comments.

References

1. Abdul, A., Vermeulen, J., Wang, D., Lim, B.Y., Kankanhalli, M.: Trends and trajectories for explainable, accountable and intelligible systems: an HCI research agenda. In: Proceedings of the 2018 CHI Conference on Human Factors in Computing Systems, pp. 1–18 (2018)
2. Araujo, T., Helberger, N., Kruikemeier, S., de Vreese, C.H.: In AI we trust? Perceptions about automated decision-making by artificial intelligence. AI Soc. **35**(3), 611–623 (2020). https://doi.org/10.1007/s00146-019-00931-w
3. Bailey, P.E., Leon, T., Ebner, N.C., Moustafa, A.A., Weidemann, G.: A meta-analysis of the weight of advice in decision-making. Current Psychology, pp. 1–26 (2022)
4. Bonaccio, S., Dalal, R.S.: Advice taking and decision-making: an integrative literature review, and implications for the organizational sciences. Organ. Behav. Hum. Decis. Process. **101**(2), 127–151 (2006)
5. Bonnefon, J.F., Rahwan, I.: Machine thinking, fast and slow. Trends Cogn. Sci. **24**(12), 1019–1027 (2020)
6. Booch, G., et al.: Thinking fast and slow in AI (2020)
7. Castelo, N., Bos, M.W., Lehmann, D.R.: Task-dependent algorithm aversion. J. Mark. Res. **56**(5), 809–825 (2019)
8. Chen, D.L., Schonger, M., Wickens, C.: oTree-an open-source platform for laboratory, online, and field experiments. J. Behav. Exp. Financ. **9**, 88–97 (2016)
9. Daniel, K.: Thinking, fast and slow (2017)
10. De Graaf, M.M., Malle, B.F.: How people explain action (and autonomous intelligent systems should too). In: 2017 AAAI Fall Symposium Series (2017)
11. De Winter, J.C., Dodou, D.: Why the fitts list has persisted throughout the history of function allocation. Cogn. Technol. Work **16**(1), 1–11 (2014)

12. Dietvorst, B.J., Simmons, J.P., Massey, C.: Algorithm aversion: people erroneously avoid algorithms after seeing them err. J. Exp. Psychol. Gen. **144**(1), 114 (2015)
13. Efendić, E., Van de Calseyde, P.P., Evans, A.M.: Slow response times undermine trust in algorithmic (but not human) predictions. Organ. Behav. Hum. Decis. Process. **157**, 103–114 (2020)
14. Enholm, I.M., Papagiannidis, E., Mikalef, P., Krogstie, J.: Artificial intelligence and business value: a literature review. Inf. Syst. Front. **24**(5), 1709–1734 (2022)
15. Gaudiello, I., Zibetti, E., Lefort, S., Chetouani, M., Ivaldi, S.: Trust as indicator of robot functional and social acceptance. an experimental study on user conformation to iCub answers. Comput. Hum. Behav. **61**, 633–655 (2016)
16. Gino, F., Brooks, A.W., Schweitzer, M.E.: Anxiety, advice, and the ability to discern: feeling anxious motivates individuals to seek and use advice. J. Pers. Soc. Psychol. **102**(3), 497 (2012)
17. Gino, F., Moore, D.A.: Effects of task difficulty on use of advice. J. Behav. Decis. Mak. **20**(1), 21–35 (2007)
18. Glikson, E., Woolley, A.W.: Human trust in artificial intelligence: review of empirical research. Acad. Manag. Ann. **14**(2), 627–660 (2020)
19. Hancock, P.A., Billings, D.R., Schaefer, K.E., Chen, J.Y., De Visser, E.J., Parasuraman, R.: A meta-analysis of factors affecting trust in human-robot interaction. Hum. Factors **53**(5), 517–527 (2011)
20. Hofheinz, C., Germar, M., Schultze, T., Michalak, J., Mojzisch, A.: Are depressed people more or less susceptible to informational social influence? Cogn. Ther. Res. **41**(5), 699–711 (2017). https://doi.org/10.1007/s10608-017-9848-7
21. Hou, Y.T.Y., Jung, M.F.: Who is the expert? reconciling algorithm aversion and algorithm appreciation in AI-supported decision making. Proceed. ACM Hum.-Comput. Interact. **5**(CSCW2), 1–25 (2021)
22. Jussupow, E., Benbasat, I., Heinzl, A.: Why are we averse towards algorithms? A comprehensive literature review on algorithm aversion. In: Proceedings of the 28th European Conference on Information Systems (ECIS), pp. 1–16 (2020)
23. Lee, M.K.: Understanding perception of algorithmic decisions: fairness, trust, and emotion in response to algorithmic management. Big Data Soc. **5**(1), 2053951718756684 (2018)
24. Logg, J.M., Minson, J.A., Moore, D.A.: Algorithm appreciation: people prefer algorithmic to human judgment. Organ. Behav. Hum. Decis. Process. **151**, 90–103 (2019)
25. Mahmud, H., Islam, A.N., Ahmed, S.I., Smolander, K.: What influences algorithmic decision-making? a systematic literature review on algorithm aversion. Technol. Forecast. Soc. Chang. **175**, 121390 (2022)
26. Makridakis, S.: The forthcoming artificial intelligence (AI) revolution: its impact on society and firms. Futures **90**, 46–60 (2017)
27. McBride, M., Carter, L., Ntuen, C.: The impact of personality on nurses' bias towards automated decision aid acceptance. Int. J. Inf. Syst. Change Manage. **6**(2), 132–146 (2012)
28. Miller, T.: Explanation in artificial intelligence: insights from the social sciences. Artif. Intell. **267**, 1–38 (2019)
29. Park, J.S., Barber, R., Kirlik, A., Karahalios, K.: A slow algorithm improves users' assessments of the algorithm's accuracy. Proceed. ACM Hum.-Comput. Interact. **3**(CSCW), 1–15 (2019)
30. Prahl, A., Van Swol, L.: Understanding algorithm aversion: when is advice from automation discounted? J. Forecast. **36**(6), 691–702 (2017)

31. Rahwan, I., et al.: Machine behaviour. Nature **568**, 477–486 (2019). https://doi. org/10.1038/s41586-019-1138-y
32. Rossi, F., Loreggia, A.: Preferences and ethical priorities: thinking fast and slow in AI. In: Proceedings of the 18th International Conference on Autonomous Agents and MultiAgent Systems, pp. 3–4. AAMAS 2019, International Foundation for Autonomous Agents and Multiagent Systems, Richland, SC (2019)
33. Schoonderwoerd, T.A., Jorritsma, W., Neerincx, M.A., Van Den Bosch, K.: Human-centered XAI: developing design patterns for explanations of clinical decision support systems. Int. J. Hum Comput Stud. **154**, 102684 (2021)
34. Sharan, N.N., Romano, D.M.: The effects of personality and locus of control on trust in humans versus artificial intelligence. Heliyon **6**(8), e04572 (2020)
35. Wang, X., Yin, M.: Are explanations helpful? a comparative study of the effects of explanations in AI-assisted decision-making. In: 26th International Conference on Intelligent User Interfaces, pp. 318–328 (2021)
36. Yeomans, M., Shah, A., Mullainathan, S., Kleinberg, J.: Making sense of recommendations. J. Behav. Decis. Mak. **32**(4), 403–414 (2019)

Unvoiced Vowel Recognition Using Active Bio-Acoustic Sensing for Silent Speech Interaction

Kousei Nagayama[✉] and Ryosuke Takada

Kobe City College of Technology, Kobe, Japan
{r117229,kcct-rtakada}@g.kobe-kosen.ac.jp

Abstract. In this study, we propose a silent speech recognition technique using Active Bio-Acoustics Sensing. The proposed method attaches a piezoelectric buzzer and a piezoelectric microphone to the skin surface around one ear. By sending ultrasonic swept sine signals with a frequency range of 20 kHz to 48 kHz between the piezoelectric elements, the shape of the mouth is recognized based on the frequency transfer characteristics and Support Vector Machine (SVM) classifier. We conducted experiments with seven volunteers to evaluate the recognition accuracy of a mouth forming the five Japanese vowels ('a', 'i', 'u', 'e', 'o') and a closed mouth. The results show an average recognition accuracy of 88.4% for the six types of mouth shapes. The proposed method enables the hands-free operation of computers while maintaining privacy and being hidden from others, even when wearing a mask or similar covering.

Keywords: Silent Voice Recognition · Kana input · Active Bio-Acoustic Sensing · Piezoelectric element

1 Introduction

Voice interfaces have the advantage of being hands-free and reducing the risk of infectious diseases as they don't require touching public equipment. However, their usage is limited due to privacy and security concerns [1–3]. Additionally, the accuracy of speech recognition is affected by surrounding noise. Therefore, silent speech recognition is being researched as an alternative to voice interface [4]. Silent speech recognition is a method of sensing speech gestures without vocal cord vibrations and estimating speech. Silent speech recognition input methods are a promising alternative to voice interfaces [5,6] and many users prefer them to traditional voice interfaces [7].

Several silent speech recognition methods have been proposed, including using RGB images [8], skin motion sensing [9], electrostatic sensor arrays [10], ultrasonic imaging [11], and electromyography of the mouth area for gesture recognition [12]. However, these methods have problems such as being affected by surrounding light, having devices that stand out and look unnatural, and interfering with daily life activities such as eating and talking. In particular, imaging methods face the occlusion problem when the mouth is hidden by a mask.

In this study, we successfully propose a silent speech recognition technique using Active Bio-Acoustic Sensing(ABAS). The proposed method uses a piezo-electric buzzer and a microphone that are attached to the skin surface around one ear. These piezoelectric electrodes can be mounted on a headphone-like device that is worn on the ear, making it less noticeable. The proposed method also uses the frequency transfer characteristics of the human body surface to perform silent speech recognition, so it does not suffer from occlusion problems or lighting effects like imaging-based methods.

In this research, we recognized six types of mouth shapes, including five Japanese vowels ('a', 'i', 'u', 'e', 'o') and a closed mouth using ABAS. Japanese kana characters can be represented by combinations of 10 consonants and 5 vowels. Therefore, if the vowels can be recognized, the approximate content of the speech can be estimated [13]. In addition, it is also can be used for shortcut input.

2   Related Work

Silent speech recognition has been approached through various methods, such as utilizing cameras and other types of sensors. This study highlights the distinction from these existing techniques by utilizing ABAS. Furthermore, relevant studies employing the same method are discussed.

2.1   Silent Speech Recognition Method

Silent speech recognition is realized through various methods, including lip-reading of the speaker using cameras [6,14] and recognizing oral gestures through monochrome images of the mouth region while obtaining the density histograms [15]. However, these methods require cameras to be placed in front of the speaker's face, causing occlusion problem when the speaker is wearing a mask or covering their mouth with their hand.

There have been other studies that estimate speech content by measuring the reflection time of ultrasound radiated into the body by attaching an ultrasonic probe on the skin of the jaw and using ultrasonic imaging [11,16]. The probe for ultrasonic imaging is very expensive, and to obtain an accurate internal image, gel must be applied to the skin.

Silent speech recognition using a microphone [17,18] has been proposed using techniques such as Non-audible Murmur (NAM) and External Ear Canal Trans-fer Function (ECTF) [19]. NAM refers to the breathing sound (whispering voice) without vibrating the vocal cords, which can be recorded by a micro-phone attached to the user's throat for silent speech recognition. However, for the system to accurately recognize silent speech, the user must speak in a cer-tain volume of whispers, which may be heard by others nearby. The technique using ECTF [19] employs a microphone embedded in the earbuds to analyze the reflected sound of the signals emitted from the earbuds to recognize the Facial Expressions. However, this method requires manual fitting calibration of the device for improved accuracy.

Silent speech recognition using muscles near the mouth has been proposed. These methods require attaching multiple sensors to measure the complex stretching state of the muscles near the mouth, and the elements attached to the face are noticeable. A method of placing sensors inside or around the mouth has also been proposed. Derma [9] performs speech recognition using acceleration and gyro sensors attached to the skin under the jaw, which can be recognized with high accuracy. However, the sensor under the jaw is noticeable, like the EMG method. SilentMask [20] also performs gesture recognition by sensing the movement of the mask along with the shape change of the mouth using similar sensors. It has high information confidentiality because the mouth movements are not visible while wearing the mask. However, there is a problem of decreased recognition accuracy when the mask slips. TongueBoard [10] recognizes speech and tongue gestures using a static sensor array placed in the oral cavity, but this hinders daily conversations and eating.

The proposed method does not suffer from occlusion problems as it utilizes the frequency transmission characteristics of ultrasonic waves on the surface of the face. Furthermore, by attaching sensors around the ears, it is easy to integrate with devices such as headphones worn on the ears.

2.2   Active Acoustic Sensing

Active acoustic sensing technique refers to a sensing method that uses the inherent resonant characteristics and frequency transfer characteristics determined by the shape, material, and boundary conditions of an object. Touch & Activate [21] can recognize how an object is touched by using changes in the resonant spectrum of sound due to changes in the boundary conditions of the object. Also, AudioTouch [22] performs hand gesture recognition by using changes in the acoustic frequency transfer characteristics of the hand as bones and muscles move when changing the position of the fingers. The sensors used in AudioTouch consist of only two piezoelectric elements, which are attached to the back of the hand. As sensors are not attached to the palm or fingertips, it has low invasiveness. The Sound of Touch [23] recognizes finger movements and gripping gestures, and estimates touch pressure, using piezoelectric buzzers and a piezoelectric microphone attached to the arm and the finger. Bitey [24], which uses passive acoustic sensing, recognizes the sound produced by biting the teeth together with a bone conduction microphone, and uses it as input. By differentiating the sounds produced by biting different teeth together, the input vocabulary can also be increased. These studies have shown that human behavior can be recognized using active acoustic sensing technique, and this research is different from previous studies in that it uses the technique to sense changes in a mouths shape.

3   Vowel Recognition Using ABAS

Prior works [22, 23] have shown that the on-body propagation of ultrasound changes due to the deformation of muscle, skin, and bones. In this study, we focus on analyzing the changes in the frequency transfer characteristics of the facial surface to recognize silent speech.

The proposed method attaches a piezoelectric speaker and a piezoelectric microphone around one ear, and the recognition of silent speech is accomplished through the examination of the propagation characteristics of the ultrasonic waves between the piezoelectric elements. To evaluate the feasibility of the proposed method, we conducted experiments to investigate the recognition accuracy of five Japanese vowels ('a', 'i', 'u', 'e', 'o') and the closed mouth state, using ABAS.

In this section, we'll describe the hardware and software components of the system.

Hardware

In this system, two piezoelectric elements (Murata 7BB-20-6L0, 20 mm) as shown in Fig. 1 were utilized as the speaker to vibrate the surrounding of the ear and the microphone to measure the propagated vibration on the facial surface. The surface of each piezoelectric element was covered with a 0.5 mm thick polystyrene plate to prevent damage to the element, and the back was covered with hot bonding to prevent noise from short-circuits.

These elements were connected to a computer (HP ENVY Laptop 15-ep, CPU: Intel Core i9) via an audio interface (Roland Octa-Capture UA-1010) and the computer was used for sound playback and recording (Fig. 2).

Fig. 1. Piezo Elements

Software

First, a signal was generated on a computer and the signal's playback and recording used the Python SoundDevice library. The signal used in this study is a swept sine signal that linearly transitions from 20 kHz to 48 kHz with 4096 samples (approximately 43 ms) generated at a sampling frequency of 96 kHz. This

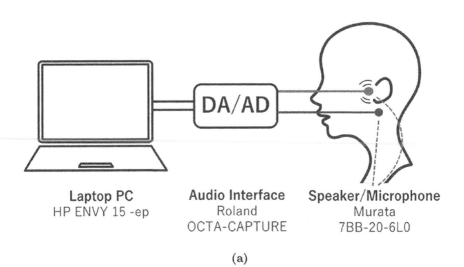

Laptop PC   **Audio Interface**   **Speaker/Microphone**
HP ENVY 15 -ep   Roland   Murata
                     OCTA-CAPTURE   7BB-20-6L0

(a)

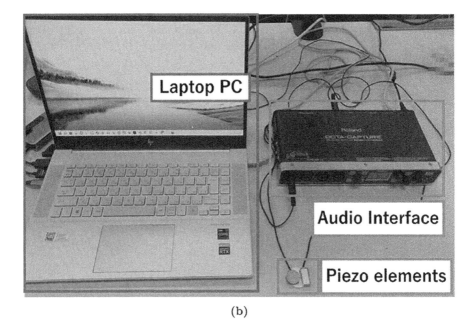

(b)

Fig. 2. System overview

frequency was determined based on previous studies [21]. The input signal from the piezoelectric microphone was performed using Fast Fourier Transform (FFT) to obtain the spectrum. The system obtained the FFT spectrum from the input signal from the piezoelectric microphone. Considering the period of the swept sine signal, the size of the window function was set to 16,384 samples and a Hann window was used. According to the Nyquist theorem, the number of effective samples is 8,192 samples. Additionally, the bandwidth used was 28 kHz since lower bandwidths below 20 kHz are not used. Therefore, the number of FFT samples used was $4,778 = 16,384 \times 28 \div 48$ samples. Furthermore, by calculating the moving average for every 150 samples, the noise contained in the signal was removed. The noise-removed spectrum was displayed on the screen, allowing the changes in the spectrum accompanying the speech motion to be confirmed. By pressing the Enter key while the program is running, the spectrum was saved in CSV format.

Next, we generated an SVM classifier using the recorded signal. The reason for using SVM is the same as in AudioTouch [22], which is capable of achieving high-accuracy classification with limited data. Additionally, it is possible to retrain the classifier for each user. In the program for generating the SVM classifier, we normalized the spectrum to the 0–1 range and used them as features to compensate for the decrease in input signal volume from changes in the fit of the piezoelectric elements. We determined the hyperparameters for learning using the Optuna library. The SVM model used was the Scikit-Learn library, which was also utilized to split the test data and the training data. The split was performed for each recorded round, and we evaluated the accuracy of the classification model using K-fold cross-validation. Finally, we output the results of the validation as the recognition accuracy for each mouth shape.

4   Silent Speech Recognition Using Active Bio-Acoustic Sensing

Evaluation

The following steps were taken to evaluate the proposed method and investigate the recognition accuracy of each gesture

4.1   Setup

We administered our proposed method on 7 volunteers (6 male and 1 female; average age 24 years, SD = 16.3). Based on pre-verification by the author, the piezoelectric elements were attached to the position shown in Fig. 3. The proposed method recognizes 6 mouth shapes, including 5 vowels with a closed mouth state, as shown in Fig. 4. The volunteers were first instructed on these gestures. To ensure the stability of the signal characteristics, the volunteers were instructed to fix their head posture while observing the PC screen. The swept sine signals were played back and recorded, and the recording signal spectrum was displayed on the screen throughout the experiment.

4.2 Procedure and Task

In the experiment, volunteers were asked to repeat the procedure of maintaining the indicated mouth shape on the screen, confirming changes in the displayed spectrum, and saving the data by pressing a key. 6 different mouth shape patterns were indicated in a random order to eliminate the order effect. This procedure was defined as one set and was repeated 25 times to form one task. Each volunteer completed the task twice, resulting in a total of 300 data points (6 mouth shapes × 25 sets × 1 task) collected for each volunteer. The piezoelectric elements were removed once during the task, and volunteers took a break of approximately 5 min between tasks.

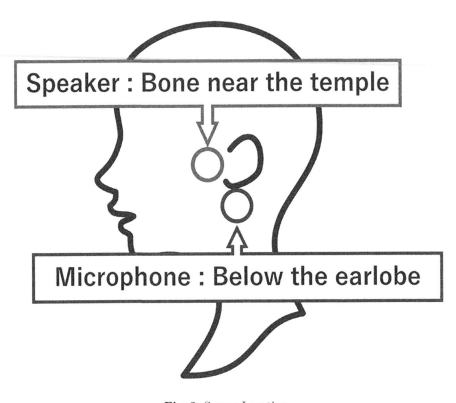

Fig. 3. Sensor Locations

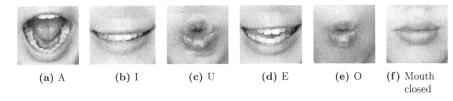

(a) A   (b) I   (c) U   (d) E   (e) O   (f) Mouth closed

Fig. 4. Mouth Shapes

The accuracy of the SVM classifier was evaluated using the collected data. Given that previous tests showed that participant-specific classifiers performed better, individual classifiers were created for each participant in the experiment. The classifier performance was evaluated through cross-validation and the results were summarized in a confusion matrix and F-value.

4.3   Results

Figure 5 displays the total confusion matrix output for each volunteer, while Table 1 shows the recognition accuracy of the constructed SVM classifier. In Table 1, P^{ave} represents the average recognition accuracy of each participant in the experiment. The participant with the highest recognition accuracy was 95.4%, while the overall average was 88.4%. P^2's recognition rate was significantly lower than others, with an average of 65.0%. The reason for P^2's low recognition rate is that the data tended to have a low volume and high noise,

Predicted Values

	a	i	u	e	o	Mouth closed
a	306	0	3	23	18	0
i	0	317	7	13	0	13
u	3	2	302	3	13	27
e	20	10	6	306	4	4
o	26	1	10	6	306	1
Mouth closed	1	9	17	4	0	319

(Actual Values)

Fig. 5. Confusion Matrix

Table 1. Recognition Accuracy[%]

Volunteers	P^1	P^2	P^3	P^4	P^5	P^6	P^7	P^{ave}
F-score	94.7	65.0	89.3	93.0	90.1	91.3	95.4	88.4

and it is likely that the piezoelectric sensors were not well attached to the skin. This suggests that the recognition accuracy of the proposed method may be greatly affected by errors that can occur when attaching the piezoelectric sensors.

5   Discussion and Future Work

5.1   Installation Error

Through the experiments, it was found that the recognition errors due to the attachment state of piezoelectric elements were significant. Figure 6 shows the change in spectrum when the piezoelectric elements were reattached five times. The graph shows that the sound volume input to the piezoelectric microphone is affected by the tightness of the piezoelectric element. Therefore, when actually using the proposed method, it is necessary to calibrate the SVM classifier each time the piezoelectric elements are attached, or to investigate a piezoelectric element installation method that attaches with stable conditions.

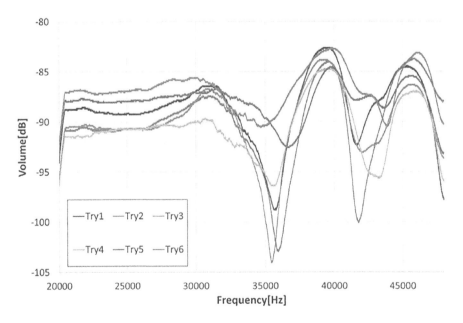

Fig. 6. Variation of amplitude spectrum with the removal of the piezoelectric element (Mouth closed)

5.2   Application Examples

This section describes application examples using the proposed method. First, as shown in Fig. 7, the proposed method allows the operation of music players. When going out and having both hands occupied, the device can still be accessed even when wearing a mask, which is excellent in terms of information confidentiality and convenience.

In addition, Japanese Kana characters consists of combinations of 5 vowels and 15 consonants. Therefore, it is possible to estimate the speech content from recognition of only 5 vowels [13], and it is possible to input existing voice AI commands.

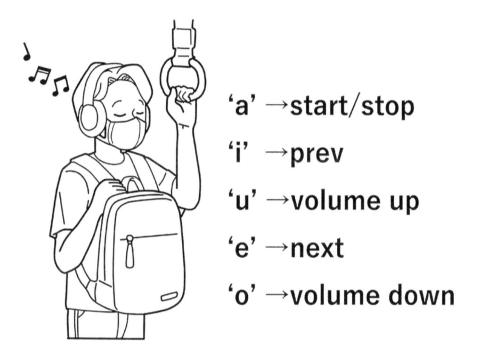

Fig. 7. Example of music player application

6   Conclusion

In this study, we focused on the deformation of the jaw joint, skin, and muscles around the masseter and temporalis muscles, and bones during speech movements. Then, we proposed a method for recognizing the Japanese vowels 'a', 'i', 'u', 'e', and 'o' using ABAS. By implementing a prototype system and conducting evaluation, we found that the vowels can be recognized with an average accuracy of 88.4%.

References

1. Moorthy, A.E., Vu, K.-P.L.: Privacy concerns for use of voice activated personal assistant in the public space. Int. J. Hum.-Comput. Interact. **31**(4), 307–335 (2015)
2. Efthymiou, C., Halvey, M.: Evaluating the social acceptability of voice based smartwatch search. In: Ma, S., et al. (eds.) AIRS 2016. LNCS, vol. 9994, pp. 267–278. Springer, Cham (2016). https://doi.org/10.1007/978-3-319-48051-0_20
3. Prabhakar, S., Pankanti, S., Jain, A.K.: Biometric recognition: security and privacy concerns. IEEE Secur. Privacy **1**(2), 33–42 (2003)
4. Denby, B., Schultz, T., Honda, K., Hueber, T., Gilbert, J.M., Brumberg, J.S.: Silent speech interfaces. Speech Commun. **52**(4), 270–287 (2010)
5. Ruan, S., Wobbrock, J.O., Liou, K., Ng, A., Landay, J.A.: Comparing speech and keyboard text entry for short messages in two languages on touchscreen phones. In: Proceedings of ACM Interaction Mobile Wearable Ubiquitous Technology, vol. 1, no. 4 (2018)
6. Sun, K., Yu, C., Shi, W., Liu, L., Shi, Y.: Lip-Interact: improving mobile device interaction with silent speech commands. In: Proceedings of the 31st Annual ACM Symposium on User Interface Software and Technology, UIST 2018, New York, NY, USA, pp. 581–593. Association for Computing Machinery (2018)
7. Pandey, L., Hasan, K., Arif, A.S.: Acceptability of speech and silent speech input methods in private and public. In: Proceedings of the 2021 CHI Conference on Human Factors in Computing Systems. ACM, May 2021
8. Assael, Y.M., Shillingford, B., Whiteson, S., De Freitas, N.: LipNet: end-to-end sentence-level lipreading. arXiv preprint arXiv:1611.01599, p. 13 (2016)
9. Rekimoto, J., Nishimura, Y.: Derma: silent speech interaction using transcutaneous motion sensing. In: Augmented Humans Conference 2021, AHs 2021, New York, NY, USA, pp. 91–100. Association for Computing Machinery (2021)
10. Li, R., Wu, J., Starner, T.: TongueBoard: an oral interface for subtle input. In: Proceedings of the 10th Augmented Human International Conference 2019, AH2019, New York, NY, USA. Association for Computing Machinery (2019)
11. Csapó, T.G., Grósz, T., Gosztolya, G., Tóth, L., Markó, A.: DNN-based ultrasound-to-speech conversion for a silent speech interface. In: INTERSPEECH (2017)
12. Kapur, A., Kapur, S., Maes, P.: AlterEgo: a personalized wearable silent speech interface. In: 23rd International Conference on Intelligent User Interfaces, IUI 2018, New York, NY, USA, pp. 43–53. Association for Computing Machinery (2018)
13. Koguchi, Y., Oharada, K., Takagi, Y., Sawada, Y., Shizuki, B., Takahashi, S.: A mobile command input through vowel lip shape recognition. In: Kurosu, M. (ed.) HCI 2018. LNCS, vol. 10903, pp. 297–305. Springer, Cham (2018). https://doi.org/10.1007/978-3-319-91250-9_23
14. Wand, M., Koutník, J., Schmidhuber, J.: Lipreading with long short-term memory. In: 2016 IEEE International Conference on Acoustics, Speech and Signal Processing (ICASSP), pp. 611–6119. IEEE Press (2016)
15. Watanabe, M., Nishi, N.: Research of daily conversation transmitting system based on mouth part pattern recognition. IEEJ Trans. Electron. Inf. Syst. **124**, 680–688 (2004)
16. Kimura, N., Kono, M., Rekimoto, J.: SottoVoce: an ultrasound imaging-based silent speech interaction using deep neural networks. In: Proceedings of the 2019 CHI Conference on Human Factors in Computing Systems, CHI 2019, New York, NY, USA, pp. 1–11. Association for Computing Machinery (2019)

17. Nakajima, Y., Kashioka, H., Shikano, K., Campbell, N.: Non-audible murmur recognition input interface using stethoscopic microphone attached to the skin. In: 2003 IEEE International Conference on Acoustics, Speech, and Signal Processing. Proceedings. (ICASSP 2003), vol. 5, pp. 708–711 (2003)
18. Hirahara, T., et al.: Silent-speech enhancement using body-conducted vocal-tract resonance signals. Speech Commun. **52**(4), 301–313 (2010)
19. Amesaka, T., Watanabe, H., Sugimoto, M.: Facial expression recognition using ear canal transfer function. In: Proceedings of the 23rd International Symposium on Wearable Computers, ISWC 2019, New York, NY, USA, pp. 1–9. Association for Computing Machinery (2019)
20. Hiraki, H., Rekimoto, J.: SilentMask: mask-type silent speech interface with measurement of mouth movement. In: Augmented Humans Conference 2021, AHs 2021, New York, NY, USA, pp. 86–90. Association for Computing Machinery (2021)
21. Ono, M., Shizuki, B., Tanaka, J.: Touch & activate: adding interactivity to existing objects using active acoustic sensing. In: Proceedings of the 26th Annual ACM Symposium on User Interface Software and Technology, UIST 2013, New York, NY, USA, pp. 31–40. Association for Computing Machinery (2013)
22. Kubo, Y., Koguchi, Y., Shizuki, B., Takahashi, S., Hilliges, O.: AudioTouch: minimally invasive sensing of micro-gestures via active bio-acoustic sensing. In: Proceedings of the 21st International Conference on Human-Computer Interaction with Mobile Devices and Services, MobileHCI 2019, New York, NY, USA. Association for Computing Machinery (2019)
23. Merrill, D., Raffle, H., Aimi, R.: The sound of touch: physical manipulation of digital sound. In: Proceedings of the SIGCHI Conference on Human Factors in Computing Systems, CHI 2008, New York, NY, USA, pp. 739–742. Association for Computing Machinery (2008)
24. Ashbrook, D., et al.: Bitey: an exploration of tooth click gestures for hands-free user interface control. In: Proceedings of the 18th International Conference on Human-Computer Interaction with Mobile Devices and Services, MobileHCI 2016, New York, NY, USA, pp. 158–169. Association for Computing Machinery (2016)

Is It Possible to Measure Real-Time VR Motion Sickness with EDA Wavelet Features?

Sujin Seong🆔 and Jaehyun Park[✉]🆔

Department of Industrial Management Engineering, Incheon University, Incheon, Korea
jaehpark@inu.ac.kr

Abstract. Virtual reality (VR) has emerged as a more commercial mainstream, and the number of users complaining of VR motion sickness is increasing rapidly. As a result, many methods, physiological indicators: electrogastrography (EGG), heart rate (HR), temperature, electrodermal activity (EDA), subjective measurement methods, simulator sickness questionnaire (SSQ), virtual reality symptom questionnaire (VRSQ), fast motion sickness score (FMS), have been studied to quantify VR motion sickness. Consequently, this study attempted to track motion sickness using EDA (sweat). The study group consisted of ten female and ten male participants who have access to VR (average age: 21.2 years; standard deviation: 2.07 years) with no physical or visual health problems. The VR environment was designed by wearing a head-mounted display (HMD) through a simple operation method. Subjects wore an EDA sensor (Empatica E4) in a VR environment and were asked to respond to SSQ, VRSQ, and FMS questionnaires. For all items of FMS and SSQ (nausea, oculomotor, disorientation, and total) and Total of VRSQ, the coefficient of determination was high in the order of 1st trial $> 2^{nd}$ trial $>$ Rest. Overall, the motion sickness score was rated the lowest during the rest period. The coefficient of determination of EDA (sweat) in rest was low in all except Disorientation in VRSQ. And VR motion sickness may have different symptoms complaining to the user depending on the VR environment. Hence, this study suggests that the EDA (sweat) signal may be suitable depending on the user's immersion interval and the symptoms.

Keywords: HMD · VR motion sickness · EDA · VRSQ · SSQ · FMS

1 Introduction

Virtual Reality (VR), a three-dimensional virtual world, has come to the fore in recent years [1]. The availability of good quality and affordable VR systems laid the foundation for the spread of VR platforms [2]. In particular, the prolonged COVID-19 has further strengthened public acceptance of non-face-to-face cultures [3]. Accordingly, VR has emerged as a more commercial and mainstream platform, and at the same time, the number of users complaining of VR motion sickness has been increasing rapidly. It points out that it may limit the effective use of training, rehabilitation, or gaming tools in using VR.

H. Degen and S. Ntoa (Eds.): HCII 2023, LNAI 14050, pp. 162–171, 2023.
https://doi.org/10.1007/978-3-031-35891-3_11

1.1 VR Sickness

The difference between general motion sickness and VR motion sensitivity is clearly present [4]. VR sensitivity is a very similar sensation to motion sickness, and the difference is that physical movement is usually limited or absent during VR exposure [5]. Many researchers conducted user experiments using VR to determine the cause of abnormal symptoms [5, 6]. The popular theory of motion sickness is as follows.

1) Sensory conflict theory is the oldest and most accepted theory related to motion sickness. It explains that motion sickness occurs because the senses that provide information on the body's direction and the body's autonomic nervous system do not match. 2) Postural instability theory focuses on causing motion sickness in the process of maintaining postural stability. 3) Poison theory explains why motion sickness occurs from an evolutionary perspective [7]. Sweating is a symptom that supports the theory of poison and is a typical symptom of motion sickness. The human body lowers the temperature the body to remove toxic substances and sweat in the process [7].

1.2 Related Work

Various methods have been studied to quantify VR motion sickness. Motion sickness measurement methods using physiological indicators (EGG, HR, Temperature, and EDA) are widely adopted [8–11]. To date, motion sickness measurements using physiological indicators cannot reliably measure motion sickness in real time [12, 13].

However, some indicators showed correlations with motion sickness and identified physiological indicators used for typical motion sickness measurements [14]. A prior study by [15] confirmed the need to develop cost-effective and objective physiological measurements.

Subjective measurement methods are also widely used to quantify motion sickness. The simulator motion sickness questionnaire SSQ [16], derived from the motion sickness assessment questionnaire MSAQ [17], is commonly used for motion sickness measurements. VRSQ [18], a measurement index for motion sickness specialized in VR situations, is also used to measure motion sickness. And FMS can measure motion sickness in real time [19].

This study attempted to track VR motion sickness using EDA (sweat) and subjective measurement methods among physiological measurements.

2 Method

2.1 Participants

The study group consisted of 10 female and 10 male participants (average age: 21.2 years; standard deviation: 2.07 years) with no physical or visual health problems.

2.2 VR Environment

The VR environment was implemented using Samsung Gear VR (SM-R325) and Samsung Galaxy Note 8. The screen resolution was 1280 × 1440 for each eye. For the

VR environment, the maze escape game "Need for Jump" was selected, designed to have an appropriate level of interaction with users. The VR environment aims to create a dynamic situation by wearing an HMD (Head Mounted Display) through a simple operation method (① directly adjusting the tilt of the head, ② jumping up and down) (Fig. 1).

Fig. 1. How to operate HMD (left), VR environment "Need for Jump" (right).

In this game, "coins" exist at each stage. All the subjects obtained the "coins" and were able to go to the next stage. They also were asked to obtain as many coins as possible during the game. There were no final stages and no game-overs in this game (Fig. 1).

2.3 EDA

Wearable Electrodermal activity (EDA) measurements in immersive simulation, such as VR, can increase emotional perception [20, 21]. In this study, we adopted wearable Empatica E4 so that participants would not be disturbed in the performance of the game.

2.4 Questionnaire

Displayed equations are centered and set on a separate line. Subjective motion sickness was measured using a total of three methods: 1) SSQ, 2) VRSQ, and 3) Fast Motion Sickness Scale (FMS). 1) For the SSQ questionnaire, there are three categories: nausea, eye movement, and disorientation. In this case, the degree of motion sickness is expressed as 0 (none), 1 (slightly), 2 (normal), and 3 (severe). The scores for each component are calculated and weighted to calculate four SSQ scores: nausea (N), oculomotor (O), disorientation (D), and total (T). 2) Some questionnaire items in SSQ were indicated as not suitable for VR environments; therefore, a VRSQ survey was developed to complement this [18]. Nausea items were removed from the existing SSQ, resulting in two components: ocular motion and disorientation. Weighing these two components is calculated by a total of three scores: ocular motion, disorientation, and total. Motion sickness score is expressed as 0 to 3, just like SSQ. 3) FMS is a real-time questionnaire method that allows measuring 'sickness' on a verbal scale of 1–20 scales every minute. FMS provides improved MS measurements and has the advantage of being fast and efficient. It can also be done online in virtual reality-like environments [19].

2.5 Procedure

Firstly, the subjects were explained the entire experiment procedure. Next, the participants were given a description of the questionnaire (SSQ, VRSQ, FMS) items and each numerical scale according to the symptoms. After that, the subjects wore EDA sensors and VR devices on their wrists and had enough practice time of about 3 to 5 min to learn the movements for smooth VR game progress. After all the preparations were completed, the subjects' bio-signal was stabilized through sufficient rest time (Fig. 2).

Next, after wearing the VR device, the subjects took a one-minute break to stabilize the bio-signal. After that, the game was repeated for five minutes and then rested for one minute. At this time, the FMS survey was conducted verbally at the same time as the game progressed.

Finally, a subjective questionnaire (SSQ and VRSQ) on the VR environment was conducted, and the experiment was completed after all data extraction was confirmed.

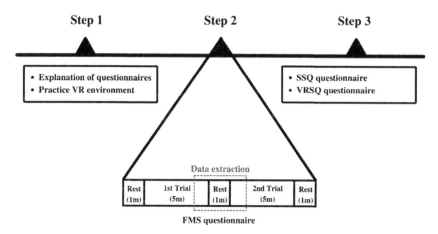

Fig. 2. Experiment process.

3 Results

3.1 EDA Signal Wavelet

Most of the subjects answered that they experienced VR motion sickness after wearing VR devices. All of them showed similar results, and #subject8 represents the subjects. The following table and graph are the EDA signal (Fig. 3) and questionnaire results of #subject8 (Table 1).

Although there are differences between individuals, EDA signals also showed an upward trend. The increase was slightly reduced in the Rest section between the first and second games.

In addition, both SSQ and VRSQ have the highest scores for Disorientation (D). The FMS score was higher in the order of 1st trial > 2nd trial > Rest. The score was measured the highest during the first game and gradually increased over time. In addition, the growth rate decreased slightly during rest. Most of the subjects showed similar patterns.

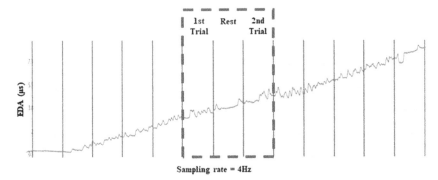

Fig. 3. EDA signal according to interval (subject#8)

Table 1. Questionnaire results (subject #8).

	1st Trial	Rest	2nd Trial
FMS	2	0	1
SSQ (N)	47.70		
SSQ (O)	30.32		
SSQ (D)	55.68		
SSQ (T)	48.62		
VRSQ (O)	8.33		
VRSQ (D)	13.33		
VRSW (T)	10.83		

3.2   Relationship Between EDA Indicators and VR Motion Sickness

In this study, the correlation between the indicators was attempted through the Polynomial Regression model. The independent and dependent variables used at this time were set as follows (Table 2).

A total of 13 independent variables were set by setting the 12 variables (2 indicators × 6 representative values) extracted from the EDA data and the number of "coins" acquired by each subject as the "performance" variable.

The subjective survey results from FMS, SSQ (Nausea, Oculomotor, Disorientation, Total), and VRSQ (Oculomotor, Disorientation, Total) were set as dependent variables.

And we applied Stepwise Regression to modeling. The following (Fig. 5) shows the results corresponding to "1st trial, Rest and 2nd trial", which are the coefficient of determination.

For all items of FMS and SSQ (Nausea, Oculomotor, Disorientation, Total) and Total of VRSQ, the order of coefficient of determination from high to low is 1st trial > 2nd trial > Rest (Fig. 4).

However, the items corresponding to the Oculomotor in VRSQ showed the 2nd trial having the largest coefficient of determination. We also confirmed that for disorientation,

Table. 2. Description of the independent and dependent variables.

Variable	Name	Description
Independent variable	MeanOD	Mean of all ODs
	StdOD	The standard deviation of all ODs
	SizeOD	Size of all ODs
	SumOD	The sum of all ODs
	MaxOD	Max of all ODs
	MinOD	Min of all ODs
	MeanOM	Mean of all OMs
	StdOM	The standard deviation of all OMs
	SizeOM	Size of all OMs
	SumOM	The sum of all OMs
	MaxOM	Max of all OMs
	MinOM	Min of all OMs
	Performance	Number of coin acquisition
Dependent variable	FMS	FMS
	SSQ (N)	Nausea of SSQ
	SSQ (O)	Oculomotor of SSQ
	SSQ (T)	Disorientation of SSQ
	VRSQ (O)	Oculomotor of VRSQ
	VRSQ (D)	Disorientation of VRSQ
	VRSQ (T)	Total of VRSQ

the coefficient of determination in rest is higher than in the 2nd trial, with the order 1st trial > Rest > 2nd trial.

4   Discussion

4.1   Comparison of EDA (Sweat) by Intervals

In this study, the EDA (sweat) showed a higher coefficient of determination of motion sickness in the 1st trial than in the 2nd trial. The results were the same for all but the Oculomotor in the VRSQ. However, the coefficient of determination of EDA in Rest was low in all except Disorientation in VRSQ.

SSQ and VRSQ are post-survey methods that take place after exposure to VR environments. All the subjects reported that they had experienced VR motion sickness. In particular, the subjects reported experiencing motion sickness in real time using FMS. At this time, subjects had rest between the end of the 1st trial and the start of the 2nd trial and evaluated the motion sickness differently before and after rest. Although there are

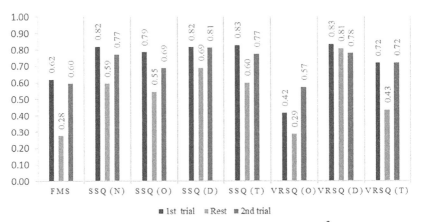

Fig. 4. Comparison of the dependent variable modeling results (Adj. R^2). Boldface means the most competitive model in terms of adjusted R^2 in each dependent variable.

some individual differences between subjects, overall, the motion sickness score was rated the lowest during rest.

Therefore, in the Rest section, EDA is not suitable to represent general motion sickness. In addition, it seems appropriate to track motion sickness using EDA when users are most immersed in the situation rather than the starting point of the VR environment. Thus, it can be concluded that the timing of measurement is important for tracking motion sickness using EDA, depending on the user's interval.

4.2   Comparison of EDA (Sweat) by Symptoms

Disorientation items can measure items such as disorientation and dizziness, as mentioned in the Theory of Postural Instability [22], which are the causes of VR motion sickness. In the VR environment of this study, EDA was the highest coefficient of determination about "Disorientation" in all 1st trials, rest, and 2nd trials. This result was consistent with both SSQ and VRSQ. And it suggests that EDA may not be an appropriate indicator for some motion sickness symptoms (general discomfort of MS, changes in eye movement, paleness, body temperature, and postural instability).

However, among the various motion sickness symptoms, symptoms such as disorientation and dizziness can be tracked through EDA. In addition, EDA had a relatively low coefficient of determination for Oculomotor compared to other survey items. Therefore, it seems difficult to track symptoms such as eye fatigue using EDA. This result was also consistent in both SSQ and VRSQ. As a result, we found that fast and efficient VRSQ can replace SSQ, just like in the previous study [18]).

Also, we confirmed that EDA explained nausea well. Nausea includes symptoms such as sweating and nausea [16]. This confirms that EDA is a suitable method for tracking symptoms such as sweating and nausea. VR motion sickness may have different symptoms complaining to the user depending on the VR environment.

Hence, this study used EDA for the tracking of motion sickness in dynamic VR environments. At this time, we checked the coefficient of determination of each VR motion sickness. Therefore, it shows that the wearable EDA sensor can be used to measure specific motion sicknesses depending on the user's symptoms.

4.3 Significance and Limitations

This paper looked to build upon the previous literature [15], which suggests the need to develop cost-effective and objective physiological measurements to track VR motion sickness. In particular, sweat is a typical symptom of motion sickness [7], and there were attempts how to measure motion sickness by using skin conductance (EDA) [11]. So, this study attempted to track VR motion sickness using EDA and subjective measurement methods among physiological measurements.

We confirmed that EDA could estimate VR motion sickness depending on the user's VR environment immersion and symptoms. This comparison uses a dynamic VR environment for the first time.

However, there are some limitations to this study. The findings in this paper are not entirely in support of a clear-cut coefficient of determination by using EDA the whole time in a VR environment. Also. It would seem from the coefficient of determination that EDA has a slight edge in tracking VR motion sickness by using physiological measurements, yet it would be wrong to conclude that using only EDA.

Using physiological measurement (EDA) is the propensity for these measures to be impacted by external factors. It is known that various states of arousal can induce a physiological change [23, 24]. And the user may have felt sweat from the physical activity felt during the VR game. So, these factors may certainly not be independent of one another.

5 Conclusion

The virtual space is still unfamiliar to most users, but as interest and demand for Metaverse increase, more improvements to VR sickness are needed. In this study, we tried to track motion sickness using EDA and various quantitative methods, which are typical motion sickness symptoms. Depending on the symptoms (i.e., disorientation, dizziness, sweating, and nausea), EDA has been identified as an indicator to measure/predict motion sickness. However, it raises many questions regarding the timing of data extraction to use the indicator alone. Also, this study may not have considered the minimum duration of motion sickness or optimal rest time.

Therefore, the next study aims to derive an optimal solution regarding the timing of EDA data extraction. In addition, group-specific VR motion sickness with various combinations should be measured to illustrate the measurement of motion sickness using quantitative methods.

Acknowledgment. This work was supported by the National Research Foundation of Korea (NRF) grant funded by the Korea government (MSIT) (No. NRF-2021R1A2C4002641). Also, this work was supported in part by the Unmanned Vehicles Core Technology Research and Development Program through the National Research Foundation of Korea (NRF), and in part by the Unmanned Vehicle Advanced Research Center (UVARC) by the Ministry of Science and ICT, Republic of Korea, under Grant 2020M3C1C1A01084900.

References

1. Jeon, J.: The effects of user experience-based design innovativeness on user-metaverse platform channel relationships in South Korea. J. Distrib. Sci. (JDS) **19**, 81–90 (2021)
2. Gaggioli, A.: Virtually social. Cyberpsychol. Behav. Soc. Netw. **21**(5), 338–339 (2018)
3. Park, J.Y., Lee, K., Chung, D.R.: Public interest in the digital transformation accelerated by the COVID-19 pandemic and perception of its future impact. Korean J. Int. Med. **37**(6), 1223–1233 (2022)
4. Laviola Jr., J.J.: A discussion of cybersickness in virtual environments. ACM Sigchi Bull. **32**(1), 47–56 (2000)
5. Keshavarz, B., Riecke, B.E., Hettinger, L.J., Campos, J.L.: Vection and visually induced motion sickness: how are they related? Front. Psychol. **6**, 472 (2015)
6. Duh, H.B., Parker, D.E., Furness, T.A.: An independent visual background reduced simulator sickness in a driving simulator. Presence Teleoper. Virtual Environ. **13**(5), 578–588 (2004)
7. Treisman, M.: Motion sickness: an evolutionary hypothesis. Science **197**(4302), 493–495 (1977)
8. Stern, R.M., Koch, K.L., Leibowitz, H.W., Lindblad, I.M., Shupert, C.L., Stewart, W.R.: Tachygastria and motion sickness. Aviat. Space Environ. Med. **56**(11), 1074–1077 (1985)
9. Hu, S., Grant, W.F., Stern, R.M., Koch, K.L.: Motion sickness severity and physiological correlates during repeated exposures to a rotating optokinetic drum. Aviat. Space Environ. Med. **64**(4), 308–314 (1991)
10. Nalivaiko, E., Rudd, J.A., So, R.H.: Motion sickness, nausea and thermoregulation: the "toxic" hypothesis. Temperature **1**(3), 164–171 (2014)
11. Golding, J.F., Stott, J.R.R.: Comparison of the effects of a selective muscarinic receptor antagonist and hyoscine (scopolamine) on motion sickness, skin conductance and heart rate. Br. J. Clin. Pharmacol. **43**(6), 633–637 (1997)
12. Hussain, M., Park, J., Kim, H.K., Lee, Y., Park, S.: Motion sickness indexes in augmented reality environment. ICIC Express Lett. Part B Appl. Int. J. Res. Surv. **12**(12), 1155–1160 (2021)
13. Kim, J., Park, J., Park, J.: Development of a statistical model to classify driving stress levels using galvanic skin responses. Hum. Factors Ergon. Manuf. Serv. Ind. **30**(5), 321–328 (2020)
14. Smyth, J., Birrell, S., Woodman, R., Jennings, P.: Exploring the utility of EDA and skin temperature as individual physiological correlates of motion sickness. Appl. Ergon. **92**, 103315 (2021)
15. Davis, S., Nesbitt, K., Nalivaiko, E.: A systematic review of cybersickness. In: Proceedings of the 2014 Conference on Interactive Entertainment, pp. 1–9 (2014)
16. Kennedy, R.S., Lane, N.E., Berbaum, K.S., Lilienthal, M.G.: Simulator sickness questionnaire: an enhanced method for quantifying simulator sickness. Int. J. Aviat. Psychol. **3**(3), 203–220 (1993)
17. Gianaros, P.J., Muth, E.R., Mordkoff, J.T., Levine, M.E., Stern, R.M.: A questionnaire for the assessment of the multiple dimensions of motion sickness. Aviat. Space Environ. Med. **72**(2), 115 (2001)
18. Kim, H.K., Park, J., Choi, Y., Choe, M.: Virtual reality sickness questionnaire (VRSQ): motion sickness measurement index in a virtual reality environment. Appl. Ergon. **69**, 66–73 (2018)
19. Keshavarz, B., Hecht, H.: Validating an efficient method to quantify motion sickness. Hum. Factors **53**(4), 415–426 (2011)
20. Estupiñán, S., Rebelo, F., Noriega, P., Ferreira, C., Duarte, E.: Can virtual reality increase emotional responses (arousal and valence)? A pilot study. In: Marcus, A. (ed.) DUXU 2014. LNCS, vol. 8518, pp. 541–549. Springer, Cham (2014). https://doi.org/10.1007/978-3-319-07626-3_51

21. Bitkina, O.V., Kim, J., Park, J., Park, J., Kim, H.K.: Identifying traffic context using driving stress: a longitudinal preliminary case study. Sensors **19**(9), 2152 (2019)
22. Riccio, G.E., Stoffregen, T.A.: An ecological theory of motion sickness and postural instability. Ecol. Psychol. **3**(3), 195–240 (1991)
23. Warwickevans, L.A., Church, R.E., Hancock, C., Jochim, D., Morris, P.H., Ward, F.: Electrodermal activity as an index of motion sickness. Aviat. Space Environ. Med. (1987)
24. Bitkina, O.V., Kim, J., Park, J., Park, J., Kim, H.K.: User stress in artificial intelligence: modeling in case of system failure. IEEE Access **9**, 137430–137443 (2021)

Explainability, Transparency,
and Trustworthiness

How Do AI Explanations Affect Human-AI Trust?

Lam Bui, Marco Pezzola, and Danushka Bandara$^{(\boxtimes)}$ (iD)

Fairfield University, Fairfield, CT 06825, USA
dbandara@fairfield.edu

Abstract. We conducted a study to explore the effect of different types of Artificial intelligence (AI) explanations on the human trust in AI systems. An in person user study was conducted (n = 7) and the trust condition was induced by varying the accuracy of AI response. The human trust was measured by surveys administered after each trial. The participants physiological data was also collected during the experiment. Our results show that image based explanations induced higher level of arousal in the participants, and the participants preferred image based explanations. We also found that the AI response accuracy had an effect on the user acceptance of AI's decision in the following trial. We also found that Photoplethysmography results had statistically significant correlation with the level of trust. The implications of this study are that AI performance and type of explanations both have an effect on the level of user trust in AI. Also this work could be extended to develop an objective measure of trust using physiological data.

Keywords: Human AI interaction · Trust · Physiological measures

1 Introduction

Most of human life today is integrated into Machine Learning (ML) and Artificial Intelligence (AI) systems, with more complex and accurate algorithms being developed each day. So much of our lives are influenced through AI, whether it be our car's GPS giving us the fastest route home, smart homes adjusting our thermostat, or even the advertisements we see online relating to a product we just searched on the internet. In many past studies, researchers have studied human interaction with ML/AI. This paper will discuss our own research between humans and ML, we study this relationship using physiological sensors and self report surveys.

Human trust in machine learning refers to the confidence and reliance that individuals place in the ability of ML systems to make accurate predictions and decisions. Building trust in ML systems is important for their successful deployment and adoption in various industries and applications. According to literature, there are several aspects that affect human trust in ML systems.

- Explainability or the ability to understand the internal logic behind the decision [1, 2].
- Performance: People are more likely to trust a ML system when it demonstrates high accuracy and low error rates [3].

© The Author(s), under exclusive license to Springer Nature Switzerland AG 2023
H. Degen and S. Ntoa (Eds.): HCII 2023, LNAI 14050, pp. 175–183, 2023.
https://doi.org/10.1007/978-3-031-35891-3_12

- Control and autonomy: People are more likely to trust a system when they have control over it and can override its decisions [4].

Yang, Huang, Scholtz, and Arendt [5] found that subjects demonstrated higher trust when both understandability and layout of the explanation is provided, with 95% bootstrap confidence intervals; where image-based explanations outperformed rose chart-based explanations since image-based explanations "increase appropriate trust, decrease overtrust and undertrust, improve self-confidence, and show more usability". In another study, Yin, Vaughan, and Wallach [3] demonstrated that high user trust comes most commonly when models observe or state a higher accuracy percentage than the user and decrease their trust otherwise. This demonstrates that subjects are biased to believe in a machine's prediction so long as it exceeds their own.

1.1 Physiological Manifestations of Trust

Heart Rate Variability
Trusting environments or individuals may be associated with increased heart rate variability, which is a measure of the variation in the time interval between heartbeats. Higher heart rates would imply a higher level of trust due to the correlation with higher levels of expectations [6, 7].

Cortisol Levels
Trusting environments or individuals may be associated with lower cortisol levels, which is a hormone associated with stress. In a study conducted by Ditzen, Schaer, Gabriel, Bodenmann, Ehlert, and Heinrichs [8], both men and women would have reduced cortisol levels while in a state of positivity.

Skin Conductance
Trusting environments or individuals may be associated with changes in skin conductance, which is a measure of electrical conductance of the skin. Showing trust in ML that concludes with a negative or uncomfortable result should increase conductance. Such an example is with self driving vehicles deciding on routes to take [9]. Researchers found that Skin Conductance would be higher prior to highly rewarding and risky decisions; meaning "if the participant had not registered the fact that the decision was risk, skin conductance did not increase."

Brain Activity
Trusting environments or individuals may be associated with changes in brain activity, specifically in regions related to social cognition, emotion regulation, and decision-making [10].

2 Study Design

2.1 Measurement of Trust

The aim of this study is to explore the concept of trust in ML systems and investigate the physiological, performance and explainability factors that contribute to building trust between humans and ML. We will discuss the implications of our findings for the design, development and deployment of ML systems. In our study, subjects were presented with a task of classifying authentic and non authentic (doctored) images. The trust and distrust conditions were induced by a simulated AI system providing correct or incorrect suggestions.

- If the participant accepted the AI decision, we consider that the participant trusted the AI.
- If the participant rejected the AI decision, we consider that the participant distrusted the AI.

We analyzed the data through different statistical techniques to show the relationship between different variables in the experiment and trust.

2.2 Experimental Design

We conducted an experiment where seven subjects participated in a 'Human AI Interaction' experiment. The participants were approximately 20 years of age and were from a university in the northeast United states. Participants completed a pre-experiment questionnaire to gauge their base level of trust in computers. We adopted the disposition to trust inventory [11] and adjusted the questions to reflect human-computer trust. When participants arrived for the experiment, they were seated in front of the computer and presented various images consecutively with 10 s of rest between each trial. Their job was to judge whether the images were authentic or 'doctored' (manipulated in any way). We used the CASIA [12] dataset as the source for the images (Fig. 1).

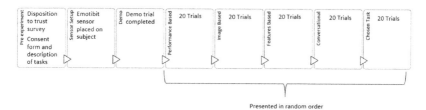

Fig. 1. Experimental design

In addition to the images, participants saw the AI decision of whether the image was authentic or not authentic. We used a 'wizard of oz' methodology for this study (i.e., we simulated the AI response) to show the participants a variety of AI responses. We also administered a trust measurement survey during the experiment to gauge how trust varies subjectively [13].

2.3 Types of Explanations

We used four types of explanations in this experiment.

1. Image-based explanations: In case of non-authentic images from the CASIA dataset, the image was occluded and the part of the image relevant to the decision was uncovered. For authentic images, the whole image was shown.

2. Performance based explanations: Had a textual description of the machine learning model performance and the performance metrics such as Area Under the Curve (AUC), Precision, Recall, Accuracy.
3. Feature-based explanations: The features (Color and noise patterns, dense field copy move, JPEG dimples, self consistency splice, splicebuster) were chosen to display the contribution of different features to the AI decision.
4. Conversational explanations: A representation of the AI agent was shown with a short sentence about the confidence level of the AI in the answer (Figs. 2 and 3).

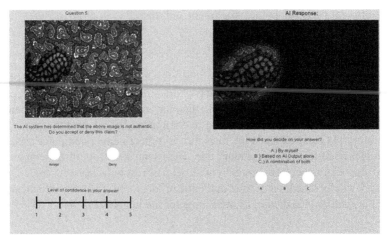

Fig. 2. An example trial with an image based explanation for a non-authentic image.

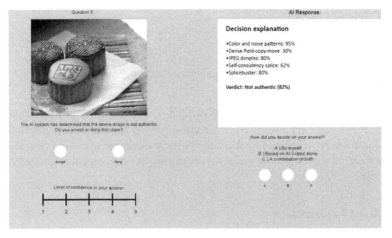

Fig. 3. An example trial with a feature based explanation.

2.4 Collected Data

Throughout our study, we collected physiological data from participants utilizing emotibit, an open-source biosensor that measures the following data,

- Electrodermal activity

  - EDA-Electrodermal Activity
  - EDL-Electrodermal Level
  - Skin Conductance Response (SCR) Amplitude
  - Skin Conductance Response (SCR) Rise Time
  - Skin Conductance Response (SCR) Frequency

- Heart Rate

  - Heart Rate
  - Heart Inter-beat Interval

- Photoplethysmography (PPG)

  - PPG-Infrared
  - PPG-Red
  - PPG-Green

- Body movement (Using accelerometer, gyroscope and magnetometer)

  - Accelerometer (X, Y, Z)
  - Gyroscope (X, Y, Z)
  - Magnetometer (X, Y, Z)

- Temperature

  - Temperature via Medical-grade Thermopile

After each question/trial, the participants were presented with several questions relating to their trust perspective. The questions include,

- Do you accept or Deny the AI decision?
- How confident are you about your answer?
- How did you arrive at your answer? (By myself, Based on AI output alone, A combination of both)

2.5 Research Questions

RQ1: Effect of the AI explanation types (image based, performance based, feature based, conversational) on trust

RQ2: How does the AI's previous performance affect trust?

RQ3: What are the physiological measures most correlated with participant trust level?

3 Results

3.1 RQ1

See Figs. 4 and 5.

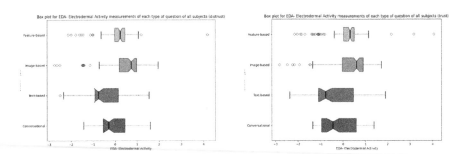

Fig. 4. EDA values for the distrust (left) vs trust (right) conditions do not show a noticeable difference. However, we do see a noticeable difference between the types of explanations. The image based explanations induced the maximum EDA levels in both conditions. Feature based explanations induced the next highest EDA levels.

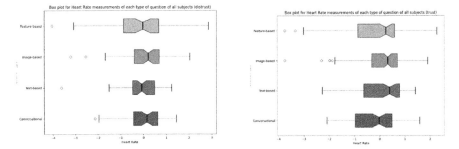

Fig. 5. Text based (performance based) explanations induced a higher heart rate in the trust condition (right) than the distrust condition (left).

3.2 RQ2

See Fig. 6.

3.3 RQ3

The physiological measures having highest correlation with trust level are, PPG green ($p < 0.005$), PPG infrared ($p < 0.05$) and PPG red ($p < 0.1$).

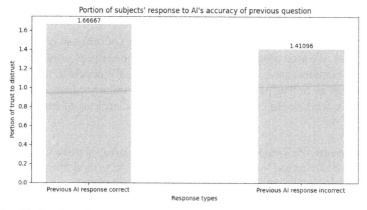

Fig. 6. Considering the ratio of trust to distrust, we can see that the participants had a higher ratio of trust if the AI provided the correct suggestion in the previous question vs if AI had provided an incorrect suggestion in the previous question.

4 Discussion

The results show that the various types of explanations do induce different physiological responses among the participants. Specifically, image based explanations induced higher EDA levels which is correlated with arousal. This could be due to the fact that images elicit a visceral reaction compared to the other methods of explanations.

Surprisingly, we did not notice a large difference between the heart rate variability for the trust and distrust conditions. It could possibly be due to the fact that our stimulus was not enough duration to create a difference in stress response in the subjects.

We did find that the AI's previous performance has an influence of the trust level. If the AI had given the correct answer to a question, the participants were more likely to trust the AI in the following question.

We also found that the Photoplethysmography data show statistically significant variation with the trust levels. Since PPG is an indicator of cardiovascular and respiratory activity, this could mean that it is capable of capturing the physiological response to trust vs distrust conditions.

Our findings indicate that image based explanations seem to have a larger effect on the participants, creating a higher level of arousal (Electrodermal activity). We also found that given a choice, participants preferred the image based explanations. Out of the seven subjects, all but one subject chose the image based explanation over the others. These results show that AI designers should pay attention to the type of explanations provided by AI as it has implications for trust in the AI and for human acceptance of AI decisions. Although we have a limited dataset, we can still see that trust and distrust conditions can be observed in the physiological data. Further studies could explore this further using machine learning models.

5   Conclusion

We designed and conducted a study to measure the effect of different types of AI explanations on trust. We used subjective surveys as well as objective physiological measures to develop a comprehensive view of human AI trust. We conclude that the types of AI explanations as well as past performance of the AI influence human trust in the AI system. Future work could explore the physiological correlates of trust with a larger dataset.

Acknowledgements. We would like to acknowledge the contribution to the trust testbed development by Robert Dillon and Noor Khattak. We would also like to thank Hien Tran and Miguel Cuahuizo for their contributions to the data analysis phase of the project.

References

1. Markus, A.F., Kors, J.A., Rijnbeek, P.R.: The role of explainability in creating trustworthy artificial intelligence for health care: a comprehensive survey of the terminology, design choices, and evaluation strategies. J. Biomed. Inform. **113**, 103655 (2021)
2. Chatzimparmpas, A., Martins, R.M., Jusufi, I., Kucher, K., Rossi, F., Kerren, A.: The state of the art in enhancing trust in machine learning models with the use of visualizations. Comput. Graph. Forum **39**(3), 713–756 (2020)
3. Yin, M., Wortman Vaughan, J., Wallach, H.: Understanding the effect of accuracy on trust in machine learning models. In: Proceedings of the 2019 CHI Conference on Human Factors in Computing Systems, pp. 1–12, May 2019
4. Israelsen, B.W., Ahmed, N.R.: "Dave...I can assure you ...that it's going to be all right ..." a definition, case for, and survey of algorithmic assurances in human-autonomy trust relationships. ACM Comput. Surv. **51**, 6, Article no. 113 (2019), 37 p. https://doi.org/10.1145/326 7338
5. Yang, F., Huang, Z., Scholtz, J., Arendt, D.L.: How do visual explanations foster end users' appropriate trust in machine learning? In: Proceedings of the 25th International Conference on Intelligent User Interfaces, pp. 189–201, March 2020
6. Mitkidis, P., McGraw, J.J., Roepstorff, A., Wallot, S.: Building trust: Heart rate synchrony and arousal during joint action increased by public goods game. Physiol. Behav. **149**, 101–106 (2015)
7. Merrill, N., Cheshire, C.: Trust your heart: assessing cooperation and trust with biosignals in computer-mediated interactions. In: Proceedings of the 2017 ACM Conference on Computer Supported Cooperative Work and Social Computing, pp. 2–12, February 2017
8. Ditzen, B., Schaer, M., Gabriel, B., Bodenmann, G., Ehlert, U., Heinrichs, M.: Intranasal oxytocin increases positive communication and reduces cortisol levels during couple conflict. Biol. Psychiatry **65**(9), 728–731 (2009)
9. Morris, D.M., Erno, J.M., Pilcher, J.J.: Electrodermal response and automation trust during simulated self-driving car use. In: Proceedings of the Human Factors and Ergonomics Society Annual Meeting, vol. 61, no. 1, pp. 1759–1762. SAGE Publications, Los Angeles, September 2017
10. Zak, P.J.: The neuroscience of trust. Harv. Bus. Rev. **95**(1), 84–90 (2017)
11. McKnight, D.H., Choudhury, V., Kacmar, C.: Developing and validating trust measures for e-commerce: an integrative typology. Inf. Syst. Res. **13**(3), 334–359 (2002). Modified to cater to trust in AI instead of trust in people. Disposition to trust inventory

12. Pham, N.T., Lee, J.W., Kwon, G.R., Park, C.S.: Hybrid image-retrieval method for image-splicing validation. Symmetry **11**(1), 83 (2019)
13. Madsen, M., Gregor, S.D.: Measuring human-computer trust (2000)

The Thousand Faces of Explainable AI Along the Machine Learning Life Cycle: Industrial Reality and Current State of Research

Thomas Decker[1,2], Ralf Gross[1], Alexander Koebler[1,3], Michael Lebacher[1(✉)], Ronald Schnitzer[1,4], and Stefan H. Weber[1]

[1] Siemens AG, Munich, Germany
{thomas.decker,ralf.gross,alexander.koebler,michael.lebacher,
ronald.schnitzer,stefan_hagen.weber}@siemens.com
[2] Ludwig Maximilians Universität Munich, Munich, Germany
[3] Goethe University Frankfurt, Frankfurt, Germany
[4] Technical University of Munich, Munich, Germany

Abstract. In this paper, we investigate the practical relevance of explainable artificial intelligence (XAI) with a special focus on the producing industries and relate them to the current state of academic XAI research. Our findings are based on an extensive series of interviews regarding the role and applicability of XAI along the Machine Learning (ML) lifecycle in current industrial practice and its expected relevance in the future. The interviews were conducted among a great variety of roles and key stakeholders from different industry sectors. On top of that, we outline the state of XAI research by providing a concise review of the relevant literature. This enables us to provide an encompassing overview covering the opinions of the surveyed persons as well as the current state of academic research. By comparing our interview results with the current research approaches we reveal several discrepancies. While a multitude of different XAI approaches exists, most of them are centered around the model evaluation phase and data scientists. Their versatile capabilities for other stages are currently either not sufficiently explored or not popular among practitioners. In line with existing work, our findings also confirm that more efforts are needed to enable also non-expert users' interpretation and understanding of opaque AI models with existing methods and frameworks.

Keywords: Explainable AI · Interpretable Machine Learning · Human-centered Computing · Machine Learning Life Cycle · Human-Computer-Interaction

1 Introduction

Artificial Intelligence (AI) has become increasingly pervasive in the industry and proved to be successful in multiple applied industrial use cases [71, 107, 113]. However, it is still a challenging step from providing first Proof of Concepts (PoCs) to actually deployed Machine Learning systems (e.g., [93]). While the causes for this problem are

---

All authors contributed equally and are listed in alphabetic order.

H. Degen and S. Ntoa (Eds.): HCII 2023, LNAI 14050, pp. 184–208, 2023.
https://doi.org/10.1007/978-3-031-35891-3_13

manifold, one potential reason is the notorious black-box nature of AI, which prevents AI developers from understanding and communicating their models, hampers the trust-building process, impedes efficient communication with stakeholders, and complicates monitoring and maintenance. Therefore, the problem of opaque AI poses challenges along the entire AI life cycle [101].

For this reason, explainable Artificial intelligence (XAI) has established itself as a multifaceted research field covering a vast variety of approaches and incorporating perspectives from different academic areas. We define explainability, in accordance with [28] as *"any technique that provides the ability to explain or present the outcomes or predictions of AI systems in understandable terms to humans"*. The relevance of such techniques is mirrored by the fast-growing interest in academia and the industry's demand. One manifestation is the number of research papers published in the area of XAI as shown in Fig. 1, see also [2]. Given this rapid growth in research interest, the field has already accumulated an enormous amount of methods and tools for models applied to image data [99], text data [38,86], tabular data [44,68], time series data [88] and reinforcement learning [111]. For a more encompassing view on the topic, we refer to [28,76].

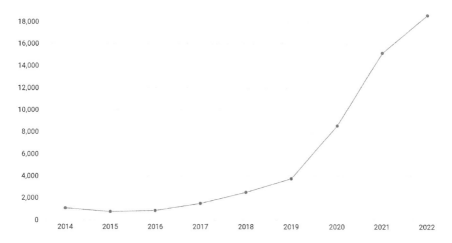

Fig. 1. Number of publications related to 'Explainable AI' from 2014 to 2022. Source: dimensional.ai, accessed 2023/20/01

However, most current academic research effort is still directed towards researchers and AI developers and does not focus on other end users or the role of explainability along the whole machine learning life cycle. Notable exceptions are the studies by [13], and [27] that concern the role of XAI for deployment and across the ML life cycle, respectively. The researchers in [13] conducted 50 interviews in domains such as Finance, Insurance, and Content Moderation, finding that ML experts and developers increasingly use XAI techniques for error tracing and debugging. They highlight that XAI currently bears no benefit to other stakeholders, and a general gap exists between the potential usage scenarios and the actual practice of XAI. In [27], 30 interviews have been conducted with a focus on natural language processing (NLP) researchers, pointing on the finding that XAI rarely addresses challenges along the full AI life cycle in practice.

We aim to extend and supplement these findings by providing a real-world perspective from the industry with a comprehensive coverage of the role of XAI in the ML life cycle. Based on a qualitative analysis of semi-structured interviews, we integrate the different views and perspectives on this topic in a consistent picture and set our findings in the context of the current literature. This allows us to highlight challenges not yet addressed and research gaps. Our contributions to the literature are as follows:

- We conducted 36 semi-structured interviews with practitioners and various stakeholders to identify the current relevance of XAI along the ML life cycle with a focus on the producing industries.
- We surveyed current XAI research and allocated it to the best matching ML life cycle stage.
- We juxtaposed and compared both perspectives to identify alignments and mismatches.

It is clear that this paper cannot summarize the findings of the enourmous XAI literature as a whole and is, therefore, restricted to the research works we found most fitting in the context of our interviews and the respective life cycle stages.

In the remainder of the paper, we will provide background on the interviews and methodology in Sect. 2. This is followed by Sect. 3, presenting a broad perspective on how the need for XAI is motivated in academia, in applied industrial use cases, and how this topic relates to regulations. Then, in Sect. 4, we shed a light on the relevance of XAI along the ML life cycle. We end the paper with a summary on our research hypothesis in Sect. 5 and a conclusion in Sect. 6.

2   Background on the Interviews and Methodology

We conducted 36 remote interviews ranging from 45 to 60 min with employees from Siemens AG, startups, technical associations, and research institutes. The main focus, with 19 persons in the sample, is on the role of *data scientists*, defined here as well-trained but applied working persons that solve practical problems with machine learning in the domain of industrial automation and autonomous vehicles. The focus on the data scientists stems from the fact that this role usually needs to provide support at all stages of the ML life cycle. However, we also integrate the views from (applied) academia with three *machine learning researchers* from public research institutes. Furthermore, we interviewed two *certification and standardization engineers* from public institutions and two *safety engineers* to integrate their views. In order to cover the organizational and business perspective, we also interviewed *machine learning team leads*, *sales persons*, *machine learning product and project managers*, and even two *chief technology officers*. These persons are subsumed in the role of *managers*. Lastly, we interviewed two *machine learning and IT service technicians* as well as one *domain expert* working in close collaboration with data scientists. Hence, we can roughly separate two groups,

Table 1. Number of Interviews by domains (columns) and roles (rows)

Role/Domain	Industrial Automatization	Technical Associations	Autonomous Vehicles	Startups	Research Institutes	$\sum$
Data Scientist	7	-	1	3	-	11
ML Researcher	-	-	-	-	3	3
Sales	3	-	-	-	-	3
Safety Engineer	2	-	1	-	-	3
ML Team Lead	1	-	-	2	-	3
ML Service Technician	2	-	-	-	-	2
Certification Engineer	-	2	-	-	-	2
Manager	3	-	3	2	-	7
Domain Expert	1	-	-	-	-	1
$\sum$	19	2	5	7	3	36

a technically oriented group and a group of team leads and managers. See Table 1 for a comprehensive overview of the covered roles, expertises, and domains.

We ensured all our interview partner anonymity. Hence, except for Siemens AG, we do not list companies or names of interview partners, and we refrain from direct quotes. Similar to [13, 27, 48], we rely on semi-structured interviews that are guided by underlying hypotheses for the different roles under study. See Table 2 for our main guiding hypotheses for data scientists and machine learning researchers (first four rows). We further investigated the hypotheses in rows five to eight for interview partners responsible for monitoring and maintaining AI systems. Finally, the hypotheses for the more business-oriented group are shown in the last three rows. The formulation of the hypotheses was guided by the idea of covering multiple stages of the Machine Learning life cycle as well as typical tasks that are presumably relatable to XAI.

Where appropriate, we also asked which XAI tools are currently used and which obstacles concerning the scaling of XAI have been encountered. Based on the transcribed protocols, we extracted main insights and matched them along the ML life cycle based on CRISP-ML [101]. This life cycle model builds upon the CRISP-DM model, first introduced in 2000 [112]. Although being relatively old, the CRISP-DM process is still considered the most widely used analytical methodology for data mining and knowledge discovery projects [70]. CRISP-ML can be interpreted as an adoption of the CRISP-DM model towards the particular requirements of machine learning applications, especially concerning the full coverage of the whole life cycle. It divides the life cycle into six stages, which are:

1. *Business and Data Understanding*, covering the scoping of ML applications, including building success criteria and feasibility concerns, as well as collecting and verifying the quality of the data.
2. *Data Preparation*, considering all necessary data preparation steps, such as selecting, cleaning, and standardizing the data.
3. *Modelling*, addressing any required step for bringing up the model, including model selection, training, and potentially pruning.

4. *Evaluation*, concerning the validation of the model performance and having in mind deficiencies of the model such as lack of robustness as well as the success criteria defined in the first stage. On top of that, explainability for AI practitioneers and end users is explicitly mentioned.
5. *Deployment*, addressing the implementation of the model into the appropriate hardware and validating the model again under production conditions.
6. *Monitoring and Maintenance*, considering possible changes in the environment or the application itself, possibly influencing the model performance. Thus, it is required to monitor the model and potentially adapt it to changes in production conditions.

For a more detailed explanation of the individual stages of the CRISM-ML model, we refer to [101]. Figure 2 provides a summary of our main findings along the ML life cycle.

Apart from the life cycle we also included the general motivation for using XAI as a focust category, covering business aspects and the role of XAI in regulation, standardization, and safety aspects (see Sect. 3). The reason for this additional section is that, during the interviews, we learned that these aspects are important as a general motivation for XAI in real-world applications but cannot be directly allocated to the ML life cycle.

Table 2. Guiding hypotheses for the interviews related to different roles

Hypotheses Data Scientists	XAI support the communication with domain experts
	XAI improves the development process
	XAI improves AI testing
	XAI relives from the lack of trust in the developed models.
Hypotheses Monitoring	XAI supports the task of monitoring
	XAI can support the task of maintaining AI
	XAI can support root cause analysis, commissioning, and other tasks
	XAI can support audits.
Hypotheses Business	XAI and AI are among the strategic priorities
	XAI bridges gaps in cross-functional teams
	XAI is needed as a distinguishing factor (from competitors)

3   Motivation for Explainability

3.1   Insights from the Interviews

The Need for Distinguishing Factors. According to our interviews, companies that try to sell AI products or solutions are increasingly confronted with their customers' growing AI maturity, which changed their expectations towards AI products and solutions. Consequently, competition became more fiercely and the pressure to provide distinguishing factors increased in order to match the demands of customers and their expectations regarding the extent of AI offering packages. It is important, however, to note that the demand for distinguishing factors has the precondition that customers have already achieved a certain degree of AI maturity, and the placement of distinguishing factors can also be a matter of market timing. Among the most important distinguishing factors are *transparency, traceability* and *explainability*, that promise to improve trust and acceptance of AI solutions and products. Forerunners for setting this trend are companies such as Google, Meta, Amazon, and Microsoft, which started activities to provide explainability, robust AI, trustworthy AI offerings, and software.[1]

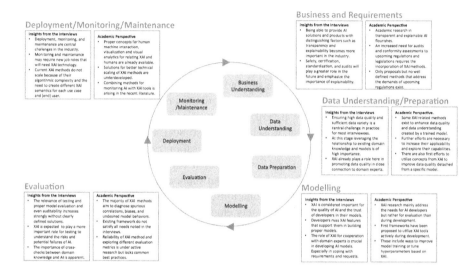

Fig. 2. CRISP-ML life cycle with summarized findings. For each stage, we display insights from the interviews contrasted with the academic perspective.

Although transparency and explainability are important factors, we also found that trust in the data business is not only of technical nature but also related to general factors such as business habits, trust in customer relations, and brand perception. Even companies with well-established and trustworthy brands can struggle with mistrust concerning their AI business models.

Standards, Regulation and Safety. Besides the need for distinguishing factors, the topic of upcoming regulations and standards can also drive the need for XAI. Although these topics were of high interest to many interviewees, their views on future standards were in conflict. However, common ground was that currently, almost no, only bad, or too lax external (and internal) standards are in place and that the future will hold standards, regulations, and even regular audits for AI.

---

[1] Examples are, e.g., the explainable AI frameworks and tools by Google for the Google Cloud, the Captum library [60] by Meta/Facebook, Amazon Lookout as well as Amazon SageMaker Clarify Model Explainability and Microsofts InterpretML [83] python library (Comments of the authors and not part of the interview responses).

Regarding the expected scope of formal AI certification, we learned that safety-critical domains, such as *healthcare, public transport, public services, industrial automation* and *shopfloor control* are likely to be subject to certification in the future.

Looking at the certification methodology, some persons advocated black box testing, e.g., with pre-defined and hidden datasets available only to certification authorities. This is also in line with the argumentation that certifying units do not need to understand (X)AI and any details besides functionality, performance or statistical arguments do not matter to them. In contrast, other interviewed persons argued that certification authorities will assume and demand that the developers understand their models in depth - which gives a strong pointer towards explainability. This explains why using XAI for certification was promoted by some interviewees. One approach would be that certification authorities use XAI methods to understand the AI to be certified, meaning that XAI will become an own component in the certification process. Another approach is to place the explainability on the side of the developers, where employment of XAI methodology is a mandatory feature to satisfy regulatory requirements.

Focusing on the more specific area of AI safety, we found that it is hard to evaluate AI systems with classical safety approaches (see also Sect. 4.2). The main issue is the fact that AI suffers from the *correlation versus causation problem* while safety arguments typically rely on causation. XAI was credited with providing a valuable set of tools for identifying errors, safety verification, and support for safety audits. Regarding the limitations of XAI for safety argumentations, we learned that XAI is currently not known to relevant stakeholders such as safety engineers and cannot guarantee the safety or achieve a safety claim on its own. Hence, in the future, it is likely that XAI tooling will not support safety argumentations solely but in combination with other approaches.

3.2   Academic Perspective on Regulation and XAI

Current Proposals for Regulation. Essentially, we learned from the interviews that conflicting views and even confusion concerning standards, regulations, and safety requirements for AI were predominant among the interviewed persons. This was somewhat surprising as there already exist quite concrete proposals. The European Commission (EC) has presented a draft for the legislation and regulation of Artificial Intelligence [32] (AIA). Similar approaches exist in other parts of the world, such as the United States. For example, the Algorithmic Accountability Act of 2022 (AAA US) [1], which is compared to the AIA in the literature, see [43, 75]. Even though compared to the AIA, the AAA US is less concrete and ambitioned [43], it is expected that the European AI regulations will implicitly expand globally. This phenomenon, also called *de facto Brussels Effect*, describes global business being conducted under unilateral EU rules even when other states continue to maintain their own rules [15]. The proposed regulation on AI causing a de facto Brussels Effect is expected to be likely [98]. The European efforts are severe and according to [35], it is evident that this will result in a legal framework based on the values of *trustworthy AI* as laid out by the High-Level Expert Group (HLEG) on Artificial Intelligence, which aims to lay the foundation for the development of lawful, ethical, and robust AI systems [30, 31].

Risk-Based Regulation. Fundamentally, the proposal classifies AI systems into three risk-based classes: *Unacceptable risk, high risk,* and *low- or no risk.* See the Cap AI publication [36] for an informative summary. This risk-based approach has concrete consequences as AI systems classified as a potential source of *unacceptable risk* will be prohibited. In contrast, for *low or no risk* AI systems, no further action has to be taken. However, a substantial part of AI systems already on the market or intended to be deployed in the future will likely be classified in the high-risk category, as every AI system referred to in Annex III of the European regulation shall be considered as high risk. Examples of criteria from Annex III are AI systems intended to be used *as safety components for recruitment or selection of natural persons to evaluate the creditworthiness of natural persons.* Note that these examples represent only a small share of all affected AI systems. For further details including the full list in Annex III, see [32].

The Role of XAI in Regulation. For all AI systems classified as high-risk, an extensive set of requirements is declared in Chap. II of the European regulation. These requirements can be relatively straightforward and directly touch upon transparency and explainability, among other points. Art 10 demands AI systems to ensure that they *operate transparently and enable users to interpret the system's output appropriately* [32], which is a direct call for XAI tooling in high-risk AI use cases. However, regarding the concrete implementation, there are currently no standardized solutions but various approaches that may achieve these goals with XAI methods [69,85]. For example, XAI can improve model bias understanding and promotes fairness [26] or increase transparency and detect adversarial examples [63].

To sum up, there are concrete proposals for regulation, and a place is reserved for XAI to fulfill them. However, currently, we see only a few examples of how explainable AI can contribute to the development of trustworthy AI systems. Much future research remains to be done to enable XAI to be useful in certification and conformity assessments towards regulations, as the EC proposes. A result that is in line with the findings from our interviews

4   XAI Along the ML Life Cycle

4.1   Data Collection and Understanding

Insights from the Interviews. Collecting data for an industrial AI project is a complex task involving many roles, but the most important interaction is between data scientists and domain experts. The domain experts are expected to support data selection and the definition of the "right" data and play an essential role in supporting data scientists with data understanding and data quality evaluation. However, in industrial reality, data with the necessary variety, coverage, quantity, and quality is often scarce or restricted for internal or external reasons.

While XAI typically plays its role during or after modeling, it was mentioned multiple times that XAI tools help in the iterated cycles between model building, data collection, and exchange with domain experts. Typical applications, where XAI is expected to support, in this context are investigating whether the available amounts and variety of data suffice and identifying issues with data quality, data bias, and wrong labels. One concrete approach mentioned is to detect relevant features via XAI methods and inspect the corresponding data quality more closely.

Academic Perspective on the Role of XAI for Data Collection and Quality. The interviews revealed that the interaction with domain experts is important (which is extensively discussed from an academic perspective in Sect. 4.2) and that XAI is already recognized as a framework that can enhance data quality, collection, and understanding in practice. However, many relevant explainability techniques proposed by the academic literature do not seem prevalent. More specifically, a variety of methods aim to evaluate the influence of particular training data point on predictions, model performance, or the final model parameters. Note that such information can be utilized to address different challenges related to data quality and collection, like data valuation, noisy label detection, data subset selection, or guiding further data acquisition.

Typically, corresponding methods either utilize the knowledge created by an already trained model or evaluate models at different checkpoints during training. One line of work for this purpose uses the concept of Shapley values to identify the importance of individual training data points for the model performance [41,52], which can also be extended to entire training distributions [40,64]. Since such approaches suffer from high computational costs, improving their scalability and effectiveness is an area of active research [51,53,108,109].

Another way to identify influential data points for a given model is by considering influence functions [23,58], which were initially designed to approximate the effects of Leave-One-Out (LOO) retraining. While multiple variations and adaptations have been proposed [11,55,59], influence functions have successfully been applied to various tasks that can improve data quality, collection, and understanding. This includes training set subsampling [110], detecting memorized examples [34], interactive relabeling [104], resolving training set bias [61] or to assist data augmentation [65]. Although these methods come with restrictive assumptions and have been demonstrated to be potentially unreliable [10], recent results by [9] suggest that they still might be useful in practice. If one has access to the training stage or intermediary model checkpoints, additional techniques can be utilized to identify influential or particularly difficult examples [3,47,84,118]. A last category of methods explains predictions on test data based on the similarity to certain training data points [19,46,56,117]. Understanding decisions via similarity can also increase data understanding through the lense of an AI model and can help to detect data set quality issues.

Overall, many XAI-related approaches exist that can help at the data collection and understanding stage based on an already trained model, but according to our interviews they are not yet popular among practitioners. Apart from that, some concepts related to XAI can also help increase data quality in the absence of any AI model. For example, in [94], Shapley values are applied directly to database queries to identify causal tuples. How the interplay of AI and XAI can help at the level of databases to improve overall data quality is also an interesting direction for future work [12].

4.2   Modelling

Insights from the Interviews.   We found that developers of AI systems have a strong intrinsic need to understand their models and algorithms from a mathematical and algorithmic perspective. The majority of the interviewed data scientists reported that they want to understand how an AI model reaches its decisions, a fact that touches directly upon explainability. While the interviewees acknowledged that a broad magnitude of XAI methods for debugging, error tracing, etc., exists, lack of development support with XAI became apparent. Examples are, e.g., XAI-guided hyperparameter search, selection of network architectures, and model selection in general. However, in practice, by embedding XAI in the development and evaluation process, we have clear evidence that model analysis with XAI is not a one-off task but a continuous iterative process switching between development and evaluation.

Besides the relevance of XAI for the developers themselves, we found a clear consensus that applied industrial AI development critically depends on collaboration with domain experts. This is important for selecting features, understanding model limitations, and incorporating domain knowledge into AI. Because the data alone often does not convey the domain expert's knowledge, data scientists are confronted with tremendous challenges if they have no access to domain knowledge, and it can take months to build up the necessary expertise. According to our findings, XAI can play its strengths for the cooperation between data scientists and domain experts. It bears significant advantages over classical approaches, such as communicating model results with descriptive statistics. However, these benefits come with the prerequisite that the XAI presents itself in the 'language' of the domain (expert). This means that explainability should be intuitive and must come in the semantics familiar to the domain expert.

Academic Perspective on the Role of XAI for Modeling.   There already exist first approaches to support the development process with the help of XAI. In this section, we focus explicitly on the task of XAI-aided development, in contrast to XAI support for evaluation and testing, which forms the main body of research and is addressed in the following section.

One of the most crucial and also individual points during the development of an ML solution is finding appropriate hyperparameters for the model and application at hand. There are numerous efforts to automatize this process. However, the choice of a specific parameter and its effect is often opaque, even for highly experienced AI experts. Methods such as [77,97] try to explain the influence of specific hyperparameters making the selection process more interpretable and lowering the level of required experience during the development phase. Also, model compression can be aided similarly by explainability techniques [119].

Some interviewees further reported that the integration of domain expertise during the development process is regarded as an essential step. Multiple approaches exist trying to combine visual explanations generated by a model with prior knowledge [87,90]. This can offer an interpretable interface to formalize domain knowledge and also communicate the effect of the knowledge integration to domain experts. This concept has also been transferred to other data modalities such as text [66]. A significant benefit of informing machine learning models with this kind of prior knowledge can be achieved by removing known spurious correlations in the training data set, which helps to increase the interpretability and robustness of the trained model [89].

However, preliminary to an extensive evaluation of a trained machine learning model, it is often unknown if spurious correlations are included in the data set to be used during training. Model explanations interpreted by human domain experts can indicate if a model has learned spurious correlations. Those might not be detected by data scientists, as mentioned in the interview responses, relying solely on (simple) performance metrics. Thus, in recently developed frameworks such as eXplainatory Interactive Learning (XIL) [105] and eXplainable Active Learning (XAL) [39], the explanations of an intermediate state of the model are presented to domain or subject matter experts during an iterative training phase. This enables non-AI experts to argue with the model via an interpretable interface [96]. As with the previously described non-iterative methods, the form of this interface depends strongly on the task and, in particular, on the data format [103]. An interface consisting of rule-based explanations [4] might be especially suited to tabular data, whereas visual explanations [92] are more useful for image data. However, approaches such as those proposed by [100] also try to correct computer vision machine learning models by using rules based on high-level concepts and thus allow domain experts to argue on a semantic level they are used to.

[39] note that the continuous observation of the explanations of AI models during the training process can not only increase the trust in the system once it is deployed, but it also offers the opportunity for the non-AI-expert to calibrate their trust in the system during the learning process. This allows to estimate better in which situation the AI systems might fall short.

Moreover, also optimizing higher-level properties of explanations during training can help to increase the final model performance [29].

4.3 Evaluation

Insights from the Interviews. Testing AI is reportedly a challenging task, and the non-availability of realistic operation environments was a major pain point for the interviewees. More generally, we learned that the quality of AI testing suffers from a lack of established test procedures. Currently, developers experiment with multiple approaches to test AI. One approach is black-box tests which care only about input-output relations. If possible, however, it was advocated to define edge cases in combination with the synthetic generation of test data or careful collection of test data in cross-functional teams, including domain experts. Especially the last point is strongly related to the vital importance of interaction with domain experts. Those need to set the baseline, help to confirm whether a model decides correctly, and define relevant test cases and scenarios.

For those data scientists that advocate XAI for evaluation, we learned that they already make extensive use of state-of-the-art XAI methods to globally debug models, trace down specific errors and conduct root cause reasoning. Among the named XAI tool stack are techniques such as Saliency Maps [99], LIME [86] or GradCam [95].[2]

---

[2] References are given by the authors and were not part of the interview responses.

Many developers would welcome additional XAI methods if they are conveniently available open source and provide extra benefits for their domain. We also noted a need for unified interfaces that allow to combine the multitude of different XAI methods. In contrast to these findings, we also received doubts regarding the technical feasibility of XAI methods to cope with complex models and critiques regarding the strict assumptions needed for many XAI methods. This helps to explain why some data scientists still place a focus solely on performance metrics and black-box testing.

Testing and validation are not only crucial tasks for ensuring the quality of AI but also touch upon the responsibility and liability that developers, product managers, product owners, or even whole companies take for their machine learning systems. Consequently, there is a need for risk control, ownership, and responsibility.

This is relevant because a central outcome from our focus group, the data scientists, is that they tend to dislike taking responsibility for their development because they struggle with accurately testing ML and the difficulties of understanding the risks associated with AI. The fact that XAI can support here was mentioned multiple times. The central part that XAI plays in this context is support for understanding the risks and potential failures associated with AI, identification of weak points, and partly relieving data scientists from their (perceived) burden of responsibilities.

Academic Perspective on the Role of XAI for Evaluation. From an academic perspective, the need for explainability for evaluation can be derived from many motivations. Many of them circle, in accordance with our findings from the interviews, centrally around the central problem of debugging and evaluating AI systems.

For evaluation purposes, XAI can help on multiple levels. The most important distinction between the methods is commonly between *intrinsically interpretable models* (sometimes called *pre-hoc models* that are interpretable because of their simple structure or because of special architectural designs) and *post-hoc methods* (that take a trained machine learning model as given). Especially for pre-hoc models, the separating line between modeling and evaluation becomes blurry.

Examples for *pre-hoc models* are methods that allow being interpreted because of their relatively simple mathematical structure, such as linear regression, generalized additive models, and tree-based models [76]. For this kind of model, the explanation coincides with the model itself, which can be a very convenient feature for the developer but restricts the choice of model to relatively simple ones. However, there also exists intrinsically interpretable components in more advanced models. For deep neural networks, leading examples are models with self-attention techniques, and especially transformers via attention maps [20] as well as concept-based approaches where latent representations can be interpreted in a meaningful way [33].

Post-hoc methods can be divided into *model-agnostic methods* that do not require a specific model for explanations and *model- or framework-specific methods* that are explicitly designed for a class or family of models. These approaches can again be subdivided into *local and global techniques*. While local methods can support the developer in explaining AI models based on single instances, or data points, the global approach typically tries to reveal aspects or concepts that hold for the model as a whole. Leading examples for global methods in the context of neural networks are activation maximization approaches [81], concept-based approaches [57] and knowledge extraction methods [37, 114]. Popular local methods for neural networks are feature attribution methods such as Saliency Maps [99], Layer-wise Relevance Propagation (LRP) [8], and information-theoretic approaches [21]. Leading examples for model-agnostic perturbation-based approaches include, in particular, local interpretable model-agnostic explanations (LIME) [86] and Shapley additive explanations (SHAP) [68]. Furthermore, a whole literature on the identification of influential instances [58], and adversarial examples [42, 102] exists.

The doubts expressed by some interview partners concerning the fidelity and reliability of the generated explanations are also an increasingly debated issue in academia. The lack of evaluation metrics to quantify the fidelity of different explanation methods makes it difficult even for data scientists to estimate which method to use for a particular application. [62] describing the *disagreement problem*, demonstrating that different XAI methods can generate contradicting explanations for a given prediction, underpins this problem. To tackle the issue [91] proposes to use intrinsically interpretable pre-hoc models instead of post-hoc explanations for black-box models. On the other hand, efforts such as by [14] establish a holistic topology and comprehensive benchmarking to ease the choice of applying XAI methods in practice. With this in mind, explaining something depends not only on the transmitter but also on the interpretation and, therefrom, drawn conclusions of the human recipient. However, there is currently only a little work trying to take the latter part into consideration [116].

4.4   Deployment and Productivization

Insights from the Interviews. Regarding deployment, our interview partners strongly emphasized the inclusion of end users. At best, AI systems should be designed to integrate seamlessly into existing systems without too many changes compared to current systems that should be replaced or enhanced. We also gathered evidence that acceptance of the new ML system increases if the ML system provides guidance for the user, drill-down possibilities, and root-cause reasoning. Hence, although the AI should often be concealed to the end user, so that the user does not percieves the black box so obviously, it is highly useful to use XAI functionalities to enable user-friendly systems that do not appear as black-box AI. This applies mainly to AI agnostic end users whoe are not interested in the model details.

Generally, it was noted multiple times that the customer and users need to understand the model before deployment. A requirement that strengthens if the end users have some responsibility which increases their need to explain why an error or decision occurred in their system. However, this raises the need for building suitable XAI interfaces. Additionally, we received many recommendations on what measures should be taken to ensure that the XAI comes in the required form. Motivations for these recommendations are that currently, it is often unclear how XAI should be used and which level of granularity is needed for the user. First and foremost, the importance of integrating the user in the design of XAI systems was highlighted. This includes user studies, user tests, user feedback, and carefully designed user experience (UX) for the interfaces. Hence, depending on the user and the use case, it is of vital importance that XAI comes in the form and semantics a user is used to, to bring real benefit.

Another issue of tremendous importance for deployment is whether current XAI methods scale for actual deployment. We gathered many insights showing that scaling XAI comes with multiple challenges that are not only of technical nature. First, many interview partners highlighted that XAI is computationally complex, which hinders XAI in deployment. Furthermore, it was noted that XAI does not scale to other data structures besides images. Another reason that prevents scaling is the lack of experts to interpret XAI methods' outcomes. On the other hand, we gained the insight that XAI itself can be an enabler of scaling ML if it enables non-AI experts to build, understand and use AI models.

Academic Perspective on the Role of XAI for Deployment and Scaling of XAI. Current research is in line with our findings insofar that, e.g., [2] highlights that academic research in XAI is strongly biased towards algorithmic improvements but lacks the human aspects. However, the central finding above is that XAI can only enfold its full strength if the explanations are presented in the 'language' of the domain experts and end users. To be precise, this can mean that the explanations need to undergo a semantic transformation (see, e.g., [72]) such that a model is explained in another semantic domain as it was trained in. An industrial example could be, e.g., a model is trained on raw time series data but explained in the frequency domain. Alternatively, more generally, in the domain, a user feels comfortable instead of simply taking the one it was trained on.

The Role of Human-Machine Interaction and Visual Analytics

Independently of the semantics, visualization has a crucial role to play in the communication of XAI. However, using state-of-the-art visualization techniques, often shipped with publications and packages for local and global XAI, such as waterfall, force, or bar chart feature importance plots, is often insufficient to achieve this goal. The reason is that the methods and corresponding visualizations are designed generically for data scientists and AI researchers from various domains instead of non-AI experts. Hence, a presentation of explanations tailored to the end user's mental model of the domain is needed to ensure highly effective workflows that enable seamless and intuitive insight-gaining. This conforms with the principles of the Visual Analytics (VA) design and implementation process that aims to create the most efficient, expressive, and appropriate visualization methods by taking the major factors of the design triangle into account: data, users, and tasks [73].

According to the nested model of [80], the first level of visualization design characterizes the problems, tasks, and data for the target users. Following this model, highly specific XAI visualizations need to be implemented for each particular domain, user, and data combination. Consequently, a scalability problem arises since new effort must be spent for each new combination. However, from another perspective, there is hope that common VA principles, best practices, and theories will "provide economies of scale" [54]. However, those can only be reached at higher, more general levels and therefore do not solve the scalability issues as discussed above.

Commercial off-the-shelf visualization software such as Tableau or Power BI offers this scalability with powerful, reusable visualization techniques that can be combined to create individual dashboards. However, domain experts usually are not willing or able to create their own complex dashboards to visualize the XAI output as discussed in [7].

Furthermore, much XAI expertise is needed anyhow to create meaningful output from the results of these methods.

Recently the combination of VA and XAI, Visual-based XAI (vXAI), is picking up more and more traction in the research community. However, until now, no common, standardized visual approaches to present local or global explanations for XAI methods for different types of data, models, and domains emerged [45]. Consequently, it remains an open research challenge whether the generalization of domain-specific vXAI solutions can solve the inherent scalability problem.

XAI for Deployment and Scaling of XAI

The problem of poor scalability of many XAI methods was mentioned multiple times in the interviews and indeed constitutes a significant restriction in practice. While gradient-based methods applicable to differentiable models typically can be computed fairly efficiently on modern GPUs [5], scalability is particularly problematic for model-agnostic techniques that require a multitude of model evaluations. A prominent example is, for instance, Shapley values which also belong to the most popular approaches among practitioners [13]. In [16], the authors show that the computation of Shapley values is intractable even for simple, commonly used models such as logistic regression. Therefore, appropriate computation and approximation strategies have been proposed in the academic literature [18,25,68]. Moreover, knowledge about a particular graph structure within the data can also be leveraged to speed up computation [22]. Model-specific versions also exist to increase the efficiency for deep neural networks further [6,68,106] or for tree ensembles [67,74,115,121]. Another way to address scalability is by considering XAI methods that learn a separate model to create explanations [21,49,120]. Once trained, such an explanation model allows to retrieve explanations quickly at inference time, enabling better scalability during deployment. This idea can also be used to learn the estimation of Shapley values explicitly [24,50]. Nevertheless, more research and implementation efforts are needed to increase the overall scalability of different XAI methods in general via more efficient computations or hardware utilization.

4.5 Monitoring and Maintenance

Insights from the Interviews. We received very diverse feedback on who is currently, or will be, responsible for monitoring and maintaining ML systems. The following roles of non-AI experts have been named: Application and automation engineers, service technicians, operators, or even a new job profile (e.g., in analogy to DevOps engineers). Since these roles are, per se, not necessarily equipped with ML expertise, the persons filling the roles will need training, well-designed interfaces, dashboards, and further tooling to do their job.

In contrast to the listed persons above, it was often noted that non-experts could not master the range of tasks and responsibilities needed for monitoring and maintenance without profound AI knowledge, shifting the role again towards AI engineers and data scientists. The main reason for placing this role for monitoring and maintenance is their competencies since monitoring and maintaining AI comprises many tasks only data

Table 3. Requirements towards XAI systems that support monitoring and maintenance

Enablement for monitoring	XAI needs to support communication with domain experts
	XAI should enable an understanding of the model functionality
	XAI should enable an understanding of the decisions of the model.
Incident handling support for monitoring	Providing root cause analysis for errors
	Indicating the type of error/incident
	Indicating the criticality of errors/incidents and their urgency
	Providing recommended actions
	Supporting with what-if scenarios if an action is not initiated.
Support for ad hoc questions/requests	Explaining why a certain result/decision is given
	Enabling drill-down possibilities
	Representing the certainty of the results/decisions.
Support for maintenance	Highlighting important features
	Identifying distribution shifts
	Suggesting how to adjust the model

scientists can do. It was also mentioned that the tasks associated with monitoring and maintaining ML are too broad for a single person, and instead, whole teams will be involved. This brings the advantage that teams do not depend on the knowledge and skills of one person and enables specialization. E.g., there will likely be a split between teams because the job profiles and needed skills for monitoring and maintenance differ strongly. However, an obvious obstacle to this proposal is the current lack of skilled and educated AI experts.

For the question of how to concretely monitor AI systems, no standard solutions exist. On the contrary, there are fundamentally distinct views on the topic. Some persons recommend monitoring the functionality of a model, while on the other hand, it is also argued that monitoring is rather about the data than the model. We even gained the insight that for some use cases, neither the model nor the data should be monitored but a higher-level business metric, such as throughput. This would imply that AI investigation and maintenance are only conditional to the failure of the higher-level business metric.

We found that the relevance of XAI is especially pronounced for supporting running AI systems and monitoring tasks. The reasons are manifold, but the key arguments are AI maintainability, keeping trust high, and safety concerns for critical systems/decisions.

Regarding the required form of XAI in monitoring and maintenance, we received various requirements and examples summarized in Table 3. Centrally, we learned that any person who needs to monitor AI systems needs to be enabled when it comes to an understanding of the model to monitor and efficient communication with domain experts on the one hand and AI developers on the other hand. Furthermore, incident handling is a non-trivial task that needs to be supported with tooling that enables the analysis of incidents with XAI as well as semi-automated action initiation. Furthermore, persons that monitor need to be able to give ad hoc answers to requests. Again, XAI can hereby play a vital role in explaining results, showing drill-downs, and demonstrating uncertainty measures. Lastly, the maintenance of AI models relies on knowing which features are important in what way and suggestions on how the model should be adjusted after a breakdown of the AI system.

Academic Perspective on Monitoring/Maintanence. Even though the link between monitoring ML models and explaining their predictions is quite compelling, which is also reflected in the interviews, there are only a few dedicated approaches in academia working on that intersection. The existing methods can be split by their intention of using explainability methods during the monitoring process.

The authors in [82] use the shift in the explanations of a model as an early indicator for a potential performance degradation. Furthermore, they claim that by monitoring the attention and maintenance, ML-model attributes to certain features can be used to identify emerging biases in its predictions with respect to fairness requirements. Similarly, [78] evaluates the connection between the change of a model's explanations and its performance.

On the other hand, [17] is trying to explain a detected decline in performance by providing actionable insights about its cause. Rather than directly explaining the decline in performance, [122] use XAI methods to investigate a complex data drift. Both approaches require a causal graph of the underlying data generation process. The authors in [79] claim to attribute model deterioration to individual features without needing a causal graph of the data generation process or labels for incoming data. Explanations hinting at the reason for the degrading model performance can be utilized to mitigate the cause of a performance drop and facilitate the communication with domain experts to reestablish a reliable predictive system jointly.

5   Findings Regarding Intital Hypotheses

Since our research and interviews was guided by the hypotheses outlined in Table 2 we provie a summary of our central learnings with respect to these hypotheses below.

5.1   Hypotheses Data Scientists

XAI Support the Communication with Domain Experts is a hypothesis we can confirm. We indeed gathered much evidence that interaction with domain experts is vital, especially for data understanding, modeling, and testing, and is already in practice supplemented with XAI methods. However, while the potential is clear, many data scientists would like more tools to improve on this point.

XAI Improves the Development Process also is supported by our interviews. The main issue here is, nevertheless, that XAI primarily supports for evaluation of models but is not recognized as being helpful for the modeling part itself by practitioners.

XAI Improves AI Testing may appear to be already answered by our notes on the previous hypothesis. However, although, in theory, a considerable research body for evaluation with XAI exists in the real-world industries, testing often has another connotation. I.e., while data scientists agree that XAI methods help to evaluate whether a model captures meaningful relationships, it often fails to support them with the critical decision of whether the model is really ready for deployment. A question that also invokes challenges such as model behavior on out-of-distribution data, feature drift, etc., which cannot be solved solely with XAI.

5.2   Hypotheses Monitoring

XAI Supports the Task of Monitoring. We gathered much evidence that explainability will be very relevant for the task of monitoring AI. Mainly because proper monitoring potentially requires functionalities such as root cause reasoning, etc. Furthermore, we learned from the interviews that the task of monitoring will be potentially be filled by diverse roles which do not necessarily come with a data science and machine learning background and hence need support in understanding the reasoning of AI systems.

XAI Can Support the Task of Maintaining AI. With respect to maintaining, we also learned that XAI will be relevant in order to highlight which features are relevant, e.g., for declining performance but also to guide the persons that need to mainten the model how to do this most efficiently.

XAI Can Support Root Cause Analysis, Commissioning, and Other Tasks. Similar as above we found mcuh evidence that these tasks could strongly benefit from XAI tooling.

XAI Can Support Audits. Here, we cannot report too much evidence because we found that among the interviewees it is still unclear to which extent there will be regulation, standardization or regular audits for industrial AI.

5.3   Hypotheses Business

AI and XAI Are Among the Strategic Priorities. While AI is definitively among the strategic priorities of many industrial companies it is harder to confirm this for XAI. This is mainly because from a business or management perspective trustworthy AI is more than a technical issue but also related to bussiness habits and other factors such as branding.

XAI Bridges Gaps in Cross-Functional Teams. Here, we can at least confirm the strong need for bridging gaps between data scientists, domain experts and end users at various stages of the life cycle together with evidence that XAI lowers barriers for interactions between those roles.

XAI Is Needed as a Distinguishing Factor (from Competitors). This hypotheses can be confirmed in the sense that we learned that transparency and explanability rank high among the features demanded by the AI market.

6   Conclusion

In this paper, we represent the findings of 36 interviews regarding the relevance of XAI in an industrial context in contrast with the current state-of-the-art academic research. We found that XAI already plays a vital role at various stages of the AI life cycle and is expected to grow in importance. Furthermore, we found that tangible business requirements such as the need for distinguishing factors and potentially upcoming regulations are a driver for XAI in the industries.

The interviews and our literature research also allows us to confirm the findings of previous studies. It still holds that most attention of academia is on the data scientists and their main task of iterating between model development and evaluation. However we also found that there already exists a non-negible body of literature that tries to address other stakeholders and stages of the ML life cycle.

Lastly, we also identified the need for more research along the ML life cycle being a demand of our interview partners. This holds especially for the interplay between XAI, AI, data collection and cleansing as well as XAI enhanced monitoring and maintenance of AI models. Generally, we see two central mismatches as central outcomes of our research. On the one hand, is appears as if the academic XAI toolbox is not yet fully utilized in practice. On the other hand, practioneers demand techniques and tools that do not yet exist. Hence, our findings can be interpreted as a call for practitioneers to widen their view on the available methods but also for directing more research effort into enabling explainability for different stakeholders such that XAI can unfold its full potential wherever needed at the ML life cycle.

References

1. A bill. The Lancet 34(873), 316–317 (May 2022). https://doi.org/10.1016/S0140-6736(02)37657-8
2. Adadi, A., Berrada, M.: Peeking inside the black-box: a survey on explainable artificial intelligence (XAI). IEEE Access 6, 52138–52160 (2018)
3. Agarwal, C., D'souza, D., Hooker, S.: Estimating example difficulty using variance of gradients. In: Proceedings of the IEEE/CVF Conference on Computer Vision and Pattern Recognition, pp. 10368–10378 (2022)
4. Alkan, O., Wei, D., Mattetti, M., Nair, R., Daly, E., Saha, D.: Frote: feedback rule-driven oversampling for editing models. In: Marculescu, D., Chi, Y., Wu, C. (eds.) Proceedings of Machine Learning and Systems, vol. 4, pp. 276–301 (2022). https://proceedings.mlsys.org/paper/2022/file/63dc7ed1010d3c3b8269faf0ba7491d4-Paper.pdf
5. Ancona, M., Ceolini, E., Öztireli, C., Gross, M.: Gradient-based attribution methods. In: Samek, W., Montavon, G., Vedaldi, A., Hansen, L.K., Müller, K.-R. (eds.) Explainable AI: Interpreting, Explaining and Visualizing Deep Learning. LNCS (LNAI), vol. 11700, pp. 169–191. Springer, Cham (2019). https://doi.org/10.1007/978-3-030-28954-6_9
6. Ancona, M., Oztireli, C., Gross, M.: Explaining deep neural networks with a polynomial time algorithm for shapley value approximation. In: International Conference on Machine Learning, pp. 272–281. PMLR (2019)

7. Arbesser, C., Muehlbacher, T., Komornyik, S., Piringer, H.: Visual analytics for domain experts: challenges and lessons learned. In: Science, V.K.T., Technology CO., L. (eds.) Proceedings of the second international symposium on Virtual Reality and Visual Computing, pp. 1–6. VR Kebao (Tiajin) Science and Technology CO., Ltd (2017). https://www.vrvis.at/publications/PB-VRVis-2017-019

8. Bach, S., Binder, A., Montavon, G., Klauschen, F., Müller, K.R., Samek, W.: On pixel-wise explanations for non-linear classifier decisions by layer-wise relevance propagation. PLoS ONE **10**(7), e0130140 (2015)

9. Bae, J., Ng, N.H., Lo, A., Ghassemi, M., Grosse, R.B.: If influence functions are the answer, then what is the question? In: Oh, A.H., Agarwal, A., Belgrave, D., Cho, K. (eds.) Advances in Neural Information Processing Systems (2022)

10. Basu, S., Pope, P., Feizi, S.: Influence functions in deep learning are fragile. arXiv preprint arXiv:2006.14651 (2020)

11. Basu, S., You, X., Feizi, S.: On second-order group influence functions for black-box predictions. In: International Conference on Machine Learning, pp. 715–724. PMLR (2020)

12. Bertossi, L., Geerts, F.: Data quality and explainable AI. J. Data Inf. Qual. (JDIQ) **12**(2), 1–9 (2020)

13. Bhatt, U., et al.: Explainable machine learning in deployment. In: Proceedings of the 2020 Conference on Fairness, Accountability, and Transparency, pp. 648–657 (2020)

14. Bodria, F., Giannotti, F., Guidotti, R., Naretto, F., Pedreschi, D., Rinzivillo, S.: Benchmarking and survey of explanation methods for black box models. arXiv preprint arXiv:2102.13076 (2021)

15. Bradford, A.: The brussels effect. Nw. UL Rev. **107**, 1 (2012)

16. Van den Broeck, G., Lykov, A., Schleich, M., Suciu, D.: On the tractability of shap explanations. J. Artif. Intell. Res. **74**, 851–886 (2022)

17. Budhathoki, K., Janzing, D., Bloebaum, P., Ng, H.: Why did the distribution change? In: Banerjee, A., Fukumizu, K. (eds.) Proceedings of The 24th International Conference on Artificial Intelligence and Statistics. Proceedings of Machine Learning Research, vol. 130, pp. 1666–1674. PMLR (13–15 Apr 2021)

18. Castro, J., Gómez, D., Tejada, J.: Polynomial calculation of the shapley value based on sampling. Comput. Oper. Res. **36**(5), 1726–1730 (2009)

19. Charpiat, G., Girard, N., Felardos, L., Tarabalka, Y.: Input similarity from the neural network perspective. Advances in Neural Information Processing Systems 32 (2019)

20. Chefer, H., Gur, S., Wolf, L.: Transformer interpretability beyond attention visualization. In: Proceedings of the IEEE/CVF Conference on Computer Vision and Pattern Recognition, pp. 782–791 (2021)

21. Chen, J., Song, L., Wainwright, M., Jordan, M.: Learning to explain: an information-theoretic perspective on model interpretation. In: International Conference on Machine Learning, pp. 883–892. PMLR (2018)

22. Chen, J., Song, L., Wainwright, M.J., Jordan, M.I.: L-shapley and c-shapley: efficient model interpretation for structured data. In: International Conference on Learning Representations (2019)

23. Cook, R.D.: Detection of influential observation in linear regression. Technometrics **19**(1), 15–18 (1977)

24. Covert, I., Kim, C., Lee, S.I.: Learning to estimate shapley values with vision transformers. arXiv preprint arXiv:2206.05282 (2022)

25. Covert, I., Lee, S.I.: Improving kernelshap: practical shapley value estimation using linear regression. In: International Conference on Artificial Intelligence and Statistics, pp. 3457–3465. PMLR (2021)

26. Das, A., Rad, P.: Opportunities and challenges in explainable artificial intelligence (xai): a survey. arXiv preprint arXiv:2006.11371 (2020)

27. Dhanorkar, S., Wolf, C.T., Qian, K., Xu, A., Popa, L., Li, Y.: Who needs to know what, when?: broadening the explainable ai (XAI) design space by looking at explanations across the ai lifecycle. In: Designing Interactive Systems Conference 2021, pp. 1591–1602 (2021)

28. Doshi-Velez, F., Kim, B.: Towards a rigorous science of interpretable machine learning. arXiv preprint arXiv:1702.08608 (2017)

29. Erion, G., Janizek, J.D., Sturmfels, P., Lundberg, S.M., Lee, S.I.: Improving performance of deep learning models with axiomatic attribution priors and expected gradients. Nature Mach. Intell. **3**(7), 620–631 (2021)

30. EU, H.L.E.G.o.A.: Ethic guidelines for trustworthy ai (2019)

31. EU, H.L.E.G.o.A.: Policy and investment recommendations for trustworthy ai (2019)

32. European Commission: Proposal for a regulation of the european parliament and the council: Laying down harmonised rules on artificial intelligence (artificial intelligence act) and amending certain union legislative acts, com/2021/206 final (2021)

33. Feifel, P., Bonarens, F., Köster, F.: Leveraging interpretability: Concept-based pedestrian detection with deep neural networks. In: Computer Science in Cars Symposium, pp. 1–10 (2021)

34. Feldman, V., Zhang, C.: What neural networks memorize and why: discovering the long tail via influence estimation. Adv. Neural. Inf. Process. Syst. **33**, 2881–2891 (2020)

35. Floridi, L.: Establishing the rules for building trustworthy ai. Nature Mach. Intell. **1**(6), 261–262 (2019)

36. Floridi, L., Holweg, M., Taddeo, M., Amaya Silva, J., Mökander, J., Wen, Y.: capai-a procedure for conducting conformity assessment of ai systems in line with the eu artificial intelligence act. Available at SSRN 4064091 (2022)

37. Frosst, N., Hinton, G.: Distilling a neural network into a soft decision tree. arXiv preprint arXiv:1711.09784 (2017)

38. Galassi, A., Lippi, M., Torroni, P.: Attention in natural language processing. IEEE Trans. Neural Networks Learn. Syst. **32**(10), 4291–4308 (2020)

39. Ghai, B., Liao, Q.V., Zhang, Y., Bellamy, R., Mueller, K.: Explainable active learning (xal): Toward ai explanations as interfaces for machine teachers. Proc. ACM Hum.-Comput. Interact. **4**(CSCW3) (2021). https://doi.org/10.1145/3432934

40. Ghorbani, A., Kim, M., Zou, J.: A distributional framework for data valuation. In: International Conference on Machine Learning, pp. 3535–3544. PMLR (2020)

41. Ghorbani, A., Zou, J.: Data shapley: Equitable valuation of data for machine learning. In: International Conference on Machine Learning, pp. 2242–2251. PMLR (2019)

42. Goodfellow, I.J., Shlens, J., Szegedy, C.: Explaining and harnessing adversarial examples. arXiv preprint arXiv:1412.6572 (2014)

43. Gstrein, O.J.: European ai regulation: Brussels effect versus human dignity? Zeitschrift für Europarechtliche Studien (ZEuS) 4 (2022)

44. Guidotti, R., Monreale, A., Ruggieri, S., Pedreschi, D., Turini, F., Giannotti, F.: Local rule-based explanations of black box decision systems. arXiv preprint arXiv:1805.10820 (2018)

45. Gulsum, A., Bo, S.: A survey of visual analytics for explainable artificial intelligence methods. Comput. Graph. **102**, 502–520 (2022). https://doi.org/10.1016/j.cag.2021.09.002. https://www.sciencedirect.com/science/article/pii/S0097849321001886

46. Hanawa, K., Yokoi, S., Hara, S., Inui, K.: Evaluation of similarity-based explanations. In: International Conference on Learning Representations (2021)

47. Hara, S., Nitanda, A., Maehara, T.: Data cleansing for models trained with sgd. Advances in Neural Information Processing Systems 32 (2019)

48. Holstein, K., Wortman Vaughan, J., Daumé III, H., Dudik, M., Wallach, H.: Improving fairness in machine learning systems: what do industry practitioners need? In: Proceedings of the 2019 CHI Conference on Human Factors in Computing Systems, pp. 1–16 (2019)

49. Jethani, N., Sudarshan, M., Aphinyanaphongs, Y., Ranganath, R.: Have we learned to explain?: how interpretability methods can learn to encode predictions in their interpretations. In: International Conference on Artificial Intelligence and Statistics, pp. 1459–1467. PMLR (2021)
50. Jethani, N., Sudarshan, M., Covert, I.C., Lee, S.I., Ranganath, R.: Fastshap: real-time shapley value estimation. In: International Conference on Learning Representations (2021)
51. Jia, R., et al.: Efficient task-specific data valuation for nearest neighbor algorithms. arXiv preprint arXiv:1908.08619 (2019)
52. Jia, R., et al.: Towards efficient data valuation based on the shapley value. In: The 22nd International Conference on Artificial Intelligence and Statistics, pp. 1167–1176. PMLR (2019)
53. Jia, R., Wu, F., Sun, X., Xu, J., Dao, D., Kailkhura, B., Zhang, C., Li, B., Song, D.: Scalability vs. utility: do we have to sacrifice one for the other in data importance quantification? In: Proceedings of the IEEE/CVF Conference on Computer Vision and Pattern Recognition, pp. 8239–8247 (2021)
54. Keim, D., Andrienko, G., Fekete, J.-D., Görg, C., Kohlhammer, J., Melançon, G.: Visual analytics: definition, process, and challenges. In: Kerren, A., Stasko, J.T., Fekete, J.-D., North, C. (eds.) Information Visualization. LNCS, vol. 4950, pp. 154–175. Springer, Heidelberg (2008). https://doi.org/10.1007/978-3-540-70956-5_7
55. Khanna, R., Kim, B., Ghosh, J., Koyejo, S.: Interpreting black box predictions using fisher kernels. In: The 22nd International Conference on Artificial Intelligence and Statistics, pp. 3382–3390. PMLR (2019)
56. Kim, B., Khanna, R., Koyejo, O.O.: Examples are not enough, learn to criticize! criticism for interpretability. In: Lee, D., Sugiyama, M., Luxburg, U., Guyon, I., Garnett, R. (eds.) Advances in Neural Information Processing Systems, vol. 29. Curran Associates, Inc. (2016)
57. Kim, B., Wattenberg, M., Gilmer, J., Cai, C., Wexler, J., Viegas, F., et al.: Interpretability beyond feature attribution: quantitative testing with concept activation vectors (tcav). In: International Conference on Machine Learning, pp. 2668–2677. PMLR (2018)
58. Koh, P.W., Liang, P.: Understanding black-box predictions via influence functions. In: International Conference on Machine Learning, pp. 1885–1894. PMLR (2017)
59. Koh, P.W.W., Ang, K.S., Teo, H., Liang, P.S.: On the accuracy of influence functions for measuring group effects. Advances in neural information processing systems 32 (2019)
60. Kokhlikyan, N., et al.: Captum: a unified and generic model interpretability library for pytorch. arXiv preprint arXiv:2009.07896 (2020)
61. Kong, S., Shen, Y., Huang, L.: Resolving training biases via influence-based data relabeling. In: International Conference on Learning Representations (2021)
62. Krishna, S., Han, T., Gu, A., Pombra, J., Jabbari, S., Wu, S., Lakkaraju, H.: The disagreement problem in explainable machine learning: a practitioner's perspective. arXiv preprint arXiv:2202.01602 (2022)
63. Kurakin, A., Goodfellow, I., Bengio, S.: Adversarial machine learning at scale. arXiv preprint arXiv:1611.01236 (2016)
64. Kwon, Y., Rivas, M.A., Zou, J.: Efficient computation and analysis of distributional shapley values. In: International Conference on Artificial Intelligence and Statistics, pp. 793–801. PMLR (2021)
65. Lee, D., Park, H., Pham, T., Yoo, C.D.: Learning augmentation network via influence functions. In: Proceedings of the IEEE/CVF Conference on Computer Vision and Pattern Recognition, pp. 10961–10970 (2020)
66. Liu, F., Avci, B.: Incorporating priors with feature attribution on text classification. In: Annual Meeting of the Association for Computational Linguistics (2019)

67. Lundberg, S.M., Erion, G.G., Lee, S.I.: Consistent individualized feature attribution for tree ensembles. arXiv preprint arXiv:1802.03888 (2018)
68. Lundberg, S.M., Lee, S.I.: A unified approach to interpreting model predictions. Advances in neural information processing systems 30 (2017)
69. Marques-Silva, J., Ignatiev, A.: Delivering trustworthy ai through formal xai. In: Proc. of AAAI, pp. 3806–3814 (2022)
70. Martínez-Plumed, F., et al.: Crisp-dm twenty years later: from data mining processes to data science trajectories. IEEE Trans. Knowl. Data Eng. **33**(8), 3048–3061 (2019)
71. Meng, L., et al.: Machine learning in additive manufacturing: a review. JOM **72**(6), 2363–2377 (2020). https://doi.org/10.1007/s11837-020-04155-y
72. de Mijolla, D., Frye, C., Kunesch, M., Mansir, J., Feige, I.: Human-interpretable model explainability on high-dimensional data. arXiv preprint arXiv:2010.07384 (2020)
73. Miksch, S., Aigner, W.: A matter of time: applying a data-users-tasks design triangle to visual analytics of time-oriented data (2013)
74. Mitchell, R., Frank, E., Holmes, G.: Gputreeshap: massively parallel exact calculation of shap scores for tree ensembles. PeerJ Comput. Sci. **8**, e880 (2022)
75. Mökander, J., Juneja, P., Watson, D.S., Floridi, L.: The us algorithmic accountability act of 2022 vs. the eu artificial intelligence act: what can they learn from each other? Minds and Machines, pp. 1–8 (2022)
76. Molnar, C.: Interpretable machine learning. Lulu. com (2020)
77. Moosbauer, J., Herbinger, J., Casalicchio, G., Lindauer, M., Bischl, B.: Explaining hyperparameter optimization via partial dependence plots. Adv. Neural. Inf. Process. Syst. **34**, 2280–2291 (2021)
78. Mougan, C., Broelemann, K., Kasneci, G., Tiropanis, T., Staab, S.: Explanation shift: detecting distribution shifts on tabular data via the explanation space. arXiv preprint arXiv:2210.12369 (2022)
79. Mougan, C., Nielsen, D.S.: Monitoring model deterioration with explainable uncertainty estimation via non-parametric bootstrap. arXiv preprint arXiv:2201.11676 (2022)
80. Munzner, T.: A nested model for visualization design and validation. IEEE Trans. Visual Comput. Graphics **15**(6), 921–928 (2009). https://doi.org/10.1109/TVCG.2009.111
81. Nguyen, A., Dosovitskiy, A., Yosinski, J., Brox, T., Clune, J.: Synthesizing the preferred inputs for neurons in neural networks via deep generator networks. Advances in neural information processing systems 29 (2016)
82. Nigenda, D., et al.: Amazon sagemaker model monitor: a system for real-time insights into deployed machine learning models. In: Proceedings of the 28th ACM SIGKDD Conference on Knowledge Discovery and Data Mining, KDD 2022, pp. 3671–3681. Association for Computing Machinery, New York (2022). https://doi.org/10.1145/3534678.3539145
83. Nori, H., Jenkins, S., Koch, P., Caruana, R.: Interpretml: a unified framework for machine learning interpretability. arXiv preprint arXiv:1909.09223 (2019)
84. Pruthi, G., Liu, F., Kale, S., Sundararajan, M.: Estimating training data influence by tracing gradient descent. Adv. Neural. Inf. Process. Syst. **33**, 19920–19930 (2020)
85. Rai, A.: Explainable ai: From black box to glass box. J. Acad. Mark. Sci. **48**(1), 137–141 (2020)
86. Ribeiro, M.T., Singh, S., Guestrin, C.: "Why should i trust you?" explaining the predictions of any classifier. In: Proceedings of the 22nd ACM SIGKDD International Conference on Knowledge Discovery and Data Mining, pp. 1135–1144 (2016)
87. Rieger, L., Singh, C., Murdoch, W., Yu, B.: Interpretations are useful: penalizing explanations to align neural networks with prior knowledge. In: International Conference on Machine Learning, pp. 8116–8126. PMLR (2020)

88. Rojat, T., Puget, R., Filliat, D., Del Ser, J., Gelin, R., Díaz-Rodríguez, N.: Explainable artificial intelligence (xai) on timeseries data: a survey. arXiv preprint arXiv:2104.00950 (2021)
89. Ross, A., Doshi-Velez, F.: Improving the adversarial robustness and interpretability of deep neural networks by regularizing their input gradients. In: Proceedings of the AAAI Conference on Artificial Intelligence, vol. 32 (2018)
90. Ross, A.S., Hughes, M.C., Doshi-Velez, F.: Right for the right reasons: Training differentiable models by constraining their explanations. In: Proceedings of the Twenty-Sixth International Joint Conference on Artificial Intelligence, IJCAI-17, pp. 2662–2670 (2017). https://doi.org/10.24963/ijcai.2017/371
91. Rudin, C.: Stop explaining black box machine learning models for high stakes decisions and use interpretable models instead. Nature Mach. Intell. **1**(5), 206–215 (2019)
92. Schramowski, P., et al.: Making deep neural networks right for the right scientific reasons by interacting with their explanations. Nature Mach. Intell. **2**(8), 476–486 (2020)
93. Sculley, D., et al.: Hidden technical debt in machine learning systems. Advances in neural information processing systems 28 (2015)
94. Sebag, M., Kimelfeld, B., Bertossi, L., Livshits, E.: The shapley value of tuples in query answering. Logical Methods in Computer Science 17 (2021)
95. Selvaraju, R.R., Cogswell, M., Das, A., Vedantam, R., Parikh, D., Batra, D.: Grad-cam: visual explanations from deep networks via gradient-based localization. In: Proceedings of the IEEE International Conference on Computer Vision, pp. 618–626 (2017)
96. Shao, X., Rienstra, T., Thimm, M., Kersting, K.: Towards understanding and arguing with classifiers: recent progress. Datenbank-Spektrum **20**(2), 171–180 (2020). https://doi.org/10.1007/s13222-020-00351-x
97. Sharma, A., van Rijn, J.N., Hutter, F., Müller, A.: Hyperparameter importance for image classification by residual neural networks. In: Kralj Novak, P., Šmuc, T., Džeroski, S. (eds.) DS 2019. LNCS (LNAI), vol. 11828, pp. 112–126. Springer, Cham (2019). https://doi.org/10.1007/978-3-030-33778-0_10
98. Siegmann, C., Anderljung, M.: The brussels effect and artificial intelligence: How eu regulation will impact the global ai market. arXiv preprint arXiv:2208.12645 (2022)
99. Simonyan, K., Vedaldi, A., Zisserman, A.: Deep inside convolutional networks: Visualising image classification models and saliency maps. arXiv preprint arXiv:1312.6034 (2013)
100. Stammer, W., Schramowski, P., Kersting, K.: Right for the right concept: revising neuro-symbolic concepts by interacting with their explanations. In: Proceedings of the IEEE/CVF Conference on Computer Vision and Pattern Recognition, pp. 3619–3629 (2021)
101. Studer, S., Bui, T.B., Drescher, C., Hanuschkin, A., Winkler, L., Peters, S., Müller, K.R.: Towards crisp-ml (q): a machine learning process model with quality assurance methodology. Mach. Learn. Knowl. Extraction **3**(2), 392–413 (2021)
102. Su, J., Vargas, D.V., Sakurai, K.: One pixel attack for fooling deep neural networks. IEEE Trans. Evol. Comput. **23**(5), 828–841 (2019)
103. Teso, S., Alkan, Ö., Stammer, W., Daly, E.: Leveraging explanations in interactive machine learning: an overview. arXiv preprint arXiv:2207.14526 (2022)
104. Teso, S., Bontempelli, A., Giunchiglia, F., Passerini, A.: Interactive label cleaning with example-based explanations. Adv. Neural. Inf. Process. Syst. **34**, 12966–12977 (2021)
105. Teso, S., Kersting, K.: Explanatory interactive machine learning. Proceedings of the 2019 AAAI/ACM Conference on AI, Ethics, and Society (2019)
106. Wang, G., et al.: Accelerating shapley explanation via contributive cooperator selection. In: International Conference on Machine Learning, pp. 22576–22590. PMLR (2022)
107. Wang, J., Ma, Y., Zhang, L., Gao, R.X., Wu, D.: Deep learning for smart manufacturing: methods and applications. J. Manuf. Syst. **48**, 144–156 (2018)

108. Wang, T., Yang, Y., Jia, R.: Improving cooperative game theory-based data valuation via data utility learning. arXiv preprint arXiv:2107.06336 (2021)
109. Wang, T., Zeng, Y., Jin, M., Jia, R.: A unified framework for task-driven data quality management. arXiv preprint arXiv:2106.05484 (2021)
110. Wang, Z., Zhu, H., Dong, Z., He, X., Huang, S.L.: Less is better: unweighted data subsampling via influence function. In: Proceedings of the AAAI Conference on Artificial Intelligence, vol. 34, pp. 6340–6347 (2020)
111. Wells, L., Bednarz, T.: Explainable ai and reinforcement learning-a systematic review of current approaches and trends. Front. Artif. Intell. **4**, 550030 (2021)
112. Wirth, R., Hipp, J.: Crisp-dm: towards a standard process model for data mining. In: Proceedings of the 4th International Conference on the Practical Applications of Knowledge Discovery and Data Mining, vol. 1, pp. 29–39. Manchester (2000)
113. Wuest, T., Weimer, D., Irgens, C., Thoben, K.D.: Machine learning in manufacturing: advantages, challenges, and applications. Production Manufacturing Res. **4**, 23–45 (2016). https://doi.org/10.1080/21693277.2016.1192517
114. Yang, C., Rangarajan, A., Ranka, S.: Global model interpretation via recursive partitioning. In: 2018 IEEE 20th International Conference on High Performance Computing and Communications; IEEE 16th International Conference on Smart City; IEEE 4th International Conference on Data Science and Systems (HPCC/SmartCity/DSS), pp. 1563–1570. IEEE (2018)
115. Yang, J.: Fast treeshap: accelerating shap value computation for trees. arXiv preprint arXiv:2109.09847 (2021)
116. Yang, S.C.H., Folke, N.E.T., Shafto, P.: A psychological theory of explainability. In: International Conference on Machine Learning, pp. 25007–25021. PMLR (2022)
117. Yeh, C.K., Kim, J., Yen, I.E.H., Ravikumar, P.K.: Representer point selection for explaining deep neural networks. Advances in neural information processing systems 31 (2018)
118. Yeh, C.K., Taly, A., Sundararajan, M., Liu, F., Ravikumar, P.: First is better than last for training data influence. arXiv preprint arXiv:2202.11844 (2022)
119. Yeom, S.K., Seegerer, P., Lapuschkin, S., Binder, A., Wiedemann, S., Müller, K.R., Samek, W.: Pruning by explaining: a novel criterion for deep neural network pruning. Pattern Recogn. **115**, 107899 (2021)
120. Yoon, J., Jordon, J., van der Schaar, M.: Invase: instance-wise variable selection using neural networks. In: International Conference on Learning Representations (2018)
121. Yu, P., Xu, C., Bifet, A., Read, J.: Linear treeshap. arXiv preprint arXiv:2209.08192 (2022)
122. Zhang, H., Singh, H., Joshi, S.: "Why did the model fail?": attributing model performance changes to distribution shifts. In: ICML 2022: Workshop on Spurious Correlations, Invariance and Stability (2022)

How to Explain It to a Model Manager?

A Qualitative User Study About Understandability, Trustworthiness, Actionability, and Action Efficacy

Helmut Degen[1]([✉]) [iD], Christof Budnik[1] [iD], Ralf Gross[2] [iD],
and Marcel Rothering[3] [iD]

[1] Siemens Technology, 755 College Road East, Princeton, NJ 08540, USA
{helmut.degen,christof.budnik}@siemens.com
[2] Siemens AG, Gleiwitzer Str. 555, 90475 Nuremberg, Germany
ralf.gross@siemens.com
[3] Siemens AG, Siemenspromenade 1, 91058 Erlangen, Germany
marcel.rothering@siemens.com

Abstract. In the context of explainable AI (XAI), little research has been done to show how user role specific explanations look like. This research aims to find out the explanation needs for a user role called "model manager", a user monitoring multiple AI-based systems for quality assurance in manufacturing. The question this research attempts to answer is what are the explainability needs of the model manager. By using a design analysis technique (task questions), a concept (UI mockup) was created in a controlled way. Additionally, a causal chain model was created and used as an assumed representation of the mental model for explanations. Furthermore, several options of confidence levels were explored. In a qualitative user study (cognitive walkthrough) with ten participants, it was investigated which explanations are needed to support understandability, trustworthiness, and actionability. The research concludes four findings: F1) A mental model for explanations is an effective way to identify uncertainty addressing explanation content that addresses target user group specific needs. F2) "AI domain" and "application domain" explanations are identified as new explanation categories. F3) "show your work" and "singular" explanations are identified as new explanation categories. F4) "actionability" is identified as a new explanation quality.

Keywords: Human-centered AI · explainable AI · explainability · understandability · trustworthiness · actionability · mental model · qualitative user research · cognitive walkthrough · design analysis technique

1 Introduction

Artificial intelligence (AI) is used in many consumer and industrial applications. Many challenges of making AI-based systems ethical, fair, and human-centered still exists [6,19]. One of them is the need for explanations. This research is looking into explainable AI (XAI) for an industrial anomaly detection and diagnostics application. The application under research is called "Explainable Model Manager."

© The Author(s), under exclusive license to Springer Nature Switzerland AG 2023
H. Degen and S. Ntoa (Eds.): HCII 2023, LNAI 14050, pp. 209–242, 2023.
https://doi.org/10.1007/978-3-031-35891-3_14

The original need for explainable AI (XAI) and its explanations comes from a quality inherent to AI-based systems, particularly machine-learning based systems: uncertainty [40]. It is not certain that an intended outcome of an AI-based system is accurate. This is particularly a challenge for industrial and safety-critical systems [38]. To address uncertainties, we apply an explainable AI approach for AI-based systems "that can explain their rationale to a human user, characterize their strengths and weaknesses, and convey an understanding of how they will behave in the future" [24, p. 44].

When we discuss explanations here, we refer to content that explains why a (non-deterministic) computational method has determined an outcome. This kind of explanation focuses on the process of a computational method and is called here "uncertainty addressing explanation."

Such an explanation should not be confused with the outcome itself, here called "intended outcome", or with an explanation of an intended outcome ("intended outcome explanation"). An intended outcome is the reason why a computational method was developed in the first place. An intended outcome explanation explains an intended outcome, like an online help, but not its determination process. It means that an (uncertainty addressing) explanation is content provided to the user *in addition* to the intended outcome (or parts of it) and potentially in addition to an intended outcome explanation.

The application domain in this research study is anomaly detection and diagnostics of multiple AI systems ("monitored systems"). Each of those monitored systems performs quality assurance in the manufacturing of printed circuit boards (PCBs). In case the monitored systems deviate from defined quality ranges (i.e., an anomaly), or tend to exceed defined quality ranges, the XMM application informs the target user, a model manager, so s/he can initiate a responsive action. The XMM application is currently envisioned as an AI-based system itself. When the XMM application detects an anomaly and reports it to the model manager, at least in theory the model manager only needs to select a suggested responsive action (intended outcome) on which s/he should act upon. The question is which uncertainty addressing explanations does the model manager need in addition to the intended outcome to trust, accept, and initiate the XMM suggested action.

Explanations are categorized today as global and local [1,7,26] as well as black box and white box [37]. They are intended to justify, control, improve, and discover [1, p. 52142–52143]. Known explainability qualities are trustworthiness, causality, transferability, informativeness, confidence, fairness, accessibility, interactivity, privacy awareness [7, p. 8–10], understandability, and predictability [33, p. 8].

The known explainability categories and types seem to be quite technology-centric. The main research question this research attempts to address is whether the known explanation categories and qualities are sufficient or require an extension. To answer that question, several more specific research questions are formulated.

Many scholars address XAI related research question (for literature surveys see for instance [1,5,17,23,27,28,34,41]). Many research papers report the evaluation and/or comparison of different kind of explanation content and/or representation to understand the influence on understandability, trustworthiness, effectiveness, efficiency and other qualities. In general, most publications do not reveal why and how an explanation content was selected. Even if a behavioral study determined a positive influence on effectiveness or efficiency for an explainability content under research, it raises the question whether the explanation content is the most appropriate ones for a given target user group, its user goal and user task. It is suspected that many explanations content have been selected because they are simply available from a technical perspective. It is unknown whether such content is the most appropriate ones.

To ensure that uncertainty addressing explanations are useful and usable for our target users, we assume in this research that such explanations need to be motivated by the mental model [30] of the target user group. Hence, we need to understand which uncertainty addressing explanations a model manager need to perform its user task(s) in order to achieve its user goal(s) (research question 1).

Explanations can be created with content from the AI domain and from the application domain (in our case the manufacturing of PCBs). A quality deviation can have multiple causal factors. We want to know whether explainability content for a model manager should be from the AI domain, the application domain, or from both domains (research question 2).

To gain a deeper understanding of explainability for an industrial anomaly detection and diagnostics system, it would be useful to understand which design elements and views of a user interface concept help to create an understanding about what happened and why, to create trust, to select and initiate a suggested action and to monitor the efficacy of an initiated action (research question 3).

The deeper understanding also includes whether a confidence level per suggested item is needed, and if so, which content it should contain (research question 4).

In a summary, this research addresses the following research questions for the selected user role "model manager":

- RQ 1: Which explanations are needed in addition to a suggested responsive action?
  - Hypothesis 1.1 : We expect that all elements of the causal chain model are needed as explanations for a suggested responsive action.
- RQ 2: Is explanation content needed from the application domain, the AI domain, or both domains?
  - Hypothesis 2.1: Due to the user role "model manager", we expect that explanations from both domains are needed.
- RQ 3: Which views, controls, and/or content elements contribute to explainability for understandability, trustworthiness, and actionability?
  - Hypothesis 3.1: We expect that one set of design elements support understandability/trustworthiness and a different set of design elements support actionability.

- Hypothesis 3.2: We expect that the same design elements support under-standability and trustworthiness.
- Hypothesis 3.3: We expect that view 3 (suggested causes mapped to symp-tom) is more relevant than view 2 (symptom only) for understandability and trustworthiness.
- RQ 4: Is displaying a confidence level important? If so, which content should it contain?
  - Hypothesis 4.1: We expect that an explicitly displayed confidence level for suggested items (e.g., causes, actions) is relevant.
  - Hypothesis 4.2: We expect that a quantitative confidence level is needed.
  - Hypothesis 4.3: We expect that a confidence level is more relevant for trustworthiness than understandability.

In Sect. 2 of the paper, related work is discussed. Section 3 introduces the application domain and the target user role "model manager" with its user goals and user tasks. Section 4 introduces the techniques to create the concept and the causal chain model. Section 5 describes the design of the qualitative user study, and Sect. 6 reports the study results. Section 7 summarizes the discussion, findings, limitations, and outlines future work.

2   Related Work

2.1   Explanations for Anomaly Detection and Diagnostics

A monitoring and control system is a system that monitors the behavior of another system, detects deviations from defined quality ranges or criteria, reports those deviations and optionally proposes responsive actions to a user. Here, we review related XAI research against the following criteria: C1) Was explainable AI used in the context of an anomaly detection and diagnostic system with a user-centered focus? C2) Does the anomaly detection monitor one or multiple AI-based systems?

[14] performed a user study to evaluate the explanation needs for a building management system, a monitoring and control system. The building manage-ment system was not using machine-learning technologies (not complying with C2). [39] investigates the use of explainable AI for fault detection and diagnos-tics for chillers in buildings. The paper reports the possibility for field personnel to understand the explanations. The report does not mention that a systematic evaluation of the explanations by field personnel took place (not complying with C1).

[8] proposes a feature importance as explanations for anomaly detection. Users were not involved in the research (not complying with C1). [10] uses an explainable artificial intelligence (XAI) approach of convolutional neural net-works (CNNs) for the classification in vibration signals analysis. The study was performed without user involvement (not complying with C1). [18] investigates explanation capabilities for predictive maintenance, so that predictive KPIs not only show "what" but also "why" it has been predicted. The paper applies the

game theory of Shapley Values. The study does not involved users (not complying with C1). [36] investigates the use of a Shapley-based anomaly detection scheme. Machine learning-based anomaly detection models are used to identify anomalies of a pressure control valve that is critical for heat-using facilities. To make the monitored data useful, a Shapley additive explanation-based explainable anomaly detection scheme is used. This is a technical study that without user involvement (not complying with C1). [11] proposes model-agnostic post-hoc explanations of detected anomalies by using textual summaries. The textual summaries are not evaluated with users (not complying with C1).

We conclude that none of the reviewed research complies with both review criteria C1 and C2.

2.2 Derivation of Mental Models for Uncertainty Addressing Explanations

A mental model is a "representation of some domain or situation that supports understanding, reasoning, and prediction" [20]. Explanations and mental models have a close relationship. Mental models can help to identify which content is needed for explanations. This is the approach utilized in this research. We want to use the user's mental model to identify uncertainty addressing explanations (not explanations for the intended outcome) that are placed on a concept (UI mockup). When we look through related XAI research, we review it against the following criteria: C3) Does the research focus on one or more uncertainty addressing explanations? C4) Is a process described to derive a mental model of the target user group for explanations? C5) Was the derived mental model validated by the target user group? C6) Was the content identified in the mental model used in a user interface to support a target user group in accomplishing a specified user goal?

[16] investigates the way so called "shoutcasters" comment real-time strategy games to an audience (like a TV soccer / football moderator comments a soccer / football game to a TV audience). The research uses the information foraging theory as an explanation framework. It shows an example how a mental model can be used. However, the research has some limitations. Shoutcasters use explanations to explain gamers' decision after the gamers made a decision, and not as an explanation to support gamers for their decision making. The gamers are comparable to our user role "model manager," not the shoutcasters. it is not clear from the research whether the explanations according to the information foraging theory explain the intended outcome (decision making) or uncertainties (it is uncertain whether C3 is met). The process of deriving the information foraging theory as an explanation model is not described (C4 not met). A validation of the elicited mental model by the target user group (i.e., gamers) is not reported in the research (not meeting C5).

[15] investigated different ways how a reinforcement learning agent explains itself to domain experts (non-AI experts). It was part of the research to measure "their mental model" [15, p. 2] by presenting different types of explanations and collecting feedback. The research includes uncertainty addressing explanations

(meet C3). It seems that the research has not elicited a mental model of the user that was used as an input to select and evaluate explanations (not meeting C4). A representation of a mental model was not evaluated by users (not meeting C5).

[31] shows visualization samples of mental models for case study 1 (PREDICT) and case study 3 (operating room). For case study 1 (PREDICT), the decision table (see [31, p., Fig. 2]) is an example of a mental model to explain risk levels for patients. The risk table looks like an intended outcome explanation, not an uncertainty addressing explanation (not meeting C3). The publication does not disclose how it was identified (not meeting C4) and whether it was validated by target users (not meeting C5). Under the assumption that the decision table is an established and hence validated mental model for the target user group, the study does not disclose how the table is "translated" into an explanation presented to users on a user interface to support them in accomplishing their user goals, and the validation of the user interface design (not meeting C6). For case study 3 (operation room), it is not clear what the mental model is, so an assessment of case study 3 against the criteria cannot be performed.

[14] performed a user study to evaluate the explanation needs for an AI-based system for energy engineers who respond to deviations reported by a building management system. A "causal chain story" was created that includes uncertainty addressing explanations (meeting C3). The causal chain story was derived with task questions (meeting C4), However, it was not used as an explicit mental model to represent explanations and was not validated by target users (not meeting C5).

[2] demonstrated that showing counterfactual examples help users to adjust their mental models. The work does not show whether and how a mental model of the target users was elicited and used to conclude that counterfactual examples would be an effective way to explain uncertainties to the target users. Therefore, criteria C4 and C5 are considered as not met.

We conclude that none of the reviewed research complies with the review criteria C3, C4, C5, and C6. The authors conclude that the systematic derivation, creation, validation, and use a mental model for uncertainty addressing explanations and particularly explanations for an anomaly detection and diagnostics system of AI-based systems are a novelty.

3   Application Domain: Quality Assurance in Manufacturing

3.1   Manufacturing

Manufacturing is the transformation of raw material into parts and parts into products. At each manufacturing step, errors can occur. Therefore, during manufacturing, quality assurance steps are used to ensure that manufactured parts comply with defined quality criteria. Today, standard technology and manual quality inspections are used for quality assurance. In this paper, we refer to manufacturing as the "application domain."

It is the intent to replace some of the cost-intensive manual quality inspections by what is called here an AI solution. An AI solution consists of components needed including but not limited to hardware, software, hardware and software connectivity elements (incl. fire wall policies), ML-models, ML-training data, ML-pipeline and others. It is expected that the use of an AI solution will lead to a faster time to detect a quality issue and to reduce costs. Subsequently, we refer to the AI solution as the "AI domain."

One of the unique characteristics of the AI solution is their uncertainties, due to the training of ML-models. Therefore, it is needed to monitor that the AI solution works within a defined quality range. An incident is defined when (1) a quality attribute of the AI solution is trending outside that quality range or (2) if a quality attribute is actually outside that quality range. In such a case, an incident will be reported to a professional, called here the model manager.

3.2   User Role: Model Manager

A model manager (MM) monitors an AI-based application called "Explainable Model Manager" (XMM) that is used to notify the model manager about detected quality deviations that occur during the manufacturing process. The model manager as a user role does not exist today. It is a new job role, comparable to a manufacturing operator. The idea is that a model manager does not require the education and experience of a data scientist, like an operator does not require the education and experience of a programmer or a software engineer. To be effective as a model manager, some knowledge of the application and the AI domain is assumed.

Together with two individuals familiar with the role model manager, the following user goals and user tasks have been identified:

- UG 1: Optimize up time of effective AI-solutions
- UG 2: Ensure expected quality goal

To achieve the two goals, the MM has the following user tasks:

- UT 1: Understand incident
- UT 2: Troubleshoot incident
- UT 3: Verify efficacy of troubleshooting
- UT 4: Response to customer requests (directly or indirectly interacting with customers)

The model manager is a role that acts as an interface between the manufacturing world (application domain) and the AI world (AI domain). The model manager also interacts with a user role "quality assurance" in the application domain who needs to ensure that the used machines, tools, and outcomes comply with the defined quality goals. Such quality goals include the goals of the AI-based system. The model manager also interacts with a user role "data scientist". A data scientist takes care of the AI domain. For instance, if an AI component needs to be changed (e.g., retrained), the data scientist needs to execute such a task.

3.3   Selected Scenario

For our study, we have a selected a specific manufacturing scenario, the manufacturing of printed circuit boards (PCBs). For the manufacturing process, a soldering paste is used to provide soldered joints. In our case, the soldering paste was changed. This event caused an anomaly. The viscosity of the new soldering paste is different from the original soldering paste. The detection of viscosity is not a feature of the current AI solution which is the reason why the f1-score dropped below the defined threshold of 50%. This drop is detected as a quality deviation and reported to the model manager.

One responsive action to address the problem is to change the soldering paste, back to the original one. Another responsive action is to add a feature "soldering paste viscosity" to the ML-model. A third option is to reduce the f1-score threshold, e.g., to 30%.

4   Controlled Concept Creation

4.1   Task Question Technique for Concept Creation

Before we conduct the user study, we had to create a concept that can be used as stimulus material for the study. The underlying assumption is that the quality of the study and its findings depends significantly on the quality of the used concept. It should be avoided that a concept is used in the study that is not optimized to support the selected user role (i.e., a model manager) to achieve its goals [35, section 4.1, third paragraph]. Therefore, a person was recruited with sufficient experience in the application domain as well as in the AI domain. This person is called here the "concept co-creator."

Since the topic of incident detection and diagnostics for AI solutions for manufacturing is complex and rather new, the technique used for creating the concept is the task question technique [13, p. 393f]. The task question technique is a design analysis technique. It builds a bridge between the user tasks (application domain) and the design elements (involvement domain). It helps to identify necessary design elements and to avoid unnecessary ones.

The core idea of the technique is to formulate questions that reflect needs of the target user role to be able to perform a specific user task. It is essential that task questions are formulated from the application domain perspective and that they do not contain design elements. Mentioning design elements in the answer would be a self-answering task question.

Each task question will be answered with at least one content or function that will be represented by a design element. The answers help to identify and group task specific design elements. By applying the task question technique, it is almost guaranteed that the derived design concept at least contains all relevant design elements and becomes effective (in the sense of ISO 9241-110 [29]).

Together with the concept co-creator, the task questions per user task were identified, together with their answers. The task question technique was only applied to user tasks UT 1, UT 2, and UT 3. UT 4 is a user task that does not require the XMM application to be directly involved and was therefore excluded from the mockup (and applying task questions). Table 1 lists the task questions for the three mentioned user tasks and its answers.

Table 1. Task questions and its answers (design elements) per user task

User task	Task question	Task answers (design element(s))
UT 1: Understand incident	What is the criticality of an incident?	Defined incident categories
	What is the urgency to take an action of a reported incident?	Defined urgency categories
	What are incident types (e.g., hardware, software, model)?	Defined incident types
	What is the incident?	Incident description and data
	What are the possible root causes?	List of root causes with likelihood per root cause
	Where did the root cause occur?	Location of root cause (e.g., a specific HW or SW component)
UT 2: Troubleshoot incident	What are recommended actions?	List of recommended actions; likelihood of each recommended action
	What is the consequence if the action is not initiated now?	Description of consequence
	When should the action be initiated?	Time frame
	What are the required resources for each recommended action?	List of resources per action
	What are the possible root causes?	List of root causes with likelihood per root cause
UT 3: Verify efficacy of troubleshooting	Have the incidents been resolved?	Simple answer and back-up data
	How much effort did it take to resolve it?	Involved resources and effort per resources
	How was the feedback from the customer?	Customer feedback

4.2   Causal Chain Model as Mental Model

Based on the user tasks, its task questions and answers, a causal chain model was selected as an assumed mental model for explanations. A causal chain [3] is a structure that shows the causal relationships between individual causal factors. It often includes a root cause, causal factors, a symptom (sometimes called a fault), and a responsive action.

In our case, the causal chain consists of the six elements (see Fig. 1).

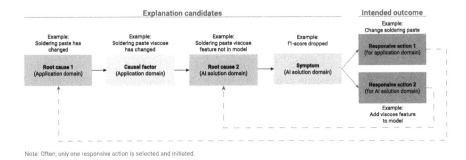

Fig. 1. Causal chain model as mental model representation

A root cause 1 (application domain) is an event that leads to a quality deviation in the AI domain. A root cause 1 example is the use of new manufacturing material or the use of a new component. A causal factor is a consequence of root cause 1, typically located in the application domain. It is often a change quality that is relevant for the AI domain. In our example, the viscosity of the new soldering paste is different than the viscosity of the original soldering paste. A root cause 2 is allocated in the AI domain. It is a deficiency of an AI component that is discovered as a result to root cause 1. In our study, an example of root cause 2 is an ML-model that does not possess a feature to detect the viscosity of a soldering paste. A symptom is a deviation in the AI domain. It represents the existence of a deviation indirectly. In our study, a symptom example is the drop of the f1-score below a defined threshold. A responsive action can be a corrective action (e.g., a model quality is already outside a defined quality range) or a preventive action (e.g., a model quality is still within the quality range, but is trending outside the quality range). A responsive action addresses one of the identified root causes. In many cases, it can be assumed that root cause 1 is business-motivated necessity. Therefore, many responsive actions will address root cause 2, a deficiency of the AI solution. In our study, an example of a responsive action is adding a feature "soldering paste viscosity" to the ML-model, addressing root cause 2.

The intended outcome of the XMM application is one or more suggested actions. The root causes, the causal factor, and the symptom are explanation candidates that the model manager may need to know to understand why the XMM application has suggested an action and to trust it. One of the research questions is which explanation content does the model manager need for understandability, trustworthiness, and actionability (RQ 1).

An incident is defined as a set of causal factors, including context information (e.g., time of occurrence, location of occurrence, machine, priority), a life cycle status (e.g., new, in progress, completed, canceled), an owner and potentially other attributes, like criticality, Return-on-Investment (ROI), customer. The intent of a model manager is to understand the incident ("time to insights") and to initiate an effective responsive action ("time to action") in a timely manner.

The causal chain as an assumed mental model should help to answer another research question: whether explanations from the application domain, the AI domain, or both domains are needed (RQ 2).

4.3 Resulting Concept

An initial concept was created, informed by the user goals, the user tasks, the task questions and the corresponding design elements and the causal chain model. The initial concept was iterated twice with the concept co-creator. The five views of the concept with a short description per view are depicted in the Appendix A.2.

To understand whether a confidence level for a number of suggested items (e.g., suggested causes) is useful as explanations, we have explored eight different variations to display a confidence level. They are shown and briefly described in the Appendix A.3.

5 Study Design

5.1 Study Participants

We used seven screening criteria for the selection of participants, reflected by the following questions (see Appendix A.1). Since the role "model manager" does not exist in its full extent today, we accept candidates that answer "yes" to at least five questions.

To reach saturation with a homogeneous study sample, the target sample size is set to twelve participants [25, p. 7] [22, p. 74].

5.2 Study Context

The study uses a semi-guided interview. Each interview session had the following agenda:

- Step 1: Introduction
- Step 2: Job experience
- Step 3: Open feedback for presented concept (What do you like? What would you like to change?)
- Step 4: Explainability questions (focus of this research)
- Step 5: Wrap-up questions

5.3   Study Method

In step 3, the concepts were shown and two open questions (What do you like? What would you like to change?) per view were asked. To gather participant's feedback for proposed concepts, we applied a cognitive walkthrough with representatives of the target user group [21]. This open session was a warm-up to get familiar with the concept.

In step 4, the same concepts were shown again. Due to the limited number of participants, qualitative research was conducted [12]. The questions are shown in Appendix A.4.

5.4   Result Analysis

Per aforementioned questions, the selected views and design elements will be summed up per question. The top three most often identified views and design elements per question are considered to be the main contributors to the respective explainability qualities understandability, trustworthiness, and actionability.

Due to the small sample size, inferential statistical analysis was not used.

6   Study Results

6.1   Participants

In total, we recruited ten participants. All participants answered at least five (out of seven) screener questions (see Appendix A.1) with "yes." The participants are Siemens employees and did not receive a monetary incentive for the interview participation. All participants have given their explicit consent to participate in the study. The interview was conducted remotely, using Microsoft®Teams. All interviews were recorded.

A single interview session lasted from 90 to 120 min. Step 1 and step 2 have been conducted without showing the concept. The HCI researcher introduced the participant into the concept the first time in step 3. After introducing each view with open feedback (What do you like? What would you like to change?), the HCI researcher asked the interviewees explainability questions (step 4), the focus of this research. This paper reports the results from step 4 only. The explainability questions are shown in Appendix A.4.

Eight participants are based in Germany, one in India, and one in China. All ten participants were male.

The participants have industrial work experience from four to 25 years. The participants have experience working with AI solutions from three to thirteen years. They perform varies levels of operation, from standard level (restart application, monitor resource consumption) to advanced (analyze standard log messages automatically analyzed) and expert level (request and analyze log messages manually). Currently, there is no online monitoring supported. After deployment, interventions take place twice per month through once per six month.

Eight participants support manufacturing of electronics processes. Three participants support automotive manufacturing. Participants also support food and beverage, photovoltaic, cranes, mechatronics, logistics, and safety. The participants' customer base is in Europe and in Asia.

6.2   Results

RQ 1: Which Explanations Are Needed for a Suggested Responsive Action? The participants were asked to rate the statement "The causal chain model reflects the key elements of an incident very well." in reference to the presented causal chain model (see Fig. 1). Six participants agree and two strongly agree that the causal chain model reflects the key elements of an incident very well (see Table 2).

Table 2. Representation of causal chain as mental model (n = 10)

Likert scale values	1 (Strongly disagree)	2 (Disagree)	3 (Neutral)	4 (Agree)	5 (Strongly agree)
"The causal chain model reflects the key elements of an incident very well."	1	0	1	6	2

Participants made individual comments about the causal chain model. One participant mentioned that the causal chain looks like the result of applying the why-why technique. It could include even more elements, e.g., including the reason why the soldering paste was changed. Another participant mentioned that a causal chain could have multiple root causes. One participant commented that "root cause 2" should not be called "root cause" because there can only be one root cause in a causal chain. One participant mentioned that one suggested action can have an effect on both root causes. One participant said that the symptom should be the beginning of the causal chain that motivates root cause 1, and not between the root cause 2 and the responsive actions.

Based on the feedback, we consider the causal chain model as a representation of the mental model of the participants.

The next question was about the elements of the causal chain model that help the participants to understand what happened and why (see Table 3). The participants could select one or multiple answer options. With the exception of option E, all other answer options refer to elements of the causal chain model.

All participants have selected either the root cause 1 or the causal factor from the application domain. Eight participants have selected the root cause 2 and/or the symptom from the AI domain. Seven participants have selected at least one element of the application domain (root cause 1 and/or causal factor) and one element of the AI domain (root cause 2 and/or symptom).

One participant said that the dependencies between the elements of the causal chain are important, too for the understanding what happened and why.

Table 3. Needed content to understand what happened and why (n = 10)

Causal chain element	Selections
Root cause 1 (application domain)	8
Example: Soldering paste was changed.	
Causal factor (application domain)	6
Example: Viscosity of soldering paste changed.	
Root cause 2 (AI domain)	7
Example: ML-Model does not possess viscosity of soldering paste.	
Symptom (AI domain)	5
Example: f1-score dropped.	
Something else	1

Reading example: Eight participants have selected "Root cause 1 (application domain)" as a content needed to understand what happened and why.

Another participant mentioned that he wants a domain expert to confirm the causal relationship between the suggested root causes, causal factor, symptom, and suggested action.

The participants' selection of explanation content indicates that content from the application domain and the AI domain are needed to understand what happened and why.

The next question was about the elements of the causal chain model that help the participants to trust the outcome of the application (see Table 4). The participants could select one or multiple answer options. With the exception of option E, all other answer options refer to elements of the causal chain model.

Table 4. Needed content to trust the outcome of the application (n = 10)

Causal chain element	Selections
Root cause 1 (application domain)	8
Example: Soldering paste was changed.	
Causal factor (application domain)	5
Example: Viscosity of soldering paste changed.	
Root cause 2 (AI domain)	9
Example: ML-Model does not possess viscosity of soldering paste.	
Symptom (AI domain)	4
Example: f1-score dropped.	
Something else	2

Reading example: Three participants have selected "Symptom (AI domain)" as a content needed to trust the outcome of the application.

Nine participants have selected at least one element of the application domain (root cause 1 and/or causal factor). All participants have selected one element of the AI domain (root cause 2 and/or symptom). Eight participants have selected at least one element of the application domain (root cause 1 and/or causal factor) and at least one element of the AI domain (root cause 2 and/or symptom).

The participants' selection of explanation content indicates that content from the application domain and the AI domain are needed to trust the outcome of the application.

Not all participants have selected all elements of the causal chain. The two root causes are the elements that provide most value when it comes to understandability and trustworthiness. Therefore, hypothesis 1.1 (all elements of the causal chain model are needed as explanations for a suggested responsive action) can be rejected.

RQ 2: Is Explanation Content Needed from the Application Domain, the AI Domain, or both Domains? Table 5 shows how important the mapping of content between the application domain and the AI domain is for the participants. View 3 and view 5 with the mapping lines are depicted in Appendix A.2.

Table 5. Importance of mapping between the application domain and the AI domain (n = 10)

Likert scale values	1 (Strongly disagree)	2 (Disagree)	3 (Neutral)	4 (Agree)	5 (Strongly agree)
View 3: "The mapping between the application domain and the AI domain is important for me to understand what happened and why."	0	0	0	5	5
View 5: "The mapping between the application domain and the AI domain is important for me to understand whether the initiated action was effective or not."	0	0	2	6	2

For all participants, the mapping of content between the application domain and the AI domain is important for understandability. For most participants (eight out of ten), the mapping of content between the two domains is important for trustworthiness. Therefore, we cannot reject hypothesis 2.1 (we expect that explanations from both domains are needed).

RQ 3: Which Views, Controls, And/or Content Elements Contribute to Explainability for Understandability, Trustworthiness, and Actionability?

Design Elements. Per explainability quality, the participants could select no, one, or multiple design elements from all views. The design elements are depicted in Appendix A.2. The top three selected design elements that help a model

Table 6. Top three selected design elements (n = 10)

Top three	Understandability	Trustworthiness	Initiate action	Check efficacy
Most often selected design element	Element 3.5 (App, AI) (8 times selected)	Element 3.5 (App, AI) (5)	Element 4.4 (8)	Elements 5.3 (AI, App), 5.4 (AI, App) (5)
Second most often selected design element	Element 3.4 (App, AI) (6)	Element 3.4 (App, AI) (4)	Element 4.3 (Application domain) (2)	Elements 5.5 (AI, App) (3)
Third most often selected design element	Element 3.3 (AI) (5)	Element 4.3 (App) (2)	Elements 3.3 (AI), 3.5 (App, AI), 4.1 (App, AI) (1)	n/a

Reading example: Element 3.5 (containing application domain and AI domain content) was selected eight times and is the most often selected design element that helps the user to understand what happened and why. AI: AI domain; App: Application domain

manager best to understand what happened and why, to gain trust, to initiate an action, and to check the efficacy of an initiated action are shown in Table 6.

The most often selected element for understandability is element 3.5 (suggested causes, eight times selected), followed by element 3.4 (vertical lines that connect the timelines of the symptom with the timeline of the suggested cause, six times selected), followed by element 3.3 (symptom, five times selected). It is interesting to see that the top two elements include content from the application and the AI domain.

The most often selected elements for trustworthiness are element 3.5 (suggested causes, five times selected), followed by element 3.4 (vertical lines that connect the timelines of the symptom with the timeline of the suggested cause, four times selected), and followed by element 4.3 (severity, twice selected), 4.4 (suggested actions, twice selected). Also here, the top two elements include content from the application and the AI domain.

The most often selected element to initiate an action are element 4.4 (suggested actions, eight times selected), followed by element 4.3 (immediate action, twice selected), and elements 3.3 (symptom), 3.5 (suggested cause), and 4.1 (criticality), each once selected.

The most often selected element to check the efficacy of an initiated action are element 5.3 (event summary) and 5.4 (list of key events), each five times selected. It is followed by element 5.5 (list of individual events, three times selected).

The selected design elements, support understandability and trustworthiness on one side and actionability on the other side are different. Therefore, hypothesis 3.1 (one set of design elements support understandability/trustworthiness and a different set of design elements support actionability) cannot be rejected. The selected design elements, supporting understandability and trustworthiness are not identical but similar. Therefore, hypothesis 3.2 (the same design elements support understandability and trustworthiness) can be rejected.

Views. Per explainability quality, the participants could select one view. The views are depicted in Appendix A.2. The top three selected views that help a model manager best to understand what happened and why, to gain trust, to initiate an action, and to check the efficacy of an initiated action are shown in Table 7.

Table 7. Top three selected views (n = 10)

Top three ranking	Understandability	Trustworthiness	Initiate action	Check efficacy
Most often selected view	View 3: Symptom and suggested causes (8 times selected)	View 3: Symptom and suggested causes (8)	View 4: Suggested actions (9)	View 5: Efficacy of initiated actions (10)
Second most often selected view	View 2: Symptom (1); View 5: Efficacy of initiated actions (1)	View 5: Efficacy of initiated actions (1)	View 1: Incident overview (1)	n/a
Third most often selected view	n/a	n/a	n/a	n/a

Reading example: View 3 was selected eight times and is the most often selected view that helps the user to understand what happened and why.

For understandability, most participants (eight out of ten) have selected view 3 (symptom and suggested causes). One participant has selected view 2 (symptom) and one participant has selected view 5 (efficacy of initiated action).

Most participants (eight out of ten) have selected view 3 (symptom and suggested cause) as the best view to gain trust. One participant selected view 5 (efficacy of initiated action). One participant has not selected a view because for the participants, trust is not gained by a specific view, but by consistent delivery of meaningful results over time.

For actionability, most participants selected view 4 (suggested actions) and for checking the efficacy, all participants selected view 5 (efficacy of initiated action).

The selection of view 3 for understandability and trustworthiness is a confirmation that an effective explanation requires several elements of the causal chain from the application and the AI domain. It also supports a hypothesis, that understandability and trust go hand-in-hand [14]. Overall, we cannot reject hypothesis 3.3 (view 3 is more relevant than view 2 for understandability and trustworthiness).

RQ 4: Is Displaying a Confidence Level Important? If So, Which Content Should It Contain? Each participant could select one confidence level option only. Table 8 shows the selected confidence level options. The confidence level options are depicted in Appendix A.3.

Table 8. Top three selected options for the confidence level (n = 10)

Top three ranking	Confidence level option
Most often selected option	Option 4c (5 times selected)
Second most often selected option	Option 3c (2)
Third most often selected option	Option 2 (1), Option 3a (1), Option 4a (1)

Nine participants have selected an option that explicitly displays a confidence level (options 3a, 3c, 4a, 4c). Six participants have selected a confidence level option that displays a quantitative confidence level (options 4a and 4c). Nine participants have selected an option that breaks down an aggregated confidence level (qualitative or quantitative) into a checklist that explains how the score was determined (options 3a, 3c, 4a, 4c). Seven participants have selected an option that provides explanations from the application domain and the AI domain (options 3c, 4c).

One participant mentioned that a model manager needs to look at both checklists (from the application domain and the AI domain). Another participant mentioned that the AI domain checklist is too technical. One participant mentioned that having access to both checklists help to understand whether the action need to take place in the application domain or the AI domain. One participant mentioned that particularly access to both checklists is important for "critical problems."

Overall hypothesis 4.1 (explicitly displayed confidence level for suggested item) cannot be rejected. Hypothesis 4.2 (quantitative confidence level is needed) can be rejected.

Table 9 shows the how much a selected confidence level option supports understandability and trustworthiness.

Table 9. Influence of selected confidence level option on understandability and trust (n = 10)

Likert scale values	1 (Strongly disagree)	2 (Disagree)	3 (Neutral)	4 (Agree)	5 (Strongly agree)
"The selected option for showing and explaining the confidence level is important for me to understand what happened and why."	0	0	1	6	3
"The selected option for showing and explaining the confidence level is important for me to trust the outcome of the application."	0	0	3	4	3

Nine participants expressed that their selected confidence level option is important to understand what happened and why. Seven participants expressed this for trustworthiness. Hypothesis 4.3 (confidence level is more relevant for trustworthiness than for understandability) can probably be rejected which is a surprise. Further research is needed.

7 Discussion, Limitations, and Future Work

7.1 Discussions

The research aimed at identifying which explainability content a model manager needs to effectively and efficiently use an industrial anomaly detection and diagnostics application called "Explainable Model Manager" (XMM). The intended use of the XMM application is to monitor one or multiple AI-based systems that perform quality assurance in manufacturing. If one or multiple of the monitored system exceed a defined quality range over a certain time, or they trend to exceed a quality range over time, the XMM should automatically create an incident to inform a model manager about the detected quality deviation. An incident may include one or more suggested actions. Each suggested action has uncertainties. The model manager should then select one or multiple suggested responsive actions to reconcile the detected and reported quality deviation. The research focuses on uncertainty addressing explanations as support for the model manager to achieve the specified user goals. The question is which explanations does the model manager need to understand what happened and why, to trust the outcome of the application, to initiate a responsive action, and to check the efficacy of an initiated responsive action.

To conduct the research, we used three research stimuli. One is a concept (UI mockup) that was created in a controlled way with the task question technique [13, p. 393f]. The second stimulus was a causal chain model that was used as an assumed representation of the user's mental model for incidents and included the needed explanations. It was derived from user goals, user tasks, and answers to the task questions. The third stimulus was a set of options that communicate and explain confidence levels for application determined suggestions (e.g., root causes and actions in our study example) to the target users. Two research stimuli (concept and confidence level options) are depicted in the Appendices A.2 and A.3. The third stimulus, the causal chain model, is depicted in Fig. 1.

We conducted semi-structured interview sessions with ten participants. All participants are Siemens employees and meet at least five out of seven screening criteria. Each interview took about 90 - 120 min and was conducted as a remote interview with Microsoft®Teams.

The broader question of this research was whether current explanation categories and types are sufficient. The assumption that the current explanation categories and types are quite technology-centric can be considered as confirmed. Based on the results of a user-centered design research for explainable AI, the following findings are derived:

Finding 1: A Mental Model for Explanations is an Effective Way to Identify Uncertainty Addressing Explanation Content that Addresses Target User Group Specific Needs. Looking at published XAI research results, it is not always clear whether an explanation was used because an underlying AI technology made it (easily) available (technology-centric approach) or it was selected to address an identified user need (user-centric approach). In other words, a selected explanation should be the outcome of applying a user-centered design approach and not only an input into such a process. The paper suggests to consider explanations as "design material" that should comply with established usability quality criteria [29]. Explanations should be user role specific and support such a user role in achieving a specified user goal by performing specified user tasks.

A validated mental model for explanations can assist in identifying needed explanation content. It can also help to distinguish between application outcomes that can be identified as the "intended outcome" of the application (in our case: suggested actions) and "uncertainty addressing explanations" (in our case: root causes, causal factor, and symptom). This separation is usually not described in XAI research. A mental model for explanations should be target user group, user goal(s), and user task(s) specific. Depending on the target users, it may contain content from the AI domain and/or from the application domain. To the best of the authors' knowledge, the elicitation of uncertainty addressing explanation content based on a mental model with representatives of the target user group is a novelty in the XAI research community.

Finding 2: "AI Domain" and "Application Domain" Explanations Identified as New Explanation Categories. Many explanations in the literature are from the AI domain. This is reflected in established categories of explanations, such as global and local explanations, or black box and white box explanations. The use of self-explanatory models [24, p. 50, Fig. 5] seems to assume that explanations from the AI domain alone address sufficiently existing explanation needs. Such an assumption does not seem to consider that different user groups may have different explanations needs, some closer to the AI domain and some closer to the application domain. [32, p. 4] uses anatomy properties of arthropods as explanations (application domain explanations) why an intelligent agent has selected a certain arthropod type. Miller did not introduce an explicit distinction between application domain explanations and AI domain explanations.

This study showed that explanations from the AI domain and from the application domain are needed, at least for certain user roles (e.g., model manager). Even more, the study shows that a mapping of application domain explanations to AI domain explanations is essential for users to achieve their user goals. A mapping allows users to check the existence of a causal relationship. Therefore, the paper proposes the introduction of new explanation categories "application domain" and "AI domain" explanations.

Finding 3: "Show Your Work" and "Singular" Explanations Identified as New Explanation Categories. In the literature, mostly single explanations are discussed and categorized as global, local, black box, and white box explanations.

The causal chain model can be considered as an explanation that explains step-by-step how the AI-based system determined the intended outcome, so that a domain expert can reproduce the steps and validate them at the same time. In our study, the intended outcome is a suggested action, and the explanations are the causal factors that describe why a suggested action was selected. This is similar to a math problem where a student writes down each step, so a math teacher can reproduce and validate the student's work. In math, this approach is called "show your work." Therefore, we call this type of explanation "show your work" explanation. "show your work" explanations can be used for rather complex explanation structure like the one used in this research. It can also be applied to pattern recognition tasks, where the criteria that are used to identify a pattern are disclosed (show your work).

The "show your work" explanation is different from a "singular" explanation. A singular explanation is a single fact or reason, often disconnected from a context. A user has often difficulties to validate the accuracy of an intended outcome based on a singular explanation. "show your work" explanations are singular explanations, connected by their causal relationships. "show your work" explanations provide context for the intended outcome and allow users to validate the system determined intended outcome. If "show your work" explanations are derived from the mental model of the target user group, they have the opportunity to be usable in accordance with [29]. The paper proposes the introduction of new explanation categories "show your work" and "singular" explanations.

Show your work and singular explanations are different from the global or local explanations [1,7,26]. Both new explanation categories can be applied to a global explanations as shown in this research study (e.g., f1-score is an example of a global explanation); it can also be applied to local explanations for an single prediction. A show your work explanation is different from a black box or white box explanation [37]. Some elements of the causal chain may require black box (e.g., f1-score) and some may require white box (e.g., feature contribution) content.

Finding 4: "Actionability" Identified as a New Explanation Quality
As shown in this study, the provided explanation should help the user to select and initiate a suggested action. The user has also the possibility to automate the execution of suggested immediate actions. "Actionability" of explanations could not be found in the related work as an explanation quality. Therefore, this paper proposed the introduction of "actionability" as a new explainability quality.

7.2   Limitations and Future Work

This research has some limitations. One is the few numbers of participants. With ten participants, the target number of twelve participants was not reached. Although it is not easy to recruit participants, the research should be extended to involve more professionals to reach the saturation level. It is also recommended to apply similar research to a different application domain to validate the findings.

Another limitation is the exploration nature of the research (cognitive walkthrough). It was necessary to understand the mental model of the interviewed participants. However, behavioral research (e.g., summative usability test) should also be conducted to evaluate that the identified explanation content is indeed effective, efficient, and satisfactory in accordance with ISO 9241-110 [29] for our target user group.

A mental model allows to consider a broad spectrum of possible explanations and assists in not falling into the trap of thinking too narrow or even technology-centric when it comes to explanations. It helps to design AI systems that "afford effective explanations" [9, p. 75] before cost-intensive research and development starts. Looking at different user groups for the same AI-based system, their mental models are probably different and somehow connected. This is also known as a shared mental model [4]. It would be worthwhile to conduct research about shared mental models for explainability and derive connected explanations that simplify communication between different user roles. Such research would help to identify user role specific explanations and shared explanations. Another topic for future work is the content and presentation of a confidence level.

Acknowledgment. The authors want to thank Andrea D'zousa for her support designing parts of the concept. The authors also thank Mike Little for fruitful discussions and term recommendations. We thank Tian Eu Lau for contributions to define the Model Manager role. We thank Michael Lebacher and Stefan-Hagen Weber for inspiring discussions throughout the project. Finally, we thank all participants for their interview time and shared insights.

A   Appendix

A.1   Screener Questions

In your current job:

- Do you work with AI solutions? (general fit)
- Do you aim to optimize the up-time of an AI-solution? (reflection of user goal UG 1)
- Do you aim to ensure a defined quality goal of an AI solution? (reflection of user goal UG 2)

- Do you identify quality deviations of an AI solution? (reflection of user task UT 1)
- Do you troubleshoot quality deviations of an AI solution? (reflection of user task UT 2)
- Do you check that the troubleshooting of an AI solution was successful? (reflection of user task UT 3)
- Do you respond to customer requests? (reflection of user task UT 4)

A.2   Concept

View 1 (Fig. 2 in Appendix) shows a list of automatically reported incidents. Each incident is described with several attributes. One attribute is an incident number to identify an incident. The second attribute is a customer name. We assume that a model manager is responsible for several customers and incidents have been reported from one customer. The third attribute is the host which is a hardware device on which the incident occurred. Each incident has a category. In our examples, we distinguish here between model, hardware, and software incidents. An incident has a date and a time of occurrence. Furthermore, an incident has a criticality level that indicates the severity of an incident. An incident has a status and an owner.

Fig. 2. View 1: Overview about reported incidents

The following views show details of the incident with the incident number IN-0001 (the first one of the incident list). On the left-hand side, key incident attributes are shown, as they have been used in view 1. The incident category has a more refined description. On our case, "hidden feature draft" was added as a detail. The incident has four detailed views, represented by views 2 through view 5. View 2 shows the symptom (see also "symptom" in Fig. 1) and view 3 shows the suggested causes (see also "root cause 1" and "root cause 2" in Fig. 1). View 4 shows suggested actions (see also "suggested action 1" and "suggested action 2" in Fig. 1) and view 5 shows the efficacy of the selected and initiated action.

We now look at each view more in detail. View 2 (see Fig. 3 in Appendix) shows the symptom of the incident. The symptom is from the AI domain. In our example, the f1-score was selected as the metric for the symptoms. Other metrics can be used, too. The detailed view show that the f1-score dropped from 61% to 37% at a certain date and time.

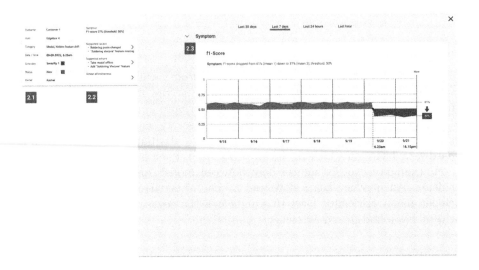

Fig. 3. View 2: Symptom

View 3 (see Fig. 4 in Appendix) shows suggested causes. On the left-hand side, one or several suggested causes are displayed, and they are sorted by a automatically determined confidence level. The suggested cause with the highest confidence level is listed first. The detailed view for a suggested cause shows root cause 1 (application domain) and root cause 2 (AI domain). For the root cause 1, a time series chart is displayed to visualize when the event occurred. In our case, the event was the change of the soldering paste. A mapping of the root cause 1 time series chart (change of soldering paste) and the symptom time series chart (drop of f1-score) is explicitly mapped (see dotted vertical lines, marked as 3.4). The suggested cause (root cause 1, application domain) and the root cause 2 (AI domain) are described.

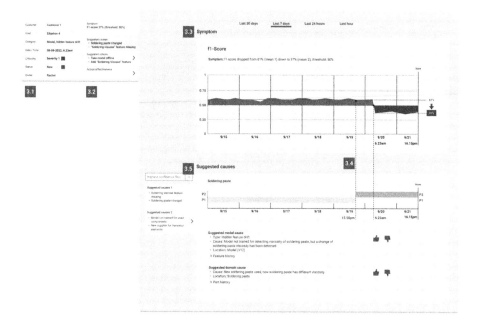

Fig. 4. View 3: Symptom and suggested causes

View 4 (see Fig. 5 in Appendix) shows suggested actions. The suggested actions refer to one of the suggested causes. One element in view 4 shows how the criticality of the incident is determined (see element 4.3). The area with suggested actions (element 4.4) is separated into two parts. The first part shows an immediate action to reduce additional damages from the symptom and the suggested causes. The second group are suggested actions that have the intend to resolve the selected suggested cause. Several suggested actions can be listed and ranked by their confidence level. For each suggested action, the action, the estimated time, the return of investment is shown, including people that need to be involved when a suggested action is selected to be initiated.

After an initiated action was fully executed, View 5 (see Fig. 6 in Appendix) shows whether the action was effective. Effective means that it has resolved the root cause and that the symptom has disappeared. View 5 is separated into two parts. In the top part (elements 5.3 and 5.4), the efficacy of the initiated action is summarized. The event overview (element 5.5) shows all events along several time series charts with synchronization lines across the charts (element 5.6). The efficacy chart top bar is a summary of the sequence of events that provides a

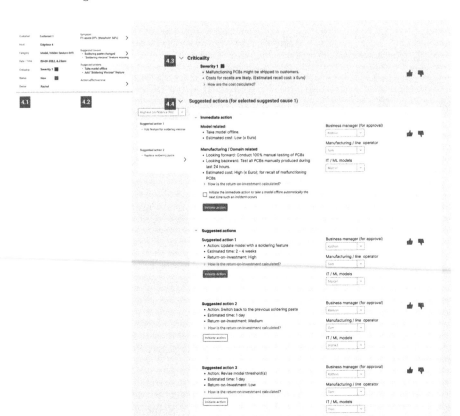

Fig. 5. View 4: Suggested actions

binary visual clue whether the action was successful (green check mark, as shown here) or not (red cross, not shown here). It also shows the key start event (root cause 1) and finish event (last action), the change of the metric values (here f1-score) and a graphical overview about the f1-score across the timeline. The event overview shows for the application domain and the AI domain all events across the timelines and synchronization lines for application events (change of soldering paste) and AI solution events (f1-score dropped, "old" model retired, "new" model launched in shadowing mode).

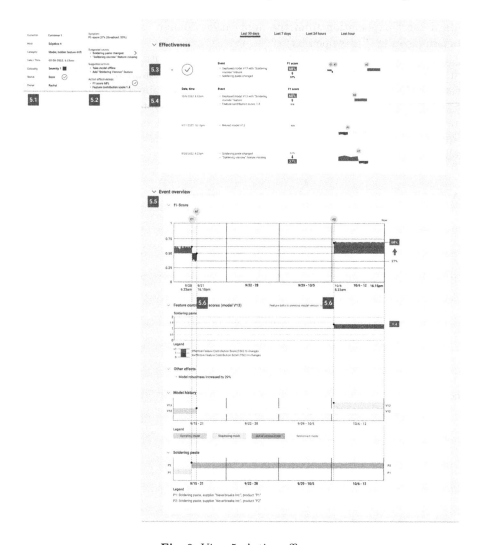

Fig. 6. View 5: Action efficacy

A.3 Confidence Level Options

Option 1 does not show a confidence level to the user at all. The system automatically selects the item with the highest confidence level, without further explanations. Option 2 shows several suggested items without a confidence level for the user. The item with the highest confidence level is selected automatically. An additional explanation for each item is not given. Option 3 uses a qualitative confidence level, with three variations. Option 3a shows a qualitative confidence level (e.g., high, medium, low) and a short explanation from the application domain is given. Option 3b shows a qualitative confidence level with a short explanation from the AI domain. Option 3c shows a qualitative confidence level with a short explanation from the application domain as well as from the AI domain (see Fig. 7 in Appendix).

Another option shows a confidence level with a quantitative confidence level, with three variations. Option 4a shows a quantitative confidence level as a percentage value and a checklist from the application domain. The relative number of met checkpoints determines the percentage value. Option 4b shows a quantitative confidence level with a checklist from the AI domain. Option 4c shows a quantitative confidence level with a checklist from the application domain as well as from the AI domain (see Fig. 8 in Appendix).

Fig. 7. View 6: Confidence level, options 1, 2, 3a, 3b, 3c

Options 4
- Short explanation
- All suggested causes above a defined threshold are displayed.
- Each suggested cause has a quantitative indicator.
- There is an explanation checklist per indicator that justifies the calculated number.

Option 4a
- Checklist explanations from the application domain.

		Why is the confidence level 83%?	
Suggested causes 1 · Soldering viscose feature missing · Soldering paste changed	83%	1 Baking time and temperature have been changed.	⊘
		2 Conductivity for all measurments has changed.	⊘
Suggested causes 2 · Model not trained for used components. · New supplier for transistor elements	34%	3 Printer settings have been changed.	⊘
		4 Volume transfer of soldering paste onto PCB has increased.	⊘
		5 New stencil has been used.	⊘
		6 Material change is acknowledged.	⊗
		Total 5 / 6 = 83%	

Option 4b
- Checklist explanations from the AI solution domain.

		Why is the confidence level 83%?	
Suggested causes 1 · Soldering viscose feature missing · Soldering paste changed	83%	1) 20% point drop on the f1 score is attributed to the feature 'conductivity'.	⊘
		2) The feature importance of the feature 'conductivity' changed since the drop in the f1 score.	⊘
Suggested causes 2 · Model not trained for used components. · New supplier for transistor elements	34%	3) A uniform shift in all feature related to 'viscosity' (e.g., conductivity) changes the prediction distribution.	⊘
		4) The confidence of the model for class 'defect' has decreased strongly as a function on variables correlated to 'viscosity'.	⊘
		5) If the feature 'conductivity' is set to value X the f1 score will be higher by 10% point.	⊘
		6) The current input datapoints are out-of-sample according to energy-based OOD scoring that can be attributed most strongly to the feature 'conductivity'.	⊗
		Total 5 / 6 = 83%	

Option 4c
- Checklist explanations from the application domain and from the AI solution domain.

		Why is the confidence level 83%?			
		Application domain explanations		AI solution explanations	
Suggested causes 1 · Soldering viscose feature missing · Soldering paste changed	83%	1) Baking time and temperature have been changed	⊘	1) 20% point drop on the f1 score is attributed to the feature 'conductivity'.	⊘
Suggested causes 2 · Model not trained for used components. · New supplier for transistor elements	34%	2) Conductivity for all measurments has changed.	⊘	2) The feature importance of the feature 'conductivity' changed since the drop in the f1 score.	⊘
		3) Printer settings have been changed.	⊘	3) A uniform shift in all feature related to 'viscosity' (e.g., conductivity) changes the prediction distribution.	⊘
		4) Volume transfer of soldering paste onto PCB has increased.	⊘	4) The confidence of the model for class 'defect' has decreased strongly as a function on variables correlated to 'viscosity'.	⊘
		5) New stencil has been used.	⊘	5) If the feature 'conductivity' is set to value X the f1 score will be higher by 10% point.	⊘
		6) Material change is acknowledged.	⊗	6) The current input datapoints are out-of-sample according to energy-based OOD scoring that can be attributed most strongly to the feature 'conductivity'.	⊗
		Subtotal 5 / 6		Subtotal 5 / 6	
		Total 10 / 12 = 83%			

Fig. 8. View 6: Confidence level, options 4a, 4b, 4c

A.4   Questions

Topic 1: Understandability

- Question 1.1: Which element(s) of any views help you best to understand what happened and why? (Answer options: no element, one or multiple elements)
- Question 1.2: Which view helps you best to understand what happened and why? (Answer option: one selected view (out of five presented views))
- Question 1.3: Why have you selected this view?

Topic 2: Trustworthiness

- Question 2.1: Which element(s) of any views help you best to trust the outcome of the application? (Answer options: no element, one or multiple elements)
- Question 2.2: Which view helps you best to trust the outcome of the application? (Answer option: one selected view (out of five presented views))
- Question 2.3: Why have you selected this view?

Topic 3: Initiate Action

- Question 3.1: Which element(s) of any view help you best to initiate a responsive action? (Answer options: no element, one or multiple elements)
- Question 3.2: Which view helps you best to initiate a responsive action? (Answer option: one selected view (out of five presented views))
- Question 3.3: Why have you selected this view?

Topic 4: Check Efficacy of Initiated Action

- Question 3.1: Which element(s) of any view help you best to check the effectiveness of the initiated action? (Answer options: no element, one or multiple elements)
- Question 3.2: Which view helps you best to check the effectiveness of the initiated action? (Answer option: one selected view (out of five presented views))
- Question 3.3: Why have you selected this view?

Topic 5: Mapping of Application Domain Explanations to AI Domain Explanations

- Question 5.1: Rate the following statement: The mapping of the AI solution information to the application domain information is important for me to understand what happened and why. (Answer options: 5-point Likert scale)
- Question 5.2: Rate the following statement: The mapping of the AI solution information to the application domain information is important for me to understand that the initiated action was effective or not. (Answer options: 5-point Likert scale)

Topic 6: Validate the Causal Chain Model as the Assumed Mental Model

- Question 6.1: The causal chain model reflects the key elements of an incident very well. (Answer options: 5-point Likert scale)
- Question 6.2: In addition to the responsive action: Which other content do you need to see to understand what happened and why per incident? (Answer options: root cause 1, causal chain, root cause 2, responsive action, none, something else; multiple selections are possible)

– Question 6.3: In addition to the responsive action: Which other content do you need to see to trust the outcome of the application? (Answer options: root cause 1, causal chain, root cause 2, responsive action, none, something else; multiple selections are possible)

Topic 7: Confidence Level

– Question 7.1: Which option to present one or more system selected options do you prefer? (Answer option: one confidence level option)
– Question 7.2: Why have you selected this option?
– Question 7.3: Rate the statement: The selected option for showing and explaining the confidence level is important for me to understand what happened and why. (Answer options: 5-point Likert scale)
– Question 7.4: Rate the statement: The selected option for showing and explaining the confidence level is important for me to trust the outcome of the application. (Answer options: 5-point Likert scale)

References

1. Adadi, A., Berrada, M.: Peeking inside the black-box: a survey on explainable artificial intelligence (XAI). IEEE Access **6**, 52138–52160 (2018). https://doi.org/10.1109/ACCESS.2018.2870052
2. Alipour, K., Ray, A., Lin, X., Cogswell, M., Schulze, J.P., Yao, Y., Burachas, G.T.: Improving users' mental model with attention-directed counterfactual edits (2021). https://doi.org/10.48550/ARXIV.2110.06863
3. Andersen, B.S., Fagerhaug, T.: Root cause analysis: simplified tools and techniques. ASQ Quality Press, 2 edn. (2006). https://asq.org/quality-press/display-item?item=H1287
4. Andrews, R.W., Lilly, J.M., Divya, S., Feigh, K.M.: The role of shared mental models in human-AI teams: a theoretical review. Theoret. Issues Ergon. Sci. **24**(2), 1–47 (2022). https://doi.org/10.1080/1463922X.2022.2061080
5. Angelov, P.P., Soares, E.A., Jiang, R., Arnold, N.I., Atkinson, P.M.: Explainable artificial intelligence: an analytical review. WIREs Data Min. Knowl. Discov. **11**(5), e1424 (2021). https://doi.org/10.1002/widm.1424
6. Antona, M., Margetis, G., Ntoa, S., Degen, H.: Special Issue on AI in HCI. Int. J. Hum.-Comput. Interact. 39(9), 1–4 (2023). https://doi.org/10.1080/10447318.2023.2177421
7. Barredo Arrieta, A., et al.: Explainable artificial intelligence (xai): concepts, taxonomies, opportunities and challenges toward responsible AI. Inf. Fus. **58**, 82–115 (2020). https://doi.org/10.1016/j.inffus.2019.12.012. http://www.sciencedirect.com/science/article/pii/S1566253519308103
8. Carletti, M., Masiero, C., Beghi, A., Susto, G.A.: Explainable machine learning in industry 4.0: evaluating feature importance in anomaly detection to enable root cause analysis. In: 2019 IEEE International Conference on Systems, Man and Cybernetics (SMC), pp. 21–26 (2019). https://doi.org/10.1109/SMC.2019.8913901
9. Carroll, J.M.: Why should humans trust AI? Interactions **29**(4), 73–77 (2022). https://doi.org/10.1145/3538392

10. Chen, H.Y., Lee, C.H.: Vibration signals analysis by explainable artificial intelligence (xai) approach: application on bearing faults diagnosis. IEEE Access **8**, 134246–134256 (2020). https://doi.org/10.1109/ACCESS.2020.3006491

11. Chouhan, S., Wilbik, A., Dijkman, R.: Explanation of anomalies in business process event logs with linguistic summaries. In: 2022 IEEE International Conference on Fuzzy Systems (FUZZ-IEEE), pp. 1–7 (2022). https://doi.org/10.1109/FUZZ-IEEE55066.2022.9882673

12. Creswell, J.S., David, C.J.: Research Design. Qualitative, quantitative, and mixed method approaches. SAGE Publications, Los Angeles, CA, USA, 5 edn. (2018)

13. Degen, H.: Respect the user's time: experience architecture and design for efficiency. Helmut Degen, Plainsboro, NJ, USA, 1 edn. (2022). https://www.designforefficiency.com

14. Degen, H., Budnik, C., Conte, G., Lintereur, A., Weber, S.: How to explain it to energy engineers? A qualitative user study about trustworthiness, understandability, and actionability. In: Stephanidis, C., et al. (eds.) HCI International 2022 - Late Breaking Papers: Multimodality, eXtended Reality, and Artificial Intelligence. 24th HCI International Conference, HCII 2022, Virtual Event, 24–01 June 2022, Proceedings, pp. 1–23. Springer, Cham (2022). https://doi.org/10.1007/978-3-031-21707-4_20

15. Dodge, J., et al.: From "no clear winner" to an effective explainable artificial intelligence process: an empirical journey. Appl. AI Lett. **2**(4), e36 (2021). https://doi.org/10.1002/ail2.36. https://onlinelibrary.wiley.com/doi/abs/10.1002/ail2.36

16. Dodge, J., Penney, S., Hilderbrand, C., Anderson, A., Burnett, M.: How the experts do it: assessing and explaining agent behaviors in real-time strategy games. In: Proceedings of the 2018 CHI Conference on Human Factors in Computing Systems, pp. 1–12. CHI 2018, Association for Computing Machinery, New York, NY, USA (2018). https://doi.org/10.1145/3173574.3174136

17. Došilović, F.K., Brčić, M., Hlupić, N.: Explainable artificial intelligence: a survey. In: 2018 41st International Convention on Information and Communication Technology, Electronics and Microelectronics (MIPRO), pp. 0210–0215 (2018). https://doi.org/10.23919/MIPRO.2018.8400040

18. Galanti, R., Coma-Puig, B., Leoni, M.d., Carmona, J., Navarin, N.: Explainable predictive process monitoring. In: 2020 2nd International Conference on Process Mining (ICPM), pp. 1–8 (2020). https://doi.org/10.1109/ICPM49681.2020.00012

19. Garibay, O.O., et al.: Six human-centered artificial intelligence grand challenges. Int. J. Hum.–Comput. Inter. **39**(3), 391–437 (2023). https://doi.org/10.1080/10447318.2022.2153320

20. Gentner, D.: Mental models, psychology of. In: Smelser, N.J., Baltes, P.B. (eds.) International Encyclopedia of the Social & Behavioral Sciences, pp. 9683–9687. Pergamon, Oxford (2001). https://doi.org/10.1016/B0-08-043076-7/01487-X. https://www.sciencedirect.com/science/article/pii/B008043076701487X

21. Granollers, T., Lorés, J.: Incorporation of users in the evaluation of usability by cognitive walkthrough. In: Navarro-Prieto, R., Vidal, J.L. (eds.) HCI related papers of Interacción 2004, pp. 243–255. Springer, Dordrecht (2006). https://doi.org/10.1007/1-4020-4205-1

22. Guest, G., Bunce, A., Johnson, L.: How many interviews are enough?: An experiment with data saturation and variability. Field Methods **18**(1), 59–82 (2006). https://doi.org/10.1177/1525822X05279903

23. Guidotti, R., Monreale, A., Ruggieri, S., Turini, F., Giannotti, F., Pedreschi, D.: A survey of methods for explaining black box models. ACM Comput. Surv. **51**(5), 1–42 (2018). https://doi.org/10.1145/3236009

24. Gunning, D., Aha, D.: DARPA's Explainable Artificial Intelligence (XAI) Program. AI Magaz. **40**(2), 44–58 (2019). https://doi.org/10.1609/aimag.v40i2.2850. https://ojs.aaai.org/index.php/aimagazine/article/view/2850

25. Hennink, M., Kaiser, B.N.: Sample sizes for saturation in qualitative research: a systematic review of empirical tests. Soc. Sci. Med. **292**, 114523 (2022). https://doi.org/10.1016/j.socscimed.2021.114523. https://www.sciencedirect.com/science/article/pii/S0277953621008558

26. Hoffman, R.R., Miller, T., Mueller, S.T., Klein, G., Clancey, W.J.: Explaining explanation, part 4: a deep dive on deep nets. IEEE Intell. Syst. **33**(03), 87–95 (2018). https://doi.org/10.1109/MIS.2018.033001421

27. Hu, Z.F., Kuflik, T., Mocanu, I.G., Najafian, S., Shulner Tal, A.: Recent studies of XAI - review. In: Adjunct Proceedings of the 29th ACM Conference on User Modeling, Adaptation and Personalization, pp. 421–431. UMAP 2021, Association for Computing Machinery, New York, NY, USA (2021). https://doi.org/10.1145/3450614.3463354

28. Islam, M.R., Ahmed, M.U., Barua, S., Begum, S.: A systematic review of explainable artificial intelligence in terms of different application domains and tasks. Appl. Sci. **12**(3), 1353 (2022). https://doi.org/10.3390/app12031353. https://www.mdpi.com/2076-3417/12/3/1353

29. ISO 9241–110:2020(E): ergonomics of human-system interaction - Part 110: dialogue principles. Standard, International Organization for Standardization, Geneva, CH (2020). https://www.iso.org/obp/ui/#iso:std:iso:9241:-110:ed-2:v1:en

30. Johnson-Laird, P.N.: Mental Models: Towards a Cognitive Science of Language, Inference, and Consciousness. Harvard University Press, USA (1986)

31. Merry, M., Riddle, P., Warren, J.: A mental models approach for defining explainable artificial intelligence. BMC Med. Inf. Dec. Making **21**(1), 344 (2021). https://doi.org/10.1186/s12911-021-01703-7

32. Miller, T.: Explanation in artificial intelligence: insights from the social sciences. Artif. Intell. **267**, 1–38 (2019)

33. Mohseni, S., Zarei, N., Ragan, E.D.: A multidisciplinary survey and framework for design and evaluation of explainable AI systems. ACM Trans. Interact. Intell. Syst. **11**(3–4), 3387166 (2021). https://doi.org/10.1145/3387166

34. Mueller, S.T., Hoffman, R.R., Clancey, W., Emrey, A., Klein, G.: Explanation in human-AI systems: a literature meta-review, synopsis of key ideas and publications, and bibliography for explainable AI (2019). https://doi.org/10.48550/ARXIV.1902.01876

35. Panigutti, C., Beretta, A., Giannotti, F., Pedreschi, D.: Understanding the impact of explanations on advice-taking: a user study for AI-based clinical decision support systems. In: CHI Conference on Human Factors in Computing Systems. CHI 2022, Association for Computing Machinery, New York, NY, USA (2022). https://doi.org/10.1145/3491102.3502104

36. Park, S., Moon, J., Hwang, E.: Explainable anomaly detection for district heating based on shapley additive explanations. In: 2020 International Conference on Data Mining Workshops (ICDMW), pp. 762–765 (2020). https://doi.org/10.1109/ICDMW51313.2020.00111

37. Rudin, C.: Stop explaining black box machine learning models for high stakes decisions and use interpretable models instead. Nat. Mach. Intell. **1**(5), 206–215 (2019). https://doi.org/10.1038/s42256-019-0048-x

38. Saraf, A.P., Chan, K., Popish, M., Browder, J., Schade, J.: Explainable artificial intelligence for aviation safety applications. In: AIAA Aviation 2020 Forum (2020). https://doi.org/10.2514/6.2020-2881. https://arc.aiaa.org/doi/abs/10.2514/6.2020-2881

39. Srinivasan, S., Arjunan, P., Jin, B., Sangiovanni-Vincentelli, A.L., Sultan, Z., Poolla, K.: Explainable AI for chiller fault-detection systems: gaining human trust. Computer **54**(10), 60–68 (2021)

40. Turek, M.: Explainable Artificial Intelligence (XAI) (2016). https://www.darpa.mil/program/explainable-artificial-intelligence. Accessed 3 Mar 2020

41. Vilone, G., Longo, L.: Explainable artificial intelligence: a systematic review (2020). https://doi.org/10.48550/ARXIV.2006.00093

Application of Reinforcement Learning for Intelligent Support Decision System: A Paradigm Towards Safety and Explainability

Calogero Maiuri[1], Milad Karimshoushtari[1], Fabio Tango[2], and Carlo Novara[1](✉)

[1] Politecnico di Torino, Corso Duca degli Abruzzi 24, 10129 Torino, Italy
`carlo.novara@polito.it`
[2] Centro Ricerche Fiat, strada Torino 50, 10043 Orbassano, Italy

Abstract. Artificial Intelligence (AI) offers the potential to transform our lives in radical ways. In particular, when AI is combined with the rapid development of mobile communication and advanced sensors, this allows autonomous driving (AD) to make a great progress. In fact, Autonomous Vehicles (AVs) can mitigate some shortcomings of manual driving, but at the same time the underlying technology is not yet mature enough to be widely applied in all scenarios and for all types of vehicles. In this context, the traditional SAE-levels of automation (J3016B: Taxonomy and Definitions for Terms Related to Driving Automation Systems for On-Road Motor Vehicles—SAE International. Available online: https://www.sae.org/standards/content/j3016_201806/) can lead to uncertain and ambiguous situations, so yielding to a great risk in the control of the vehicle. In this context, the human drivers should be supported to take the right decision, especially on those edge-cases where automation can fail. A decision-making system is well designed if it can augment human cognition and emphasize human judgement and intuition. It is worth to noting here that such systems should not be considered as teammates or collaborators, because humans are responsible for the final decision and actions, but the technology can assist them, reducing workload, raising performances and ensuring safety. The main objective of this paper is to present an intelligent decision support system (IDSS), in order to provide the optimal decision, about which is the best action to perform, by using an explainable and safe paradigm, based on AI techniques.

Keywords: Decision Making · Human-Centered Artificial Intelligence · Autonomous Driving

1 Introduction

The mobility sector has been revolutionized in the latest years when we consider that Artificial Intelligence (AI) offers the potential to transform our lives in radical ways. In fact, when it is combined with the rapid development of mobile communication and advanced sensors, AI can make autonomous driving (AD) a great process and improvement. A good AD system must accomplish the driving task in a safe and effective way, to correctly replace the human behavior and possibly also to improve it.

H. Degen and S. Ntoa (Eds.): HCII 2023, LNAI 14050, pp. 243–261, 2023.
https://doi.org/10.1007/978-3-031-35891-3_15

1.1 The Context and the Problem Addressed

Autonomous Vehicles (AVs) can mitigate some shortcomings of manual driving: reduction of human-caused accidents and the realization of a more efficient driving task in terms of energy consumption, traffic flow and driver's workload [1, 2]. However, the underlying technology is not yet mature enough to be widely applied in all scenarios and for all types of vehicles, due to complex transportation environments, imperfect road infrastructure and even legal issues (for example, automation cannot cope with highly complex traffic situations, e.g., dense urban traffic, for perception difficulties) [3, 4]. What happens in AD mode? As described in [11], the automation of the dynamic driving task removes humans from the control loop, leaving to the driver the monitoring loop. If we consider the Skills, Rules, Knowledge framework of Rasmussen in manual operation of a vehicle [14], we can say that moving from the skill-based behavior to the rule-based behavior up to the knowledge-based behavior makes the workload and the probability of errors more likely to increase.

In this context, the traditional SAE-levels of automation can lead to uncertain take-over request (TOR) time, so yielding to a great risk in the process of control transfer[1] [2, 5–8]. In order to avoid the drawbacks of automation, minimizing its disadvantages and, at the same time, maximizing its advantages, many works in literature have proposed the concept of human-machine shared control, which ensures that the driver is always inside the control loop (for example, see [9, 10]), so regarded as a promising solution to improve road safety. Moreover, as long as the human driver is responsible for at least some parts of the driving task – even during the automated driving – the driver and the machine are actually sharing the driving task. This leads to sharing control, where the cooperation between driver and automation is essential. In fact, it is important for safe operation to not only have insight into the capabilities and limitations of the individual parties, but also in the quality of their cooperation (such as described by the joint cognitive system of Woods & Hollnagel). For example, some studies showed that the limited driver–vehicle interaction in conditionally automated driving (SAE-L3) increases the difficulty for drivers to take over control when requested. In this perspective, the human-machine co-driving systems represent a key-technology of intelligent vehicles, to improve safety and reliability [13].

To realize this type of shared system, intelligent support to the driver's decision can help a lot, especially if it can ensure finer human control, or can extend someway the human faculties (e.g., perception and overcome human senses limitations[2]). In fact, a

---

[1] In other words, while AVs aims at revolutionizing our "consolidated concept" of transportation, at the same time they introduce new challenges. One of them is the takeover transitions in conditionally automated driving (SAE-L3), where drivers are no longer required to actively monitor the driving environment and can be allowed to fully engage in non-driving-related tasks (NDRTs), but at the same time they are still regarded as a fallback mechanism for the automation, requiring to take the control of the vehicle back, when the automation reaches the limits of its ODD (Operational Design Domain), considering that the situational understanding and prediction capabilities of AVs are at the moment far less sophisticated than the capabilities of human drivers.

[2] Taking into account that there is also the risk that humans lose some skills, thus fundamental changes can occur to what humans are expected to learn.

decision support system should augment human cognition, emphasizing human judgement and intuition, as well as supporting him/her to take the proper decision in the right terms and time. It is worth to noting here that such systems (decision-making support plus shared control) should not be considered as teammates or collaborators, because humans are responsible for the final decision and actions, but the technology can assist them, reducing workload, raising performances and ensuring safety. In addition, human users/drivers are more likely to accept autonomous driving technology if they are (or feel) in control of the vehicle, have a mental model to predict future actions, and can intervene to stop the activity of AD if not comprehensible or clear [12, 15].

1.2 Contribution of Our Work

In this paper we propose an intelligent decision support system (IDSS), to provide the optimal decision about which is the best action to perform, by using an explainable and safe paradigm, based on AI techniques. In our previous work [11], we described a supervisor agent together with dedicated Human-Machine Interaction (HMI) strategies able to make "transparent" the recommendation process. Here, starting from that previous work, we propose a high-level support system for autonomous driving, to decide the best action to do (e.g., change the lane / overtake, or keep the speed / follow the car ahead).

In order to achieve that, we considered a combination of Feed Forward Neural Networks (FFNN) and Markovian Decision Process (MDP), solved with a Reinforcement Learning (RL) approach, which is one of the three broad categories of ML. This method is safe and explainable (optimization criteria and reward/cost functions are defined in explicit way) and moreover it provides a good trade-off between computational cost and versatility. Quoting from the book "Reinforcement Learning: An Introduction" of Sutton and Barto, we can say that "RL is learning what to do—how to map situations to actions—so as to maximize a numerical reward signal. The learner is not told which actions to take, but instead must discover which actions yield the most reward by trying them". The consequence is that systems trained with this method can find the best action to take, in environment with large state and action spaces, imperfect world information, and uncertainty around how short-term actions pay off in the long run, which is exactly our case (the decision if it is better to keep or change the lane, in an unstructured and dynamic environment, such as a high-speed motorway, where many different unforeseen situations may happen).

2 Material and Methods

In this section, we describe the methodology followed in our work, mainly to collect the data.

2.1 Definition of Use-Cases and Scenarios

The first step is the definition of the scenario of interest and of the related use-cases. We focused on a motorway scenario, where different situations can happen, as represented in the following figure (Fig. 1):

a)   *b)*

Fig. 1. Sketch of a simple overtaking use-case in a motorway scenario, using the Driving Scenario Designer app implemented in MATLAB. In a), it is illustrated the overtaking scenario, with bird's eye view; in b), the same overtaking scenario is presented, with egocentric view, in 3D environment simulated in Unreal.

In this work, we focus particularly on the scenario illustrated in the figure: the AV is travelling with a predetermined speed and approaches a slower vehicle. In this case, the driver has to take the best decision. Specifically, the driver must choose between two possible maneuvers: the first one being to follow the car ahead (Car Following, CF, maneuver) or alternatively, to change lane (Lane Change, LC, maneuver) and then overtake the slower vehicle. Determining which of these maneuvers is optimal requires considering several factors, such as safety, travel time optimization, fuel consumption minimization, and even the cognitive state of the driver. In this regard, an Intelligent Decision Support System (IDSS) could be beneficial by guiding the driver toward the best possible course of action or by taking over the vehicle's actuators to perform the maneuver (even together with the driver in shared control mode).

To design the scenario of interest, we utilized the "Driving Scenario Designer" app in MATLAB, which facilitates the creation of synthetic driving scenarios that can be used to test specific autonomous driving functions. Within this platform, a designated environment is simulated, wherein the behavior of the ego-vehicle (EV) is observed alongside other vehicles (actors) and road boundaries. Our use case involved the creation of several such scenarios, one of which is a simple overtaking scenario.

2.2 The System Architecture

The AV system architecture can be categorized into three sections: perception, high-level decision making and low-level control. In this work, our primary focus is on the high-level decision-making section, and as a starting point, we utilize a Simulink model previously described in [11] and outlined in Fig. 2.

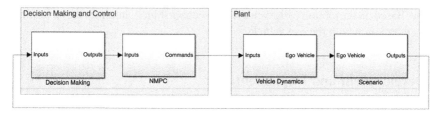

Fig. 2. Starting SIMULINK model, used as base.

The Simulink model comprises two macro-blocks and several sub-blocks, each serving a distinct purpose within the simulation. Below, we provide a brief overview of each of these blocks.

Decision Making. The Decision-Making (DM) block receives inputs from the scenario through a feedback bus signal and is responsible for handling high-level decision making and trajectory planning. The feedback bus signal contains various variables, including ego vehicle state (speed, acceleration, yaw rate, lateral offset from center of the lane), scenario information (road curvature, number of lanes, lane width, position of the vehicle in the road), obstacles information (position, speed). A state machine implemented in a MATLAB/STATEFLOW chart handles the conditional logic based on the type of the maneuver to be executed (action) and the input variables. The possible actions are Lane Keeping, Stop, Left Lane Change, Right Lane Change, and Emergency Stop. Once an action is determined, this block generates a collision free reference trajectory for the vehicle to follow.

Nonlinear Model Predictive Controller. Nonlinear Model Predictive Control (NMPC) is a widely used methodology for control and trajectory optimization of complex non-linear systems. In the Simulink model an MPC approach is adopted for low level control of the AV. The methodology is based on two fundamental operations: prediction of the behavior of the system of interest over a finite time interval, and optimization of the system trajectory based on its predicted behavior. The main advantage of MPC is that it can perform local trajectory planning and control simultaneously. The planned trajectories are optimal over a finite time interval, and they are consistent with the vehicle dynamics. Trajectory planning is performed online, allowing the ego vehicle to adapt in real-time to the road scenario and react promptly to unexpected events. MPC can systematically deal with constraints such as command saturations, obstacles, and boundaries in the trajectory domain. Additionally, MPC can efficiently manage the trade-off between performance and energy consumption. This is achieved by minimizing an objective function that describes maneuver precision and command effort, characterized by suitable weight matrices that can be designed to manage the trade-off.

Vehicle Dynamics and Scenario. The output of the "NMPC" block is then the input for the "Vehicle Dynamics" block, which simulates the behavior of the vehicle using a 3-degree of freedom dual-track model. The command from the NMPC block is the steering angle and throttle commands to control the longitudinal, lateral, and yaw motion of the vehicle. Based on the motion of the vehicle, the scenario block simulates the environment and its interaction with the ego vehicle.

3 Development and Implementation

To develop a decision-making model that is simple yet effective in aiding drivers to choose the best action to take, this work evaluates and explores two approaches to the problem. The first approach is the "*Finite State Machine*", while the second is "*Reinforcement Learning*", which is based on the Markov Decision Processes framework.

3.1 Finite State Machine Approach

A first and simple approach to automate the decision-making process was carried out by means of a finite state machine. This is a computational model used in mathematics, useful to describe the transitions between states of a system, following the change of some internal or external variables. In MATLAB this method was implemented trough a STATEFLOW Chart (more details in [11], summarized here), as showed (Fig. 3):

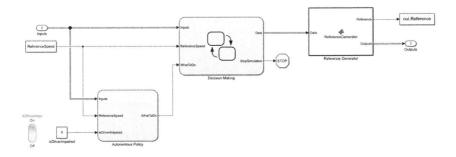

Fig. 3. DM STATEFLOW Chart

This block uses different inputs and data from the simulation to define the state of the EV and to determine whether or not a transition is needed by means of conditional logic. In the overtaking use case, the used inputs were defined as following (Table 1):

Table 1. State machine variables

Variables	Meaning
OtherVehicleDistance	Distance [m] from preceding vehicle
ReferenceSpeed	Selected speed [m/s] to be followed
CurrentLane	Number of the lane
isDriverImpaired	Check on driver's ability to drive

Using these variables, the states and the transitions can also be defined:

- State 0: Lane Keeping
- State 1: Overtaking
- State 2: Emergency Stop

The transitions between these states are managed by constantly checking the distance from the vehicle to overtake, the reference speed and the current lane in which the EV is moving forward.

While this approach is simple to implement, this only depends on the use case. The overtake is a simple maneuver in an ideal situation, but it can become quite complicated quite soon, when external and internal factors start being taken into considerations. For example, we could add the information about a third or fourth vehicle approaching, the presence of a curve or a straight road, people on the sidewalk or crossing the street and so on. So, while a fully hard-coded approach is quick and easy to implement, it's not always useful due to the lack of versatility.

3.2 Markov Decision Processes Approach

To develop a more complex model of autonomous decision making, the Markov Decision Processes (MDP) are introduced. These are used in mathematics as a clear way to define and model partly stochastic decision making by using states, actions, rewards and probabilities.

In particular, a MDP is defined as a tuple of 4 different elements:

$$(S, \ A, \ P_a, \ R_a), \tag{1}$$

where:

- S is the state space
- A is the action space
- P_a is the probability of transition from a state to another state, given an action a
- R_a is the reward obtained by performing a transition

A general policy π is a mapping from the state space S to the action space A. The objective, in a defined MDP framework, is to find the optimal policy π^* that also maximizes a cumulative reward function, typically the expected discounted sum of the rewards, over a potentially infinite horizon.7

After defining all the possible states of the system (in our case, the EV), we also need to identify which are the actions that allow the system to go from one state to another. These actions may have a certain probability of leading to a state, thus introducing a stochastic factor in the modeling. Finally, each transition from one state to another, must give back a reward, that is used by the training algorithm to understand which way to accomplish the task is desirable or not.

MDP State Space. The simulated scenarios, where the algorithm has to optimize the policy, is composed by several vehicles moving in both directions on a three lanes road (two main lanes, one emergency lane). As already reported in [11], the lanes are numbered as follow, from right to left: L0: emergency lane; L1: main lane; L2: overtaking lane.

The involved vehicles (actors) are defined as: *EV* (ego vehicle), starting in lane 1; *PV* (preceding vehicle), moving in lane 1; *OV* (oncoming vehicle), moving in lane 2, but opposite direction.

Before defining the states of the EV and actors, it's useful to introduce some variables: v_{EV}: longitudinal speed of EV; v_{PV}: longitudinal speed of PV; v_{ref}: reference speed for EV; $v_{th} \leq v_{ref}$: threshold speed, below which it's convenient to overtake; x_{OV}: relative distance between the OV and EV; d_{saf}: safety distance.

The states are described as following:

- State S_{EV} of *EV*:

  $-EV1$: *EV* in L0, car stopped
  $-EV2$: *EV* in L1
  $-EV3$: *EV* in L2

- State S_{EVd} of *EV*'s driver:

  - *NS*: normal state, able to drive
  - *IS*: impaired state, unable to drive (where this state is eventually used to trigger the emergency stop action)

- State S_{PV} of *PV*:

  $-PV1$: no preceding vehicle is present, lane 1 is free
  $-PV2$: preceding vehicle is present and $v_{PV} < v_{th}$
  $-PV3$: preceding vehicle is present and $v_{PV} \geq v_{th}$

- State S_{OV} of *OV*:

  $-OV1$: no oncoming vehicle is present, lane 2 is free
  $-OV2$: oncoming vehicle is present and $|x_{OV}| < d_{saf}$
  $-OV3$: oncoming vehicle is present and $|x_{OV}| \geq d_{saf}$

The total state ST of the system is the combination of the individual states of the elements of the system, that is $S_T = (S_{EV}, S_{EVd}, S_{PV}, S_{OV})$. This would bring the total number of possible combinations to $N = card(S_T) = 3 \times 2 \times 3 \times 3 = 54$.

While a complete state definition could give a more precise overview of the model behavior, this is not useful on a computational level. Some of the states are not useful for our purpose, because they may lead to the same preferable output. For this reason, it is advisable to collapse the state-space S_T to a subset S of the same, aggregating the single states, as shown in the following table (Table 2):

Table 2. State space for the overtaking maneuver.

States	Definition
S11	EV traveling in L1, not possible or useful to overtake
S0	Emergency Stop in L0, terminal state
S12	EV in L1, overtake possible
S21	EV in L2, re-entry in L1 not possible
S22	EV in L2, re-entry in L1 possible
S3	EV in L1, overtake complete, terminal state

The simulation always starts in state S11; the decision-making system should aim at obtaining the full transition to state S3 using the minimum number of steps to avoid redundancy of states and to minimize the control effort.

MDP Action Space. Even if the base model allowed for several action outputs, some of those can be redundant. For example, the overtaking action was just a combination of left lane change, lane keeping and right lane change. In order to have a more meaningful notation and to simplify the training, the possible actions have been reduced to just three basic behaviors: *llc*: left lane change; *lk*: lane keeping; *rlc*: right lane change. In this way, the action space A is defined as following: $A = \{llc, lk, rlc\}$.

The correct definition of the MDP framework is necessary, but not sufficient. In fact, in a real road environment, with two (or multiple cars) it is important to take into account non-deterministic aspects: for example, different drivers may have different driving skills or behaviors (likelihood to complete an overtake or to keep following the preceding car), a possible overtake may become risky or dangerous if a third vehicle appears in the opposite direction, the re-entry in the main lane may be impossible due to a group of preceding vehicles and so on.

Therefore, to have a more comprehensive model (but not excessive complex), some environmental probabilities have been implemented, as following:

- *p0*: left lane change success
- *p1*: right lane change success
- *p2*: probability of a PV appearing and becoming possible the overtaking maneuver
- *p3*: probability that the PV disappears
- *p4*: re-entering possibility

- *p5*: probability that if the EV doesn't re-enter when allowed, re-entry becomes impossible

These probabilities help to model the states transitions and are useful to understand how the training process changes when these are altered. As it can be noticed, to correctly define the framework, it must hold true that:

$$\sum_{i=1}^{N} p_i^x = 1 \qquad (2)$$

where N is the number of outgoing state transitions from state x.

In addition, the technological implementation of this modeling requires that a transition must exist from each state for every possible action. This does may not be true in the reality: for instance, in most of the cases it is not possible (or recommended) to perform a left lane change while the EV is proceeding in the left lane L2. To manage these borderline cases, the model will assume that performing those actions in those states will reward with a negative loss and the transition will keep the state unchanged.

The modeling explained up to now can be visualized on the following sketched graph (Fig. 4):

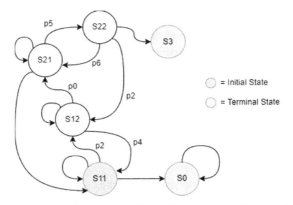

Fig. 4. MDP states and transitions, where the main states, transitions and probabilities are highlighted.

To improve the readability, only the aggregated states are showed and not every transition is reported.

3.3 Reinforcement Learning

Markov Decision Processes (MDP) allow for a formal definition in mathematical terms of systems or environment. Once the states and transitions are defined, it's also important to develop an optimal policy that an automated agent can use to pick the best action to perform, given a certain state. Instead of using a manually input policy, a good alternative is represented by the use of Reinforcement Learning (RL) to pick a suitable and optimal one.

RL uses machine learning to deal with sequential decision-making optimization problems [17]. In the RL paradigm, an intelligent agent learns a control strategy by mainly interacting with the environment. Because of each action, the agent steps from one state to another and generates and immediate reward, visible to the agent. The goal of the agent is to learn a mapping from states to actions that maximizes a cumulative function of rewards. The agent then searches for the best sequence of actions and not for decisions that are locally optimal [17] (Fig. 5).

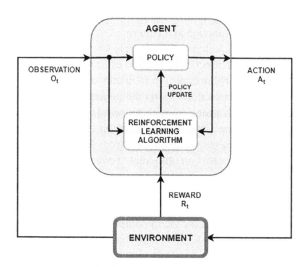

Fig. 5. RL general Scheme.

As illustrated in the figure, the general RL scheme is composed by two main blocks, the *environment* and the *agent*, which includes: a policy, used to pick an action; a RL algorithm, used to update the policy.

In our case, the environment is already defined as a Markov Decision Process, with the respective state space as observation domain and the action-space as possible output of the agent. The reward is also defined by means of a n by n by m reward matrix, where n is the dimension of the state space and m is the one of the action-space.

The process of designing a properly trained agent consists in two phases:

1. training phase during which the agent can explore the environment and learn the best actions path through it
2. testing and validation phase during which an already trained agent is deployed inside a real or simulated environment to check performance.

During the training phase, the algorithm must tune the policy in order to maximize the cumulative reward received by the environment. This can be done either through a model-based or model-free approach. While the first is a more efficient way of proceeding, it is also more complex and requires a precise knowledge of the environment under testing. This could be possible in some cases, but not always. Besides, a model-free approach is easier to adapt to unseen states, simply by extending the training and updating the policy.

Since the model has been developed with the aim of maintaining a low computational effort throughout the design, train and testing process, the resulting choice has been to use a Q-learning algorithm.

3.4 Q-Learning

Among the possible ways for determining the optimal policy π^*, Dynamic Programming (DP) [17] uses the Q-learning function as an intermediate in the case where the transition probabilities and the reward function are completely known. Q-learning is a model-free method for RL, where a critic function is used to estimate the expected reward. In the case of a finite MDP, this algorithm is proven to maximize the expected reward [18] and to find an optimal policy. This section reports the general structure of the optimization algorithm used during the Q-learning training process [19, 20].

Given a discrete state space S and a discrete action space A, the agent at time step t can move in the world environment transitioning from state s_t to state s^{t+1}, by picking the action a_t. Doing this, it receives an immediate reward r_t that can either be positive, negative or zero. These steps are repeated for $t+1, t+2, t+3...$ Until the agent reaches a terminal state s_{ts} (defined a priori).

In order to maximize the total reward obtained by the environment over a simulation episode, the algorithm has to solve for the maximum of the *discounted expected return function* G_t:

$$G_t = r_{t+1} + \gamma \cdot r_{t+2} + \cdots = \sum_{k=0}^{\infty} \gamma^k \cdot r_{t+k+1} \tag{3}$$

where r is the reward at each time step t, and $\gamma \in (0,1)$ is the discount factor that increases the value for early rewards and decreases it for later ones.

In summary, the step-by-step process is the following:

1. The Q-value critic function $q(s, a, \phi)$ (where ϕ are the learnable parameters) is initialized (at zero, or random values).
2. For each training episode:
   a. Observe the initial state s.
   b. Choose an action, either the best one or random, using Eq. (7)
   c. Observe the received reward r and final state s'.
   d. Compute the value function target, using Eq. (8):

$$a(t) = \begin{cases} r + \gamma \cdot max_a q(s', a, \emptyset) - if \ s' \ is \ not \ a \ terminal \ state \\ r - if \ s' \ is \ a \ terminal \ state \end{cases} \tag{4}$$

3. Compute the temporal difference ΔQ between the target and actual value:

$$\Delta Q = vft - q(s, a, \emptyset) \tag{5}$$

4. Update the critic function using ΔQ and α:

$$q(s, a) = q(s, a, \emptyset) + \alpha \cdot \Delta q \tag{6}$$

5. Set the new observation state $s = s'$.

Now, we detail points 2b) and 2d). During the training, the agent may assume two kinds of behavior, when picking the action to perform exploration or exploitation.

The first, *exploration*, is the preferred method during the initial phase: the critic is not trained or poorly trained and it is better to select a random action to perform, checking the resulting reward and the end-state after the transition. This is necessary to store new information and to update the *q-value*. After some time, a preferable path may appear, in the form of a higher probability of best outcome for one specific action with respect to the others. In this case, the *exploitation* leads to the best results in terms of reward, leading the agent to use the stored experience instead of relying on trial and error. This trade-off can be formalized with the introduction of the $\epsilon \in (0,1]$ variable and the *Epsilon Greedy* algorithm:

$$a(t) = \begin{cases} any\ a(t)\ with\ probability\ \varepsilon \\ arg_a\big[\max(q_t(s, a))\big]\ with\ probability\ 1 - \varepsilon \end{cases} \tag{7}$$

By tuning the value of ϵ it's possible to promote a more explorative or cautious behavior, avoiding getting stuck in local optima.

Finally, we report here the Eq. (8), as indicated in point 2d):

$$q^*(s, a) = E\big[R_{t+1} + \gamma \cdot max_{a'} q^*(s', a')\big] \tag{8}$$

Under the optimal policy π^* the Bellman Optimality Equation is satisfied by (8). Its meaning is that for any state-action pair, the *Q-value* function is equal to the sum of the next immediate reward obtained and the maximum discounted expected return of any possible state-action pair. During the training, the critic is instructed to find the optimal values of the *Q-value* function by updating them iteratively using the Bellman equation. For not too large environment dimensions, it is possible to store the value of the critic function in a human-readable table format, called *Q-table*.

It is still important to spend few words on the parameter α, which appears in the above equations. It represents the learning rate and $\alpha \in (0,1]$. "α" is an important hyperparameter to tune since it appears as a weight in the equation. It largely conditions the convergence and speed of the training process.

4   Data Analysis and Simulation Results in Realistic Road Scenarios

The trained agent has been tested by means of a simulated MATLAB-SIMULINK environment. Different road scenarios were used to test the reliability of the agent policy obtained through the Q-learning approach described above and the stability of the control algorithm. The scenarios were created using the Driving Scenario Designer app, that offers a user-friendly graphical interface to setup the road geometry and boundaries, the EV initial position and speed, and additional actors if needed. The EV was simulated using the 3-degree of freedom dual-track model available in the SIMULINK libraries. The considered scenarios are variations of increasingly complexity of an overtaking maneuver, where the agent has to make the best decision, taking into consideration several external factors. The scenarios and the obtained simulation results are now described. At the end of this section, the results obtained in a Monte Carlo campaign where the vehicles initial conditions were randomized are also presented.

Use Case 1. Basic Overtake. A simple overtaking maneuver is considered, where the goal is to minimize the maneuver travel time. Figure 6 shows a sequence of three frames for this maneuver. When the EV approaches the PV, the agent transitions from state S11 to state S12. A reference is generated for the controller and the overtaking manoeuvre starts. From state S21, the re-entry is allowed, and the controller performs the right lane change. Figure 7 shows the MDP state and action. It can be noted that the correct action is performed a short after state recognition.

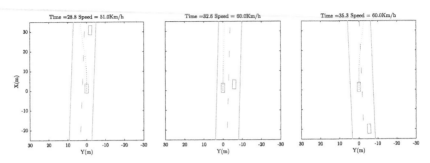

Fig. 6. Use case 1. Basic overtake.

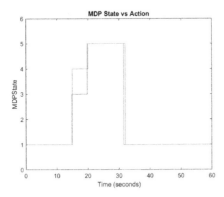

Fig. 7. Use case 1. Basic overtake. MDP state (blue) and action (red). (Color figure online)

Use Case 2. Overtake/Car Following. This use case involves a preceding vehicle, but the agent is instructed to choose a more convenient policy, either an overtaking action or a car following action, based on the speed of the actor. The overtake threshold has been set to $v_{th} = 0.7v_{ref}$ of the reference speed. The goal is to minimize a suitable trade-off between travel time and fuel consumption. Figure 8 shows the situation where the overtake is not recommended due to the PV having an acceptable speed, and the agent decides to work in a car-following modality. The EV approaches the preceding car and switch to the Adaptive Cruise Control (ACC) mode, the speed is higher than the policy threshold so there is no state transition. The check on the preceding speed is computed during the switch from Cruise Control (CC) to ACC. As a result, the MDP state and action do not change during the simulation. The case where the agent decides to overtake is not reported, since very similar to Use Case 1.

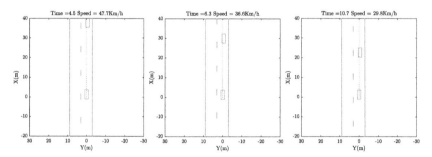

Fig. 8. Use case 2. Car-following/Adaptive Cruise Control.

Use Case 3. Overtake Sequence with Vehicles Coming in the Opposite Direction. This scenario involves a sequence of two overtakes, where the second one requires a stricter safety procedure due to a third vehicle approaching the group in the opposite direction. The agent is required to understand and act accordingly, checking for safety distance before attempting to complete the manoeuvre. The safety distance is computed according to two parameters d_1 and d_2, that represent the front and rear distance with respect to the EV inside which the left lane is required to be clear of incoming vehicles. The simulations results are shown in Figs. 9, 10 and 11. It can be seen that the EV performs the first overtake since no vehicles are coming in the opposite direction. After the first overtake, a vehicle is coming in the opposite direction. The agent decides to wait until the left lane is clear and then performs the overtaking manoeuvre. The corresponding MDP state and action are shown in Fig. 11.

Monte Carlo Campaign. A Monte Carlo campaign has been carried out, where 50 simulations were run for each of the three use cases described above, resulting in a total of 150 simulations. In each simulation of this campaign, the initial conditions (positions and velocities) of the EV and the other vehicles were chosen randomly. The agent shown a 100% success rate in decision making, without any error or unexpected behaviour.

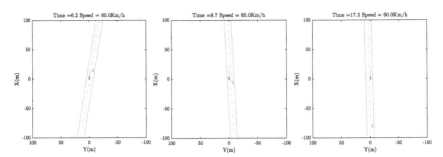

Fig. 9. Use case 3. First overtake. The left lane is clear.

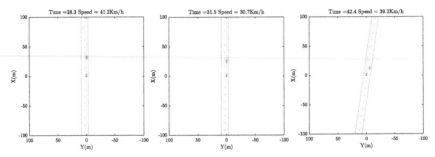

Fig. 10. Use case 3. Second overtake. The EV waits for the left lane to be clear and then accomplishes the overtaking maneuver.

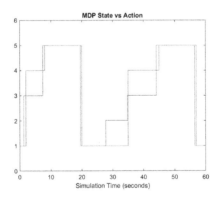

Fig. 11. Use case 3. Duble overtake. MDP state (blue) and action (red). (Color figure online)

5 Discussions and Conclusions

Advances in sensing, computing, machine learning, and intelligent supporting systems have driven the rapid growth of connected autonomous driving applications around the world [21]. Connected and autonomous vehicles (CAVs) have become intelligent mobility spaces carrying rich functions and services. However – as side-effects – these CAVs pointed out some new problems, first the so-called "irony of automation" [22].

In this perspective, our research aimed at developing an intelligent support system for (optimal) decision, to realize safe, efficient, comfortable and pleasant human-vehicle interaction, meaning that the drivers or the automated systems are helped to take the proper decision in the right time.

To achieve that, we considered the Markov Decision Processes (MDPs), which are one possible way to solve this type of problems. There are some reasons why this method is preferable, with respect to others. By defining the environment as a framework of states and transitions, we are effectively shifting from a model defined in the continuous domain, to a discrete one. This decoupling is extremely useful to simplify the process of decision making, but some elements have to be taken into account. First, the state definition must be complete, in the sense that every possible situation should be included as main state or aggregate state, to avoid incurring in unexpected behaviors. This is of course hard to predict "a priori", but it can be improved by time through simulation, specifically by simulating extreme or uncommon cases or by using customized explorative policy functions. As a second factor, the transitional probabilities are defined, but not fixed. This means that it is possible to understand how the model changes when a certain state transition is made "more or less" probable. While it is not useful to simulate an unrealistic environment, it may be useful to check the immediate and cumulative reward variation of when a certain case changes its appearance frequency. This could allow the manufacturer for a more precise and reliable risk assessment, already in the training phase of the process. Another crucial advantage of using an MDP state approach is the low requirement in computational effort. Since the work is carried on in a decoupled discrete domain, there is a remarkable reduction in training time and usage of the processor units. This element is of paramount importance if these decision-making systems must be used in real-time and on-line applications (such as on the intelligent transportation systems).

Finally, we want to discuss here the deterministic vs stochastic approach. The proposed supporting system is exploiting the first one. In a real human-driven scenario, each choice is based not only on rational factors but also on some other elements that have an important weight in the decision-making process. It is easy to imagine, for instance, how a human driver could approach in extremely different ways the same scenario, at different times. While it is intuitive to think that it is not possible to predict the outcome of an action where a human is involved, it is questionable if this is the result of real stochastic process. In fact, this could just be related to the small quantity of information about the system that the observer could have. Imagine predicting the answer to the question: "Will a human driver try to overtake the next vehicle?", this could be a much easier or harder task to complete based on the amount of knowledge we have about the related subject. There are factors that could be fundamental to make an optimal prediction and at the same time they contribute to reduce greatly the stochastic aspect of the system, bringing it much closer to a deterministic function (examples are "is the subject on time or late with respect to the scheduled arrival time?", "is the subject a skilled driver?", and so on). When trying to replicate or substitute that same human driver, the consequences need to be taken into consideration. AI methods analyze a certain number of variables to understand the state of the system and then use an optimal policy (that can either be static and previously trained or dynamic and subject to constant updating) to pick the best output. While it is possible to largely increase the dimension of the input space to better characterize the status of the system (for instance, using as input advanced sensors data like mood-detection cameras or neural interfaces) or, on the other hand, to use neural networks that can simulate random elements, using stochastic weights or transfer functions [23], we are still far away from matching the complexity of a human-level decision process.

An unpredictable artificial intelligence may not be safe or efficient in some cases: this issue is already of great importance in the autonomous driving field, bringing up ethical and moral aspects. In fact, one of the main concerns in applying AI to cars is of course related to the safety of driver and passengers, but also how the car should behave in the world environment under critical situations, considering that the automotive environment is completely unregulated, unpredictable and strictly tied to the human sphere (this is reduced in other types of environment, for example in aeronautics or in space exploration rover, which operate in human-free or human-restricted settings). On the other hand, the development of a deterministic policy, considering every possible variation that could cause a system fault, is an impossible task; so, how and when the automated vehicles actually contribute to reduce (even eliminate) the road accidents is still not clear [24], involving also ethical and acceptance problems [25].

As a very last note, authors want to declare their awareness that some contents have been reported again from our previous work [11]. This has been done for the sake of readability and comprehensibility, assuming that not all readers are necessarily familiar with MDP and RL topics.

Acknowledgment. This work was supported by the NewControl project, within the Electronic Components and Systems For European Leadership Joint Undertaking (ESCEL JU) in collaboration with the European Union's Horizon2020 Framework Programme and National Authorities, under grant agreement N° 826653–2.

References

1. Chu, D., Li, H., Zhao, C., Zhou, T.: Trajectory tracking of autonomous vehicle based on model predictive control with pid feedback. IEEE Trans. Intell. Transp. Syst. **23**, 1–12 (2022). https://doi.org/10.1109/TITS.2022.3150365
2. Marcano, M., et al.: From the concept of being "the Boss" to the idea of being "a Team": the adaptive Co-Pilot as the enabler for a new cooperative framework. Appl. Sci. **11**(15), 6950 (2021). https://doi.org/10.3390/app11156950
3. Huang, C., Lv, C., Hang, P., Hu, Z., Xing, Y.: Human–machine adaptive shared control for safe driving under automation degradation. IEEE Intell. Transp. Syst. Mag. **14**(2), 53–66 (2021)
4. Deng, H., Zhao, Y., Feng, S., Wang, Q., Lin, F.: Shared control for intelligent vehicle based on handling inverse dynamics and driving intention. IEEE Trans. Veh. Technol. **71**(3), 2706–2720 (2022)
5. Russell, H.E.B., Harbott, L.K., Nisky, I., Pan, S., Okamura, A.M., Christian Gerdes, J.: Motor learning affects car-to-driver handover in automated vehicles. Sci. Robot. **1**(1), eaah5682 (2016). https://doi.org/10.1126/scirobotics.aah5682
6. Flemisch, F., Schieben, A., Schoemig, N., Strauss, M., Lueke, S., Heyden, A.: Design of human computer interfaces for highly automated vehicles in the EU-project HAVEit. In: Stephanidis, C. (ed.) UAHCI 2011. LNCS, vol. 6767, pp. 270–279. Springer, Heidelberg (2011). https://doi.org/10.1007/978-3-642-21666-4_30

7. Flemish, F.O., Goodrich, K.H., Adams, A.A., Conway, S.R., Palmer, M.T., Schutte, P.C.: The H-Metaphor as a guideline for vehicle automation and interaction. University of Munich: Munich, Germany (2003). http://www.sti.nasa.gov. Accessed 24 May 2021

8. Bainbridge, L.: Ironies of automation. Automatica **19**, 775–779 (1983). https://doi.org/10. 1016/0005-1098(83)90046-8

9. Benloucif, A., Nguyen, A.-T., Sentouh, C., Popieul, J.-C.: Cooperative trajectory planning for haptic shared control between driver and automation in highway driving. IEEE Trans. Industr. Electron. **66**(12), 9846–9857 (2019)

10. Wang, W., et al.: Decision-making in driver-automation shared control: a review and perspectives. IEEE/CAA J. Automatica Sinica **7**(5), 1289–1307 (2020)

11. Castellano, A., Karimshoushtari, M., Novara, C., Tango, F.: A supervisor agent-based on the markovian decision process framework to optimize the behavior of a highly automated system. In: Schmorrow, D.D., Fidopiastis, C.M. (eds.) Augmented Cognition. Lecture Notes in Computer Science (Lecture Notes in Artificial Intelligence), vol. 12776, pp. 351–368. Springer, Cham (2021). https://doi.org/10.1007/978-3-030-78114-9_24

12. Shneiderman, B.: Human-centered artificial intelligence: reliable, safe & trustworthy. Int. J. Hum. Comput. Inter. **36**(6), 495–504 (2020). https://doi.org/10.1080/10447318.2020.174 1118

13. Madl, T., Baars, B.J., Franklin, S.: The timing of the cognitive cycle. PLoS ONE **6**(4), e14803 (2011). https://doi.org/10.1371/journal.pone.0014803

14. Rasmussen, J.: Skills, rules, and knowledge; signals, signs, and symbols, and other distinctions in human performance models. IEEE Trans. Syst. Man Cybern. **SMC-13**(3), 257–266 (1983). https://doi.org/10.1109/TSMC.1983.6313160

15. Shneiderman, B.: Human-centered artificial intelligence: three fresh ideas. AIS Trans. Hum. Comput. Inter. **12**, 109–124 (2020). https://doi.org/10.17705/1thci.00131

16. Poler, R., Mula, J., Díaz-Madroñero, M.: Dynamic Programming. In: Operations Research Problems, pp. 325–374. Springer, London (2014). https://doi.org/10.1007/978-1-4471-557 7-5_9

17. Barto A.G.: Reinforcement learning: an introduction (Adaptive Computation and Machine Learning), 3rd ed. The MIT press (1998) (cit. on p. 18)

18. Olivier, P., Tango, F.: A reinforcement learning approach to optimize the longitudinal behavior of a partial autonomous driving assistance system. In: ECAI 2012. IOS Press, pp. 987–992 (2012) (cit. on p. 20)

19. Melo, F.S.: Convergence of q-learning: a simple proof. in: institute of systems and robotics. Tech. Rep, pp. 1–4 (2001) (cit. on p. 20)

20. Dayan, P., Watkins, C.J.C.H.: Q-learning. Mach. Learn. **8**(3), 279–292 (1992)

21. ERTRAC: "Connected automated driving roadmap." https://www.ertrac.org/uploads/docume ntsearch/id57/ERTRAC-CAD-Roadmap-2019.pdf (2019)

22. Jerry, W.: By what Hubris? The readiness of the human operator to take over when the automation fails or hands over control. In: Proceedings of the DDI2018 6th International Conference on Driver Distraction and Inattention, Gothenburg, Sweden, 15–17 October 2018, pp. 182–184 (2018)

23. Turchetti, C.: Stochastic models of Neural Networks. IOS Press (2004) (cit. on p. 28)

24. Insurance Institute for Highway Safety. Self-driving vehicles could struggle to eliminate most crashes (2020). https://www.iihs.org/news/detail/self-driving-vehicles-could-struggle-to-eli minate-most-crashes

25. Bonnefon, J.F., Shariff, A., Rahwan, I.: The social dilemma of autonomous vehicles. Science **352**(6293), 1573–1576 (2016). https://doi.org/10.1126/science.aaf2654

INFEATURE: An Interactive Feature-Based-Explanation Framework for Non-technical Users

Yulu Pi[✉]

University of Warwick, Coventry, UK
yulu.pi@warwick.ac.uk

Abstract. The field of explainable artificial intelligence (XAI) aims to make AI systems more understandable to humans. However, current XAI research often produces explanations that convey only one aspect of the information, ignoring the complementary nature of local and global explanations in the decision-making process. To address this issue, this study introduces an interactive interface based on feature-based explanations generated by SHAP. The interface presents feature-based explanations in an interactive and staggered manner, bridging the gap between local explanations and the overall understanding of the model. It allows users to explore datasets, models, and predictions in a self-discovery process that yields insights into model behavior in interaction with visual and verbal explanations. The interface also displays the confusion matrix in an intuitive way that takes the underlying data distributions into account.

Keywords: XAI · HCI · Interactivity · Confusion Matrix

1 Introduction

The interdisciplinary field of Explainable Artificial Intelligence (XAI) focuses on making AI more understandable to humans. It is proposed as a remedy to increase system understanding, facilitate Human-AI collaboration, and calibrate system trust [26]. However, in many cases, XAI research makes the implicit assumption that explanations are static and there is a single message to convey through the explanation [1]. This view is also reflected in the emphasis on the distinction between local and global explanations while ignoring their complementarity in the current XAI literature. As Miller remarked that explainability is a dynamic social process that connects the explainer-who asks for explanations and the explainee-who provides them with the transfer of knowledge [19]. Therefore, the process of explaining a model and its outputs to users via XAI techniques should not be a static one. Once a single aspect of the model is given by providing related information, the user may ask many successive questions, which requires interactivity to enable a continuous dialogue between the user and the explanatory interface. Injecting interactivity into XAI research has the potential to help align it more

© The Author(s), under exclusive license to Springer Nature Switzerland AG 2023
H. Degen and S. Ntoa (Eds.): HCII 2023, LNAI 14050, pp. 262–273, 2023.
https://doi.org/10.1007/978-3-031-35891-3_16

closely with real-world decision-making scenarios, where people may be responsible for a particular decision, and they may have multiple follow-up questions before deciding to accept or reject a system prediction [6].

Feature-based explanations produce the importance scores of features to quantify their contributions to the model predictions [4]. We refer to the features as individual independent variables that are used as inputs to the model. In XAI research, feature importance is by far the most widely studied approach [25]. In addition, in their recent study, X. Wang and M. Yin found that showing how different features affect model predictions can improve understanding of AI models, help people recognize model uncertainty, and support trust in model calibration, while other explanatory methods, such as Nearest Neighbors and Counterfactual explanations, produce less satisfying results [27]. Therefore, we chose feature-based explanation as our first step to explore interactive XAI for non-technical end users. We present INFEATURE, a web-based interactive interface that based on feature-based explanations generated by SHAP. As part of my ongoing PhD research, this prototype offers users the opportunity to self-discover the characteristics of the model and the training dataset. We make INFEATURE available online[1]. The interface shows a main bar chart that displays a prediction's most important features as horizontal bars, users can click each bar to get an another chart showing the related feature distribution, label distribution and model performance on the training set. We anticipate multiple benefits from our interface. Firstly, this interface presents feature-based explanations in a dynamic and interactive way, allowing users to explore and understand the dataset, the model, and certain predictions. Secondly, it allows users to explore the model performance at the training set globally from the lens of the given important features of the investigated local instance, bridging the local explanations to the global explanations. Our interface aims to provide users with a deeper understanding of the estimated important features for the analyzed instance. Additionally, in our future work, we will test how INFEATURE can enable users to incrementally gain a comprehensive understanding of the model's behavior through interactive exploration, utilizing the provided important features as a starting point. Finally, although it was not our initial design intention, we found that using the model performance as a legend to show the feature distribution improves the display of the confusion matrix. Confusion matrices are a useful tool for evaluating the performance of AI models, but they can be difficult to interpret and do not consider the underlying data distributions. Our interface also displays confusion matrices in an intuitive and visual way, showing how the model behaves differently with the data distribution.

2 Explorable Explanations with Interactivity

In practical terms, a single explanation cannot possibly address all of the user's concerns. Users may have many follow-up questions when using an explaination generated by XAI methods. For instance, Belle and Papantonis illustrates

---

[1] https://nikipi-infeature-app-becfsw.streamlit.app/.

how different XAI techniques can be used to respond to the many queries posed by users with a real-world example [7]. Jane, a data scientist, built a Random Forests model used for loan approvals. She needed to come up with methods that would help her explain to stakeholders how the model operates. At first, she applied SHAP method and found out that the model heavily relies on an applicant's salary. She would like to know if all other elements of the current application remain the same, what is the salary threshold that differentiates between approval and rejection of the application. To answer this question, she employed Individual Conditional Expectation(ICE) plots and Partial Dependence Plots to inspect how the model's behavior changes with salary when other features are fixed. While the stakeholders found the explanations useful, there is a new issue to address. In contrast to what several bank experts believed ought to happen, the model in the test set rejected one application. Stakeholders were left wondering why the model made the choice it did and whether the model would have approved an application that was somewhat different. Jane made the choice to tackle this problem using a counterfactual approach and discovered that the applicant's failure to make one payment was what caused this outcome; otherwise, the application would have been approved. To externalize her finding with easy-to-understand 'if-then' rules, Jane used Anchors to generate the resulting rule 'if salary is greater than 20 k e and there are no missed payments, then the loan is approved." As we can see from the example, a series of XAI techniques were used to understand different facets of the model. By having the opportunity to explore various aspects of the model through the insights gained from different explanation methods, a user can achieve a deeper and more comprehensive understanding of the system.

There is a growing recognition of the significance of interactive XAI, which provides users with a combination of XAI methods with a means of interaction that goes beyond a single explanation [10]. Adadi et al. state that "explainability can only happen through interaction between human and machine" [2]. Cheng et al's work provided empirical evidence that interactive visual explanations are effective at improving non-expert users' comprehension of algorithmic decisions [9]. Weld and Bansal outlined a vision of an interactive explanation system, which should support the user's follow-up questions and drill-down actions, such as redirecting answers or requesting more details [28]. A number of dashboard-like frameworks for interactive explanations have been developed. Baniecki and Biecek introduced the concept of interactive explanation of the model analysis, proposing "multi-threaded customizable story about the blackbox model" rather than single aspect model explanations [6]. They also provided a modelStudio software package for interactive model interpretation. ModelStudio can automatically compute various model-agnostic explanations and display them visually through dashboards, which allow user-friendly and interactive full customization of the visual grid and productive model inspection. While the package's functionality makes it easy to save and share dashboard documentation and allows for easy communication with non-technical users, generating visual explanations through ModelStudio still requires some programming skills. Additionally, the What-If Tool (WIT), an open-source application that supports interactivity, automation, and customization, enables practitioners to comprehend and analyze ML systems through various complementary visualizations with minimal coding [29]. With the Datapoint Editor, WIT allows customizable analysis of input data and model results to examine how general variations in data points affect model interference. It allows users to test model performance in hypothetical situations through counterfactual reasoning. WIT also allows practitioners to visualize model behavior across multiple models and subsets of input data and measure the system against multiple ML fairness metrics. Our work contributes to the visual and interactive exploration of XAI research by introducing a web-used interactive interface based on feature-based explanations that enables users' self-discovery of the model and training dataset starting from a local level.

We leverage SHAP (SHapley Additive exPlanations), a well-studied post hoc explanation generation method, to extract important features at the instance level as our explaining first step and then enable users to explore the distribution of these features and model performance on the training set via interactive graphs. Although SHAP is vulnerable to adversarial attacks [22] and has potential infidelity [12], it is a promising starting point to explore interactive XAI for the following reasons. For starters, it unifies existing feature attribution methods (e.g., LIME, DeepLIFT and QII) and links them to additive Shapley values linkage [10]. Moreover, it allows the generation of mutually consistent local and global interpretations, since they both use Shapley values as atomic units. Multiple SHAP local explanations can be combined to create contrastive and counterfactual explanations [21]. It is also a model-agnostic approach that allows XAI designers to provide a unified format for explanations, even if the underlying ML model is different. However, previous research has shown that even experienced ML engineers have difficulty in using the current visualization of SHAP to effectively validate their assumptions about the ML model under examination [15]. We choose to use a web-based interface to reduce the technical barriers for non-technical end-users. Shapley values estimations can provide users with a list of important features for an individual prediction. However, only knowing the contribution of each feature to a certain prediction does not give users a satisfying picture of the model. For example, a user might ask the question: If feature 1, feature 2, and feature 3 are considered important for an instance prediction, what does this mean for the performance of the overall model. Our interface enables users to ask such questions.

3   Functionality of INFEATURE

We build upon the local feature importance plot provided by the SHAP framework to allow users to further explore the model and dataset at the global level as shown in Fig. 2. Firstly, for a given individual prediction, we used SHAP to estimate feature contributions. We display the feature contributions as a bar chart that displays a prediction's most important features as horizontal bars. Users can click each bar to get the histogram for the selected feature on the training set. Besides showing the feature distribution, the histogram has two other important functions: firstly, it will show the label distribution and model performance of the training set based on the chosen feature. It can help users develop their understanding of the training dataset as well as the global behavior of the model from the point of the chosen feature. Moreover, below the histogram, we generated verbal explanations using the template-based Natural Language Generation (NLG) method to provide information about the model performance given the chosen feature and the feature value of the instance under investigation (Fig. 1).

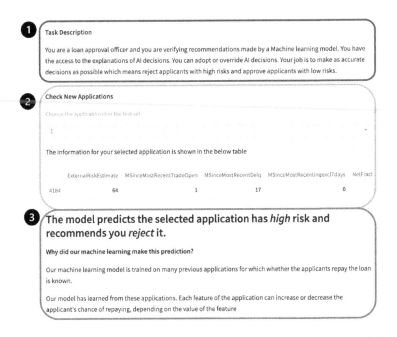

Fig. 1. Overview of the INFEATURE interface that gives the context of the task, instances and model predictions.

The interface allows users to explore the model performance at the training set globally from the lens of the given important features of the investigated local instance, bridging the local explanations to the global understanding of the model. Human preferences for a combination of global and local explanations of AI have been found through a number of empirical studies. For instance, the researchers found that in addition to the explanations of the individual predictions of the model, clinicians wanted global information about the model [8]. Our interface can not only help users have a deeper understanding of estimated important features for the investigated instance, but they can also develop global insight incrementally into the model's behavior through interactive exploration.

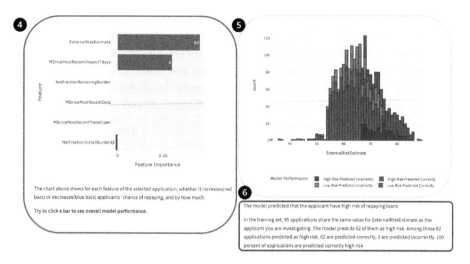

Fig. 2. UI prototype of interactive feature-based-explanation in INFEATURE: (4) The feature contributions are displayed as a bar chart. (5)Users can click each bar to get the histogram for the selected feature on the training set. It will show the label distribution and model performance of the training set based on the chosen feature. (6) Verbal explanations are given with Natural Language Generation (NLG) method to provide information about the model performance given the chosen feature and the feature value of the instance under investigation.

The most important features estimated by SHAP can draw users' attention from the high-dimensional data space to a more accessible number of features, facilitating their understanding of the dataset as well as the model behavior. Furthermore, by exploring the model performance based on the subset of the features, users can conduct their own validation of the model prediction, giving them more information about the model and dataset than solely relying on feature importance. Through guided interactive drill down of the local feature-based explanations, users can have a richer understanding of the model's behavior. In addition, our language explanations relate model performance to the specific range of data in which the feature values of the selected instances are located, allowing for narrower and more targeted validation of the instance prediction. In natural language, we provide the contextual information between the instance's value and model behavior tightly coupling the explanation with the subject. However, the impact of this deeper understanding on user trust, satisfaction with the model, and on the decision-making process is unknown and will be further investigated in our future research.

4   From Local Explanations to Global Insights

One of the main XAI approaches consists of applying post hoc techniques that explain which features are more relevant to the prediction of a model [14]. The most prevalent way to classify post-hoc feature-based explanations is their explanation scales. They can show trends in how variables are related to the models' prediction at the scale of global and local. For example, an explanation can be as thorough as describing the entire machine learning model(global explanations). Alternatively, it can only partially explain the model, or be limited to explaining a certain input-output chain(local explanations) [20]. Global explanations explore which patterns exist in general, while local explanations provide the reasons for a specific decision. Local explanations label the most dominant features and feature dimensions in the model decisions for each data point. Conversely, global explanations aim to identify the most sensitive features of the model as a whole in the data. Due to the different focus, i.e., local explanations focus on explaining model decisions based on specific instances or subgroups, while global explanations reveal inferences about the entire model, global and local explanations can provide different perspectives for understanding the model.

A local explanation is helpful to understand the reasoning behind a certain prediction made by the model by explaining the relationship between specific input-output pairs. Users tend to care more about what leads to those predictions that affect their interests, and in this sense, local explanations are very valuable. A local explanation that describes one instance does not necessarily apply to other instances in the same way, which means that it is personalized for different users depending on the selected instance. Moreover, local explanations can particularly facilitate the monitoring and detection of inappropriate use or anomalies by investigating edge cases [13]. According to a study of 381 published papers, this type of explanation is considered less overwhelming for novices, and it is the most widely developed approach [17]. Local explanations help to understand, question, or correct individual cases, but lack the ability to validate the overall consistency of AI systems. Focusing on the explainability of the entire model and its operating mechanism, global explanations provide the general logic of how the overall model works to the users. Therefore, global explanation helps to validate the consistency of the model across domains and scenarios. In addition, global explanations can be part of the toolbox of regulators and compliance officers to interrogate and prove the suitability of the system [18]. However, it has the risk of revealing trade secrets, thus hindering innovation. In addition, global interpretation is technically more difficult to obtain, especially for complex models, such as deep neural networks.

Many studies currently view the local and global explanations as two separate methods, lacking the perspective that they can be complementary while interacting with each other. Providing both global and local explanations of an AI model can allow users to understand the model's overall functioning as well as delve into specific instances for more detailed analysis. It can also help users understand how the model operates in different parts of the feature space, so that they don't mistakenly assume that their understanding of the model based on one instance applies to all instances. For example, a local explanation of a medical diagnostic model might highlight the specific symptoms and test results that were most influential in making a particular diagnosis, while a global explanation of the same model might show the overall relationship between different symptoms and diagnoses, allowing medical practitioners to understand the general behavior of the model. While local explanations are useful for users to investigate and validate a certain instance, without some level of understanding of the model itself, users may find it hard to trust their reliability, and cannot apply such information to meet their explanatory needs. Alqaraawi et al. showed that the local explanations bring new information to the user, but the model behavior remains unpredictable and unintelligible to the participants [5]. Human preferences for a combination of global and local explanations of AI have been found through a number of empirical studies. Cai and colleagues [8] studied how clinicians interact with an AI model that can assist in cancer diagnosis and their needs in terms of model explanations. They found in addition to explanations about the model's individual predictions, clinicians also wanted information about the model as a whole. The empirical study by Chromik et al. showed that humans have difficulty in abstracting their local insights into global understanding. The participants comprehended the local justifications given for individual observations, but struggled to determine how representative they were of the overall model behaviour [11]. Lundberg et al. proposed a technique for tree-based models that used many local explanations as building blocks to establish the understanding of global model structure [16]. Our interface addresses the detachment of local and global explanations by enabling users to gain global insights including feature distribution, label distribution and model performance from given important features of an instance at a local level, through interactive charts. Our interface enables users to examine the model's performance on the training set from the perspective of the important features of a specific instance, linking local explanations to a global understanding of the model. In addition to helping users gain a deeper understanding of the estimated important features for a particular instance, the interface also allows them to incrementally build global insights into the model's behavior through interactive exploration using those important features as a starting point (Fig. 3).

5   Visualising Model Performance with Underlying Data Contribution

When providing feature importance for a certain model prediction without conveying the overall model performance, it leads to incorrect conclusions or misunderstandings about the model's ability resulting in mistrust or overreliance [24]. Stowers et al. noted that it is of great importance that uncertainties should be made explicit [23]. Communicating uncertainties gives users a more complete picture of the model's abilities and limitations, allowing them to utilize their domain knowledge to compensate for the AI systems' lack of knowledge. A confusion matrix (Kohavi and Provost, 1998) is considered as a useful tool for

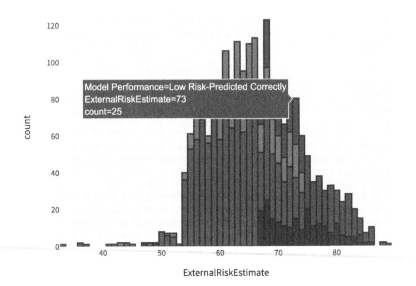

Fig. 3. A closer look at feature distributions to convey uncertainty in model performance

evaluating the performance of an AI model helping users understand the uncertainty of the model's predictions. It can help users understand that the model is not always able to make a correct prediction, and that there may be a level of uncertainty in its predictions. However, there is growing criticism around the misleading effect of the confusion matrix in conveying incomplete information about the model to users [3]. One of the main reasons why the confusion matrix can be misleading is that it does not take into account the underlying distribution of the data and how the behavior of the model changes with the data distribution. For example, if the data used to train the model is skewed, with a large fraction of the sample having low values for an important feature considered by the model, then the model is likely to make different predictions for low and high values, and high accuracy can be achieved simply by predicting the most common categories of low-value data. Our interface shows the data distribution with model performance labels, showing how the model behaves differently with the data distribution, compensating for confusion matrix's lack of consideration of data distribution. Each bar is a confusion matrix of a small subset of the training data, which together form a composite picture of the model behavior. This will provide a more complete picture of model performance, making it possible for users to make informed decisions based on model performance over the specific range of data associated with the instance under investigation. However, this preliminary prototype does not consider what is a suitable number of bars in the chart, and how the different number of bars affects the information about the model performance. We intend to delve into these questions more thoroughly through user testing in the future.

6 Furture Work

In this work, we investigate only one possible way to make feature-based explanations interactive; however, the lens of interactivity can also be applied to connect different explanations methods, such as Individual Conditional Expectation, counterfactual explanations and rule-based explanations. Having the chance to explore different aspects of the model by learning varying information provided by different explanation methods, a user can have a deeper and more complete understanding of the system.

This is the preliminary part of my ongoing doctoral research. In future research, INFEATURE will be extended to incorporate other explanation methods and to explore how interactive explanations can help users gain a deeper and more comprehensive understanding of AI. We plan to design a non-technical user-friendly interface to explain different aspects of the model by using various XAI techniques, such as SHAP, ICE graphs, partial dependency graphs, counterfactual explanations, and rule-based explanations (e.g., Anchors).

References

1. Abdul, A., Vermeulen, J., Wang, D., Lim, B.Y., Kankanhalli, M.: Trends and trajectories for explainable, accountable and intelligible systems: an HCI research agenda. In: Proceedings of the 2018 CHI Conference on Human Factors in Computing Systems, pp. 1–18. ACM. ISBN 978-1-4503-5620-6. https://doi.org/10.1145/3173574.3174156
2. Adadi, A., Berrada, M.: Peeking inside the black-box: A survey on explainable artificial intelligence (XAI). **6**, 52138–52160. ISSN 2169–3536. https://doi.org/10.1109/ACCESS.2018.2870052. https://ieeexplore.ieee.org/document/8466590/
3. Akosa, J.: Predictive accuracy: A misleading performance measure for highly imbalanced data
4. Alicioglu, G., Sun, B.: A survey of visual analytics for explainable artificial intelligence methods, p. 19
5. Alqaraawi, A., Schuessler, M., Weiß, P., Costanza, E., Berthouze, N.: Evaluating saliency map explanations for convolutional neural networks: a user study. http://arxiv.org/abs/2002.00772
6. Baniecki, H., Parzych, D., Biecek, P.: The grammar of interactive explanatory model analysis. http://arxiv.org/abs/2005.00497
7. Belle, V., Papantonis, I.: Principles and practice of explainable machine learning. http://arxiv.org/abs/2009.11698
8. Cai, C.J., Winter, S., Steiner, D., Wilcox, L., Terry., M.: "hello AI": uncovering the onboarding needs of medical practitioners for human-AI collaborative decision-making. 3:1–24. ISSN 2573–0142. https://doi.org/10.1145/3359206
9. Cheng, H.-F., et al.: Explaining decision-making algorithms through UI: Strategies to help non-expert stakeholders. In Proceedings of the 2019 CHI Conference on Human Factors in Computing Systems, pp. 1–12. ACM. ISBN 978-1-4503-5970-2. https://doi.org/10.1145/3290605.3300789. https://dl.acm.org/doi/10.1145/3290605.3300789

10. Chromik, M.: reSHAPe: a framework for interactive explanations in XAI based on SHAP. ISSN 2510–2591. https://doi.org/10.18420/ECSCW2020_P06. https://dl.eusset.eu/handle/20.500.12015/3710. Publisher: European Society for Socially Embedded Technologies (EUSSET)

11. Chromik,M., Eiband, M., Buchner, F., Krüger, A., Butz, A.: I think i get your point, AI! the illusion of explanatory depth in explainable AI. In: 26th International Conference on Intelligent User Interfaces, pp. 307–317. ACM. ISBN 978-1-4503-8017-1. https://doi.org/10.1145/3397481.3450644.https://dl.acm.org/doi/10.1145/3397481.3450644

12. Gosiewska, A., Biecek, P.: Do not trust additive explanations. http://arxiv.org/abs/1903.11420

13. Hacker, P., Passoth, J.-H.: Varieties of AI explanations under the law. from the GDPR to the AIA, and beyond, p. 32

14. Jin, W., Fan, J., Gromala, D., Pasquier, P., Hamarneh, G.: EUCA: practical prototyping framework towards end-user-centered explainable artificial intelligence. http://arxiv.org/abs/2102.02437

15. Kaur, H., Nori, H., Jenkins, S., Caruana, R., Wallach, H., Vaughan, J.W.: Interpreting interpretability: understanding data scientists' use of interpretability tools for machine learning. In: Proceedings of the 2020 CHI Conference on Human Factors in Computing Systems, pp. 1–14. ACM. ISBN 978-1-4503-6708-0. https://doi.org/10.1145/3313831.3376219. https://dl.acm.org/doi/10.1145/3313831.3376219u

16. Lundberg, S., Lee, S.-I.: A unified approach to interpreting model predictions. http://arxiv.org/abs/1705.07874

17. Maltbie, N., Niu, N., Van Doren, M., Johnson, R.: XAI tools in the public sector: a case study on predicting combined sewer overflows. In: Proceedings of the 29th ACM Joint Meeting on European Software Engineering Conference and Symposium on the Foundations of Software Engineering, pp. 1032–1044. ACM. ISBN 978-1-4503-8562-6. https://doi.org/10.1145/3468264.3468547. https://dl.acm.org/doi/10.1145/3468264.3468547

18. McDermid, J.A., Jia, Y., Porter, Z., Habli, I.: Artificial intelligence explainability: the technical and ethical dimensions, p. 18

19. Miller, T.: Explanation in artificial intelligence: Insights from the social sciences. http://arxiv.org/abs/1706.07269

20. Mohseni, S., Zarei, N., Ragan, E.D.: A multidisciplinary survey and framework for design and evaluation of explainable AI systems. http://arxiv.org/abs/1811.11839

21. Rathi, S.: Generating counterfactual and contrastive explanations using SHAP. http://arxiv.org/abs/1906.09293

22. Slack, D., Hilgard, S., Jia, E., Singh, S., Lakkaraju, H.: Fooling LIME and SHAP: Adversarial attacks on post hoc explanation methods. http://arxiv.org/abs/1911.02508

23. Stowers, K., Kasdaglis, N., Newton, O., Lakhmani, S., Wohleber, R., Chen, J.: Intelligent agent transparency: The design and evaluation of an interface to facilitate human and intelligent agent collaboration. 60(1):1706–1710. ISSN 2169–5067. https://doi.org/10.1177/1541931213601392. Publisher: SAGE Publications Inc

24. Vasconcelos, H., Jörke, M., Grunde-McLaughlin, M., Gerstenberg, T., Bernstein, M., Krishna, R.: Explanations can reduce overreliance on AI systems during decision-making. http://arxiv.org/abs/2212.06823

25. Vilone, G., Longo, L.: Explainable artificial intelligence: a systematic review. http://arxiv.org/abs/2006.00093

26. van der Waa, J., Nieuwburg, E., Cremers, A., Neerincx, M.: Evaluating XAI: A comparison of rule-based and example-based explanations. 291, 103404. ISSN 00043702. https://doi.org/10.1016/j.artint.2020.103404.   https://linkinghub.elsevier.com/retrieve/pii/S0004370220301533
27. Wang, X., Yin, M.: Effects of explanations in AI-assisted decision making: Principles and comparisons. **12**(4), 1–36. ISSN 2160–6455, 2160–6463. https://doi.org/10.1145/3519266. https://dl.acm.org/doi/10.1145/3519266
28. Weld, D.S., Bansal, G.: The challenge of crafting intelligible intelligence. **62**(6), 70–79. ISSN 0001–0782, 1557–7317. https://doi.org/10.1145/3282486. https://dl.acm.org/doi/10.1145/3282486
29. Wexler, J., Pushkarna, M., Bolukbasi, T., Wattenberg, M., Viegas, F., Wilson, J.: The what-if tool: Interactive probing of machine learning models, pp. 1–1. ISSN 1077–2626, 1941–0506, 2160–9306. https://doi.org/10.1109/TVCG.2019.2934619. http://arxiv.org/abs/1907.04135

A Quantitative Comparison of Causality and Feature Relevance via Explainable AI (XAI) for Robust, and Trustworthy Artificial Reasoning Systems

Atul Rawal[1]([⊠])(iD), James McCoy[1], Adrienne Raglin[2], and Danda B. Rawat[1](iD)

[1] Center of Excellence in AI/ML (CoE-AIML), Department of Electrical Engineering and Computer Science, Howard University, Washington D.C. 20059, USA
atul.rawal@ieee.org
[2] DEVCOM Army Research Laboratory, Adelphi, MD 20783, USA

Abstract. Challenges related to causal learning remain a major issue for artificial reasoning systems. Similar to other ML approaches, robust and trustworthy explainability is needed to support the underlying tasks. This paper aims to provide a novel perspective on causal explainability, creating a model which extracts quantitative causal knowledge and relationships from observational data via Average treatment effect (ATE) estimation to generate robust explanations through comparison and validation of the ranked causally relevant features with results from correlation-based feature relevance explanations. Average treatment effect estimation is calculated to provide a quantitative comparison of the causal features to the relevant features from Explainable AI (XAI). This approach provides a comprehensive method to generate explanations via validations from both causality and XAI to ensure trustworthiness, fairness, and bias detection from both within the data, as well as the AI/ML models themselves for artificial reasoning systems.

Keywords: Causality · Explainable AI · Artificial Reasoning

1 Introduction

Artificial Intelligence (AI) systems are seamlessly woven into many aspects of our daily lives, from simple recommendation systems such as the song recommendations in Spotify, to major prediction systems such as cancer predictions in medical imaging. Due to the increased adaption of AI systems the ongoing challenges for trust and robustness have a center-stage. Especially, for AI systems that have an impact on human lives such as those used within the healthcare field. Towards this goal of trustworthy AI, numerous sub-fields of research have seen growth as well. Fields such as Explainable AI (XAI) and causal

This work was supported in part by the DoD Center of Excellence in AI and Machine Learning (CoE-AIML) at Howard University under Contract Number W911NF-20-2-0277 with the U.S. Army Research Laboratory.

H. Degen and S. Ntoa (Eds.): HCII 2023, LNAI 14050, pp. 274–285, 2023.
https://doi.org/10.1007/978-3-031-35891-3_17

learning (CL) have seen a growth in research interest within the past decade. Used together XAI and causal learning can help AI systems detect and mitigate bias, provide fairness, transparency and explainability of the AI systems.

Challenges related to causal learning remain a major area of interest for artificial reasoning research. Both explicit and implicit information is needed for robust AI/ML models, where implicit information is traditionally obtained from participants via field experiments. A major challenge for AI/ML engineers is the availability of implicit information from observational datasets. Thus, the scarcity of observational datasets with available ground-truth is a hindrance for causal-learning research. While some datasets are available with ground-truth, extending ground-truth with additional information to support explainability can make the models more robust. As the saying goes, the whole is greater than the sum of parts, combining XAI and causal relationships provides models with enhanced performance and greater explainability. Similar to other ML approaches, robust and trustworthy explainability is needed to support underlying tasks. In this study we present a novel causal explainability model by applying both causality and explainability from observational data via treatment effect estimation to generate robust explanations through comparison and validation of the ranked causally relevant features with results from correlation-based feature relevance explanations.

Future AI/ML systems that use causal learning will be considered more intelligent and results should be more transferable. Causal learning may help make AI/ML systems more efficient. Currently there are multiple readily available and open-source causal-learning packages for ML applications, such as EcomML, DoWHY, and CausalML [3,20,23]. For this paper we utilized an open source dataset from the U.S. Census. For XAI, the study utilized feature relevance via SHAP. SHAP, is an open-source algorithm based on Shapley values to generate feature relevance for ML models [11]. Feature relevance supports explanations of the AI/ML systems by generating a relevance score of the managed variables. The comparison of the scores for each different variable then provides the emphasis of each of the variables on the results generated by the system. This study provides a novel new method of comparing the robustness and fairness of models by utilizing both causality and explainability. The paper is organized as follows. Section 2 provides the background into causal learning and XAI, Sect. 3 provides the proof of concept example, while Sect. 4 provides the results and discussion. Section 5 includes concluding remarks.

2   Overview of Explainable AI (XAI) and Causal Learning

2.1   Explainable AI (XAI)

While prediction systems have been around for quite some time, there has been an increase in explainability for these types of systems. This is in-part due to the ubiquity of AI/ML systems in a plethora of applications that act as a black-box model, which has caused for an increased demand in more robust, trustworthy, explainable and transparent systems. One such example of the keen interest in

XAI, is the The U.S Defense Advanced Research Projects Agency's (DARPA) XAI program started in 2017. It defined XAI as "AI systems that can explain their rationale to a human user, characterize their strengths and weakness, and convey an understanding of how they will behave in the future" [8]. This section gives a brief overview of XAI, for an in-depth review of XAI, readers are encouraged to read the survey by the authors on XAI [17]. Explainability is a vital part of trustworthiness for AI/ML systems. An explainable system is also a vital part of ensuring accountability for AI/ML systems, aiding in identification and mitigation of biases. For a system to be accountable, Madalina Busuioc listed the following criteria [2, 17]:

– Fairness via bias identification and mitigation.
– Explainable decisions.
– Consequences for the predictions/recommendations, which includes imposing of sanctions and addressing those negatively affected by the predictions/recommendations.

From transparent models to post-hoc explainability, there have been numerous studies on making ML models more explainable. Numerous post-hoc explainable techniques for ML models exist such as LIME, LIFT, DeepLIFT, SHAP, DeepSHAP [11,18,19,21].

Lundberg et al., presented SHapley Additive exPlanations (SHAP), a unified framework for interpreting predictions. It calculates feature relevance where an importance value is assigned to each feature for specific predictions, to provide explainability for the model. To get insights into how much of an impact each feature made in the model's predictions, SHAP provides additive feature importance values for accurate and consistent explainable predictions [11].

Riberio et al., presented Local Interpretable Mode-Agnostic Explanations (LIME) for trustworthy explanations of classifier prediction models. It generates local explainable model prediction model by utilizing explanation by simplification and local explanations [18,19].

DeepLIFT (Learning Important FeaTures) presented by Shrikumar et al., generated explanations for deep neural networks. By computing the variance between the activation and reference activation for each neuron, DeepLIFT generates importance scores for the neural networks [21].

2.2   Causality

Causality can be explained as the relationship between a cause and an effect. Though, it must be noted that causation differs from statistical association. For AI/ML systems, causal learning can be done by estimating the changes in the prediction made by the model when another variable is modified. *Treatment* refers to the variable that is modified, whereas the *outcome* is the variable whose change is being observed. In addition to the treatment and outcome, other terms for causal learning include *covariates*, the background variables and *confounders*, variables that affect both the treatment and outcome on a causal level.

Causality within data can be classified into three separate categories that make up Judea Pearl's causal hierarchy: *association, intervention,* and *counterfactuals* [13–15]. The first level of the hierarchy *association* defines the statistical relations within the data. Here traditional statistical techniques are used to derive correlation within the data. Machine learning is based on the association level of causality, where statistical correlations from data are derived from the raw data without causal information. The second level *intervention* estimates the effects of each action based on the causal structure. Here the specific treatment is modified to derive the causality by understanding the causal structure of the different variables. This involves going further than calculating simple correlations based on statistical methods. Finally, the highest level of causality is called *counterfactuals*, which comprise of both associative and interventive questions. Counterfactuals can be used to infer information from both associative and intervention level questions, and predictions can be made from unobserved outcomes. For machine learning, causality can aid in a plethora of applications by helping answer questions that are categorized into two main forms:

- To what extent is the outcome affected by modifications to the treatment?
- Which treatment needs to be modified to yield a change in the outcome?

The first category of questions are referred to as *causal inference,* and the second type of questions are referred to as *causal discovery.* Causal discovery and causal inference are central to studying causal information for machine learning [7,16]. Causal inference can aid in investigating causal effects, whereas causal discovery can aid in deriving causal relations from the data.

Two formal frameworks are available to investigate causality and derive causal information. The first is the *structural causal models (SCMs)* and the other is the *potential outcomes framework.* Structural causal models incorporate causal graphs and structural equations, and provide an extensive causal theory [9,13,27]. *Causal graphs* are directed acrylic graphs representing the causal effects between the various variables within a dataset. Here each node within the graph represents an individual variable, and directed lines between nodes indicate the causal effect of one variable on the other. For example, A → B indicates the causal effect of A on B. Structural equations indicate the direct effect of the treatment on an outcome, where causal effects can be derived from the directed edges in a causal graph.

The potential outcomes framework links causality to the modification/manipulation of treatment(feature) applied to an outcome(label), where the potential outcomes of the treatments is the treatment effect. The framework is commonly applied to investigate the causal effect within a treatment-outcome pair. Here the potential outcome is defined as the outcome that results from the received treatment. For estimating the causal effects of treatments, there are three different methods that can be applied. The first *individual treatment effect* (ITE) is commonly assumed as a binary treatment and defined as the difference between the outcomes of a given instance with two different treatments. Building on the ITE, the *average treatment affect* can be derived by extending the treatment effect from the individual level to the population level. Finally, the *conditional average treatment effect* (CATE) can be applied for sub-populations [9,13,27]. For the current study, we estimate the average treatment effect to compare it with the results from XAI based feature relevance.

2.3 Related Works

Because the fields of causal learning and XAI are both fairly new, there is a gap in literature for the use of both in conjunction with one another. Even though there are a few studies that have presented the use of causal learning as a method for explainability, there is a need for studies using both. A few studies where causal learning and explainability are used are discussed in brief below.

Cui et al., proposed stable learning as an intermediary between causal inference and black-box approaches for machine learning [5]. They present the advantages of using casual inference for machine learning to aid in fairness and explainability issues.

Smith et al., proposed extracting counterfactuals as a method for explainabilty in image based models [22]. They trained a counterfactual generative model to create modifications to known inputs for classification and regression.

Frye et al., presented the Asymmetric Shapley Values (ASVs) framework that is less restrictive than SHAP and incorporates causal structures into the explainability of the model [6]. The approach provided greater explainability, fairness and robustness compared to traditional shapley values.

Xian et al., proposed the Policy-Guided Path Reasoning (PGPR) approach for designing an interpretable causal inference model based on reinforcement learning [25]. They presented reinforcement learning over knowledge graphs for generating recommendations and also explaining the recommendations based on its reasoning.

Moraffah et al., presented a survey of current causal interpretable models, which highlighted methods and evaluation metrics for causal interpretability [12].

Causal learning presents invaluable insights for the development of transparent explainable systems, to provide trustworthiness. Various studies have investigated explainability via causal learning [1,10,24,26]. Chou et al., highlighted the significance of causally understandable explanations to emphasize the impact of causal learning for generating human-like explanations [4].

3 Proof of Concept Example

3.1 Data Source

The dataset for this study, the Census Income Dataset was derived from the UC Irvine Machine Learning Repository (https://archive.ics.uci.edu/ml/datasets/census+income). The Census Income Dataset includes information from the 1994 census data with different variables to predict whether an individual makes an income of above or below $50,000. The dataset includes different features such as age, education, occupation, relationship/marital status, race, sex, and the country. The dataset itself included fourteen different features, which were filtered down to six features for model simplification. The final dataset included variables that made logical correlation with the income label: age, education, occupation, relationship status, sex, and race. The final filtered dataset included information for 32561 individuals.

3.2   Methods

Upon finalizing the dataset, the data was imported into a python notebook using pandas DataFrame. Data visualization was performed using different plots imported from the matplotlib.pyplot libraries to analyze the raw data. The data was numerically encoded as the dataset contained both numerical and categorical variables. The encoded dataset was then randomly split for training and testing at a 80%-20% split with 80% of the dataset used for training the model and 20% used for validation. The training dataset was then applied to the different ML classification models to compare and pick the top performing model.

For income prediction, classification models are suitable as they can make binary classification predictions based on the datasets. Different ML classification models were generated by importing libraries such as Scikit-learn (sklearn), pandas, NumPy, and Keras into the Python notebook. The data were processed and trained with multiple ML classification models to identify top performing models. For the current study we included the following ML classification models: Logistic Regression (LR), Random Forest (RF), Gradient Boosting (GB), Light Gradient Boosting (LGBM), Extreme Gradient Boosting (XGB), and CatBoost (CB) classifiers.

Upon completion of the training and validation the models were evaluated for performance using metrices for accuracy, precision, recall, and F1-score. The top performing model was then chosen to apply XAI via SHAP, (SHapley Additive exPlanations) to identify the variables critical for the income prediction. LR, RF, and GB classifiers were imported from sklearn. LGBM, XGB and CB classifiers were imported from LightGBM, XGBoost and CatBoost respectively. Other libraries such as auto encoders, CausalML, and SHAP were installed directly for the notebook using pip. To evaluate the top performing models metrics of accuracy, precision, recall, and F1-score were used.

- Accuracy - The base metric used for model evaluation is often Accuracy, describing the number of correct predictions over all predictions.

$$Accuracy = \frac{TruePositive + TrueNegative}{TruePositive + TrueNegative + FalsePositive + FalseNegative}$$

- Precision - Precision is a measure of how many of the positive predictions made are correct.

$$Precision = \frac{TruePositive}{TruePositive + FalsePositive}$$

– Recall - Recall is a measure of how many of the positive cases the classifier correctly predicted, over all the positive cases in the data.

$$Recall = \frac{TruePositive}{TruePositive + FalseNegative}$$

– F1-Score - F1-Score is a measure combining both precision and recall. It is generally described as the harmonic mean of the two. It is between 0 and 1, where 0 is the worst score and 1 indicates that the model predicts each observation correctly.

$$F1 - score = 2 * \frac{Precision \times Recall}{Precision + Recall}.$$

Upon completion of model evaluations, the top performing model was chosen for further analysis using XAI. As mentioned in the earlier section SHAP is an open-source post-hoc explanation method used for explaining ML and DL models, where explanations can be provided via feature relevance. An importance value is assigned to each feature for specific predictions based on the impact of the feature on the model's prediction. For this study a linear explainer was used for explaining the logistic regression model and the tree explainer was used for explaining the rest of the models.

Finally, once the ML models were analyzed and explained via SHAP, causal learning was performed on the raw observational dataset using CausalML. Average treatment effect (ATE) estimation was calculated for each variable by assigning each variable as a treatment for the outcome of the income classification. The average treatment effect (ATE) was calculated for a ranked listing of the effect each treatment had on the classification. This ranked listing was then compared to the correlation-based ML classifiers via SHAP feature relevance listing.

4   Results and Discussion

Figure 1 displays the cross validation accuracy for all six ML models used in the study. Additionally, Table 1, highlights the performance metrics for all six ML classifiers. Confusion matrices from all six ML classifiers are displayed in Fig. 2. Even though the ML classifiers were not able to achieve a perfect score of 1 for the performance metrics, the LGBM classifier with a 0.97 F1-score was deemed good for this proof of concept study.

As mentioned in the previous section, upon completion of model evaluations, the top performing model was chosen for further analysis using XAI. For this study, the top model was identified as the LGBM model, to which XAI was applied via SHAP. Explainability of the models were visualized using a feature relevance plot, and a beeswarm plot as seen in Figs. 3 and Fig. 4. Table 2 lists the calculated ATEs for all the features in the dataset. Figure 5 displays the ranked

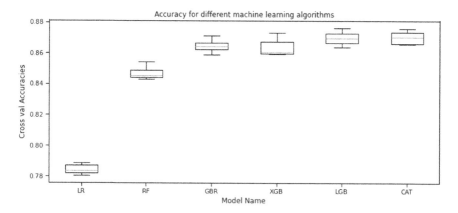

Fig. 1. Accuracy for different classifiers.

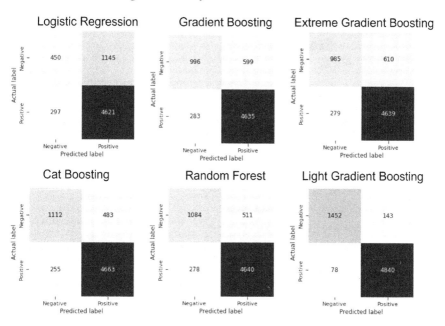

Fig. 2. Confusion matrices for different classifiers.

treatment variables(features) based on the calculated average treatment effect for income classification.

When comparing the causality based treatment effect estimations to the correlation based ML-classifiers feature relevance, the features are listed in an almost identical rank/order. However, the ranking for education varies between the two methods with SHAP based feature relevance ranking it in the bottom three (4th) features, whereas the CausalML based ATE calculation ranking it in the top three (2nd) features. While it is intuitive for humans to relate a higher

Table 1. Model performance metrics for different classifiers.

Model	Accuracy	Precision	Recall	F1 Score
Logistic Regression	0.7844	0.76	0.76	0.76
Gradient Boosting	0.8647	0.86	0.87	0.86
Extreme Gradient Boosting	0.8640	0.86	0.86	0.86
CAT Boosting	0.8704	0.89	0.89	0.89
Random Forest	0.8471	0.88	0.88	0.88
Light Gradient Boosting	0.8700	0.97	0.97	0.97

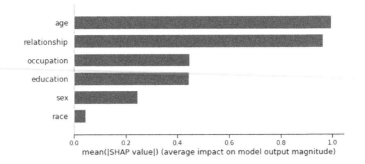

Fig. 3. Feature relevance plot for light gradient boosting classifier.

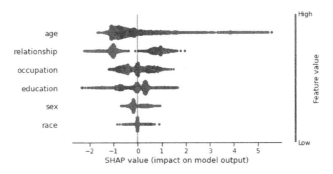

Fig. 4. SHAP beeswarm plot for light gradient boosting classifier.

education to a higher salary, the correlation based ML classifiers fail to make such observations. This result, while only a proof-of-concept, highlights the need of causal learning for artificial reasoning systems to obtain a human-like thinking. With ML-classifiers and current XAI systems providing explanations and predictions based on correlations, the addition of causal learning provides the additional layer of robustness to the explanations by providing feature relevance based on causation and not simply correlation. With future AI/ML systems required to be more robust against a variety of challenges, providing causal

Table 2. Average treatment effect estimation for all features.

Feature	Treatment Effect Estimation
Age	0.8078
Education	0.7976
Relationship	0.7255
Occupation	0.5015
Sex	0.4794
Race	0.1348

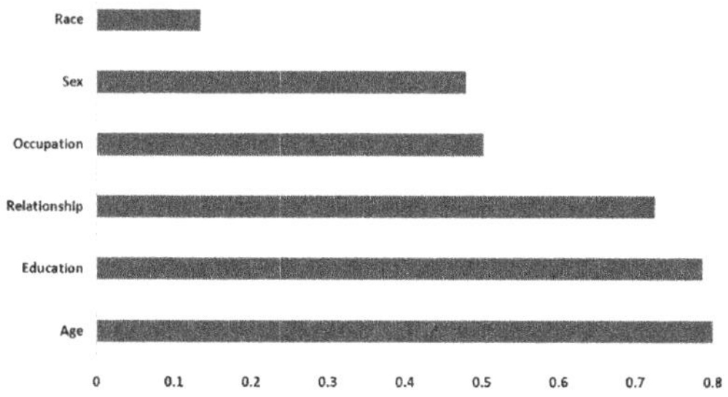

Fig. 5. Average treatment effect estimation for all the features.

explanations based on average treatment effect can provide these systems with the needed robustness and trustworthiness.

In this paper we have provided a novel comparison of causal features from an XAI perspective. This provides a more robust AI/ML model where trustworthiness is achieved via both causality and XAI. Even though XAI is a great approach for achieving trustworthiness in AI/ML systems, sometimes it is not sufficient. Thus, providing an extra layer of robustness to the models via causal learning is an easy and effective method to ensure the trustworthiness of these systems. Causal learning provides the first layer of fairness via bias detection within the data, whereas XAI provides the additional layer of the same for both the model and the data as a whole. We have provided a simple and efficient novel method to ensure the use of observational data for trustworthy AI/ML systems. This paper, simply presented an ad-hoc method for making AI/ML models trustworthy by applying explainability and causality to observational data. For datasets when the ground-truth is not present, causal graphs can be generated via causal discovery and compared to feature relevance from XAI. Directed causal graphs can display the features that are causally relevant for the predictions, and these causally relevant features can be directly compared to the features listed from correlation based explanations from XAI.

5   Conclusion

Artificial reasoning systems have come a long way in the past decade. For these systems to be robust and trustworthy, causality and explainability have to be integrated within them. Causal learning and explainability together can provide a robust system where fairness and bias detection & mitigation are achieved seamlessly. In this paper we have presented a novel new perspective of applying explainability and causality to observational data. For AI/ML systems using causal data the application of XAI via post-hoc methodologies can provide an extra layer of robustness to ensure fairness and trustworthiness.

References

1. Beckers, S.: Causal explanations and xai. arXiv preprint arXiv:2201.13169 (2022)
2. Busuioc, M.: Accountable artificial intelligence: holding algorithms to account. Public Adm. Rev. **81**(5), 825–836 (2021)
3. Chen, H., Harinen, T., Lee, J.Y., Yung, M., Zhao, Z.: Causalml: python package for causal machine learning. arXiv preprint arXiv:2002.11631 (2020)
4. Chou, Y.L., Moreira, C., Bruza, P., Ouyang, C., Jorge, J.: Counterfactuals and causability in explainable artificial intelligence: theory, algorithms, and applications. Inf. Fusion **81**, 59–83 (2022)
5. Cui, P., Athey, S.: Stable learning establishes some common ground between causal inference and machine learning. Nature Mach. Intell. **4**(2), 110–115 (2022)
6. Frye, C., Rowat, C., Feige, I.: Asymmetric shapley values: incorporating causal knowledge into model-agnostic explainability. Adv. Neural. Inf. Process. Syst. **33**, 1229–1239 (2020)
7. Gelman, A.: Causality and statistical learning (2011)
8. Gunning, D., Aha, D.: Darpa's explainable artificial intelligence (xai) program. AI Mag. **40**(2), 44–58 (2019)
9. Guo, R., Cheng, L., Li, J., Hahn, P.R., Liu, H.: A survey of learning causality with data: problems and methods. ACM Comput. Surv. (CSUR) **53**(4), 1–37 (2020)
10. Janzing, D., Minorics, L., Blöbaum, P.: Feature relevance quantification in explainable ai: a causal problem. In: International Conference on Artificial Intelligence and Statistics, pp. 2907–2916. PMLR (2020)
11. Lundberg, S.M., Lee, S.I.: A unified approach to interpreting model predictions. Advances in Neural Information Processing Systems 30 (2017)
12. Moraffah, R., Karami, M., Guo, R., Raglin, A., Liu, H.: Causal interpretability for machine learning-problems, methods and evaluation. ACM SIGKDD Explorations Newsl **22**(1), 18–33 (2020)
13. Pearl, J.: Causal inference in statistics: an overview. Stat. Surv. **3**, 96–146 (2009)
14. Pearl, J.: Theoretical impediments to machine learning with seven sparks from the causal revolution. arXiv preprint arXiv:1801.04016 (2018)
15. Pearl, J.: The seven tools of causal inference, with reflections on machine learning. Commun. ACM **62**(3), 54–60 (2019)
16. Peters, J., Janzing, D., Schölkopf, B.: Elements of causal inference: foundations and learning algorithms (2017)
17. Rawal, A., Mccoy, J., Rawat, D.B., Sadler, B., Amant, R.: Recent advances in trustworthy explainable artificial intelligence: status, challenges and perspectives. IEEE Trans. Artif. Intell. **1**(01), 1–1 (2021)

18. Ribeiro, M.T., Singh, S., Guestrin, C.: "Why should i trust you?" explaining the predictions of any classifier. In: Proceedings of the 22nd ACM SIGKDD International Conference on Knowledge Discovery and Data Mining, pp. 1135–1144 (2016)
19. Ribeiro, M.T., Singh, S., Guestrin, C.: Nothing else matters: model-agnostic explanations by identifying prediction invariance. arXiv preprint arXiv:1611.05817 (2016)
20. Sharma, A., Kiciman, E.: Dowhy: an end-to-end library for causal inference. arXiv preprint arXiv:2011.04216 (2020)
21. Shrikumar, A., Greenside, P., Kundaje, A.: Learning important features through propagating activation differences. In: Precup, D., Teh, Y.W. (eds.) Proceedings of the 34th International Conference on Machine Learning. Proceedings of Machine Learning Research, vol. 70, pp. 3145–3153. PMLR (06–11 Aug 2017)
22. Smith, S.C., Ramamoorthy, S.: Counterfactual explanation and causal inference in service of robustness in robot control. In: 2020 Joint IEEE 10th International Conference on Development and Learning and Epigenetic Robotics (ICDL-EpiRob), pp. 1–8. IEEE (2020)
23. Syrgkanis, V., et al.: Causal inference and machine learning in practice with econml and causalml: Industrial use cases at microsoft, tripadvisor, uber. In: Proceedings of the 27th ACM SIGKDD Conference on Knowledge Discovery & Data Mining, pp. 4072–4073 (2021)
24. Wang, H.X., Fratiglioni, L., Frisoni, G.B., Viitanen, M., Winblad, B.: Smoking and the occurence of Alzheimer's disease: cross-sectional and longitudinal data in a population-based study. Am. J. Epidemiol. 149(7), 640–644 (1999)
25. Xian, Y., Fu, Z., Muthukrishnan, S., De Melo, G., Zhang, Y.: Reinforcement knowledge graph reasoning for explainable recommendation. In: Proceedings of the 42nd International ACM SIGIR Conference on Research and Development in Information Retrieval, pp. 285–294 (2019)
26. Xu, S., et al.: Learning causal explanations for recommendation. In: The 1st International Workshop on Causality in Search and Recommendation (2021)
27. Yao, L., Chu, Z., Li, S., Li, Y., Gao, J., Zhang, A.: A survey on causal inference. ACM Trans. Knowl. Discovery Data (TKDD) 15(5), 1–46 (2021)

Evaluating Explainable AI (XAI) in Terms of User Gender and Educational Background

Samuel Reeder, Joshua Jensen, and Robert Ball[✉]

Weber State University, 3848 Harrison Blvd, Ogden, UT 84408, USA
{joshuajensen1,roberball}@weber.edu

Abstract. Artificial intelligence (AI) and machine learning (ML) have become ubiquitous tools in the modern era. As more technologies become dependent on AI and ML, there is a greater push to understand how to use Explainable AI (XAI) to help human users understand the underlying decision processes of the technology. We report on a laboratory-controlled experiment focused on trust and understanding comparing different types of XAI explanations with a recommendation system while controlling for participant gender and educational background. We found statistically significant interactions of both gender and educational background. As a result, we conclude that there is not one particular way to show explanations that is best for all audiences because both gender and the person's education and professional background play a part in determining their trust and understanding in the system. In addition, although a number of publications have promoted visual word clouds as a way to show XAI, our participants rejected that type of explanation and preferred textual explanations.

Keywords: Recommender Systems · Machine Learning · Artificial Intelligence · Usability Testing · Explainable AI

1 Introduction

In 1950 Alan Turing published his landmark paper titled "Computing Machinery and Intelligence" where he proposed the question "Can machines think?" [1]. Since then artificial intelligence (AI) has now become a part of everyday life in the modern world with AI-driven systems being developed all around us. The use of AI powered systems has taken many forms ranging from machines that play chess better than humans [2] to complex networks that drive cars [3].

For the purposes of this paper, unless specified, we will include both Machine Learning (ML) and Artificial Intelligence into one single label of "AI."

Of particular concern to many people in the private, public, and military sectors is the use of AI in recommendation systems. Recommendation systems are the primary drivers for billions of dollars annually. From Amazon.com to Google.com, recommendation engines suggest and steer billions of people to particular products or search results.

If Alan Turing asked if machines can think then we ask the following question: How do machines reach their conclusions, particularly in recommendation systems?

© The Author(s), under exclusive license to Springer Nature Switzerland AG 2023
H. Degen and S. Ntoa (Eds.): HCII 2023, LNAI 14050, pp. 286–304, 2023.
https://doi.org/10.1007/978-3-031-35891-3_18

This question is answered by the subfield of Explainable AI (XAI). Explanations for recommendations from recommendation systems are important for a number of reasons, from legal compliance, de-bugging the system, curiosity about how the system works, etc.

In our related works section we show that there has been a large amount of work done to create many different types of explanations. However, little work has been done to take these explanations and evaluate how effective they are with actual people.

In this paper we share the results of an in-depth study that compares how people empirically react to different types of XAI, particularly different types of textual explanations and word clouds. Specifically, the purpose of this research is to investigate how explanations in recommendation engines affects a user's trust and comprehension in a recommendation system.

We found that gender and educational background had an interactive effect on both trust and under-standing and that different explanations were preferred by different groups. However, the word cloud XAI was overwhelmingly rejected by all groups.

In other words, we conclusively found that different types of XAI are preferred based on gender and educational background. In particular, we found that women's trust and understanding of the explanations did not vary significantly based on educational background, but that men's trust and understanding of explanations did statistically differ based on their backgrounds.

Although the study focused on recommendation engines, the results most likely generalize to all XAI.

Explaining why a decision was made by a person is a daunting task and not easily explained [4]. A study of history shows that even with all or most of the facts present, different motivations and accompanying explanations are posited for why individuals or groups made the choices that they did. Research into how people make decisions is an active topic (e.g., [5] and [6]).

In addition, distrust in technology and online technologies is a particular problem in today's world. Recent research shows that trust in online content can be based on simple things like the graphics and structure of websites [7]. Also, distrust in content, like in Facebook with terms like "misinformation," is a problem for many users [8].

Given many people's mistrust and non-understanding of how most technologies work, we address the following question: How effective are XAI solutions for actual people? We will show in the related works section that extensive amounts of work has been put into creating AI and ML algorithms and creating accompanying XAI, but little research in comparison has been done in evaluating how effective XAI is for actual people.

In this paper we answer that question by reporting on trust and understanding in a laboratory-controlled experiment. We exposed users to an explainable recommendation system and gauged the effects of the explanations through a series of questions. We utilized three approaches to demonstrating the explanations: simple textual, technical textual, and visual explanations.

We particularly focused on how people's back-grounds (STEM [Science, Technology, Engineering, and Mathematics] vs non-STEM [e.g., humanities, arts, etc.]) and gender (male vs female) affected their trust and understanding of the explanations given by the recommendation system.

2 Related Works

The importance of XAI cannot be overstated. For ex-ample, Dattner, et al. explain in the Harvard Business Review that there are legal and ethical implications of using artificial intelligence-based systems to aid in the hiring process for businesses. The authors points out that since the underlying AI is not well understood it is unclear if these systems comply with nondiscrimination laws, the ADA (American with Disabilities Act), as well as others [9].

Another area where AI accountability is particularly important is when these systems are used for military applications. David Gunning and David W. Aha describe a system that can account for choices made as well as inform users of its shortcomings so that AI systems that could provide justification for the suggestions that were made. The purpose of this type of AI system is to provide a tool to the military that could help in making strategic choices while at the same time providing enough transparency to justify its use [10].

In the end, there are numerous examples that make the case that XAI is important and needed. Some ML algorithms, like neural networks, are not explainable and certain properties, such as the use of randomized neuron weights, as well as other factors contribute to this [11].

There are many other types of machine learning algorithms that suffer from this same issue in the con-text of comprehensibility. In general, the issue of comprehensibility in machine learning and AI is known as the "black box problem." In an exhaustive survey of this issue Guidotti, et al. defines the black box problem as follows: "In recent years, many accurate decision support systems have been constructed as black boxes, that is as systems that hide their in-ternal logic to the user. This lack of explanation constitutes both a practical and an ethical issue" [12].

There have been attempts to make black box ML algorithms more comprehensible. For example, by using decision trees, which are considered white box algorithms and are comprehensive, to mimic the behavior of neural networks output [13]. This can be difficult, but others have proposed solutions with pruning the nodes in decision trees to improve comprehensibility [14].

Others have proposed using the concept of a rule set. The idea is that a black box model could be explained by generating a set of rules that humans can understand that dictate a prediction for a given input [15]. Support Vector Machines (SVM) have also been used with the concept of a rule set (e.g., [16] and [17]). Another example of complex models that can be explained via a rule set is tree ensembles [18].

An interesting example of this type of explanation is given in the work of Xu et al. In this work a system that automatically generates captions describing an image is given. The system writes one word per pass over the picture. The algorithm provides an explanation for why each word in the caption is included by showing the portion of the picture that was used to generate the word [19].

Zhang, et al. present a survey of explainable recommendation systems. The paper breaks down XAI into two subgroups: the method of explanation and the models the generate them. The paper also breaks down the types of explanations into five categories: based on relevant users/items, feature based explanations, textual based explanations, visual explanations, and social explanations [20].

The key idea with sentiment analysis is to deter-mine if a user feels negatively or positively about a product. One of the challenges with doing this is a lack of labeled training data for recommendation systems to learn from. This problem is highlighted in by Guan, et al. They introduce a method for deriving a larger labeled set of training data for algorithms to train on. They use a semi-supervised model to add sentiment labels to unlabeled data [21].

There are many types of recommendation engines. A good overview of these systems can be found in [22]. At a high level, the idea is that a user will likely be interested in items that are similar to ones that they have indicated a preference for. Recommendation systems generally rely on prior knowledge about users and provide suggestions to the user based on that history.

Explanations are sometimes visual. The concept of a visual explanation is when a product is recommended and the justification is provided in a visual format. This can take the form of a picture or a picture accompanying a textual explanation.

Wu and Ester provide an example of this principle in action. They describe an algo-rithm called Factorized Latent ModEL (FLAME) that attempts to solve the problem of personalized latent aspect rating analysis. The FLAME model presents the explanation for the recommendation as a word cloud. The word clouds generated aims to give the user a sense of what features are most prominent for the recommended product [23].

Visual aids may also be used to help augment text-based explanations as shown in the work of Lin, et al. The authors provide a system that pairs images of products with a sentence explaining the recommendation [24].

Another suggested presentation idea for XAI is by using graph-based models. He, et al. propose a system that utilizes a tripartite graph to rank aspect opinion data about items based on users' reviews. This graph is used to create the explanations that ac-company recommendations. This approach was de-vised to address the shortcomings of matrix factorization models that are often used in collaborative filtering recommendation systems [25].

There are numerous other papers that suggest different ways to produce XAI for various ML algorithms. For example, the use of gradient boosted decision trees combined with matrix factorization they produce recommendations as well as generating hu-man comprehensible explanations for them [30] to various deep learning neural networks (e.g., [26] and [27]).

It is clear from the above works that there is a lot of interest in explainable rec-ommendations. The overarching assumption is that that explainable recommendations are valuable because they increase a user's trust in the recommendation system. It is understandable why many people make that particular assumption. However it shouldn't simply be assumed. In the rest of this paper we will present re-search that attempts to provide some verification for this claim.

Our experiment was heavily impacted by the description text-based explainable recommendation systems as was shown in [21]. The concept of using the sentiment found in reviews to generate explanations is a good basis for comparing to other types of explanations. We also used the concept of using a word cloud as a means of explanation a recommendation as a form to incorporate some visual explanations. We used the technique from [23].

The recommendation system strategies that have been discussed so far represent the foundation of recommendation systems. In practice, these strategies are mixed and combined with many forms of advanced machine learning to create reliable recommendations. One of the more famous examples of this can be found in the "Netflix Prize" competition. In 2006 the video streaming company Netflix announced a coding challenge. The premise was that Netflix wanted to see if a team could develop an algorithm better than their Cinematch recommendation system. Any team who could produce a system that made a 10% or more improvement over the Cine-match system would be awarded one million dollars. The winning team that to beat the native Netflix recommendation engine had many different statistical and machines learning algorithms were blended to get the improved performance [24].

There have been many papers published on creating XAI and creating frameworks that provide direction for explanations. Gilpin, Leilani H., et al. provide a general survey of 87 XAI papers for numerous types of ML algorithms. They conclude that "for machine learning systems to achieve wider acceptance among a skeptical populace, it is crucial that such systems be able to provide or permit satisfactory explanations of their decisions" [25].

One fair question to ask about these systems is can these complicated systems be decomposed such that individual recommendations be explained in a meaningful way? Furthermore, if they can be explained, does it matter to the users of the recommendation?

The goal of this paper is to provide some insight into the question of whether XAI matters or not to the user.

3   Experiment and Methodology

As stated above, the purpose of this research is to investigate how explanations in recommendation engines affects a user's trust and comprehension in a recommendation system based on their gender and educational and professional background. To do this we designed an experiment that exposes participants to a series of recommendations where each recommendation is paired with a collection of explanations. After viewing each recommendation, a participant was asked to respond to a series of questions.

The purpose of the questions was to gather information about how trust and comprehension develop over time as the participant progresses through the experiment. After viewing all the recommendations, the participants were asked to respond to a final set of questions.

3.1   Experimental Format

The experiment was delivered via website to each participant. There were three distinct parts: The tutorial stage, the recommendations stage, and the final survey.

The purpose of the tutorial section was twofold. First, to make sure that each participant was familiar with the mechanics of the experiment. The tutorial was designed with the goal of answering any questions a participant might have about how the experiment was to be taken. Each participant was given a phone number to call in the event they encountered any issues. The tutorial was delivered in the form of a video that each participant was invited to watch. The video presented a live walk-through of the pages in the tutorial section as well as commentary on the purpose of the experiment. The provided commentary and instructions were carefully designed not to introduce any bias towards our research questions.

During the tutorial, the participants were told that they were helping to validate the performance of a recommendation engine designed to recommend cookie recipes. To help with this task, participants were introduced to a current user of the recommendation software named "Steve," who was introduced via his user profile. The profile shows a list of Steve's favorite types of cookies, a list of his favorite ingredients, and a final list showing the names of Steve's favorite recipes that he had found through the recommendation software. Participants were told that they were supposed to imagine that they were Steve while they were viewing the recommendations and explanations. The purpose of this was to remove the need for each participant to have to create their own profile with enough data to overcome the cold-start problem.

The main feature of the tutorial was showing the participant how they were supposed to view recommendations as well as how to take the survey that accompanies each recommendation. During this part of the tutorial a demonstration recommendation was shown, each button on the screen explained, with emphasis given to the buttons that show the explanations. The survey was explained question by question with an explanation given for what individual questions mean as well as how the responses are to be input. This also included the necessary IRB disclaimers, and explanations required by our institution's IRB.

The last stage of the experiment involved collecting demographic data about each participant. Each participant was asked to provide their gender, age, and status as a technical or non-technical person. The definition of a technical person was given as any person who meets one of more of the criteria listed below:

- Earned a degree in a STEM field,
- Currently enrolled in a university level computer science program,
- Or currently employed in a STEM related job.

Each step of the tutorial was shown in the recorded video, but participants were required to visit each page of the tutorial section to make sure that they understood the content of the video as well.

3.2   The Recommendation State

During the actual experiment, users viewed 25 different recommendations. Each recommendation had three explanations given as justifications for the recommendation. An example of how recommendations appear is given in Fig. 1 below.

Participants were encouraged to view all the explanations for each recommendation, but the testing software did not require it. After each recommendation, participants were required to answer six questions.

Fig. 1. An Example of an experimental recommendation. This is the layout of an experimental recommendation. Each recommendation displays a picture of the recommended cookie. Meta data about the cookie given. Users can click on buttons bellow the nutrition facts section to see directions for the recipe and ingredients (not shown in the figure). Explanations are viewed by clicking the buttons on the right-hand side of the screen.

The last step of the experiment involved asking participants to give some feedback on the recommendation software. This feedback was collected in the form of four open-ended questions. The purpose of this last section was to gather information about each participant's perspective on key elements of the experiment. The hope was that this feedback could provide some insight and context to the results of the experiment.

3.3   The Recommendation System

The recommendation system used in this experiment provided recommendations about cookie recipes to its users. The recipe data was extracted from an online recipe website. For each recommendation, three types of explanations were provided to the user. These explanations are categorized as simple, technical, and visual.

A simple explanation represents a basic type of explanation for a recommendation that a participant should be familiar with from using real recommendation engines. A simple explanation is one to two sentences long. The goal of the explanation is to show the user how the recommendation ties back to Steve's profile. Figure 2 and Fig. 3 give examples of simple explanations that were used in the experiment.

The intent of this recommendation type is to provide an explanation that is more understandable and substantive than something like a star rating that you might encounter when looking at suggested products like on Amazon.com. The other goal of the simple explanation is to be basic enough that anyone would be able to understand it and connect it to Steve's profile. This type of explanation was inspired by some of the papers related works section, specifically [21].

This recipe is recommended to you because it is one of the highest rated cookies containing chocolate.

Fig. 2. An example of a simple explanation for "Carmel Filled Chocolate Cookies".

This recipe is recommended to you because it is a highly rated oatmeal cookie recipe, this type of cookies matches one of your favorites.

Fig. 3. Another example of a simple explanation given for a recipe called "Delicious Raspberry Oatmeal Cookie Bars."

The technical explanations build off the simple explanations by attempting to give some insight into how the recommendation engine may have generated the explanation by exposing the internal mechanism of the software. These explanations are still text based but provide an additional technical vantage point. Figure 4 and Fig. 5 provide examples of these explanations.

Users who are similar to you gave this recipe an average star ratting of 4.9. The most common positive feature of this recipe was the carmel center of the cookie. This feature was extracted using a sentence level analysis of reviews from users most similar to you.

Fig. 4. An example of a technical explanation. This is the technical explanation given for the recipe "Carmel Filled Chocolate cookies."

Users who are similar to you gave this recipe an average star rating of 4.7. The most common positive feature of this recipe was how surprised other users were at the inclusion of turkey. This feature was extracted using a sentence level analysis of reviews from users most similar to you.

Fig. 5. Another example of a technical explanation.

The motivation for this explanation type stems from research around feature sentiment-based explanations such as those described in [21]. The other motivating factor is to provide the participants some signals about different types of data and analysis strategies that could have been used to generate the explanation. For instance, the mention of similar users hints at the use of some type of collaborative filtering method. The last sentence of each explanation gives a clue that some type of natural language processing might have been used as well.

The last type of explanation were visual explanations. For this explanation type we took inspiration from [23] and used word clouds as visual explanation.

There are some draw backs to this approach. For instance, the word clouds do not do a great job of associating a sentiment with the features. Each of the words on its own could hold positive or negative sentiment for a participant and it is not clear what the sentiment of reviews that generated the world cloud are for the emphasized features.

3.4   Experimental Mechanics

For the purposes of experimentation and focusing on evaluating the explanations, each recommendation and the accompanying explanations were hard coded. This was so that the system used in the experiment would not introduce any additional variables to the experiment.

The hard-coded set of recommendations allowed the experiment to focus on the research questions without concern over recommendation variance or the accuracy of programmatically generated recommendation. If the experimental recommendation system generated a new set of recommendations for each participant there is no way to guarantee that each participant would have the same experience.

As mentioned above, the premise of the experiment given to the participant is that they were being asked to help validate a recommendation engine that gives recommendations about cookie recipes.

The goal of presenting this scenario to participants was to encourage them to pay attention while at the same time mask the primary purpose of the experiment. Since the experiment is aimed at gauging trust, we presented the experiment in a way that provided as little bias as possible where the software is concerned. The hope was that by asking the participants to validate the system it will give them some feeling of obligation to view at least some of the explanations.

The open nature of the experiment was meant to give each participant the opportunity for their trust and understand of the system to develop as organically as possible.

3.5   False Explanations

One of the key features of the experimental recommendation system was that five of the twenty-five recommendations provided false explanations. At a high level the purpose of these false explanations was to test participants to see if being presented with false explanations for an otherwise correct recommendation had an impact on their trust and comprehension.

For a recommendation that has false explanations each of the three types of explanations are explanations that are for a different recipe. Figures 6 and 7 show a set of false recommendations.

This recipe is recommended to you because it is a highly rated pulled pork recipe.

Fig. 6. An example of a false simple explanation. This simple explanation was given for a recipe called Beth's Spicy Oatmeal Raisin Cookies.

Users who are similar to you gave this recipe an average star rating of 4.7. The most common positive feature of this recipe was how surprised other users were at the inclusion of turkey. This feature was extracted using a sentence level analysis of reviews from users most similar to you.

Fig. 7. An example of a false technical explanation. This technical explanation was given for a recipe called Beth's Spicy Oatmeal Raisin Cookies.

The false explanations shown in Figs. 6 and 7 were inspired from a pulled pork recipe. The goal of these false explanations is to give the impression that the software was experiencing a bug.

One of the assumptions that the experiment had is that each participant has some level of trust in, and understanding of, recommendation engines. False explanations were given to provide a way to better understand how explanations were changing participants trust and understanding.

The other purpose of the false explanations was to provide a check to verify if the participants were paying attention to the explanations. The false explanations were obviously wrong so when analyzing the results if participants did not indicate that they had seen some questionable data then we could conclude that they had not read the explanations.

The false explanations were also important in measuring trust. Specifically, we tested this is by attempting to establish trust in the recommendations and then challenge that trust with a false explanation. To do this the experimental system presented the first five recipe recommendations with true explanations. The hope is that the participant would develop some level of trust while viewing these recommendations. Then on the sixth recipe recommendation the participant was given a set of false explanations. After that the remaining 4 false explanations were given at different intervals to the participants so as to appear to be random bugs in the system.

3.6 Measuring Trust and Understanding

In order to measure trust and comprehension, participants were presented with a series of questions. After each recommendation a participant was required to give an answer to six questions. The first four questions were based on a Likert scale and follow (The bold words were part of what was presented to the users):

- How did the recommendation you just saw affect your **trust** in the recommendation software?

- Based on **all** the recommendation you have seen **up to this point**, how much do you **trust** the recommendation software currently?
- How did the explanation of the recommendation affect your **understanding** of the recommendation software?
- Based on **all** the recommendation you have seen **up to this point**, how much do your **understand** the recommendation currently?

The general idea with these questions is that over time the different values reported can be interpreted as a trend for how the participants' trust changes over time. This change in time is a critical measure of participants use of the system coupled with the false explanations.

The last two questions, which were multiple choice, revisit trust and understanding by asking the participant about which explanation method had the most impact on their understanding and trust. The second to last question was, "Which explanation increases **trust** the most?" with the following options: Simple Explanation, Technical Explanation, Visual Explanation or None of Them. The last question was, "Which explanation did you find the most useful when trying to **understand** the recommendation?" with the same options as the previous question.

The purpose of these two questions is to get a sense of how participants were responding to the different types of explanations.

In addition to the multiple-choice questions, we collected quantitative data about the behavior of the participants as they interacted with the recipe recommendations. We recorded how many times the users clicked on each of the buttons on each page.

At the end of the experiment each participant was asked to provide qualitative data by giving feedback about the experiment by answering four open-ended questions about the recommendation engine in general. The questions asked about their final levels of trust, understanding, inconsistencies that they found, and asked if they understood how the recommendation engine worked internally.

The experiment had sixty participants after erroneous submissions were removed. As previously mentioned, the goal was to get an even distribution of male and female and well as between technical (STEM) and non-technical people.

Table 1 summarizes the population of the participants.

Table 1. Participants' demographics.

Gender	Total	Technical (STEM)	Non-Technical
Male	30	15	15
Female	30	15	15

4 Results

The results of this experiment show that trust and understanding are clearly affected by the presence of explanations. To show this we show the analysis of each set of questions presented to the participants.

For all analysis where a P value is used we chose to consider all results with a P value less than 0.05 as significant. This value was selected previous to data analysis.

4.1 Trust

The first survey question states, "How did the recommendation you just saw affect your trust in the recommendation software?" The participants were asked to answer this question using a Likert scale of 1–5 where 1 represented a significant reduction in trust and 5 indicated a significant increase. The first thing to note is the general trend of how the participants answered this question. This trend is given below in Fig. 8.

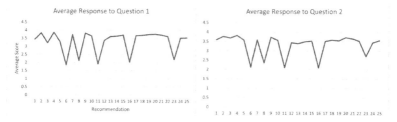

Fig. 8. Average responses to question 1 and question 2. The graph shows the responses to survey question 1 and question 2 for each recommendation averaged over all the participants.

The main feature of this graph is that is shows that false recommendations did affect trust. This can be seen by the dips at recommendations 6, 8, 11, 16, and 23 which used false explanations. Each time a false recommendation was encountered, on average participants reported that they had less trust in the recommendation software. This leads to the following question: Does the presence of false explanations damage trust over time? Fig. 8, which summarizes question 2 on the right, measuring trust over time gives some insight into this.

Survey question two states, "Based on all the recommendations you have seen up to this point, how much do you trust the recommendation software?" We can see from Fig. 8 that the trends in question two follow nearly identically the trend in question one. This leads to the conclusion that exposure to faulty recommendations does not impact trust negatively over the long term.

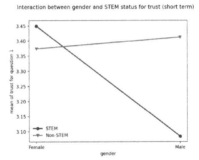

Fig. 9. Statistically significant interaction between gender and STEM status of participants for question one.

Performing a two-way ANOVA on gender and STEM status for question one results in a statistically significant interaction with an F score of $F(11.1979, 1) = 0.0144$. The interaction is visualized in Fig. 9. The interaction in the graph shows insight into the difference in the genders relative to trust. The graph shows that, on average, men have a larger variance in their trust than women do, but both genders are affected by their educational and professional background. Specifically, men's trust factor is negatively affected and women's trust is positively affected by their STEM background, but non-STEM participants had approximately the same amount of trust regardless of gender.

Performing a two-way ANOVA on gender and STEM status for question 2 also results in a statistically significant interaction with an F score of $F(11.1979, 1) = 0.0144$. The interaction is visualized in Fig. 10.

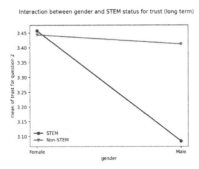

Fig. 10. Statistically significant interaction between gender and STEM status of participants for question two.

It is important to also note that there is an interaction between participants' STEM status and their trust as affected by false explanations. Performing a two-way ANOVA on STEM status and trust found results in an interaction with an F-score of $F(9.1811, 1) = 0.0025$. The interaction is shown in Fig. 11. Specifically, participants' trust not in the STEM field had a greater variance based on bad or false explanations.

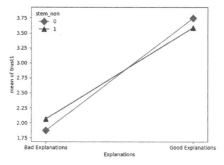

Fig. 11. Statistically significant interaction between STEM status of participant and explanation type for question 1.

4.2 Understanding

Questions three and four relate to understanding. These trends are shown in Fig. 12.

Question three states, "How did the explanation of the recommendation affect your understanding of the software?" The main result from this trend is that after participants see a false recommendation that their average understanding decreases. The highest average understanding occurs during the first five recommendations. Interestingly, after each recommendation that has a false explanation the understanding of future recommendations is impacted. This is especially true after recommendation 11. It appears that the false explanations create lingering confusion about how correct explanations were being generated.

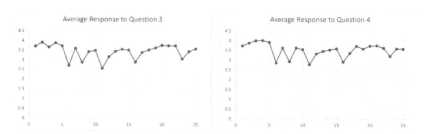

Fig. 12. Average response to question 3 and question 4. The graph shows the response to survey question 3 and question 4 for each recommendation averaged over all the participants.

The trend for question four is similar to that of question three. Question four was "Based on all the recommendations you have seen up to this point, how much do you understand the recommendation software?".

Performing a two-way ANOVA for STEM status and gender for question three and four resulted in a statistically significant interactions with a F score of $F(5.3545, 1) = 0.0003$ for question three and an F score of $F(4.1216, 1) = 0.0425$ for question four. The interactions are visualized in Fig. 13.

These results are consistent with the two-way ANOVA results from questions one and two. This leads to the conclusion that for both trust and understanding an important factor was the interaction of STEM status and gender. In other words, men and women react differently in regard to trust and understanding to explanations based on their educational and professional background.

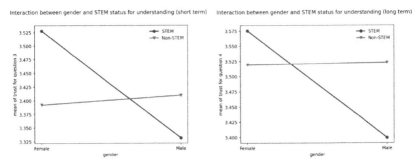

Fig. 13. Statistically significant interaction between gender and STEM status of participants for question 3 and question 4 (left and right respectively).

4.3 Explanation Types

We now analyze the explanation types. There were three types of explanations: simple text, technical text, and visual word clouds.

Question five asks, "Which Explanation increases your trust the most?" Participants are asked to select which of the three types of explanations helped the most or if none of them were helpful.

Table 2 shows the results of a statistically significant Chi-squared analysis for question 5.

Table 2. Question 5 (explanation trust) chi-squared analysis results.

Gender	Female		Male	
Stem	No	Yes	No	Yes
Simple	194	203	180	191
Technical	196	104	116	149
Visual	9	14	7	17
None	67	62	74	71
P Value	0.00034			

Table 2 shows a summary of how each participant answered question 5, broken down by gender and STEM status.

The visual word cloud explanation was viewed by participants as far less effective at increasing trust when compared to the simple and technical explanations. Despite this, it is interesting to note that both men and women who were considered STEM preferred the visual explanations when compared to their not STEM counterparts.

For the technical text explanations, we see that non-technical women preferred the technical explanation over STEM women. In men it was the opposite, STEM men preferred the technical explanations more than non-STEM men.

Simple text explanations are preferred roughly the same between men and women as well as their STEM and non-STEM groups. These findings continue the theme that the main factors affecting participant trust and understanding is the interaction of gender and STEM status that is present in the findings from the first 4 questions.

These patterns also appear, with some variation in the results of the Chi-squared analysis of question six. Survey question six states, "which explanation did you find the most useful when trying to understand the recommendation?" Table 3 shows the results of the analysis.

Again, we see that the visual word cloud explanations were the least preferred type when participants were trying to understand the recommendation software. We again see that STEM women preferred the visual explanations vs non-STEM women. However, for the men, we see that non-STEM men prefer the visual explanations more than STEM men did. In terms of the technical explanations, the results show that STEM men preferred technical explanations far more than non-STEM men. This preference is reversed for the STEM/non-STEM women. Interestingly, non-STEM women found the simple explanation much more useful than STEM women did, meanwhile, the men were roughly even as they were in question five.

Table 3. Question 6 (explanation understanding) Chi-squared analysis results.

Gender	Female		Male	
Stem	No	Yes	No	Yes
Simple	181	106	140	148
Technical	213	189	115	208
Visual	15	36	62	18
None	57	52	60	54
P Value	5.20e-15			

4.4 Qualitative Results

The concepts of trust and understanding can be hard to quantify. Because of this, the comments made by participants provide useful insight into the results in the previous section.

The final section of the survey asked open-ended questions. The first question asked participants about which explanation did the best job of increasing their trust and why. Of the STEM females who replied, the consensus was that the simple textual explanations were best. A few examples responses included conciseness, clarity, and simplicity as to their reasons.

There were a few responses where STEM females note that it was a combination of the simple and technical explanations but only stated that the technical explanations were best at increasing their trust.

Non-STEM females who responded were evenly split between the simple and technical. In general, there was concern that the simple textual explanation was too simple or condescending, while the technical textual explanation was sometimes more detailed than needed.

This feedback is consistent with the outcome of the Chi-squared analysis of question 5. It also gives valuable context to what participants may have been thinking as they went through the experiment.

For STEM males the responses were more split. However, the participants who responded seemed to favor the simple textual explanations as well.

Non-STEM males were also somewhat divided between technical and simple explanations, but they leaned more towards the simple explanations.

The second open-ended question asked participants to indicate which explanation method was most helpful in understanding the recommendations and asked the participants to give their best guess as to how the software was generating recommendations.

STEM females who responded preferred the technical explanations generally. Almost all the participants who responded were able to give a high-level description of how hybrid recommendation systems work.

Non-STEM females also tended to prefer the technical explanations.

STEM males had a response like the females in that they generally also preferred technical explanations. This group was also able to provide well educated guesses for how the software might be working.

Non-STEM males who responded, were more divided between technical and simple explanations being the best for increasing understanding. Most of the non-STEM males who responded were able to make a good guess, but some of them were less specific and in one case, a participant admits that they did not know.

4.5 Summary of Results

We have shown that the trust and understanding users have in recommendation engines is influenced by the presence of explanations. Specifically, we found that there is an interaction between a participant's education and professional background (STEM status) and their gender.

We also found that the presence of explanations was impactful to a user's trust of the system overall. The consistent appearance of the STEM status and gender interaction across the first four questions provides an explanation of what factors are important in influencing users trust and explanation in a recommendation system.

We also found that different explanation methods have different impacts on participants based on their STEM status and gender. In general, we found that simple explanations were best at increasing trust while technical explanations were best at aiding in understanding the recommendation system. It was also shown that visual explanations, as they were expressed in the experiment, were by far the least useful for increasing trust and understanding.

5 Conclusion

In this paper we report on an experiment to understand how trust and understanding in a recommendation engine are affected by explainable AI (XAI). We specifically tested 60 people divided into different categories, namely STEM status (educational and professional STEM background) and gender, which resulted in 15 people per category. Based on related works, we also tested two text-based explanations and one visual explanation, specifically a word cloud. We also introduced false explanations, explanations that were obviously wrong, for the purpose of more deeply seeing if explanations mattered to participants.

We found the following summarized results:

Gender and STEM status had an interactive effect on both trust and understanding.

Different explanations were preferred by different groups; however, the visual word cloud was overwhelmingly rejected.

The results section overwhelmingly show that the gender and STEM status of the participant were important factors in determining trust and understanding. In other words, there is not one particular way to show explanations that is best for all audiences because both gender and the person's education and professional background play a part in determining their trust and understanding in the system.

In addition, although a number of publications have promoted visual word clouds as a way to show XAI, our participants rejected that type of explanation and preferred textual explanations.

Acknowledgments. This work was supported in part by a grant from AFRL contract #FA 8650–20-F-1956.

References

1. Turing, A.: Computing machinery and intelligence. Mind **59**, 433–460 (1950)
2. Silver, D., et al.: A general reinforcement learning algorithm that masters chess, shogi, and Go through self-play. Science **362**(6419), 1140–1144 (2007)
3. S. Grigorescu, et al.: A survey of deep learning techniques for autonomous driving. J. Field Robot **37**, 21918 (2019)
4. Klein, G.: Sources of power: how people make decisions. MIT press (2017)
5. Reyna, V.: How people make decisions that involve risk: a dual-processes approach. Curr. Dir. Psychol. Sci. **13**(2), 60–66 (2004)
6. Glöckner, A., Betsch, T.: Do people make decisions under risk based on ignorance? an empirical test of the priority heuristic against cumulative prospect theory. Organ. Behav. Hum. Decis. Process. **107**(1), 75–95 (2008)
7. Seckler, M., et al.: Trust and distrust on the web: user experiences and website characteris-tics. Comput. Hum. Behav. **45**, 39–50 (2015)
8. Cheng, Y., Zifei, F.: Encountering misinformation online: antecedents of trust and dis-trust and their impact on the intensity of Facebook use. Online Inf. Rev. (2020)

9. Dattner, B., et al.: The legal and ethical implications of using AI in hiring. Harvard Business Review, vol. 25 (2019)
10. Gunning, D., Aha, D.: DARPA's explainable artificial intelligence (XAI) program. AI Mag. **40**(2), 44–58 (2019)
11. Cao, W., et al.: A review on neural networks with random weights. Neurocomputing **275**, 278–287 (2018)
12. Craven, M., Shavlik, J.: Extracting tree-structured representations of trained networks, In: Proceedings of the Conference on Advances in Neural Information Processing System, pp. 24–30 (1996)
13. Boz, O.: Extracting decision trees from trained neural networks. In: Proceedings of the 8th ACM SIGKDD International Conference on Knowledge Discovery and Data Mining, pp. 456–461 (2002)
14. Augasta, M., Kathirvalavakumar, T.: Reverse engineering the neural networks for rule extraction in classification problems. Neural Process. Lett. **35**(2), 131–150 (2012)
15. Barakat, N., Bradley, A.P.: Rule extraction from support vector machines: a review. Neurocomputing **74**(1), 178–190 (2010)
16. Martens, D., et al.: Comprehensible credit scoring models using rule extraction from support vector machines. Eur. J. Oper. Res. **183**(3), 1466–1476 (2007)
17. Deng, H.: Interpreting tree ensembles with intrees. Int. J. Data Sci. Analytics **7**(4), 277–287 (2019)
18. Barakat, N., Bradley, A.P.: Rule extraction from support vector machines: a review. Neurocomputing **74**, 178–190 (2010)
19. Xu, K., et al.: Show, attend and tell: Neural image caption generation with visual attention. In: Proceedings of the International Conference on Machine Learning, pp. 2048–2057 (2015)
20. Zhang, Y., Xu, C.: Explainable recommendation: a survey and new perspectives. arXiv preprint arXiv:1804.11192 (2018)
21. Guan, X., et al.: Attentive aspect modeling for review-aware recommendation. ACM Trans. Info. Sys. (TOIS) **37**(3), 1–27 (2019)
22. Aggarwal, C.: Recommender Systems: The Textbook. Springer (2016). https://doi.org/10.1007/978-3-319-29659-3
23. Zhang, Y., et al.: Explicit factor models for explainable recommendation based on phrase-level sentiment analysis. In: Proceedings of the 37th International ACM SIGIR Conference on Research & Development in Information Retrieval (2014)
24. Lin, Y., et al.: Explainable outfit recommendation with joint outfit matching and comment generation. IEEE Trans. Knowl. Data Eng. **32**(8), 1502–1516 (2020)
25. He, X., et al.: Trirank: Review-aware explainable recommendation by modeling aspects. In: Proceedings of the 24th ACM International on Conference on Information and Knowledge Management (2015)
26. Wang, X, et al.: TEM: Tree-enhanced Embedding Model for Explainable Recommendation. In: Proceedings of the 2018 World Wide Web Conference (WWW 2018) (2018)
27. Wang, N., et al.: Explainable recommendation via multi-task learning in opinionated text data. In: The 41st International ACM SIGIR Conference on Research & Development in Information Retrieval (SIGIR 2018), pp. 165–174 (2018)
28. Seo, S., et al.: Interpretable convolutional neural networks with dual local and global attention for review rating prediction. In: Proceedings of the Eleventh ACM Conference on Recommender Systems (2017)
29. Koren, Y., et al.: Matrix factorization techniques for recommender systems. Computer **42**(8), 30–37 (2009)
30. Leilani, G., et al.: Explaining explanations: an overview of interpretability of machine learning. In: 2018 IEEE 5th International Conference on Data Science and Advanced Analytics (DSAA). IEEE (2018)

AI Explainability, Interpretability, Fairness, and Privacy: An Integrative Review of Reviews

Aimee Kendall Roundtree[(✉)] [iD]

Texas State University, San Marcos, TX 78666, USA
akr@txstate.edu

Abstract. This integrative review incorporates findings from reviews on AI explainability, interpretability, fairness, and privacy to synthesize and understand the concepts. There is synergy between these concepts. Increasing explainability, interpretability, and privacy might help increase fairness. Explainability is necessary to ensure AI is interpretable, fair, and private AI. AI cannot be fair if it is incomprehensible or does not involve consent. Explainable and interpretable AI affords transparency to help counteract biases. This review integrates knowledge and applicability of results of significant studies to inform practice. Human and non-human coding was used for interpretation and analysis. A total of 42 reviews were included in the integrative review. The four domains converged often regarding the need for human-centeredness, trustworthiness, and transparency. Although real-world implementation was a persistent theme for all domains, global models, transfer learning, neural and genetic networks, and machine and federated learning were the strategies most mentioned. These strategies rely on metaphorical and deductive logic that risks underfitting, overfitting, and untethering from real-world grounding and complexity. The review significantly contributes to new thinking by integrating all conceptual findings. Overall, consensus definitions are needed on all terms, as are multi-disciplinary and multi-perspectival analyses.

Keywords: explainability · interpretability · fairness · privacy · reviews

1 Introduction

This integrative review incorporates findings from reviews on AI explainability, interpretability, fairness, and privacy to synthesize and understand the concepts. AI explainability, interpretability, fairness, and privacy are interrelated concepts of great interest to AI developers and policymakers. Explainability is the active part of the learning model that can clarify the inner workings of the model to the point where users can understand why or how it reaches conclusions [1, 2]. Interpretability is the extent to which a learning model makes sense on its face and a general understanding of how it works [1, 2]. Explainability and interpretability are achieved through methods that help humans comprehend and trust output [3]. Fairness is sought by using mathematical tools to avoid discrimination when algorithms make decisions [4]. However, achieving fairness to individuals is different than fairness to groups, particularly when using quantitative

© The Author(s), under exclusive license to Springer Nature Switzerland AG 2023
H. Degen and S. Ntoa (Eds.): HCII 2023, LNAI 14050, pp. 305–317, 2023.
https://doi.org/10.1007/978-3-031-35891-3_19

approaches [5]. Privacy includes limitations on data collection, use, quality, purpose, accountability, and participation [6]. The European Union's General Data Protection Regulations are currently the most comprehensive set of laws requiring privacy and security through upholding the right to explanation, fairness, human oversight, robustness, and security [6]. These laws demonstrate the interrelatedness of explainability, interpretability, fairness, and privacy. They also illustrate the rhetorical challenges of holding non-human agents like algorithms to human ethical standards [7, 8].

AI models use consumer and social media data, raising questions about privacy and ownership. AI fairness attempts to correct algorithmic bias in automated decision processes. Explainable AI helps humans comprehend and trust the results and output created by machine learning, and interpretability helps increase explainability. There is synergy between these concepts. Increasing privacy, interpretability, explainability might help increase fairness. Explainability and interpretability are necessary to ensure fair and private AI. AI cannot be fair if it is incomprehensible or does not involve consent. Explainability and interpretability afford transparency to help counteract biases. Users are wary of automated technologies that obtain and use their data without consent, transparency, or clarity. While public knowledge about AI and algorithms is generally low, the areas where AI has an impact—including health, justice, commerce, and politics—make a big impact on public life, and human control, dignity and fairness have been found as important to the public as is AI accuracy [9]. The public considers trade-offs between privacy concerns and perceived social, persona, and reciprocal benefits when opting-in and adopting AI intentions [10]. Understanding the state of the field on AI explainability, interpretability, fairness, and privacy is important to human factors surrounding implementations of AI technology. As the technology pervades more aspects of human life, it becomes increasingly important to uphold the technology to standards that would increase their responsibility and trustworthiness.

This review will synthesize the findings from reviews about AI explainability, interpretability, fairness, and privacy to categorize and translate the mathematical and programming strategies in terms of their approach and logical assumptions underpinning the approaches. Natural language rhetorical categories such as deduction (or inference based on general or overall premises), induction (or inference based on a local observation), and abduction (or inference based on intuition) underpin computational logical strategies, and these similarities are important to identify as they are more intuitive and accessible for consumption and use by programmers in training, the public, and policymakers [11]. This review integrates knowledge and applicability of results of significant studies to inform practice. It also uses rhetorical terms to help synthesize how the articles explain the objectives, strategies, and evaluation methods for AI explainability, interpretability, fairness, and privacy.

2 Methods

Methods included searching major databases using keywords (such as AI, artificial intelligence, explainability, explainable, interpretability, fairness, fair, privacy, survey, review, etc.) in the titles of articles. These terms were used, and the term list were extended as new articles revealed additional concepts. The key term list reached saturation when article abstracts yielded no new search terms Sources were downloaded from databases, and findings were organized in spreadsheets. We eliminated duplicates, manuscripts in languages other than English, and manuscripts for which the keywords were not the manuscript focus. Data were analyzed using human and natural language processing coding.

Integrative literature reviews require systematic search and analysis processes. Searches were conducted in Scopus, ScienceDirect, Web of Science, PubMed, ERIC, IEEE Xplore, ACM, ERIC, JSTOR, and Google Scholar, which cover cross-disciplinary peer-reviewed research. Abstracts and methods sections were scanned for article focus. Articles were included only if the title, abstract, or methods section self-designated as a review. Peer reviewed articles were included; theses, manuscripts in languages other than English, and inaccessible articles were excluded. Articles with a primary focus on the subject matter at hand were included. Focus was determined by searching for the keywords within the article; keywords must have occupied the top ten percent of reoccurring themes and terms in the article to be included. Frequencies were determined using Orange.si., an open-source machine learning and data visualization tool that builds data analysis workflows using a large, diverse toolbox. Data was extracted using Microsoft Excel for extracting and organizing the content that provided definitions, objectives, strategies, problems, and evaluations of strategies used for AI explainability, interpretability, fairness, and privacy reported in each article. The spreadsheet facilitated machine learning data analysis.

Human and non-human coding was used for interpretation and analysis. Using text mining in reviews can help reduce workload and streamline screening [12]. Human coding included three iterations of coding and close reading that took place at three different time periods over the course of three months—one open coding iteration to extract content by definitions, objectives, strategies, problems and evaluation strategies, another to confirm extraction and assign alignment with rhetorical terms, and yet another to confirm the rhetorical codes. Orange.si was used to verify foci of content. Orange was used to create a corpus of text documents tagged with categories (i.e., definitions, objectives, strategies, problems, evaluation techniques). Orange was also used to preprocess the text, including removing stop words, numbers, URLs and other nonessential terms. Orange tracked n-grams, or shared text strings, ranging in length from two to five terms. Orange facilitated using term frequency-inverse document frequency, TF-IDF, which measures how relevant words are to a document in a collection of documents. It also was enlisted for topic modelling, which analyzes text data to determine cluster words that typify a set of documents. Hierarchal Dirichlet processing was used to cluster grouped data; it infers the number of topics from data. Close reading and text mining were used to identify and confirm categories and major topics.

3   Results

3.1   Study Characteristics

A total of 42 reviews were included in the integrative review (23 explainability, 3 interpretability, 5 fairness, and 11 privacy) [13–54]. These 42 reviews reviewed a total of 4,766 reviewed articles. Articles were excluded from this review for incorrect focus and methods, lack of access, and duplication. See Table 1. Most articles were from the following industries: medical (n = 12), healthcare (n = 8), security (n = 5), and education (n = 7). The reviews were cited an average of 151 times (median = 8, range = 0 to 3863). There were 22 systematic reviews, 19 narrative reviews, and 1 integrative review included.

Table 1. Inclusion and Exclusion.

Inclusion/Exclusion	E	I	F	P
total	161	121	48	30
not focus, methods	131	116	39	15
no access	2	0	4	0
duplicates	5	2	0	4
included	23 [13–35]	3 [36–38]	5 [39–43]	11 [44–54]

E = explainability, I = interpretability, F = fairness, P = privacy.

3.2 Definitions

Definitions of explainability usually included interpretability [14, 15, 19–21, 24, 25, 27, 30, 32, 33, 35]), transparency [13, 15–17, 19, 24, 28, 32, 35], understandability [15, 16, 18, 28, 32, 35], fairness [14, 16, 17, 25, 28, 35], human perspective [28, 31, 34], privacy [28, 35], responsibility [14, 30, 32, 35], and trustworthiness [13, 14, 16, 25, 28, 30, 32, 35]. Some definitions explicitly defined explainability as a post hoc condition of AI—post hoc meaning a characteristic of products of AI rather than AI processes [21, 32]. Definitions of interpretability included references to human need [38], trust [36, 38], uncertainty [36, 38], and explainability [37]. Definitions of fairness included concerns about discrimination [39, 42], social prejudice [39, 43], bias [39–43], law [39], understandability [39, 40], and justice [39, 40]. Finally, definitions of privacy usually included concerns about personal information [45, 48, 53], confidentiality [48], responsibility [45, 54], ethical concerns [45, 47–49, 52, 54], and understandability [45]. The importance of transparency, human-centeredness, and trustworthiness were shared across all domains—explainability, interpretability, fairness, and privacy. Topic modelling revealed that objectivity, reliability, transparency, and functionality were also keywords around which topics clustered (topic coherence = 0.72) across all domains.

3.3 Objectives

Regarding the objective of explainability, articles mentioned revealing the reasoning underpinning the "black box" that complex algorithms can create [14, 17, 19, 21, 23, 25, 26, 35]. They also acknowledged that explainability was important given how algorithms are used in real-world decision-making [14–16, 18–21, 23, 25, 27, 31–35], particularly in clinical settings where health, safety, life, and death are at stake [13, 21, 25–27, 30,

32]. Some also acknowledged the limitations of AI [23, 25–27, 31, 33]. Others also centered on stakeholders [14, 18, 19, 21, 23, 27, 30, 34] and human needs [15, 18–21, 26, 27, 32, 33] as to why explainability is important. The objectives of interpretability included explaining algorithms and AI systems [36–38], making real world decisions [38], reducing uncertainty [36, 38], and increasing transparency [37]. Fairness objectives included meeting stakeholder needs [41] and real-world tools [40, 41] and decisions [39, 40, 42, 43]. Privacy objectives also included addressing data [44, 46, 48, 50–54], research [44, 45, 47, 49, 50, 52, 54], and security [48–50] needs and sectors. Common objectives across all domains—explainability, interpretability, fairness, and privacy— included opening black boxes and explaining algorithms as well as a focus on practice and real-world implementation. Topic modelling identified ethics, consequences, and translation as common key words for topics (topic coherence = 0.71) across all domains.

3.4 Strategies

Rhetorical, logical, and argumentative structures underpin the strategies used for AI explainability, interpretability, fairness, and privacy [11, 55, 56]. See Table 2. Ensemble and feature importance models use accumulation and composition strategies, insofar as they rely on combining multiple models with different features, unifying structures obtained from different data sources, and scoring features for importance. Regression employs conditional logic because it traces relationships between variables (if A happens, then B happens). Global, imagenet, and transfer learning models use deductive logic. They move from general to specific claims when they use single classifiers based on large sets of data and image identification based on training from large-scale object recognition models. Probabilistic and counterfactual models employ hypothetical logic insofar as they indicate degrees of uncertainty and describe what did not happen and why. Sector-specific and object detection models employ inductive logic. They move from specific to general claims when they identify industry specific trends and objects in defined classes. Game theory and constraint models employ rule-based logic by defining strategic interactions within predefined rules. Performance overhead and economic models employ material logic because they track excesses in financial investment and computation time, memory, bandwidth, or other resources. Neural networks, machine and federated learning, and genetic models employ metaphorical logic. They use brain and other biological processes to design interconnected nodes and decentralized models. Intrinsic models and auto encoders employ metonymic (or reductive) logic by reducing representations of input data. Model-specific, social, and human models use subjective logic unique to contexts and specific to a single model or group of models. Local models and relevance propagation methods use synecdoche logic. They take a part of the program for the whole when they explain individual predictions and output from local groupings or use a particular path to observe how the model works. Finally, model agnostic approaches are tautological by attempting to apply to all models.

Table 2. Strategies by Citation.

Strategy	Code	E	I	F	P
ensemble, feature importance	accumulation, composition	[13–15, 19, 21, 22, 24–27, 29–36]	[37]	[40, 42]	[47–50, 53]
regression	conditional	[12, 19, 24]		[40, 42]	[48, 53]
global, imagenet, transfer learning	deductive	[13, 21–25, 27, 28, 30, 31, 35]	[37]	[40, 43]	[49–51, 53, 54]
probabilistic, counterfactual	hypothetical	[13, 19, 20, 25, 27, 29, 30]	[36, 37]	[42]	[50]
sector-specific, object detection	inductive	[19, 20, 24, 27, 29, 30]	[37, 38]	[39, 43]	[47–50, 53, 54]
game theory, constraint	rule-based	[17, 18, 20, 26, 30]			[50, 54]
performance overhead, economic	material		[36]	[43]	[48–50, 53]
neural networks, genetic, machine learnng, federated learning	metaphorical	[13, 14, 19, 21–24, 26, 28, 30, 32–34]	[36, 40]	[42, 44]	[46, 48, 50, 52–54]
intrinsic, auto encoders	metonymic	[19, 20, 22, 24, 27, 30, 34, 35]			
model-specific, social, human models	subjective	[13, 15, 19, 21, 22, 25, 26, 28, 29, 30, 31 33, 34, 35]	[37, 38]	[39, 43]	[51, 54]
local, relevance propagation	synecdoche	[13–15, 20–23, 25–31, 35]	[36, 37]		[46, 50, 53]
model-agnostic	tautological	[13, 14, 20–22, 25, 26, 30, 36]	[37]		[53]

E = explainability, I = interpretability, F = fairness, P = privacy.

Each model or approach falls prey to the inherent limitations of the logical and rhetorical approach. Accumulation and composition are limited by the data accumulated. Conditional, deductive, and inductive logic fall prey to underfitting and overfitting. Hypothetical and tautological approaches risk untethering from real-world grounding and complexity, as do metonymy, metaphor, and synecdoche. Material, subjective, and rule-based approaches risk specificity over generalizability, in addition to overfitting and underfitting. Induction and deduction risk under- and overfitting, distortion, and oversimplification.

Strategies used for explainability included all but neural and genetic networks and machine and federated learning. See Table 3. Table 3 tracks mentions of the methods across all reviews and domains. Strategies for interpretability included all but regression and game theory models. Strategies for fairness included all but performance overhead, economic, neural, and genetic networks and machine and federated learning, intrinsic models, auto encoders, local models, relevance propagation, and model-agnostic approaches. Strategies for privacy included all but intrinsic models and auto encoders. Game theory and constraint models (n = 10), regression (n = 31), probabilistic and counterfactual models (n = 34), performance overhead and economic models (n = 35), and auto encoders and intrinsic models (n = 37) were least mentioned. Global models and transfer learning (n = 125), as well as neural and genetic networks and machine and federated learning (n = 108), were most mentioned Topic modeling revealed that tuning, logit, schemas, convolution, accumulators, and transformers were keywords for topics (topic coherence = 0.64). Game theory was least mentioned (n = 10) across all domains.

Table 3. Strategies by Mention Frequency.

Strategies	E	I	F	P
ensemble, feature importance	18	15	6	15
regression	22		6	3
global, imagenet, transfer learning	61	8	2	54
probabilistic, counterfactual	27	5	1	1
sector-specific, object detection	6	6	16	55
game theory, constraint	5			5
performance overhead, economic		1	9	25
neural networks, genetic, machine learning, federated learning	39	3	5	61
intrinsic, auto encoders	35	2		
model-specific, social, human models	32	10	11	31
local, relevance propagation	71	15		3
model-agnostic	33	8		1

E = explainability, I = interpretability, F = fairness, P = privacy.

3.5 Problems

Problems achieving explainability included lingering questions about the real-world implementations [13, 17–19, 29, 32, 33], inaccurate explanations [13, 15, 17, 18, 21, 22, 24, 27, 29–33] and interpretations [15, 22, 30, 32, 35], difficulties putting methods into practice [15–23, 26, 27, 29–32, 34, 35], limitations of datasets [13, 15, 16, 18, 26, 27, 31, 32, 34], and lingering distrust [17]. Learning methods was a concern for interpretability [36–38], as were real world implementations [38]. For fairness methods, concerns about practitioners learning and appropriately using the methods [41–43] were reported issues. Ethics [39, 41] and fairness in decision making [39–43] also emerged as fairness concerns. Privacy methods concerns also included practical implementations [44, 45, 48–54], dataset limitations [44, 46, 49–54], and lingering questions regarding consent [52] and personal information [45, 47, 51–54]. Real world analogs and applications were a common concern across domains, as were limitations of datasets. Topic modelling confirmed that threats, standards, and researcher and practitioner use were key terms for topics (topic coherence = 0.64) across all domains.

3.6 Evaluation

When evaluating explainability methods, reviews reported using iteration [13, 16–19, 30] and human centered design and usability strategies such as patient annotations and mapping [16–25, 27–33]. Interpretability methods called for calibration and sensitivity [37, 38], evaluations grounded in human factors [36–38], and monitoring for bias [37, 38] and robustness [37]. Evaluating fairness methods included concerns about how practitioners use the methods [39–43], understanding and implementing algorithms [39–43], limitations of the dataset [39–43], and protection from bias [40–43]. Finally, the reviews reported that evaluating privacy methods most often called for user-centeredness [45, 48–50, 53], data rights [44–46, 48–54], and detection [47, 48, 54] and protection from attack [48, 50]. Human centeredness and protection against bias and attack were common themes across domains. Topic modelling confirmed that user centeredness and transferability were important topic keywords (topic coherence $= 0.71$) across all domains.

4 Discussion

The literature calls for a multi-perspectival approach to AI explainability, interpretability, privacy, and fairness. Regarding explainability, studies show that more interdisciplinary work is needed, and more attention to perspectives other than designers and technicians is required. There are different definitions of AI explainability. Furthermore, there are different justifications for why we need explainability. There are calls for increased understandability, trustworthiness, transparency, controllability, and fairness and for incorporating end-user feedback to understand methods. Recommendations include offering personalized and on-demand explanations. Explainability depends on the algorithm. The simpler the algorithm, the easier it is to be understood by humans. Furthermore, the definition of explainability should come from the public standpoint to better reflect a broad range of perspectives. Findings stress the importance of user experience and users' perspectives in rendering explanations more precise. Questions linger about how to standardize and formalize the definition of explainability, how to navigate the trade-off between explainability and efficiency of models, how to use visual explanations, and which graphic descriptions are most effective. Furthermore, it is important to distinguish who is the receiver of the explanation, why it is needed, and in which context and other situated information.

Regarding interpretability, definitions incorporate explainability, but focused on human need and trust, and the objectives of interpretability gravitated toward concerns about making real world decisions and reducing uncertainty, as well as ethical and consequential results of interpretability. Interpretability methods did not employ conditional, rule-based, or metonymic logical approaches as much as the other domains, such as accumulation logic (compositionensemble, feature importance), subjective logic (model-specific, social, human models) and synecdoche logic (local, relevance propagation), thereby potentially avoiding underfitting and overfitting but still risking results that are distant and different from real world scenarios and outcomes. Interpretability efforts underscored limitations implementing methods in practice. Therefore, calibration and sensitivity were of importance when evaluating interpretability.

Regarding AI fairness, individual perception of AI fairness is context-dependent and influenced by transparency, trust, and individual moral concepts. Most definitions are from the designer's perspective and focused on the public services sector—law, immigration, and the health sector—as well as technical and social/human aspects over the economic factors. There are calls to develop formal standards clearly defining AI terminology in plain language globally and involves intertwining reason and emotion that have yet to be explored. Drawing from AI cases used in the real world might help contextualize and frame the discussion around fairness. A multi-perspectival approach is necessary to address these complex matters. AI can often reinforce structural inequities if applied in social contexts, and diversity and representation are essential to consider throughout the design process. Inductive methods (sector-specific, object detection) and subjective models (model-specific, social, human models) were most often mentioned, therefore the methods run the risk of fitting errors. Reviews reported that practitioner learning and using these methods were a concern, so human factors are important to consider when evaluating which methods to use.

Regarding AI privacy, studies call for more attention to personal and social value systems. Public datasets often need to be more balanced and suitable training grounds for AI. Integrating work and research from other domains is important. Basic principles of focus data collection and minimization can reduce many privacy risks. Privacy definitions included aspects like understandability (resembling explainability and interpretability) as well as confidentiality and responsibility. Privacy objectives acknowledged the limitations of data practices in honoring privacy. Intrinsic models and auto-encoders were not discussed for privacy methods, perhaps to achieve the most transparency possible. Data rights and human factors were the aim of privacy evaluations.

The four domains converged often regarding the need for human centeredness, trustworthiness, and transparency. Although real world implementation was a persistent theme for all domains, global models, transfer learning, neural and genetic networks and machine and federated learning were strategies most mentioned. These strategies rely on metaphorical and deductive logics that risk underfitting, overfitting, and untethering from real-world grounding and complexity. Definitions of the four domains stressed the importance of transparency, human-centeredness, and trustworthiness, as well as objectivity, reliability, transparency, and functionality. The shared themes prioritize human factors and outcomes. Deductive logics (global models and transfer learning) and metaphorical models (neural and genetic networks and machine and federated learning) were most mentioned, therefore problems with underfitting and overfitting might limit accuracy even as deduction and metaphor help contextualize the methods and definitions for the public. On the other hand, limited datasets emerged as an important shared theme that also may reduce accuracy by underrepresenting real world dynamics due to missingness. Overall, how explanations, interpretations, fairness, and privacy are achieved, validated, and evaluated should be as intuitive, transparent, and clear as possible.

5   Conclusion

The review significantly contributes to new thinking by integrating all four conceptual findings. Overall, consensus definitions are needed on all terms, as are multidisciplinary and multi-perspectival analyses. The public should be more involved in approaches, and evidence-based communication tools and templates would help developers and decision-makers increase transparency, representativeness, and equity. Such tools would also help educate and train designers and policymakers before, during, and after the AI design and marketing process. Although access to reviews and broad scope limited this integrative review from providing operational details of the methods, the integrative review provides a broad synthesis of the findings from several reviews for gaining an overview perspective of definitions, objectives, strategies, problems, and evaluations of explainability, interpretability, fairness, and privacy. Future work must pay attention to data representativeness and transparency about bias, increase explainability, interpretability, fairness, and privacy, and map lines of accountability and recourse for misinformation and erroneous predictions. Future work should explore these concepts more fully with all stakeholders involved.

Acknowledgement. This study was conducted with support from a research gift from the NEC Foundation.

References

1. Gandhi, M.: What exactly is meant by explainability and interpretability of AI? Medium. https://medium.com/analytics-vidhya/what-exactly-is-meant-by-explainability-and-interp retability-of-ai-bcea30ca1e56. Accessed 15 Feb 2023
2. The Royal Society, Explainable AI: The Basics, https://royalsociety.org/-/media/policy/pro jects/explainable-ai/AI-and-interpretability-policy-briefing.pdf. Accessed 15 Feb 2023
3. IBM, Explainable AI (XAI). https://www.ibm.com/watson/explainable-ai (2023). Accessed 15 Feb 2023
4. Ceurstemont, S.: Finding the Fairness in AI. Communications of the ACM. https://cacm.acm.org/news/261047-finding-the-fairness-in-ai/fulltext. Accessed 15 Feb 2023
5. Smith, G., Kohli, N., Rustagi, I.: What does "fairness" mean for machine learning systems? Center for Equity, Gender & Leadership (EGAL). Berkeley Haas. https://haas.berkeley.edu/wp-content/uploads/What-is-fairness_-EGAL2.pdf. Accessed 15 Feb 2023
6. Koerner, K.: Privacy and Responsible AI. The Privacy Advisor. https://iapp.org/news/a/pri vacy-and-responsible-ai/. Accessed 15 Feb 2023
7. Roundtree, A.: ANT ethics in professional communication: an integrative review. Am. Commun. J. **22**(1), 1–13 (2020)
8. Roundtree, A.: Ethics and facial recognition technology: an integrative review. In: 3rd World Symposium on Artificial Intelligence, pp. 10–19. IEEE, New York (2021)
9. Araujo, T.: Automated decision-making fairness in an AI-driven world: public perceptions, hopes and concerns. Digital Communication Methods Lab (2018)
10. Hong, S.J., Cho, H.: Privacy management and health information sharing via contact tracing during the COVID-19 pandemic: a hypothetical study on AI-based technologies. Health Commun. **38**, 913–924 (2021)
11. Roundtree, A.K.: Computer Simulation, Rhetoric, and the Scientific Imagination: How Virtual Evidence Shapes Science in the Making and in the News. Lexington Books, Lanham (2013)
12. O'Mara-Eves, A., Thomas, J., McNaught, J., Miwa, M., Ananiadou, S.: Using text mining for study identification in systematic reviews: a systematic review of current approaches. Syst. Rev. **4**(1), 1–22 (2015)
13. Albahri, A.S.: A systematic review of trustworthy and explainable artificial intelligence in healthcare: assessment of quality, bias risk, and data fusion. Inf. Fusion (2023). https://doi.org/10.1016/j.inffus.2023.03.008

14. Alsaigh, R., Mehmood, R., Katib, I.: AI explainability and governance in smart energy systems: a review. arXiv preprint arXiv:2211.00069 (2022)
15. Arrieta, A.B., et al.: Explainable artificial intelligence (XAI): concepts, taxonomies, opportunities and challenges toward responsible AI. Inf. fusion **58**, 82–115 (2020)
16. Cabiddu, F., Moi, L., Patriotta, G., Allen, D.G.: Why do users trust algorithms? A review and conceptualization of initial trust and trust over time. Eur. Manag. J. **40**, 685–706 (2022)
17. Chazette, L., Brunotte, W., Speith, T.: Explainable software systems: from requirements analysis to system evaluation. Requirements Eng. **27**, 457–487 (2022). https://doi.org/10.1007/s00766-022-00393-5
18. Chen, H., Gomez, C., Huang, C.M., Unberath, M.: Explainable medical imaging AI needs human-centered design: guidelines and evidence from a systematic review. Digit. Med. **5**(1), 156–163 (2022)
19. Chou, Y.L., Moreira, C., Bruza, P., Ouyang, C., Jorge, J.: Counterfactuals and causability in explainable artificial intelligence: theory, algorithms, and applications. Inform. Fusion **81**, 59–83 (2022)
20. Dey, S., et al.: Human-centered explainability for life sciences, healthcare, and medical informatics. Patterns **3**(5), 100493 (2022)
21. Gevaert, C.M.: Explainable AI for earth observation: a review including societal and regulatory perspectives. Int. J. Appl. Earth Obs. Geoinformation **112**, 102869 (2022). https://doi.org/10.1016/j.jag.2022.102869
22. Groen, A.M., Kraan, R., Amirkhan, S.F., Daams, J.G., Maas, M.: A systematic review on the use of explainability in deep learning systems for computer aided diagnosis in radiology: limited use of explainable AI? Eur. J. Radiol. **157**, 110592 (2022). https://doi.org/10.1016/j.ejrad.2022.110592
23. Hall, O., Ohlsson, M., Rögnvaldsson, T.: A review of explainable AI in the satellite data, deep machine learning, and human poverty domain. Patterns **3**(10), 100600 (2022)
24. Bahalul Haque, A.K.M., Najmul Islam, A.K.M., Mikalef, P.: Explainable Artificial Intelligence (XAI) from a user perspective: a synthesis of prior literature and problematizing avenues for future research. Technol. Forecast. Soc. Chang. **186**, 122120 (2023). https://doi.org/10.1016/j.techfore.2022.122120
25. Linardatos, P., Papastefanopoulos, V., Kotsiantis, S.: Explainable AI: a review of machine learning interpretability methods. Entropy **23**(1), 1–18 (2020)
26. Loh, H.W., Ooi, C.P., Seoni, S., Barua, P.D., Filippo Molinari, U., Acharya, R.: Application of explainable artificial intelligence for healthcare: a systematic review of the last decade (2011–2022). Comput. Methods Programs Biomed. **226**, 107161 (2022). https://doi.org/10.1016/j.cmpb.2022.107161
27. Markus, A.F., Kors, J.A., Rijnbeek, P.R.: The role of explainability in creating trustworthy artificial intelligence for health care: a comprehensive survey of the terminology, design choices, and evaluation strategies. J. Biomed. Inform. **113**, 103655 (2021)
28. Mohseni, S., Zarei, N., Ragan, E.D.: A multidisciplinary survey and framework for design and evaluation of explainable AI systems. ACM Trans. Interact. Intell. Syst. (TiiS) **11**(3–4), 1–45 (2021)
29. Nauta, M., et al.: From anecdotal evidence to quantitative evaluation methods: a systematic review on evaluating explainable AI. arXiv preprint arXiv:2201.08164 (2022)
30. Nazir, S., Dickson, D.M., Akram, M.U.: Survey of explainable artificial intelligence techniques for biomedical imaging with deep neural networks. Comput. Biol. Med. **156**, 106668 (2023). https://doi.org/10.1016/j.compbiomed.2023.106668
31. Okolo, C.T., Dell N., Vashistha, A.: Making AI explainable in the global south: a systematic review. In: ACM SIGCAS/SIGCHI Conference on Computing and Sustainable Societies (COMPASS) Jun 29, pp. 439–452 (2022)

32. Saleem, R., Yuan, B., Kurugollu, F., Anjum, A., Liu, L.: Explaining deep neural networks: a survey on the global interpretation methods. Neurocomputing **513**, 165–180 (2022)
33. Tiddi, I., Schlobach, S.: Knowledge graphs as tools for explainable machine learning: A survey. Artif. Intell. **302**, 103627 (2022)
34. Vo, T.H., Nguyen, N.T.K., Kha, Q.H., Le, N.Q.K.: On the road to explainable AI in drug-drug interactions prediction: a systematic review. Comput. Struct. Biotechnol. J. **20**, 2112–2123 (2022)
35. Yang, G., Ye, Q., Xia, J.: Unbox the black-box for the medical explainable AI via multi-modal and multi-centre data fusion: a mini-review, two showcases and beyond. Inf. Fusion **77**, 29–52 (2022)
36. McCrindle, B., Zukotynski, K., Doyle, T.E., Noseworthy, M.D.: A radiology-focused review of predictive uncertainty for AI interpretability in computer-assisted segmentation. Radiol. Artif. Intell. **3**(6), e210031 (2021)
37. Salahuddin, Z., Woodruff, H.C., Chatterjee, A., Lambin, P.: Transparency of deep neural networks for medical image analysis: a review of interpretability methods. Comput. Biol. Med. **140**, 105111 (2022)
38. Tomsett, R., et al.: Rapid trust calibration through interpretable and uncertainty-aware AI. Patterns **1**(4), 100049 (2020)
39. Baleis, J., Keller, B., Starke, C., Marcinkowski, F.: Cognitive and emotional response to fairness in AI–A systematic review (2019)
40. Birzhandi, P., Cho, Y.S.: Application of fairness to healthcare, organizational justice, and finance: a survey. Expert Syst. Appl. **216**, 119465 (2022)
41. Richardson, B., Gilbert, J.E.: A framework for fairness: A systematic review of existing fair AI solutions. arXiv preprint arXiv:2112.05700 (2021)
42. Rieskamp, J., Hofeditz, L., Mirbabaie, M., Stieglitz, S.: Approaches to improve fairness when deploying AI-based algorithms in hiring–using a systematic literature review to guide future research. In: Hawaii International Conference on System Sciences (2023)
43. Xivuri, K., Twinomurinzi, H.: A systematic review of fairness in artificial intelligence algorithms. In: Dennehy, D., Griva, A., Pouloudi, N., Dwivedi, Y.K., Pappas, I., Mäntymäki, M. (eds.) Responsible AI and Analytics for an Ethical and Inclusive Digitized Society. I3E 2021. Lecture Notes in Computer Science, vol. 12896, pp. 271–284 . Springer, Cham (2021). https://doi.org/10.1007/978-3-030-85447-8_24
44. Aslan, A., Greve, M., Diesterhöft, T.O., Kolbe L.M.: Can Our Health Data Stay Private? A Review and Future Directions for IS Research on Privacy-Preserving AI in Healthcare (2022)
45. Augustin, Y., Carolus, A., Wienrich, C.: Privacy of AI-based voice assistants: understanding the users' perspective. In: Salvendy, G., Wei, J. (eds.) Design, Operation and Evaluation of Mobile Communications. HCII 2022. Lecture Notes in Computer Science, vol. 13337, pp. 309–321. Springer, Cham (2022). https://doi.org/10.1007/978-3-031-05014-5_26
46. Duda, S., Geyer, D., Guggenberger, T., Principato, M., Protschky, D.: A systematic literature review on how to improve the privacy of artificial intelligence using blockchain. In: Pacific Asia Conference on Information Systems, pp. 1–17 (2022)
47. Giordano, G., Palomba, F., Ferrucci, F.: On the use of artificial intelligence to deal with privacy in IoT systems: a systematic literature review. J. Syst. Softw. **193**, 111475 (2022)
48. Hameed, S.S., Hassan, W.H., Latiff, L.A., Ghabban, F.: A systematic review of security and privacy issues in the internet of medical things; the role of machine learning approaches. PeerJ Computer Science **7**, e414 (2021)
49. Himeur, Y., Sohail, S.S., Bensaali, F., Amira, A., Alazab, M.: Latest trends of security and privacy in recommender systems: a comprehensive review and future perspectives. Comput. Secur. **118**, 102746 (2022)

50. Mothukuri, V., Parizi, R.M., Pouriyeh, S., Huang, Y., Dehghantanha, A., Srivastava, G.: A survey on security and privacy of federated learning. Future Gener. Comput. Syst. **115**, 619–640 (2021)
51. Smidt, H.J., Jokonya, O.: The challenge of privacy and security when using technology to track people in times of COVID-19 pandemic. Procedia Comp. Sci. **181**, 1018–1026 (2021)
52. Taitingfong, R., et al.: A systematic literature review of Native American and Pacific Islanders' perspectives on health data privacy in the United States. J. Am. Med. Inform. Assoc. **27**(12), 1987–1998 (2020)
53. Xu, J., et al.: Data-Driven Learning for Data Rights, Data Pricing, and Privacy Computing. Engineering (2023)
54. Zhang, Yi., Mengjia, Wu., Tian, G.Y., Zhang, G., Jie, Lu.: Ethics and privacy of artificial intelligence: Understandings from bibliometrics. Knowl.-Based Syst. **222**, 106994 (2021)
55. Howard, G.T.: A Glossary of Rhetorical Terms. Accessed Corporation, Bloomington (2018)
56. Simpson, R.L.: Essentials of Symbolic Logic. Broadview Press, New York (2008)

Emotional Debiasing Explanations for Decisions in HCI

Christian Schütze[1,2]($\boxtimes$) , Olesja Lammert[3] , Birte Richter[1,2] ,
Kirsten Thommes[3] , and Britta Wrede[4]

[1] Medical Assistance Systems, Medical School OWL, Bielefeld University,
Universitätsstraße 25, 33615 Bielefeld, Germany
[2] Center for Cognitive Interaction Technology, CITEC, Bielefeld University,
Universitätsstraße 25, 33615 Bielefeld, Germany
{christian.schuetze,birte.richter}@uni-bielefeld.de
[3] Faculty of Business Administration and Economics, Department of Management,
Paderborn University, Warburger Str. 100, 33098 Paderborn, Germany
{olesja.lammert,kirsten.thommes}@uni-paderborn.de
[4] Software Engineering for Cognitive Robots and Systems, University of Bremen,
Am Fallturm 1, 128359 Bremen, Germany
bwrede@techfak.uni-bielefeld.de

Abstract. Emotions play an important role in human decision-making.
However, first approaches to incorporating knowledge of this influence
into AI-based decision support systems are only very recent. Accordingly,
our target is to develop an interactive intelligent agent that is capable of
explaining the recommendations of AI-systems while taking emotional
constraints into account. This article addresses the following research
questions based on the emotions of happiness and anxiety: (1) How do
induced emotions influence risk propensity in HCI? (2) To what extent
does the explanation strategy influence the human explanation recipient in a lottery choice? (3) How well can an HCI system estimate the
emotional state of the human? Our results showed that (1) our emotion
induction strategy was successful. However, the trend took the opposite direction of ATF predictions. (2) Our explanation strategy yielded a
change in the risk decision in only 26% of the participants; in some cases,
participants even changed their selection in the opposite direction. (3)
Emotion recognition from facial expressions did not provide sufficient
indications of the emotional state - because of head position and a lack
of emotional display - but heart rate showed significant effects of emotion induction in the expected direction. Importantly, in individual cases,
the dynamics of facial expressions followed the expected path. We concluded that (1) more differentiated explanation strategies are needed,
and that temporal dynamics may play an important role in the explanation process, and (2) that a more interactive setting is required to elicit
more emotional cues that can be used to adapt the explanation strategy
accordingly.

Keywords: Emotions · Emotion Recognition · Risk-decision making ·
Explanation Strategy · Human-centered XAI

H. Degen and S. Ntoa (Eds.): HCII 2023, LNAI 14050, pp. 318–336, 2023.
https://doi.org/10.1007/978-3-031-35891-3_20

1   Introduction

Emotions have been identified as a significant and reliable factor influencing our behavior, memory [15], and decisions [20] in everyday situations. Up to now, however, systems designed to support human decisions by drawing on artificial intelligence (AI) are generally largely ignorant about their interaction partner's emotional state. Hence, equipping AI systems with the ability to take the user's emotional states into account when providing support in decision-making processes would be a desirable feature for better decision-making, and this would open up a range of new research questions.

AI systems can be especially helpful if they take human interaction partners seriously. Importantly, in our research agenda, we follow the idea that AI support requires explanations to empower users to incorporate AI advice into their task-related actions, and that a successful interaction requires both interaction partners to respond to each other actively [30].

In this research, we will address the following questions as a first step toward assessing the effect of AI explanations on decision-making. How is AI advice recognized by the explainee? How do an individual's emotions change during interaction with an AI system? How can both interaction partners shape this process actively?

In this work, we will start a first investigation into the reaction of humans to a risk decision dependent on their current emotion, as well as the first influence of a simple explanation and recommendation by an AI support system. To study this, we induced the emotions of "Happiness" or "Anxiety" in our study participants.

We present two studies: In the first, the main focus was on emotion induction, the understanding of the risk game that was used, and the influence of the induced emotion on decision-making. For the second study, we added the collection of physiological data. We used a first rough explanation and recommendation by a social agent to test the impact of a simple explanation dependent on the induced emotion.

2   Related Work

Risk decisions are especially prone to emotional confluence [20]. From a rational point of view, individuals should choose the level of risk that best reflects both what is at stake and the probability of making the wrong decision and losing. However, behavioral theorists [26] acknowledge that individuals feel differently when losing: For some individuals, the potential joy of winning does not compensate for the fear of losing. Such individuals avoid risks and are generally better off with less risky decisions. Other individuals enjoy the prospect of a potential win more than they fear a loss. These individuals are risk-prone and better off with risky decisions. Thus, an optimal level of risk can be identified for each individual, depending on the positive or negative utility of gains and losses along with the associated feelings. Two factors prevent individuals from adopting their optimal level of risky choices and, therefore, from making optimal decisions: (1) They may not be able to reflect thoroughly on all factors and forecast the possible outcomes. This is a cognitive problem, and, in such cases, individuals may be better off using AI assistance. (2) Emotions can bias an individual's perceptions and thus also her or his choice. For instance, happiness leads to a tendency to underestimate risk [40], whereas fear increases low risk-taking tendencies [21,32]. In both cases, the resulting action and even the process of understanding may yield a result with which the decision-maker may not be happy under normal circumstances. Cognition and emotion have long been considered separately in decision research. However, it is now clear that emotions evoke changes in cognitive processes such as attention, perception, or memory and impact action [19].

Nonetheless, no reliable statements can currently be made on how distinct emotions influence such decision-making under risk. The theoretical foundation of this work is based on the Appraisal Tendency Framework (ATF) [18,19]. This states that emotions of equal valence (e.g., fear and anger) can have different influences on risk appraisal, whereas emotions that have opposing valences (e.g., anger and joy) can exert similar influences [20]. A systematic review has shown that there is indeed a highly significant correlation between emotion-related impulsivity and risky decision-making [8]. Because emotions alter how explanations about risk are perceived, and explanations also, in turn, alter emotions [25], we need to understand how an explainable AI can identify and respond to humans' emotions. As such, explainable AI must somehow adapt to the human factor and consider non-rationalities. Thus, a good recommender system would strive to give the best recommendation and explain the associated risk in line with the explainee's emotions.

There seems to be an upcoming trend toward recommendation systems that involve the current emotion of the user in interesting areas such as in a web-shop to support the recommendation of products [14] or for music recommendations [24]. But there appears to be a lack of research on human-agent interaction, especially in risky decisions. More specifically, methods are missing that comprehensively incorporate humans into explainable AI [29,39]. In line with research indicating that machines are capable of altering emotions during an interaction [4,25], it might be important to include a recognition system to track the emotions and emotion changes during interaction with agents. Good AI systems, therefore, need not only to address the cognitive component but also to take into account the emotional component of their interaction partner.

For the emotion recognition process, some promising models have already been developed. For example, Emonet is able to continuously detect valence and arousal as well as up to eight discrete emotions under naturalistic conditions [38]. Another approach is deepface [33], a more lightweight python framework that can detect discrete emotions and even age, gender, and race by facial attribute analysis. Besides face and video analysis, another method is opensmile. Its interpretation of audio can extract the current emotion from the voice [9].

Whereas the subjective perception of a person's own emotions is an important source of information, such subjective ratings have been complemented by a whole plethora of objective measures ranging from directly observable cues such as voice or facial expressions to physiological correlates such as skin conductance, heart rate, or EEG. Facial expressions have often been considered to provide a direct window into a person's emotional state, and facial expressions of the basic emotions are universal [7]. However, it has been substantiated that the emotional display is also affected by the social context, that is, the communicative situation, the persons, and the relationships to these [6,12]. Hence, investigations of the effect of emotions in explaining situations need to take the role of interactivity and social context into account.

Research on how AI assistants alter the emotional state of the individual and also how AI systems can monitor human emotions is not just important for risky decisions. The dynamics of emotions may also play an important role in what and how scaffolding strategies can affect an emotional interaction partner's understanding and action processes. Information about such dynamics comes from clinical research investigating different therapeutical strategies that enable patients who have mostly emotional problems related to anxiety to control their emotional responses. The most relevant strategies in this context are diversion and re-appraisal. The strategy of diverting attention away from the emotional aspect of a stimulus is applied early in the interaction with the stimulus and yields less emotional processing [37]. In contrast, the cognitive re-appraisal strategy aims at re-evaluating the meaning underlying an emotional stimulus and thus affects the emotion-generating process at a later stage.

To gain a basic understanding of the interplay between AI assistants, emotions, and human decision-making, we conducted two consecutive studies: In Study 1, we induced emotions in the lab and measured how emotions alter decisions in a decision-making task. After confirming that our procedure actually induced emotions and gaining an understanding of emotional bias in the decision-making task, Study 2 analyzed basic principles regarding how emotions can be monitored, and how the interaction with an AI assistant affects emotional states and subsequent decision-making.

3   Study 1 - Emotion Induction

In Study 1, we conducted a laboratory experiment to test the effectiveness of emotion induction. Furthermore, we investigated whether a biased risk decision arises when participants are in an emotional state. Between May and June 2022, a randomized controlled experiment based on a 2×1 design was conducted with student participants at Paderborn University. Participants were randomly assigned to one of two different treatment groups, "Happiness" or "Anxiety". Experiments took place onsite at the university and in a strictly controlled environment. One person per session participated in the experiment. A neutral condition was intentionally not established, because neutral conditions are not necessarily a requirement for experiments in which emotions are induced [1]. We expected that happiness and anxiety would induce larger differences in effects on decision-making and that the causes of these differences in decision-making could be attributed to emotion.

3.1   Method

Experimental Task. To assess participants' risk-taking behavior, we used the widely used Holt and Laury Lottery [13]. This lottery is particularly suitable for investigating the decision-making behavior of individuals in connection with emotional states because the participants make real decisions in the lottery and have an opportunity to win money. In this context, the participants had to choose between lottery A and B. The prize, as well as the associated risk of each lottery, differed. The risk propensity was determined by the moment at which the participant switched from the safe lottery A to the riskier lottery B. The Holt and Laury Lottery involves a total of ten decision situations. The graphical representation of the lottery has been processed in such a way that the participants can only switch once from the left (lottery A) to the right (lottery B). Figure 1 shows exemplarily the two lotteries four and five. In decision situation four the probability of winning 2.00 € is 40% and the probability of winning 1.60 €. is 60%. In contrast, in lottery B, in the aforementioned decision situation, participants can win 3.85 € with a probability of 40% and 0.10 € with a 60% probability. Lotteries A and B differ in the expected value, and a risk-averse person would therefore stay with lottery A until lottery five. As shown in the figure, each decision situation changes in 10% steps until the tenth situation, where the probabilities for lottery A are 100% for 2.00 € and for lottery B 100% for 3.85 €. Each lottery was additionally represented visually with balls to help the participants' understanding of the probabilities and risks.

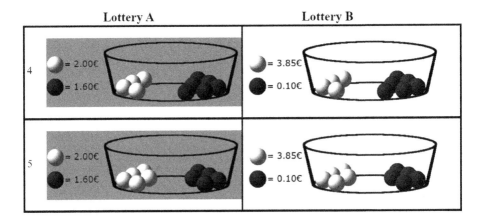

Fig. 1. Visualization of lottery 4 and 5 in the Holt and Laury lottery game.

Sample. Five participants who did not switch from lottery A to lottery B at all were excluded because this indicates a lack of understanding of the game. This left a final sample of N = 32. In total, 12 male and 20 female participants were paid for participating in the study. The average age of participants was 24 years ($SD = 3.6$). Most had a high school diploma ($N = 18$) or a technical college/university degree ($N = 8$). In addition, six participants reported having received an intermediate school-leaving certificate, completed vocational training, or another degree. Participants received a 5.00 € show-up fee and had the opportunity to additionally receive up to 3.85 €, depending on their decision in the lottery game. The study was carried out in accordance with the Helsinki Declaration of 1975 and all participants provided written informed consent to participate in the experimental study prior to participation. Good general health status was mandatory for participation, and participants were required to confirm that they had no history of neurological or psychiatric disorders (e.g., depression, anxiety, etc.) and currently have no hearing or visual impairments that could not be corrected [28].

Procedure. Subjects were distributed almost equally across the two treatment groups (treatment group "Happiness" $N = 15$, treatment group "Anxiety" $N = 17$). After providing demographic data and written consent, participants could begin the computer-assisted experiment on a touch monitor. They first completed the scales assessing emotions (SAM, mDES, STAI) before the treatment. In addition, they were asked about their general willingness to take risks in different areas of life. This was followed by a 5-minute relaxation phase as well as a 5-minute autobiographical recall phase of the emotion induction. For this task, participants were provided with a blank sheet of paper and a pencil so that they could write down the memory related to the emotion induction (happiness vs. anxiety). Participants were asked to write down detailed information about that memory so that an external person could reconstruct their experience [23]. To avoid any effect of social desirability, this paper was not collected. The emotion induction was followed by a manipulation check that reassessed the participants' emotional states. Finally, they participated in the Holt and Laury lottery. After they made a decision, a random number generator was used to determine the reward. On average, each session lasted 23 min.

Emotion Induction. A review of recent studies showed that the autobiographical procedure is a suitable method for eliciting emotions such as happiness and anxiety [34]. Therefore, we chose this procedure for emotion induction. Participants were asked to recall a past situation in which they felt either happy or anxious, depending on which treatment group they were assigned to. For the memory task, the participants had five minutes. Following Smith and Ellsworth [35], the following questions were used for this emotion recall task: "What happened in this situation to make you feel happy/anxious? Why did these things make you feel happy/anxious? How did you know that you were happy/anxious in this situation? What did it feel like for you to be happy/anxious in this situation? What did you do in this situation where you were happy/anxious?"

Manipulation Check. To verify that the emotion manipulation was successful, we used 5-point-Likert scales to determine the extent to which participants felt certain emotions. The scales were identical for both treatment groups. They included the modified Differential Emotions Scale (mDES) [11], the Self-Assessment Manikin (SAM) [3] for valence and arousal as well as the short version of the State-Trait-Anxiety Inventory (STAI) [36].

3.2   Results

Manipulation Check. As noted above, various scales were used before and after emotion induction to assess the participants' emotional states. To check the effectiveness of the self-generated emotions in inducing the respective emotion, we conducted paired samples Wilcoxon tests for the different Likert scales.

The valence (SAM) in the "Happiness" condition was rated higher after the emotion induction ($Mdn = 5$, $SD = 0.83$) than before the induction ($Mdn = 4$, $SD = 0.68$, $z = -2.12$, $p = .0703$, $r = .55$). Moreover, in the "Anxiety" condition, the valence was rated lower after the emotion induction ($Mdn = 3$, $SD = 1.10$) than before the induction ($Mdn = 4$, $SD = 1.01$, $z = 3.53$, $p < .001$, $r = .86$).

The autobiographical recall in the "Happiness" treatment group did not significantly affect the participants' arousal ($z = 1.27$, $p = .266, r = .33$). In contrast, the arousal measure of the treatment group "Anxiety" showed a significant difference ($z = -2.55$, $p = .0176$, $r = .62$). Participants in this treatment group reported feeling more aroused after emotion induction ($Mdn = 3$, $SD = 1.03$) than before induction ($Mdn = 2$, $SD = 0.66$).

To determine a positive and a negative total score for the mDES, we calculated the mean of ten positive and ten negative emotions, respectively. The treatment group "Happiness" showed a significant difference ($z = -2.47$, $p = .0107$, $r = .64$) between the mDES positive score before ($Mdn = 2.5$, $SD = 0.57$) and after the emotion induction ($Mdn = 3.1$, $SD = 0.77$). A significant difference was also found in the treatment group "Anxiety" ($z = -3.07$, $p = .001$, $r = .74$).

The same procedure was used for the other Likert scales. Table 1 summarizes the results of all paired samples Wilcoxon tests. Although not all differences are significant, which may be due to the small sample, all scales show a higher rating of the corresponding emotion in the related treatment group. Hence, the subjective emotional experience results show that emotion induction was successful in both treatment groups. Therefore, it could be assumed that recalling a happy (anxious) event effectively induces happiness (anxiety) and thus represents a suitable procedure for designing further studies we planned to conduct.

Table 1. Median of the respective Likert scale.

Variable	Before (Mdn, SD)	After (Mdn, SD)	Wilcoxon-test
	Treatmentgroup "Happiness"		
Valence (SAM)	4 (0.68)	5 (0.83)	z = -2.12, p = .0703*
Arousal(SAM)	2 (1.29)	2 (1.16)	z = 1.27, p = .266
mDES-positive	2.5 (0.57)	3.1 (0.77)	z = -2.47, p = .0107**
mDES-negative	0.5 (0.51)	0.2 (0.72)	z = -1.49, p = .145
STAI	2.2 (0.88)	1.8 (.93)	z = 1.19, p = .2465
	Treatmentgroup "Anxiety"		
Variable	Before (Mdn, SD)	After (Mdn, SD)	Wilcoxon-test
Valence (SAM)	4 (1.01)	3 (1.10)	z = 3.53, p < .001***
Arousal(SAM)	2 (0.66)	3 (1.03)	z = -2.55, p = .0176**
mDES-positive	2.3 (0.57)	1.5 (1.03)	z = 3.07, p = .001***
mDES-negative	0.2 (0.50)	0.9 (0.92)	z = -3.37, p < .001***
STAI	2.0 (0.54)	2.6 (0.92)	z = -3.03, p < .001***

*** p<.01, ** p<.05, *p<.1

Risk Behavior. With regard to the participants' risk behavior, the two-sample Wilcoxon rank-sum test (see Fig. 2) revealed significant differences between the treatment groups of "Happiness" ($Mdn = 7$, $SD = 2.49$) and "Anxiety" ($Mdn = 4$, $SD = 2.74$, $z = 2.80$, $p = .0041$, $r = .49$). According to the Holt

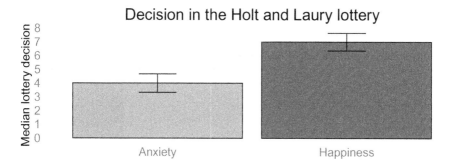

Fig. 2. Risk behavior by treatment (error bar = standard error).

and Laury Lottery [13], high scores are associated with higher risk aversion. Thus, participants in the treatment group "Anxiety" made more risk-seeking decisions than those in the group "Happiness". The distribution in Fig. 3 visualizes these results. It can be seen that about one-half of the participants in the "Anxiety" treatment group showed risk-seeking behavior, according to Holt and Laury, because they had already switched to lottery B on the first lottery.

All participants in the "Happiness" treatment group did not switch to lottery B until lottery four or later, indicating risk-averse behavior. In particular, the last one, i.e., the lottery, which indicates the highest risk aversion, was chosen most frequently by the participants of this treatment group (33%). However, these results showed the opposite behavior than predicted by the ATF [17]. Overall, our results indicated that the autobiographical recall task was effective as an emotion induction: the risk distribution of the participants was not normally distributed, and the medians of the two treatment groups differed significantly. Anxious participants took higher risks, whereas happy participants avoided risk. Thus, we showed that participants made a biased decision due to emotion induction.

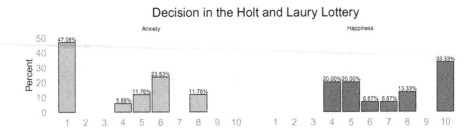

Fig. 3. Percentage distribution of risk behavior by treatment.

4   Study 2 - Explicit Emotional Debiasing

The results of Study 1 show that the autobiographical emotion induction was successful. Therefore, in Study 2, we also implemented the social agent Floka in the design and used it to provide an explicit emotional debiasing explanation to the explainee depending on their emotional state. The detailed extensions to Study 1 will be described below. Otherwise, Study 2 used the same procedure as that in Study 1.

4.1   Method

As in Study 1, participants who did not switch from lottery A to lottery B at all were excluded from the data set. In total, 23 students (7 male, 16 female) participated in the study for pay. On average, each session lasted 33 min. The average age of participants was 26 years ($SD = 7.3$). Thirteen participants had graduated with a high school diploma, and ten participants graduated with a technical college or university degree. Fourteen participants were assigned to the "Happiness" treatment group; nine to the "Anxiety" treatment group. As in Study 1, participants received a 5.00 € show-up fee and had the opportunity to additionally receive up to 3.85 € in lottery winnings. As a follow-up to Study 1, a randomized controlled experiment following a 2×1 design with student participants was conducted at Bielefeld University in July 2022. The questionnaire used in Study 1 was extended to include the technology interaction scale (ATI) [10] and a test of the Big Five personality characteristics [27].

Setup Changes. Besides the small changes in the questionnaire, we added a two-minute relaxation phase while keeping the five minutes of the autobiographical memory task. We also added the virtual social agent Floka, the visually improved version of Flobi [22]. This agent was used to interact directly with the participant. First, Floka led the participants through the same emotion induction phases as Study 1 by reading the task aloud. After the first decision in the lottery, Floka gave a recommendation and explanation before the participants had the opportunity to change their decision. To simulate an intelligent virtual agent, an experimenter in a nearby room controlled Floka following a pre-defined action sequence. To time the interaction, the experimenter could see the whole touchscreen as well as the webcam feed with the participant's face on their screen. The webcam feed was used to calculate and log the current emotions using the emotion recognition framework deepface [33]. To also collect the current heart rate of the participant, we used a Samsung Watch 3 with a specially developed application to log the current heart rate with the timestamp. Both emotion recognition and heart rate were collected only for later interpretation and had no direct influence on the study.

Procedure. The experiment took place in two rooms, with a participant in one room and the experimenter in the other. During the experiment, the participant sat in front of a touchscreen and was filmed with a webcam. One-half of the screen was used for the questionnaire, implemented in SoSci Survey [16]. Thus, the entire interaction part of the experiment took place with the help of this questionnaire. The other half was used to display Floka (see Fig. 4).

Fig. 4. A visualization of the setup. The participant sat in front of a screen, while the social agent Floka was controlled from another room by the experimenter.

At the beginning of the experiment, participants were told to put on the smartwatch and take a seat in front of the touch monitor. After a short introduction of Floka, triggered by the experimenter, demographic information was collected in the questionnaire along with the ATI and the Big Five. We then collected current emotions with the STAI, mDES, and a visual question about valence and arousal. Next, the emotion induction started. For this, Floka told the participant to first relax for two minutes and then spend five minutes recalling a situation in which they felt especially either happy or anxious. To control the induction, the STAI, mDES, and items on valence and arousal were asked again. This was followed by the Holt and Laury lottery. Floka told participants how the lottery worked, and then they had to make a decision. After that decision, Floka explained that depending on the group, the current emotions might lead to higher ("Happiness" treatment)/lower ("Anxiety" treatment) risk-taking than normal and that participants should rethink their decision. They were then given another chance to change their decision. In the end, the lottery was randomly chosen to calculate the additional payout.

4.2 Results

Manipulation Check. To examine the efficiency of the self-generated emotions in relation to the induction of the respective emotion, we conducted Wilcoxon tests with paired samples for the different Likert scales, as in Study 1. In total, positive feelings in the "Happiness" condition were higher after the emotion induction ($Mdn = 2.70$, $SD = 1.02$) than before the induction ($Mdn = 2.35$, $SD = 0.36$, $z = -2.70$, $p = .0044$, $r = .72$). Negative feelings in the anxiety condition were higher after the emotion induction ($Mdn = 0.80$, $SD = 0.71$) than before ($Mdn = 0.40$, $SD = 0.36$, $z = -2.03$, $p = .0469$, $r = .68$). Though not all differences attained significance due to the small sample size, all scales show a higher rating of the respective emotion in the associated treatment group (see Table 2). In total, our results suggest that our emotion induction was effective.

Risk Behavior. A Wilcoxon matched-pairs signed-rank test was calculated for the first and second decisions during the Holt and Laury lottery per treatment. In the treatment group "Happiness," this showed no significant difference between the first lottery decision ($Mdn = 6.5$, $SD = 2.20$) and the second decision ($Mdn = 6.5$, $SD = 1.82$, $z = 0.62$, $p = .75$, $r = .17$) (see Fig. 5). In the treatment group "Anxiety," the participants' willingness to take risks was higher after ($Mdn = 6$, $SD = 2.51$) than before Floka's explanation ($Mdn = 7$, $SD = 2.60$, $z = 1.72$, $p = .25$, $r = .57$). This difference did not attain significance, which may have been due to the small sample size. Looking at the attention paid to Floka's explanation, 6 out of the 23 participants (26%) changed their second lottery choice compared to the first one.

Heart Rate. Results were calculated with data from only 20 participants, because of too few data points and other technical issues for some participants.

Table 2. Median of the respective Likert scale.

Variable	Before (Mdn, SD)	After (Mdn, SD)	Wilcoxon-test
	Treatmentgroup "Happiness"		
Valence (SAM)	4 (0.83)	5 (0.99)	z = -2.63, p = .00156***
Arousal(SAM)	2 (0.83)	1.5 (0.65)	z = 2.33, p = .0391**
mDES-positive	2.35 (0.36)	2.7 (1.02)	z = -2.70, p = .0044***
mDES-negative	0.15 (0.49)	0.0 (0.26)	z = 2.77, p = .0078***
STAI	2.3 (0.64)	2.0 (0.38)	z = 3.02, p = .0010***
	Treatmentgroup "Anxiety"		
Variable	Before (Mdn, SD)	After (Mdn, SD)	Wilcoxon-test
Valence (SAM)	4 (0.71)	3 (1.05)	z = 1.67, p = .1875
Arousal(SAM)	2 (0.83)	2 (1.12)	z = -1.23, p = .3594
mDES-positive	1.7 (0.67)	1.1 (1.02)	z = 2.14, p = .0313**
mDES-negative	0.4 (0.36)	0.8 (0.71)	z = -2.03, p = .0469**
STAI	2.5 (0.63)	2.8 (0.88)	z = -1.90, p = .0625*

*** p < .01, ** p < .05, *p < .1

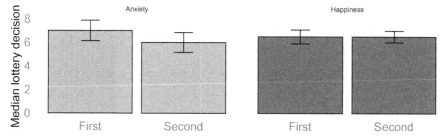

Decision in the Holt and Laury lottery

Fig. 5. Comparison of the first and second decision in the lottery by treatment (error bar = standard error).

To compare the different heart rate (HR) data of the participant, we calculated delta of the heart rate: $\Delta\,HR = HR_{Induction} - Mean(HR_{Relax})$. For both the mean of the relax phase and the HR during the induction, we used only the time after Floka's explanations. Therefore, HR was analyzed only during the task itself. In Fig. 6, results showed a trend of the "Anxiety" treatment group getting a higher delta overall, with nearly all being above zero, while the $\Delta\,HR$ of the "Happiness" treatment group gathers around zero and some below.

The $\Delta\,HR$, grouped by treatment, were tested for significance using the two-sample Wilcoxon rank test. Results showed a highly significant difference between the treatments ($z = 6.84$, $p < .001$, $r = .111$). Therefore, participants in the "Anxiety" treatment group have on average a higher $\Delta\,HR$ ($Mdn = 2.29$, $SD = 6.75$) than participants in the "Happiness" group ($Mdn = 1.56$, $SD = 4.46$).

Anxiety Induction Phase

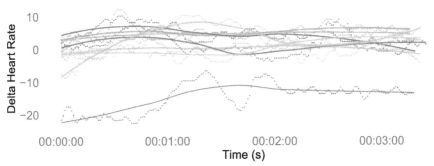

Happiness Induction Phase

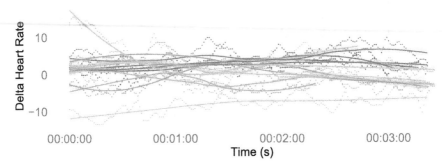

Fig. 6. ΔHR during the induction phase for each participant grouped by treatment with smoothed curve.

When calculating the same Wilcoxon rank test using the mean ΔHR for each participant (see Fig. 7), results were not significant ($z = 0.77$, $p = .472$, $r = .172$).

Descriptive Emotion Recognition Results. During the experiment, participants' faces were recorded and interpreted by deepface.

Figure 8 illustrates these results for one participant in each treatment group. The x-axis depicts the time passed since the start of the study; and on the y-axis, is the precentral result of the discrete emotion output of the deepface analysis. Dots represent the actual output and the percentage of the detected emotion at that time. In contrast, the lines are the smoothed result using the generalized additive model (GAM) set within the confidence interval. The vertical annotations represent the start of the different sections of the study. During the induction phase, participants were asked to write on paper. Because some participants rested their heads on their hands, the recognition often could not detect their emotions. Especially for the "Happiness" treatment, emotion recognition could not recognize happiness during the emotion phase. For the "Anxiety" group,

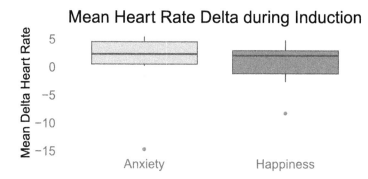

Fig. 7. Comparison of the mean ΔHR of each participant during the induction phase by treatment.

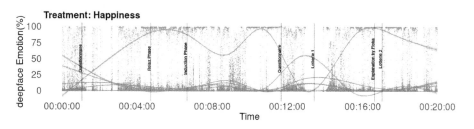

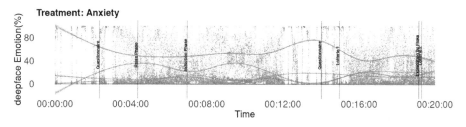

Fig. 8. Exemplary emotion recognition via deepface over the full time with discrete emotions in the percentage of one participant per treatment. The colored points represent the recognized emotion in that timeframe, while the curves are the smoothed results over one emotion. The different sections of the study are labeled with vertical lines.

when a change was visible, it was recognized more as sadness than as anxiety. The emotion recognition data had no clear pattern over all participants. In the given exemplary visualization of two participants, for the "Anxiety" treatment, the sadness grows; for the happiness example, the neutral emotion rises at some points up to nearly 100%. The angry emotion rises during the induction for other participants with the "Happiness" treatment. Assumptions as to why this was the case and how this possibly could be improved will be addressed in the discussion.

5 Discussion

This study used the Holt and Laury lottery to examine the influence of the discrete emotions of happiness and anxiety on a financial risk decision. In addition, we tested the autobiographical procedure as a form of emotion induction under laboratory conditions. The respective emotion ratings in the treatment group were higher after emotion induction than before, indicating the success of the autobiographical memory task. This is consistent with the results of other studies showing that this procedure is suitable for eliciting the emotions of happiness and anxiety [34]. Following the ATF [19], we hypothesized that happiness would elicit more risk-seeking behavior and anxiety would elicit more risk-averse behavior. Contrary to the ATF, results from both studies showed that happiness is associated with risk-averse and anxiety is associated with risk-seeking decisions. Furthermore, the risk distribution of the participants did not follow a normal distribution. Hence, we were able to show that the participants made a biased decision due to emotion induction. The risk behavior results are in contrast to the results of Schulreich et al. [32]. In their study, the authors showed that loss aversion increased in individuals who were shown incidental fear cues. In their experiment, they used emotional priming with the help of visual imagery. To measure risk aversion, participants were asked to accept or reject a series of mixed gambles. The probability of winning or losing was equal. These contrasting results may be because a different emotion induction procedure, as well as a different measure of risk-taking behavior, was chosen than in our studies. In the Holt and Laury lottery we used in our studies, participants choose one risk choice, whereas the experiment of Schulreich et al. [32] consists of 200 trials. Furthermore, the authors suggest that the participants' personality plays a moderating role in this context and should be included for more specific predictions about risk behavior in further studies.

In the next step, we investigated whether we could use Floka as an intervention and as an explicit emotional debiasing explanation to influence risk behavior of the participants. Only six participants changed their decision after the explanation, indicating that the strategy we applied is not yet successful. This result is in line with the current state of research, which states that until now, it has not yet been sufficiently investigated what constitutes a good explanation from a human perspective [29]. A theory-driven conceptual framework exists for explanations and reasoning methods [39]. So far, this has been related to the medical context and, therefore, still needs to be adapted to a human-computer interaction considering emotions, especially in risk-decision. We consider experiments under laboratory conditions especially suitable for further investigations.

The emotional data were not able to show much of a consistent difference between the treatments and even between the different sections of the study itself. One reason for this could be the lack of interaction with Floka. Other studies have shown that spontaneous smiling happens much more often during interaction [31]. Therefore, participants could have felt the emotion triggered by the treatment during the emotion induction, but had no social reason to adapt their appearance, e.g., facial expressions, to their feelings. This makes it hard for the facial emotion recognition to detect the right emotion.

With the ΔHR, we were able to show a significant difference between conditions when each ΔHR point is compared instead of the mean of the ΔHR per participant. The mean of the ΔHR might not be significant. This could be due to the small sample size. But also, in Fig. 6 visible, are the reactions to the inductions more in waves and concentrated in the "Anxiety" treatment group in the first minute. With the same physical task of writing down memories, emotions seemed to have a relevant impact on the heart rate. In our results, the "Anxiety" treatment group had a higher mean ΔHR than the "Happiness" group. Another study presented facial expressions while collecting brain activity and heart rate data. Here as well, sad expressions enhanced the heart rate compared to happiness expressions [5]. Furthermore, the relation between the heart rate and the arousal intensity was shown in another study [2]. Therefore, sadness or anxiety has a higher arousal than relaxed happiness and so a higher ΔHR. As a methodological improvement, we need to ensure the watch is correctly positioned to prevent data loss. Even with this small amount of data, differences between the treatment were visible. Therefore, it still could be possible that the heart rate is a good indicator of emotional changes when compared to the baseline.

6   Conclusion and Outlook

Using a laboratory setting, our studies investigated how induced emotions influence the risk propensity in HCI. We also investigated how far the first explanation strategy we chose - explicit emotional debiasing - influences the human explainee in a lottery decision, and how well the emotional state can be estimated during this process. We found experimental evidence that the emotion induction was successful and that induced emotions (happiness vs. anxiety) influence risk behavior in a lottery choice game, although the risk behavior proves to be different from that expected. More precisely, individuals in the treatment group "Happiness" show higher risk aversion, whereas individuals in the treatment group "Anxiety" take a higher risk. The small percentage of participants (26%) who changed their lottery choice after Floka's explanation suggests that further explanatory strategies should be explored and adapted to humans. We plan to conduct a variety of follow-up studies with a stronger interaction between Floka and human explainees that will address the following questions: How do different explanation strategies by AI recommender systems influence the human explainee in decision-making? Which explanation strategies are appropriate for the successful co-construction of explanations? How do emotions influence the process of perception and understanding of the human receiver of explanations? Increasing awareness of the influence of emotions on financial risk decisions might help to overcome harmful decision biases in the future. Accordingly, our future work has the potential to expand the general literature on human-centered explainable AI and provide approaches for designing intelligent systems capable of helping humans understand their decision when they are emotionally aroused. Moreover, practical recommendations can be made for developers of computer-aided decision systems.

The calculated ΔHR showed the presence of changes, but these were only temporary. Upcoming studies will calculate ΔHR during the study to get an indicator of arousal changes, because of the finding that ΔHR primarily reflects arousal intensity [3]. The current emotion should still be monitored within some emotion recognition framework. This could lead to fast and more direct reactions to emotionally relevant situations of the social agent - in this case, Floka. The emotion recognition framework deepface collected some interesting data but was unable to register the right emotion during the induction. Further research will test how other frameworks and models fit the collected video data as a comparison. But we expect similar results due to the lack of interaction and therefore the non-display of emotions. To see whether we can overcome the effect of emotions being displayed more in social contexts and collect suitable information from facial expressions, we are also planning an upcoming study in which participants interact with Floka directly.

Acknowledgements. We would like to thank Maryam Alizadeh (Bielefeld University) and Anamaria Cubelic (Paderborn University) for their assistance with data collection in their master theses. The work described in this paper was supported by a grant from the Deutsche Forschungsgemeinschaft (DFG, German Research Foundation): TRR 318/1 2021 - 438445824.

References

1. Angie, A.D., Connelly, S., Waples, E.P., Kligyte, V.: The influence of discrete emotions on judgement and decision-making: a meta-analytic review. Cogn. Emotion **25**(8), 1393–1422 (2011)
2. Azarbarzin, A., Ostrowski, M., Hanly, P., Younes, M.: Relationship between arousal intensity and heart rate response to arousal. Sleep **37**(4), 645–653 (2014)
3. Bradley, M.M., Lang, P.J.: Measuring emotion: the self-assessment manikin and the semantic differential. J. Behav. Ther. Exp. Psychiatry **25**(1), 49–59 (1994)
4. Chaminade, T., Zecca, M., Blakemore, S.J., Takanishi, A., Frith, C.D., Micera, S., Dario, P., Rizzolatti, G., Gallese, V., Umiltà, M.A.: Brain response to a humanoid robot in areas implicated in the perception of human emotional gestures. PLoS ONE **5**(7), e11577 (2010)
5. Critchley, H.D., Rotshtein, P., Nagai, Y., O'Doherty, J., Mathias, C.J., Dolan, R.J.: Activity in the human brain predicting differential heart rate responses to emotional facial expressions. Neuroimage **24**(3), 751–762 (2005)
6. Crivelli, C., Fridlund, A.: Facial displays are tools for social influence. Trends Cognitive Sci. **22**(5) (2018)
7. Ekman, P.: Universal and cultural differences in facial expressions of emotions. Nebraksa Symposium Motivation **19**, 207–283 (1971)

8. Elliott, M.V., Johnson, S.L., Pearlstein, J.G., Lopez, D.E.M., Keren, H.: Emotion-related impulsivity and risky decision-making: a systematic review and meta-regression. Clinical Psychol. Rev., 102232 (2022)
9. Eyben, F., Wöllmer, M., Schuller, B.: Opensmile: the Munich versatile and fast open-source audio feature extractor. In: Proceedings of the 18th ACM International Conference on Multimedia, pp. 1459–1462 (2010)
10. Franke, T., Attig, C., Wessel, D.: A personal resource for technology interaction: development and validation of the affinity for technology interaction (ati) scale. Int. J. Hum.-Comput. Interact. **35**(6), 456–467 (2019)
11. Fredrickson, B.L.: Positive emotions broaden and build. In: Advances in Experimental Social Psychology, vol. 47, pp. 1–53. Elsevier (2013)
12. Hess, U., Banse, R., Kappas, A.: The intensity of facial expression is determined by underlying affective state and social situation. J. Personlaity Soc. Psychol. **69**(2), 280–288 (1995)
13. Holt, C.A., Laury, S.K.: Risk aversion and incentive effects. Am. Econ. Rev. **92**(5), 1644–1655 (2002)
14. Jaiswal, S., Virmani, S., Sethi, V., De, K., Roy, P.P.: An intelligent recommendation system using gaze and emotion detection. Multimed. Tools Appl. **78**, 14231–14250 (2019)
15. Kensinger, E.A.: Remembering the details: effects of emotion. Emot. Rev. **2**(1), 99–113 (2009). https://doi.org/10.1177/1754073908100432
16. Leiner, D. J.: Sosci survey. https://www.soscisurvey.de
17. Lerner, J.S., Han, S., Keltner, D.: Feelings and consumer decision making: extending the appraisal-tendency framework. J. Consum. Psychol. **17**(3), 181–187 (2007)
18. Lerner, J.S., Keltner, D.: Beyond valence: toward a model of emotion-specific influences on judgement and choice. Cogn. Emotion **14**(4), 473–493 (2000)
19. Lerner, J.S., Keltner, D.: Fear, anger, and risk. J. Pers. Soc. Psychol. **81**(1), 146 (2001)
20. Lerner, J.S., Li, Y., Valdesolo, P., Kassam, K.S.: Emotion and decision making. Annu. Rev. Psychol. **66**, 799–823 (2015)
21. Lerner, J.S., Tiedens, L.Z.: Portrait of the angry decision maker: how appraisal tendencies shape anger's influence on cognition. J. Behav. Decis. Mak. **19**(2), 115–137 (2006)
22. Lütkebohle, I., et al.: The bielefeld anthropomorphic robot head "flobi". In: 2010 IEEE International Conference on Robotics and Automation, pp. 3384–3391 (2010). https://doi.org/10.1109/ROBOT.2010.5509173
23. Mills, C., D'Mello, S.: On the validity of the autobiographical emotional memory task for emotion induction. PLoS ONE **9**(4), e95837 (2014)
24. Moscato, V., Picariello, A., Sperlí, G.: An emotional recommender system for music. IEEE Intell. Syst. **36**(5), 57–68 (2021). https://doi.org/10.1109/MIS.2020.3026000
25. Rosenthal-von der Pütten, A.M., Krämer, N.C., Hoffmann, L., Sobieraj, S., Eimler, S.C.: An experimental study on emotional reactions towards a robot. Int. J. Soc. Robot. **5**(1), 17–34 (2013)
26. Rabin, M., Thaler, R.H.: Anomalies: risk aversion. J. Econ. Perspectives **15**(1), 219–232 (2001)
27. Rammstedt, B., Kemper, C.J., Klein, M.C., Beierlein, C., Kovaleva, A.: Big five inventory (bfi-10). Zusammenstellung sozialwissenschaftlicher Items und Skalen (ZIS) (2014). https://doi.org/10.6102/zis76,https://zis.gesis.org/DoiId/zis76

28. Ribeiro, F.S., Santos, F.H., Albuquerque, P.B., Oliveira-Silva, P.: Emotional induction through music: measuring cardiac and electrodermal responses of emotional states and their persistence. Front. Psychol. **10**, 451 (2019)
29. Riedl, M.O.: Human-centered artificial intelligence and machine learning. Hum. Behav. Emerg. Technol. **1**(1), 33–36 (2019)
30. Rohlfing, K.J., et al.: Explanation as a social practice: toward a conceptual framework for the social design of AI systems. IEEE Trans. Cogn. Dev. Syst. **13**(3), 717–728 (2020)
31. Ruiz-Belda, M.A., Fernández-Dols, J.M., Carrera, P., Barchard, K.: Spontaneous facial expressions of happy bowlers and soccer fans. Cogn. Emot. **17**(2), 315–326 (2003)
32. Schulreich, S., Gerhardt, H., Heekeren, H.R.: Incidental fear cues increase monetary loss aversion. Emotion **16**(3), 402 (2016)
33. Serengil, S.I., Ozpinar, A.: Hyperextended lightface: a facial attribute analysis framework. In: 2021 International Conference on Engineering and Emerging Technologies (ICEET), pp. 1–4. IEEE (2021). https://doi.org/10.1109/ICEET53442. 2021.9659697
34. Siedlecka, E., Denson, T.F.: Experimental methods for inducing basic emotions: a qualitative review. Emot. Rev. **11**(1), 87–97 (2019)
35. Smith, C.A., Ellsworth, P.C.: Patterns of cognitive appraisal in emotion. J. Pers. Soc. Psychol. **48**(4), 813 (1985)
36. Spielberger, C.D.: Manual for the state-trait anxietry, inventory. Consulting Psychologist (1970)
37. Thiruchselvam, R., Blechert, J., Sheppes, G., Rydstrom, A., Gross, J.J.: The temporal dynamics of emotion regulation: an eeg study of distraction and reappraisal. Biol. Psychol. **87**(1), 84–92 (2011). https://doi.org/10.1016/j.biopsycho.2011.02. 009. https://www.sciencedirect.com/science/article/pii/S0301051111000391
38. Toisoul, A., Kossaifi, J., Bulat, A., Tzimiropoulos, G., Pantic, M.: Estimation of continuous valence and arousal levels from faces in naturalistic conditions. Nature Mach. Intell. (2021). https://www.nature.com/articles/s42256-020-00280-0
39. Wang, D., Yang, Q., Abdul, A., Lim, B.Y.: Designing theory-driven user-centric explainable AI. In: Proceedings of the 2019 CHI Conference on Human Factors in Computing Systems, pp. 1–15 (2019)
40. Yang, Q., Zhou, S., Gu, R., Wu, Y.: How do different kinds of incidental emotions influence risk decision making? Biol. Psychol. **154**, 107920 (2020)

Exploring Mental Models for Explainable Artificial Intelligence: Engaging Cross-disciplinary Teams Using a Design Thinking Approach

Helen Sheridan[✉] 📧, Emma Murphy 📧, and Dympna O'Sullivan 📧

School of Computer Science, TU Dublin, Grangegorman, Dublin, Ireland
{helen.sheridan,emma.x.murphy,dympna.osullivan}@tudublin.ie

Abstract. Exploring end-users' understanding of Artificial Intelligence (AI) systems' behaviours and outputs is crucial in developing accessible Explainable Artificial Intelligence (XAI) solutions. Investigating mental models of AI systems is core in understanding and explaining the often opaque, complex, and unpredictable nature of AI. Researchers engage surveys, interviews, and observations for software systems, yielding useful evaluations. However, an evaluation gulf still exists, primarily around comprehending end-users' understanding of AI systems. It has been argued that by exploring theories related to human decision-making examining the fields of psychology, philosophy, and human computer interaction (HCI) in a more people-centric rather than product or technology-centric approach can result in the creation of initial XAI solutions with great potential. Our work presents the results of a design thinking workshop with 14 cross-collaborative participants with backgrounds in philosophy, psychology, computer science, AI systems development and HCI. Participants undertook design thinking activities to ideate how AI system behaviours may be explained to end-users to bridge the explanation gulf of AI systems. We reflect on design thinking as a methodology for exploring end-users' perceptions and mental models of AI systems with a view to creating effective, useful, and accessible XAI.

Keywords: Artificial Intelligence · Explainable Artificial Intelligence · Human Computer Interaction · Design Thinking

1 Introduction

The use of AI across almost every facet of society, including healthcare, education, recruitment, financial services, entertainment, and social media, to list but a few domains, has revolutionised many industries where sophisticated algorithms process large data sets and vast quantities of information beyond the capacity of humans [1]. As such most end-users who interact with information technology engage with AI powered systems at some stage in their lives, whether knowingly or unknowingly [2]. Recent advancements in AI powered technologies have garnered public and media attention [3, 4] giving the

H. Degen and S. Ntoa (Eds.): HCII 2023, LNAI 14050, pp. 337–354, 2023.
https://doi.org/10.1007/978-3-031-35891-3_21

public an insight into how powerful modern AI has become [5]. What viral media and public attention does, in relation to AI, is spark a public conversation about what AI can do, what AI should do and how do we trust the outputs of systems which sometimes, even those that develop them, have difficulty in explaining [6]. In recent years research into and interest in the necessity to explain the decisions of AI systems has given rise to explainable artificial intelligence (XAI) where human-comprehensible explanations of AI based systems are produced as a means of enhancing acceptance and trust in AI systems decisions and outputs [7]. The EU's General Data Protection Regulation (GDPR) calls for the "right to explanation" [8] and where users' data is processed by an automated decision-making system, the right to "meaningful information about the logic involved" [8] allowing for ethical and transparent AI. The USAs Algorithmic Accountability Act states similar requirements seeking "transparency, explainability, contestability, and opportunity for recourse" [9] and goes further seeking access for users to information as to which factors contributed to a particular decision and if changed, how this may result in a different decision [9]. The "right to explanation" in theory and its meaningful implementation in practice has given rise to "explosive" [10–12] public debate questioning what legislation envisages as an explanation which allows users to verify and understand their interaction with an automated decision making system and what constitutes a "meaningful" explanation when the diverse range of end users are taken into account [13].

Explanations in XAI can be defined by certain criteria including the explanation scope either global or local, making the entire infernal process comprehensible versus explaining each inference [14]. Explanation stage either ante-hoc or post hoc, considering explanations from the beginning and during training versus explanations post training using an external explainer including factual, counterfactual, and semi-factuals [15]. Explanations can also be defined by problem type either classification or regression, by input data, usually numerical, pictorial, textual and times series and finally by output format including numerical, rules, textual, visual or mixed [14].

Explorations in the incorporation of virtual agents into explainable artificial intelligence has shown an increase in user trust in an AI system [16], analysis of users' mental models in recommender systems (RS) such as Netflix and the use of explainable RS has been shown to increase users' confidence in these systems [17, 18], and the use of visual explanations in the detection of skin cancer has been investigated in the integration of AI models in clinical practice [19, 20]. What these studies show is that XAI increases users' trust in the outputs of AI systems bringing accountability and transparency into systems limited by their inability to explain their operations to end users [21].

However, while the use of explanations in AI is a positive development, it has been argued that many AI developers build explanatory agents for themselves rather than for the end-user and that considerations from wider areas of expertise as well as more user-centric rather than technology focused approaches should be adopted in order for XAI to succeed [22]. Miller et al. argues that those experts who understand the decisions of AI systems the best may not be in the right position to judge the usefulness of explanations for end-users. An understanding of how people explain, what constitutes an explanation, what is their function and structure seems imperative [23] and leveraging methods and processes from user experience (UX) design and human computer interaction (HCI) [23] can be used as a step towards designing and developing more meaningful XAI.

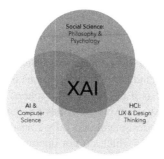

Fig. 1. Our "Scope of Explainable Artificial Intelligence" [23] engages experts in the fields of AI and Computer Science, Philosophy and Psychology and HCI, specifically UX and Design thinking.

In this paper we present the findings of a cross-disciplinary workshop taking methods from HCI and UX design in the form of Design Thinking, concentrating on the empathise, define and ideate modes. Where expertise in computer science and AI systems development, psychology and philosophy and UX and HCI intersect can more meaningful understanding and mental models of AI be explored? See Fig. 1. Following Miller's "Scope of Explainable Artificial Intelligence" [23] our study explored this by:

- Engaging a cross-collaborative team of 14 participants with expertise in psychology and philosophy, computer science and AI systems development in a design thinking workshop.
- Workshop led by 2 experts in HCI, UX and Design Thinking.
- Leveraging the use of personas and scenarios of two typical users of an AI driven system to facilitate empathising, defining and ideation related to users' frustrations around opaque areas of the system.
- Defining pain points in each personas' experience which reflect opaque areas of the system's decision making and outputs.
- Designing big ideas (possible XAI solutions) to ease this pain.

These results form part of a larger programme of work which engages diverse AI stakeholders examining the perspectives of users from AI experts to non-expert end users. These include participants having recently faced CV rejection with backgrounds in computer science and participants with a background in design together with computer scientists [24]. In future research we envisage combining and contrasting these results to gain a more holistic understanding of mental models and XAI as an initial stage in the development of XAI solutions.

2 Related Work

2.1 Challenges of XAI for the UX Designer

AI is now a well-established technology with diverse applications across many domains combining the expertise of computer and data scientists in conjunction with UX designers. However, AI has not experienced the same level of design and UX innovation which other technologies have experienced perhaps due to this material being considered difficult to work with and understand [25]. With less focus on interaction by users, as the AI system computes outputs "as if by magic", the role of UX designer may have traditionally been omitted. In a similar vein, XAI has proven a complicated problem for AI systems developers and UX designers especially considering the range of users who engage with complex AI systems which do not operate in the same manner as traditional UI applications. It has been argued that optimisation and efficiency, quantitative metrics, are primarily the realm of developers versus ethical concerns and context of use, qualitative metrics which are primarily the concern of UX designers. UX designers usually enter the AI project lifecycle after the developers have concentrated on making the technology work, adding the window dressing or as Dove et al. state "putting lipstick on the pig" [25]. Since the inner workings and outputs of AI systems are not fully understood by many UX designers who find it "difficult to articulate what AI can/cannot do" [26] and as such find it "difficult to understand a working AI system's design potential" [26]. Further human-AI interaction design challenges within a technology-driven design process include "Cannot envision AI uses that do not yet exist", "HCI/design experts often joined AI teams late in the design/dev process" and "Do not know how HCI/design and AI experts should collaborate" [26].

Similar challenges apply to the design and development of XAI where many current solutions rely on developers' own intuition of what embodies a useful explanation rather than basing explanations on the understanding of the end user or taking into account the expertise of diverse stakeholders throughout the lifecycle of the XAI project [23]. Some of these challenges may be mitigated through the engagement of cross-disciplinary teams collaborating early in the design and development process [22] and in UX designers working with skilled technologists, computer scientists and AI developers [25]. In addition, drawing from human reasoning using teachings from philosophy and psychology alongside the technical features of AI can be used to develop more user-centric XAI [27].

2.2 Design Thinking

Design thinking can be best described as a problem-solving approach, or more comprehensively as a non-linear, collaborative approach for identifying, defining and creatively solving problems [28]. Implemented and advocated over at least the last 50 years within business [29, 30] and fostered by those in research and education [31], design thinking simply facilitates approaching problems and their prospective solutions as a designer might, helping non-designers to think like designers [32]. Drawing from theories and teaching in HCI and UX, design thinking can be described as an iterative approach which asks that participants put themselves in the users' shoes to better understand their needs, experiences and behaviours [33]. Design thinking is considered as having 5 distinct modes; empathise, define, ideate, prototype and test [31]. In our experience, as a method to engage stakeholders at the early design and development stages of a project and to facilitate collaboration between disparate team members such as HCI/UX designers and developers, design thinking has been shown to be particularly beneficial [34]. One key mode, definition can be accomplished using the concept of pain points, areas of frustration for users or in the case of an AI powered system areas of opacity requiring ideation or big ideas development in the form of explanations. Novel approaches to pain point definition and ideation have emerged from UX research including the technology-as-monster approach where unknowns or concerns in a system are embodied in the form of a monster. Once identified and described workshop participants can tame or domesticate these monsters allowing for mitigation of concerns [35]. Essentially, by defining monsters / pain points and ideating on taming monsters / big ideas development, workshop participants can visualise and articulate concepts usually difficult to describe and converge on how best to alleviate users' pain.

2.3 Mental Models

A mental model can be described as a belief that a user has about a software system such as a website, interface or other information system and how users understand how something can, does or should function in the world [36]. Described as a model of what users' know or think they know about a system, each users' mental model is unique in some way as it is an internal construct within a users' brain. Ultimately designers of information systems aim to communicate a system's function reasonably well so that end-users' can build accurate and as a result useful mental models [37]. One common predicament is the gap in the mental models formed between the designers and developers of a system and those of its users. Those that design and build the system cannot unknow what they know whereas end-users are often more deficient in their knowledge of a system [37]. Basically, mental models reflect how a user expects a system to work rather than how it actually works [38]. Within many information technology disciplines including user interface design and website design the theory of mental models have been used to great effect [39]. However, within less predictable systems such as AI systems the theory of mental models can be more difficult to apply or obtain but are an integral step in developing accessible XAI. AI systems tend to be less transparent, more complex and changeable compared to traditional systems, as such end-users may find it difficult to visualise or articulate their understanding of how these systems work. Mental models for AI have been described as a model of how end-users perform a function whilst using an AI system and how AI might anticipate end-users' actions and update the output accordingly [40]. This can be further explained by Norman's gulf of execution, the difference between a user's intentions and what the system allows them to actually do or whether the system supports those actions in its output [41]. Without an understanding of how an algorithm might reason and what a user might do to achieve an accurate or useful output, an AI system might not produce a state or output which makes sense to the user. User interface designers refer to this as the gulf of evaluation, the degree to which the system displays representations which are aligned with the intentions and expectations of the user [41]. We posit there also exists an explanation gulf for AI systems including a lack of explanation as to how they behave and how they compute outputs which is crucial in developing accessible XAI solutions for end-users.

3   Methods

3.1   Participants

We conducted a design thinking workshop with 14 participants with expertise in philosophy, psychology, computer science and AI systems development and facilitated by experts in human computer interaction, user experience and design thinking. Invitation to participate was distributed via email with a pre-workshop survey distributed via Microsoft Forms and university ethical approval was sought prior to workshop delivery.

A range of nationalities were represented with participants from Ireland, Italy, Nigeria, Sweden, Iran, Greece, France and Spain in attendance and a gender representation of 8 males and 6 females participating and 2 females facilitating. To ensure participants satisfied our cross-collaborative approach, inclusion criteria included expertise in AI, computer science, philosophy or psychology and HCI and UX design. Inclusion criteria for facilitators included expertise in design thinking, UX and HCI to ensure that participants were successfully guided through the design thinking modes.

3.2   Persona and Scenario Design

The problem domain, employment, which we explored in this workshop and as part of our larger study, including two further workshops, was considered suitable given the demographics of all participants. Considering the increasing role AI driven systems play in the lifecycle of the employment process, from a candidate perspective and from that of a recruiter, we identified an employment domain as one which participants would most closely empathise with and one which gave us sufficient scope to examine mental models of both expert and non-expert end users. Additionally, when we consider the extensive use of AI particularly in CV filtering systems resulting in the puzzling phenomenon of recruiters struggling to find suitable talent whilst job seekers apply for multiple open jobs [42] and recent media attention in relation to AI recruitment systems which have been proven to discriminate against women or those with disabilities [43–45]. AI in the recruitment domain calls for further research and exploration regarding XAI.

As such, following interviews with a recruitment manager employed in the IT sector and interviews with recent graduates struggling to find employment, two personas and scenarios were designed to reflect two typical, but different users of an AI driven recruitment system. See Fig. 4. Andrew Wilson, a recent graduate of a computer science programme designed as an atypical candidate in that his comparatively older age profile and CV gaps are likely to exacerbate biases observed in many CV filtering AI applications [46]. Maria Atkins, a recruiter, was designed as a typical user experiencing the flipside of Andrew's frustrations in that she is struggling to understand the outputs of a CV filtering AI tool and with little or no explanation is losing confidence in the AI system [42]. A broad problem statement was presented "How can we explain AI systems decisions, making them more transparent and understandable to users?" which was further specified for each persona with an accommodating scenario.

Maria Atkins Scenario

Maria is 32 year old talent acquisition specialist working in a HR department of a multinational company in Dublin, Ireland.

Maria has been working in talent acquisition since graduating from college 9 years ago. She has recently been promoted to head of talent acquisition in a large, multinational company in the docklands area of Dublin. In her previous job she worked for a small recruitment company where she filtered CVs of applicants manually. This was a slow process, but it did allow Maria to feel like she connected with applicants and really feel like she was a part of the selection process. In her new role a piece of AI powered software is used to screen applicants. Maria isn't sure how this software arrives at its conclusions and has noticed that all of the results seem very similar. Maria has no way of telling if some worthy applicants are slipping through the net.

How can we help Maria understand the CV filtering systems being used and ensure possible suitable candidates aren't slipping through the net (Fig. 2)?

Fig. 2. Maria Atkins and Andrew Wilson Personas referenced during the workshop.

Andrew Wilson Scenario

Andrew is a 42 year old recent graduate of a computer science degree from a well respected University in Ireland. Andrew is currently looking for a job within the computer science field but so far has had no success.

Andrew's route into education would be considered non-traditional in that he left school early to start work as an apprentice plumber as he needed to contribute to the household income. Also, with fees of thousands of pounds in the 1990's his parents couldn't afford to send him to college. He never completed his leaving certificate but was a bright student in school. Andrew decided to return to education, having always had an interest in computers even though he only actually bought one recently. He achieved excellent results in his degree and can't understand why he isn't being screened for interviews. He believes that if he could attend an interview and if the recruiter could meet him in person, he would get many of the jobs he has applied for.

How can we help Andrew understand the AI powered process involved in how his CV is being screened for selection for interview and increase his chances of success?

3.3 Design Thinking Workshop

The design thinking modes examined included empathise, define, and ideate with prototype and testing modes being reserved for further research and analysis post-workshop. Tools used included large paper sheets, black markers, sticky notes and sticky dots.14 participants in total were divided into 2 groups of 5 participants and 1 group of 4 participants.

Group 1: 1 psychology, 1 philosophy, 2 computer science & 1 AI with computer science, 2 females & 3 males: Maria Atkins Persona.

Group 2: 1 philosophy & 1 computer science, 1 philosophy with computer science and 2 AI with computer science, 2 females & 3 males: Andrew Wilson Persona.

Group 3: 1 computer science and 3 AI with computer science, 2 females & 2 males: Maria Atkins Persona.

Empathise
Empathy in UX design is an integral part of understanding the needs and frustrations of possible end users [47] and in design thinking we explored this using two methods. 1. Empathy mapping where participants considered what their given persona might say, think, feel or do with regard to the problem statement and 2. As-is-scenario design. This task calls for participants to break their personas engagement with the AI system into steps and further empathise considering what their persona might think, feel and do during each step [48].

Define
Apart from facilitating understanding a persona's frustrations with a system, empathising in the form of empathy mapping and as-is-scenario design, aids in the definition of pain points, possible opaque or problem areas in users' understanding of the system outputs [49]. Participants voted using 5 sticky dots applied to the as-is-scenario on areas of most pain for their persona. This stage of the workshop is considered an important milestone where each group nominates one participant to playback or present their findings with an emphasis on describing pain points identified.

Ideate
Ideation was explored in the form of big ideas development followed by prioritisation or evaluation of these ideas. The format of these tasks included, grouping of similar pain points and establishment of four main pain points based on the location of sticky dots on the as-is-scenario. A grid with four quadrants is used with one quadrant for each pain point. Four solutions are designed to ease each pain point with one considered an absurd solution. A round of voting using 5 sticky dots per participant follows considering the most important and feasible solutions. Finally, those big ideas with the most sticky dots

are prioritised using an XY grid where X axis = feasibility for us, Y Axis = importance to the user. This categorises big ideas as follows.

- High importance to the user + High feasibility for us = No brainer
- High importance to the user + Low feasibility for us = Big bets
- Low Importance for the user + Low Feasibility for us = Unwise
- Low Importance for the user + High Feasibility for us = Utilities

A second playback or presentation followed the ideation stage where each group introduced the results of their big ideas and prioritisation grid. A closing group interview and debrief session followed with questions designed to identify any further mental models in relation to XAI.

3.4 Data Collection and Analysis

Data collection included the use of digital photography to document participants' work sheets including sticky notes and sticky dots, audio recordings of playbacks or presentations and closing interview and debrief. Audio recordings were subsequently transcribed for further analysis.

4 Results

First, our results were divided into two parts; those regarding the Andrew Wilson persona and those regarding the Maria Atkins persona and further grouped by design thinking activities. Empathise and define (empathy mapping, as-scenario design and identification of pain points) and ideation (big ideas generation and prioritisation). Our rationale was to identify common and contrasting pain points for each persona, reflecting opacity in understanding AI outputs and to examine related big ideas which may offer clarity and scope for further development of XAI solutions.

4.1 Empathise and Define: Andrew Wilson Persona

During the empathise step of the design thinking process, group 2 described Andrew's engagement with a CV filtering AI system with little or no explanation as making him feel "confused", "underappreciated" and "like giving up" and he might think "What am I doing wrong?" and "How can I do better?" along with "sending out thousands of CVs that are all alike" and "tries again and again". During the as-is-scenario activity, participants broke Andrew's steps into; writing cvs, search for jobs, apply for jobs, waiting for response and learn & revise. Here too the experience was predominantly confusing and frustrating for Andrew resulting in the identification of the following pain points; lack of feedback, repeating the same process, feeling anxious and not understanding what he is doing wrong.

4.2 Empathise and Define: Maria Atkins Persona

For Maria engaging with a CV filtering AI system was also complex leading to mistrust and confusion related to how the system computes outputs. Group 1 described Maria feeling "out of control" but "eager to learn" and saying, "Is there a human left?" and "sampling rejected CVs randomly". Group 2 expressed "anger" and that "systems can be frustrating". She might "analyse successful applications to see patterns" and say, "she and candidates should have meaningful feedback".

During the as-is-scenario activity participants in group 1 broke Maria's steps into; Log in & read email, learn / frame the question, understand the system decision, communicate the problem and realisation. Through further empathising participants described Maria's eagerness to understand by comparing "other person's CVs data" to see how the system deals with data. At a given point she says "I hate AI because I cannot find the information" leading to Maria communicating to those in charge but unfortunately finally accepting that "she cannot find any information for the system, for now". Pain points identified included, talking to company managers, checking CVs & imitating the AI process manually, filtering the database.

Group 2 defined steps Maria might take as; log in to PC, view list of top applicants, manually view each of 10 candidates, contact candidates, interview top 3 candidates, send congratulations & offer to some candidates and send rejection letters. Further empathising revealed that Maria might feel that "that the system is opaque to her, and she feels it can be improved upon". She would require "transparency overall because she doesn't understand what's going on behind the scenes in how the top lists are made" and feeling "frustration, being powerless". As such pain points identified included, opacity of the system, missing good candidates and filtering data.

4.3 Ideation

For our purpose and to more comprehensively assess the outcomes of our workshop we sought to map participant big ideas to a taxonomy of XAI solutions which reflect existing XAI techniques and explanation methods [50]. Using the "category of methods" presented by Liao et al. see Fig. 3 [50] as a starting point we utilised the taxonomy or categories shown in the fourth column of Tables 1 and 2. Global (1), local (2), counterfactual (3) and example-based explanations (4).

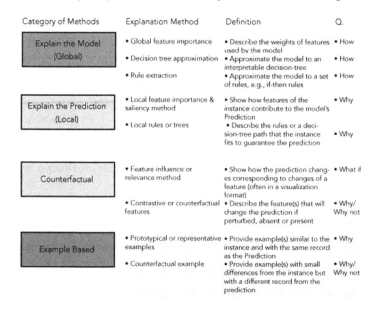

Fig. 3. Liao et al. Taxonomy of XAI methods mapping to user question types

What Liao et al. Taxonomy of XAI and user question types facilitated is the grounding of big ideas developed during the workshop in real-world, widely accepted methods of explaining AI. Mapping our big ideas to this taxonomy with corresponding questions not only confirms that our workshop helped participants to explain opaque areas of an AI system using XAI methods which are already acknowledged but also provides XAI methods to consider and questions to ask during the next phase of our research, prototype, and test. An example of how our results (pain points, big ideas and priority) maps to the taxonomy of XAI methods and question types (category, question and XAI method) can be seen in Fig. 4.

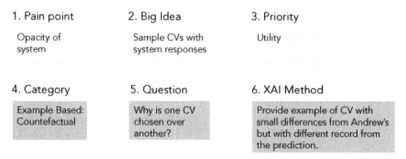

Fig. 4. Design Thinking Pain points, Big Ideas & Priority mapped to Category, Question and XAI method.

Global explanations: included those that attempt to mimic how humans explain in one instance taking the form of a digital concierge or motivator technology (Group 2, P1) *"It's not very common to have an employer tell you the reasons why you are rejected [Andrew could have] some kind of motivator technology that pops into your life and tells you if you are doing well or not"* which might be achieved using global feature importance, decision tree approximation or rule extraction [50].

Descriptions of **Local explanations:** included: (Group 3, P1) *"We thought at this point that it would be very helpful to show Maria the weights of each aspect of the CV if you have technical experience, how much does it contribute to the overall decision."* This method of explanation might take the form of local feature importance and saliency methods or local rules or trees [50].

Counterfactual explanations: included feature manipulation and how feature(s) might change the prediction: (Group 3, P2) *"So, play around with the criteria, if I change say Male to Female randomly what's the impact on the results? If I change 5 years of C + + to 6 years of C + + what's the results? So you can identify the criteria that the machine thinks have no importance that end up having a big impact....to interrogate the excluded candidates it would be helpful to have a certain percentage of them randomly selected and shown to Maria their weight score and why they are not selected"*. Explanation methods to achieve this might include feature influence or relevance method and contrastive or counterfactual features [50].

For **example explanations:** providing samples similar to the instance: (Group 1, P2) *"Maria, if she doesn't understand how the algorithm works maybe she can play with the system a little bit. Provide some fake (example) CVs and see how the system responds to them"*. This form of explanation might be accomplished in two ways, using prototypical or representative examples or counterfactual examples [50].

Table 1. Ideation Results for Andrew Wilson Persona

Pain Point	Big Idea	Priority	Category
Lack of feedback	Digital Mentor/feedback watch	Big Bet	Global
	Employer has to communicate output in person	Big Bet	Global
Repeating Process	Inclusion check for algorithm	Big Bet	Local
	Help to work with algorithm e.g. change these words etc	Utilities	Counterfactual
What am I doing wrong?	Rejection should list 3 motivations	No brainer	Counterfactual/Example
	Typical mistakes	Big Bet	Counterfactual/Example
	Tips to look better	Utilities	Counterfactual/Example
	Ranking Ranking	Utilities	Local
Feeling anxious	Digital mentor/fit watch monitors mood	Big Bet	Global/Local

Table 2. Ideation Results for Maria Atkins Persona

Pain Point	Big Idea	Priority	Category
Missing good candidates	Random Filtering	Utilities	Local
	Roll a dice, Number corresponds to candidate	Utilities	Global
	Distribution model	Utilities	Global/Local
Communicate to those in charge	Collaborate with developers	No Brainer	All Categories
	Build communication channels	No Brainer	All Categories
Manually replicating AI process	Neurolink	Big Bet	Global
	Download AI into Maria/Download Maria into AI	Big Bet	Global
	AI sorting hat	Big Bet	Global
Opacity of system	Destroy AI	Unwise	All categories
	Criteria manipulation with visual results	No Brainer	Counterfactual
	Visualisation tool	Utilities	Global/Local
	Fake/sample CVs with system responses	Utilities	Example
Filtering data/database	See weight/score for factors that contribute to decision	Utilities	Local
	Enable/Apply filters on system	Utilities	Counterfactual

5   Discussion

We sought to explore cross-disciplinary participants' (experts in AI, computer science, psychology and philosophy) understanding and mental models of AI using methods from HCI, specifically the design thinking modes, empathise, define and ideate, to consider AI as an early stage in the development of XAI solutions. From our analysis we believe design thinking, as a method of exploration and problem solving specifically with cross-disciplinary groups, has been shown to be effective especially whilst exploring ideation of AI systems. Developing a better understanding of mental models for AI systems can help bridge the explanation gulf of AI systems and aid in development of novel and accessible explanations for XAI. By engaging workshop participants in empathising with a view to identifying pain points, participants converged on areas of most opacity for users. By developing big ideas to solve pain points or opaque areas, participants presented solutions which might enhance understanding of AI.

We mapped participants' big ideas to pre-existing taxonomies of XAI techniques and methods as an initial stage or a guide in the design and development of more meaningful XAI in real world AI products [50]. For the scope of this paper, we considered the general mechanism of the system such as scope of the explanation, be that global, making the entire process of the AI model transparent and explainable or local, explaining a single prediction [51]. Together with explanations which consider how the system output might change with instance changes in the form of counterfactual explanations along with example-based explanations [52] as a distinct explanation style. Our reasoning for employing this four-part taxonomy was to consider the "How?", "Why?", What if?" and "Why not?" of cross-collaborative participants' big ideas. Further research in the form of supplementary design thinking workshops, facilitating prototype and test research stages, will examine and evaluate the "What format?" and "When?" of XAI. For this early stage of a larger study, we were concerned with the nature of the explanations rather than, at this point, what output format these explanations might take (numerical, rules, textual, visual, mixed) [14] and at what stages of a user interaction an explanation might be necessary [53]. By mapping cross-collaborative (AI, computer science, psychology, philosophy) participant's big ideas to existing taxonomies of XAI we can infer that engaging HCI methods to obtain design thinking workshop outputs successfully facilitated meaningful and shared understanding of an AI system. This aided understanding emotional responses [54] to AI and subsequently mental models of AI and potential XAI solutions.

6 Limitations

Limitations of this study centre around two areas; participant profile and domain examined. Our "Scope of Explainable Artificial Intelligence" [23] by engaging experts in the fields of AI and Computer Science, Philosophy and Psychology and HCI, specifically UX and design thinking, did not engage end users in a strict sense. By engaging experts in 3 disciplines and by empathising with two personas and corresponding scenarios, which reflected the experience of typical end users of an AI recruitment system, we cannot claim that this is an exhaustive examination of end user needs for XAI. Future work could include participants employed in recruitment, those having faced CV rejection and those employed in other roles along the AI development lifecycle such as UI designers or data scientists. Additionally, subsequent research has shown that by engaging designers as participants in design thinking workshops encourages the use of drawing, an integral part of the design thinking process [55] which can help participants visualise AI concepts and mental models which are usually difficult to articulate [24].Our chosen domain, recruitment, is one which is well understood by cross-disciplinary participants and it is not inconceivable that our findings might be applied to other domains such as financial services or within the criminal justice system. Here also, AI powered decisions can exhibit bias and discriminatory outcomes based on users data and/or individual characteristics [56] and in conjunction with AI driven recruitment decisions these outcomes aren't transparent to users. Personas and scenarios which explore more high-stakes decisions such as those within the medical domain where decisions are life or death [57], technologies with limited (fitbit) or "invisible user interfaces" (Alexa / Siri) [58] should be considered in future research.

7 Conclusion

The requirement for more user-friendly XAI is well documented [59] and one approach in the journey towards developing more meaningful XAI is in the engagement of cross-disciplinary teams, particularly at the early stages of an AI project [22, 50]. We took the position that by examining where UX, AI and Social Sciences converge, in the form of cross-disciplinary participants engaging in a design thinking workshop, uncovering opaque areas in the understanding of AI systems decisions (pain points) and their respective solutions (big ideas) has facilitated human understanding of machine learning and AI. By mapping our results to already established taxonomies of XAI solutions [50] we illustrated possible explanations to the "How?", "Why?", "What if?" and "Why not?" of an early-stage AI driven recruitment system. This equipped participants with tools to articulate and explain their understanding and mental models for AI systems thus providing the opportunity for further research and to develop better solutions for XAI.

Acknowledgements. The support of the TU Dublin Scholarship Programme is gratefully acknowledged.

References

1. Executive Office of the President. Big Data: a report on algorithmic systems, opportunity, and civil rights. Executive Office of the President, The White House, Washington, pp. 8–9 (2016)
2. IBM, IBM Global AI Adoption Index 2022. https://www.ibm.com/downloads/cas/GVA GA3JP. Accessed 02 Oct 2023
3. OpenAI, ChatGPT: optimising language models for dialogue. https://openai.com/blog/cha tgpt/. Accessed 02 Oct 2023
4. Vallance, C.: AI image creator faces UK and US legal challenges, BBC. https://www.bbc. com/news/technology-64285227. Accessed 02 Oct 2023
5. Piper, K.: OpenAI's ChatGPT is a fascinating glimpse into the scary power of AI – Vox. https://www.vox.com/future-perfect/2022/12/15/23509014/chatgpt-artificial-intell igence-openai-language-models-ai-risk-google. Accessed 02 Oct 2023
6. IBM, Explainable AI (XAI). https://www.ibm.com/watson/explainable-ai. Accessed 02 Oct 2023
7. Ahmed, I., Jeon, G., Piccialli, F.: From artificial intelligence to explainable artificial intelligence in industry 4.0: a survey on what, how, and where. IEEE Trans. Ind. Inf. **18**(8), pp. 5031–5042 (2022)
8. EPRS | European parliamentary research service scientific foresight unit (STOA). The impact of the general data protection regulation (GDPR) on artificial intelligence. https://www.eur oparl.europa.eu/RegData/etudes/STUD/2020/641530/EPRS_STU(2020)641530_EN.pdf. Accessed 02 Oct 2023
9. Federal trade commission, algorithmic accountability act of 2022. https://www.congress.gov/ bill/117th-congress/house-bill/6580/text. Accessed 02 Oct 2023
10. Goodman, B., Flaxman, S.: European union regulations on algorithmic decision-making and a "right to explanation." AI Mag. **38**(3), 50–57 (2017)
11. Wachter, S., Mittelstadt, B., Floridi, L.: Why a right to explanation of automated decision-making does not exist in the general data protection regulation. Int. Data Priv. Law **7**(2), 76–99 (2017)

12. Selbst, A., Powles, J.: Meaningful information and the right to explanation. In: Conference on Fairness, Accountability and Transparency (p. 48). PMLR (2018)
13. Casey, B., Farhangi, A., Vogl, R.: Rethinking explainable machines. Berkeley Technol. Law J. **34**(1), 143–188 (2019)
14. Vilone, G., Longo, L.: Classification of explainable artificial intelligence methods through their output formats. Mach. Learn. Knowl. Extract **3**(3), 615–661 (2021)
15. Kenny, E.M., Delaney, E.D., Greene, D., Keane, M.T.: Post-hoc explanation options for XAI in deep learning: the insight centre for data analytics perspective. In: Del Bimbo, A., et al. (eds.) ICPR 2021. LNCS, vol. 12663, pp. 20–34. Springer, Cham (2021). https://doi.org/10.1007/978-3-030-68796-0_2
16. Weitz, K., Schiller, D., Schlagowski, R., Huber, T., André, E.: "Let me explain!": exploring the potential of virtual agents in explainable AI interaction design. J. Multimodal User Interfaces **15**(2), 87–98 (2020). https://doi.org/10.1007/s12193-020-00332-0
17. Ngo, T., Kunkel, J., Ziegler, J.: Exploring mental models for transparent and controllable recommender systems: a qualitative study. In: Proceedings of the 28th ACM Conference on User Modeling, Adaptation and Personalization (pp. 183–191) (2020)
18. Tsai, C.H., Brusilovsky, P.: Explaining recommendations in an interactive hybrid social recommender. In: Proceedings of the 24th International Conference on Intelligent User Interfaces (pp. 391–396) (2019)
19. Saarela, M., Geogieva, L.: Robustness, stability, and fidelity of explanations for a deep skin cancer classification model. Appl. Sci. **12**(19), 9545 (2022)
20. Hauser, K., et al.: Explainable artificial intelligence in skin cancer recognition: a systematic review. Eur. J. Cancer **167**, 54–69 (2022)
21. Shin, D.: The effects of explainability and causability on perception, trust, and acceptance: Implications for explainable AI. Int. J. Hum Comput Stud. **146**, 102551 (2021)
22. Miller, T., Howe, P. Sonenberg, L.: Explainable AI: beware of inmates running the asylum or: how I learnt to stop worrying and love the social and behavioural sciences (2017). arXiv preprint arXiv:1712.00547
23. Miller, T.: Explanation in artificial intelligence: Insights from the social sciences. Artif. Intell. **267**, 1–38 (2019)
24. Sheridan, H, O'Sullivan, D., Murphy, E.: Ideating XAI: an exploration of user's mental models of an ai-driven recruitment system using a design thinking approach. In: Proceedings IARIA, CENTRIC, International Conference on Advances in Human-oriented and Personalized Mechanisms, Technologies, and Services, Lisbon (2022)
25. Dove, G., Halskov, K., Forlizzi, J., Zimmerman, J.: UX design innovation: challenges for working with machine learning as a design material. In: Proceedings of the 2017 Chi Conference on Human Factors in Computing Systems (pp. 278–288) (2017)
26. Yang, Q., Steinfeld, A., Rosé, C., Zimmerman, J.: Re-examining whether, why, and how human-AI interaction is uniquely difficult to design. In: Proceedings of the 2020 Chi Conference on Human Factors in Computing Systems (pp. 1–13) (2020)
27. Wang, D., Yang, Q., Abdul, A., Lim, B.Y.: Designing theory-driven user-centric explainable AI. In: Proceedings of the 2019 CHI conference on human factors in computing systems (pp. 1–15), Brown, T., Katz, B., 2011. Change by design. J. Product Innov. Manage. **28**(3), pp. 381–383 (2019)
28. Luchs, M.G., Swan, S., Griffin, A.: Design thinking: New product development essentials from the PDMA. John Wiley & Sons (2015)
29. IBM, learn the enterprise design thinking framework - enterprise design thinking. https://www.ibm.com/design/thinking/page/framework/keys/playbacks. Accessed 02 Oct 2023] [Ideo this work can't wait, IDEO | Global design & innovation company | This work can't wait. https://cantwait.ideo.com/. Accessed 02 Oct 2023

30. Han, E.: 5 Examples of design thinking in business | HBS Online. https://online.hbs.edu/blog/post/design-thinking-examples. Accessed 02 Oct 2023
31. Stanford, Hasso Plattner, Institute of design at stanford, an introduction to design thinking process guide. https://web.stanford.edu/~mshanks/MichaelShanks/files/509554.pdf. Accessed 02 Oct 2023
32. Brown, T., Katz, B.: Change by design. J. Prod. Innov. Manag. **28**(3), 381–383 (2011)
33. Luchs, M.G.: A brief introduction to design thinking. Design thinking: New product development essentials from the PDMA, pp.1–12 (2015)
34. Jensen, M.B., Lozano, F., Steinert, M.: The origins of design thinking and the relevance in software innovations. In: Abrahamsson, P., Jedlitschka, A., Nguyen Duc, A., Felderer, M., Amasaki, S., Mikkonen, T. (eds.) PROFES 2016. LNCS, vol. 10027, pp. 675–678. Springer, Cham (2016). https://doi.org/10.1007/978-3-319-49094-6_54
35. Dove, G., Fayard, A.L.: Monsters, metaphors, and machine learning. In: Proceedings of the 2020 CHI Conference on Human Factors in Computing Systems (pp. 1–17) (2020)
36. Holtrop, J.S., Scherer, L.D., Matlock, D.D., Glasgow, R.E., Green, L.A.: The importance of mental models in implementation science. Front. Public Health **9**, 680316 (2021)
37. Nielsen, J.: Mental models and user experience design (2010). https://www.nngroup.com/articles/mental-models/. Accessed 02 Oct 2023
38. Johnson-Laird, P.N.: Mental Models. Cambridge University Press, Cambridge (1983)
39. Norman, D.A.: Some observations on mental models. In: Mental Models, pp. 15–22. Psychology Press (2014)
40. Kaur, H., Williams, A., Lasecki, W.S.: Building shared mental models between humans and AI for effective collaboration. CHI 2019, May 2019, Glasgow, Scotland (2019)
41. Interaction design foundation, gulf of evaluation and gulf of execution | The glossary of human computer interaction. https://www.interaction-design.org/literature/book/the-glossary-of-human-computer-interaction/gulf-of-evaluation-and-gulf-of-execution. Accessed 02 Oct 2023
42. Schellman, H.: Finding it hard to get a new job? Robot recruiters might be to blame | Work & careers | The Guardian (2022). https://www.theguardian.com/us-news/2022/may/11/artitifical-intelligence-job-applications-screen-robot-recruiters. Accessed 02 Oct 2023
43. Pessach, D., Shmueli, E.: Algorithmic fairness (2020). arXiv preprint arXiv:2001.09784
44. Dastin, J.: Amazon scraps secret AI recruiting tool that showed bias against women (2018). https://www.reuters.com/article/us-amazon-com-jobs-automation-insight/amazon-scraps-secret-ai-recruitingtool-that-showed-bias-against-women-idUSKCN1MK08G. Accessed 02 Oct 2023
45. Nugent, S., et al.: Recruitment AI has a disability problem: questions employers should be asking to ensure fairness in recruitment (2020)
46. Pessach, D. and Shmueli, E., 2020. Algorithmic fairness. arXiv preprint arXiv:2001.09784.][Jeffrey Dastin. 2018. Amazon scraps secret AI recruiting tool that showed bias against women. Retrieved September 6, (2022). https://www.reuters.com/article/us-amazon-com-jobs-automation-insight/amazon-scraps-secret-ai-recruitingtool-that-showed-bias-against-women-idUSKCN1MK08G
47. Krueger, A.E.: Two methods for experience design based on the needs empathy map: persona with needs and needs persona. Mensch und Computer 2022-Workshopband (2022)
48. IBM, learn the enterprise design thinking framework - enterprise design thinking. https://www.ibm.com/design/thinking/page/framework/keys/playbacks. Accessed 02 Oct 2023
49. NNGroup, three levels of pain points in customer experience. https://www.nngroup.com/articles/pain-points/. Accessed 02 Oct 2023
50. Liao, Q.V., Gruen, D., Miller, S.: Questioning the AI: informing design practices for explainable AI user experiences. In: Proceedings of the 2020 CHI Conference on Human Factors in Computing Systems, pp. 1–15 (2020)

51. Aechtner, J., Cabrera, L., Katwal, D., Onghena, P., Valenzuela, D.P., Wilbik, A.: Comparing user perception of explanations developed with XAI methods. In: 2022 IEEE International Conference on Fuzzy Systems (FUZZ-IEEE), pp. 1–7. IEEE (2022)

52. Markus, A.F., Kors, J.A., Rijnbeek, P.R.: The role of explainability in creating trustworthy artificial intelligence for health care: a comprehensive survey of the terminology, design choices, and evaluation strategies. J. Biomed. Inform. **113**, 103655 (2021)

53. Dhanorkar, S., Wolf, C.T., Qian, K., Xu, A., Popa, L., Li, Y.: Who needs to know what, when?: Broadening the Explainable AI (XAI) design space by looking at explanations across the AI lifecycle. In: Designing Interactive Systems Conference 2021, pp. 1591–1602 (2021)

54. Sperrle, F., et al.: A survey of human-centered evaluations in human-centered machine learning. Comput. Graph. Forum **40**(3), 543–568 (2021). https://doi.org/10.1111/cgf.14329

55. Becker, C. R, UX sketching: the missing link. I recognize this will make me sound… I by Chris R Becker I UX Collective, https://uxdesign.cc/ux-sketching-the-missing-link-4ac2f5bcc8be. Accessed 02 Oct 2023

56. Executive Office of the President, Big Data: A Report on Algorithmic Systems, Opportunity, and Civil Rights, Executive Office of the President. The White House, Washington, pp. 8–9 (2016)

57. Law Society of Ireland, Rationale for High-Stakes AI Decisions must be Public and Transparent. https://www.lawsociety.ie/gazette/top-stories/2021/08-august/rationale-for-high-stakes-ai-decisions-must-be-public-and-transparent. Accessed 02 Oct 2023

58. Schwarz, J.: No user interface and data-driven design: how AI is changing the UI/UX landscape I software development company in NYC. https://www.dvginteractive.com/no-user-interface-and-data-driven-design-how-ai-is-changing-the-ui-ux-landscape/. Accessed 02 Oct 2023

59. Arrieta, A.B., et al.: Explainable Artificial Intelligence (XAI): Concepts, taxonomies, opportunities and challenges toward responsible AI. Inf. Fusion **58**, 82–115 (2020)

Requirements for Explainability and Acceptance of Artificial Intelligence in Collaborative Work

Sabine Theis[1]($\boxtimes$)(iD), Sophie Jentzsch[1](iD), Fotini Deligiannaki[2](iD),
Charles Berro[2](iD), Arne Peter Raulf[2](iD), and Carmen Bruder[3](iD)

[1] Institute for Software Technology, Linder Höhe, 51147 Cologne, Germany
{sabine.theis,sophie.jentzsch}@DLR.de
[2] Institute for AI Safety and Security, Rathausallee 12, 53757 Sankt Augustin, Germany
{fotini.deligiannaki,charles.berro,arnepeter.raulf}@DLR.de
[3] Institute for Aerospace Medicine, Sportallee 5a, 22335 Hamburg, Germany
carmen.bruder@DLR.de

Abstract. The increasing prevalence of Artificial Intelligence (AI) in safety-critical contexts such as air-traffic control leads to systems that are practical and efficient, and to some extent explainable to humans to be trusted and accepted. The present structured literature analysis examines $n = 236$ articles on the requirements for the explainability and acceptance of AI. Results include a comprehensive review of $n = 48$ articles on information people need to perceive an AI as explainable, the information needed to accept an AI, and representation and interaction methods promoting trust in an AI. Results indicate that the two main groups of users are developers who require information about the internal operations of the model and end users who require information about AI results or behavior. Users' information needs vary in specificity, complexity, and urgency and must consider context, domain knowledge, and the user's cognitive resources. The acceptance of AI systems depends on information about the system's functions and performance, privacy and ethical considerations, as well as goal-supporting information tailored to individual preferences and information to establish trust in the system. Information about the system's limitations and potential failures can increase acceptance and trust. Trusted interaction methods are human-like, including natural language, speech, text, and visual representations such as graphs, charts, and animations. Our results have significant implications for future human-centric AI systems being developed. Thus, they are suitable as input for further application-specific investigations of user needs.

Keywords: Artificial intelligence · Explainability · Acceptance · Safety-critical contexts · Air-traffic control · Structured literature analysis · Information needs · User requirement analysis

1 Introduction

Humans will collaborate with *artificial intelligence (AI)* systems in future living and working environments. In particular, this will characterize aviation,

© The Author(s) 2023
H. Degen and S. Ntoa (Eds.): HCII 2023, LNAI 14050, pp. 355–380, 2023.
https://doi.org/10.1007/978-3-031-35891-3_22

medicine or space travel activities. These outstanding safety-critical application areas require – more than others – the consideration of individual requirements of human operators in the design of collaborative assistance systems. In this context, the German Aerospace Center (DLR) is developing guidelines for the human-centered collaboration design between users and AI systems. The focus is on tasks and contexts where operators, such as *air traffic controllers (ATCOs)*, medical professionals, or operators of space systems work collaboratively with AI to achieve efficient and safe operation. Especially humans as the operators of AI systems form a thematic priority, together with the question of how explainability and acceptance can be assured for the users of AI systems. To develop an explainable and acceptable AI pilot and AI air traffic co-controller, this article examines previously noted *user requirements* in collaboration with artificial intelligence. In general, *user requirement analysis* denotes an iterative process in which one identifies [80], specifies, and validates functional and non-functional characteristics of an IT system [40,66] together with individual users and user groups. The main goal of this user requirement engineering process is to ensure that the system to be developed meets the needs of its users [10,67]. This requires a deep understanding of user characteristics, goals, and tasks, as well as the context in which the software or system will be used [26,71]. User requirement engineering is a critical part of the software development process, as it can significantly impact the success or failure of the final product [40].

One variable within the context of requirements engineering of data-driven systems refers to the data and information that a user requires in order to achieve their goals or perform their tasks [99,102,103]. A focus on *users' information needs (IN)* and seeking behavior during user requirement engineering focuses the development process less on technology and more on the essential result of information technology, namely the transfer of information to the human, which is especially relevant for human-AI interaction or data visualization systems [18, 100]. Information needs essentially describe the gap between a current and the desired state of knowledge that needs to be filled to achieve a goal which in the present case is to understand an AI [114]. IN is defined by an individual and can vary in specificity, complexity, and urgency while being induced by social, affective, and cognitive needs.

The main contribution of the present article is a brief and understandable overview of the technical background of AI, *explainable artificial intelligence (XAI)*, and *human-in-the-loop (HITL)* in AI development. Through an interdisciplinary synthesis of computer science and psychological knowledge the present article address the need for human-centered explainable and trusted artificial intelligence by eliciting user requirements through a structured analysis of previous work on human-AI interaction.

2   Background

The following paragraphs briefly introduce related technological aspects to establish a common understanding of the broader context. First, challenges and state-of-the-art of XAI are discussed from a technical perspective in Sect. 2.1. Section 2.2 then provides a human perspective on explainability in intelligent systems. Finally, Sect. 2.3 brings both perspectives together by discussing the HITL paradigm.

2.1   Technical Perspective

AI is an umbrella term for a wide variety of different systems and techniques. When AI first emerged in the 1950s, the main focus was on symbolic AI, where real-world concepts are represented by symbolic entities, and human behavior is expressed by explicitly formulated logical rules. However, with exponentially growing computational resources and a stronger focus on statistical approaches, AI went through a sharp paradigm shift in the 1990's: from a logic-based to a data- and representation-driven doctrine [87]. This was the start of the era of *machine learning (ML)* and later *deep learning (DL)*, which is a subdomain of ML using (deep) neural networks [73]. ML has reached multiple milestones in various domains [7,85,86], exploiting massive amounts of data with sophisticated algorithms.

Nowadays, the field of AI is strongly dominated by ML and DL, turning the vast majority of concrete XAI implementations towards ML-based sub-problems. Understanding ML-based systems is especially challenging and relevant for several reasons, outlined in the following paragraphs.

ML and Explainability. XAI is a constantly growing research field, yet there exists no single established definition of explainability and related concepts such as transparency or interpretability [6]. The EASA defines *explainability* as the *"capability to provide the human with understandable and relevant information on how an AI/ML application is coming to its results."* [36]. A strongly related term in literature is *interpretability* as it is often defined similarly, e.g., the users' ability to *"correctly and efficiently predict the method's results"* [60].

Achieving system explainability is a relevant requirement for numerous reasons, essentially though because ML-based systems' decisions affect many aspects of our daily lives and need to be proven reliable. While empirical evidence on the effects of system explainability on users' trust remains inconclusive, explainability certainly supports *trustworthiness* [58]. In addition, Gerlings et al. outline a comprehensive list of motivations for XAI which are, among others, generation of trust and transparency, following compliance and regulations (e.g. GDPR), social responsibility and risk avoidance [44].

Although it is evident that XAI is a fundamental requirement it comes along with multiple technical and systemic obstacles. In a standard ML pipeline, enormous amounts of data are fed into an algorithm that autonomously identifies and encodes relevant patterns into a model. In contrast to symbolic AI, state-of-the-art ML models encode real-world information and human knowledge implicitly into inherently opaque models. It is, therefore, especially challenging to retrace their latent reasoning and portraying their insights rationally, which is why they are frequently referred to as *black boxes*.

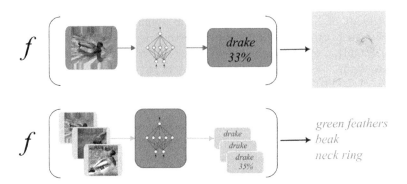

Fig. 1. The concept of a local (top) and global (bottom) explanation function f is depicted. LRP [77], the former explanation method[4], solely depends on the specific input/output pair. The output highlights the useful to the network image area (as seen in red, the duck's head). The later yields abstract features/concepts, targets the AI model in itself and explains what features are used in its decision. The input images are taken from the ImageNet data set [31].

Explanation Characteristics. Technically, explanation approaches can be divided by a row of characteristics [36, 75]:

Global vs. Local. While global explanation approaches seek to describe the overall model, answering the question *what information does the model utilize to answer?*, local approaches are designed to explain specific model outputs or the role of particular input samples, i.e, *why did the model yield a specific output from a specific input?*. Both approaches are illustrated in Fig. 1.

Model-Specific vs. Model-Agnostic. Depending on the specific system or the types of input data, different explanation techniques can be appropriate. Other approaches claim to be model agnostic. That means they can be applied to every type of underlying ML model.

Intrinsic vs. Post-Hoc Explainability. Some ML models, e.g., linear and logistic regression or decision trees, are intrinsically interpretable. These models can be explained by restricting the models' complexity [76]. In contrast, models that do not possess that characteristic can be explained through so-called posthoc approaches, i.e, generating explanations for contemplation after the training process [56].

Explainee. The explainee, i.e. the recipient of the explanation, plays a central role; consequently, system's explanations require a different level of detail for an expert or a developer compared to a naive, non-expert user.

Tools and Approaches for XAI. In the ML community, a row of explanation approaches has been established recently. These approaches mainly bear on ML models not intrinsically interpretable [76], such as deep neural networks.

Many XAI methods aim at highlighting the most relevant (to a certain outcome) features of the input data. In the case of neural networks, *Layer-wise relevance propagation (LRP)* [77] works by propagating the prediction backward through the system and can be used to unmask correct predictions being made for the wrong reasons [68]. Similarly, *LIME* and *SHAP* are python data visualization libraries. All mentioned approaches generate local post-hoc explanations and are model-agnostic.

A method partially related to unveiling correct decision being taken for false reasons are *counterfactual explanations*, that determine and highlight which features need to be different to receive a different system outcome [110]. *Concept-based* explanations aim to identify relevant higher-level concepts instead of features specific to the input data. As such, they focus on meaningful human concepts, establishing human-understandable explanations [46,61]. A non-technical measure to enhance the explainability and responsible deployment of intelligent systems is the convention of *model cards*. This framework specifies relevant details regarding the model's training, evaluation, and intended usage, which helps practitioners to understand the context and conclude assumptions about inner workings [72].

The fusion of modern ML approaches with symbolic AI yields methods depicting learned representations from neural networks symbolically in an inherently intuitive structure. They appear highly effective for achieving interpretability, trust and reasoning (also see Sect. 5). Primary methods of *neural-symbolic learning* [117] aim at injecting semantics, as seen in [1], or expert knowledge in the form of knowledge graphs [34].

2.2   Human Perspective

Following the preceding description of the technical perspective on the collaboration between humans and artificial intelligence, this section provides an overview of important concepts from human factors research on the collaboration and coordination between human operators and AI in domains where safety is critical.

Collaboration at Work. *Collaboration* is based on the human's ability to participate with others in collaborative activities with shared goals and intentions, as well as the human's need to share emotions, experiences, and activities with each other [104]. This enables people to work together and understand each other. As a consequence, human-centered integration of AI should address humans' expectations on their human partners as well as digital partners.

In domains where safety is of critical importance and human error can have severe consequences [51,89], human operators often work together in control centers [98] to achieve efficient and safe operation. Examples are airport operational centers, air traffic control centers, nuclear power plants, and military control centers. In control centers, teams of human operators have to work under time pressure to supervise complex dynamic processes as well as decide for remedy. Supervisory control is the human activity involved in initiating, monitoring, and adjusting processes in systems that are otherwise automatically controlled [24]. Being a supervisor takes the operator out of the inner control loop for short periods or even for significantly longer periods, depending on the level at which the supervisor chooses to operate [112]. Workshops with experienced pilots and ATCOs, which were conducted in order to gather their expectations about future tasks, roles, and responsibilities, indicated that task allocation, teamwork, and monitoring in a highly automated workplace pose challenges [16]. As supervisory control is one of the core tasks in control rooms, teams of operators are required to monitor the systems appropriately [91]. Through interactions, operators in a team can dynamically modify each other's perceptual and active capabilities [49]. However, when monitoring a system, it is essential that human operators work together effectively and cooperatively [23,89]. With this in mind, communication in control operations is of high importance. Communication as a "meta-teamwork process that enables the other processes" [82] provides indications for the coordinative activities while monitoring. Especially in critical situations, "it is not only critical that teams correctly assess the state of the environment and take action, but how this is accomplished" [22]. As a consequence, a team's communication provides insight into how the team members deal with critical situations.

Trust and Acceptance. Especially in domains where safety is of critical importance, both *trust* of the users in human-human interactions and trust in human-technology interactions is of vital importance [14]. Trust as a psychological concept is defined as a belief in the reliability, truth, ability, or strength of someone or something [5]. Trust influences interpersonal relationships and interaction and plays a fundamental role in decision-making [33] and risk perception [35]. Trust can be influenced by past experiences [20], communication [13], and behaviors.

Trust in automation can be conceptualized as a three-factor model consisting of the human trustee, the automated trustee, and the environment or context. In this model, qualities of the human (such as experience), work with qualities of the autonomous agent (such as form) in an environment that also influences the nature of the interaction. Since trust is constantly evolving, time itself is also a facet of trust in human-automation interactions. Measurement of trust is challenging because trust itself is a latent variable, and not directly observable. [65]. To make the complexity of the concept more manageable, technical perspectives often consider it as the extent to which a human believes the AI's outputs are correct and useful for achieving their current goals in the current situation [105].

Trust and *acceptance* are related in that a person is more likely to accept something if they trust it, which is investigated for users' trust in AI technologies by [21]. Trust can provide a sense of confidence and security, which can make it easier for a person to accept something. In addition to the concept of trust, human acceptance of technology plays an important role. Technology acceptance is the extent to which individuals are willing to use and adopt new technological innovations [28,93]. It is a multi-dimensional concept that takes into account various factors that influence an individual's decision to use a particular technology. The concept of technology acceptance is rooted in the theory of reasoned action [50] and the theory of planned behavior [3]. Technology acceptance is influenced by a range of factors, including the perceived usefulness and perceived ease of use of the technology, social influence, trust, compatibility with existing technologies and practices, perceived risks, and anxiety about using the technology.

To summarize the human perspective, it can be stated that a successful integration of AI in control centers' operations has to consider humans' expectations on their human partners and digital partners. To address the humans' expectations on their human partners and digital partners, AI systems should:(1) support teamwork in safety critical situations, (2) facilitate situation awareness, (3) consider the requirements of supervisory control, (4) support communication between team members, and (5) consider both interpersonal trust and trust in technology.

2.3   Human-in-the-Loop Methods

The information flow in AI-based automated systems can be represented as a loop: the *environment* is recorded using sensors; the *data* produced by the recordings is consumed by the *algorithm* to either train a *model* or to use the model to infer a *result*; the result is used as a command for an automation to modify the environment. In order to trust the system in safety critical applications, humans must have the oversight and understanding of the various elements of the loop. It is therefore natural to place the human in the loop (also see Fig. 2).

Definition. The *Human-in-the-loop* (HITL) paradigm is a set of human oversight mechanisms on systems running AI models. Such mechanisms implement human-computer interaction methods at different levels of the AI-based system life-cycle such as data collection, model design, training process, model evaluation or model inference [25,39,116]. Overall, HITL brings together research fields from computer science, cognitive science and psychology [116].

Approaches. The implementation of HITL in a ML system primarily depends on the degree and nature of human knowledge to be injected. This can take place throughout the entire ML pipeline as seen in Fig. 2. Following the categorization in [116] an initial approach is performing data processing with HITL. The goal is obtaining a valid data set, i.e. which is accurately labeled (with the help of human annotators) essentially at key/representative data samples, stemming from a pool of unlabeled data. The above method employs expert feedback before the ML model training and inference take place. During training, feedback can be used to push the model to map its knowledge as closely as

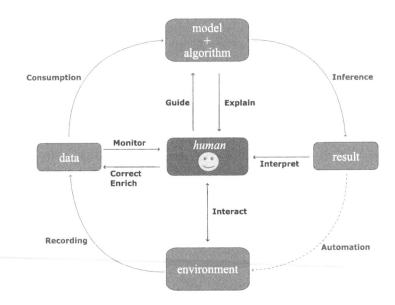

Fig. 2. A figure depicting the data/information/knowledge/command flow – showed as directional arrows – in a classical *human-in-the-loop* approach. The AI-based system is abstractly depicted as consisting of the data – recorded from the environment – given as training/inference input; the model architecture and learning algorithm; followed lastly by its results (dependent on the AI's task). The results might be used as commands for an automated system to act on the environment. The blue arrows should be interpreted as the human - either a developer or a non-expert user - performing the action (e.g. "the human guides the model", or "the human interprets the result").

possible to humans' (i.e., rewarding alignment with their decisions) or by learning through imitation [25] in the case of *reinforcement learning (RL)* agents. Finally, HITL coupled with model inference is best described by the application areas where the outcomes of ML models are used or processed by humans (occasionally interactively and iteratively). Collaboration is mostly imagined in this setting since the human has multiple abilities to interact with the outputs such as choosing between or observing multiple outcomes, to ask for explanations on what they represent or to further refine them by accepting/rejecting the AI's assistive input [7].

Applications. A HITL system shows great results in domains where the human creativity and fine understanding of the context is combined with the machine's data-analysis to reach performance superior to the human alone or the machine alone [7]. Trust and acceptance can be built as well, as seen in [106] where HITL for data labeling is employed to improve automatic conflict resolution suggestions within the air traffic management. Specifically, claiming that modern methods are not fully trusted by human operators, such as ATCOs and pilots, the authors enhance their acceptance by combining human-generated resolutions with RL algorithms.

The collaboration of human and AI-based systems – as a hybrid team – is particularly relevant in safety critical applications where the strengths of the machine on data-analysis and tasks repetitiveness are combined to the context understanding and adaptability to new scenarios of the human operator. As in a *4-Eyes Principle* team organization, it is expected for the hybrid team to be less prone to missing relevant information or to overlooking effective solutions. On top of that, in collaborative RL schemes the safety of the human teaching the AI-based system is naturally prioritized. Consequently, random and/or dangerous actions of this system can be mitigated by sophisticated on-the-fly guidance from humans, as noted in [37].

Concerning the current and future focus in HITL systems, the authors in [116] indicate that existing methods need to learn more effectively from expert human experience, essentially by moving towards more complex and less simplistic and superficial human intervention.

3   Problem and Research Questions

XAI techniques provide information that describes how ML or DL models generate results based on data or processes. Depending on the model type, its results can be explained either by reducing complexity or by looking back at its training or evaluation. These techniques aim to demonstrate the effectiveness of models for developers of ML and DL models. However, to what extent information resulting from XAI methods aligns with the users' requirements remains unclear. Although HITL approaches allow for human input, their purpose rather addresses improving the life cycle of the AI model, including its data collection, model design, training, and evaluation. So far, less attention is given to explanations serving the user and contextual goals. Human-computer interaction and user-centered design have long addressed the challenges of developing technical systems that meet user needs. Eliciting the requirements of different user groups may provide valuable insights for developing accepted and trusted AI. In the run-up to requirements analysis, the following research question arises:

RQ1: What information do people need to perceive an AI system as explainable or understandable?

RQ2: What information do people need to accept an AI system?

RQ3: Which interaction/ information representation methods are trustworthy?

4   Method

In order to answer the aforementioned research questions, a structured literature review was conducted. Its methodological procedure is described in the following section, following the general methodological framework of the *Preferred Reporting Items for Systematic reviews and Meta-Analyses (PRISMA)* statement published in 2009 [74] and updated in 2020 [81].

4.1   Databases and Search Query

Accordingly, a comprehensive literature search was conducted in the "Web of Science" and "Google Scholar" databases, the DLR repository "eLib," the "DLR Library Catalog", the "NASA Technical Report Server", as well as the "Ebook Central" portal, and the database of German national libraries. We identified search terms and used Boolean operators to generate the following query strings for searching each of the mentioned sources the search term combination (("explainability" OR "traceability" OR "acceptance") AND ("artificial intelligence") AND ("reasoning" OR "problem solving" OR "knowledge representation" OR "automatic planning" OR "automatic scheduling" OR "machine perception" OR "computer vision" OR "robotics" OR "affective computing")).

4.2   Identification and Screening

Here, relevant articles in mentioned data sources were identified from 01.08.22 to 08.10.22. In total, $n = 244$ articles identified as relevant were returned from the "Web of Science Core Collection", $n = 240$ relevant articles from a total of $n = 18,700$ Google scholar results, and $n = 27$ from the DLR search consisting of $n = 16$ from NASA Technical Reports, $n = 5$ from eLib publications, and $n = 6$ articles originating from the DLR library catalog. The latter were not included because source details were not available. The search results of all three queries were saved to .ris files and imported into the browser-based literature management program Paperpile, and data source tags were added here. When exporting the Web of Science Core Collection results, there was a loss of $n = 10$ records that were presumed duplicates. In addition, another record was recognized as a duplicate in Paperpile and removed from the initial records set. This resulted in $n = 521$ initially identified records as input for screening.

4.3   Inclusion and Exclusion Criteria

During the screening, each reference was screened first by machine filtering and then by manually checking the titles and abstracts for the following a priori inclusion and exclusion criteria: (1) the language of the article is in English, (2) the publication date of the article is between the years 1950 and 2022 inclusive, (3) the article contains results on explainability, and user acceptance of systems where humans interact and collaborate with AI, (4) the AI systems perform at least one of the following tasks: reasoning, problem-solving, knowledge representation, automated planning, and scheduling, ML, natural language processing, machine perception (computer vision), machine motion and manipulation (robotics), or emotional or social intelligence (affective computing). After excluding $n = 412$, banned records $n = 109$ could be retrieved and assessed in detail for mentioned inclusion and exclusion criteria.

4.4   Content Assessment

In the subsequent systematic review of $n = 48$ reports, two different content assessments were made: (a) the implicit or explicit perspective of humans and (b) the quality of evidence for the outcome of interest. In addition, qualitative narrative analysis and synthesis through tabulation were performed. Of the 48 articles subjected to close examination, 32 were journals, 13 were conference papers, and 3 were technical reports-articles from 1980–2022. While early articles focus on describing technical implementation and function, the proportion of empirical evaluation of technical systems and inclusion of the user perspective increases over time.

5   Results

The following section presents the key findings of previously described literature review, highlighting the information needed for explainability and acceptance together with trustworthy methods for humans interaction with AI systems, as well as trustworthy information representation methods.

5.1   Information Needed for Explainability

In this section, we explore the information needs of different users in understanding the results and behavior of AI systems. Analysis additionally revealed characteristics of explanations that are most effective in supporting human reasoning.

Information Explaining the Model. A much-regarded user group in the development of explainable AI are its developers, who have extensive technical and AI-specific background knowledge [11,12,30,41,84,90]. For AI development, developers require information to understand the data and the model in terms of its internal operations, such as the weighting of individual parameters, features, or nodes, as well as information about the relation between input and output variables [27,56]. Such model-specific information can largely be generated through model-specific, global, and local XAI methods, as described in the background section of this paper. In addition, the contextual information of the use case or the development process may be important. However, these are rarely addressed by common XAI methods [27,56,111] and require at least HITL approaches. While model-specific XAI can enhance the explainability of AI techniques to developers [43,47,97], these effects do not necessarily carry over to non-expert end users we subsequently shed light onto their requirements. However, explaining an AI through accessible raw data, code, or details about the AI models can also entail disadvantages, such as code manipulation and restrictions on the inventor's potential for innovation. In this regard, a balance needs to be found between the need for transparency and the demand for ownership [107]. [107] argue in their position paper to put more effort into understanding the requirements of all relevant user groups of an AI system to ensure that information for explaining the AI can be understood and thereby increase efficiency and effectiveness of the system.

Information Explaining Results. Most important information non-expert users require is information explaining the results as output or behavior of an AI system [32,53,63,94,119] by answering the "WHY?"-question. This is often addressed by providing the raw data from which the results were derived from [8,15,79,92,94,111] as well as through access to additional data used to generate the results, such as user interaction data [119]. Beyond that, users require information that explains why specific properties are assigned to certain result [4,27,53,57] and to which extent features [27,115], rules and decisions contributed to a specific result [19]. As with technical users, non-technical users need model-specific statistical information, data sources, and their biases or quality in terms of six dimensions, which are completeness, uniqueness, timeliness, validity, accuracy, and consistency [17,57], and algorithmic information [53].

Characteristics of Understandable Explanations. Information that explains the results or actions of an AI is particularly effective for humans if it supports logical inductive and deductive reasoning [4,53,111,119]. Humans generally understand explanatory information best if they are presented in a contrasting manner [17,57,108]. Thereby, different properties of a result, different results with other properties, and results with different properties at different points in time should be compared to each other [27].

However, most model-agnostic, local XAI methods provide far more detail than what an end-user requires for a satisfactory explanation [19]. Explanatory information should therefore include various levels of detail represented conditionally to context, explanation capability of the AI, and temporal, perceptual, and cognitive resources of the user.

Contextual information, domain knowledge, and meta-information such as time and location are vital for domain experts, e.g., in healthcare [42]. Regarding security-critical scenarios, information should be communicated at conflict-free and less work-intensive times [63]. When representing model-specific statistics often discrete in nature, it has to be considered that human understanding and explanation of phenomena invariably utilize categories together with relationships among them, describing, for example, the relation between model predictors and the target as the relationship between entities and the target [70]. Such relationships might contain probabilistic information even if these are not as crucial for humans as causal links [17,108]. Recent work even points out that most humans struggle to deal with uncertain information [17]. Causal information, in turn, supports humans, especially in decision-making in unfamiliar situations, but it has to be considered when individuals have prior experience with a domain, causal information can reduce confidence and lead to less accurate decisions [17,120].

As humans prefer rare events, explanations should focus on odd reasons and be concise, meaning that shorter explanations are not considered interpretive. Form and explanation content interact largely with what is understandable [17]. To make it even more challenging, relevant contextual information extends to the person's social context, considering assumptions about the users' beliefs about themselves and their environment [17]. When including contextual information in an explanation, different users and situations have to be considered [59].

Application-Specific Information Needs. Since 2019, consideration of the user perspective has been increasing in the development of XAI. The outcome of a conversational agent supporting criminal investigations, for example, revealed that investigators want to have a clear understanding of the data, system processes, and constraints to make informed decisions and continue the investigation effectively [52].

Furthermore, different user perspectives of autonomous surface vehicles (ASV) included AI developers, engineers, and expert users, who required information about the ASV models and training data used. Operators, crew, and safety attendants wanted to get information about the current state and intention of the ASV, as well as the definition of the AI-human control boundary and when to intervene. Passengers instead needed confirmation that the ASV can see and avoid collisions with other objects [109].

Last but not least, domain experts' and lay users' trust in a robotic AI system increased by providing relevant reasons for each of its decision together with explanations of the systems' autonomous policy and the underlying reinforcement learning model through natural language question-answer dialogue [55].

5.2   Information Needed for Acceptance

To increase the chances of humans accepting an AI, it is essential to understand what information they require for acceptance. The acceptance of artificial intelligence (AI) systems is considered a proxy measure for trust [111], but can also emerge as a barrier to it [109]. Further details about the relation of both concepts are described in the Background section.

Goal-Supporting Information. Literature suggests that information for acceptance strongly relates to the system's functions and performance, demonstrating and emphasizing the use so that the perceived usefulness of an AI system increases [54,63]. Information supporting usefulness of a system is the goal-supporting information needed to successfully complete tasks contributing to the user's goal. For example, if an AI as part of a guidance and control system for a spacecraft provides erroneous information about system states, key functions cannot be performed, resulting in direct user rejection of the system [64]. In case of an AI recommending health decisions, correct general medical and patient-specific information together with best practice procedures are required [94] while for the acceptance of air traffic control systems, goal-supporting information include route information, air traffic information, sequential position and velocity information of other vehicles, clearance, events, vehicle responses, altitude, position of own vehicle, positions of other aircraft or information for contingencies, such as diagnosis of vehicle subsystems [69]. As with information for explainability, goal-supporting information strongly depends on the domain, task, and context of an AI system [94,96]. However, it has been shown that across application domains, the acceptance of an AI system can be increased by making the scope and limitations of AI methods and information about potential system failures [64] known to users beforehand [29,96].

Reliability Information. The acceptance of AI results benefits from attached quality or reliability indicators such as error margins, uncertainties or confidence intervals, especially in high-stakes contexts [96,111]. All information provided must be tailored to their individual preferences and should, in general, include how data about the user is collected and processed, and how privacy is protected [111,119]. In particular, information about the extent to which other users trust the system plays a vital role in positively influencing its acceptance, especially if these are actors having a high social significance for the user, such as friends, family, work colleagues, or professional experts [111]. Arguments, for example applied to explain an AI and its results or actions [108], are accepted if they have the support that makes them acceptable to the participants in a conversation. Similarly, information that establishes perceived usefulness and ease of use is related to user acceptance [92]. The greater the coherence of a proposition with other propositions the greater its acceptability. If a proposition is highly coherent with a person's beliefs, then the person will believe the proposition with a high degree of confidence and the other way around, also known as confirmation bias [17,101].

5.3   Information Representations and Interaction Methods

Methods for representing information and interacting with those in the context of human-AI collaboration are trusted if they exhibit a certain anthropomorphism such as natural language and speech [9,27,32,42,52,83,105,108], text [17,88] or human like visual appearances, for example in the context of robotics [38,48,92].

Textual and Speech Representations. The former include text-based, as well as speech-based input and output. Especially domain experts expect system feedback in natural language to domain specific language [32] and be presented within 3–4 s [48,69] to ensure a cognitive and emotional linkage through realistic, social interaction. Social quality of a dialogue through emotionally intelligent interaction can profit from closed-loop interaction with cognitive human models [48]. In order to address the previously described information need by answering "why" questions, but also "how" and "why not" questions, natural language should be expressed easily understandable in a narrative style [9].

Dialectic explanations have for example been generated based on a log file with internal steps an AI performed to reach a certain recommendation [108].

Data and Information Visualizations. In addition to natural language and speech interaction, data and information visualizations such as graphs [8,52,115], charts [79], and animations [17] are especially suitable for efficiently conveying information from statistical [78] and model-specific data [42,108] such as intermediate network layers of DNNs [115], neuron activation and weights or token embedding in 2D and gradient based methods [57]. In addition, visualizations suitable for the representation of structural information such as CNN feature maps or DNNs graph structures [27,57] or conceptual and semantic information [42,57]. Features impact such as words impact on the classification outcome could effectively be represented through color-coding [115], especially when coding is based on relations relevant grammars [70]. Even though, speech is frequently used to represent explanatory information and multi-modal data contains persistent inconsistencies and biases [57], combining graphic narratives with natural language can be even more effective [9,79,92,108,118], reduce human workload or increase human performance [113]. Visual representations are particularly suitable for target groups with little background knowledge; analogies that correspond to the mental model can reinforce this [109].

Interaction Quality. Regardless of modality, safety-critical contexts often require interactive and reciprocal information exchanges and learning among humans and machines (HITL) [57,64], while answers are expected to be fast and accurate [119]. Depending on user task and context touch and gesture-based interaction methods have also demonstrated to be powerful and effective [63] while emotion-aware mechanisms, especially when combined with human-like appearance support user satisfaction and adherence[92]. In any case suitability of a representation or interaction method is strongly dependent on age, culture and gender of the user group [54]. Examples for effective and efficient information representations and interaction methods include logged interactions to handle lost link procedures and error-free resumption of interaction after interrupted communication for an artificial pilot. This system applied natural language interaction to interact with the terminal crew, to enable automated reasoning and decision making, to coordinate autonomous operations and basic pilot procedures with variable autonomy [69].

6   Discussion and Conclusion

This article aims to bridge the gap between technical and human perspectives in developing AI systems that are understandable, acceptable, and trustworthy. To achieve this, user needs are identified and transformed into requirements for AI system design, constituting an initial step for requirements engineering. These requirements must be validated and refined for various application domains to serve as the foundation for development activities.

6.1   Contribution

The results show that the existing methods for explaining AI (see Sect. 2.1) correspond to the needs and requirements of people with extensive background knowledge about AI, ML and DL models and whose task is to develop and improve AI models. In contrast, people who have little AI background knowledge use an AI system to achieve their individual goals and to process application-related tasks. They mainly expect the results and behavior of the system to be explained. Only occasionally the latter group would like to use the statistical parameters of an AI model to understand the system result or behavior. However, for this purpose, a lower and more flexible level of detail is required than for the former group. Relevant to either group yet is the questionable reliance of certain XAI methods, with many being prone to manipulation and adversarial attacks [95]. Arguably, multiple well-established explanation algorithms are criticized in [2] revealing that some fail to depict accurate mappings from input features to model outcomes [45, 62, 95]. To further provide explanations that fit the user needs, their requirements have to be taken into account during the development but also within AI applications (as described in Sect. 2.3). Since explanations should maximize the user's mental model of explanatory information, human feedback should be incorporated to a greater extent to iteratively improve development outcomes and AI result. As an example, such an approach was followed in [46] and appears highly promising.

A particular user group for AI systems collaborating with humans, are domain experts, such as ATCOs, medical professionals, or scientific personnel as crew and operators of space systems. They have extensive domain knowledge but restricted background knowledge of AI technologies. They also mainly need information that explains system results and behavior, aiming to understand a system outcome and behavior by information of the professional context rather than the technology. For medical professionals, this means, for example, that they want to interpret a result based on its relevance for different patient groups or based on its validity and relevance for other experts. Regarding the requirements for an AI system for air traffic control in terms of explainability, it can be stated that the needs of AI developers, as well as non-expert users, have to be considered: The former require information about the data and the model in terms of internal operations and the relationship between input and output variables. Essentially, the latter profit from information about the results and behavior of the AI system, why certain properties are assigned to specific results, and the contribution of features, rules, and decisions to a specific result. In general, the information should be presented in a contrasting manner and include various levels of detail depending on the context of each user group, the explanation capability of the AI, and the temporal, perceptual, and cognitive resources of individual users. For security-critical scenarios such as air traffic control, information should be communicated at conflict-free and less work-intensive times. Designing a comprehensible AI system requires various functionalities and modules that detail the individual needs and characteristics of all important user groups.

With respect to the information users require to accept an AI system, it can be stated that acceptance for AI systems profits from task-related information supporting users in achieving their goals, information demonstrating the performance and usefulness of the AI and information about privacy and ethical considerations. It has to be stated that information alone are not sufficient for acceptance the system in general needs to be useful in a user-friendly way also providing control over their data and data processing.

Regarding trustworthy information representation and interaction methods, results revealed that natural language and visual information representations are most suitable for human AI-collaboration, especially their combination. Effective interaction in safety-critical contexts, such as air traffic control, primarily require fast and accurate information exchange and learning between humans and machines. However, the suitability of a representation or interaction method is dependent on factors such as task and its context, the user's age, culture, and gender.

6.2 Limitations

Results presented describe user needs and requirements for a system only to the extent that these were included in the literature. In this context, the underlying data is subject to time-dependent biases towards technology-centered development methods, limited result validity, and biases due to the topicality of applied models. Early work, for example, developed models with much smaller data sets which is why the users' need to access these data might be more valid for earlier than for present systems. Literature analysis and synthesis was guided by the three research questions formulated in Sect. 3. In order to provide the most comprehensive and generally valid information possible, no restrictions were placed on the fields of application, user groups, technologies, or research methods/questions. Accordingly, considered papers exhibit a high level of heterogeneity regarding these characteristics. Nevertheless, contextual and methodological variance among studies examined must be acknowledged as a potential limitation. However, its effect is reduced by the fact that the user requirements formulated here are validated, refined, and supplemented for the air traffic control application context.

6.3 Future Work

This literature analysis demonstrated that, with respect to interdisciplinary perspectives in developing AI systems, different frameworks for considering humans are exploited which are not being integrated enough. On the one hand, the human-in-the-loop paradigm as a set of human oversight mechanisms on systems running AI models is well-known within the technical community. On the other hand, human factors specialists and psychologists have adopted a human-centered design approach, in a framework that develops socio-technical systems by involving the human perspective in all steps of the design process. Finally, in safety-critical contexts such as air traffic control, research and development focuses on shifting from manual control where the human is *in* the loop, to supervisory control where the human operator is *on* the loop. By having integrated automation in aviation some decades ago, the human operator no longer needs to be in direct control of the system. As a result operators are supervising many aspects of the system, which changes the role of the human in a system.

Therefore, one main topic of future work is to share and integrate the different perspectives and methods for designing understandable, acceptable, and trustworthy AI systems in an interdisciplinary development team. Another topic for further research lies on investigating and validating the presented findings for AI integration in air traffic control systems. A first step is to conduct user workshops as to assess their expectations on tasks to be allocated between human and AI system, on information needed from AI systems, user-friendly interaction and use of personal data. In doing so, a two-day workshop with nine ATCOs from German air navigation service provider (DFS) and Austro Control GmbH is currently being conducted. Furthermore, it is planned to research and validate prototypes of AI systems with users throughout the design process of AI systems in aviation. To achieve this, experimental studies will be conducted in laboratory settings simulating a control-center task environment, as well as large-scale simulations of air traffic control with experienced operators. In doing so, guidelines for effective and safe collaboration between AI systems and human operators in safety-critical contexts will be investigated, which will finally lead to recommendations for the development of AI systems.

References

1. Explaining Trained Neural Networks with Semantic Web Technologies: First Steps, July 2017 (2017). http://daselab.cs.wright.edu/nesy/NeSy17/
2. Adebayo, J., Gilmer, J., Muelly, M., Goodfellow, I., Hardt, M., Kim, B.: Sanity checks for saliency maps. In: Proceedings of the 32nd International Conference on Neural Information Processing Systems. NIPS 2018, Red Hook, NY, USA, pp. 9525–9536. Curran Associates Inc. (2018)
3. Ajzen, I.: The theory of planned behavior. Organ. Beh. Hum. Dec. Proc. **50**(2), 179–211 (1991). https://doi.org/10.1016/0749-5978(91)90020-T
4. Alshammari, M., Nasraoui, O., Sanders, S.: Mining semantic knowledge graphs to add explainability to black box recommender systems. IEEE Access **7**, 110563–110579 (2019). https://doi.org/10.1109/ACCESS.2019.2934633
5. American Psychological Association and others: APA dictionary of psychology online (2020)
6. Arrieta, A.B., et al.: Explainable artificial intelligence (XAI): concepts, taxonomies, opportunities and challenges toward responsible AI. Inf. Fus. **58**, 82–115 (2020). https://doi.org/10.1016/j.inffus.2019.12.012
7. Assael, Y., et al.: Restoring and attributing ancient texts using deep neural networks. Nature **603**(7900), 280–283 (2022). https://doi.org/10.1038/s41586-022-04448-z
8. Atkinson, D.J.: SHARP: spacecraft health automated reasoning prototype. In: NASA. Johnson Space Center, Control Center Technology Conference Proceedings, August 1991. https://ntrs.nasa.gov/citations/19920002802

9. Baclawski, K., et al.: Ontology summit 2019 communiqué: explanations. Appl. Ontol. **15**(1), 91–107 (2020). https://doi.org/10.3233/ao-200226

10. Bano, M., Zowghi, D.: Users' involvement in requirements engineering and system success. In: 2013 3rd International Workshop on Empirical Requirements Engineering (EmpiRE), pp. 24–31. IEEE (2013). https://doi.org/10.1109/EmpiRE.2013.6615212

11. Beno, M.: Robot rights in the era of robolution and the acceptance of robots from the slovak citizen's perspective. In: 2019 IEEE International Symposium on Robotic and Sensors Environments (ROSE), pp. 1–7, June 2019. https://doi.org/10.1109/ROSE.2019.8790429

12. Beyret, B., Shafti, A., Faisal, A.A.: Dot-to-Dot: explainable hierarchical reinforcement learning for robotic manipulation. In: 2019 IEEE/RSJ International Conference on Intelligent Robots and Systems (IROS), pp. 5014–5019, November 2019. https://doi.org/10.1109/IROS40897.2019.8968488

13. Blöbaum, B., et al.: Trust and Communication in a Digitized World. Models and Concepts of Trust Research. Springer, Heidelberg (2016). http://dx.doi.org/10.1007/978-3-319-28059-2

14. Bonini, D.: ATC do i trust thee? referents of trust in air traffic control. In: CHI 2001 Extended Abstracts on Human Factors in Computing Systems, pp. 449–450 (2001). https://doi.org/10.1145/634067.634327

15. Braun, M., Bleher, H., Hummel, P.: A leap of faith: is there a formula for "trustworthy" AI? Hastings Cent. Rep. **51**(3), 17–22 (2021). https://doi.org/10.1002/hast.1207

16. Bruder, C., Jörn, L., Eißfeldt, H.: When pilots and air traffic controllers discuss their future (2008)

17. Burkart, N., Huber, M.F.: A survey on the explainability of supervised machine learning. JAIR **70**, 245–317 (2021). https://doi.org/10.1613/jair.1.12228

18. Cai, C.J., Winter, S., Steiner, D., Wilcox, L., Terry, M.: "Hello AI": uncovering the onboarding needs of medical practitioners for human-AI collaborative decision-making. In: Proceedings of the ACM on Human-computer Interaction **3**(CSCW), 1–24 (2019). https://doi.org/10.1145/3359206

19. Calvaresi, D., Mualla, Y., Najjar, A., Galland, S., Schumacher, M.: Explainable multi-agent systems through blockchain technology. In: Calvaresi, D., Najjar, A., Schumacher, M., Främling, K. (eds.) EXTRAAMAS 2019. LNCS (LNAI), vol. 11763, pp. 41–58. Springer, Cham (2019). https://doi.org/10.1007/978-3-030-30391-4_3

20. Chen, Y.H., Chien, S.H., Wu, J.J., Tsai, P.Y.: Impact of signals and experience on trust and trusting behavior. Cyberpsychol. Beh. Soc. Network. **13**(5), 539–546 (2010). https://doi.org/10.1089/cyber.2009.0188

21. Choung, H., David, P., Ross, A.: Trust in AI and its role in the acceptance of AI technologies. Int. J. Hum.-Comput. Interact. 1–13 (2022). https://doi.org/10.1080/10447318.2022.2050543

22. Cooke, N.J., Gorman, J.C., Myers, C.W., Duran, J.L.: Interactive team cognition. Cognit. Sci. **37**(2), 255–285 (2013). https://doi.org/10.1111/cogs.12009

23. Cooke, N.J., Salas, E., Cannon-Bowers, J.A., Stout, R.J.: Measuring team knowledge. Hum. Factors **42**(1), 151–173 (2000). https://doi.org/10.1518/001872000779656561

24. Council, N.R., et al.: Research and modeling of supervisory control behavior: report of a workshop (1930)

25. Cui, Y., et al.: Understanding the relationship between interactions and outcomes in human-in-the-loop machine learning. In: Zhou, Z.H. (ed.) Proceedings of the Thirtieth International Joint Conference on Artificial Intelligence, IJCAI-21, pp. 4382–4391. International Joint Conferences on Artificial Intelligence Organization, August 2021. https://doi.org/10.24963/ijcai.2021/599, survey Track

26. Dalpiaz, F., Niu, N.: Requirements engineering in the days of artificial intelligence. IEEE software **37**(4), 7–10 (2020). https://doi.org/10.1109/MS.2020.2986047

27. Dam, H.K., Tran, T., Ghose, A.: Explainable software analytics. In: Proceedings of the 40th International Conference on Software Engineering: New Ideas and Emerging Results. ICSE-NIER 2018, New York, NY, USA, pp. 53–56. Association for Computing Machinery, May 2018. https://doi.org/10.1145/3183399.3183424

28. Davis, F.D.: A technology acceptance model for empirically testing new end-user information systems: Theory and results. Ph.D. thesis, Massachusetts Institute of Technology (1985). http://dspace.mit.edu/handle/1721.1/7582

29. Day, D.: Application of AI principles to constraint management in intelligent user interfaces. In: Association for Information Systems, Proceeding of the Americas Conference on Information Systems, pp. 730–732 (1997). http://aisel.aisnet.org/amcis1997/54?utm_source=aisel.aisnet.org

30. De, T., Giri, P., Mevawala, A., Nemani, R., Deo, A.: Explainable AI: a hybrid approach to generate Human-Interpretable explanation for deep learning prediction. In: Complex Adaptive Systems, vol. 168, pp. 40–48 (2020). https://doi.org/10.1016/j.procs.2020.02.255

31. Deng, J., Dong, W., Socher, R., Li, L.J., Li, K., Fei-Fei, L.: Imagenet: a large-scale hierarchical image database. In: 2009 IEEE Conference on Computer Vision and Pattern Recognition, pp. 248–255 (2009). https://doi.org/10.1109/CVPR.2009.5206848

32. Dominick, W.D., Kavi, S.: Knowledge based systems: a preliminary survey of selected issues and techniques. Technical report, DBMS.NASA/RECON-5, May 1984. https://ntrs.nasa.gov/citations/19890005582

33. Dunning, D., Fetchenhauer, D.: Understanding the Psychology of Trust. Psychology Press (2011)

34. Díaz-Rodríguez, N., et al.: Explainable neural-symbolic learning (x-nesyl) methodology to fuse deep learning representations with expert knowledge graphs: the monumai cultural heritage use case. Inf. Fusion **79**, 58–83 (2022). https://doi.org/10.1016/j.inffus.2021.09.022

35. Earle, T.C., Siegrist, M., Gutscher, H.: Trust, risk perception and the TCC model of cooperation. In: Trust in Risk Management, pp. 18–66. Routledge (2010)

36. EASA: EASA concept paper: first usable guidance for level 1 machine learning applications (2021)

37. Eder, K., Harper, C., Leonards, U.: Towards the safety of human-in-the-loop robotics: challenges and opportunities for safety assurance of robotic co-workers. In: The 23rd IEEE International Symposium on Robot and Human Interactive Communication, pp. 660–665 (2014). https://doi.org/10.1109/ROMAN.2014.6926328

38. Ene, I., Pop, M.I., Nistoreanu, B.: Qualitative and quantitative analysis of consumers perception regarding anthropomorphic AI designs. In: Proceedings of the International Conference on Business Excellence, vol. 13, pp. 707–716 (2019). https://doi.org/10.2478/picbe-2019-0063

39. European Commission, Directorate-General for Communications Networks, Content and Technology: The Assessment List for Trustworthy Artificial Intelligence (ALTAI) for self assessment. Publications Office (2020). https://doi.org/10.2759/002360
40. Finkelstein, A., Kramer, J.: Software engineering: a roadmap. In: Proceedings of the Conference on the Future of Software Engineering, pp. 3–22 (2000)
41. Garibaldi, J.M.: The need for fuzzy AI. IEEE/CAA J. Automatica Sinica **6**(3), 610–622 (2019). https://doi.org/10.1109/JAS.2019.1911465
42. Gaur, M., Faldu, K., Sheth, A.: Semantics of the Black-Box: can knowledge graphs help make deep learning systems more interpretable and explainable? IEEE Internet Comput. **25**(1), 51–59 (2021). https://doi.org/10.1109/MIC.2020.3031769
43. Gerdes, A.: The quest for explainable AI and the role of trust (work in progress paper). In: Proceedings of the European Conference on the impact of Artificial Intelligence and Robotics (ECIAIR), pp. 465–468 (2019). https://doi.org/10.34190/ECIAIR.19.046
44. Gerlings, J., Shollo, A., Constantiou, I.: Reviewing the need for explainable artificial intelligence (XAI). In: 54th Annual Hawaii International Conference on System Sciences, HICSS 2021, pp. 1284–1293. Hawaii International Conference on System Sciences (HICSS) (2021). https://doi.org/10.24251/HICSS.2021.156
45. Ghorbani, A., Abid, A., Zou, J.: Interpretation of neural networks is fragile. Proc. AAAI Conf. Artificial Intell. **33**(01), 3681–3688 (2019). https://doi.org/10.1609/aaai.v33i01.33013681
46. Ghorbani, A., Wexler, J., Zou, J.Y., Kim, B.: Towards automatic concept-based explanations. In: Advances in Neural Information Processing Systems, vol. 32 (2019)
47. Gilpin, L.H., Bau, D., Yuan, B.Z., Bajwa, A., Specter, M., Kagal, L.: Explaining explanations: an overview of interpretability of machine learning. In: 2018 IEEE 5th International Conference on Data Science and Advanced Analytics (DSAA), pp. 80–89. ieeexplore.ieee.org, October 2018. https://doi.org/10.1109/DSAA.2018.00018
48. Goodman, P.H., Zou, Q., Dascalu, S.M.: Framework and implications of virtual neurorobotics. Front. Neurosci. **2**(1), 123–129 (2008). https://doi.org/10.3389/neuro.01.007.2008
49. Gorman, J.C., Cooke, N.J., Winner, J.L.: Measuring team situation awareness in decentralized command and control environments. In: Situational Awareness, pp. 183–196. Routledge (2017)
50. Hale, J.L., Householder, B.J., Greene, K.L.: The theory of reasoned action. Persuasion Handbook: Dev. Theory Pract. **14**(2002), 259–286 (2002). https://dx.doi.org/10.4135/9781412976046
51. Hauland, G.: Measuring individual and team situation awareness during planning tasks in training of EN route air traffic control. Int. J. Aviation Psychol. **18**(3), 290–304 (2008). https://doi.org/10.1080/10508410802168333
52. Hepenstal, S., Zhang, L., Kodagoda, N., Wong, B.l.W.: Developing conversational agents for use in criminal investigations. ACM Trans. Interact. Intell. Syst. **11**(3–4), 1–35 (2021). https://doi.org/10.1145/3444369
53. Ibrahim, A., Klesel, T., Zibaei, E., Kacianka, S., Pretschner, A.: Actual causality canvas: a general framework for Explanation-Based Socio-Technical constructs. In: ECAI 2020: 24th European Conference on Artificial Intelligence, vol. 325, pp. 2978–2985 (2020). https://doi.org/10.3233/FAIA200472

54. Ismatullaev, U.V.U., Kim, S.H.: Review of the factors affecting acceptance of AI-Infused systems. Hum. Factors (2022). https://doi.org/10.1177/00187208211064707

55. Iucci, A., Hata, A., Terra, A., Inam, R., Leite, I.: Explainable reinforcement learning for Human-Robot collaboration. In: 2021 20th International Conference on Advanced Robotics (ICAR), pp. 927–934, December 2021. https://doi.org/10.1109/ICAR53236.2021.9659472

56. Jentzsch, S.F., Hochgeschwender, N.: Don't forget your roots! using provenance data for transparent and explainable development of machine learning models. In: 2019 34th IEEE/ACM International Conference on Automated Software Engineering Workshop (ASEW), pp. 37–40. IEEE (2019)

57. Joshi, G., Walambe, R., Kotecha, K.: A review on explainability in multimodal deep neural nets. IEEE Access 9, 59800–59821 (2021). https://doi.org/10.1109/ACCESS.2021.3070212

58. Kästner, L., et al.: On the relation of trust and explainability: why to engineer for trustworthiness. In: 2021 IEEE 29th International Requirements Engineering Conference Workshops (REW), pp. 169–175. IEEE (2021)

59. Kästner, L., Langer, M., Lazar, V., Schomäcker, A., Speith, T., Sterz, S.: On the relation of trust and explainability: why to engineer for trustworthiness. In: 2021 IEEE 29th International Requirements Engineering Conference Workshops (REW), pp. 169–175, September 2021. https://doi.org/10.1109/REW53955.2021.00031

60. Kim, B., Khanna, R., Koyejo, O.O.: Examples are not enough, learn to criticize! criticism for interpretability. In: Advances in Neural information Processing Systems, vol. 29 (2016)

61. Kim, B., et al.: Interpretability beyond feature attribution: quantitative testing with concept activation vectors (TCAV). In: Dy, J., Krause, A. (eds.) Proceedings of the 35th International Conference on Machine Learning. Proceedings of Machine Learning Research, vol. 80, pp. 2668–2677. PMLR, 10–15 July 2018. https://proceedings.mlr.press/v80/kim18d.html

62. Kindermans, P.-J., et al.: The (Un)reliability of saliency methods. In: Samek, W., Montavon, G., Vedaldi, A., Hansen, L.K., Müller, K.-R. (eds.) Explainable AI: Interpreting, Explaining and Visualizing Deep Learning. LNCS (LNAI), vol. 11700, pp. 267–280. Springer, Cham (2019). https://doi.org/10.1007/978-3-030-28954-6_14

63. Klumpp, M., Hesenius, M., Meyer, O., Ruiner, C., Gruhn, V.: Production logistics and human-computer interaction—state-of-the-art, challenges and requirements for the future. Int. J. Adv. Manuf. Technol. 105(9), 3691–3709 (2019). https://doi.org/10.1007/s00170-019-03785-0

64. Kraiss, F.: Decision making and problem solving with computer assistance. Technical report, NASA-TM-76008, January 1980. https://ntrs.nasa.gov/citations/19800007713

65. Krueger, F.: The Neurobiology of Trust. Cambridge University Press, Cambridge (2021)

66. Kujala, S., Kauppinen, M., Lehtola, L., Kojo, T.: The role of user involvement in requirements quality and project success. In: 13th IEEE International Conference on Requirements Engineering (RE 2005), pp. 75–84. IEEE (2005). https://doi.org/10.1109/RE.2005.72

67. Kujala, S.: Effective user involvement in product development by improving the analysis of user needs. Beh. Inf. Technol. 27(6), 457–473 (2008). https://doi.org/10.1080/01449290601111051

68. Lapuschkin, S., Wäldchen, S., Binder, A., Montavon, G., Samek, W., Müller, K.R.: Unmasking clever Hans predictors and assessing what machines really learn. Nature Commun. **10**(1), 1–8 (2019). https://doi.org/10.1038/s41467-019-08987-4
69. Lowry, M., et al.: Design considerations for a variable autonomy executive for UAS in the NAS. Technical report, ARC-E-DAA-TN51256, January 2018. https://ntrs.nasa.gov/citations/20180004247
70. Lukyanenko, R., Castellanos, A., Storey, V.C., Castillo, A., Tremblay, M.C., Parsons, J.: Superimposition: augmenting machine learning outputs with conceptual models for explainable AI. In: Grossmann, G., Ram, S. (eds.) Advances in Conceptual Modeling, LNCS, vol. 12584, pp. 26–34. Springer, Cham (2020). https://doi.org/10.1007/978-3-030-65847-2_3
71. Maalej, W., Nayebi, M., Ruhe, G.: Data-driven requirements engineering-an update. In: 2019 IEEE/ACM 41st International Conference on Software Engineering: software Engineering in Practice (ICSE-SEIP), pp. 289–290. IEEE (2019). https://doi.org/10.1109/ICSE-SEIP.2019.00041
72. Mitchell, M., et al.: Model cards for model reporting. In: Proceedings of the conference on fairness, accountability, and transparency, pp. 220–229 (2019). https://doi.org/10.1145/3287560.3287596
73. Mitchell, M.: Why AI is harder than we think. In: Proceedings of the Genetic and Evolutionary Computation Conference, pp. 3–3 (2021). https://doi.org/10.1145/3449639.3465421
74. Moher, D., Liberati, A., Tetzlaff, J., Altman, D.G., PRISMA Group*, t.: Preferred reporting items for systematic reviews and meta-analyses: the prisma statement. Ann. Internal Med. **151**(4), 264–269 (2009). https://doi.org/10.7326/0003-4819-151-4-200908180-00135
75. Mohseni, S., Zarei, N., Ragan, E.D.: A multidisciplinary survey and framework for design and evaluation of explainable AI systems. ACM Trans. Interactive Intell. Syst. (TiiS) **11**(3-4), 1–45 (2021). https://doi.org/10.1145/3387166
76. Molnar, C.: Interpretable Machine Learning (2019). https://christophm.github.io/interpretable-ml-book/
77. Montavon, G., Binder, A., Lapuschkin, S., Samek, W., Müller, K.-R.: Layer-wise relevance propagation: an overview. In: Samek, W., Montavon, G., Vedaldi, A., Hansen, L.K., Müller, K.-R. (eds.) Explainable AI: Interpreting, Explaining and Visualizing Deep Learning. LNCS (LNAI), vol. 11700, pp. 193–209. Springer, Cham (2019). https://doi.org/10.1007/978-3-030-28954-6_10
78. Munzner, T.: Visualization Analysis and Design. CRC Press (2014)
79. Murphy, R.R.: Human-robot interaction in rescue robotics. IEEE Trans. Syst. Man Cybern. C Appl. Rev. **34**(2), 138–153 (2004). https://doi.org/10.1109/TSMCC.2004.826267
80. Nuseibeh, B., Easterbrook, S.: Requirements engineering: a roadmap. In: Proceedings of the Conference on the Future of Software Engineering, pp. 35–46 (2000). https://doi.org/10.1145/336512.336523
81. Page, M.J., et al.: The Prisma 2020 statement: an updated guideline for reporting systematic reviews. Int. J. surgery **88**, 105906 (2021). https://doi.org/10.1016/j.ijsu.2021.105906
82. Papenfuss, A.: Phenotypes of teamwork–an exploratory study of tower controller teams. In: Proceedings of the Human Factors and Ergonomics Society Annual Meeting, Los Angeles, CA, vol. 57, pp. 319–323. SAGE Publications Sage CA (2013). https://doi.org/10.1177/1541931213571070

83. Pierrard, R., Poli, J.P., Hudelot, C.: Spatial relation learning for explainable image classification and annotation in critical applications. Artif. Intell. **292**, 103434 (2021). https://doi.org/10.1016/j.artint.2020.103434

84. Prentzas, N., Nicolaides, A., Kyriacou, E., Kakas, A., Pattichis, C.: Integrating machine learning with symbolic reasoning to build an explainable AI model for stroke prediction. In: 2019 IEEE 19th International Conference on Bioinformatics and Bioengineering (BIBE), pp. 817–821, October 2019. https://doi.org/10.1109/BIBE.2019.00152

85. Raffel, C., et al.: Exploring the limits of transfer learning with a unified text-to-text transformer (2019). https://doi.org/10.48550/ARXIV.1910.10683

86. Ravuri, S., et al.: Skilful precipitation nowcasting using deep generative models of radar. Nature **597**(7878), 672–677 (2021). https://doi.org/10.1038/s41586-021-03854-z

87. Rumelhart, D.E., Hinton, G.E., Williams, R.J.: Learning representations by back-propagating errors. Nature **323**, 533–536 (1986). https://doi.org/10.1038/323533a0

88. Sachan, S., Yang, J.B., Xu, D.L., Benavides, D.E., Li, Y.: An explainable AI decision-support-system to automate loan underwriting. Expert Syst. Appl. **144**, 113100 (2020). https://doi.org/10.1016/j.eswa.2019.113100

89. Salas, E., Cooke, N.J., Rosen, M.A.: On teams, teamwork, and team performance: discoveries and developments. Human factors **50**(3), 540–547 (2008). https://doi.org/10.1518/001872008X288457

90. Shafik, R., Wheeldon, A., Yakovlev, A.: Explainability and dependability analysis of learning automata based AI hardware. In: 2020 26th IEEE International Symposium on On-line Testing and Robust System Design (IOLTS) (2020). https://doi.org/10.1109/IOLTS50870.2020.9159725

91. Sharma, C., Bhavsar, P., Srinivasan, B., Srinivasan, R.: Eye gaze movement studies of control room operators: a novel approach to improve process safety. Comput. Chem. Eng. **85**, 43–57 (2016). https://doi.org/10.1016/j.compchemeng.2015.09.012

92. Shin, D.: Embodying algorithms, enactive artificial intelligence and the extended cognition: you can see as much as you know about algorithm. J. Inf. Sci. Eng. (2021). https://doi.org/10.1177/0165551520985495

93. Silva, P.: Davis' technology acceptance model (tam) (1989). Information seeking behavior and technology adoption: theories and trends, pp. 205–219 (2015). http://dx.doi.org/10.4018/978-1-4666-8156-9.ch013

94. Simpson, J., Kingston, J., Molony, N.: Internet-based decision support for evidence-based medicine. Knowl.-Based Syst. **12**(5), 247–255 (1999). https://doi.org/10.1016/S0950-7051(99)00014-3

95. Slack, D., Hilgard, S., Jia, E., Singh, S., Lakkaraju, H.: Fooling lime and shap: adversarial attacks on post hoc explanation methods. In: Proceedings of the AAAI/ACM Conference on AI, Ethics, and Society, pp. 180–186 (2020). https://doi.org/10.1145/3375627.3375830

96. Sousa, P., Ramos, C.: A distributed architecture and negotiation protocol for scheduling in manufacturing systems. Comput. Ind. **38**(2), 103–113 (1999). https://doi.org/10.1016/S0166-3615(98)00112-2

97. Spreeuwenberg, S.: Choose for AI and for explainability. In: Debruyne, C., et al. (eds.) OTM 2019. LNCS, vol. 11878, pp. 3–8. Springer, Cham (2020). https://doi.org/10.1007/978-3-030-40907-4_1

98. Suchman, L.: Centers of coordination: a case and some themes. In: Resnick, L.B, Säljö, R., ontecorvo, C., Burge, B. (eds.) Discourse, Tools and Reasoning: Essays on Situated Cognition, pp. 41–62. Springer, Heidelberg (1997). https://doi.org/10.1007/978-3-662-03362-3_3

99. Sutcliffe, A.: Scenario-based requirements analysis. Requirements Eng. J. **3**(1), 48–65 (1998). https://doi.org/10.1007/BF02802920

100. Taggart Jr, W., Tharp, M.O.: A survey of information requirements analysis techniques. ACM Comput. Surv. (CSUR) **9**(4), 273–290 (1977). https://doi.org/10.1145/356707.356710

101. Thagard, P.: Explanatory coherence. Behav. Brain Sci. **14**(4), 739–739 (1991). https://doi.org/10.1017/S0140525X00057046

102. Theis, S., et al.: Predicting technology usage by health information need of older adults: Implications for ehealth technology. Work **62**(3), 443–457 (2019). https://doi.org/10.3233/WOR-192878

103. Theis, S., et al.: What do you need to know to stay healthy? – health information needs and seeking behaviour of older adults in Germany. In: Bagnara, S., Tartaglia, R., Albolino, S., Alexander, T., Fujita, Y. (eds.) IEA 2018. AISC, vol. 822, pp. 516–525. Springer, Cham (2019). https://doi.org/10.1007/978-3-319-96077-7_55

104. Tomasello, M., Carpenter, M., Call, J., Behne, T., Moll, H.: In search of the uniquely human. Beh. Brain Sci. **28**(5), 721–735 (2005). https://doi.org/10.1017/S0140525X05540123

105. Tomsett, R., et al.: Rapid trust calibration through interpretable and Uncertainty-Aware AI. Patterns (N Y) **1**(4), 100049 (2020). https://doi.org/10.1016/j.patter.2020.100049

106. Tran, P.N., Pham, D.T., Goh, S.K., Alam, S., Duong, V.: An interactive conflict solver for learning air traffic conflict resolutions. J. Aerospace Inf. Syst. **17**(6), 271–277 (2020). https://doi.org/10.2514/1.I010807

107. Umbrello, S., Yampolskiy, R.V.: Designing AI for explainability and verifiability: a value sensitive design approach to avoid artificial stupidity in autonomous vehicles. Int. J. Soc. Robot. **14**(2), 313–322 (2021). https://doi.org/10.1007/s12369-021-00790-w

108. Vassiliades, A., Bassiliades, N., Patkos, T.: Argumentation and explainable artificial intelligence: a survey. Knowl. Eng. Rev. **36**, e5 (2021). https://doi.org/10.1017/S0269888921000011

109. Veitch, E., Alsos, O.A.: Human-Centered explainable artificial intelligence for marine autonomous surface vehicles. J. Mar. Sci. Eng. **9**(11), 1227 (2021). https://doi.org/10.3390/jmse9111227

110. Verma, S., Arthur, A., Dickerson, J., Hines, K.: Counterfactual explanations for machine learning: a review https://arxiv.org/abs/2010.10596

111. Vorm, E.S.: Assessing demand for transparency in intelligent systems using machine learning. In: 2018 Innovations in Intelligent Systems and Applications (INISTA), pp. 1–7, July 2018. https://doi.org/10.1109/INISTA.2018.8466328

112. Wickens, C., Mavor,A., McGee, J.E.: Flight to the future: humans factors in air traffic control (1997)

113. Wickens, C.D., Helton, W.S., Hollands, J.G., Banbury, S.: Engineering Psychology and Human Performance. Routledge (2021). https://www.routledge.com/Engineering-Psychology-and-Human-Performance/Wickens-Helton-Hollands-Banbury/p/book/9781032011738

114. Wilson, T.D.: On user studies and information needs. J. Doc. **37**(1), 3–15 (1981)

115. Winkler, J.P., Vogelsang, A.: "What Does My Classifier Learn?" a visual approach to understanding natural language text classifiers. In: Frasincar, F., Ittoo, A., Nguyen, L.M., Métais, E. (eds.) NLDB 2017. LNCS, vol. 10260, pp. 468–479. Springer, Cham (2017). https://doi.org/10.1007/978-3-319-59569-6_55

116. Wu, X., Xiao, L., Sun, Y., Zhang, J., Ma, T., He, L.: A survey of human-in-the-loop for machine learning. Futur. Gener. Comput. Syst. **135**, 364–381 (2022). https://doi.org/10.1016/j.future.2022.05.014

117. Yi, K., Wu, J., Gan, C., Torralba, A., Kohli, P., Tenenbaum, J.B.: Neural-symbolic VQA: disentangling reasoning from vision and language understanding. In: Advances in Neural Information Processing Systems (NIPS) (2018). https://doi.org/10.48550/ARXIV.1810.02338

118. Yokoi, R., Nakayachi, K.: Trust in autonomous cars: exploring the role of shared moral values, reasoning, and emotion in Safety-Critical decisions. Hum. Factors **63**(8), 1465–1484 (2021). https://doi.org/10.1177/0018720820933041

119. Zarka, R., Cordier, A., Egyed-Zsigmond, E., Lamontagne, L., Mille, A.: Trace-based contextual recommendations. Expert Syst. Appl. **64**, 194–207 (2016). https://doi.org/10.1016/j.eswa.2016.07.035

120. Zheng, M., Zhang, S., Zhang, Y., Hu, B.: Construct food safety traceability system for people's health under the internet of things and big data. IEEE Access **9**, 70571–70583 (2021). https://doi.org/10.1109/ACCESS.2021.3078536

Exploring the Effect of Visual-Based Subliminal Persuasion in Public Speeches Using Explainable AI Techniques

Klaus Weber[(⊠)] [iD], Lukas Tinnes, Tobias Huber[iD], and Elisabeth Andre[iD]

University of Augsburg, Augsburg, Germany
{klaus.weber,tobias.huber,elisabeth.andre}@uni-a.de, tinnes-lukas@gmx.de

Abstract. When it comes to persuading other people, non-verbal cues play an important role in order to be successful. Mostly, people use these non-verbal cues subconsciously and, from the perspective of the persuadee, are not aware of the subliminal impact of them. To raise awareness of subliminal persuasion, we analyzed videos of different political public speeches. We used the labels of three annotators to train three subjective neural networks capable of predicting their degree of perceived persuasiveness based on the images as input only. We then created visualizations of the predictions for each network/annotator to draw conclusions about what the annotators have most likely focused on. For that, we employed layer-wise relevance propagation (LRP) that highlights the most relevant image sections for each prediction. Our results show that techniques like LRP can help uncover existing subliminal bias.

Keywords: Explainable Artificial Intelligence · Subliminal Persuasion

1 Introduction

The opinion-building process strongly depends on subliminal persuasion and subliminal persuasive cues; therefore, people can be manipulated very easily without noticing.

For instance, a study by Légal et al. [22] showed that subliminal goal priming of trust could significantly enhance the persuasiveness of a conveyed message.

Subliminal persuasion defines *"the presentation of information in a manner that may change people's attitudes without their conscious awareness of the content of the information to which they have been exposed."*[1], however, in the context of this paper, we also denote the persuasion by means of *persuasive cues* as *subliminal persuasion*. This subliminal persuasion can refer both to the addressee, who is subliminally persuaded, and the sender of the message, who tries to persuade the addressee by using subliminal persuasive techniques. In the latter case, these techniques can be manipulative if the sender deliberately

---

[1] https://dictionary.apa.org/subliminal-persuasion.

H. Degen and S. Ntoa (Eds.): HCII 2023, LNAI 14050, pp. 381–397, 2023.
https://doi.org/10.1007/978-3-031-35891-3_23

uses them. As per Buss [8], manipulation concerns *"the ways in which individuals intentionally or purposefully [...] alter, change, influence, or exploit others"*, although he also said that *"the mechanism of manipulation need imply no evil, malicious, or pernicious intent"*.

Consequently, subliminal persuasion can be subconscious and deliberate from the sender's perspective, but this requires long training. The best political speakers have trained themselves for years to persuade their voters. Therefore, it is not surprising that many politicians are genuinely charismatic and know how to engage the audience successfully and (subliminally) make them believe their speeches, most just with logical arguments.

People often use far more subliminal persuasive techniques in changing opinions or attitudes than logical and rational ones. There is much evidence from the literature that the persuasive power of arguments significantly depends on appropriate body language [3,7,19,37]. Consequently, if arguments that are content-wise identical are presented differently, i.e., with different non-verbal behaviors, the persuasive power of an argument can be different. These findings apply to humans and robots as several studies have also demonstrated that body language and verbal cues significantly influence the perceived persuasiveness of robots similarly to humans [5,11,16].

However, these are often unconsciously perceived by people, i.e., they are unaware of this subliminal persuasion or do not pay much attention to these cues.

A comprehensive understanding of these cues bears two advantages: 1) People can use this knowledge to be more persuasive in debates, speeches, or job interviews, and 2) using this knowledge makes people less susceptible to subliminal persuasion.

In this paper, we present an extension of our previously presented approach [39], in which we explored how explainable artificial intelligence techniques can be used to make persuasive cues visible to demonstrate the importance of the persuasive power of body-language-based argumentation. In this paper, we go beyond simply explaining the learning process of a neural network in general. We explicitly investigate the subjective markers of perceived persuasiveness among different annotators of public speeches using explainable AI (XAI). This approach is motivated by perceived persuasion being highly subjective [18,27], and the question arises if we can highlight these differences employing XAI. With that, our overall goal is to raise awareness of the power of subliminal persuasive cues and demonstrate the different influences that those cues have on people.

First, we trained a model for each annotator (three in total) to predict the perceived persuasiveness based on the annotated political public speeches utilizing the visual (image) channel only (i.e., without the audio channel). We then employed an explainable artificial intelligence (XAI) visualization technique to uncover the image's most relevant parts for predicting the degree of perceived convincingness. This enables us to conclude what each annotator has most likely focused on.

Our post-hoc analysis reveals that our neural networks have learned to focus on the person's hands which is the most thriving factor for perceived persuasiveness. While this effect seems less intense for rater one and two, rater three was focused on dynamic hand movements, which can be made visible by using LRP (Layer-wise Relevance Propagation), revealing an unyielding focus on the hand positions for the neutral class compared to the other two raters. This leads us to conclude that rater three paid more attention to the body language than the content of the speeches, unlike rater one and two. For rater one and two, we identified a trend of note-reading as being *neutral*, which is also highlighted in the generated saliency maps.

2   Related Work

Related work of this research can be divided into two parts: (1) The effect of non-verbal cues in persuasive messages and (2) Explainable Artificial Intelligence.

2.1   The Effect of Persuasion and Classifiers

The Effect of Non-verbal Cues in Persuasive Messages. The theory of persuasion goes back to Aristotle. He identified three means of persuasion: logos, pathos, and ethos. Logos defines the logical and rational aspects, i.e., the content of the argument, and pathos, the emotional engagement between the speaker and the listener. Finally, ethos describes the personality of the speaker, their character, and how the speaker is perceived by the audience [20].

According to psychological models, there are two cognitive routes (*central* and *peripheral*) through which a persuasive message can be processed. Petty and Cacioppo [28] developed the Elaboration Likelihood Model (ELM) describing the influence of information processing on the result of a persuasive message depending on the listeners "*need for cognition*" (NFC). If the listener's NFC is low, a message is more likely processed via the *peripheral route*; otherwise, *central processing* takes place. Chaiken et al. [10] extended this model (Heuristic-Systematic Model – HSM), claiming that people do not process information in isolation via one of the two routes. Instead, peripheral processing always takes place, to which central processing is added when an elaboration threshold is reached (depending on the listener's *need for cognition*).

Consequently, researchers have investigated the effect of non-verbal cues on perceived persuasiveness. DeSteno et al. [12] showed that persuasive messages are more successful if they are framed with emotional overtones that correspond to the recipient's emotional state. Wang et al. [38] showed that perceived persuasiveness of emotions depends on the speaker's and listener's level of power. Further, Van Kleef et al. [19,37] showed that people use the source's emotions as an information channel when they form their attitudes.

In addition, researchers have investigated the effect of gestures and gaze. Maricchiolo et al. [23] investigated the effect of hand gestures concerning the speaker's perceived persuasiveness, revealing that hand gestures affect the evaluation of a message's persuasiveness, the speaker's style effectiveness, and their composure and competence. Poggi et al. [29] further investigated the use of gestures and gaze in political discourse concerning their persuasive import.

In short, much evidence suggests that persuasiveness largely depends on body-language-based argumentation and persuasive cues. Thus, by taking away the audio channel, a neural network can learn these cues to predict perceived persuasiveness successfully, as shown in [anonymized]. However, the authors should have explored the subjectivity of those cues and the potential differences between several annotators, which we, therefore, investigate in this paper by training different models of different people.

Persuasive Classifiers. Some work previously investigated the practicability of the development of a persuasive classifier.

Strapparava et al. [36] assessed the persuasiveness of transcript tagged with different labels (intensity of applause, spontaneous demonstration, standing- ovations, sustained-applause, cheers, and booing) employing text categorization. Nojavanasghari et al. [26] used deep learning to analyze persuasiveness based on a deep learning architecture. They used visual, audio, and text features to compute a prediction of persuasiveness. Overall, they achieved an accuracy of about 90%.

In this work, we do not aim to outperform these results (which is likely not even possible using visual input only). Most works on persuasive classifiers focused on development alone but not on the analysis of subliminal persuasion. In contrast, we explicitly explore the effect of subliminal persuasion of different annotators based on subjectively annotated videos employing explainable AI.

2.2   Explainable Artificial Intelligence

Since artificial intelligent systems are becoming increasingly complex, there is an increasing need to increase the explainability of these systems. Understanding how a system works is crucial for working with and building trust in artificial, intelligent systems.

XAI is especially important when the system is inferring personality traits of humans, such as persuasiveness, which is a highly subjective task that might include biases. For this reason, earlier works used XAI on several subjective tasks. For example, Escalante et al. [14] developed a challenge to test different explainable systems used for first impression analysis in job applications. Weitz et al. [40] and Prajod et al. [30] investigated XAI methods on facial pain and emotion recognition models.

In the context of persuasion and XAI, recent work mainly investigated explainable recommendation systems persuading humans [13,42].

XAI is often split into several subcategories. In this work, we do not, for example, deal with developing more interpretable model architectures. Instead, we focus on *post hoc* explanations that are created after the model was trained

[24]. Furthermore, we focus on local explanations that analyze single predictions of a system instead of global explanations that try to shed light on the general behavior of a system. The most common local post-hoc explanation method for neural networks is the generation of saliency maps [1]. Saliency maps are heat maps that highlight areas of the input that were relevant to a system's decision in a certain way.

One of the first kinds of saliency maps was based on the gradient. Simonyan et al. [34] used backpropagation to calculate the gradient with respect to each input unit to measure how much a small change in this input affects the prediction. Selvaraju et al. [32] made this approach more class discriminatory by stopping the backpropagation after the fully connected layers and using the gradient with respect to the output of the last convolutional layer.

A different kind of saliency map estimates how much each input is attributed to a neural network's final decision. Lapushkin et al. [6, 21] introduced layer-wise relevance propagation (LRP) that assigns a relevance value to each neuron in a neural network, measuring how relevant this neuron was for a particular prediction. For this assignment, they defined different rules based on the intermediate outputs of the neural network during the forward pass. One of those rules introduced by Huber et al. [17] tries to create more selective saliency maps by only propagating the relevance to the neuron with the highest activation in the preceding layer. Montavon et al. [25] put the LRP concept into the theoretical framework of the Taylor decomposition.

Another take on saliency maps comes with occlusion or perturbation-based visualizations. Zeiler et al. [41] zero out windows inside the input image and measure how much this changes the model's prediction. The more the output changes, the more relevant this window is for this particular prediction. Greydanus et al. [15] uses a similar approach but perturbs the windows with noise to see how much the introduced uncertainty affects the prediction. The LIME framework from [31] first separates the input picture into super-pixels by a segmentation algorithm. Afterward, a more interpretable model is trained to estimate which super-pixels are the most relevant for a given decision. One of the advantages of those methods is that they are independent of the structure of the model, but this comes with the drawback of not being as precise as some model-specific methods.

Recently, Adebayo et al. [2] introduced a sanity check that showed that some gradient-based saliency maps were not analyzing the learned weights of a neural network. The original saliency maps from [34] and the Grad-CAM maps passed the test. In follow-up work, Sixt et al. [35] tested different LRP variants more in-depth. They concluded that most LRP variants lose information about the last fully connected layers of very deep neural networks. However, this only slightly affects very shallow neural networks, like the ones in our work.

While in Weber et al. [39] we analyzed the general feasibility of using XAI to highlight persuasive markers, we still needed to analyze and compare different raters by analyzing networks trained on single raters rather than a gold standard across all raters

Fig. 1. Some example frames taken from the dataset.

3 Approach

In this Section, we describe the data annotation process and the model architecture, including the training process of the neural network, in detail.

3.1 Data Collection and Annotations

In order to obtain a diverse dataset, 30 public speeches were annotated. Figure 1 shows some example frames taken from the dataset, whereas Fig. 2 shows the distribution of those speeches according to gender and party affiliation. Most of the speeches in the dataset come from the German Bundestag, and a small part from other countries, for example, America and Austria. About every fourth speech was chosen to be of a woman to account for gender biases. In addition, care was taken to ensure that the speeches covered as many political directions as possible, i.e., that the speeches did not belong to just one political direction. The speeches' main topic was the ongoing COVID-19 Pandemic; other topics included the Deutsche Bahn (german railway), agriculture, and healthy food.

We had the corpus annotated by three labelers continuously with a sample rate 25 Hz. They were asked to rate how convincing the speaker appeared, distinguishing between five different levels (ranging from *not convincing at all* to *very convincing*)

An overview of the class distributions of the annotators is displayed in Fig. 3, showing a general imbalance between classes. We applied Oversampling to counteract imbalance during the learning process. It is also noteworthy that the two lowest classes were barely present because expert politicians made the speeches. Thus, the two lowest classes were omitted from the learning process.

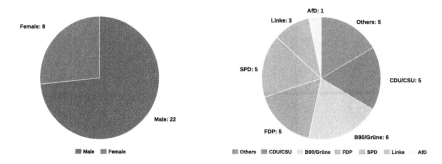

Fig. 2. Data set properties; Left: Male-Female-Ratio; Right: Party affiliation of the speakers. Speeches were chosen to obtain a relatively diverse dataset. Non-German politicians have been included in *Others*.

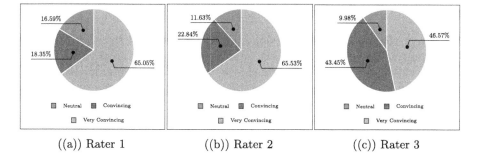

| ((a)) Rater 1 | ((b)) Rater 2 | ((c)) Rater 3 |

Fig. 3. Class distributions per annotator showing an imbalance between classes.

3.2   OpenPose Feature Extraction

To bypass skin color or background noise-related errors described in [39], the model is trained on OpenPose features. Openpose is a library for the multi-person body, face, hand, and foot keypoint detection [9,33]. It allows the extraction of body, hand, and foot key points from videos, images, and webcam feeds. An image is first used as input to a convolutional neural network (CNN) to predict confidence maps and partial affinity fields (PAFs) for specific body parts such as the nose, shoulders, etc. The PAFs are used to determine, given an unknown number of people in the image, which recognized body points belong to a particular person. Finally, the detected key points are matched with other associated body parts to obtain a complete body pose of all persons in the image. Examples of the features extracted by OpenPose are shown in Fig. 4. OpenPose outputs a vector of key points of the form (x, y, c), where x and y are the normalized coordinates within the image, and c defines the confidence. For our approach, we use the model $BODY\_25$, which generates 67 keypoint triples, of which we used 54 because the speakers' feet were never visible, and therefore, this data was omitted from the learning process.

Fig. 4. Example features extracted by OpenPose, visualized and overlayed on the original input. LTR: Sebastian Kurz, Bernie Sanders, Johann Saathoff

3.3 Model Architecture and Training

To prevent the models from overfitting on the dataset and thus not providing representative relevance values in the later analysis, ten-fold cross-validation (27 training videos and three validation videos) was performed, and it was checked at which epoch overfitting was detectable. The final models were trained only up to this number of epochs, which was found to be five.

Different from our previous work [39], where a CNN was used on raw images, we use a fully connected neural network with five layers as we use OpenPose features as input. As initial training results were unsatisfactory, we applied a hyper-parameter search for each of the three models to obtain the best-practical model for each annotator.

Table 1. Hyperparameters for each Rater (h_n describes the nth hidden layer). Adam parameters: Learning rate 0.00001, $\beta_1 = 0.9$, $\beta_2 = 0.999$

	Neurons h_1/h_2	Neurons $h_3/h_4/h_5$	Optimizer	Dropout
Rater 1	1024	256	adam	0.1
Rater 2	256	1024	adam	0.1
Rater 3	256	1024	adam	0.1

Figure 2 shows the precision, recall, and F1-Score of all three final models trained on all data showing that the networks could predict the perceived persuasiveness to a sufficient degree for our analysis of subliminal persuasive cues. We did not intend to train a perfect predictor but only used the trained network to analyze the learned cues; thus, we trained the network on all 30 videos.

Table 2. Training results of the final model for each rater.

		Precision	Recall	F1-Score	Accuracy
Rater 1	Neutral	0.28	0.61	0.39	
	Convincing	0.75	0.68	0.72	
	Very Convincing	0.60	0.41	0.49	
	Weighted Average	0.66	0.61	0.63	0.61
Rater 2	Neutral	0.65	0.88	0.75	
	Convincing	0.82	0.85	0.84	
	Very Convincing	0.77	0.44	0.56	
	Weighted Average	0.79	0.78	0.77	0.78
Rater 3	Neutral	0.59	0.84	0.70	
	Convincing	0.71	0.26	0.38	
	Very Convincing	0.34	0.73	0.47	
	Weighted Average	0.62	0.56	0.53	0.56

3.4 Layer-Wise Relevance Propagation

To visualize what the network paid the most attention to, we use LRP. LRP assigns a relevance value R_k to each neuron in a neural network. Let a_k be the activation of the k-th neuron during the forward pass, and let w_{jk} be the weight that connects neuron j and neuron k. After the forward pass, the relevance propagation starts in the output layer. Here, the activation responsible for the prediction gets assigned its activation as relevance, and every other neuron gets set to zero. That is

$$R_k = \begin{cases} a_k & \text{if } k = argmax\{a_k\} \\ 0 & \text{if not.} \end{cases} \tag{1}$$

From there, relevance gets propagated from each layer l to each preceding layer $l-1$ according to different rules (see Fig. 5). In our experiments, we used the z^+- or $\alpha1\beta0$-rule. This rule calculates the relevance of the neuron j in the preceding layer $l-1$ as follows:

$$R_j = \sum_k \frac{(a_j w_{jk})^+}{\sum_i (a_i w_{ik})^+} R_k, \tag{2}$$

where the index k goes over all neurons in layer l, the index i goes over all neurons in the preceding layer $l-1$, and $(a_j w_{jk})^+$ is defined as $\max(a_j w_{jk}, 0)$.

Using the relevance values R_x, R_y and R_c for each key point $k = (x, y, c)$, we aggregated the relevance values per key point to get a normalized value R_k for each key point k to be mapped onto the original image.

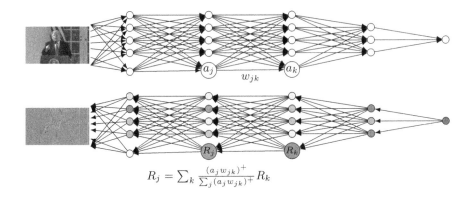

$$R_j = \sum_k \frac{(a_j w_{jk})^+}{\sum_j (a_j w_{jk})^+} R_k$$

Fig. 5. Relevance propagation using the z^+-Rule (Eq. 2).

4   Results and Discussion

In the following, we present an in-depth analysis of all three raters. We computed the relevance values using LRP using iNNvestigate [4]. Then, we generated saliency maps for input images x with sufficiently high confidence (≥ 0.8) that were correctly predicted by the network.

4.1   Rater 1

Table 3. Images of rater one.

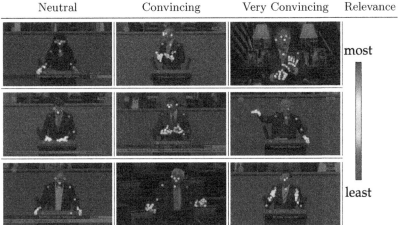

First, we analyzed which cues rater 1 found persuasive based on the annotated data and identified trends. Then we observed the saliency maps to see if we could also find those trends in the saliency maps. Example saliency maps for rater one are shown in Table 3.

Trend 1: Although this pose is was frequently seen in the *convincing* class, rater 1 tends to see reading notes as *neutral*. Looking at the saliency maps, we can see this trend that the network has learned to focus on the eyes for class *neutral*. Additionally, specific instances of clasped hands labeled as *neutral* can be found in the data. This pose suggests an unbiased and objective view of the speaker.

Trend 2: More dynamic gestures can be found within the class *convincing*. A speaker who makes active gestures and motions and does not constantly read from his notes appears prepared and confident to speak without overly relying on their notes. This is again highlighted in the saliency maps as we can see a stronger focus on the hands and less on the gaze for the *convincing* class compared to class *neutral*.

Trend 3: The *very convincing* class has a definite trend toward precise hand gestures and dynamic body language. Clear, dynamic body language makes a speaker seem very persuasive. Consequently, the network has learned a focus on shoulders and arms which indicate a big gesture.

4.2   Rater 2

The same applies to rater two. Note-reading with a bowed head was often labeled as *neutral* or *convincing*, which is yet again (**Trend 1**) highlighted in the saliency maps by a network's focus on the eyes. The *very convincing* class tends toward more dynamic, energetic poses and movements, while both the classes *convincing* and *very convincing* contain images with hand motions in general (**Trend 2**). Both raters one and two concur that engaging and active speakers are more convincing than those who appear stiff or who appear to read the majority of their speech from notes. See Fig. 4 for examples of rater two's saliency maps.

4.3   Rater 3

Rater three disagrees with the other raters. The reading notes and bowed-head poses can be seen once more in the *neutral* class (**Trend 1**). However, compared to raters one and two, these poses are far less common in the class *convincing*. While we can again identify a focus on the eyes for class *neutral*, there seems to be a specific new focus on the hands lying on the notes, which is revealed by the salience maps. The *convincing* class primarily consists of poses with overt gestures or body language. Nearly all images of the class *very convincing*

Table 4. Images of rater two.

Neutral	Convincing	Very Convincing	Relevance

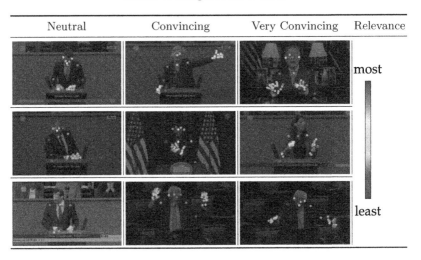

Table 5. Images of rater three.

Neutral	Convincing	Very Convincing	Relevance

contain expressive gestures and lively body language (**Trend 2**); thus, we can often see a focus on the hands in saliency maps. It seems that rater three was more influenced by body language than other elements, such as tone and speech content. Examples of saliency maps of rater three can be found in Table 5.

Table 6. Comparison of raters.

	Neutral	Convincing	Very Convincing	Relevance
Rater 1				most
Rater 2				
Rater 3				least

4.4 Comparison

Comparing the saliency maps of the raters (see Table 6 for examples), we can see one trend again: The third rater's network puts a lot more focus on the hands for the *neutral* class, which is not surprising as previously we generally identified a stronger focus on gaze for rater one and two. This suggests that the gestures, the pose, and the perceived persuasiveness are related. As analyzed earlier, this trend is weaker for raters one and two. While we can again see the highlighted hands in the saliency maps for class *very convincing* across all raters in the salience maps, the trend that rater three pays more attention to the hands is somewhat reversed in the example above for class *convincing*. This is likely because of the particular body posture (gaze to the left) and thus suggests that rater three overall paid more attention to specific body language, such as directly facing someone, which the network seems to have learned.

5 Limitations

Finally, we summarize below some limitations that are worth mentioning.

5.1 Time-Consuming Annotation Process

First, to use this approach to validate and highlight reflection bias, subjective annotations from each person are required. To get a reasonable ground truth, much data must be collected, and annotating that data takes much effort.

5.2 Time-Consuming Training Process

Second, the network needs to be optimized for each person individually because no baseline network produced satisfactory training results for every annotator.

5.3   OpenPose

Any background person would result in the detection of additional people by OpenPose. OpenPose allows limiting detection to only one individual, which the model is the most certain about. Though, that this is the speaker whom we want to analyze cannot be assumed in general. Therefore, applying this method to a speech with numerous bystanders in the background would be pretty tedious and complicated because the key points are just a list of coordinate values from an input image, and it needs to be manually filtered out so that key points are not from bystanders. A false example can be seen in Table 7.

Table 7. Examples: Openpose recognition errors. **Left**: Wrong person detected - **Middle**: Object wrongly classified as body part - **Right**: Undetected body parts.

	1	2	3
Errors			

6   Conclusion

In this paper, we presented an extended approach to highlight the effect of subliminal persuasiveness in public speeches of single raters using LRP (Layer-wise Relevance Propagation). We first collected 30 videos, annotated them by three raters, and trained three neural networks for each rater on OpenPose features. We then identified trends in data and investigated if we could see them in the highlighted saliency maps. Results show that we could highlight the note-reading posture as a strong indicator for *neutral* persuasiveness. While this effect seems less intense for rater one and two, rater three focused on dynamic hand movements, which we made visible by using LRP (Layer-wise Relevance Propagation), revealing a firm focus on the hand positions for the neutral class compared to the other two raters. A direct comparison further showed that rater three not only paid attention to hand movements in general but specifically to body language and unique posture, such as *direct-gazing*.

Acknowledgements. This work has been funded by the Deutsche Forschungsgemeinschaft (DFG) within the project "BEA - Building Engaging Argumentation", Grant Number 455911629, as part of the Priority Program "Robust Argumentation Machines (RATIO)" (SPP-1999).

References

1. Adadi, A., Berrada, M.: Peeking inside the black-box: a survey on explainable artificial intelligence (XAI). IEEE Access **6**, 52138–52160 (2018)
2. Adebayo, J., Gilmer, J., Muelly, M., Goodfellow, I., Hardt, M., Kim, B.: Sanity checks for saliency maps. In: Advances in Neural Information Processing Systems 31, pp. 9505–9515. Curran Associates, Inc. (2018)
3. Ahmad, W.N.W., Ali, N.M.: A study on persuasive technologies. The relationship between user emotions, trust and persuasion. Int. J. Interact. Multimedia Artif. Intell. **5**(1), 57 (2018). https://doi.org/10.9781/ijimai.2018.02.010. http://www.ijimai.org/journal/node/2156
4. Alber, M., et al.: iNNvestigate neural networks! J. Mach. Learn. Res. **20**(93), 1–8 (2019). http://jmlr.org/papers/v20/18-540.html
5. Andrist, S., Spannan, E., Mutlu, B.: Rhetorical robots: making robots more effective speakers using linguistic cues of expertise. In: 2013 8th ACM/IEEE International Conference on Human-Robot Interaction (HRI), pp. 341–348. IEEE (2013)
6. Bach, S., Binder, A., Montavon, G., Klauschen, F., Müller, K.R., Samek, W.: On pixel-wise explanations for non-linear classifier decisions by layer-wise relevance propagation. PLOS ONE **10**(7), e0130140 (2015)
7. Burgoon, J.K., Birk, T., Pfau, M.: Nonverbal behaviors, persuasion, and credibility. Hum. Commun. Res. **17**(1), 140–169 (1990). https://doi.org/10.1111/j.1468-2958.1990.tb00229.x. https://academic.oup.com/hcr/article/17/1/140-169/4575795
8. Buss, D.M.: Selection, evocation, and manipulation. J. Pers. Soc. Psychol. **53**(6), 1214–1221 (1987)
9. Cao, Z., Hidalgo Martinez, G., Simon, T., Wei, S., Sheikh, Y.A.: OpenPose: real-time multi-person 2d pose estimation using part affinity fields. IEEE Transactions on Pattern Analysis and Machine Intelligence (2019)
10. Chaiken, S.: Heuristic and systematic information processing within and beyond the persuasion context. Unintended Thought, pp. 212–252 (1989)
11. Chidambaram, V., Chiang, Y.H., Mutlu, B.: Designing persuasive robots: how robots might persuade people using vocal and nonverbal cues. In: Proceedings of the Seventh Annual ACM/IEEE International Conference On Human-robot Interaction, pp. 293–300 (2012)
12. DeSteno, D., Petty, R.E., Rucker, D.D., Wegener, D.T., Braverman, J.: Discrete emotions and persuasion: the role of emotion-induced expectancies. J. Pers. Soc. Psychol. **86**(1), 43 (2004)
13. Donadello, I., Dragoni, M., Eccher, C.: Persuasive explanation of reasoning inferences on dietary data. In: Demidova, E., et al. (eds.) Joint Proceedings of the 6th International Workshop on Dataset PROFILing and Search & the 1st Workshop on Semantic Explainability co-located with the 18th International Semantic Web Conference (ISWC 2019), Auckland, New Zealand, 27 October 2019. CEUR Workshop Proceedings, vol. 2465, pp. 46–61. CEUR-WS.org (2019)
14. Escalante, H.J., et al.: Design of an explainable machine learning challenge for video interviews. In: 2017 International Joint Conference on Neural Networks, IJCNN 2017, Anchorage, AK, USA, 14–19 May 2017, pp. 3688–3695. IEEE (2017)
15. Greydanus, S., Koul, A., Dodge, J., Fern, A.: Visualizing and understanding Atari agents. In: Proceedings of the 35th International Conference on Machine Learning, ICML 2018, Stockholmsmässan, Stockholm, Sweden, pp. 1787–1796 (2018)

16. Ham, J., Bokhorst, R., Cuijpers, R., van der Pol, D., Cabibihan, J.-J.: Making robots persuasive: the influence of combining persuasive strategies (gazing and gestures) by a storytelling robot on its persuasive power. In: Mutlu, B., Bartneck, C., Ham, J., Evers, V., Kanda, T. (eds.) ICSR 2011. LNCS (LNAI), vol. 7072, pp. 71–83. Springer, Heidelberg (2011). https://doi.org/10.1007/978-3-642-25504-5_8

17. Huber, T., Schiller, D., André, E.: Enhancing explainability of deep reinforcement learning through selective layer-wise relevance propagation. In: Benzmüller, C., Stuckenschmidt, H. (eds.) KI 2019. LNCS (LNAI), vol. 11793, pp. 188–202. Springer, Cham (2019). https://doi.org/10.1007/978-3-030-30179-8_16

18. Kaptein, M., Lacroix, J., Saini, P.: Individual differences in persuadability in the health promotion domain. In: Ploug, T., Hasle, P., Oinas-Kukkonen, H. (eds.) PERSUASIVE 2010. LNCS, vol. 6137, pp. 94–105. Springer, Heidelberg (2010). https://doi.org/10.1007/978-3-642-13226-1_11

19. van Kleef, G.: Emotions as agents of social influence. In: The Oxford Handbook of Social Influence. Oxford University Press (2019)

20. Krapinger, G.: Aristoteles: Rhetorik. Reclam, Übersetzt und herausgegeben von Gernot Krapinger. Stuttgart (1999)

21. Lapuschkin, S., Wäldchen, S., Binder, A., Montavon, G., Samek, W., Müller, K.R.: Unmasking clever Hans predictors and assessing what machines really learn. Nat. Commun. 10(1), 1096 (2019)

22. Légal, J.B., Chappé, J., Coiffard, V., Villard-Forest, A.: Don't you know that you want to trust me? Subliminal goal priming and persuasion. J. Exper. Soc. Psychol. 48(1), 358–360 (Jan 2012). https://doi.org/10.1016/j.jesp.2011.06.006. https://linkinghub.elsevier.com/retrieve/pii/S0022103111001673

23. Maricchiolo, F., Gnisci, A., Bonaiuto, M., Ficca, G.: Effects of different types of hand gestures in persuasive speech on receivers' evaluations. Lang. Cognit. Process. 24(2), 239–266 (2009)

24. Molnar, C.: Interpretable machine learning. http://lulu.com/ (2019)

25. Montavon, G., Samek, W., Müller, K.: Methods for interpreting and understanding deep neural networks. Dig. Sig. Process. 73, 1–15 (2018)

26. Nojavanasghari, B., Gopinath, D., Koushik, J., Baltrušaitis, T., Morency, L.P.: Deep multimodal fusion for persuasiveness prediction. In: Proceedings of the 18th ACM International Conference on Multimodal Interaction, pp. 284–288 (2016)

27. O'Keefe, D.J., Jackson, S.: Argument quality and persuasive effects: a review of current approaches. In: Argumentation and values: In: Proceedings of the Ninth Alta Conference on Argumentation, pp. 88–92. Speech Communication Association Annandale (1995)

28. Petty, R.E., Cacioppo, J.T.: The elaboration likelihood model of persuasion. In: Communication and Persuasion. Springer Series in Social Psychology, pp. 1–24. Springer, NY (1986). https://doi.org/10.1007/978-1-4612-4964-1_1

29. Poggi, I., Vincze, L.: Gesture, gaze and persuasive strategies in political discourse. In: Kipp, M., Martin, J.-C., Paggio, P., Heylen, D. (eds.) MMCorp 2008. LNCS (LNAI), vol. 5509, pp. 73–92. Springer, Heidelberg (2009). https://doi.org/10. 1007/978-3-642-04793-0_5

30. Prajod, P., Schiller, D., Huber, T., André, E.: Do deep neural networks forget facial action units?-exploring the effects of transfer learning in health related facial expression recognition. In: Shaban-Nejad, A., Michalowski, M., Bianco, S. (eds.) AI for Disease Surveillance and Pandemic Intelligence. W3PHAI 2021. Studies in Computational Intelligence, vol. 1013, pp. 217–233. Springer, Cham (2022). https://doi.org/10.1007/978-3-030-93080-6_16

31. Ribeiro, M.T., Singh, S., Guestrin, C.: "why should I trust you?": Explaining the predictions of any classifier. In: Krishnapuram, B., Shah, M., Smola, A.J., Aggarwal, C.C., Shen, D., Rastogi, R. (eds.) Proceedings of the 22nd ACM SIGKDD International Conference on Knowledge Discovery and Data Mining, San Francisco, CA, USA, 13–17 August 2016, pp. 1135–1144. ACM (2016)
32. Selvaraju, R.R., Cogswell, M., Das, A., Vedantam, R., Parikh, D., Batra, D.: Grad-CAM: Visual explanations from deep networks via gradient-based localization, vol. 128, pp. 336–359 (2020). https://doi.org/10.1007/s11263-019-01228-7
33. Simon, T., Joo, H., Matthews, I., Sheikh, Y.: Hand keypoint detection in single images using multiview bootstrapping. In: Conference on Computer Vision and Pattern Recognition (2017)
34. Simonyan, K., Vedaldi, A., Zisserman, A.: Deep inside convolutional networks: Visualising Image Classification Models and Saliency Maps. CoRR abs/1312.6034 (2013)
35. Sixt, L., Granz, M., Landgraf, T.: When explanations lie: Why modified BP attribution fails. CoRR abs/1912.09818 (2019)
36. Strapparava, C., Guerini, M., Stock, O.: Predicting persuasiveness in political discourses. In: LREC (2010)
37. Van Kleef, G.A., van den Berg, H., Heerdink, M.W.: The persuasive power of emotions: effects of emotional expressions on attitude formation and change. J. Appl. Psychol. **100**(4), 1124 (2015)
38. Wang, Y., Lucas, G., Khooshabeh, P., De Melo, C., Gratch, J.: Effects of emotional expressions on persuasion. Soc. Influ. **10**(4), 236–249 (2015)
39. Weber, K., et al.: Towards demystifying subliminal persuasiveness: using XAI-techniques to highlight persuasive markers of public speeches. In: Calvaresi, D., Najjar, A., Winikoff, M., Främling, K. (eds.) EXTRAAMAS 2020. LNCS (LNAI), vol. 12175, pp. 113–128. Springer, Cham (2020). https://doi.org/10.1007/978-3-030-51924-7_7
40. Weitz, K., Hassan, T., Schmid, U., Garbas, J.U.: Deep-learned faces of pain and emotions: Elucidating the differences of facial expressions with the help of explainable AI methods. Tm-Technisches Messen **86**(7–8), 404–412 (2019)
41. Zeiler, M.D., Fergus, R.: Visualizing and understanding convolutional networks. In: Fleet, D., Pajdla, T., Schiele, B., Tuytelaars, T. (eds.) ECCV 2014. LNCS, vol. 8689, pp. 818–833. Springer, Cham (2014). https://doi.org/10.1007/978-3-319-10590-1_53
42. Zhang, Y., Chen, X.: Explainable recommendation: a survey and new perspectives. Found. Trends Inf. Retr. **14**(1), 1–101 (2020)

Ethics and Fairness in Artificial Intelligence

Assessing the Impact of Cognitive Biases in AI Project Development

Chloé Bernault[1] , Sara Juan[1] , Alexandra Delmas[2] , Jean-Marc Andre[1] ,
Marc Rodier[3] , and Ikram Chraibi Kaadoud[4(✉)]

[1] ENSC-Bordeaux INP, IMS, UMR CNRS 5218, Bordeaux, France
jean-marc.andre@ensc.fr
[2] Onepoint - R&D Department, Bordeaux, France
[3] IBM - University chair "Sciences et Technologies Cognitiques" in ENSC,
Bordeaux, France
[4] IMT Atlantique, Lab-STICC, UMR CNRS 6285, 29238 Brest, France
ikram.chraibi-kaadoud@imt-atlantique.fr

Abstract. Biases are a major issue in the field of Artificial Intelligence (AI). They can come from the data, be algorithmic or cognitive. If the first two types of biases are studied in the literature, few works focus on the last type, even though the task of designing AI systems is conducive to the emergence of cognitive biases. To address this gap, we propose a study on the impact of cognitive biases during the development cycle of AI projects. Our study focuses on six cognitive biases selected for their impact on ideation and development processes: Conformity, Confirmation, Illusory correlation, Measurement, Presentation, and Normality. Our major contribution is the realization of a cognitive bias awareness tool, in the form of a mind map, for AI professionals that address the impact of cognitive biases at each stage of an AI project. This tool was evaluated through semi-structured interviews and Technology Acceptance Model (TAM) questionnaires. User testing shows that (i) the majority admitted to being more aware of cognitive biases in their work thanks to our tool, (ii) the mind map would improve the quality of their decisions, their confidence in their realization, and their satisfaction with the work done, which impact directly their performance and efficiency, (iii) the mind map was well received by the professionals, who appropriated it by planning how to integrate it into their current work process: for awareness-raising purposes for the onboarding process of new employees and to develop reflexes in their work to question their decision-making.

Keywords: cognitive bias · AI project development · awareness · user-centered design

1 Introduction

Systems using Artificial Intelligence (AI) are taking a prominent place in our lives and in businesses. These systems have become increasingly complex and

H. Degen and S. Ntoa (Eds.): HCII 2023, LNAI 14050, pp. 401–420, 2023.
https://doi.org/10.1007/978-3-031-35891-3_24

powerful and have real implications in many major fields: health [37], biodiversity [43], justice [41] and even banking [31]. Yet some AI can lead to discriminatory practices related to gender or ethnicity [19,20]. The question of biases has thus become a major issue in AI. Their identification, management, and reduction, when possible, raise several technical, human, societal, and ethical issues related to the application of deep learning algorithms [11,24,35,39]. Many research in deep learning and human-IA interaction study the impact of humans on AI systems [6,7,35] during their design, development, and management, and conversely the impact of these systems on humans [16,25,29]. Among them, two strategies stand out [27]: those focused on data and those focused on algorithms. However, few studies examine the AI development-cognitive biases link [7].

Our work, in the area of human-IA interaction, aims to fill this gap by focusing on the people involved in developing and designing AI projects and their cognitive biases. Many definitions of the concept of cognitive bias exist [4,8,33,35,47]. In the context of our work, we choose to align ourselves with the definition of [7] which presents *"A cognitive bias such as a systematic deviation of logical and rational thinking from reality"*. This neutral definition (neither positive or negative) allows an objective approach of the subject. Cognitive biases are human, systematic, and universal. They are necessary for human reasoning to maintain consistency and to help fill in gaps when faced with the unknown. They also allow an individual to make a decision quickly according to his/her experience, his/her cognitive state at the time (mental load, state of fatigue, etc.), and the context. We define the development and design of AI projects as the following steps that lead to the completion of an AI project [1]: design, code implementation, testing, and production. In our work, we will refer to all of these steps as AI project development. We will call all actors in an AI project who can have an impact on the development stages of an AI system as AI professionals: AI researchers, managers, data scientists, data analysts, data architects, data engineers, and AI developers.

Our multidisciplinary work, in the field of Human-AI interaction at the intersection of cognitive science, and AI project management, is a continuation of studies conducted on the evaluation of the sensitivity of AI actors to cognitive biases [7] and the impact of the latter on intelligent systems. We question the impact of humans on AI systems during their design. Note that in our study, we make no distinction between AI systems. Our study focuses on all types of AI projects, not only those that exhibit discriminating or biased behavior towards a population.

Our research questions are associated with the following hypotheses:

- H1- the cognitive biases of AI professionals impact the projects these individuals work on
- H2- these individuals are unaware of their own cognitive biases
- H3- it is possible to create more ethical AI through raising awareness of cognitive biases among AI actors.

To test these hypotheses, our study focuses on six cognitive biases in particular, selected after a literature review for their impact on ideation and development processes [7,27]: (i) Conformity bias (ii) Confirmation bias (iii) Illusory correlation bias, (iv) Measurement bias (v) Presentation bias, and (vi) Normality bias.

Our major contribution is the realization of a mind map as a tool to raise awareness of these cognitive biases for AI professionals that addresses the impact of these biases at each stage of the AI project life cycle. This mind map was evaluated as follows: (1) A two-stage semi-structured interview session: (i) first to identify work habits without addressing cognitive biases, (ii) then to assess work habits in relation to these biases after introducing the biases targeted by the study to the interviewees; (2) Qualitative evaluation of the impact of this tool on their perception of their own biases, through user testing and observation of the professional-mind map interaction.

As the topic of bias in AI systems is much debated and studied within the AI community, we would like to clarify the contribution and position of the present work: we do not seek to establish any causal effect of the relationship between cognitive biases and algorithmic biases (a clearly distinct concept in the literature defined as *"Problems related to the gathering or processing of data that might result in prejudiced decisions on the bases of demographic features such as race, sex, and so forth"* [35]), nor do we seek to propose a tool for debiasing humans and in particular the actors involved in AI. Through our work we wish to question the cognitive biases that come into play in the human work involved in the development of an AI system (whether it is biased or not) and to highlight the concept of awareness of cognitive biases for these professionals.

We organize this article as follows: Sect. 2 presents related work in the area of bias analysis in AI and the methods used in prevention. Section 3 introduces the 6 cognitive biases targeted by this study. Section 4 describes the mind map, our awareness tool. In Sect. 5, we detail the evaluations carried out: the methodology followed and the associated results. We discuss these findings and the work of this study in Sect. 6, before concluding with prospective work in Sect. 7. Figure 1 presents a schematic representation of the hypothetical link between the cognitive biases of AI professionals and the possible impact on the AI systems they work on.

2   Related Work

There are several types of biases impacting AI systems: cognitive biases, algorithmic biases, and biases related to the data sets [34,45]. The latter can threaten the fairness of the system for example by systematically giving advantages to privileged groups and systematically giving disadvantages to non-privileged groups [3].

Because of the multiplicity of biases and their sources, it is difficult to successfully take them all into consideration and avoid them all [10]. Nevertheless, there are tools [3] and methodologies [15,27,38,40] that can be implemented

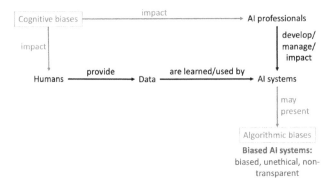

Fig. 1. Schematic representation of the hypothetical link between cognitive biases of AI professionals and the impact on AI systems.

to detect them and limit their negative consequences. For example, IBM offers "AI Fairness 360", a toolkit available in open source that ensures the fairness of an algorithm. It contains several fairness metrics for data sets and models and industry-specific tutorials to allow data scientists and others to choose the most appropriate tool for their problems. In particular, it allows to detect biases present in data sets or to evaluate the fairness of the models used [3]. As for methodologies, [15] propose a datasheet that provides a list of questions designed to obtain information about data sets. Each data set would therefore be accompanied by this datasheet to ensure transparency of the database so that users can make informed choices about how to use the data set. It would include information about its composition, collection process and recommended uses. Similarly, [27] propose to create datasheets summarizing the methods of creation, characteristics, and motivations of the data set.

There is also the SMACTR method for "Scoping, Mapping, Artifact Collection, Testing, Reflection", which allows determining the dangerous consequences that algorithms can bring before their deployment. It is an internal auditing system where developers are held accountable at each step by writing a report [40]. Finally, [38] propose a machine learning model that could handle multiple definitions of fairness and apply them. To do this, they harmonize two machine learning techniques, privileged learning [46] and distribution matching [42], to ensure that privileged characteristics such as race or gender will be information that is only used and available when the machine learning algorithms are being trained (and not in the testing or launching phase).

We have found that while the influence of human characteristics of designers on programs is known [25,29,48], there are few studies examining how cognitive biases can be concretely illustrated in the AI design process [21]. In particular, we highlight the following two works. The first work of [7], specifically addressed the issue of cognitive biases among AI professionals through a questionnaire. This study measured the sensitivity of AI professionals to three cognitive biases: conformity bias, confirmation bias, and illusory correlation bias. However, the authors do not propose any tool or framework. In the second work of [44], the authors addressed the similar-to-me bias and stereotype bias in the context of the realization of a model of the interaction between the Human Resources manager and the AI developer, in the context of the development of an AI system in the recruitment domain. This study, through interviews with 10 managers from New Zealand and Australia, examines how the cognitive biases of Human Ressources managers and developers lead to the development of biased AI. This model is specific to the recruitment domain and focuses on one part of the population involved in AI projects: managers and developers.

It is clear that if some works emerge in order to understand and detect the impact of cognitive biases, few approach the prism of human factors and focus on the whole life cycle of AI with different profiles of professionals (i.e. other than developers and managers). None, to our knowledge, proposes an awareness tool for the actors of AI systems design. We propose to carry out a study dedicated to this particular topic.

3   The 6 Studied Cognitive Biases

For a given project, the cognitive biases of the project actors can intervene in every decision making [5]: from the choice of the data, to the processing that the data must undergo, to the choice of the user interface at the end of the project or even the way to represent the information [45]. Theoretically, to have a complete study about cognitive biases impacts on AI project development, we should take into account all of the 200 biases already identified [28] in the literature. However, this is impossible without conducting an overly long or complex study.

In our work, we chose to focus on six biases that have a theoretically strong impact among AI professionals and that intervene at different stages of the AI system design chain. We chose to study the **conformity bias** which consists in abandoning one's own opinion to conform to the general opinion, consciously or not [36]. We also address the **confirmation bias**, which is a tendency to look for evidence to support/confirm a diagnosis rather than to refute it [32] and finally, the **illusory correlation bias**, which consists of trying to establish/find a correlation between two variables that are nevertheless independent [17]. We chose to work on these first three biases following the work of [7] who demonstrated that they had a singular and important impact on the AIs developed. On top of that, conformity and confirmation biases come into play during the personal choices of the different actors and during interactions within the team [22]. Placing the human being at the center of our reflection and thinking particularly about human-machine interactions, it seemed to us coherent and essential to take into account the interactions within the team and not only the code produced by the individuals. This is why we chose to study the **presentation bias** which consists in influencing the perception of information by a user according to the way it is presented [27]. This bias can occur: (i) during exchanges between members of the same team who do not always have the same qualifications or the same knowledge and (ii) also during exchanges between the machine and the user who must understand the information given by the machine without necessarily having the context of this information.

Finally, we have studied two other biases that can occur at many stages during the design of an AI. First, the **measurement bias**, which translates into subjectivity in the choice, utility and measurement of certain attributes [27,45] and which can notably lead to ethnic or gender discrimination, and second, the **normality bias**, which is a tendency to think that everything is going to happen as usual and to ignore signs indicating the opposite [2]. The role of this last bias in the field of AI is little studied. These six cognitive biases of Conformity, Confirmation, Illusory Correlation, Presentation, Measurement, and Normality are therefore at the center of our study and of the awareness tool we have created.

4   Mind Map, A Cognitive Bias Awareness Tool

In this section, we describe the design process followed to create the mind map shown in Fig. 2, as well as the mind map, its structure and functionalities, displayed in Fig. 3.

4.1   Overall Design Process

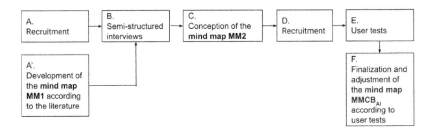

Fig. 2. Design process of the mind map

The first step of our approach was to elaborate the profile of the people we were looking for and their recruitment (Fig. 2, step A). We sought to recruit AI professionals with different profiles to participate in interviews and user testing. We identified three different professions in which to classify these actors: project managers, developers, and data scientists. It should be noted that during the recruitment process, we did not mention the subject of cognitive biases in order to avoid interviewing only professionals who were already aware of or curious about this subject. The second stage concerns the semi-structured interviews conducted (Fig. 2, stage B). We wanted to have a balance of the three professions (4 data scientists, 5 engineers, 5 project managers) so that the tool would be intended for everyone, with no disadvantaged or less well-considered professions. Thanks to these interviews, we were able to assess the sensitivity of each of the interviewees to cognitive biases and their impact on their work. Then we also briefly presented them the first mind map that represents the stages of AI project design according to the literature and which we will refer to as MM1. This step is described in detail later in Sect. 5.1. The third step (Fig. 2, step C) was the elaboration of the second mind map, that we will refer to as MM2, the version of the tool that we put forward in this work. We developed this tool based on the scientific literature and the feedback and results obtained during the interviews in the second stage. The fourth step consisted in the recruitment of participants to take user tests on the mind map MM2. This step constitutes the validation phase of our tool (Fig. 2, step D). For this purpose, we conducted a new recruitment campaign to recruit participants who had not previously been involved in our study. Our objective was to create a group of two types of participants to collect different opinions: those who participated in experiments 1 and 2 (who were aware of the project) and those who participated only in experiment 2 (who are neutral to the project). The fifth step (Fig. 2, step E) consisted in conducting user tests to test the MM2 mind map, validate it, and improve it. These tests are described in detail in Sect. 5.2. Finally, the results of the user tests allowed us to make the last modifications in order to create our final tool **MindMap for cognitive biases in AI** that we will name $MMCB_{AI}$ (Fig. 2, step E). Let us underline two points: 1) the MM1 mind map is realized in parallel to the first recruitment step. It comes from the literature. Not detailed in this work, it is an intermediary step in obtaining the MM2 mind map, the central awareness tool of this work which has been evaluated, 2) the panels of people interviewed during the second and fifth steps are different (with some exceptions discussed later).

4.2   The Mind Map: A Decision Tree for Scenarios

We developed a tool for raising awareness of cognitive biases for AI professionals, in the form of a mind map (Fig. 2, step C). It is a diagram whose objective is to reflect the functioning of thought and to visually represent the associative path of thought. It is as much a tool for visualization and representation of information as for learning new concepts [9]. Mind maps are also an effective study technique that allows for better learning performance and retention of information over time, more than if the information was present in the form of written documents [12,30].

We have thus created a mind map that takes up the design steps of a project involving statistical AI[1]. We describe here the $MMCB_{AI}$ mind map. We have

---

[1] Statistical AI is a subfield of AI that exploits probabilistic graphical models to provide a framework for both (i) efficient reasoning and learning and (ii) modeling of complex domains such as in machine learning, network communication, computational biology, computer vision and robotics [13].
Symbolic AI refers to AI research methods based on high-level symbolic representations of problems, logic, and search, that are accessible and readable by humans [14].
Hybrid AI combines approaches from symbolic AI and statistical AI. .

identified 9 design steps according to a study of the literature [1] and the feedback from interviews conducted in the second step (Fig. 2, step B) of the design chain:

1. Analyze the problem, i.e., understand the business issues and the applications of the problem to define the objectives and the data to use
2. Collect and process the data
3. Choose the learning algorithm
4. Develop the model
5. Train and test the model
6. Visualize and analyze the results
7. Deploy/Launch the program if necessary
8. Maintain the system
9. Scale up

Our $MMCB_{AI}$ mind map is therefore presented in the form of a decision tree with 83 nodes in total. It offers 3 scenarios: a contextualization, a tutorial and the awareness part, the heart of the tool. More precisely, the mind map is composed of 12 nodes for contextualization (accessible by clicking on the "How to use it?" button) which indicates the cognitive biases we focused on, as well as our main scientific references. The tutorial has 5 nodes. As for the awareness part, it has 63 nodes. To access it, the user must click on the "Let's go" button. Figure 3 shows an overview of the folded mind map, in French and in English, with the 3 scenarios accessible to the user.

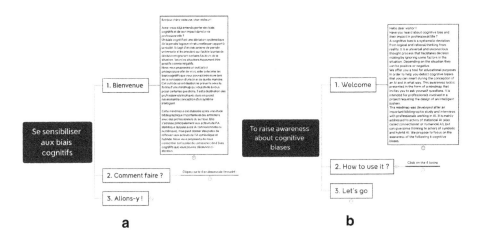

Fig. 3. Overview of the folded mind map: (a) in French, (b) in English

The awareness part focuses only on the first 6 design steps, raising questions for each of them to make users aware of the cognitive biases that can influence them. For more clarity and a better identification of the users to the problem of cognitive biases in their work, an example of a situation where cognitive biases have negatively impacted the work of an AI actor is provided as an illustration for each step. This also allows to highlight the consequences that cognitive biases can have. Figure 4 presents, in French and in English, an overview of the issues raised during the choice of the machine learning algorithm stage, during the implementation of the design stage and the associated example.

a   **b**

Fig. 4. Node level mind map extract: (a) "Choisir l'algorithme d'apprentissage" in French, (b) "Choose the learning algorithm"

Note that our $MMCB_{AI}$ mind map has two versions: the French version is the one used in our study. Our work was carried out in French, with a panel of French-speaking professionals, and the result is the version cited above. However, for the sake of sharing with the international community, we present an English translation for illustration purposes and to promote the reproducibility of this study. Here are the links to the:

- french version of $MMCB_{AI}$: https://www.xmind.net/m/m5nJVM
- english version of $MMCB_{AI}$: https://www.xmind.net/m/c8H8wb

Please note that both versions of the mind map are licensed under a CC BY-NC-SA license.

5   Evaluations

In order to evaluate the impact of cognitive biases on the AI projects development, we conducted two experimental sessions: the first one before the presentation of the awareness tool in the form of face-to-face semi-directive interviews (Fig. 2, step B), and the second one after the presentation of the tool in remote mode through a screen sharing with question and answer sessions (Fig. 2, step E). We present in the following each experiment: the methodology followed, the profile of the respondents as well as the results obtained.

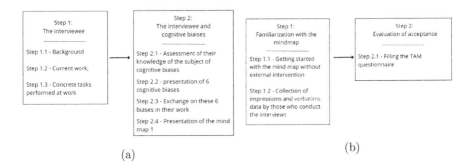

(a)   (b)

Fig. 5. Procedures follow during experiments: (a) Experiment 1: Semi-structured interviews; (b) Experiment 2: MM2 mind map user tests

5.1   Experiment 1: Semi-structured Interviews

Methodology. The purpose of the first experiment was to gather information through interviews about the reality of their practices, their knowledge of cognitive biases, and their opinions about an awareness tool. We conducted semi-structured interviews with 24 questions, 18 of them are open, thus allowing for flexibility of response. This type of interview has the advantage of focusing the discussion on specific points while leaving room for rich content of information and explanatory digressions [23]. The interviews consist of 2 phases (7 steps in total) illustrated in Fig. 5a. The first phase consists of collecting information about the interviewee (Fig. 5a, step 1): his or her background, current job, and the course of the previous day. This last point allows us to know what the interviewee does as concrete tasks and allows us to know at which moments the biases can appear, without the answer being biased by the interviewee's judgment. The second phase deals with cognitive biases. First, we assessed their knowledge on the subject (Fig. 5a, step 2.1). Then we discussed the six cognitive biases we are studying (Fig. 5a, step 2.2), and we discussed how they manifest them in their work (Fig. 5a, step 2.3): when, how, and how they try to counteract them. The last phase of the interviews is the presentation of the MM1 mind map (Fig. 5a, step 2.4), a tool for raising awareness of cognitive biases in AI developed from the literature. This phase has multiple objectives: to gather users' opinions on the tool's format, content, and acceptability.

Profile of Respondents. We interviewed 14 professionals working on projects involving statistical AI. Among them, we count 4 data scientists, 5 engineers, and 5 project managers. Table 1 details the profile of the 14 professionals, according to their gender, age, experience in AI development, job title, and area of expertise. Our panel consists of 2 women and 12 men, all working in statistical AI except one who works in hybrid AI[2]. They have on average more than 6 years of experience in the field of AI with 5 people having more than 5 years of experience and 4 people having less than 2 years of experience.

---

[2] Please refer to the footnote 1.

Table 1. Descriptive characteristics of the participants in Experiment 1

Id subject	Gender Male/Female	Age	Experience level	Job title	Field of expertise
1	F	30-40 years	10 years	Data scientist	Statistical AI
2	M	30-40 years	4 years	Data scientist	Statistical AI
3	F	18-30 years	2 years	Data scientist	Statistical AI
4	M	40-65 years	4 years	Data scientist	Statistical AI
5	M	30-40 years	3 years	AI Engineer	Statistical AI
6	M	18-30 years	1.5 years	AI Engineer	Statistical AI
7	M	18-30 years	1 year	AI Engineer	Statistical AI
8	M	18-30 years	1.5 years	AI Engineer	Statistical AI
9	M	40-65 years	1 year	AI Engineer	Statistical AI
10	M	30-40 years	8 years	AI project manager	Statistical AI
11	M	40-65 years	10 years	AI project manager	Statistical AI
12	M	40-65 years	6 years	AI project manager	Statistical AI
13	M	40-65 years	2 years	AI project manager	Statistical AI
14	M	40-65 years	34 years	AI project manager	Hybrid AI

Results. Thanks to the interviews, we were able to understand at which moments of the design of an intelligent system cognitive biases are most likely to appear. More precisely, they intervene at the level of the different choices to be made (selection of data and construction of the data set, choice of the model to be set up, choice of evaluation metrics, choice of hypotheses, choice of inputs and outputs in Machine Learning), and during the exchanges and the design phase of the algorithms. Moreover, the interviewees mentioned that there may also be existing biases in the pre-designed data sets. Through the second step of our directional interviews (Fig. 5a, step 2.3) we identified different methods to counter the effects of the cognitive biases shared by the interviewees themselves (remember that step 2.2 in Fig. 5a consists in presenting them the 6 cognitive biases targeted by our study): exchange with various people, both internal and external to the project, diversify the teams, follow a clear and precise methodology with feedback to learn from each other's mistakes.

A major result of this first step is that we were able to note that several people declared themselves not subject to certain biases. More precisely, out of 14 people, 4 do not think they are subject to conformity bias, 4 do not think they are subject to confirmation bias, 2 do not think they are subject to illusory correlation bias, 3 do not think they are subject to measurement bias, 1 does not think they are subject to presentation bias, 8 (57%) do not think they are subject to normality bias. Among them, 2 of which because they have little experience: they argued that they had not programmed several models up to that point, and therefore they were not used to favoring one model over another. Finally, only 6 (43%) of the 14 people interviewed thought they were subject to all the cognitive biases studied. However, thinking that one is not subject to cognitive biases is the result of a cognitive bias: the illusory superiority bias [18].

Finally, we collected various opinions on the MM1 mind map. For 64% (9 people) of the respondents, the form of a mind map seems to be judicious, 14% (2 people) are afraid that this form is too simplistic or linear in relation to their job, and the remaining 21% (3 people) have no clear opinion. From the point of view of the content, the interviewees told us that it should contain an explanation of cognitive biases, illustrative examples where cognitive biases interfered negatively, and the resulting discriminating consequences. On the other hand, they shared with us the ways in which they think they use the mind map: for example, integrating it into on-boarding processes to raise awareness among newcomers, using it to facilitate awareness workshops but also to check the awareness of a future employee, or displaying it in the office.

5.2   Experiment 2: User Testing

Methodology. User tests were carried out in order to evaluate the acceptance of the MM2 mind map, the quality and formulation of the questions, and finally the sensitivity of the participants to cognitive biases. We set up a test protocol taking place remotely thanks to screen sharing. We posed the following hypotheses:

H4: people who are sensitive to cognitive biases will validate and accept the tool, **vs H5:** people who are not sensitive will refuse the tool.

To collect the participants' opinions we used a questionnaire with the Likert scale (LS). This is a psychometric tool (i.e., scale) commonly used in research that employs questionnaires to measure an attitude in individuals [26]. Thus, in the first phase (Fig. 5b, step 1.1), the participants had to take in hand the MM2 mind map , and then they had to answer orally the questions of the mind map that concerned them using a LS going from 1 to 5 with 1 meaning "Totally disagree" and 5 "Totally agree" (Fig. 5b, step 1.2). This allowed assessing the participants' sensitivity to cognitive biases. In a second phase (Fig. 5b, step 2.1), participants were asked to complete a questionnaire to assess the perceived usefulness and perceived ease of use of the tool using the Technology Acceptance Model (TAM) questionnaire [49]. This TAM questionnaire is used to attempt to predict whether an individual will use or refuse to use any computer application, corporate or consumer, based on two factors: the perceived ease of use of that application and its perceived usefulness. For this questionnaire, participants were asked to rate their response on a LS ranging from 1 to 7 with 1 meaning "Strongly disagree" and 7 meaning "Strongly agree".

Profile of Respondents. Our awareness tool aims to be transmitted to a large number of AI professionals of all levels and professions in order to make them aware of cognitive biases and enable them to avoid them in their work. It must therefore respond to global issues and not be customized for a single panel of people. This is why we decided to take a different panel of testers than the one used for the interviews. Our panel for this second study is composed of 8 participants, whose profiles are detailed in Table 2: 2 women and 6 men. They have an average of 3 years of experience in the field of AI with 2 people who have more than 3 years of experience and 3 who have two or less. Of these, 3 people

Table 2. Descriptive characteristics of the participants in Experiment 2

Id subject	Gender Male/Female	Experience level	Participate to experiment 1	Trained in cognitive biases
1	M	3 years	yes	no
2	M	3 years	no	yes
3	F	1 year	no	no
4	M	6 years	no	yes
5	F	2 years	yes	no
6	M	3 years	no	no
7	M	1 year	no	yes
8	M	6 years	yes	no

Table 3. TAM questionnaire results: comparison of answers from participants (Likert scale of 1 to 7) who participated in both experiments and in experiment 2 only. "Answ." stands for answers.

	Answers of 3 participants that attended both experiments	Mean	Nb answ. <= 3	Nb answ. >=5	Answers of 5 participants that attend experiment 2	Mean	Nb answ. <= 3	Nb answ. >=5
Would this tool allow you to complete your work tasks more quickly?	5 2 2	3	2	1	2 6 2 6 6	4.4	2	3
Would using this tool allow you to improve your performance at work?	6 3 6	5	1	2	5 6 1 6 3	4.2	2	3
Would using this tool allow you to improve your productivity?	5 1 2	2.7	2	1	2 6 1 6 6	4.2	2	3
Would using this tool allow you to improve your efficiency?	6 3 4	4.3	1	1	4 6 1 6 6	4.6	1	3
Would using this tool make it easier to do your job?	6 3 1	3.3	2	1	1 6 4 7 6	4.8	1	4
Will you find this tool useful in your work?	6 4 6	5.3	0	2	6 4 5 7 6	5.6	0	4
How easy is it to learn how to use this tool?	5 6 6	5.6	0	3	6 7 6 7 7	6.6	0	5
Is your interaction with this tool clear and understandable?	5 7 7	6.3	0	3	7 5 7 5 6	6	0	5
Is the tool itself clear and understandable?	7 7 6	6.6	0	3	6 7 6 6 5	6	0	5

participated in the interviews (Fig. 2, step B) and 3 were trained in cognitive biases during their studies[3]. Note that no participant both conducted the interviews and studied cognitive biases. In total, we estimate that 6 participants

---

[3] They studied at the *Ecole Nationale Supérieure de Cognitique*, known also as ENSC which is an engineering school in Bordeaux, France that aims to provide an education that places humans at the heart of its designs by blending the fields of cognitive science, human-computer interaction, and AI.

are more aware of cognitive biases because of their training or this study. All participants answer the questions of the MM2 mind map and test the entire tool.

Results. The TAM questionnaire assesses the perceived usefulness of the tool and the perceived ease of use. We had 8 answers in total presented in Table 3.

Table 4. TAM questionnaire results: comparison of answers from participants (Likert scale of 1 to 7) sensitive and not sensitive to cognitive biases. "Answ." stands for answers.

	Answers of 3 participants trained in cognitive biases	Mean	Nb answ. <= 3	Nb answ. >=5	Answers of 5 participants NOT trained in cognitive biases	Mean	Nb answ. <= 3	Nb answ. >=5
Would this tool allow you to complete your work tasks more quickly?	6 2 6	4.6	1	2	5 2 2 2 6	3.4	3	2
Would using this tool allow you to improve your performance at work?	6 1 6	4.3	1	2	6 3 6 5 3	4.6	2	3
Would using this tool allow you to improve your productivity?	6 1 6	4.3	1	2	5 1 2 2 6	3.2	3	2
Would using this tool allow you to improve your efficiency?	6 1 6	4.3	1	2	6 3 4 4 6	4.6	1	2
Would using this tool make it easier to do your job?	6 4 7	5.6	0	2	6 3 1 1 6	3.4	3	2
Will you find this tool useful in your work?	4 5 7	5.3	0	2	6 4 6 6 6	5.6	0	4
How easy is it to learn how to use this tool?	6 7 7	6.6	0	3	5 6 6 6 7	6	0	5
Is your interaction with this tool clear and understandable?	5 7 6	6	0	3	5 7 7 7 5	6.2	0	5
Is the tool itself clear and understandable?	5 6 5	5.3	0	3	7 7 6 6 6	6.4	0	5

• **Concerning the usefulness of the MM2 mind map in their work**: For 62.5% of the participants (5 people) the MM2 mind map would be very useful in their work (6 or 7 on the LS). For the other 3 people, the MM2 mind map would perhaps be useful (4 or 5 on the LS). Above all, it would improve the performance and efficiency of AI professionals with an average of 4.5 out of 7.

• **Concerning the contribution of the mind map to facilitate work**: For two people, the MM2 mind map would not facilitate their work at all (1 out of 7 on the LS) because it requires constant back and forth between the work done and the mind map. 50% of the participants think that the MM2 mind map will slow down their work and will not improve their productivity even if it can be very useful.

• **Regarding perceived ease of use and ease of learning to use**: Regarding perceived ease of use, 87.5% of the participants (7 people) found the tool clear and understandable (6 or 7 on the LS). Of these 87.5%, 42% even thought it was extremely clear and understandable (7 on the LS). The statistics are the same for the ease of learning to use. However, for only 62.5% of the participants (5 people), the interaction with the tool is clear and understandable.

Regarding the acceptance of our tool according to the sensitivity to cognitive biases, we noted the following:

(i) Table 3 showed that having participated in the interviews (Experiment 1) does not influence either the perceived relevance/usefulness of the tool or the ease of picking up and using the tool. Similarly, not having participated in the interviews had no influence.

(ii) Table 4 showed that being trained in cognitive biases does not influence either the perceived relevance/usefulness of the tool or the perceived ease of use of the tool. Similarly, the fact of not having received such training has no influence.

In the current context, we were unable to confirm or refute our hypotheses H4 and H5. However, since the sample on which we rely is small, we can question this similarity in results.

Finally, thanks to the different verbatims of the participants, we were able to draw some remarks from these interviews concerning the MM2 mind map. First, the use of a mind map was not innate in all testers. Indeed, during the course of the mind map by the users, we noticed some misunderstandings on certain questions following reflections such as "I am not sure I understand" or "What does it mean?". Some of these misunderstandings could have been solved by reading the optional information accessible through a button on the side of the question. However, not all users knew that it was possible to click and get more content. Second, there were some misunderstandings related to the wording of the questions, which were sometimes too vague or too repetitive according to the interviewees because some questions were asked in two sections at the same time. This is the case, for example, of the question "Does the model work for all subgroups differentiated by socio-demographic characteristics?" which is present both in Sect. 5, "Training and Testing the model" and in Sect. 6, "Visualizing and Analyzing the results". We chose to keep this repetition because it ensures that the mind map user reads it, even if they skip a step. These are questions that are important to ask at different times to ensure that no bias is inadvertently introduced during the development of the tool.

The feedback from users allowed us to develop the mind map from its MM2 version to its final version $MMCB_{AI}$ presented in Sect. 4.2. Compared to MM2, this last version contains: (i) a tutorial visible from the opening of the tool so that users can learn how to use this tool; (ii) a description of the project, as well as the main sources used to inform the user and give him confidence; (iii) clarified questions that were misunderstood by the majority of the participants by rephrasing them for greater clarity.

6   Discussion

In this paper, we address the issue of assessing the impact of cognitive biases in the development of AI projects. We focus our study on AI professionals who intervene in the life cycle of an AI project, whether they are developers, data scientists or managers, with strong technical knowledge or not. The main contribution of our work is to propose a tool to raise awareness of cognitive biases for this type of population in the form of a mind map that we have named $MMCB_{AI}$. This mind map was obtained after two experiments (Fig. 2) which allowed us to 1) study the sensitivity of the panel of participants to the notion of cognitive bias, 2) collect their opinion on a tool in the form of a mind map and the criteria associated with the acceptance of this tool, and finally, 3) to design a final tool accepted and adapted to the needs of the AI professionals interviewed.

In more detail, Experiment 1(Fig. 2, step B) collected the testimony of interviewees on the potential impact of their cognitive biases on their job and thus the AI projects they have already conducted. In terms of results, 85% of the participants (12 people) identified at least one moment when cognitive biases impacted one of their projects or that of a colleague, which confirmed hypothesis H1. However, although the term bias was known by all participants, we also found that 43% (6 participants) considered themselves not subject to cognitive bias. On the other hand, 57% of them (8 interviewees) mentioned that one of the challenges of their work in carrying out their projects was to detect and correct the biases present in the data. While these results did not confirm or deny the H2 hypothesis, it is important to note that our participants were more likely to think that biases came either from the data or from other collaborators. The first point can be explained by the fact that AI professionals and especially technical profiles are probably more aware of technical and data-related biases in view of the development of techniques, works, and software libraries with the vocation of making ethical algorithms or unbiased data sets [3, 10, 15, 27, 38, 40]. Therefore, it is easier for them to think about these biases than cognitive ones. Regarding the second point, let us also point out that, in more detail, 8 of the 14 (57%) interviewees think that they are not subject to at least one of the six cognitive biases presented. This reaction, itself the result of the illusory superiority cognitive bias, and more globally the results of this first experiment, have reinforced the need to make AI professionals aware of the topic of cognitive biases in their work.

Concerning hypothesis H3, it is not possible to deny or confirm it within the framework of our study, because we did not have enough time to measure the impact of the awareness of cognitive biases on the quality of the work of AI professionals from an ethical point of view (let us emphasize that the project was carried out in 4 months), however, the results of experiment 2 show that an approach like ours would be appreciated and useful for these professionals. Experiment 2 showed that although there are areas of improvement in the ergonomics of the tool to facilitate interaction with it, none of the 8 participants interviewed expressed an unfavorable opinion on the usefulness of the MM2 mind map (62.5%, i.e. 5 people, even declared that it would be very useful). According to them, our tool would improve the quality of their decisions, confidence in their realization, and satisfaction with the work done, which would directly impact their performance and efficiency. They even point out that the mind map could potentially be a cost-saving tool for companies since by integrating work on identifying and understanding cognitive biases and their impact during the life cycle of a project, it would allow them to anticipate and avoid more complex modifications afterward, and therefore additional costs for maintenance or correction of AI projects.

Finally, it should be noted that the principle of integrating a tool to raise awareness of cognitive biases was well received by the professionals who appropriated it by planning how to integrate it into their current work processes: the panels of participants in both experiments think that it would be interesting to use the mind map for awareness purposes, for example when new employees start work, and to develop reflexes in their work to question their decision-making.

Concerning the field of application of our tool, since 13 people interviewed came from the field of statistical AI, 1 person from the field of hybrid AI and none from the field of symbolic AI, we believe that this tool was designed more specifically for people working in the field of statistical AI, even if it can participate in raising awareness of actors in hybrid AI. This reflection was confirmed during a user test carried out by a person working in symbolic AI, who did not recognize himself in the questions raised by the design stages of a project involving AI.

In conclusion, more than an evaluation, our tool seeks to reinforce sensitivity by making AI professionals aware of the biases they may introduce in their work. It is important to make AI professionals aware of all types of bias, whether data-based, algorithmic, or cognitive. Indeed, a biased algorithm, regardless of the origin of these biases, has impacts on its users. The latter will potentially be led to make biased decisions and thus generate even more biased data for the training of future AI. This then creates a user-algorithm-data feedback loop that amplifies the biases [27].

7   Conclusion

The proposed methodology and the mind map, as a tool to raise awareness of cognitive biases, contribute to the field of human-AI systems interaction through a human factor and cognitive science-based approach. We consider this work as an alliance of cognitive science and AI project management.

We showed that although the AI field suffers from the issue of bias, few professionals think about the cognitive biases they carry as impacting their work and that therefore the issue of cognitive bias awareness is a current issue in the professional world working in AI. Our methodology including professionals before and after the presentation of an awareness tool allowed us to better understand the participants, their job, and their vision of this field. By giving them a voice on this subject and the possibility to act on the tool (unlike a classic training course such as a MOOC or a school course), we encouraged the creation of a context favorable to their empowerment and the questioning of their knowledge, work habits, and prior behaviors. The interactive aspect of the mind map, by encouraging the exploration of the tool, also allowed for a better appropriation of it and a projection of the participants with it. The human-tool relationship is strengthened.

As future work areas, we think it would be interesting to increase the panel (people trained in bias and untrained, for example) to re-evaluate hypotheses H1 and H2. Another line of work is to extend our study to people in symbolic AI. We believe that a new study and a tool dedicated to the sensitization of this community should therefore be carried out. Finally, we would like to explore the impact of a more interactive tool in the form of a website or an application which we believe will be more accessible to the international community.

To conclude, we invite future research in human-IA interaction and, more globally, the AI scientific community, AI companies and educational establishments teaching AI to open up to the fields of cognitive sciences and human factors. Proposing or carrying out training at the crossroads of these multiple domains can allow for better sensitivity to cognitive biases and above all a better consideration of the human being in all its diversity. We invite the international community to test and use our $MMCB_{AI}$ mind map available online: https://www.xmind.net/m/c8H8wb. Understanding the impact of a human's cognitive sphere on its environment would allow the design of better AI tools, more adapted, and more sensitive to the different existing cognitive profiles.

Author contributions. Sara Juan and Chloé Bernault contributed equally to this work: conception and realization of the experiments, bibliographical research, and writing of the article. Alexandra Delmas, Marc Rodiez, and Jean-Marc Andre contributed to the experiments' design and the project's supervision. Ikram Chraibi Kaadoud contributed to the bibliographic research, the design of the experiments, the writing of the article, and the supervision of the project. All authors contributed to the revision of the manuscript, read and approved the submitted version.

References

1. Barenkamp, M., Rebstadt, J., Thomas, O.: Applications of AI in classical software engineering. AI Perspectives **2**(1), 1 (2020)
2. Baron, J., Ritov, I.: Omission bias, individual differences, and normality. Organ. Behav. Hum. Decis. Process. **94**(2), 74–85 (2004)
3. Bellamy, R.K., et al.: Ai fairness 360: an extensible toolkit for detecting, understanding, and mitigating unwanted algorithmic Bias. arXiv preprint arXiv:1810.01943 (2018)
4. BIAS, F.O.C.: The evolution of cognitive bias. The Handbook of Evolutionary Psychology, Volume 2: Integrations **2**, 968 (2015)
5. Bonabeau, E.: Don't trust your gut. Harv. Bus. Rev. **81**(5), 116–23 (2003)
6. Caliskan, A., Bryson, J.J., Narayanan, A.: Semantics derived automatically from language corpora contain human-like biases. Science **356**(6334), 183–186 (2017)
7. Cazes, M., Franiatte, N., Delmas, A., André, J., Rodier, M., Kaadoud, I.C.: Evaluation of the sensitivity of cognitive biases in the design of artificial intelligence. In: Rencontres des Jeunes Chercheurs en Intelligence Artificielle (RJCIA2021) Plate-Forme Intelligence Artificielle (PFIA2021) (2021)
8. Chapman, L.J., Chapman, J.P.: Genesis of popular but erroneous psychodiagnostic observations. J. Abnorm. Psychol. **72**(3), 193 (1967)
9. Cunningham, G.E.: Mindmapping: its effects on student achievement in high school biology. The University of Texas at Austin (2006)

10. Danks, D., London, A.J.: Algorithmic bias in autonomous systems. In: IJCAI, vol. 17, pp. 4691–4697 (2017)
11. Dressel, J., Farid, H.: The accuracy, fairness, and limits of predicting recidivism. Sci. Adv. **4**(1), eaao5580 (2018)
12. Farrand, P., Hussain, F., Hennessy, E.: The efficacy of themind map'study technique. Med. Educ. **36**(5), 426–431 (2002)
13. Frontiers in Robotics and AI: Statistical relational artificial intelligence (2018). https://www.frontiersin.org/research-topics/5640/statistical-relational-artificial-intelligence. Accessed 23 Feb 2023
14. Garnelo, M., Shanahan, M.: Reconciling deep learning with symbolic artificial intelligence: representing objects and relations. Curr. Opin. Behav. Sci. **29**, 17–23 (2019)
15. Gebru, T., et al.: Datasheets for datasets. Commun. ACM **64**(12), 86–92 (2021)
16. Gordon, D.F., Desjardins, M.: Evaluation and selection of biases in machine learning. Mach. Learn. **20**, 5–22 (1995)
17. Hamilton, D.L., Rose, T.L.: Illusory correlation and the maintenance of stereotypic beliefs. J. Pers. Soc. Psychol. **39**(5), 832 (1980)
18. Hoorens, V.: Self-enhancement and superiority biases in social comparison. Eur. Rev. Soc. Psychol. **4**(1), 113–139 (1993)
19. Howard, A., Borenstein, J.: The ugly truth about ourselves and our robot creations: the problem of bias and social inequity. Sci. Eng. Ethics **24**, 1521–1536 (2018)
20. Intahchomphoo, C., Gundersen, O.E.: Artificial intelligence and race: a systematic review. Leg. Inf. Manag. **20**(2), 74–84 (2020)
21. Johansen, J., Pedersen, T., Johansen, C.: Studying the transfer of biases from programmers to programs. arXiv preprint arXiv:2005.08231 (2020)
22. Kahneman, D., Lovallo, D., Sibony, O.: Before you make that big decision. Harvard Business Review (2011)
23. Lallemand, C., Gronier, G.: Méthodes de design UX: 30 méthodes fondamentales pour concevoir et évaluer les systèmes interactifs. Editions Eyrolles (2015)
24. Leavy, S.: Gender bias in artificial intelligence: the need for diversity and gender theory in machine learning. In: Proceedings of the 1st International Workshop on Gender Equality in Software Engineering, pp. 14–16 (2018)
25. Lepri, B., Oliver, N., Letouzé, E., Pentland, A., Vinck, P.: Fair, transparent, and accountable algorithmic decision-making processes: the premise, the proposed solutions, and the open challenges. Philosophy Technol. **31**, 611–627 (2018)
26. Likert, R.: A technique for the measurement of attitudes. Archives of Psychology (1932)
27. Mehrabi, N., Morstatter, F., Saxena, N., Lerman, K., Galstyan, A.: A survey on bias and fairness in machine learning. ACM Comput. Surv. (CSUR) **54**(6), 1–35 (2021)
28. Mohanani, R., Salman, I., Turhan, B., Rodríguez, P., Ralph, P.: Cognitive biases in software engineering: a systematic mapping study. IEEE Trans. Software Eng. **46**(12), 1318–1339 (2018)
29. Nelson, G.S.: Bias in artificial intelligence. N. C. Med. J. **80**(4), 220–222 (2019)
30. Nesbit, J.C., Adesope, O.O.: Learning with concept and knowledge maps: a meta-analysis. Rev. Educ. Res. **76**(3), 413–448 (2006)
31. Neves, J.M.T.D.: The impact of artificial intelligence in banking, Ph. D. thesis, Universidade Nova de Lisboa (2022)
32. Nickerson, R.S.: Confirmation bias: a ubiquitous phenomenon in many guises. Rev. Gen. Psychol. **2**(2), 175–220 (1998)

33. Nissenbaum, H.: How computer systems embody values. Computer **34**(3), 120–119 (2001)
34. Norori, N., Hu, Q., Aellen, F.M., Faraci, F.D., Tzovara, A.: Addressing bias in big data and AI for health care: a call for open science. Patterns **2**(10), 100347 (2021)
35. Ntoutsi, E., et al.: Bias in data-driven artificial intelligence systems-an introductory survey. Wiley Interdiscip. Rev. Data Mining Knowl. Discov. **10**(3), e1356 (2020)
36. Padalia, D.: Conformity bias: a fact or an experimental artifact? Psychol. Stud. **59**, 223–230 (2014)
37. Panch, T., Szolovits, P., Atun, R.: Artificial intelligence, machine learning and health systems. J. Global Health **8**(2), 020303 (2018)
38. Quadrianto, N., Sharmanska, V.: Recycling privileged learning and distribution matching for fairness. In: Advances in Neural Information Processing Systems 30 (2017)
39. Raji, I.D., Buolamwini, J.: Actionable auditing: Investigating the impact of publicly naming biased performance results of commercial AI products. In: Proceedings of the 2019 AAAI/ACM Conference on AI, Ethics, and Society, pp. 429–435 (2019)
40. Raji, I.D., et al.: Closing the AI accountability gap: defining an end-to-end framework for internal algorithmic auditing. In: Proceedings of the 2020 Conference on Fairness, Accountability, and Transparency, pp. 33–44 (2020)
41. Re, R.M., Solow-Niederman, A.: Developing artificially intelligent justice. Stan. Tech. L. Rev. **22**, 242 (2019)
42. Sharmanska, V., Quadrianto, N.: Learning from the mistakes of others: matching errors in cross-dataset learning. In: Proceedings of the IEEE Conference on Computer Vision and Pattern Recognition, pp. 3967–3975 (2016)
43. Silvestro, D., Goria, S., Sterner, T., Antonelli, A.: Improving biodiversity protection through artificial intelligence. Nat. Sustainability **5**(5), 415–424 (2022)
44. Soleimani, M., Intezari, A., Taskin, N., Pauleen, D.: Cognitive biases in developing biased artificial intelligence recruitment system. In: Proceedings of the 54th Hawaii International Conference on System Sciences, pp. 5091–5099 (2021)
45. Suresh, H., Guttag, J.: A framework for understanding sources of harm throughout the machine learning life cycle. In: Equity and Access in Algorithms. Mechanisms, and Optimization, pp. 1–9. Association for Computing Machinery, New York, NY, USA (2021)
46. Vapnik, V., Vashist, A.: A new learning paradigm: learning using privileged information. Neural Netw. **22**(5–6), 544–557 (2009)
47. Wason, P.C.: On the failure to eliminate hypotheses in a conceptual task. Quart. J. Exper. Psychol. **12**(3), 129–140 (1960)
48. West, S.M., Whittaker, M., Crawford, K.: Discriminating systems. AI Now (2019)
49. Yves Martin, N.P.: Acceptabilité, acceptation et expérience utilisateur: évaluation et modélisation des facteurs d'adoption des produits technologiques, Ph. D. thesis, Université Rennes 2 (2018)

How is the AI Perceived When It Behaves (Un)Fairly?

Yang Chu[1] ⓘ, Jiahao Li[1] ⓘ, and Jie Xu[1,2(✉)] ⓘ

[1] Center for Psychological Sciences, Zhejiang University, Hangzhou, China
xujie0987@zju.edu.cn
[2] Center for Research and Innovation in Systems Safety, Vanderbilt University Medical Center, Nashville, TN, USA

Abstract. Fairness plays a crucial role in human-human interaction, so it is expected to play a significant role in human-AI interaction as well. Integrating the principles of fairness into AI design and investigating people's perceptions of it can help improve user experience and ensure AI systems are responsible, trustworthy, ethical, and human-centered. In the current study, we simulated different human behaviors in economic games through a human fairness model and reinforcement learning approach and then conducted an experiment to investigate how people perceive AI agents with varying levels of fairness. The study was a within-subject experiment with 2 treatments (fair vs. unfair AI), in which the participants play the Alternated Repeated Ultimatum Game (ARUG) for 12 rounds with each AI agent. The results suggest that the participants evaluated fair AI as having higher levels of warmth, intelligence, animacy, likability, and safety compared to unfair AI. These findings indicate that AI that aligns with social norms is more favored by people. We discuss the theoretical implications for comprehending people's behavior and attitude towards AI fairness and the practical implications for designing AI that has the potential to increase fairness in society.

Keywords: Human-centered AI · Fairness · Alternated Repeated Ultimatum Game · Perception of AI fairness

1 Background and Significance

Since resources are rarely distributed equally, concern for fairness, justice, and equality is a fundamental feature of human society [1]. According to psychological research, fairness is one of the fundamental social norms, motives, and morals [2, 3]. Thus, fairness is not just a desirable outcome, but also a critical factor in promoting cooperation, reciprocity, and social stability.

As machines powered by AI increasingly permeate our society [4], fairness has become one of the fundamental principles of AI ethics [5, 6]. For example, fairness plays an important role in responsible and trustworthy systems [7]. Consequently, AI needs to be trained to behave with fairness. Meanwhile, humans tend to apply social rules and expectations to artificial agents [8], such as politeness [9] and reciprocity behaviors

H. Degen and S. Ntoa (Eds.): HCII 2023, LNAI 14050, pp. 421–430, 2023.
https://doi.org/10.1007/978-3-031-35891-3_25

[10, 11]. There is a need to investigate how humans perceive the fairness of AI, thereby informing the design of human-centered AI.

The current study investigated social perception of AI's fairness in a behavior modeling exercise and evaluation experiment. We situated our work in the context of economic games, where human participants interact with AI agents for different fairness levels. Participants in the study viewed "fair" AI as having more positive attributes, such as being warmer, more animate, more intelligent, and more likable, and being perceived as safer, compared to "unfair" AI. These findings demonstrated that incorporating ethics and social norms into AI design can help AI systems align with human expectations and better serve humans.

1.1 Ultimatum Game and Fairness

Economic games are rigorous models for multiple social interactions [12]. These games model situations in which the future outcomes of individuals are affected by the decisions and those of other individuals [13], derived from social conflict and interpersonal relations. As Game Theory leads to quantitative models, economic games are also ideal experimental paradigms. Researchers simplified social interactions by taking economic games, such as trust game, ultimatum game (UG), and dictator game [14, 15].

We situated our work in UG, where a range of prior work has studied how individuals perceive and act regarding fairness [16–19]. In the classic UG, two players with fixed roles (a proposer and a responder) must negotiate the partition of a pot of money. The proposer suggests a split offer, which the responder can accept or reject. If accepted, the players could get the amount of money that the proposer proposed; otherwise, neither side gets anything [20]. Under these circumstances, it would be rational and in the best interest of self-regarding proposers to offer the minimum amount to the responder, and similarly, self-regarding responders should accept any offer that is not zero. However, in UG experiments, the range of common offers that were proposed by the proposer and accepted by the responder was 10% to 70% [21]. Approximately half of the responders declined offers that were deemed unfair, in which they would receive less than 30% of the total sum [22].

Sense of fairness and other considerations, such as culture and emotions, lead responders to reject low offers [23]. Fairness concerns are regarded as the primary reason for the pattern of behavior. The conventional definition of fairness in behavioral economics states that individuals are considered fair if they behave following the norm fair [23, 24]. In the context of UG, fairness means that individuals offer a more equitable distribution of resources, such as a 50–50 split, and reject inequitable offers. These patterns have been attributed to a preference for reciprocal fairness and inequity aversion [3].

Rather than being rational and strictly self-interested, people are often influenced by social and emotional aspects of their interactions, which result in choices based on other-regarding preferences. Previous studies largely investigated how the behaviors related to fairness influenced social perceptions. For instance, Ruessmann and Unkelbach [15] found that fair people were seen as warmer and more intelligent than unfair ones. Stellar and Willer [14] proposed that breaches of fairness norms are deemed as the notion of immoral acts or moral transgressions. Thus, unfair behavior is interpreted as an indicator of lower intelligence and communion.

The computers are social actors (CASA) theory argues that humans treat computers socially and naturally as if interacting with real people [8, 25]. Research in human-computer interaction and human-robot interaction has demonstrated that people apply human social norms to artificial agents, such as reciprocating cooperative behavior when interacting with computer agents [10]. This suggests people would exhibit similar fairness concerns with AI agents as they do with human beings. Thus, designers of AI systems should take fairness into account, as AI systems are typically designed to be rational and maximize profits. It's also crucial to investigate how individuals perceive the fairness of AI, as this can significantly impact human-AI interaction and the user experience. However, previous studies have only focused on analyzing and modeling AI fairness [26, 27]. This study, on the other hand, focuses on the reactions and feelings of individuals to the fairness of AI agents.

2 Method

In the study, we first developed an AI algorithm that could simulate human actions associated with varying degrees of fairness in the UG. In the empirical experiment, we assessed the participants' perceptions of fair and unfair AI agents after they interacted with them. The experiment was a within-subject design, where the participants interacted with both the fair and unfair AI agents with counterbalancing.

2.1 Experimental Paradigm

The experiment was a variation of the classic UG, called the Alternated Repeated Ultimatum Game (ARUG) [11]. In the ARUG, players engage in multiple rounds and alternate the proposer and responder roles in each round. In our study, the participant and the AI agent negotiated the partition of 100 tokens (as depicted in Fig. 1) for 12 rounds. The participants were informed that the objective for both themselves and the AI agent was

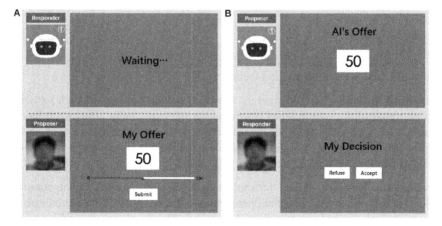

Fig. 1. User interface of the experimental platform. A depicts the participant playing as a proposer. B depicts the participant playing as a responder.

to earn the maximum amount of money possible. The participants engaged in two blocks of the experiment, each with one AI (fair or unfair) in a successive manner.

2.2 Fair and Unfair AI

Early studies of UG with artificial agents mostly used approaches to create the illusion of AI, such as the "Wizard of Oz" method and pre-programmed static scripts [19, 28, 29]. However, we implemented the algorithm to simulate human behavior in UG, enabling the real human-AI interaction and effective factors controlled.

The algorithm's design was inspired by the inequity aversion in human fairness research, which suggests that humans resist inequitable outcomes and may even be willing to give up rewards for a more equitable outcome [3]. To model inequity aversion, an extension of the traditional game-theoretic actor called the Homo Egualis [3] was introduced. Homo Egualis agents are driven by the following utility function:

$$\mu_i = x_i - \frac{\alpha_i}{n-1} \sum_{x_j > x_i} (x_j - x_i) - \frac{\beta_i}{n-1} \sum_{x_i > x_j} (x_i - x_j) \tag{1}$$

The utility of agent $i \in \{1, 2, \cdots, n\}$, denoted as μ_i, is calculated on the agent i's own payoff, x_i, and the two terms derived from the comparison to payoff, x_j, of other agents j. The utility of agent i is influenced negatively by both agents who possess a higher payoff and those who possess a lower payoff. Thus, the maximum utility u_i, is achieved when all other agents possess an equal payoff, or when $\forall j, x_j = x_i$.

The fairness of AI could be manipulated by adjusting relevant parameters according to Homo Egualis [26, 30]. At the same time, we obtained the initial value of the algorithm based on the existence of large empirical studies about human behaviors in UG. Therefore, we have implemented two AI algorithms, representing behavioral performances in fairness at high and low levels, respectively referred to as fair AI and unfair AI. We utilized reinforcement learning (RL) to develop our AI to maximize the notion of cumulative reward in the game [26].

2.3 Measurement

The behavioral game allows researchers to observe objective behavior as well as self-reports of individuals' thoughts and feelings.

Behavioral Measure. We recorded the decision-making behavior of each participant in each round of the two treatments throughout the experiment. The two behavioral measures we employ are: (1) when the participant plays as proposer, the amount of offer proposed by the participant to the AI, and (2) when the participant plays as responder, the times that the participant rejected the AI's offer.

Psychometric Measure. After interacting with one AI agent, the participants completed self-report instruments to assess their perceptions of the agent. We measured the perception and evaluation of AI agents in three dimensions. The first dimension is the perceived fairness of AI agents (hereafter referred to as "fairness"), which served as a manipulation check for our AI algorithm design. The second dimension is the perceived warmth of AI agents (hereafter referred to as "warmth"), which is one of the fundamental dimensions in navigating the social world [31]. The third dimeson is the perceived anthropomorphism, animacy, likeability, intelligence, and safety of the AI agent (hereafter referred to as "anthropomorphism", "animacy", "likeability", "intelligence", and "safety"), which are widely-used standardized measurement tools for human-robot interaction [32].

Fairness was measured with three items on a five-point Likert scale, "The AI that interacted with me is a fair AI", "I was treated fairly by the AI", "The AI acted fairly during our interaction", from "strongly disagree" = 1 to "strongly agree" = 5.

Warmth was adapted from prior research [33]. The participants rated their perception of AI's warmth using 100-point analog sliders, consistent with previous research [15, 33]. The measure contains six bipolar items: "untrustworthy/trustworthy", "dishonest/honest", "threatening/benevolent", "repellent/likable", "cold/warm", and "egoistic/altruistic".

Anthropomorphism, animacy, likeability, intelligence, and safety were adopted from Godspeed questionnaires [32]. The series of questionnaires, consisting of 24 items in total, used 5-point semantic differential scales. Each semantic differential scale was headed with the instruction, "Please rate your impression of the AI".

2.4 Participants

We recruited participants from Zhejiang University through a campus-wide job posting network. A total of 20 participants participated in this study. One of the participants was removed from the final dataset due to equipment malfunction. In total, 19 participants' responses were included in the final dataset for our analysis. The participants ranged in age from 20 to 25 years old (M = 23.16; SD = 1.34), 47.37% were female, and 52.63% were male. Each participant was paid 30 RMB (approximately 5 USD) as compensation. Each participant also had the opportunity to earn an additional 0–50 RMB bonus based on their performance in the game. The protocol of the study was approved by the institution's Institutional Review Board.

2.5 Procedure

The participants were recruited for a 20-min experiment. They were informed that they would be engaging in a two-player game with AI on the computer in the laboratory. Consent was given prior to the experiment; all participants who showed up agreed to participate. The participants were provided with instructions on how to perform the task in the game, followed by two practice trials. The experiment was divided into two blocks, each of which involved playing a 12-round ARUG with one AI, with participants assigned to either fair or unfair treatment. After each block, participants were asked to complete questionnaires evaluating the AI in that block. Finally, participants were asked to provide their basic demographic information.

3 Results

To check the fairness manipulations, three t-tests were performed on behavioral measurements and fairness using the R software. The first analysis, as illustrated in Fig. 2(A), indicated significant differences between fair and unfair conditions with regard to the

AI's rejection times ($t(18) = 3.90, p < .001$) and participants' rejection times ($t(18) = 8.94, p < .001$). The second analysis revealed a significant difference between fair and unfair conditions in terms of AI's offer ($t(18) = 30.11, p < .001$) and participants' offers ($t(18) = 3.81, p < .001$), as illustrated in Fig. 2(B). Furthermore, there was a significant difference in the subjective rating of perceived fairness, with the fair condition rated higher than the unfair condition, $t(18) = 11.54, p < .001$.

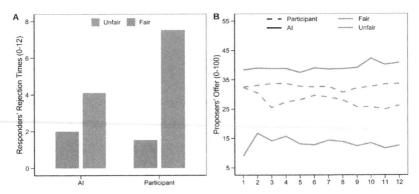

Fig. 2. The AI and human behavior data are displayed under each condition ($n = 19$). A depicts the mean rejection times of the responders in 12 rounds. B illustrates the mean offers of the proposers in 12 rounds.

To assess the impact of AI fairness on participants' perceptions, t-tests were conducted on the warmth, anthropomorphism, animacy, likeability, intelligence, and safety scales (see details in Table 1, Fig. 3). The results showed a significant difference for the warmth dimension, with participants rating the fair AI agent higher than the unfair AI agent, $t(18) = 10.35, p < .001$. The evaluations for the 4 dimensions from the Godspeed questionnaires showed significant differences between fair and unfair conditions, with the fair AI agent perceived as more animate ($t(18) = 2.10, p < .05.$), more intelligent ($t(18) = 2.27, p < .05$), more likeable ($t(18) = 10.15, p < .001$), and safer ($t(18) = 4.19, p < .001$) compared to the unfair AI agent. However, there was no significant difference between the fair and unfair conditions for the anthropomorphism, $t(18) = 1.49, p = .15$.

Table 1. The results of the paired t-tests of participants' ratings of the fair and unfair AI agents.

Rating	t	df	p
Fairness	11.54	18	< 0.001
Warmth	10.35	18	< 0.001

(continued)

Table 1. (*continued*)

Rating	t	df	p
Animacy	2.10	18	0.050
Anthropomorphism	1.49	18	0.154
Intelligence	2.27	18	0.036
Likeability	10.15	18	< 0.001
Safety	4.19	18	< 0.001

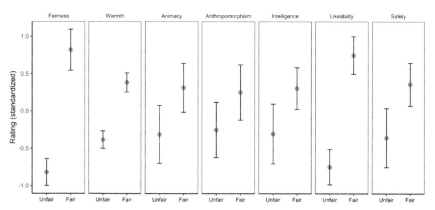

Fig. 3. Mean and 95% confidence intervals of the participants' ratings of the AI agent on fairness, warmth, anthropomorphism, animacy, likeability, intelligence, and safety under each condition.

4   Discussion

The results of the behavior measures indicated that the offer and acceptance rate of the fair AI were significantly higher than those of the unfair AI, consistent with the prediction of the human fairness model, suggesting that the model can be used to develop AI that demonstrates different levels of fairness in ARUG. Furthermore, when interacting with AI with two different levels of fairness, the offer and acceptance rates of the participants in the fair condition were also significantly higher than those in the unfair condition. This implied that the AI behavior elicited reciprocal behavior from participants, i.e., when AI behavior was fair, the participants' behavior also tended to be fairer, which is consistent with the reciprocal phenomenon found in past human-human interaction and human-AI interaction [11, 34]. In addition, from the subjective evaluation results, participants' fairness perception score for the fair AI was also higher than that for the unfair AI, further demonstrating the effectiveness of manipulating the fairness level of AI behavior.

The level of fairness in AI behavior in the ARUG impacted the participants' social perception of AI. Psychometric analysis indicated that the participants evaluated fair AI as having higher levels of warmth, intelligence, animacy, likability, and safety compared to unfair AI. The findings regarding the dimensions of warmth and intelligence are consistent with previous research conducted in the context of human-human interaction, as they demonstrate that people rate unfair dictators as cold, and less intelligent [15]. This also suggests that individuals unconsciously apply social norms and expectations to AI and form impressions of it. Additionally, the low ratings of the participants for the dimensions of likability and safety of the unfair AI, compared to fair AI, may be related to the unfair behavior violating the norm of reciprocity. Previous studies have found that participants preferred the pure reciprocal robot strategy with tit for tat and gained more benefits from the strategy [28]. The unfair behavior of the AI violated the prevailing social norms, making it hard for the perceivers to predict the actions of the AI, leading to a sense of threat to their own interests. Besides, some evidence has shown that breaches of fairness norms can affect people's evaluation of an actor's competence [14], and evaluations of AI in terms of its intelligence and animacy dimensions are typically related to its capabilities. Interestingly, anthropomorphism was not affected by the fairness of AI behaviour. We speculate that this dimension may be more related to the external features of AI, such as appearance, voice, and movements. In this experiment, since artificial intelligence does not have a physical entity and its external features are also not different under different manipulation conditions, it does not affect participants' perceptions of AI anthropomorphism.

5 Conclusions

As AI agents become increasingly prevalent in our daily lives, it's important to incorporate fairness into the AI framework. This is because AI that conforms to social norms, such as fairness, is more aligned with human expectations and performs better in situations involving social welfare or fairness. We integrated human-inspired fairness, such as inequity aversion, into algorithms and experimentally evaluated individuals' perceptions of AI with varying degrees of fairness. Our findings showed that fair AI was perceived more positively than unfair AI, which is consistent with the role of human fairness in shaping perception. These results imply that it's crucial for AI to have social emotions and norms, such as fairness. AI that follows social norms leads to a better interactive experience, and these findings should be considered for the future design of human-centered AI. However, more research is needed to explore the effects of AI fairness in more complex and real-world situations and to investigate the underlying mechanisms to guide AI design.

Acknowledgment. This work was supported by the National Natural Science Foundation of China (Grant No. T2192931).

References

1. Lamm, H., Schwinger, T.: Norms concerning distributive justice: are needs taken into consideration in allocation decisions? Soc. Psychol. Q. 425–429 (1980)
2. Hallsson, B.G., Siebner, H.R., Hulme, O.J.: Fairness, fast and slow: a review of dual process models of fairness. Neurosci. Biobehav. Rev. **89**, 49–60 (2018)

3. Fehr, E., Schmidt, K.M.: A theory of fairness, competition, and cooperation. Quart. J. Econ. **114**, 817–868 (1999)
4. Rahwan, I., et al.: Machine behaviour. Nature **568**, 477–486 (2019)
5. Jobin, A., Ienca, M., Vayena, E.: The global landscape of AI ethics guidelines. Nat. Mach. Intell. **1**, 389–399 (2019)
6. Riedl, M.O.: Human-centered artificial intelligence and machine learning. Hum. Behav. Emerging Technol. **1**, 33–36 (2019)
7. Shneiderman, B.: Responsible AI: Bridging from Ethics to Practice, vol. 64, pp. 32–35. Association for Computing Machinery, Inc (2021)
8. Nass, C., Moon, Y.: Machines and mindlessness: social responses to computers. J. Soc. Issues **56**, 81–103 (2000)
9. Nass, C., Moon, Y., Carney, P.: Are people polite to computers? Responses to computer-based interviewing systems[1]. J. Appl. Soc. Psychol. **29**, 1093–1109 (1999)
10. Li, J.H., Dong, S., Chiou, E.K., Xu, J.: Reciprocity and its neurological correlates in human-agent cooperation. IEEE Trans. Hum.-Mach. Syst. **50**, 384–394 (2020)
11. Sandoval, E.B., Brandstetter, J., Obaid, M., Bartneck, C.: Reciprocity in human-robot interaction: a quantitative approach through the prisoner's dilemma and the ultimatum game. Int. J. Soc. Robot. **8**, 303–317 (2016)
12. Camerer, C.F., Fehr, E.: Measuring social norms and preferences using experimental games: a guide for social scientists. Found. Hum. Soc.: Econ. Exper. Ethnographic Evid. Fifteen Small-scale Soc. **97**, 55–95 (2004)
13. van Dijk, E., De Dreu, C.K.W.: Experimental games and social decision making. Ann. Rev. Psychol. **72**, 415–438 (2021)
14. Stellar, J.E., Willer, R.: Unethical and inept? The influence of moral information on perceptions of competence. J. Pers. Soc. Psychol. **114**, 195–210 (2018)
15. Ruessmann, J.K., Unkelbach, C.: Rational dictators in the dictator game are seen as cold and agentic but not intelligent. Pers. Soc. Psychol. Bull. **48**, 1298–1312 (2022)
16. Boksem, M.A., De Cremer, D.: Fairness concerns predict medial frontal negativity amplitude in ultimatum bargaining. Soc. Neurosci. **5**, 118–128 (2010)
17. Harjunen, V.J., Spape, M., Ahmed, I., Jacucci, G., Ravaja, N.: Persuaded by the machine: the effect of virtual nonverbal cues and individual differences on compliance in economic bargaining. Comput. Hum. Behav. **87**, 384–394 (2018)
18. Nishio, S., Ogawa, K., Kanakogi, Y., Itakura, S., Ishiguro, H.: Do robot appearance and speech affect people's attitude? Evaluation through the ultimatum game. In: Ishiguro, H., Libera, F.D. (eds.) Geminoid Studies, pp. 263–277. Springer, Singapore (2018). https://doi.org/10.1007/978-981-10-8702-8_16
19. Heijnen, S., de Kleijn, R., Hommel, B.: The Impact of human-robot synchronization on anthropomorphization. Front. Psychol. **9**, 2607 (2018)
20. Güth, W., Schmittberger, R., Schwarze, B.: An experimental analysis of ultimatum bargaining. J. Econ. Behav. Organ. **3**, 367–388 (1982)
21. Eckhardt, A., Vojtáš, P.: Learning user preferences for 2CP-Regression for a recommender system. In: van Leeuwen, J., Muscholl, A., Peleg, D., Pokorný, J., Rumpe, B. (eds.) SOFSEM 2010. LNCS, vol. 5901, pp. 346–357. Springer, Heidelberg (2010). https://doi.org/10.1007/978-3-642-11266-9_29
22. Yamagishi, T., et al.: Rejection of unfair offers in the ultimatum game is no evidence of strong reciprocity. Proc. Natl. Acad. Sci. USA **109**, 20364–20368 (2012)
23. Murnighan, J.K., Wang, L.: The social world as an experimental game. Organ. Behav. Hum. Decis. Process. **136**, 80–94 (2016)
24. de Melo, C.M., Marsella, S., Gratch, J.: Social decisions and fairness change when people's interests are represented by autonomous agents. Auton. Agent. Multi-Agent Syst. **32**(1), 163–187 (2017). https://doi.org/10.1007/s10458-017-9376-6

25. Reeves, B.: The media equation: how people treat computers, television, and new media like real people (1996)
26. De Jong, S., Tuyls, K., Verbeeck, K.: Artificial agents learning human fairness. In: Autonomous Agents and Multiagent Systems (2008)
27. Zhong, F., Wu, D.J., Kimbrough, S.O.: Cooperative agent systems: artificial agents play the ultimatum game. Group Decis. Negot. **11**, 433–447 (2002)
28. Sandoval, E.B., Brandstatter, J., Yalcin, U., Bartneck, C.: Robot likeability and reciprocity in human robot interaction: using ultimatum game to determinate reciprocal likeable robot strategies. Int. J. Soc. Robot. **13**(4), 851–862 (2020). https://doi.org/10.1007/s12369-020-006 58-5
29. Schniter, E., Shields, T.W., Sznycer, D.: Trust in humans and robots: Economically similar but emotionally different. J. Econ. Psychol. **78,** (2020)
30. Lee, J., Hwang, S.-W., Nie, Z., Wen, J.-R.: IEEE: product entitycube: a recommendation and navigation system for product search. In: 26th IEEE International Conference on Data Engineering (ICDE), pp. 1113–1116 (2010)
31. Abele, A.E., Ellemers, N., Fiske, S.T., Koch, A., Yzerbyt, V.: Navigating the social world: toward an integrated framework for evaluating self, individuals, and groups. Psychol. Rev. **128**, 290–314 (2020)
32. Bartneck, C., Kulić, D., Croft, E., Zoghbi, S.: Measurement Instruments for the anthropomorphism, animacy, likeability, perceived intelligence, and perceived safety of robots. Int. J. Soc. Robot. **1**, 71–81 (2008)
33. Koch, A., Imhoff, R., Dotsch, R., Unkelbach, C., Alves, H.: The ABC of stereotypes about groups: agency/socioeconomic success, conservative-progressive beliefs, and communion. J. Pers. Soc. Psychol. **110**, 675–709 (2016)
34. Sanfey, A.G., Rilling, J.K., Aronson, J.A., Nystrom, L.E., Cohen, J.D.: The neural basis of economic decision-making in the ultimatum game. Science **300**, 1755–1758 (2003)

Distance Correlation GAN: Fair Tabular Data Generation with Generative Adversarial Networks

Amirarsalan Rajabi[1] and Ozlem Ozmen Garibay[1,2(✉)]

[1] Department of Computer Science, University of Central Florida, Orlando, FL 32816, USA
`amirarsalan@knights.ucf.edu, ozlem@ucf.edu`
[2] Department of Industrial Engineering and Management Systems, Orlando, FL 32816, USA

Abstract. With the growing impact of artificial intelligence, the topic of fairness in AI has received increasing attention for valid reasons. In this paper, we propose a generative adversarial network for fair tabular data generation. The model is a WGAN, where the generator is enforcing fairness by penalizing distance correlation between protected attribute and target attribute. We compare our results with another state-of-the-art generative adversarial network for fair tabular data generation and a preprocessing repairment method on four datasets, and show that our model is able to produce synthetic data, such that training a classifier on it results in a fair classifier, beating the other two methods. This makes the model suitable for applications that concern with fairness and preserving privacy.

Keywords: Fairness in AI · Human-centered AI · Generative Adversarial Networks

1 Introduction

Artificial intelligence algorithms have a significant impact on many aspects of people's lives as a result of their increased use in a wide range of software applications, particularly when they are incorporated into decision-support tools used by governmental organizations, and different industry sectors, and many institutions. In order to ensure justice and eliminate unfair biases, it is imperative to ensure that these algorithms are carefully examined. Discrimination is the term used to describe unjustified disparities made in judgments of people based on their affiliation with a certain group.

Numerous research efforts have demonstrated that the performance of machine learning algorithms is biased against some protected groups [7–9,39]. Many AI systems, like the Correlational Offender Management Profiling for Alternative Sanctions (COMPAS), have been demonstrated to be biased. The US criminal justice system uses COMPAS, an automated decision-making system, to determine a criminal defendant's chance of re-offending. This system has been proved to be prejudiced against African Americans by looking into the risk scores that are given to individuals [14]. Other examples of bias in AI decision making systems include one targeted advertising program in which highly paid positions were more frequently recommended for men than women [28].

Models trained on different modalities of data might contain bias. Bias in tabular datasets and models trained on tabular data are well-studied in the literrature [2,21,23]. Other modalities of data also contain bias. Many studies address biased image datasets [25,40,41,48], bias in models trained on and dealing with text like language models [10,12,42], and bias in recommender systems [1,13,27]. It is observed that bias present in datasets might get further amplified by the models trained on those datasets [51].

The emergence of unfairness in AI systems is mostly attributed to: 1) direct bias existing in the historical datasets being used to train the algorithms, 2) bias caused by missing data, 3) bias caused by proxy attributes, where bias against the minority population is present in non-protected attributes, and 4) bias resulting from algorithm objective functions, where the aggregate accuracy of the whole population is sought and therefore the algorithm might disregard the minority group for the sake of majority [37].

In addition to the unfairness issue, in the big data era, through sharing data with partners and releasing data to the public, data privacy is a persistent and growing concern. Some anonymization techniques have been proposed in the data privacy body of research, including removing identifiers such as social security numbers, modifying quasi-identifiers such as ZIP code, age, and gender, and data perturbation [29,30,35,46]. There are some issues attributed to the conventional privacy preserving techniques. One major drawback of these methods is that through introducing noise to the original data (data perturbation), many statistical characteristics of the original data is exposed to alteration, hence losing the ability of machine learning methods to be trained on the altered data. Another major disadvantage is the ability of adversaries to recover the identification of records through possessing background knowledge [35]. Generative Adversarial Networks have shown very promising results, and are well-suited to address both issues: fairness [43] and data privacy [35].

2   Related Work

Bias mitigation methods can be divided into three general categories of *pre-process*, *in-process*, and *post-process*. Pre-process methods include modifying the training dataset before feeding it to the machine learning model. For example, Kamiran and Calders [23] propose methods such as suppression which includes removing attributes highly correlated with the protected attribute, reweighing, i.e. assigning weights to different instances in the data, and massaging the data to change labels of some objects. In-process methods include adding regularizing terms to penalize some representation of bias during the training process. For example, [24] proposes adding a regularization term to the objective function which penalizes mutual information between the protected attributes and the classifier predictions. Finally, post-process methods include modifying the final decisions of the classifiers. For example, the work in [21] proposes a method to alter the final classification scores in order to promote equalized odds. Bias mitigation methods often come at the expense of losing some accuracy, and these preliminary methods usually entail higher fairness-utility cost.

Recently, more sophisticated methods are proposed to address fairness in a classifier. The work in [31] provides an attention-based framework to identify features' contribution to performance and fairness in a model, and then propose a post-processing method to mitigate bias. Some other studies such as [34] consider mutual information [26] to ensure independence between protected attributes and target attribute. The work in [20] shows how limiting mutual information between protected attributes and representations controls demographic parity, and proposes a method for controlling parity.

Generative adversarial networks are an emerging technique to generate synthetic datasets. GANs are found to thrive in a variety of tasks when compared to other generative models, and overcome several shortcomings in classic generative models [11]. The original GAN proposed in [18] includes two networks, *generator* and *discriminator*, where the two networks play a minimax game. The generator receives a latent vector as input, and over time learns to produce data which is from the real data distribution. The work in [4] proposed Wasserstein generative adversarial network, in which the discriminator network is replaced by *critic* network, and the model is evaluated by estimating and minimizing Wasserstein distance [38] between real and generated data, as opposed to Jenssen-Shannon divergence [22] in the original GAN.

An approach recently considered for addressing fairness is using generative models to produce *fair* data, and then use the generated data to train fair classifiers [39], or to augment a biased training dataset with unbiased data [40]. Sattigeri et al. [44] propose a novel generative adversarial network to generate fair image datasets, where the generator produces fair data conditioned on demographic parity and equality of opportunity. The work in [50] proposes a GAN to produce fair tabular datasets. Their proposed network includes a generator, and two discriminators, where one discriminator assures data quality, and the other ensure the data is discrimination free. The work in [39] proposes a Wasserstein GAN where the network includes a generator and a critic, and the generator attempts to enforce demographic parity in the generated data.

3   Methodology

3.1   Problem Statement

Consider a dataset $D = (\mathcal{X}, \mathcal{S}, \mathcal{Y})$, where $\mathcal{X} \in \mathbb{R}^n$ is the set of unprotected attributes, $\mathcal{Y} = \{+1, -1\}$ is the target attribute, and $\mathcal{S}$ is the protected attribute. Protected attribute is the attribute against which discrimination must not exist from a legal stand point [37]. As an example, consider a dataset (Adult dataset [15]) containing information about individuals, where protected attribute S is the Sex of an individual, the target attribute $\mathcal{Y}$ is whether or not their income exceeds 50K, and unprotected attributes $\mathcal{X}$ include other information about an individual including their employment status, their marital status, country of origin, etc. A fair classifier would be one which predicts an individual's income (target attribute, $\mathcal{Y}$), regardless of the individual's sex (protected attribute, S).

Our objective is to produce a synthetic dataset D which satisfies the following conditions [50]: 1) **data utility**: the synthetic generated dataset comes from the same distribution as the real data and the relationship among data attributes is preserved to some extent; 2) **data fairness**: there is no discrimination in the generated data for the target attribute, conditioned on the protected attribute; 3) **classification utility**: once the synthetic data is used to train a classifier, the trained classifier should achieve high accuracy; and 4) **classification fairness**: The trained classifier on the synthetic data must be *fair* (the main objective among all four objectives).

3.2   Demographic Parity

There are several metrics proposed in the literature to quantify fairness in a dataset or classifier. The work in [47] provides a comprehensive survey on different fairness metrics used in the fairness in AI research. Among fairness metrics, demographic parity [32] is the most widely used metric. Demographic fairness ensures that overall proportion of members with respect to protected attribute receive a positive decision identically. Demographic fairness is defined as follows:

$$P(Y = 1|S = 1) = P(Y = 1|S = -1) \tag{1}$$

Demographic unfairness, or demographic parity, is then defined as follows:

$$P(Y = 1|S = 1) - P(Y = 1|S = -1) \tag{2}$$

Considering the dataset described in Sect. 3.1, assume a biased classifier is trained $f : (\mathcal{X}, S) \to \hat{Y}$, such that the classifier's prediction for target attribute is not independent from the protected attribute, i.e. $\hat{Y} \not\perp S$. A similar demographic parity score could be outlined for the classifier, where demographic parity is defined as $P(\hat{Y} = 1|S = 1) - P(\hat{Y} = 1|S = -1)$. In this work, we try to train a generative adversarial network which generates a dataset $D = (\mathcal{X}, S, \mathcal{Y})$, where $\mathcal{Y} \perp S$. We expect that a classifier $f : (\mathcal{X}, S) \to \hat{Y}$ trained on D, results in classifications s.t. ideally $\hat{Y} \perp S$.

3.3   Independence

Although some earlier fairness studies considered decorrelating target attribute from the protected attribute, independence between the protected attribute and the target attribute must eventually be sought. The Pearson correlation coefficient [6], which is the traditional and most widely used correlation coefficient, has its disadvantage: it is straightforward to construct non-independent random variables A and B, s.t. $cor(A, B) = 0$ (e.g. any two random variables A and B where A is symmetrically distributed around zero and $B = |A|$ [16]). In their work Szekely et al. introduced the distance correlation coefficient [45], where the measure could quantify the non-linear relationship between two random variables, and does not suffer from the problem mentioned for the Pearson correlation coefficient.

Let A and B be real valued random variables with finite second moments. Let (A, B), (A', B'), and (A'', B'') denote independent and identically distributed copies, then the population value of squared distance covariance is defined as:

$$
\begin{aligned}
\mathrm{dCov}^2(A, B) :=& \mathbb{E}[\|A - A'\| \|B - B'\|] + \mathbb{E}[\|A - A'\|] \\
& \mathbb{E}[\|B - B'\|] - 2\mathbb{E}[\|A - A'\| \|B - B''\|]
\end{aligned}
\tag{3}
$$

It can be shown that random variables A and B are independent, if and only if $\mathrm{dCov}^2(A, B) = 0$ [45]. The distance variance is a special case of distance covariance when the two random variables are identical, and the square root of populating value of distance variance is calculated as:

$$
\begin{aligned}
\mathrm{dVar}^2(A) :=& \mathbb{E}[\|A - A'\|^2] + \mathbb{E}^2[\|A - A'\|] \\
& - 2\mathbb{E}[\|A - A'\| \|A - A''\|]
\end{aligned}
\tag{4}
$$

Finally, distance correlation between A and B is calculate by:

$$
\mathrm{dCor}(A, B) = \frac{\mathrm{dCor}(A, B)}{\sqrt{\mathrm{dVar}(A)\,\mathrm{dVar}(B)}}
\tag{5}
$$

In our model, we use distance correlation between the target attribute $\mathcal{Y}$ and protected attribute $\mathcal{S}$ of synthetically generated samples, to enforce independence.

4   Network

4.1   TabFairGAN

The work in [39] proposes a generative adversarial network, *TabFairGAN*, to produce fair synthetic fair datasets. The training process includes two phases of training, where in the first phase the network is being trained for accuracy, and in the second phase of training by adding an extra term which calculates demographic parity, the network is fine-tuned to achieve a balance of fairness and accuracy. Depending on whether or not second phase of training is activated, the network is able to generate data which is only accounted for accuracy, or a mixture of both accuracy and fairness.

While *TabFairGAN* is shown to outperform other models in most of cases, there are three major drawbacks in designing the model: 1) including two phases of training, adds an extra hyperparameter to the model training process, in which an optimal combination of epoch numbers is needed to achieve fair and accurate data, 2) the fairness enforcement term added to the value function of generator in the second phase of training is enforcing demographic parity. In this regard, it seems inappropriate to evaluate the model's output using demographic parity, and 3) the model is shown to be able to produce synthetic data where the generated data satisfies demographic parity, but their results show that when a classifier is trained on the synthetic data, the results of the classifier is not as impressive and fair as the generated data.

In this paper, we adopt the architecture of the network as described in [39]. We propose a new training algorithm for the network, so that the model's noted flaws are addressed.

4.2   Data Transformation

A tabular dataset contains N numerical data attributes and M categorical data attributes. Before feeding to the network, one-hot encoding transformation is performed on categorical attributes. Numerical attributes on the other hand are transformed using quantile transformation [5]:

$$c_i = \Phi^{-1}(F(c_i)) \tag{6}$$

where c_i represents the ith numerical attribute, F is the CDF of a feature c_i, and Φ is the CDF of a uniform distribution.

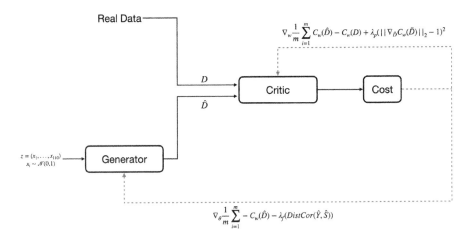

Fig. 1. The network architecture of the proposed generative adversarial network.

4.3   Network Architecture

Figure 1 is a schematic of the network structure. The network architecture is similar to TabFairGAN. the generator includes a fully-connected layer with ReLu activation function in the first layer. The second layer is formed by concatenation of multiple vectors that produce data similar to the transformed original data. A fully connected layer with a ReLu activation function is used for numerical attributes, while for each categorical attributes a fully connected layer with Gumbel softmax activation is used. In the critic, 2 fully connected layers with Leaky ReLu activation function is used. The generator's network architecture is formally defined as [39]:

$$\begin{cases} h_0 = z \\ h_1 = \text{ReLu}(\text{FC}_{r\ r}(h_0)) \\ h_2 = \text{ReLu}(\text{FC}_{r\ N}(h_1)) \oplus \text{gumbel}_{0.2}(\text{FC}_{r\ l_1}(h_1)) \oplus \\ \text{gumbel}_{0.2}(\text{FC}_{r\ l_2}(h_1)) \oplus ... \oplus \text{gumbel}_{0.2}(\text{FC}_{r\ l_M}(h_1)) \end{cases} \tag{7}$$

And the critic's network architecture is formally defined as [39]:

$$\begin{cases} h_0 = x \\ h_1 = \text{LeakyReLu}_{0.01}(\text{FC}_{r\ r}(h_0)) \\ h_2 = \text{LeakyReLu}_{0.01}(\text{FC}_{r\ r}(h_1)) \end{cases} \tag{8}$$

where r shows dimensionality of transformed data, N is the number of numerical attributes, l_i is the dimension of the ith categorical column, and $\oplus$ denotes concatenation of vectors.

4.4   Training

In this section we introduce the loss functions for network components. As Fig. 1 exhibits, the developed WGAN includes a generator and critic networks. The value function for the critic net work is [19]:

$$V_C = \mathop{\mathbb{E}}_{\hat{\mathbf{X}}\ P_g} [C(\hat{\mathbf{X}})] - \mathop{\mathbb{E}}_{\mathbf{X}\ P_r} [C(\mathbf{X})] + \lambda \mathop{\mathbb{E}}_{\bar{\mathbf{X}}\ P_{\bar{\mathbf{X}}}} [(\|\nabla_{\bar{\mathbf{X}}} C(\bar{\mathbf{X}})\|_2 - 1)^2] \tag{9}$$

where P_r and P_g are real data distribution and generated data distribution, respectively. The gradient penalty to enforce the Lipschitz constraint appears in the third term, and λ is the gradient penalty coefficient. $P_{\bar{\mathbf{x}}}$ is implicitly defined sampling uniformly along straight lines between pairs of points sampled from the data distribution P_r and the generator distribution P_g [19].

The value function for the generator is as follows:

$$V_G = - \mathop{\mathbb{E}}_{\hat{\mathbf{x}},\hat{\mathbf{y}},\hat{\mathbf{s}}\ P_g} [C(\hat{\mathbf{x}}, \hat{\mathbf{y}}, \hat{\mathbf{s}})] - \lambda_f(\text{DistCor}(\hat{\text{S}}, \hat{\text{Y}})) \tag{10}$$

where λ_f controls the accuracy-fairness trade-off. To calculate sample distance correlation, the work in [45] suggest the following:

$$dCov^2(S,Y) = \frac{1}{m^2} \sum_{j\,1}^{m} \sum_{k\,1}^{m} A_{j,k} B_{j,k}$$

$$dVar(S) = dCov^2(S,S) = \frac{1}{m^2} \sum_{k,l} A_{k,l}^2 \qquad (11)$$

$$DistCor(S,Y) = \frac{dCov^2(S,Y)}{\sqrt{dVar(S)\,dVar(Y)}}$$

where A and B are doubly centered distance matrices from samples S and Y respectively. The formal procedure of training the model is shown in Algorithm 1.

Algorithm 1. training algorithm for the proposed WGAN. We use $n_{crit} = 4$, batch size of 128, $\lambda_p = 10$

1: **for** Epoch **do**
2:     **for** t $1,\dots,n_{crit}$ **do**
3:         Sample batch m D x,y,s P_r and z P z and ϵ U $0,1$
4:         $\hat{D}$ $\hat{X},\hat{S},\hat{Y}$ G_θ z
5:         $\bar{D}$ ϵD 1 ϵ $\hat{D}$
6:         Update the critic by descending:
7:         $\nabla_w \frac{1}{m} \sum_{i\,1}^{m} C_w$ $\hat{D}$ C_w D λ_p $\nabla_{\bar{D}} C_w$ $\bar{D}$ $_2$ 1 ^{2}
8:     **end for**
9:     sample a batch m $\hat{D}$ $\hat{X},\hat{S},\hat{Y}$ P G_θ z
10:     $A_{j,k}$ doubly centered distance matrix of $\hat{S}$
11:     $B_{j,k}$ doubly centered distance matrix of $\hat{Y}$
12:     DistCor $\dfrac{\frac{1}{m^2} \sum_{j\,1}^{m} \sum_{k\,1}^{m} A_{j,k} B_{j,k}}{\sqrt{\frac{1}{m^2} \sum_{k,l} A_{k,l}^2 \frac{1}{m^2} \sum_{k,l} B_{k,l}^2}}$
13:     Update the generator by descending:
14:     $\nabla_\theta \frac{1}{m} \sum_{i\,1}^{m}$ C_w $\hat{D}$ λ_f DistCor
15: **end for**

---

5   Experiments

5.1   Certifying and Removing Disparate Impact

In addition to TabFairGAN, we compare our results with the model proposed in Feldman et al.'s work [17]. They propose a method to remove bias from training data, and preserve information for data utility. In dataset $D = \{X,S,Y\}$, For each unprotected attribute X, they take marginal distribution of X conditioned on S ($X_s = Pr(X|S = s)$). Let $F_s : X_s \to [0,1]$ show the cumulative distribution function for values $x \in X_s$, and $F_s^{-1}(u)$ be the quantile function. They modify

X in a way that its quantile function, is equal to Median of quantile function of marginalized distributions:

$$F_A{}^1 : F_A{}^1(u) = \text{median}_s\ {}_SF_s{}^1(u) \tag{12}$$

They also incorporate lambda coefficient to control the trade-off between accuracy and fairness of the model: $\bar{F}_s{}^1 = (1 - \lambda)F_s{}^1 + \lambda(F_A){}^1$. Performing this transformation, they are able to produce a new data $D = \{\bar{X}, S, Y\}$, where training a classifier on D will improve the fairness, while preserving model accuracy. Similar to [39], we call this method CRDI.

5.2 Datasets

In this section, we describe the datasets that are used in this work to compare the results of our model to that of TabFairGAN and CRDI. To provide straightforward and fair comparison, the datasets utilized here are similar to the work in [39].

UCI Adult dataset [15] is the first dataset. This dataset, which is based on data from the 1994 US Census, has 48,842 rows containing information about each person such as their employment, and degree of education, age, sex, etc. The target variable (Y) indicates if that person has an annual income of more than \$50,000. In our experiments, we define sex as the protected attribute (S).

The Bank Marketing dataset [33] is the second dataset utilized in the studies. This dataset includes data on a Portuguese banking institution's direct marketing campaign. Each row in the dataset comprises information about a specific person, including their age, profession, marital status, housing situation, etc. The target variable is whether an individual has signed up for a term deposit or not. There are 45,211 records in the collection. Similar to [39] age is regarded as the protected attribute (S) because young people are more likely to be tagged as "yes" when applying for a term deposit. A cut-off age of 25 is thought to binarize the protected attribute.

The ProPublica dataset [3] from the COMPAS risk assessment system is the third dataset used in this section. This dataset provides data on offenders from Broward County. It includes attributes about defendants such their ethnicity, marital status, and sex, as well as a score for each person indicating how likely they are to re-offend as the target attribute. We precisely adhered to preprocessing procedure described in [39] for this dataset. The binary protected attribute in the processed data is therefore ethnicity (S) and the binary target attribute is the chance of re-offending (Y).

The last dataset used in this study is the Law School dataset [49]. This dataset includes details on 21,790 law students, including their GPA, race, LSAT score, and the target attribute is a binary variable showing their first year average (Y). Following [39], we considered individuals with black and white race.

5.3 Training

In this section, we explain the experiments conducted and present the results. The purpose is to train the proposed network on each dataset, and then produce synthetic data such that the synthetic dataset is both accurate (good data utility) and fair. After training the model on training set of dataset D, a synthetic dataset D' is generated. The synthetic data D' is then used to train a Decision Tree Classifier.

To evaluate data utility (accuracy) of D', we first train a Decision Tree Classifier on D'. Then we test the trained classifier on testing set of D. We repeat this process 5 times, and record the accuracy each time. The utilized Decision Tree Classifier uses the default parameter setting in Scikit-learn [36] (gini impurity and no max depth set).

To evaluate fairness of the generated data, we use demographic parity (described in Sect. 3.2). To evaluate fairness of a generated synthetic data $D' = \{X', S', Y'\}$, we calculate $P(Y' = 1|S' = 1) - P(Y'|S' = -1)$. To evaluate fairness of the classifier trained on the synthetic data, we calculate $P(\hat{Y} = 1|S = 1) - P(\hat{Y} = 1|S = -1)$, where $\hat{Y}$ is the final decision of the classifier on test set of original data D. All the experiments are repeated 5 times, and mean and standard deviation is reported in Table 1.

In implementing the training, we use $n_{crit} = 4$, a batch size of 128, $\lambda_p = 10$, and Adam optimizer with $\alpha = 0.0002$, $\beta_1 = 0.5$, and $\beta_2 = 0.999$. For UCI Adult dataset, the Bank Marketing dataset, and ProPublica dataset, the network was trained for 200 epcohs, with $\lambda_f = 0.06$, 0.12, and 0.05, respectively. For Law School Dataset, the network was trained for 150 epochs, with $\lambda_f = 0.11$. All trainings were performed on a machine with a single NVIDIA GeForce RTX 3090, and a single training of network for each dataset, takes an average of 18 min.

Table 1. Comparing the results of our model with TabFairGAN and CRDI. Showing DP Gen. Data (Demographic Parity in generated data, lower the better), Acc. Gen. Data (Accuracy of generated data, higher the better), and DP in Classifier (Demographic Parity in the trained classifier, lower the better). Each number is the aggregate of 5 separate training.

Dataset	Ours			TabFairGAN			CRDI		
	DP Gen. Data	Acc. Gen. Data	DP in Classifier	DP Gen. Data	Acc. Gen. Data	DP in Classifier	DP Rep. Data	Acc. Rep. Data	DP in Classifier
Adult	0.01 0.001	0.793 0.011	0.073 0.03	0.009 0.027	0.773 0.013	0.082 0.038	0.165 0.048	0.786 0.011	0.121 0.024
Bank	0.001 0.004	0.773 0.03	0.012 0.04	0.001 0.011	0.854 0.004	0.060 0.056	0.122 0.004	0.776 0.004	0.050 0.017
COMPAS	0.06 0.004	0.837 0.025	0.157 0.053	0.009 0.102	0.860 0.040	0.208 0.072	0.119 0.128	0.893 0.021	0.205 0.055
Law School	0.011 0.005	0.834 0.007	0.151 0.081	0.024 0.036	0.847 0.020	0.153 0.072	0.233 0.103	0.892 0.004	0.289 0.057

5.4   Results

Table 1 shows the results of experiments. We directly report the results of TabFairGAN and CRDI from [39]. Looking into Table 1, Ours is superior in generating synthetic data such that training a classifier on the synthetic data, results in a fair classifier. Comparing demographic parity of generated dataset, ours beats TabFairGAN for banking dataset and Law School dataset, while TabFairGAN is able to produce a fairer synthetic dataset for Adult dataset and COMPAS

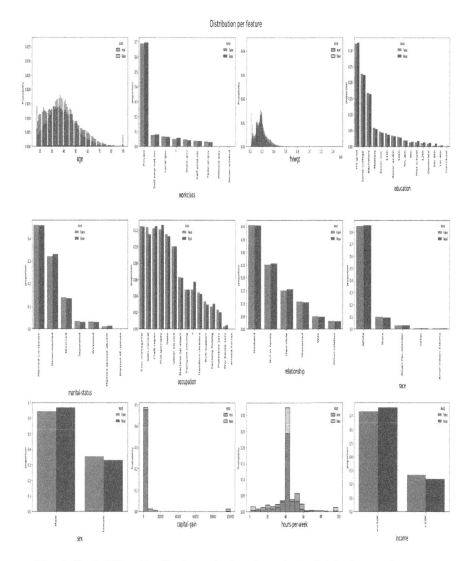

Fig. 2. Probability distributions of ral and synthetic Adult dataset features.

dataset. Comparing the accuracy columns, the results show that Ours is able to produce more accurate data for Adult dataset, while TabFairGAN is able to produce accurate data for Bank dataset, and for COMPAS and Law School dataset CRDI beats ours and TabFairGAN.

Finally, to visualize data quality, Fig. 2 compares histograms of real data D and synthetic data D for Adult dataset, for 12 numerical and categorical attributes.

6   Discussion

In this work, we proposed a generative adversarial network to generate fair synthetic tabular datasets. The experiments show the model exhibits the four mentioned objectives in Sect. 3.1, namely data utility, data fairness, classification utility, and classification fairness. While the model has the same architecture as TabFairGAN, our model makes three improvements over the previous approaches: 1) Instead of two phases of training in TabFairGAN, our model includes one single phase of training. This is important as it removes the necessity to explore for different combinations of number of epochs in the two phases of training in TabFairGAN. 2) Fairness enforcement is based on generating data where S and Y are independent, rather than solely enforcing a specific fairness metric in the loss function. 3) The model is shown to be superior in training a fair classifier, which is the most important reason for generating a fair synthetic dataset. In the future, we will explore utilizing similar approach for generating other types of datasets, such as image data.

References

1. Abdollahpouri, H., Burke, R., Mobasher, B.: Managing popularity bias in recommender systems with personalized re-ranking. In: The thirty-Second International Flairs Conference (2019)
2. Alves, G., Amblard, M., Bernier, F., Couceiro, M., Napoli, A.: Reducing unintended bias of ml models on tabular and textual data. In: 2021 IEEE 8th International Conference on Data Science and Advanced Analytics (DSAA), pp. 1–10. IEEE (2021)
3. Angwin, J., Larson, J., Mattu, S., Kirchner, L.: Machine bias propublica (2016)
4. Arjovsky, M., Chintala, S., Bottou, L.: Wasserstein generative adversarial networks. In: International Conference on Machine Learning, pp. 214–223. PMLR (2017)
5. Mark Beasley, T., Erickson, S., Allison, D.B.: Rank-based inverse normal transformations are increasingly used, but are they merited? Beh. Genet. **39**(5), 580–595 (2009)
6. Benesty, J., Chen, J., Huang, Y., Cohen, I.: Pearson correlation coefficient. In: Noise Reduction in Speech Processing, pp. 1–4. Springer, Vienna (2009). https://doi.org/10.1007/978-3-211-89836-9_1025
7. Beutel, A., Chen, J., Zhao, Z., Chi, E.H.: Data decisions and theoretical implications when adversarially learning fair representations. arXiv preprint arXiv:1707.00075 (2017)
8. Binns, R.: Fairness in machine learning: Lessons from political philosophy. In: Conference on Fairness, Accountability and Transparency, pp. 149–159. PMLR (2018)
9. Bolukbasi, T., Chang, K.-W., Zou, J.Y., Saligrama, V., Kalai, A.T.: Man is to computer programmer as woman is to homemaker? Debiasing word embeddings. In: Advances in Neural Information Processing Systems, vol. 29 (2016)
10. Bordia, S., Bowman, S.R.: Identifying and reducing gender bias in word-level language models. arXiv preprint arXiv:1904.03035 (2019)
11. Brock, A., Donahue, J., Simonyan, K.: Large scale GAN training for high fidelity natural image synthesis. arXiv preprint arXiv:1809.11096 (2018)

12. Chang, K.-W., Prabhakaran, V., Ordonez, V.: Bias and fairness in natural language processing. In: Proceedings of the 2019 Conference on Empirical Methods in Natural Language Processing and the 9th International Joint Conference on Natural Language Processing (EMNLP-IJCNLP): Tutorial Abstracts (2019)
13. Chen, J., Dong, H., Wang, X., Feng, F., Wang, M., He, X.: Bias and debias in recommender system: A survey and future directions. arXiv preprint arXiv:2010.03240 (2020)
14. Chouldechova, A.: Fair prediction with disparate impact: a study of bias in recidivism prediction instruments. Big Data 5(2), 153–163 (2017)
15. Dua, D., Graff, C.: UCI machine learning repository (2017)
16. Edelmann, D., Móri, T.F., Székely, G.J.: On relationships between the Pearson and the distance correlation coefficients. Stat. Probabil. Lett. **169**, 108960 (2021)
17. Feldman, M., Friedler, S.A., Moeller, J., Scheidegger, C., Venkatasubramanian,S.: Certifying and removing disparate impact. In: Proceedings of the 21th ACM SIGKDD International Conference on Knowledge Discovery and Data Mining, pp. 259–268 (2015)
18. Goodfellow, I., et al.: Generative adversarial nets. In: Advances in Neural Information Processing Systems, vol. 27 (2014)
19. Gulrajani, I., Ahmed, F., Arjovsky, M., Dumoulin, V., Courville, A.C.: Improved training of wasserstein GANs. In: Guyon, I., et al. (eds.) Advances in Neural Information Processing Systems, vol. 30. Curran Associates Inc (2017)
20. Gupta, U., Ferber, A.M., Dilkina, B., Ver Steeg, G.: Controllable guarantees for fair outcomes via contrastive information estimation. In: Proceedings of the AAAI Conference on Artificial Intelligence, vol. 35, pp. 7610–7619 (2021)
21. Hardt, M., Price, E., Srebro, N.: Equality of opportunity in supervised learning. In: Advances in Neural Information Processing Systems, vol. 29, pp. 3315–3323 (2016)
22. Jenssen, R.: An information theoretic approach to machine learning. Doctor Scientiarum thesis, Department of Physics, Faculty of Science, University of Tromsø (2005)
23. Kamiran, F., Calders, T.: Data preprocessing techniques for classification without discrimination. Knowl. Inf. Syst. **33**(1), 1–33 (2012)
24. Kamishima, T., Akaho, S., Asoh, H., Sakuma, J.: Fairness-aware classifier with prejudice remover regularizer. In: Flach, P.A., De Bie, T., Cristianini, N. (eds.) ECML PKDD 2012. LNCS (LNAI), vol. 7524, pp. 35–50. Springer, Heidelberg (2012). https://doi.org/10.1007/978-3-642-33486-3_3
25. Khosla, A., Zhou, T., Malisiewicz, T., Efros, A.A., Torralba, A.: Undoing the damage of dataset bias. In: Fitzgibbon, A., Lazebnik, S., Perona, P., Sato, Y., Schmid, C. (eds.) ECCV 2012. LNCS, vol. 7572, pp. 158–171. Springer, Heidelberg (2012). https://doi.org/10.1007/978-3-642-33718-5_12
26. Kraskov, A., Stögbauer, H., Grassberger, P.: Estimating mutual information. Physical Rev. E **69**(6), 066138 (2004)
27. Krishnan, S., Patel, J., Franklin, M.J., Goldberg, K.: A methodology for learning, analyzing, and mitigating social influence bias in recommender systems. In: Proceedings of the 8th ACM Conference on Recommender Systems, pp. 137–144 (2014)
28. Lambrecht, A., Tucker, C.: Algorithmic bias? an empirical study of apparent gender-based discrimination in the display of stem career ads. Manage. Sci. **65**(7), 2966–2981 (2019)
29. Lee, N.T.: Detecting racial bias in algorithms and machine learning. J. Inf. Commun. Ethics Soc. (2018)

30. Lepri, B., Oliver, N., Letouzé, E., Pentland, A., Vinck, P.: Fair, transparent, and accountable algorithmic decision-making processes. Philos. Technol. **31**(4), 611–627 (2018)
31. Mehrabi, N., Gupta, U., Morstatter, F., Ver Steeg, G., Galstyan, A.: Attributing fair decisions with attention interventions. arXiv preprint arXiv:2109.03952 (2021)
32. Mehrabi, N., Morstatter, F., Saxena, N., Lerman, K., Galstyan, A.: A survey on bias and fairness in machine learning. ACM Comput. Surv. (CSUR) **54**(6), 1–35 (2021)
33. Moro, S., Cortez, P., Rita, P.: A data-driven approach to predict the success of bank telemarketing. Decis. Support Syst. **62**, 22–31 (2014)
34. Moyer, D., Gao, S., Brekelmans, R., Galstyan, A., Ver Steeg, G.: Invariant representations without adversarial training. In: Advances in Neural Information Processing Systems, vol. 31 (2018)
35. Park, N., Mohammadi, M., Gorde, K., Jajodia, S., Park, H., Kim, Y.: Data synthesis based on generative adversarial networks. arXiv preprint arXiv:1806.03384 (2018)
36. Pedregosa, F., et al.: Scikit-learn: machine learning in python. J. Mach. Learn. Res. **12**, 2825–2830 (2011)
37. Pessach, D., Shmueli, E.: Algorithmic fairness. arXiv preprint arXiv:2001.09784 (2020)
38. Piccoli, B., Rossi, F.: Generalized wasserstein distance and its application to transport equations with source. Arch. Ration. Mech. Anal. **211**(1), 335–358 (2014)
39. Amirarsalan Rajabi and Ozlem Ozmen Garibay: Tabfairgan: fair tabular data generation with generative adversarial networks. Mach. Learn. Knowl. Extract. **4**(2), 488–501 (2022)
40. Ramaswamy, V.V., Kim, S.S.Y., Russakovsky, O.: Fair attribute classification through latent space de-biasing. In: Proceedings of the IEEE/CVF Conference on Computer Vision and Pattern Recognition, pp. 9301–9310 (2021)
41. Robinson, J.P., Livitz, G., Henon, Y., Qin, C., Fu, Y., Timoner, S.: Face recognition: too bias, or not too bias? In: Proceedings of the IEEE/CVF Conference on Computer Vision and Pattern Recognition Workshops, pp. 0–1 (2020)
42. Sahlgren, M., Olsson, F.: Gender bias in pretrained Swedish embeddings. In: Proceedings of the 22nd Nordic Conference on Computational Linguistics, pp. 35–43 (2019)
43. Sattigeri, P., Hoffman, S.C., Chenthamarakshan, V., Varshney, K.R.: Fairness GAN. arXiv preprint arXiv:1805.09910 (2018)
44. Sattigeri, P., Hoffman, S.C., Chenthamarakshan, V., Varshney, K.R.: Fairness GAN: generating datasets with fairness properties using a generative adversarial network. IBM J. Res. Dev. **63**(4/5), 3–1 (2019)
45. Székely, G.J., Rizzo, M.L., Bakirov, N.K.: Measuring and testing dependence by correlation of distances. Ann. Stat. **35**(6), 2769–2794 (2007)
46. Tolan, S., Miron, M., Gómez, E., Castillo, C.: Why machine learning may lead to unfairness: evidence from risk assessment for juvenile justice in Catalonia. In: Proceedings of the Seventeenth International Conference on Artificial Intelligence and Law, pp. 83–92 (2019)
47. Verma, S., Rubin, J.: Fairness definitions explained. In: 2018 IEEE/ACM International Workshop on Software Fairness (fairware), pp. 1–7. IEEE (2018)
48. Wang, Z., et al.: Towards fairness in visual recognition: Effective strategies for bias mitigation. In: Proceedings of the IEEE/CVF Conference on Computer Vision and Pattern Recognition, pp. 8919–8928 (2020)

49. Wightman, L.F.: LSAC national longitudinal bar passage study. LSAC Research Report Series (1998)
50. Xu, D., Yuan, S., Zhang, L., Wu, X.: Fairgan: fairness-aware generative adversarial networks. In: 2018 IEEE International Conference on Big Data (Big Data), pp. 570–575. IEEE (2018)
51. Zhao, J., Wang, T., Yatskar, M., Ordonez, V., Chang, K.-W.: Men also like shopping: reducing gender bias amplification using corpus-level constraints. arXiv preprint arXiv:1707.09457 (2017)

Through a Fair Looking-Glass: Mitigating Bias in Image Datasets

Amirarsalan Rajabi[1], Mehdi Yazdani-Jahromi[1], Ozlem Ozmen Garibay[1,2(✉)], and Gita Sukthankar[1]

[1] Department of Computer Science, University of Central Florida, Orlando, FL 32816, USA
ozlem@ucf.edu
[2] Department of Industrial Engineering and Management Systems, Orlando, FL 32816, USA

Abstract. With the recent growth in computer vision applications, the question of how fair and unbiased they are has yet to be explored. There is abundant evidence that the bias present in training data is reflected in the models, or even amplified. Many previous methods for image dataset de-biasing, including models based on augmenting datasets, are computationally expensive to implement. In this study, we present a fast and effective model to de-bias an image dataset through reconstruction and minimizing the statistical dependence between intended variables. Our architecture includes a U-net to reconstruct images, combined with a pre-trained classifier which penalizes the statistical dependence between target attribute and the protected attribute. We evaluate our proposed model on CelebA dataset, compare the results with two state-of-the-art de-biasing method, and show that the model achieves a promising fairness-accuracy combination.

Keywords: Fairness in AI · Human-centered AI · U-Net · Fair Adversarial Learning

1 Introduction

Due to their increased usage within myriad software applications, artificial intelligence algorithms now influence many aspects of people's lives, particularly when they are embedded into decision-support tools used by educators, government agencies, and various industry sectors. Thus, it is crucial to make sure that these algorithms are scrutinized to ensure fairness and remove unjust biases. Bias has been shown to exist in several deployed AI systems, including the well known Correlational Offender Management Profiling for Alternative Sanctions (COMPAS). COMPAS is an automated decision making system used by the

Supplementary Information The online version contains supplementary material available at https://doi.org/10.1007/978-3-031-35891-3_27.

US criminal justice system for assessing a criminal defendant's likelihood of re-offending. By exploring the risk scores assigned to individuals, this system has been shown to be biased against African Americans [4]. Other examples include a targeted advertising system in which highly paid jobs were advertised more frequently to men vs. women [12].

Bias in computer vision is a major problem, often stemming from the training datasets used for computer vision models [24]. There is evidence suggesting the existence of multiple types of bias, including capture and selection bias, in popular image datasets [25]. The problems arising from bias in computer vision can manifest in different ways. For instance, it is observed that in activity recognition models, when the datasets contain gender bias, the bias is further amplified by the models trained on those datasets [36]. Face recognition models may exhibit lower accuracy for some classes of race or gender [2].

This paper addresses the issue of a decision-making process being dependent on *protected attributes*, where this dependence should ideally be avoided. From a legal perspective, a protected attribute is an attribute upon which discrimination is illegal [16], e.g. gender or race. Let $D = (\mathcal{X}, \mathcal{S}, \mathcal{Y})$ be a dataset, where $\mathcal{X}$ represents unprotected attributes, $\mathcal{S}$ is the protected attribute, and $\mathcal{Y}$ be the target attribute. If in the dataset D, the target attribute is not independent of the protected attribute ($\mathcal{Y} \not\perp \mathcal{S}$), then it is very likely that the decisions $\hat{\mathcal{Y}}$ made by a decision-making system which is trained on D, is also not independent of the protected attribute ($\hat{\mathcal{Y}} \not\perp \mathcal{S}$).

We propose a model to reconstruct an image dataset to reduce statistical dependency between a protected attribute and target attribute. We modify a U-net [20] to reconstruct the image dataset and apply the Hilbert-Schmidt norm of the cross-covariance operator [6] between reproducing kernel Hilbert spaces of the target attribute and the protected attribute, as a measure of statistical dependence. Unlike many previous algorithms, our proposed method doesn't require training new classifiers on the unbiased data, but instead reconstructing images in a way that reduces the bias entailed by using the same classifiers.

In Section Methodology we present the problem, the notion of independence, and our proposed methodology. In Section Experiments we describe the CelebA dataset and the choice of feature categorization, introduce the baseline model with which we compare our results [19], our model's implementation details, and finally present the experiments and results.

2 Background

Bias mitigation methods can be divided into three general categories of *pre-process*, *in-process*, and *post-process*. Pre-process methods include modifying the training dataset before feeding it to the machine learning model. In-process methods include adding regularizing terms to penalize some representation of bias during the training process. Finally, post-process methods include modifying the final decisions of the classifiers [8]. Kamiran and Calders [11] propose methods such as suppression which includes removing attributes highly correlated with the protected attribute, reweighing, i.e. assigning weights to different instances in the data, and massaging the data to change labels of some objects. Bias mitigation methods often come at the expense of losing some accuracy, and these preliminary methods usually entail higher fairness-utility cost. More sophisticated methods with better results include using generative models to augment the biased training dataset with unbiased data [19], or training the models on entirely synthetic unbiased data [18]. [31] provide a set of analyses and a benchmark to evaluate and compare bias mitigation techniques in visual recognition models.

Works such as [26,33] suggest methods to mitigate bias in visual datasets. Several studies have deployed GANs for bias mitigation in image datasets. For example, [22] modified the value function of GAN to generate fair image datasets. FairFaceGAN [10] implements a facial image-to-image translation, preventing unwanted translation in protected attributes. Ramaswamy et al. propose a model to produce training data that is balanced for each protected attribute, by perturbing the latent vector of a GAN [19]. Other studies employing GANs for fair data generation include [3,23].

A variety of techniques beyond GANs have been applied to the problems of fairness in AI. A deep information maximization adaptation network was used to reduce racial bias in face image datasets [28], and reinforcement learning was used to learn a race-balanced network in [27]. Wang et al. propose a generative few-shot cross-domain adaptation algorithm to perform fair cross-domain adaption and improve performance on minority category [30]. The work in [32] proposes adding a penalty term into the softmax loss function to mitigate bias and improve fairness performance in face recognition. [17] propose a method to discover fair representations of data with the same semantic meaning of the input data. Adversarial learning has also successfully been deployed for this task [29,34].

3   Methodology

Consider a dataset $D = (\mathcal{X}, \mathcal{S}, \mathcal{Y})$, where $\mathcal{X}$ is the set of images, $\mathcal{Y} = \{+1, -1\}$ is the target attribute such as attractiveness, and $\mathcal{S} = \{A, B, C, ...\}$ is the protected attribute such as gender. Assume there exists a classifier $f : (\mathcal{X}) \rightarrow \mathcal{Y}$, such that the classifier's prediction for target attribute is not independent from the protected attribute, i.e. $f(\mathcal{X}) \not\perp \mathcal{S}$. Our objective is to design a transformation $g : \mathcal{X} \rightarrow \widetilde{\mathcal{X}}$, such that 1) $f(\widetilde{\mathcal{X}}) \perp \mathcal{S}$, i.e. the classifier's predictions for target attribute is independent of the protected attribute, and 2) $f(\widetilde{\mathcal{X}}) \approx f(\mathcal{X})$, i.e. the classifier still achieves high accuracy.

In other words we want to train a network to transform our original images, such that if the classifiers that are trained on the original and unmodified images, are used to predict the target attribute (attractiveness in our example) from the transformed version of an image, they still achieve high accuracy, while the predictions of those classifiers are independent of the protected attribute (gender in our example). It should be noted that we are not seeking to train new classifiers, but rather only aim to modify the input images. This is a main distinction between our methodology and most of other techniques (e.g. [17,19]), in which the process includes training new classifiers on modified new image datasets and achieving *fair classifiers*.

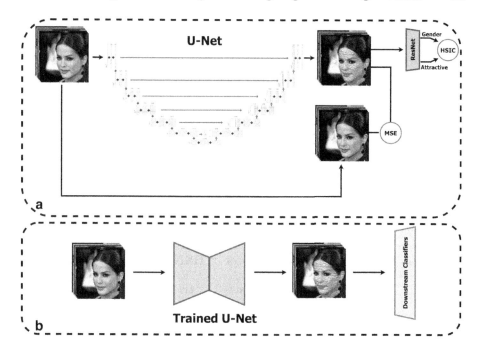

Fig. 1. Our model consists of an encoder-decoder (U-net) and a double-output pre-trained ResNet classifier. First, the output batch of the U-net (reconstructed images) is compared with the original batch of images by calculating MSE loss. Then, the output batch of the U-net passes through the ResNet and statistical dependency of the two vectors is calculated by HSIC. Detailed architecture of the U-net is described in the supplementary material.

Our proposed model consists of a U-net [20] as the neural network that transforms the original images. This type of network was originally proposed for medical image segmentation, and has been widely used since its introduction. The encoder-decoder network consists of two paths, a contracting path consisting of convolution and max pooling layers, and a consecutive expansive path consisting of upsampling of the feature map and convolutions. Contrary to [20] where each image is provided with a segmented image label, we provide our U-net with the exact same image as the label, and alter the loss function from cross-entropy to mean squared error, so that the network gets trained to produce an image as close to the original image as possible, in a pixel-wise manner.

While some previous fairness studies consider *decorrelating* the target attribute from the protected attributes, what must be ultimately sought however, is independence between the protected attribute and the target attribute. Dealing with two random variables which are uncorrelated is easier than independence, as two random variables might have a zero correlation, and still be dependent (e.g. two random variables A and B with recordings $A = [-2, -1, 0, 1, 2]$ and $B = [4, 1, 0, 1, 4]$ have zero covariance, but are apparently not independent).

Given a Borel probability distribution $\mathbf{P}_{ab}$ defined on a domain $\mathcal{A} \times \mathcal{B}$, and respective marginal distributions $\mathbf{P}_a$ and $\mathbf{P}_b$ on $\mathcal{A}$ and $\mathcal{B}$, independence of a and b ($a \perp\!\!\!\perp b$) is equal to $\mathbf{P}_{ab}$ factorizing as $\mathbf{P}_a$ and $\mathbf{P}_b$. Furthermore, two random variables a and b are independent, if and only if any bounded continuous function of the two random variables are uncorrelated [7].

Let $\mathcal{F}$ and $\mathcal{G}$ denote all real-value functions defined on domains $\mathcal{A}$ and $\mathcal{B}$ respectively. In their paper [6] define the Hilbert-Schmidt norm of the cross-covariance operator:

$$HSIC(\mathbf{P}_{ab}, \mathcal{F}, \mathcal{G}) := ||C_{ab}||^2_{HS} \tag{1}$$

where C_{ab} is the cross-covariance operator. They show that if $||C_{ab}||^2_{HS}$ is zero, then $cov(f, g)$ will be zero for any $f \in \mathcal{F}$ and $g \in \mathcal{G}$, and therefore the random variables a and b will be independent. Furthermore, they show if $\mathcal{Z} := (a_1, b_1), ..., (a_n, b_n) \in \mathcal{A} \times \mathcal{B}$ are a series of n independent observations drawn from $\mathbf{P}_{ab}$, then a (biased) estimator of **HSIC** is [6]:

$$HSIC(\mathcal{Z}, \mathcal{F}, \mathcal{G}) := (n-1)^{-2}\mathbf{tr}(KHLH) \tag{2}$$

where $H, K, L \in \mathbb{R}^{n \times n}$, K and L are Gram matrices [9], $K_{ij} := k(a_i, a_j)$, $L_{ij} := l(b_i, b_j)$, k and l are universal kernels, and $H_{ij} := \delta_{ij} - n^{-1}$ centers the observations in feature space. We use Hilbert-Schmidt independence criteria to penalize the model for dependence between the target attribute and the protected attribute.

Fig. 2. Examples of CelebA dataset original images. Images in the first row are labeled not Male and images in the second row are labeled Male. In each row, the first three images are labeled Attractive and the last three images are labeled not Attractive.

3.1   Training Loss Function

We seek to modify a set of images, such that 1) the produced images are close to the original images, and 2) the predicted target attribute is independent from the predicted protected attribute. In the optimization problem, image quality (1) is measured by pixel-wise MSE loss. For independence (2), consider our U-net network as a mapping from original image to the transformed image, i.e. $U_w(\mathbf{x}) = \widetilde{\mathbf{x}}$. Consider also a function $h : \mathcal{X} \rightarrow [0, 1] \times [0, 1]$, where $h(\mathbf{x}_i) = (h_1(\mathbf{x}_i), h_2(\mathbf{x}_i)) = (\mathrm{P}(y_i = 1|\mathbf{x}_i), \mathrm{P}(s_i = 1|\mathbf{x}_i))$. Our objective is to train the parameters of U_w such that $h_1(U_w(\mathbf{x})) \perp\!\!\!\perp h_2(U_w(\mathbf{x}))$, i.e. $h_1(U_w(\mathbf{x}))$ is independent of $h_2(U_w(\mathbf{x}))$.

Given X representing a batch of N training images and $\widetilde{X}$ representing the transformed batch, our formal optimization problem is as follows:

$$\underset{U_w}{\text{minimize}} \underbrace{\frac{1}{NCWH} \sum_{n=1}^{N} \sum_{i,j,k} (\mathbf{x}_{ijk}^n - \widetilde{\mathbf{x}}_{ijk}^n)^2}_{\text{image accuracy}}$$

$$+ \lambda \times \underbrace{HSIC(h_1(\widetilde{X}), h_2(\widetilde{X}))}_{\text{independence}} \tag{3}$$

where N is the number of samples, C is the number of channels of an image, W is the width of an image, H is the height of an image, and λ is the parameter that controls the trade-off between accuracy of the transformed images and independence (fairness). In practice, the mapping function U_w that we use is a U-net, the function $h(\cdot)$ is a pre-trained classifier with two outputs h_1 and h_2, each being the output of a Sigmoid function within the range of $[0, 1]$, where $h_1 = \mathrm{P}(Y = 1|X)$ (a vector of size N), and $h_2 = \mathrm{P}(S = 1|X)$ (also a vector of size N), and $HSIC(\cdot, \cdot)$ denotes Hilbert-Schmidt Independence Criteria.

Figure 1 shows the network architecture and a schematic of the training procedure. Consider a batch of original images X entering the U-net. The U-net then produces the reconstructed images $U_w(X) = \widetilde{X}$. To calculate the *image accuracy* part of the loss function, the original image batch X is provided as label and the Mean Squared Error is calculated to measure the accuracy of the reconstructed images. The ResNet component in Fig. 1 is our $h(\cdot)$ function as described before, which is a pre-trained ResNet classifier that takes as input a batch of images and returns two probability vectors. The second part of the loss function, *independence*, is calculated by entering the reconstructed images $\widetilde{X}$ into this ResNet classifier, and calculating the HSIC between the two vectors.

As noted before, the image dataset is reconstructed in a way that using them on the original biased classifiers, will result in an improvement in classifications. This is dissimilar to some previous works such as [17,19], in which the model training process includes augmenting the original dataset with generated images and training new fair classifiers [19], or discovering fair representations of images and subsequently training new classifiers [17].

4   Experiments

In this section, we test the methodology described in Section Methodology on CelebA dataset [13]. We first introduce the CelebA dataset and the attribute categories in CelebA. We then describe the implementation details of our model. Subsequently, the method described in the work of [19] and the two versions of it that we use as baseline models to compare our results with are introduced. Finally, we introduce evaluation metrics and present the results.

4.1   CelebA Dataset

CelebA is a popular dataset that is widely used for training and testing models for face detection, particularly recognising facial attributes. It consists of 202,599 face images of celebrities, with 10,177 identities. Each image is annotated with 40 different binary attributes describing the image, including attributes such as Black_Hair, Pale_Skin, Wavy_Hair, Oval_Face, Pointy_Nose, and other attributes such as Male, Attractive, Smiling, etc. The CelebA dataset is reported to be biased [35]. In this experiment, we consider Male attribute as the protected attribute (with Male = 0 showing the image does not belong to a man and Male = 1 showing the image belongs to a man), and Attractive to be the target attribute. We divide the dataset into train and test sets, with train set containing 182,599 and test set containing 20,000 images. In the training set, 67.91% of images with Male = 0 are annotated to be attractive (Attractive = 1), while only 27.93% of images with Male = 1 are annotated as being attractive (Attractive = 1). This shows bias exists against images with Male = 1.

In order to compare our results with [19], we follow their categorization of CelebA attributes. Leaving out Male as the protected attribute, among the rest 39 attributes in CelebA dataset, [19] eliminates some attributes such as Blurry and Bald as they contain less than 5% positive images. The remaining 26 attributes is subsequently categorized into three groups. *inconsistently-labeled* attributes are the ones that by visually examining sets of examples, the authors often disagree with the labeling and could not distinguish between positive and negative examples [19]. This group includes attributes such as Straight_Hair, and Big_Hair. The second group of attributes are the ones that are called *gender-dependent* and the images are labeled to have (or not have) attributes based on the perceived gender [19]. These include attributes such as Young, Arched_Eyebrows and Receding_Hairline. Finally, the last group of attributes are called *gender-independent*. These attributes are fairly consistently labeled and are not much dependent on gender expression. This group includes attributes such as Black_Hair, Bangs, and Wearing_Hat. The list of all attributes is provided in supplementary material.

4.2   Attribute Classifiers

For attribute classifiers, we use ResNet-18 pre-trained on ImageNet, in which the last layer is replaced with a layer of size one, along with a Sigmoid activation for binary classification. We train all models for 5 epochs with batch sizes of 128. We use the Stochastic Gradient Descent optimizer with a learning rate of 1e-3 and momentum of 0.9. We use a step learning rate decay with step size of 7 and

Fig. 3. Examples of CelebA dataset images and how the model reconstructs them. The first row shows a set of images from the original testing set, and the second row shows the reconstructed images.

factor of 0.1. After training, we will have 26 classifiers that receive an image and perform a binary classification on their respective attribute.

4.3 Implementation Details

As shown in Fig. 1, a ResNet-18 network is used to accompany the U-net to produce predictions for `Male` and `Attractive`. Prior to training the U-net, the ResNet-18 [21] which is pre-trained on ImageNet, is modified by replacing its output layer with a layer of size two, outputing the probability of attractiveness and gender. The ResNet-18 is then trained for 5 epochs on the train set, with a batch size of 128. We use the Stochastic Gradient Descent optimizer with a learning rate of 1e-3 and momentum of 0.9. We use a step learning rate decay with step size of 7 and factor of 0.1. After the ResNet is trained and prepared, we train the U-net as described in Section Methodology on the train set. The detailed architecture of the U-net is described in Supplementary Material. In our implementation of biased estimator of HSIC estimator in Eq. 2, we use Gaussian RBF kernel function for $k(\cdot, \cdot)$ and $l(\cdot, \cdot)$. The training was conducted on a machine with two NVIDIA GeForce RTX 3090, and each training of the U-Net took 1 h. When the training is complete, the U-net is ready to reconstruct images. Figure 3 shows six examples of how the U-net modifies the original images. We train our model for 5 epochs with an $\lambda = 0.07$.

4.4 Comparison with Baseline Models

We compare our results with Ramaswamy et al.'s method, described in their paper 'Fair Attribute Classification through Latent Space De-biasing' [19]. Building on work by [5] which demonstrates a method to learn interpretable image modification directions, they develop an improved method by perturbing latent vector of a GAN, to produce training data that is balanced for each protected attribute. By augmenting the original dataset with the generated data, they train target classifiers on the augmented dataset, and show that these classifiers will be fair, with high accuracy. The second model that we compare our results with is explicit removal of biases from neural network embeddings, presented in [1]. The authors provide an algorithm to remove multiple sources of variation from the feature representation of a network. This is achieved by including secondary branches in a neural network with the aim to minimize a confusion loss, which in turn seeks to change the feature representation of data such that it becomes invariant to the spurious variations that are desired to be removed.

We implement Ramaswamy et al.'s method as follows: As mentioned in their paper, we used progressive GAN with 512-D latent space trained on the CelebA training set from the PyTorch GAN Zoo. We use 10,000 synthetic images and label the synthetic images with a ResNet-18 (modified by adding a fully connected layer with 1,000 neurons). Then we trained a linear SVM to learn the hyper-planes in the latent space as proposed in the original paper. We generate $\mathcal{X}_{syn}$ (160,000 images) to generate a synthetic dataset which aims to de-bias `Male` from all 26 attributes one by one. Next, we train ResNet-18 classifiers on the new datasets consisting of augmenting $\mathcal{X}$ and $\mathcal{X}_{syn}$. We call this model as *GANDeb*. We use the implementation of [1] with the uniform confusion loss $-(1/|D|)\sum_d \log q_d$ provided in [31].

4.5   Evaluation Metrics

In evaluating the results of our model with the baseline models, three metrics are used. To capture the accuracy of the classifiers, we measure the *average precision*. This metric combines precision and recall at every position and computes the average. A higher average precision (**AP**) is desired. To measure fairness, there are multiple metrics proposed in the literature [15]. Among the most commonly used metrics is *demographic parity* (**DP**). This metric captures the disparity of receiving a positive decision among different protected groups ($|P(\hat{Y} = 1|S = 0) - P(\hat{Y} = 1|S = 1)|$). A smaller **DP** shows a fairer classification and is desired. Finally for our last fairness measure, we follow [14,19] and use *difference in equality of opportunity* (**DEO**), i.e. the absolute difference between the true positive rates for both gender expressions ($|TPR(S = 0) - TPR(S = 1)|$). A smaller **DEO** is desired.

4.6   Results

All the values reported in this section, are evaluated on the same test set. Prior to comparing the results of our method with the comparison models, to assess the original training data, the performance of baseline, i.e. classifiers being trained on the original train set, and tested on the test set is presented. The AP, DP, and DEO values of classifiers trained on the original training set is shown in Table 1 under *Baseline*. Looking into Baseline values, the AP of classifiers for gender-independent category of attributes is higher than gender-dependent category, and the AP of inconsistent category is less than the other two categories. As expected, DP and DEO for gender-dependent category of attributes is higher than the other two categories.

In Table 1, we compare our model with GAN Debiasing (GanDeb) [19], Adversarial debiasing (AdvDb) presented in [1], and the Baseline on the original data. Looking into the average precision scores, the results show that GanDeb is slightly performing better than Ours. This is anticipated, since half of the training data for GanDeb consists of the original images, and therefore a higher average precision is expected. AdvDb on the other hand is performing poorly in terms of average precision, with average precision scores far away from other models.

Looking into demographic parity scores, the results show that GanDeb falls behind the other two models in two out of three attribute categories. While Ours is performing better for gender dependent and gender independent attribute categories. Looking into the third fairness measure, difference in equality of opportunity, AdvDb and ours are performing better than GanDeb in all three categories of attributes. Ours beats AdvDb for inconsistent attributes category, AdvDb beats Ours in gender dependent category, and AdvDb slightly beats Ours for gender independent category of attributes. In summary, Ours is close to Gan-Deb in terms of maintaining high average precision scores, which means higher accuracy of prediction, while beating GanDeb in terms of fairness metrics. Also, while AdvDb performance in terms of fairness enforcement is better than ours in 3 out of 6 cases, it falls behind significantly in terms of average precision.

To explore the trade-off between fairness and precision, we perform the following experiment: λ was increased between $[0.01, 0.15]$ in steps of 0.01, and for each value of λ, the model was trained three times, each time for 1 epoch. Figure 4 shows how AP, DEO, and DP change. The results show that by increasing λ, precision decreases while fairness measures improve.

Table 1. Comparing the results of our model with Baseline, GAN debiasing (Gan-Deb), and Adversarial debiasing (AdvDb). Showing AP (Average Precision, higher the better), DP (Demographic Parity, lower the better), and DEO (Difference in Equality of Opportunity, lower the better) values for each attribute category. Each number is the average over all attributes within that specific attribute category.

	AP ↑			DP ↓			DEO ↓		
	Incons.	G-dep	G-indep	Incons.	G-dep	G-indep	Incons.	G-dep	G-indep
Baseline	0.667	0.79	0.843	0.147	0.255	0.137	0.186	0.243	0.163
GanDeb	0.641	0.763	0.831	0.106	0.233	0.119	0.158	0.24	0.142
AdvDb	0.243	0.333	0.218	0.091	0.169	0.121	0.136	0.149	0.098
Ours	0.618	0.732	0.839	0.097	0.146	0.118	0.124	0.172	0.114

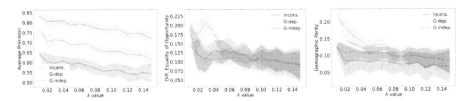

Fig. 4. Exploring the trade-off between accuracy and fairness by incremental increasing of parameter λ. Each data point is the average over three trainings, with standard deviation of the three trainings shown as confidence intervals.

4.7   Interpretation and the Effect on Other Attributes

In this section, we aim to display the correspondence between an attribute's relationship with `Attractive` attribute, and the extent to which the model modifies that attribute. To do so, for each attribute, we record two values, namely HSIC value between that attribute and the `Attractive` attribute, and the change in demographic parity. To calculate the change in demographic parity, we first calculate the demographic parity of the classifier for that specific attribute, when the classifier classifies the original testing set images (similar to *Baseline* in previous tables, but for each attribute separately). We then calculate the demographic parity of the classifier for that specific attribute, when the classifier receives the modified training images **Ours(5,0.07)**. We then subtract the two values,

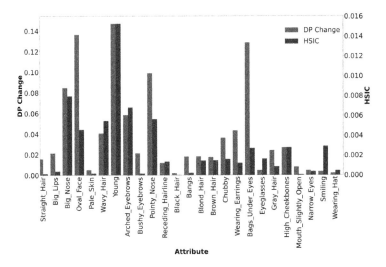

Fig. 5. Displaying the relationship between an attribute's statistical dependence on `Attractive` attribute, and the extent to which the model modifies that attribute. Blue bars show the HSIC between each attribute with `Attractive` attribute in the original data. Red bars show the absolute difference in demographic parity of each attribute's classifier, acting on original images and transformed images, respectively.

to get the change in demographic parity for that specific attribute. Figure 5 presents the results, with the red bars showing the change in demographic parity for each attribute, and the blue bars showing the statistical dependence measured by HSIC, between each attribute with `Attractive` attribute, in the original training data. The results show that the absolute change in demographic parity is positively correlated with that attribute's statistical dependence with the attribute `Attractive`, with a Pearson correlation coefficient of 0.757. For instance, we observe large changes in demographic parity for attributes such as `Young`, `Big_Nose`, `Pointy_Nose`, `Oval_Face`, and `Arched_Eyebrows`, as they are typically associated with being attractive, and therefore reflected in the CelebA dataset labels.

5   Conclusions

We proposed an image reconstruction process to mitigate bias against a protected attribute. The model's performance was evaluated on CelebA dataset and compared with an augmentation based method developed by [19]. The proposed model showed promising results in mitigating bias while maintaining high precision for classifiers. An interesting aspect of the results is that although we only explicitly train the U-net to remove dependence between the target attribute (`Attractive`) and the protected attribute (`Male`), classifiers related to many other attributes, most of which have a statistical dependency with the target attribute, become 'fairer'. An advantage of the proposed model is that it does not rely on modifying downstream classifiers, and rather includes only modifying the input data, hence making it suitable to be deployed in an automated machine learning pipeline more easily and with lower cost. As a potential future direction, we intend to consider the problem in a situation where multiple protected attributes are present, and attributes are non-binary. We also intend to apply similar methodology on other data types such as tabular data.

References

1. Alvi, M., Zisserman, A., Nellåker, C.: Turning a blind eye: explicit removal of biases and variation from deep neural network embeddings. In: Proceedings of the European Conference on Computer Vision (ECCV) Workshops (2018)
2. Buolamwini, J., Gebru, T.: Gender shades: intersectional accuracy disparities in commercial gender classification. In: Conference on Fairness, Accountability and Transparency, pages 77–91. PMLR (2018)
3. Choi, K., Grover, A., Singh, T., Shu, R., Ermon, S.: Fair generative modeling via weak supervision. In: International Conference on Machine Learning, pp. 1887–1898. PMLR (2020)
4. Chouldechova, A.: Fair prediction with disparate impact: a study of bias in recidivism prediction instruments. Big Data **5**(2), 153–163 (2017)

5. Denton, E., Hutchinson, B., Mitchell, M., Gebru, T., Zaldivar, A.: Image counterfactual sensitivity analysis for detecting unintended bias. arXiv preprint arXiv:1906.06439 (2019)
6. Gretton, A., Bousquet, O., Smola, A., Schölkopf, B.: Measuring statistical dependence with hilbert-schmidt norms. In: Jain, S., Simon, H.U., Tomita, E. (eds.) ALT 2005. LNCS (LNAI), vol. 3734, pp. 63–77. Springer, Heidelberg (2005). https://doi.org/10.1007/11564089_7
7. Gretton, A., Herbrich, R., Smola, A., Schölkopf, B., et al.: Kernel methods for measuring independence, Olivier Bousquet (2005)
8. Hardt, M., Price, E., Srebro, N.: Equality of opportunity in supervised learning. Adv. Neural. Inf. Process. Syst. **29**, 3315–3323 (2016)
9. Horn, R.A., Johnson, C.R.: Matrix Analysis. Cambridge University Press, Cambridge (2012)
10. Hwang, S., Park, S., Kim, D., Do, M., Byun, H.: Fairfacegan: fairness-aware facial image-to-image translation. arXiv preprint arXiv:2012.00282 (2020)
11. Kamiran, F., Calders, T.: Data preprocessing techniques for classification without discrimination. Knowl. Inf. Syst. **33**(1), 1–33 (2012)
12. Lambrecht, A., Tucker, C.: Algorithmic bias? an empirical study of apparent gender-based discrimination in the display of stem career ads. Manage. Sci. **65**(7), 2966–2981 (2019)
13. Liu, Z., Luo, P., Wang, X., Tang, X.: Deep learning face attributes in the wild. In: Proceedings of International Conference on Computer Vision (ICCV) (2015)
14. Lokhande, V.S., Akash, A.K., Ravi, S.N., Singh, V.: FairALM: augmented Lagrangian method for training fair models with little regret. In: Vedaldi, A., Bischof, H., Brox, T., Frahm, J.-M. (eds.) ECCV 2020. LNCS, vol. 12357, pp. 365–381. Springer, Cham (2020). https://doi.org/10.1007/978-3-030-58610-2_22
15. Mehrabi, N., Morstatter, F., Saxena, N., Lerman, K., Galstyan, A.: A survey on bias and fairness in machine learning. ACM Comput. Surv. (CSUR) **54**(6), 1–35 (2021)
16. Pessach, D., Shmueli, E.: Algorithmic fairness. arXiv preprint arXiv:2001.09784 (2020)
17. Quadrianto, N., Sharmanska, V., Thomas, O.: Discovering fair representations in the data domain. In: Proceedings of the IEEE/CVF Conference on Computer Vision and Pattern Recognition, pp. 8227–8236 (2019)
18. Rajabi, A., Garibay, O.O.: Tabfairgan: fair tabular data generation with generative adversarial networks. arXiv preprint arXiv:2109.00666 (2021)
19. Ramaswamy, V.V., Kim, S.S.Y., Russakovsky, O.: Fair attribute classification through latent space de-biasing. In: Proceedings of the IEEE/CVF Conference on Computer Vision and Pattern Recognition, pp. 9301–9310 (2021)
20. Ronneberger, O., Fischer, P., Brox, T.: U-Net: convolutional networks for biomedical image segmentation. In: Navab, N., Hornegger, J., Wells, W.M., Frangi, A.F. (eds.) MICCAI 2015. LNCS, vol. 9351, pp. 234–241. Springer, Cham (2015). https://doi.org/10.1007/978-3-319-24574-4_28
21. Russakovsky, O., et al.: Imagenet large scale visual recognition challenge. Int. J. Comput. Vis. **115**(3), 211–252 (2015)
22. Sattigeri, P., Hoffman, S.C., Chenthamarakshan, V., Varshney, K.R.: Fairness gan: generating datasets with fairness properties using a generative adversarial network. IBM J. Res. Dev. **63**(4/5), 3:1-3:9 (2019)
23. Sharmanska, V., Hendricks, L.A., Darrell, T., Quadrianto, N.: Contrastive examples for addressing the tyranny of the majority. arXiv preprint arXiv:2004.06524 (2020)

24. Tommasi, T., Patricia, N., Caputo, B., Tuytelaars, T.: A deeper look at dataset bias. In: Csurka, G. (ed.) Domain Adaptation in Computer Vision Applications. ACVPR, pp. 37–55. Springer, Cham (2017). https://doi.org/10.1007/978-3-319-58347-1_2

25. Torralba, A., Efros, A.A.: Unbiased look at dataset bias. In: CVPR 2011, pp. 1521–1528. IEEE (2011)

26. Wang, A., Narayanan, A., Russakovsky, O.: Revise: a tool for measuring and mitigating bias in visual datasets. In: European Conference on Computer Vision, pp. 733–751. Springer (2020)

27. Wang, M., Deng, W.: Mitigate bias in face recognition using skewness-aware reinforcement learning. arXiv preprint arXiv:1911.10692 (2019)

28. Wang, M., Deng, W., Hu, J., Tao, X., Huang, Y.: Racial faces in the wild: reducing racial bias by information maximization adaptation network. In: Proceedings of the IEEE/CVF International Conference on Computer Vision, pp. 692–702 (2019)

29. Wang, T., Zhao, J., Yatskar, M., Chang, K.-W., Ordonez, V.: Balanced datasets are not enough: estimating and mitigating gender bias in deep image representations. In: Proceedings of the IEEE/CVF International Conference on Computer Vision, pp. 5310–5319 (2019)

30. Wang, T., Ding, Z., Shao, W., Tang, H., Huang, K.: Towards fair cross-domain adaptation via generative learning. In: Proceedings of the IEEE/CVF Winter Conference on Applications of Computer Vision, pp. 454–463 (2021)

31. Wang, Z., et al.: Towards fairness in visual recognition: effective strategies for bias mitigation. In: Proceedings of the IEEE/CVF Conference on Computer Vision and Pattern Recognition, pp. 8919–8928 (2020)

32. Xu, X., et al.: Consistent instance false positive improves fairness in face recognition. In: Proceedings of the IEEE/CVF Conference on Computer Vision and Pattern Recognition, pp. 578–586 (2021)

33. Yang, K., Qinami, K., Fei-Fei, L., Deng, J., Russakovsky, O.: Towards fairer datasets: filtering and balancing the distribution of the people subtree in the imagenet hierarchy. In: Proceedings of the 2020 Conference on Fairness, Accountability, and Transparency, pp. 547–558 (2020)

34. Zhang, B.H., Lemoine, B., Mitchell, M.: Mitigating unwanted biases with adversarial learning. In: Proceedings of the 2018 AAAI/ACM Conference on AI, Ethics, and Society, pp. 335–340 (2018)

35. Zhang, Q., Wang, W., Zhu, S.-C.: Examining CNN representations with respect to dataset bias. In: Proceedings of the AAAI Conference on Artificial Intelligence, vol. 32, (2018)

36. Zhao, J., Wang, T., Yatskar, M., Ordonez, V., Chang, K.-W.: Men also like shopping: Reducing gender bias amplification using corpus-level constraints. arXiv preprint arXiv:1707.09457 (2017)

EthicalAI Based Decision Making to Reduce TaxRelated Debts for Governments

Savithaa Rajendran[1(✉)], Aparna Kongot[1(✉)], and Kratika Varma[2(✉)]

[1] SAP Labs India Private Limited, Bengaluru, India
{savithaa.rajendran,aparna.kongot}@sap.com
[2] Bengaluru, India
kratika.lca@gmail.com

Abstract. Piled up debts, missed revenue targets, inefficient manual processes and large data volumes in tax agencies have created a demand for intelligent systems that can assist tax agents to efficiently handle the tax recovery processes. This could help tax agents focus on strategic initiatives instead of avoidable manual tasks. Design Thinking, generative interviews, and naturalistic observation with a diverse set of user profiles were adopted to get clarity on the revenue authority's vision, business process flows and user journeys. A risk score-based machine learning application was built to combine the power of AI and human judgement for better informed decision making and explainable AI helped to put humans in the loop. Usability tests were conducted with distinct user groups to refine the user experience. With initial test results of the algorithm showing good accuracy levels, the vision is to help governments to improve overall business efficiency by reducing the tax gap and increasing revenue.

Keywords: Explainable AI · Tax payment processes · Design Thinking · Human Centered Design Process

1 Introduction

Nations often struggle with missed or delayed payments from their citizens and businesses, leading to piled-up debts for the governments and missed revenue targets [1]. This has huge implications like poor services offered to the country by the government due to lack of funding or taking loan from other nations or increase in debt owed to other nations. Governments struggle with the 'Tax Gap,' the difference between true tax liability for a given tax year and the amount that is paid on time. Extreme amounts of manual effort are required by tax administrators to uncover missed or delayed payments that contribute to the tax gap.

The revenue authority of a country in the East African region was keen on investing in machine learning solutions to optimize their business processes, empower their employees by helping them be more efficient while they make informed decisions. They shared anonymized sample data that helped train the algorithm. For the pilot machine learning product, the tax types selected were corporate tax, later followed by Value Added Tax (VAT) and Pay As You Earn (PAYE) tax. Through discussions, design thinking workshop, generative interviews and naturalistic observation with stakeholders like Business,

IT (Information Technology) and End user groups clarity was gained about the vision, current business processes and challenges faced. The final solution was built keeping in mind that the machine learning algorithm should enable the users to be efficient and quick in their work, by providing them insights and being transparent about the rationale behind the machine learning algorithms using explainable Artificial Intelligence. The solution was tested with end users before it was built into the final product. Initial test results of the algorithm have shown good accuracy levels.

2   Research Methodology and Frameworks

2.1   Initial and Revised Business Process and User Journeys

Initial discussions were conducted over remote calls with business and information technology stakeholders from the revenue authority along with product managers, user experience designers, engineers, and data scientists from the product development team at SAP. This helped trigger discussions about the revenue authority's business processes, challenges faced as an organization, their vision and high-level end user touch points. These were captured in the form of initial user journey (see Fig. 1) and initial business process flow (see Fig. 2). While this helped gain an early grasp on the problem area, there was still insufficient clarity on the personas, collaboration models, their responsibilities, and struggles. This led to the planning and execution of a week-long face-to-face design thinking [2] workshop that included generative interviews and naturalistic observation with different user groups, business heads and IT managers. A design thinking coach and user experience designer, product manager and developer were representatives from the product team.

Fig. 1. Initial tax recovery high level user journey

2.2   Design Thinking: Problem Understanding

The initial user journey and business process flow diagrams were printed out in large charts and pasted on the walls. This was then displayed in focus groups to gain a deeper understanding and rectify prior understandings (see Fig. 3) to create the revised user journeys with written insights (see Fig. 2) and revised business process flow (see Fig. 4).

Fig. 2. Revised user journeys with written insights

Business Process Flow. The following is a summary of learnings of the final business process flow.

- Training sessions are only offered for VAT tax type to educate customers
- Media campaigns are run only for personal income tax. This may be run for corporate tax in the future
- First time customers have 18 months (about 1 and a half years) to prepare account and additional 6 months to file returns and pay tax
- Cashier payment is discouraged. It is mandatory to electronically file returns and pay tax for corporate tax and VAT
- Returns with errors are reviewed by a Processing unit. First level Dunning is a mass job run to send reminders and claims for non-payment
- Second level Dunning letter is manually signed and sent by a Case officer

User Ecosystem. The following is a summary of learnings of the user ecosystem.

- Case workers handle both small (<50k) as well as large (>50k) debt cases
- Case workers report to Debt Managers and Debt Managers report to Section Heads

2.3   Design Thinking: End User Research with Generative Interviews and Naturalistic Observation

Eight end user interviews [4] were conducted with three user groups. This included three debt managers, three case workers and two tax risk management officers. The interviews were conducted in 2 parallel sessions to manage time and each interview involved one end user, one moderator who drove the interview and one note taker who captured notes and recorded the session.

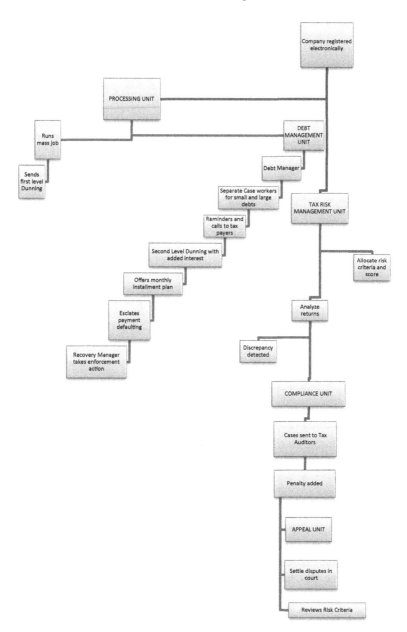

Fig. 3. Initial business process flow

Naturalistic Observation [5] were conducted with 2 case workers and one tax risk manager to gain insights into the way they work, the tools they use and get empathy for the struggles they face. There were also opportunities to converse and ask a few questions to the users at the end of this activity.

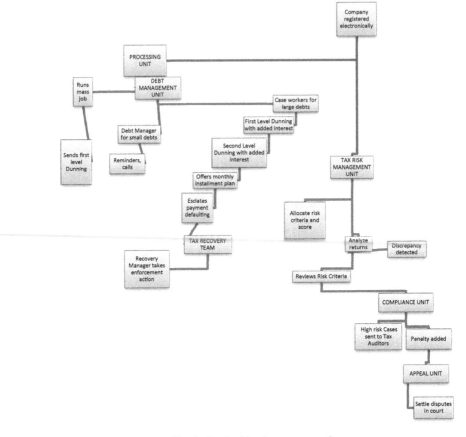

Fig. 4. Revised business process flow

2.4 Design Thinking: Synthesis and Problem Definition

This was a collaborative activity with all Business, IT, and end users from the revenue authority along with the Product stakeholders. The following Table 1 gives a summary of learnings from the End user research.

The broad themes also helped derive deeper insights into the challenges in the current business processes as detailed below and define the problem statement and personas.

Inefficient Risk Scores. The existing Risk score system is time consuming, heavily manual and relies on expert knowledge of few. Existing Risk scores are currently used only for auditing and not available for case workers to recover debt.

Manual Tasks Hinder Progress. Manual tasks take valuable time that can be used to ramp up case worker's efficiencies and skill sets. Empowered case workers can free up Debt Managers to focus on efficient business processes.

Table 1. End user research learnings

Themes	Learnings
Personas	The debt manager and Case workers are key personas working closely to recover tax payments. A debt manager oversees several case workers. Each case worker monitors a set of customers and all their tax types (VAT, CIT (Corporate Income Tax), PAYE, PIT (Personal Income Tax etc.)
Manual Tasks	Each caseworker has a physical file for a customer with scattered records of the taxes filed, payments, contact details, dunning letters, enforcement actions taken. This led to an increase in debt collection time
Lack insights	Given the limited time and large data, case workers and debt managers struggled to prioritize risky customers in excel files and this decreased chances of taking appropriate enforcement actions
Manual Risk scores	Tax Risk management unit manually allocates customers with a risk score. It works with debt managers to define risk criteria and scores, inexperienced case workers to identify new risk criteria, third party system to manually pull customers data and compare with their records in an excel, compliance team to get audit reports

Problem Statement. How can we empower the Debt managers and Case workers to monitor customers who are at risk of missing payments so that they can proactively act, recover payments on time, and reduce overall debt?

Personas. Debt manager was identified as the primary persona (see Fig. 5), Case Worker as the secondary persona and Tax risk officer was the tertiary persona.

Fig. 5. Debt manager persona

3   Formative Usability Testing

Formative usability testing [4] was conducted over 3 days with the revenue authority of a country in the East African region. The objective was to gather feedback and analyze ease of use, discoverability of the features and user's perception on intuitiveness of the overall experience to support further design iterations.

3.1   Set Up and Procedure

Each usability test [5] was conducted by a moderator and a note taker for 45 min. The test began with an introduction that explained to the participants the nature of the test and the method of thinking aloud [6]. The users were provided interactive prototypes on a laptop for the test. Each session was recorded using QuickTime Player software on an Apple MacBook Pro laptop. Real-time screen audio and video recording helped in capturing user's feedback and emotions. The test started with few background questions to deep dive into user's persona and his daily work environment. The users were then asked to complete various tasks. Moderators noted the level of assists that users needed to perform the task. User also rated each task on a scale of 0(Easy) – 5(Difficult). Post-test each user was asked to fill a post-test survey where the user had to rate the task on a scale of 0–7 on various measuring parameters like the ease of use, usefulness, consistency, terminology, recommending to others. The following Table 2 gives the details of participants from the usability testing.

Table 2.   Usability test participants.

Participant	Demographic	Tech-savviness
Case Officer 1	Female (age: 35)	Advance
Debt Manager 1	Male (age: 50)	Medium
Case Officer 2	Female (age: 35)	Advance
Case Officer 3	Female (age: 35)	Advance
Debt Manager 2	Male (age: 60)	Low

3.2   Tasks Undertaken, Results and Recommendation

Efficiency of Hierarchy of Visual Filters.   The task intent was to identify the value of visual filters to 'find top 3 customers at a high risk of receivership'. Test result showed 4 out of 5 users could complete this task with an average of 2 assists. Average task rating was 4 out of 5.

Recommendation.   The interaction of visual filters was intuitive to drilldown to the list of customers. However, the major feedback that came out was about content relevancy of donut chart filter (see Fig. 6). It was identified that instead of having 'risk distribution by customer type', a filter by 'number of customers by scenario' would be contextually relevant for an organization (see Fig. 7). Severity of this issue was recorded as high.

Fig. 6. Visual filter before test

Fig. 7. Visual filter after test

Copy and Assistive Cues. The task intent was to recognize the efficacy of terminologies used across the interface. Test result showed 3 out of 5 users could complete this task with an average of 3 assists. Average task rating was 3 out of 5.

Recommendation. There was an initial learning curve as the user started interacting with filters and tried to act upon the content. Along with the scope to introduce tooltips at certain places, the terminologies like 'number of customers' to 'number of occurrences' was preferred to be more understandable (see Fig. 8). The filters on customer pulse chart were expected to have labels for better efficiency (see Fig. 9). Severity of this issue was recorded as medium.

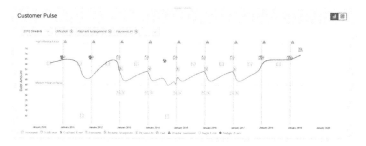

Fig. 8. Customer pulse chart before test

At-risk Customer's Overview. The task intent was to understand user's need with respect to different scenarios as they interacted with top 3 scenarios to analyze most risky customers in one view. Test result showed 4 out of 5 users could complete this task with an average of 1 assist. Average task rating was 4 out of 5.

Fig. 9. Customer pulse chart after test

Recommendation. Even though the analysis from tops 3 scenarios was appreciated, user also suggested the requirement to see the riskiest customers from all the scenarios in one view and then investigate them in different groups. This was taken as a separate dashboard application to allow the Debt Managers to proactively take collective action in a time efficient manner. Severity of this issue was recorded as high.

Content Relevancy on Customer Detail Page. The task intent was to recognize the value and need for customer's detail. Test result showed 4 out of 5 users could complete this task with an average of 3 assists. Average task rating was 4 out of 5.

Recommendation. More relevant details like 'Due date' were identified to be included at the top bar for better overview of the customer (see Fig. 10). Based on preferred hierarchy of tabs 'Events' was move as the last placed (see Fig. 11). Severity of this issue was recorded as medium.

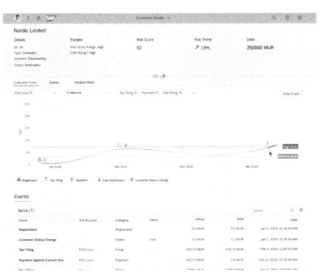

Fig. 10. Customer detail page before test

Fig. 11. Customer detail page after test

3.3 Overall Outcome

The result from the usability tests indicates that the participants were satisfied with the possibilities the application offers like Influencing Factors (AI nudge) contributions to Risk Score, Risk Trend, Visual filters, and Heat Map as ways to narrow down to the focused list of customers at risk. The most impressive aspect highlighted was the customer pulse providing one stop visualization to analyze data. The hierarchy of information from semantic trend line to the possibility of narrowing down to investigate the root cause of fluctuation helped the users to identify behavioral pattern to take proactive actions.

As the top wishes there were strong asks for providing enforcement actions for each customer to empower the debt managers to take informed decision on actions. There were also considerations to personalize the content to only show role specific allocated customers to case officers. These wishes were considered as part of future product roadmap (Fig. 12).

	Search Customer	Use of Filter	Use of Heat Map	Analyze Table	Export Customer	Navigate To Detail	Customer Details	Explore Related Risk	View Events
Participant 1	3	2	1	3	2	3	2	2	3
Participant 2	2	1	1	2	1	2	2	1	1
Participant 3	3	1	2	3	3	3	2	2	3
Participant 4	2	2	2	3	2	3	2	2	2
Participant 5	2	1	1	2	2	3	1	2	2
SUM	12	7	7	13	10	14	9	9	11

3: User can perform task quickly and with no trouble   <10: Worked as expected
2: User can perform task with probe   8 – 10: Can be enhanced
1: User can perform task, but has some struggles   >8: Needs attention

Fig. 12. Task completion matrix

4 AI-Driven Intelligent Solutions for Data Analysis and Decision Making for Tax Recovery

4.1 Explore At-Risk Customers – A Machine Learning Powered Solution with Strong Predictive Capabilities

The 'Explore At-Risk Customers' application was designed to assist the user in predicting which customers will not pay tax, or will pay late, or will run into bankruptcy. A Risk Score for each customer by scenario is generated by a machine learning algorithm, with the support of which, the Debt Manager can trigger timely reminders and plan campaigns to recover tax on time. A pulse chart is provided for each customer to help the Debt Manager analyze the tax paying behaviour and patterns of the customer. This helps the Government tax collection authorities to decrease their losses from debts through missed or delayed payments of tax. With the support of this solution, manual effort from the Debt Manager in analyzing each customer's case is also reduced, thus improving the overall efficiency of the tax collection process.

Key Features. The application can be accessed by the Debt Manager through a tile on the Fiori Launchpad. Upon selecting the tile, an analytical list page is opened (see Fig. 13).

Fig. 13. Analytical list page of the explore at-risk customers application

Visual Filter Bar. At the top of the screen, a set of visual filters in the form of bar charts can be observed. These charts display a count of the number of customers by each Scenario (Risk of Receivership, Risk of Late Payment, and Risk of Non-Filing), by Risk Score Range (High, Medium, and Low) and by Debt Range (High, Medium, and Low). Clicking of any of the bars results in all the content of the page being filtered by the selection.

Heat Map. Below the Visual Filter Bar, a heat map is provided, which plots the number of customers by Debt Range and Risk Score Range, allowing the user to gain a quick overview of the concentration of customers with respect to Debt and Risk Score Ranges. The heatmap can also act as a filter for drilling down to specific groups of customers the user wants to explore further.

Risk Score. Below the heat map is a table of all customers with their Account Name, Sub Account ID and Debt Amount provided. Each customer is also provided with a Risk Score. The risk score is calculated through a machine learning algorithm, taking into consideration several factors such as Due Amount, Status, Missed Submissions and Audit Assessment in the past, etc. It is a value between 0 to 100 that indicates the likeliness of the Customer to default on the payment of tax. The severity of the Risk Score is highlighted with semantic colours (Red, Orange, and Green) the range for which can be configured.

Risk Score Trend. A risk score trend is also provided, which indicates the net change of the Risk Score for the customer from the previous prediction run. On click, the user can also view the trend of the Risk Score over the past few predictions runs (see Fig. 14).

Fig. 14. Risk score trend popover

Customer Pulse Chart. Once the user drills down by clicking on any one of the rows of the table of Customers, a Customer Details page is opened (see Fig. 15), including a customer pulse chart of debt over time and the events that have occurred over time such as Registration, Tax Filing, Payment, etc. Events that have influenced the Risk Score are highlighted and predicted events are also displayed on click.

Robust Regression Algorithm. A robust regression algorithm with APL from the SAP HANA Predictive Analysis Library (PAL) was used in determining the Risk Scores of Customers. The data from the customers is divided into training and prediction data sets which are fed to the model to derive Risk Scores and top influencing factors for each customer with a value and a corresponding quality is assigned. Based on this, the top influencing factors are displayed to the end user.

Fig. 15. Customer details page with the customer pulse chart

Explainable AI. The Risk Score is generated by the classification algorithm robust regression based on which the users can make informed decisions on selecting tax recovery methods. When AI is used to inform decisions, the decision makers would need to understand the underlying reasons for the AI recommendation, due to which explainable AI becomes essential for users [7].

Explainable AI explains the algorithmic logic used to derive the Risk Score to the user. Several options on how to present this information to the end user in a concise manner were explored and evaluated before arriving at the final design. On clicking the Risk Score in the table, a popover is opens (see Fig. 16) displaying in a table, the Top 5 indicators that contributed to the Risk Score with their values and a contribution level. (Strong / Moderate). A high-level one-liner summary is also provided at the top of the table for the user to gain a quick insight.

Fig. 16. Explainable AI in a popover displaying top risk score indicators

4.2   At-Risk Customers Overview – A Dashboard for Tracking Customer Debts and Risk Scores

The research conducted and the regular design discussions with the end users through the design phase uncovered their need to monitor the overall tax payment and risk score trends of the customers. This would allow the Debt Managers to proactively take collective action in a time-efficient manner. To meet this need, along with the application 'Explore At-Risk Customers', which was designed for Debt Managers to monitor and study the risk score trends and debt ranges of individual customers in depth, we provided a supporting application, 'At-Risk Customers Overview.'

'At-Risk Customers Overview' is a dashboard that provides aggregated information on the total number of customers, debt amounts, risk scores, collection strategies and collection steps. The information is presented in a set of cards in the UI, each with charts that visually depict customer data, which the Debt Manager can use to gain an overview of the tax paying behaviour of the customers (see Fig. 17). The charts can be filtered based on different parameters, like scenario, tax type and date range, with the help of the filters provided. The charts are clickable, allowing the user to navigate to the 'Explore At-Risk Customers' app to view the details and to deep dive into any specific area of interest. The cards provided can also be hidden by the user in the settings if required.

The cards include Customers At-Risk, Debt Amount, Top 5 Risk Score Trends, Rising Risk Score Trend, Rising Debt Trend, Collection Analysis, Top 5 Collection Steps Trends, Top 5 Risk Reasons, High Risk Customers, Collection Strategy Trend, Customer Groups.

For the 'Customer Groups' card, machine learning with the K Means Clustering algorithm is used to identify and group customers based on predefined input parameters. Based on the grouping indicators of each cluster of customers, tax collection strategies and steps can be adopted for all the customers within the group. This saves the debt manager time and resources spent on individually analyzing the scenario, debt, and risk trends of each customer to take reformative action.

K Means Clustering. Cluster analysis is a fundamental tool used in statistical data analysis. Historically, cluster analysis has been applied for pattern recognition, information retrieval, etc. [8] The goal of clustering is to group data points and structure them into clusters within which the similarities between the data points are maximized and the similarities between data points of different clusters are minimized. K Means Clustering, being one of the simplest and most used unsupervised machine learning algorithms, can cluster large data sets efficiently, due to which it was used in the 'Customer Groups' card. The card has a scatter plot chart of Customer Groups with the Number of Customers in the x-axis and Total Customers in the y-axis. This allows the user to quickly identify the groups of customers with high debts and with many customers to prioritize for targeted tax collection strategies.

Fig. 17. At-risk customer overview application

Explainable AI. A popover with explainable AI was included for the debt manager to understand the top contributing grouping indicators and the group average of those indicators. The overall average of the indicator across all groups is also provided for reference and to gauge the customers belonging to this group and follow up on them accordingly (see Fig. 18).

Fig. 18. Explainable AI in a popover displaying top customer grouping indicators

5 Conclusion

We designed, developed, and released a Suite of SAP Fiori Enterprise Design applications for a revenue authority by following the Design Thinking Methodology. Other nations have also showed interest in adopting machine learning solutions to empower their employees with informed decisions and transform their manual business processes leading to digital maturity.

Acknowledgements. The revenue authority shared time to co-innovate, helped us with domain knowledge, anonymized sample data for training the algorithm, and providing feedback on designs. Craig Kennedy, Arun Mathew, and other engineers, data scientists from the Product Team at SAP helped shape the solution throughout the product lifecycle.

References

1. Venkataraman, R., Ghosh Kundu, S.: Preventing tax evasion of the commercial tax departments through statistical models. Adarsh J. Manage. Res. **9**(2) (2016). (ISSN 0974–7028)

2. Thoring, K., Muller, R.M.: Understand design thinking: a process model based on method engineering. In: International Conference on Engineering and Product Design Education, City University, London, UK (2011)
3. Endmann, A., Keßner, D.: User Journey Mapping – A Method in User Experience Design i-com **15**(1), 105–110(2016). https://doi.org/10.1515/icom-2016-0010
4. Hannabuss, S.: Research interviews. New Libr. World **97**(5), 22–30 (1996). https://doi.org/10.1108/03074809610122881
5. Angrosino, M.V.: Naturalistic Observation (1st ed.). Routledge (2007). https://doi.org/10.4324/9781315423616
6. Jos, N.: Formative evaluation of software usability: a case study. In: 5th International Conference on ICT Applications (AICTTRA), https://www.researchgate.net/publication/323259268_Formative_Evaluation_of_Software_Usability_A_case_study
7. Clayton, L., Rieman, J.: Task-Centered User Interface Design: A Practical Introduction, Boulder, USA (1994). http://hcibib.org/tcuid/tcuid.pdf
8. Fox, J.E.: The Science of Usability Testing, Bureau of Labor Statistics. https://nces.ed.gov/fcsm/pdf/C2_Fox_2015FCSM.pdf
9. Xu, F., Uszkoreit, H., Du, Y., Fan, W., Zhao, D., Zhu, J.: Explainable AI: a brief survey on history, research areas, approaches and challenges. In: Tang, J., Kan, M.-Y., Zhao, D., Li, S., Zan, H. (eds.) NLPCC 2019. LNCS (LNAI), vol. 11839, pp. 563–574. Springer, Cham (2019). https://doi.org/10.1007/978-3-030-32236-6_51
10. Erisoglu, M., Calis, N., Sakallioglu, S.: A new algorithm for initial cluster centers in k-means algorithm. Pattern Recogn. Lett. **32**(14), 1701–1705 (2011)

Improving Fairness via Deep Ensemble Framework Using Preprocessing Interventions

Aida Tayebi and Ozlem Ozmen Garibay[(✉)]

Department of Industrial Engineering and Management Systems,
University of Central Florida, Orlando, USA
aida.tayebi@knights.ucf.edu, ozlem@ucf.edu

Abstract. In recent years, automated decision making has grown as a consequence of wide use of machine learning models in real-world applications. Biases inherited in these algorithms might eventually result in discrimination and can significantly impact people's lives. Increased social awareness and ethical concerns in the human-centered AI community has led to responsible AI to address issues such as fairness in ML models. In this paper we propose an ensemble framework of deep learning models to improve fairness. We propose four different sampling strategies to analyze the impact of different ensemble strategies. Through experiments on two real-world datasets, we show our proposed framework achieves higher fairness than several benchmark models with minimal compromise of accuracy. Also our experiments show that a standard ensemble model without any fairness constraint does not remove bias and a proper design is necessary.

Keywords: Fairness in AI · Human-centered AI · Ensemble Learning · Explainable AI

1 Introduction

In recent decades, the use of artificial intelligence and machine learning models in real-world applications has grown, leading to automated decision making in a variety of domains such as hiring pipelines, face recognition, financial services, healthcare systems, and criminal justice. There is a common belief that these data driven approaches and automated decision making systems perform better than humans since they can handle more data and complex computations much faster. Besides, human decisions are subjective and might have biases that makes these algorithms much suitable for getting objective decisions [32], however, this idea that AI algorithms are bias free is not completely correct, since AI algorithms learn the patterns and biases inherited in the data and replicate or in some cases intensify them [33].

Bias in datasets are inevitable; they might arise from measurement bias, representation bias, selection bias, etc [35]. Bias might arise from ML algorithm itself, since the objective function of ML models aim to minimize the errors in prediction, algorithmic decision making has the potential to cause algorithmic bias toward the central population subgroup and discrimination toward the minority. A well known example is Correctional Offender Management Profiling for Alternative Sanctions (COMPAS) tool which is a recidivism risk prediction tool used by the US criminal justice system that has shown bias against African American defendants and falsely predicting re-offending twice at the rate its predicting for white race [33,34,36]. Another common example in the advertising domain is a targeted advertising shown to be biased against gender and reccomending higher paying jobs more to male than female [37,38]. Similarly in the hiring domain, a company's hiring algorithm was shown to discriminate against female candidates specially in software development positions which was due to historical bias inherited in the data [39]. Even if sensitive attributes are not directly included in the dataset, bias may still occur in the attributes correlated with sensitive attributes called proxy attributes [40,41].

These findings about fairness in AI, have increased ethical concerns since these automated decisions can significantly impact people's lives, leading to growing attention in recent years from human-centered AI research communities. Tackling these biases needs further exploration and understanding of the impact of these decision making AI systems on human and societal well-being. The AI community can benefit from novel techniques to address these biases in developing AI to incorporate human values and cultural norms into AI systems, and to allow society to regulate and control AI systems [48]. There is a growing awareness of the need for "Human-centered AI" among AI researchers that hold the viewpoint of developing and designing the AI systems with social responsibility to consider the larger system consisting of humans in mind and to address issues such as fairness, accountability, interpretability, and transparency [49]. As a consequence, there has been growing interest in the recent literature on defining, assessing, and enhancing fairness in ML algorithms [28,33,34,46,47]. The task of enhancing the fairness of ML algorithms is not simple, as there is a natural trade-off between accuracy and fairness [45].

In machine learning, ensemble methods have been successfully used in a variety of domains and have shown promising results in classification tasks particularly better performance in class imbalance cases [43,44]. The main idea behind ensemble methods is to train multiple classifiers (base/weak learners) for the same task and combine them to achieve a better performance than each individual classifier [5]. Nina et al. [4] is the first study that proposes an ensemble of unfair models can yield a fair model by averaging out the bias in these base models. The main argument they make is that even if each base model is biased, the averaged model might still be fair because the biases cancel each other out. However, their statements remain theoretical, and no experiments on real-world datasets are provided and discussion on how much fairness ensemble models can achieve is missing. Further [3,42] deploy an ensemble framework of traditional ML approaches, AdaBoost [3] and Random forest, SVM, Linear Regression, Decision Tree, KNN, and etc [42] respectively, based on Nina et al's proposed argument to improve fairness.

In this paper, we propose a deep ensemble framework to tackle the discrimination problem against minority groups and to improve fairness. Four different sampling strategies are proposed as preprocessing intervention to evaluate which strategy is more effective. In this step, we employ oversampling by generating synthetic data of the unprivileged group in favored predictions using SMOTE [26] and undersampling techniques to tackle the problems of group imbalance and class imbalance of underrepresentation of the unprivileged group by balancing the four groups in each bag of our ensemble model. We demonstrate the proposed framework achieves higher fairness than single models as well as baseline ensemble without any interventions and other state-of-the-art models through experiments on two real-world data sets. By comparing various sampling strategies, we demonstrate that ensemble models show improvement in terms of trade off between fairness and accuracy when designed properly.

The rest of the paper is organized as follows: in section two, we present related works done in the domain of fairness in AI; in section three, we present the definitions of fairness and accuracy metrics used in the comparison; in section four we present the proposed ensemble framework and different sampling strategies; experimental results are presented and discussed in section five and conclusions and future works in the last section.

2   Related Work

Fairness studies in AI focuses on eliminating unethical bias in algorithmic decision making predictions. Many approaches in this field have been proposed. They can be categorized into pre-process, in-process, and post-process. Pre-processing approaches reduce the bias through changing the input dataset before feeding it into the standard model. The bias in the input data might exist in the sensitive attribute directly or be inherited in other attributes called proxy attributes. Kamiran and Calders [2] propose methods such as suppression which include removing the sensitive attribute and its most correlated features, massaging the dataset which include detecting and correcting the unfair class labels before feeding it into model, reweighting which include assigning weights for input data, and sampling which include unified sampling and preferential sampling which remove or duplicate the data points based on a unified probability (randomly) or based on preference (closeness to borderline). Other pre-processing approaches consist of feature preprocessing meaning learning fair representations and fair features before standard model learning [13,14], other massaging methods [11,12], and other sampling methods such as over-sampling, under-sampling, and synthetic data generation like SMOTE [26] and boosting that deal with class distributions [2,9,10].

In-processing approaches modify the learning algorithm to eliminate or reduce the bias. These methods add constraint or regulating terms to objective function to penalize any bias during the learning process directly [15–17]. For example, the work in [21] proposes adding a regularization term to the objective function which penalizes mutual information [25] between the target attribute and sensitive attribute. The study proposed in [24] also utilizes the mutual information to ensure the independence between predictions and sensitive attributes. [23] proposes a method for controlling the parity and shows how demographic parity is effected through limiting the mutual information between sensitive attributes and representations. Finally, post-processing methods modify the model's predictions or decision boundary after learning the model in order to make them fair [18–20]. For example, [7] proposes a method for modifying the final classification scores to improve the equalized odds. Recently, Mehrabi and Gupta [22] propose a post-processing method that identifies each feature's contribution in the performance utilizing an attention-based framework. Most of the bias mitigating studies result in a loss in the accuracy metric, which is the trade off of having higher fairness-utility cost.

3 Background

3.1 Fairness Metrics

For the fairness in algorithmic classification problems, different definitions and metrics such as equalized odds, equal opportunity, demographic parity, etc. have been utilized [8]. *Demographic parity* also known as statistical parity, is one of the common fairness metrics utilized in the fairness literature, which is used in this paper as well. The goal of demographic parity is to ensure that the overall proportion of members in privileged group who receive a favorable decision is the same as in unprivileged group [6] or in another words, the likelihood of a favorable outcome should be the same regardless of whether the person is in the unprivileged group [8]. For the simplicity, we consider a binary classification problem with target attribute $Y \in \{1,0\}$, and one sensitive(protective) attribute $S \in \{1,0\}$ in which 1 being the favorable outcome and respectively in favor(privileged) group. For example, in a binary gender discrimination case study the value S=0 will be assigned to "Female", whereas 1 is assigned to "Male". Also, Y=1 is assigned for a favorable decision such as getting hired and Y=0 is assigned for an unfavorable decision (rejection). In such case, fairness in ideal world is defined as below [7]:

$$P(Y = 1 \mid S = 1) = P(Y = 1 \mid S = 0) \tag{1}$$

Thus discrimination or demographic parity is defined by the difference between the conditional probability and its marginal [6]. For a classifier $f : (X, S) \rightarrow Y$ the demographic parity with respect to protected attribute S, can be calculated as below:

$$DP = P(\hat{Y} = 1 \mid X, S = 1) - P(\hat{Y} = 1 \mid X, S = 0) \tag{2}$$

where $\hat{Y}$ is the predicted label by classifier f.

3.2 Accuracy Metrics

In this study, accuracy and F1 score are selected to evaluate the models. Accuracy is the overall predictive accuracy, which is the rate of accurate predicted samples to the entire number of samples. These metrics are defined as below:

$$\text{Accuracy} = P(\hat{Y} = y \mid Y = y)$$
$$\text{F1-Score} = \frac{2 * \text{Precision} * \text{Recall}}{\text{Precision} + \text{Recall}} \tag{3}$$

where in this definition recall is the true positive rate, which is the rate of accurate prediction when Y is positive. Precision shows the percentage of accurate positive predictions to all positive predictions and are calculated as below:

$$\text{Recall} = P(\hat{Y} = 1 \mid Y = 1)$$
$$\text{Precision} = P(Y = 1 \mid \hat{Y} = 1) \tag{4}$$

4 Methodology

4.1 Proposed Fair Ensemble Framework

The ensemble learning approach comprises training multiple base models(weak learner) for the same task and combining them to form a more accurate model [5]. There are different methods to ensemble base learners. Bagging and boosting are the two common approaches. Bagging (bootstrap aggregation) is an approach in which base models are homogeneous in structure and vary in training data. All the base models are then combined and averaged to form a strong model [5]. Boosting on the other hand, is another approach where each model is trained in order and sequentially based on previous model's error and then these models are averaged in a weighted fashion [3].

As mentioned earlier Nina et al. [4] is the first study that argues ensemble of unfair models can obtain a fair model since bias in these base models can be averaged out. Their main point is that even if each base model is biased, the averaged model may be fair because the biases cancel each other out. Similar to [3] an example is provided below to demonstrate this argument:

Lets consider the task of machine learning to be predicting whether to hire a person or not. The fairness goal in such situation is to remove gender bias in prediction. Suppose f_1, f_2 are two bias base models that f_1 is biased against female and f_2 is biased against male. The probability of a person to be predicted as hired by f_1 model is:

$$p_{1male} = P(Class = + \mid S = Male, f_1) = 0.5$$
$$p_{1female} = P(Class = + \mid S = Female, f_1) = 0.1 \tag{5}$$

The demographic parity of f_1 is:

$$DP_{f_1} = p_{1male} - p_{1female} = 0.4 \qquad (6)$$

Similarly the demographic parity of the f_2 is:

$$p_{2male} = P(Class = + \mid S = Male, f_2) = 0.1$$
$$p_{2female} = P(Class = + \mid S = Female, f_2) = 0.5 \qquad (7)$$
$$DP_{f_2} = p_{2male} - p_{2female} = -0.4$$

Now lets consider an ensemble model that takes the average vote of the model f_1 and f_2:

$$p_{male} = \frac{p_{1male} + p_{2male}}{2} = 0.3$$
$$p_{female} = \frac{p_{1female} + p_{2female}}{2} = 0.3 \qquad (8)$$
$$DP_f = p_{male} - p_{female} = 0.3 - 0.3 = 0$$

We can see how these two unfair base model can cancel out each other biases and form a fair ensemble model. Nina et al's arguments, however, remain theoretical, and no experiments is presented. Furthermore, their arguments provides no discussion of which ensemble strategy is more effective for learning a fair model. In this paper, we propose an ensemble model that achieves higher fairness than several baseline methods on real-world data sets. The proposed fair ensemble framework is summarized in Algorithm 1. The sampling strategies are summarized in the schematic diagram Fig. 1 and are described in the next section.

Algorithm 1. Pseudocode of Proposed Startegy

Input:
Training Set(M)
Number of Base Learners in Ensemble Model (t)
Output:
 Ensemble Model f
for $i = 1, ..., t$ **do**
1: Extract group A, B, C, D from training set(M)
2: Generate sample A', B', C', D' wrt sampling strategy
3: Bag $M' = A' \cup B' \cup C' \cup D'$
4: Train an MLP classifier f_i upon M_i
end for
Return:
Ensemble Model $f = \frac{1}{t} \sum_{t=1}^{t} f_i$

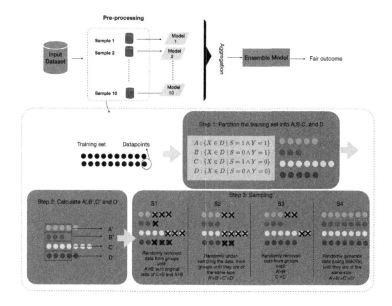

Fig. 1. The schematic diagram of fair ensemble framework

4.2   Sampling

As mentioned earlier, we consider a binary classification problem with target attribute $Y \in \{1,0\}$, and one sensitive(protective) attribute $S \in \{1,0\}$. Then the dataset is divided to four groups, PP: Privileged group with Positive class label, UP: Unprivileged group with Positive class label, PN: Privileged group with Negative class label, UN: Unprivileged group with Negative class label which are defined as follows:

$$
\begin{aligned}
PP &: \{X \in D \mid S = 1 \wedge Y = 1\} \\
UP &: \{X \in D \mid S = 0 \wedge Y = 1\} \\
PN &: \{X \in D \mid S = 1 \wedge Y = 0\} \\
UN &: \{X \in D \mid S = 0 \wedge Y = 0\}
\end{aligned}
\tag{9}
$$

The number of training points in these four groups are represented by A, B, C, and D, respectively. Then four sampling strategies are proposed to generate four different bags of A', B', C', and D'.

S1: In this strategy the criteria is to remove randomly from A, B w.r.t ratio of $A + B$ (the number of positive class in the original training dataset to total dataset) and the ratio of $C + D$ (the number of negative class in the original training dataset to total dataset) being fixed, until they are of the same size $A' = B'$. For example in the Adult dataset, 24 % of the datapoints are related to rich group($income \geqslant 50k$) and A=1179, B=6662, C=15127, D=9592. To have a sample with $A' = B'$ and to keep the ratio of $A + B$ and $C + D$ fixed we have to randomly sample A'=1179, B'=1179 and C'+D'=7467.

S2: In this strategy the criteria is to remove randomly from A, B, C, D until they are of the same size $A' = B' = C' = D'$. The expected number of A', B', C', D' are based on the size of the group with least training points($argmin(A, B, C, D)$). This sampling strategy is considered uniform sampling meaning that each data point has the same chance to be removed. As the goal of the study is to remove the bias from predictions, the expected data distribution in bags should be:

$$P(S = 1) = P(S = 0) = 0.5 \qquad P(Y = 1) = P(Y = 0) = 0.5 \qquad (10)$$

where P is the expected possibility of one point belonging to a specific group. If we want S and Y to be statistically independent, then:

$$P(Y = y \mid S = s) = P(Y = y) \times P(S = s) = 0.25 \qquad (11)$$

meaning that the expected number of points are equal and are 0.25 % of the total new bag M'.

S3: In this strategy the criteria is to remove randomly from A, B until they are of the same size $A' = B'$. Similarly remove randomly from C, D until $C' = D'$.

S4: This strategy is similar to S2. The only difference is that the datapoints are randomly generated from A, B, C, D using SMOTE(Synthetic Minority Oversampling Technique) [26] until they are of the same size $A' = B' = C' = D'$. The expected number of A', B', C', D' are based on the size of the group with most training points($argmax(A, B, C, D)$).

5   Experiments

5.1   Datasets

In our experiments we used two benchmark dataset utilized in the fairness related literature namely Adult and German Credit.

Adult. The Adult dataset (also known as Census Income dataset) available in the UCI ML repository [1], contains 48,842 instances with associate demographic information of them in which the task is to predict whether a person have income of over 50K per year or not. Each instance contains 14 attribute, 8 of them being categorical and 6 numerical. As suggested in [2], attribute fnlwgt is excluded from the dataset. We used Gender which is coded as binary, as sensitive/protected attribute with Gender=Male being the privileged group. As suggested by [29], categorical features are encoded into numbers using one-hot encoder and the numerical features are transformed using standard-scaling. The repository itself provides separate training set with 32,560 instances and testing set with 16,281 instances. The demographic parity of the whole dataset is:

$$P(Class = + \mid S = Male) - P(Class = + \mid S = Female) = 19.46\% \quad (12)$$

German Credit. The German Credit dataset available in the UCI ML repository [1], contains 1000 instances of individuals who requested credit from a bank. Each record contains 20 attribute (13 categorical and 7 numerical) and the prediction task is whether that person was good or bad in repaying their loan. We used Age as a sensitive attribute. As suggested by [28] the age attribute is binarized into two values older/younger with Age=Older being the privileged group. The threshold (25 years old) is based on analysis provided by [27] showing that this has the most discriminatory possibilities. We randomly chose 90 percent of the data for training and used the rest for testing.

On each dataset, we performed 5 trials for each experiment and reported the average performance.

5.2   Results and Discussion

Experimental results from all examined methods on two data sets are shown in Table 1. As a baseline, we trained an ensemble model without any preprocessing intervention on the original datasets. We see all the proposed sampling strategies achieved lower demographic parity compared to the original baseline ensemble model without any intervention, suggesting its improvement in learning fair models. We also observe that the compromise of accuracy to achieve better fairness in ensemble+S1, ensemble+S3, and ensemble+S4 is less than 1 % which shows better trade-off of accuracy and fairness. These results suggest that ensemble learning can improve fairness through appropriate sampling strategies. Our ensemble framework gives the best results regarding the lowest demographic parity in ensemble+S3 for both datasets. We choose this model to compare our results with other studies in the fairness domain in Table 2. We report these results as presented in their original publications. We present prior results for Fair Naive-Bayes denoted as FNB [27], Regularized Logistic Regression denoted as RLR [51], Variation Fair Auto-Encoders denoted as VFAE [52][1], and Ethical Adversaries denoted as EA [31]. As we can observe among five models, our ensemble+S3 framework gives the best results in terms of highest accuracy and lowest demographic parity in the Adult dataset. On the German dataset, compared to FNB and VFAE our ensemble+S3 framework achieves higher accuracy and lower demographic parity. Compared to RLR and EA, ensemble+S3 framework shows comparable demographic parity with less compromise in accuracy and F1 score, respectively.

---

[1] The scores of this paper was extracted and presented in [50].

Table 1. Classification results of four ensemble models on Adult and German datasets, where the protected attribute is gender and age, respectively, are compared with a base ensemble method without any fairness intervention.

	Adult			German		
	F1 score↑	Accuracy↑	$|DP|$ ↓	F1 score↑	Accuracy↑	$|DP|$ ↓
Base Ensemble	0.6529 ± 0.0092	0.8376 ± 0.0015	0.1811 ± 0.0093	0.8046 ± 0.0250	0.7260 ± 0.0324	0.2575 ± 0.0827
Ensemble+S1	0.6073 ± 0.0058	0.8330 ± 0.0017	0.0321 ± 0.0029	0.7994 ± 0.0189	0.7133 ± 0.0153	0.1389 ± 0.0439
Ensemble+S2	0.6666 ± 0.0011	0.8121 ± 0.0011	0.1673 ± 0.0055	0.7609 ± 0.0043	0.6900 ± 0.0000	0.1155 ± 0.0500
Ensemble+S3	0.4928 ± 0.0150	0.8307 ± 0.0024	0.00249 ± 0.0057	0.7953 ± 0.0292	0.7233 ± 0.0306	0.0384 ± 0.0461
Ensemble+S4	0.6680 ± 0.00140	0.8324 ± 0.0015	0.0077 ± 0.0108	0.7971 ± 0.0480	0.7200 ± 0.1033	0.0799 ± 0.0174

Table 2. Performance of various prior works with our best model. Best results are shown in bold.

	Adult			German		
	F1 score↑	Accuracy↑	$|DP|$ ↓	F1 score↑	Accuracy↑	$|DP|$ ↓
Ensemble+S3	0.4928 ± 0.0150	**0.8307 ± 0.0024**	**0.00249 ± 0.0057**	**0.7953 ± 0.0292**	0.7233 ± 0.0306	0.0384 ± 0.0461
FNB [27]	–	0.7847	0.0136	–	0.6888	0.0574
RLR [51]	–	0.6758	0.0264	–	0.5953	0.0111
VFAE [52]	–	0.8129	0.0708	–	0.7270	0.0430
EA [31]	**0.689**	0.814 ± 0.009	0.031	0.640	**0.730 ± 0.062**	**0.006**

6 Conclusion

In this paper, we propose a deep ensemble framework over two different real world datasets. We considered four different sampling strategies to make four ensemble models on top of ten multi layer perceptrons with different training bags and studied the impact of different sampling strategies on fairness. Results show that all the sampling strategies improved fairness and reduced the demographic parity compared to an ensemble model without any interventions. Our ensemble framework allows us to reduce biases of machine learning while maintaining certain accuracy compared to individual classifiers and also the baseline ensemble model without fairness constraint. These findings imply that standard ensemble strategies do not remove biases solely and for learning fair models, ensemble models should be designed properly. Improving fairness in machine learning models with low trade-off in accuracy is an on-going research and future work may benefit from combining ensemble learning with other deep learning models.

References

1. Dua, D., Graff, C.: UCI machine learning repository. (University of California, Irvine, School of Information, 2017). http://archive.ics.uci.edu/ml
2. Kamiran, F., Calders, T.: Data preprocessing techniques for classification without discrimination. Knowl. Inf. Syst. **33**, 1–33 (2012)
3. Bhaskaruni, D., Hu, H., Lan, C.: Improving prediction fairness via model ensemble. In: 2019 IEEE 31st International Conference On Tools With Artificial Intelligence (ICTAI), pp. 1810–1814 (2019)

4. Grgić-Hlača, N., Zafar, M., Gummadi, K., Weller, A.: On fairness, diversity and randomness in algorithmic decision making. ArXiv Preprint ArXiv:1706.10208 (2017)
5. Tayebi, A., et al.: UnbiasedDTI: mitigating real-world bias of drug-target interaction prediction by using deep ensemble-balanced learning. Molecules **27**, 2980 (2022)
6. Rajabi, A., Garibay, O.: Tabfairgan: fair tabular data generation with generative adversarial networks. Mach. Learn. Knowl. Extract. **4**, 488–501 (2022)
7. Hardt, M., Price, E., Srebro, N.: Equality of opportunity in supervised learning. In: Advances in Neural Information Processing Systems, vol. 29 (2016)
8. Verma, S., Rubin, J.: Fairness definitions explained. 2018 IEEE/ACM International Workshop On Software Fairness (fairware), pp. 1–7 (2018)
9. Calmon, F., Wei, D., Vinzamuri, B., Natesan Ramamurthy, K., Varshney, K.: Optimized pre-processing for discrimination prevention. In: Advances In Neural Information Processing Systems, vol. 30 (2017)
10. Iosifidis, V., Ntoutsi, E.: Dealing with bias via data augmentation in supervised learning scenarios. Jo Bates Paul D. Clough Robert Jäschke. 24 (2018)
11. Zhang, L., Wu, X.: Anti-discrimination learning: a causal modeling-based framework. Int. J. Data Sci. Anal. **4**(1), 1–16 (2017). https://doi.org/10.1007/s41060-017-0058-x
12. Luong, B., Ruggieri, S., Turini, F.: k-NN as an implementation of situation testing for discrimination discovery and prevention. In: Proceedings of the 17th ACM SIGKDD International Conference On Knowledge Discovery And Data Mining, pp. 502–510 (2011)
13. Feldman, M., Friedler, S., Moeller, J., Scheidegger, C., Venkatasubramanian, S.: Certifying and removing disparate impact. In: Proceedings of the 21th ACM SIGKDD International Conference On Knowledge Discovery and Data Mining, pp. 259–268 (2015)
14. Zemel, R., Wu, Y., Swersky, K., Pitassi, T., Dwork, C.: Learning fair representations. International Conference On Machine Learning, pp. 325–333 (2013)
15. Zafar, M., Valera, I., Gomez Rodriguez, M., Gummadi, K.: Fairness beyond disparate treatment & disparate impact: learning classification without disparate mistreatment. In: Proceedings of the 26th International Conference On World Wide Web, pp. 1171–1180 (2017)
16. Dwork, C., Hardt, M., Pitassi, T., Reingold, O., Zemel, R.: Fairness through awareness. In: Proceedings of the 3rd Innovations in Theoretical Computer Science Conference, pp. 214–226 (2012)
17. Zafar, M., Valera, I., Rogriguez, M., Gummadi, K.: Fairness constraints: mechanisms for fair classification. Artif. Intell. Statist., 962–970 (2017)
18. Kamiran, F., Calders, T., Pechenizkiy, M. Discrimination aware decision tree learning. In: 2010 IEEE International Conference On Data Mining, 869–874 (2010)
19. Fish, B., Kun, J., Lelkes, Á.: A confidence-based approach for balancing fairness and accuracy. In: Proceedings of the 2016 SIAM International Conference On Data Mining, pp. 144–152 (2016)
20. Pedreschi, D., Ruggieri, S., Turini, F.: Measuring discrimination in socially-sensitive decision records. In: Proceedings of the 2009 SIAM International Conference On Data Mining, pp. 581–592 (2009)
21. Kamishima, T., Akaho, S., Asoh, H., Sakuma, J.: Fairness-aware classifier with prejudice remover regularizer. In: Joint European Conference On Machine Learning And Knowledge Discovery In Databases, pp. 35–50 (2012)

22. Mehrabi, N., Gupta, U., Morstatter, F., Steeg, G., Galstyan, A.: Attributing fair decisions with attention interventions. ArXiv Preprint ArXiv:2109.03952 (2021)
23. Gupta, U., Ferber, A., Dilkina, B., Ver Steeg, G.: Controllable guarantees for fair outcomes via contrastive information estimation. In: Proceedings of the AAAI Conference On Artificial Intelligence, vol. 35, pp. 7610–7619 (2021)
24. Moyer, D., Gao, S., Brekelmans, R., Galstyan, A., Ver Steeg, G. Invariant representations without adversarial training. In: Advances in Neural Information Processing Systems, vol. 31 (2018)
25. Kraskov, A., Stögbauer, H., Grassberger, P.: Estimating mutual information. Phys. Rev. E **69**, 066138 (2004)
26. Chawla, N., Bowyer, K., Hall, L., Kegelmeyer, W.: SMOTE: synthetic minority over-sampling technique. J. Artif. Intell. Res. **16**, 321–357 (2002)
27. Kamiran, F., Calders, T.: Classifying without discriminating. In: 2009 2nd International Conference On Computer, Control and Communication, pp. 1–6 (2009)
28. Friedler, S., Scheidegger, C., Venkatasubramanian, S., Choudhary, S., Hamilton, E., Roth, D.: A comparative study of fairness-enhancing interventions in machine learning. In: Proceedings of the Conference on Fairness, Accountability, and Transparency, pp. 329–338 (2019)
29. Yang, K., Huang, B., Stoyanovich, J., Schelter, S.: Fairness-aware instrumentation of preprocessing undefined pipelines for machine learning. Workshop On Human-In-the-Loop Data Analytics (HILDA'20) (2020)
30. Zhou, Y., Kantarcioglu, M., Clifton, C.: Improving fairness of AI systems with lossless de-biasing. ArXiv Preprint ArXiv:2105.04534 (2021)
31. Delobelle, P., Temple, P., Perrouin, G., Frénay, B., Heymans, P., Berendt, B.: Ethical adversaries: towards mitigating unfairness with adversarial machine learning. ACM SIGKDD Explor. Newslett. **23**, 32–41 (2021)
32. Pessach, D., Shmueli, E.: Improving fairness of artificial intelligence algorithms in privileged-group selection bias data settings. Expert Syst. Appl. **185**, 115667 (2021)
33. Pessach, D., Shmueli, E.: A review on fairness in machine learning. ACM Comput. Surv. (CSUR) **55**, 1–44 (2022)
34. Chouldechova, A.: Fair prediction with disparate impact: a study of bias in recidivism prediction instruments. Big Data **5**, 153–163 (2017)
35. Mehrabi, N., Morstatter, F., Saxena, N., Lerman, K., Galstyan, A.: A survey on bias and fairness in machine learning. ACM Comput. Surv. (CSUR) **54**, 1–35 (2021)
36. Angwin, J., Larson, J., Mattu, S., Kirchner, L.: Machine bias. Ethics Of Data And Analytics, pp. 254–264 (2016)
37. Lambrecht, A., Tucker, C.: Algorithmic bias? An empirical study of apparent gender-based discrimination in the display of STEM career ads. Manage. Sci. **65**, 2966–2981 (2019)
38. Datta, A., Tschantz, M., Datta, A.: Automated experiments on ad privacy settings: a tale of opacity, choice, and discrimination. ArXiv Preprint ArXiv:1408.6491 (2014)
39. Dastin, J.: Amazon scraps secret AI recruiting tool that showed bias against women. Ethics Of Data And Analytics, pp. 296–299 (2018)
40. Barocas, S., Selbst, A.: Big data's disparate impact. California Law Review, pp. 671–732 (2016)
41. Pessach, D., Shmueli, E.: Algorithmic fairness. ArXiv Preprint ArXiv:2001.09784 (2020)

42. Kenfack, P., Khan, A., Kazmi, S., Hussain, R., Oracevic, A., Khattak, A.: Impact of model ensemble on the fairness of classifiers in machine learning. In: 2021 International Conference On Applied Artificial Intelligence (ICAPAI), pp. 1–6 (2021)
43. Sagi, O.: Rokach, L.: Ensemble learning: a survey. Wiley Interdisc. Rev.: Data Mining Knowl. Discov. **8**, e1249 (2018)
44. Galar, M., Fernandez, A., Barrenechea, E., Bustince, H., Herrera, F.: A review on ensembles for the class imbalance problem: bagging-, boosting-, and hybrid-based approaches. In: IEEE Trans. Syst. Man Cybernet., Part C (Applications And Reviews) **42**, 463–484 (2011)
45. Kleinberg, J., Mullainathan, S., Raghavan, M.: Inherent trade-offs in the fair determination of risk scores. ArXiv Preprint ArXiv:1609.05807 (2016)
46. Berk, R., Heidari, H., Jabbari, S., Kearns, M., Roth, A.: Fairness in criminal justice risk assessments: the state of the art. Sociol. Methods Res. **50**, 3–44 (2021)
47. Holstein, K., Wortman Vaughan, J., Daumé III, H., Dudik, M., Wallach, H.: Improving fairness in machine learning systems: what do industry practitioners need?. In: Proceedings of the 2019 CHI Conference On Human Factors in Computing Systems, pp. 1–16 (2019)
48. Lee, M., et al.: Human-centered approaches to fair and responsible AI. Extended Abstracts of the 2020 CHI Conference on Human Factors in Computing Systems, pp. 1–8 (2020)
49. Riedl, M.: Human-centered artificial intelligence and machine learning. Hum Behav. Emerg. Technol. **1**, 33–36 (2019)
50. Raff, E., Sylvester, J.: Gradient reversal against discrimination: a fair neural network learning approach. In: 2018 IEEE 5th International Conference On Data Science and Advanced Analytics (DSAA), pp. 189–198 (2018)
51. Kamishima, T., Akaho, S., Sakuma, J.: Fairness-aware learning through regularization approach. In: 2011 IEEE 11th International Conference On Data Mining Workshops, pp. 643–650 (2011)
52. Louizos, C., Swersky, K., Li, Y., Welling, M., Zemel, R.: The variational fair autoencoder. ArXiv Preprint ArXiv:1511.00830 (2015)

AI-Supported User Experience Design

TextureAda: Deep 3D Texture Transfer for Ideation in Product Design Conceptualization

Rgee Wharlo Gallega[1]() , Arnulfo Azcarraga[2], and Yasuyuki Sumi[1]

[1] Future University Hakodate, Hakodate 041-8655, Hokkaido, Japan
r-gallega@sumilab.org
[2] De La Salle University, 922 Manila, Metro Manila, Philippines

Abstract. In the product design life-cycle, the conceptual design stage is an important and time-consuming phase where designers ideate in the form of sketches and 3D renderings of a product. Specifically, with 3D renderings, the choice of material texture and color is an important aspect that is often critiqued by designers because it impacts the product's visual aesthetic and the impression it evokes in the customer when first viewing the product; thus, making material selection and the conceptual design stage, overall, challenging. In this study, we turn to deep texture synthesis for generating material textures and propose a novel method, TextureAda. TextureAda creates high-fidelity textures by performing adaptive instance normalization between multiple layers of a texture generator and a pre-trained image encoder. Our experiments show that our method beats previous methods in texture synthesis visually and quantitatively. Lastly, we show how TextureAda can be applied for ideation in product design conceptualization by material texturing 3D models of furniture.

Keywords: Texture synthesis · Texture transfer · Product design

1 Introduction

Product design deals with developing physical items like furniture and electronic appliances to address specific customer needs and improve quality of life. In order to conceptualize, create, and sell a product, product designers undergo the following stages [26]: research, brief specification, conceptual design, design development, detailed design, and production, as in Fig. 1. Notably, in the conceptual design stage, designers ideate product designs in the form of 3D renderings where they are critiqued based on many aspects, especially in material choice. The material's texture and color are driving factors of the product's personality which comprises its aesthetics, associations with certain concepts, and perceptions evoked by the customer [1]. Choosing the right colors and material textures is critical in product design, and exploring alternatives can be time-consuming for designers. As a result, design critique sessions can iterate for days

H. Degen and S. Ntoa (Eds.): HCII 2023, LNAI 14050, pp. 493–505, 2023.
https://doi.org/10.1007/978-3-031-35891-3_30

or even weeks until the product's 3D rendering reaches a desirable look, making design conceptualization a challenging process.

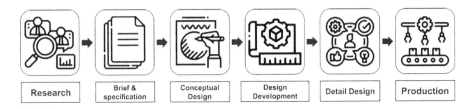

| Research | Brief & specification | Conceptual Design | Design Development | Detail Design | Production |

Fig. 1. The product design life-cycle and its stages from Rodgers & Milton [26].

In generative artificial intelligence, texture synthesis has been a longstanding task of creating image textures from real-life exemplars using deep generative models. Previous works train decoders that generate a single texture [12,13, 28,35,38] or a wide variety of textures [2,22,23,31,32] in a single feed-forward pass. Other studies take a step further in applying generated textures onto 3D objects by inputting exemplar object images [14,27,40,43] or textual descriptions [16,17,25].

In this study, we propose to leverage deep texture synthesis and traditional 3D rendering for material texturing parts of 3D models during product design conceptualization. Building on previous deep texture synthesis methods, we introduce TextureAda, a generative model that performs adaptive instance normalization [15] from multiple layers of a pre-trained VGG-19 [36] feature extractor onto multiple layers of a modified Texture Net [38] to synthesize high-fidelity textures. Results from our experiment in texture synthesis, show that TextureAda beats previous methods visually and quantitatively based on Single Frechet Inception Distance (SIFID) [11,35]. Furthermore, we show its application in the material texturing of 3D furniture for product design conceptualization. Overall, the main contributions of this study are (1) TextureAda, a novel deep generative model for texture synthesis and material texturing of 3D models, and (2) results of a quantitative study where TextureAda outperforms previous methods in texture synthesis based on SIFID.

2   Generative AI for Texture Synthesis and Transfer

2.1   Texture Synthesis

Texture synthesis is the task of inferring image textures or patterns based on real-world examples. Pioneering studies proposed non-parametric methods in texture generation by predicting neighboring pixels [9,41] or texture patches [8,21] from a given sample of exemplar pixels. With the advent of deep learning, many studies have used neural networks to synthesize textures. Based on neural style transfer, the early work of Gatys et al. [10] optimizes a noise image on exemplar texture image features from a pre-trained VGG-19 [36] that are represented as Gram matrices. Subsequent works train decoders on texture images for rapid generation [12,13,28,35,38]. Rather than optimizing an image, Ulyanov et al. [38] propose Texture Net, a convolutional generator trained on an exemplar texture in order to generate texture variants in a single feed-forward pass. Similarly, Shaham et al. [35] utilize generative adversarial networks (GANs) to create images including textures by learning on a single example. Recently, the works of Houdard et al. [12,13] use optimal transport from local exemplar texture patches for detailed texture synthesis, and demonstrate applying this technique on both optimizing a noise image and training a generative model. On the other hand, Mordvintsev et al. [28] rely on neural cellular automata for high-fidelity texture generation.

Other studies have proposed deep generative models to synthesize multiple types of textures [2,22,23,31,32]. For instance, PSGAN [2] is an extension of GAN that can generate different types of image textures, and interpolate between samples. Lin et al. [23] uses a similar approach by building on top of StyleGAN-2 and integrating a texton broadcasting module for a more accurate and broader synthesis of textures. Lately, several works have introduced text-to-image models [31–33] that are trained on large image datasets [34], allowing near-universal texture synthesis by simply inputting text. With textures synthesis having advanced over the past several years, this study investigates how these methods can be integrated into material texture synthesis for product design conceptualization.

2.2   3D Texture Transfer

There has also been a line of research that deals with synthesizing and applying textures to 3D shapes by inputting images [14,27,40], 3D shapes [43], or text [6,16,17,25]. Initial studies [3,40] develop pipelines to extract texture patches from input images of objects and map them onto untextured 3D models. Using neural networks, other studies propose differentiable renderers [5,19,24] that have demonstrated 3D texture transfer from a single image of an object while also reshaping the 3D model accordingly. Similarly, 3DStyleNet [43] trains two neural networks to transfer textures from a source 3D model to a target model, while also reshaping the target. With a focus on furniture, Hu et al. [14] devise a pipeline of neural networks that are trained to semantically transfer material textures from an image onto corresponding parts of a 3D model. Studies that focus on interior scenes enable transferring materials from an interior image to a 3D room [42] and between 3D interior scenes [29].

With the introduction of CLIP [30], there has also been an emergence of methods for texturing 3D objects using textual descriptions. ClipMatrix [16] textures an SMPL 3D model according to a text prompt by using differentiable rendering and minimizing a loss between the embeddings of the 3D rendering image and the input text. Succeeding works like Text2Mesh [25] and TANGO [6] also utilize differentiable rendering to texture 3D meshes while also adjusting their topology to match the input description. The work of Jin et al. [17]

performs semantic style transfer onto 3D indoor scenes by also using natural language. Despite these methods being able to perform language-guided texture transfer, most of them use differentiable rendering which is time-consuming and unsuitable for quick ideation during product design conceptualization.

3   TextureAda

We adopt a novel texture synthesis method called TextureAda, which uses a modified Texture Net [38] generator and a pre-trained VGG-19 [36] encoder. TextureAda also involves another technique: adaptive instance normalization (AdaIN). Adaptive instance normalization was proposed by Huang et al. [15] for style transfer in order to transfer styles from an arbitrary number of image sources in real-time. This is done by normalizing the intermediate features of an image generator according to the features of a style image that is encoded using the VGG-19. While the study of Huang et al. [15] performs AdaIN at a single layer of their generator, in this study, AdaIN is performed several times at multiple layers of Texture Net in order to create higher-fidelity image textures.

3.1   Network Architecture

TextureAda uses a Texture Net generator and VGG-19 encoder for texture synthesis, where their architectures are shown in Fig. 2.

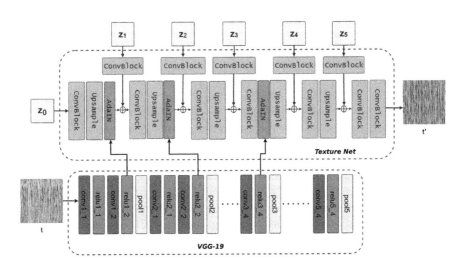

Fig. 2. Overview of TextureAda. TextureAda uses the Texture Net architecture and performs adaptive instance normalization from multiple layers of a pre-trained VGG-19.

The inputs to TextureAda are a tensor Z, which contains noise images z_0 to z_n, and a reference texture image t. t is inputted into the VGG-19 to encode its features, and the noise images of Z are sequentially inputted into Texture Net. We use 6 noise images as the generator's input and set the largest noise image of Z to 256 square pixels. AdaIN is then performed between the intermediate features of Texture Net and the extracted features from VGG-19. AdaIN is calculated using the following equation,

$$x' = \sigma(y) \left(\frac{x - \mu(x)}{\sigma(x)} \right) + \mu(y) \tag{1}$$

where x represents the intermediate features in TextureAda at a certain layer, y represents the features of texture t extracted using VGG-19 at a certain layer, and x' represents the outputted intermediate features after the operation. μ and σ calculate the mean and standard deviation, respectively. Specifically, we use the features from VGG-19 layers 'relu1_2', 'relu2_2', and 'relu3_4'. The output to TextureAda is a generated image texture t' that aims to resemble reference texture t.

In order to perform multiple AdaIN operations, the following modifications are made to the Texture Net architecture:

- All instance normalization layers are removed.
- AdaIN is performed after each upsampling block or convolutional block in Texture Net.
- For all convolutional blocks, the number of hidden features is increased from multiples of 8 to multiples of 64.

3.2   Training Details and Implementation

TextureAda is trained for 500 epochs using the Adam optimizer [20] at a fixed learning rate of $1e-4$. The covariance matrix loss [39] is used as the training loss function. In calculating the loss, we utilize the pre-trained VGG-19 to extract the features of both the real and generated image textures at layers 'relu1_2', 'relu2_2', 'relu3_4', and 'relu4_4'. The system was implemented using the PyTorch deep learning library.

4   Experiments

We evaluate TextureAda based on its performance in texture synthesis with previous methods and show how it can be applied in the material texturing of 3D models of products during design conceptualization. For texture synthesis, TextureAda was compared with the following benchmarks: Texture Nets [38], the feed-forward style transfer network [18], and the vanilla AdaIN network [15].

All texture synthesis methods were tested on two datasets: a dataset of textures of furniture and a subset of the Describable Textures Dataset [7]. The furniture textures dataset (FTD) is comprised of 35 material texture images that were segmented from images of furniture scraped from the internet. The entire Describable Textures Dataset (DTD) [7] comprises 5640 in-the-wild texture images across 47 categories. However, for this experiment, we only used categories that contain material textures such as the "braided" and "woven" categories, and removed duplicates and images that were not material textures (e.g., faces). The DTD subset that was used in this experiment contains 319 texture images across 17 categories. All images were resized to 256×256 pixels. The other benchmark methods were trained using their respective configurations.

To quantitatively compare the quality of the generated textures, the Single Image Frechet Inception Distance (SIFID) metric [11,35] is used. SIFID measures the similarity between the features of a generated image texture and real image texture that are encoded using the Inception Network [37].

Lastly, we propose applying texture synthesis methods such as TextureAda in texturing 3D models for product design conceptualization. For the scenario of choosing materials for furniture design, we transferred TextureAda's generated textures onto 3D models of chairs and tables from ShapeNet [4]. All chair and table models were manually segmented by their parts. The Blender API was used in applying the textures and rendering the 3D models.

5   Results and Discussion

For evaluating TextureAda with other benchmarks on texture synthesis, we show visual comparisons of their generated textures and also their average SIFID scores. For the furniture textures dataset, a sample of the texture images is in Fig. 3. Visually, the textures from our proposed method, TextureAda, resemble much more closely to the ground truth textures in comparison to the other methods and are of higher fidelity. For instance, in row 1 of Fig. 3, the textures of the vanilla Texture Net and AdaIN network contain discolorations while the texture of our method does not. Additionally, in row 4, the textures of both the Texture Net and AdaIN network exhibit blurs in some regions, while our method's texture does not. The textures created by the Feedforward Style Transfer network do not show any visual artifacts, our method creates much more detailed textures. It is also worth mentioning that TextureAda does not exactly copy the ground truth textures, yet is able to capture their patterns and styles.

For the DTD subset, we present a visual comparison of generated textures in Figs. 4 and 5. All methods can perform texture synthesis on non-stochastic textures. Interestingly in Fig. 5, for textures that repeat by larger image patches such as in rows 2 and 3, and the non-stochastic texture in row 4, our method is shown to learn local patterns and repeat them, whereas the other methods are not able to. However, some textures from TextureAda exhibit artifacts such as color jitters on rows 1, 2, and 4, and also lines on row 3; thus, there can be room for improvement in TextureAda.

We also present the SIFID scores for texture synthesis on both the furniture textures dataset and Describable Textures Dataset in Tables 1 and 2, respectively. Our method outperforms all previous methods based on the average SIFID of all generated textures from both datasets.

Lastly, to show the application of our method in material texturing for product design conceptualization, we semantically apply the generated textures of

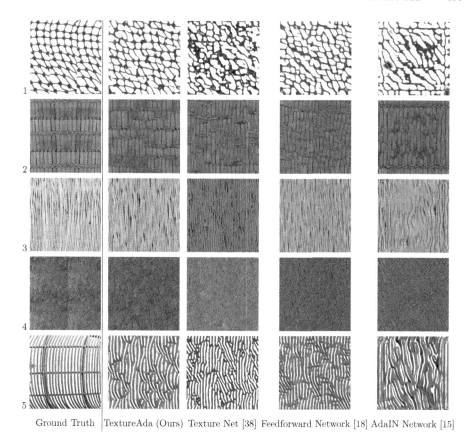

Ground Truth | TextureAda (Ours) Texture Net [38] Feedforward Network [18] AdaIN Network [15]

Fig. 3. Visual comparisons of generated textures from the furniture images dataset between our method and previous deep texture synthesis methods.

Table 1. Texture synthesis performance comparisons on the furniture images dataset based on average SIFID. The bolded value indicates the method with the lowest score which indicates a higher similarity to the ground truth texture.

Deep Texture Synthesis Method	Average SIFID
TextureAda (Ours)	**0.00009**
Texture Net [38]	0.16270
Feedforward Network [18]	0.00014
AdaIN Network [15]	0.20840

TextureAda from the furniture images dataset onto chairs and tables from the ShapeNet dataset. Figures 6 and 7 show combinations of similar and drastically different textures mapped onto parts of different types of chairs, respectively.

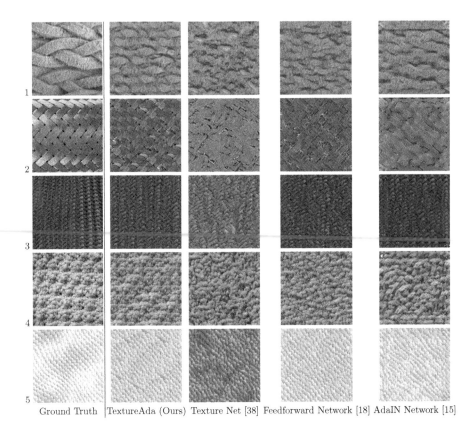

Ground Truth |TextureAda (Ours) Texture Net [38] Feedforward Network [18] AdaIN Network [15]

Fig. 4. Visual comparisons of generated textures from the subset of the Describable Textures Dataset between our method and previous deep texture synthesis methods. The textures shown are from the "braided" and "bumpy" categories.

Table 2. Texture synthesis performance comparisons on the subset of the Describable Textures Dataset [7] based on average SIFID. The bolded value indicates the method with the lowest score which indicates a higher similarity to the ground truth texture.

Deep Texture Synthesis Method	Average SIFID
TextureAda (Ours)	**0.000079**
Texture Net [38]	0.000105
Feedforward Network [18]	0.000145
AdaIN Network [15]	0.000192

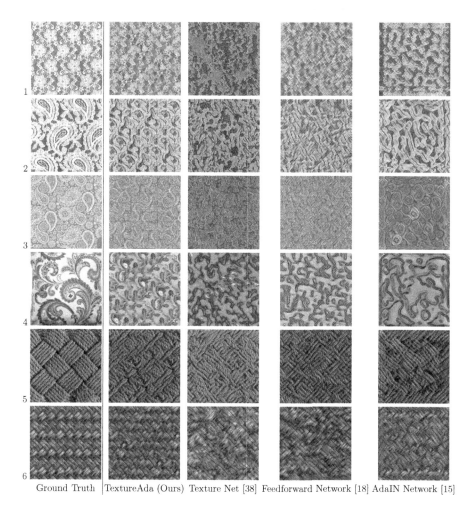

Ground Truth | TextureAda (Ours) Texture Net [38] Feedforward Network [18] AdaIN Network [15]

Fig. 5. Visual comparisons of generated textures from the subset of the Describable Textures Dataset between our method and previous deep texture synthesis methods. The textures shown are from the "lacelike", "paisley", and "woven" categories.

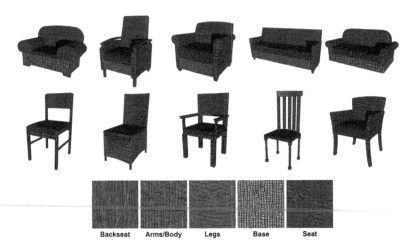

Fig. 6. 3D part-based texture transfer using similar-looking textures created by TextureAda.

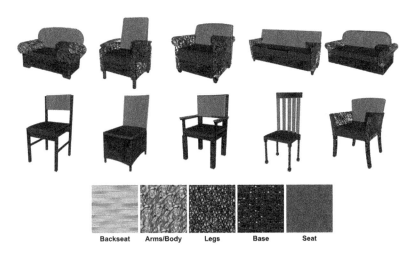

Fig. 7. 3D part-based texture transfer using different textures created by TextureAda.

6 Conclusion and Future Work

TextureAda is a novel texture synthesis method that is based on Texture Net [38] and performs adaptive instance normalization (AdaIN) [15] between multiple layers of Texture Net and a pre-trained VGG-19 [36] with the goal of creating higher-fidelity textures. Texture synthesis experiments on two datasets show that TextureAda beats previous methods visually and based on SIFID. Most importantly, we show how it can be potentially adopted for ideating in product design conceptualization by applying generated material textures to 3D models of furniture.

For future work, in order for TextureAda to be usable by designers, we plan to incorporate it into an application that allows designers to further post-process the generated textures such as changing their color and pattern sizes and also removing undesirable textures. We believe that utilizing deep texture synthesis methods like TextureAda would ease the task of quickly ideating and choosing material textures for 3D models in product design conceptualization.

References

1. Ashby, M., Johnson, K.: The art of materials selection. Mater. Today **6**(12), 24–35 (2003). https://doi.org/10.1016/S1369-7021(03)01223-9
2. Bergmann, U., Jetchev, N., Vollgraf, R.: Learning texture manifolds with the periodic spatial GAN. In: 34th International Conference on Machine Learning, ICML 2017, vol. 1, pp. 722–730 (2017)
3. Bi, S., Kalantari, N.K., Ramamoorthi, R.: Patch-based optimization for image-based texture mapping. ACM Trans. Graph. **36**(4) (2017). https://doi.org/10.1145/3072959.3073610
4. Chang, A.X., et al.: ShapeNet: an information-rich 3D model repository. arXiv preprint arXiv:1512.03012 (2015)
5. Chen, W., et al.: Learning to predict 3D objects with an interpolation-based differentiable renderer, pp. 1–12 (2019). https://nv-tlabs.github.io/DIB-R/
6. Chen, Y., Chen, R., Lei, J., Zhang, Y., Jia, K.: TANGO: text-driven photorealistic and robust 3D stylization via lighting decomposition. In: NeurIPS, pp. 1–13 (2022). http://arxiv.org/abs/2210.11277
7. Cimpoi, M., Maji, S., Kokkinos, I., Mohamed, S., Vedaldi, A.: Describing textures in the wild. In: Proceedings of the IEEE Computer Society Conference on Computer Vision and Pattern Recognition, pp. 3606–3613 (2014). https://doi.org/10.1109/CVPR.2014.461
8. Efros, A.A., Freeman, W.T.: Image quilting for texture synthesis and transfer. In: Proceedings of the 28th Annual Conference on Computer Graphics and Interactive Techniques, SIGGRAPH 2001 (August), pp. 341–346 (2001). https://doi.org/10.1145/383259.383296
9. Efros, A.A., Leung, T.K.: Texture synthesis by non-parametric sampling. In: Proceedings of the IEEE International Conference on Computer Vision **2**(September), 1033–1038 (1999). https://doi.org/10.1109/iccv.1999.790383
10. Gatys, L., Ecker, A.S., Bethge, M.: Texture synthesis using convolutional neural networks. Advances in Neural Information Processing Systems, vol. 28 (2015)

11. Heusel, M., Ramsauer, H., Unterthiner, T., Nessler, B., Hochreiter, S.: GANs trained by a two time-scale update rule converge to a local nash equilibrium. In: Advances in Neural Information Processing Systems, vol. 30 (2017)

12. Houdard, A., Leclaire, A., Papadakis, N., Rabin, J.: Wasserstein generative models for patch-based texture synthesis, pp. 269–280 (2021)

13. Houdard, A., Leclaire, A., Papadakis, N., Rabin, J.: A generative model for texture synthesis based on optimal transport between feature distributions. J. Math. Imaging Vis. (2022). https://doi.org/10.1007/s10851-022-01108-9

14. Hu, R., Su, X., Chen, X., Van Kaick, O., Huang, H.: Photo-to-shape material transfer for diverse structures. ACM Trans. Graph. 41(4) (2022). https://doi.org/10.1145/3528223.3530088

15. Huang, X., Belongie, S.J.: Arbitrary style transfer in real-time with adaptive instance normalization. In: 2017 IEEE International Conference on Computer Vision (ICCV), pp. 1510–1519 (2017)

16. Jetchev, N.: ClipMatrix: Text-controlled creation of 3D textured meshes (2021). http://arxiv.org/abs/2109.12922

17. Jin, B., Tian, B., Zhao, H., Zhou, G.: Language-guided semantic style transfer of 3D indoor scenes, pp. 11–17 (2022). https://doi.org/10.1145/3552482.3556555

18. Johnson, J., Alahi, A., Fei-Fei, L.: Perceptual losses for real-time style transfer and super-resolution, pp. 694–711 (2016)

19. Kato, H., Ushiku, Y., Harada, T.: Neural 3D mesh renderer, pp. 3907–3916 (2018). https://doi.org/10.1109/CVPR.2018.00411

20. Kingma, D.P., Ba, J.L.: Adam: a method for stochastic optimization. In: 3rd International Conference on Learning Representations, ICLR 2015 - Conference Track Proceedings, pp. 1–15 (2015)

21. Kwatra, V., Schödl, A., Essa, I., Turk, G., Bobick, A.: Graphcut textures: image and video synthesis using graph cuts. ACM Trans. Graph. 22(3), 277–286 (2003). https://doi.org/10.1145/882262.882264

22. Li, Y., Fang, C., Yang, J., Wang, Z., Lu, X., Yang, M.H.: Diversified texture synthesis with feed-forward networks (2017)

23. Lin, J., Sharma, G., Pappas, T.N.: Towards universal texture synthesis by combining Texton broadcasting with noise injection in StyleGAN-2 (2022). http://arxiv.org/abs/2203.04221

24. Liu, S., Chen, W., Li, T., Li, H.: Soft rasterizer: a differentiable renderer for image-based 3D reasoning 2019-Octob, 7707–7716 (2019). https://doi.org/10.1109/ICCV.2019.00780

25. Michel, O., Bar-On, R., Liu, R., Benaim, S., Hanocka, R.: Text2Mesh: text-driven neural stylization for meshes, 13492–13502 (2022). https://arxiv.org/abs/2112.03221

26. Milton, A., Rodgers, P.: Product design. Laurence King Publishing (2011)

27. Mir, A., Alldieck, T., Pons-Moll, G.: Learning to transfer texture from clothing images to 3D humans. In: 2020 IEEE/CVF Conference on Computer Vision and Pattern Recognition (CVPR), pp. 7021–7032 (2020). https://doi.org/10.1109/CVPR42600.2020.00705

28. Mordvintsev, A., Niklasson, E., Randazzo, E.: Texture generation with neural cellular automata (2021). http://arxiv.org/abs/2105.07299

29. Perroni-Scharf, M., Sunkavalli, K., Eisenmann, J., Hold-Geoffroy, Y.: Material swapping for 3D scenes using a learnt material similarity measure. In: IEEE Computer Society Conference on Computer Vision and Pattern Recognition Workshops, pp. 2033–2042 (2022). https://doi.org/10.1109/CVPRW56347.2022.00221

30. Radford, A., et al.: Learning transferable visual models from natural language supervision (2021). http://arxiv.org/abs/2103.00020
31. Ramesh, A., Dhariwal, P., Nichol, A., Chu, C., Chen, M.: Hierarchical text-conditional image generation with clip latents. ArXiv abs/2204.06125 (2022)
32. Rombach, R., Blattmann, A., Lorenz, D., Esser, P., Ommer, B.: High-resolution image synthesis with latent diffusion models, 10674–10685 (2022). https://doi.org/10.1109/cvpr52688.2022.01042
33. Saharia, C., et al.: Photorealistic text-to-image diffusion models with deep language understanding (2022). http://arxiv.org/abs/2205.11487
34. Schuhmann, C., et al.: LAION-400M: open dataset of CLIP-Filtered 400 million image-text Pairs, 1–5 (2021). http://arxiv.org/abs/2111.02114
35. Shaham, T.R., Dekel, T., Michaeli, T.: SinGAN: learning a generative model from a single natural image 2019-Octob, 4569–4579 (2019). https://doi.org/10.1109/ICCV.2019.00467
36. Simonyan, K., Zisserman, A.: Very deep convolutional networks for large-scale image recognition. CoRR abs/1409.1556 (2015)
37. Szegedy, C., et al.: Going deeper with convolutions. In: Proceedings of the IEEE Conference on Computer Vision and Pattern Recognition, pp. 1–9 (2015)
38. Ulyanov, D., Lebedev, V., Vedaldi, A., Lempitsky, V.S.: Texture networks: feed-forward synthesis of textures and stylized images (2016)
39. Virtusio, J.J., Tan, D.S., Cheng, W.H., Tanveer, M., Hua, K.L.: Enabling artistic control over pattern density and stroke strength. In: IEEE Transactions on Multimedia (2020)
40. Wang, T.Y., Su, H., Huang, Q., Huang, J., Guibas, L., Mitra, N.J.: Unsupervised texture transfer from images to model collections. ACM Trans. Graph. **35**(6) (2016). https://doi.org/10.1145/2980179.2982404
41. Wei, L.Y., Levoy, M.: Fast texture synthesis using tree-structured vector quantization. In: Proceedings of the ACM SIGGRAPH Conference on Computer Graphics, pp. 479–488 (2000). https://doi.org/10.1145/344779.345009
42. Yeh, Y.Y., et al.: PhotoScene: photorealistic material and lighting transfer for indoor scenes. In: Proceedings of the IEEE/CVF Conference on Computer Vision and Pattern Recognition, pp. 18541–18550 (2022). https://doi.org/10.1109/cvpr52688.2022.01801
43. Yin, K., Gao, J., Shugrina, M., Khamis, S., Fidler, S.: 3DStyleNet: creating 3D shapes with geometric and texture style variations. In: Proceedings of the IEEE International Conference on Computer Vision, pp. 12436–12445 (2021). https://doi.org/10.1109/ICCV48922.2021.01223

Scatter Plots Based on Fuzzy Logic in Supporting the Design of Graphical Interfaces

Jerzy Grobelny [ID] and Rafał Michalski[✉] [ID]

Faculty of Management, Wroclaw University of Science and Technology,
27 Wybrzeże Wyspiańskiego Street, 50-370 Wrocław, Poland
{jerzy.grobelny,rafal.michalski}@pwr.edu.pl

Abstract. This article shows the possibilities of applying the concept of scattered plots in the process of constructing graphical interfaces. A special feature of the proposed approach is the use of linguistic variables represented by fuzzy sets and elements of fuzzy logic to stimulate the movement of virtual agents on the plane that represent interface components. The result of the wandering of the randomly distributed, related elements in the first step are layouts with scattered objects. They represent the interface structure corresponding to the requirements of an expert interface designer. This approach makes it possible to find the arrangement of GUI elements in an arbitrarily defined area that correspond to the desired design features formulated by the expert in a form close to natural language. On the basis of practical examples, the essence of the behavior of the proposed tool was shown. In particular, the process of creating objects distribution on the plane was compared depending on the parameters that govern the behavior of agents which correspond to interface components.

Keywords: User interface design · Scatter plots · Agent-based modelling · Linguistic variables · Expert knowledge

1 Introduction

Human-machine interaction occurs through an interface that can be physical or virtual and includes signaling components and control devices. Human-centered design of such interaction aims, among other things, to create interface of high usability. According to the ISO 9241 standard [2], a usable interface enables the operator to perform tasks efficiently, effectively and, in addition, to increase the level of satisfaction. Plenty of research has been done on finding optimal arrangements of control panel components. Among the most known, there is the work of McCormick [12] where he formulated the main principles of interface components' arrangement, that is:

1. Placing the most important elements of the interface (panel) in the most convenient areas of the operator's workspace, e.g. in the central field of vision.
2. Placing the elements most frequently used in the locations most convenient for the operator.
3. Arranging the components used in sequences close to each other.

© The Author(s), under exclusive license to Springer Nature Switzerland AG 2023
H. Degen and S. Ntoa (Eds.): HCII 2023, LNAI 14050, pp. 506–518, 2023.
https://doi.org/10.1007/978-3-031-35891-3_31

4. Grouping objects that serve similar purposes or perform comparable functions.

Since in practice meeting all of the above criteria can be very challenging, researchers have started developing methods that support the interface design process. Some of the ideas referred to the use of formal models from the field of Facilities Layout Problems (FLP) [9, 10, 14, 18]. The problem in the context of interface design can be defined as follows:

Given the relations between interface components, arrange them in available locations as to minimize the overall cost or effort of operating the interface.

The links between control elements can be represented by hand, finger or pointer-cursor movement. There are several optimization techniques for this type of problem which vary in the relationship definitions, criteria considered, and object representation. Some approaches only consider the frequency of use, while others also take into account the importance of objects and the order of use. For example, Bonney M, Williams [3] proposed a multi-criteria and multi-stage model based on heuristics, where relationship data is defined by the designer using subjective rating scales. Sargent et al. [16], on the other hand, introduced a multi-stage methodology for optimizing a panel operated by a single operator. Interestingly, the relationships between interface components were determined through subjective evaluations within the Analytic Hierarchy Process (AHP) framework [15]. The pairwise comparisons employed in this approach are considered to improve assessment accuracy [1].

In addition to purely measurable criteria for arranging the objects of interaction systems, there is also an interesting strand of research that focuses on the influence of aesthetics on interface quality. Moshagen et al. [13] and Sondereger and Sauer [19] presented very convincing results were in this regard. Their experiments showed a significant positive effect of aesthetics (of websites and mobile applications, respectively) on the speed of task execution and the reduction of errors. Subsequently, studies have attempted to build measures of interface aesthetics based on classical art criteria [4], as well as to explore the relationship between objective interface features (structure and colors) and the subjective feeling of aesthetics [17]. More recently, Wang et al. [20] convincingly documented the role of aesthetic layout formation at the neural response level. The study revealed that interfaces with strong emotional appeals still manage to attract more user attention and elicit unconscious aesthetic inclinations.

The main aim of the approach presented in this work is to suggest the use of scatter plots as a support tool in the design of graphical interfaces. Unlike in previous studies, here the basis for obtaining these plots is the concept of *wandering agents* introduced in [8]. Dissimilar to traditional optimization approaches for interaction systems, the scatter plots obtained using this approach are not the final, optimal solution for arranging interface elements. Instead, they provide a general suggestion of the spatial relationships of the components required the interaction system being designed. Additionally, the linguistic, close-to-natural language, way of defining project requirements encourages the use of experienced expert knowledge.

In the following sections, we first present the idea of creating scatter plots through agent wandering and then demonstrate the most relevant capabilities of our approach on subsequent examples. Finally, we show the effect of applying our methodology to the analysis of a real project: a control panel for a nuclear power plant, which has been the subject of previous optimization attempts. In the discussion, we outline the possibilities for further development and application of our proposal.

2   The Idea of Wandering Agents in Creating Scattered Plots

The proposed approach in this work uses the concept presented in detail in reference [8]. This idea involves defining the relationship between each pair of agents in the system under study, deploying all agents randomly in a rectangular area, and then simulating their movements (wandering) based on criteria formulated as linguistic patterns of optimal position in the group of agents. The movement of each agent in each step of the simulation aims to improve the degree of fulfillment of the defined patterns, which are in the form of logical expressions that can be assigned a degree of truth. The linguistic nature of these patterns has led to the use of the term *Linguistic Patterns* (LP). LP is defined as a logical expression that specifies the desired state of the link-distance relationship for each pair of components as follows:

$$\textbf{P1}: \textbf{IF } \text{LINK\_BETWEEN } (i, j) \text{ is POSITIVE}$$
$$\textbf{THEN } (j) \text{ is in a SMALL\_DISTANCE from } (i) \tag{1}$$

We determine the truth values of the LINK is POSITIVE pattern in experiments as the linear relationship Truth_value = LINK(i, j)/maximum[LINK(i, j)]. Thus, the POSITIVE expression is defined as the fuzzy set shown in Fig. 1.

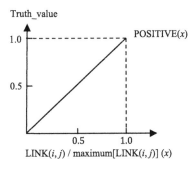

Fig. 1. Schematic definition of the truth values for the pattern expression POSITIVE(x).

Meanwhile, the method of determining SMALL_DISTANCE from (i) is shown in Fig. 2.

Neutral zone (*NeutralZ*) in this definition corresponds to the radius of the circle determining the size of the zone occupied by each object on the plane. An additional, simple pattern that acts analogously to P1 generates a repulsive force between each pair of agents, preventing them from sticking together. It can be defined in the following way:

$$\textbf{P2}: \text{DISTANCE\_BETWEEN\_OBJECTS is greater than NEUTRAL\_ZONE} \tag{2}$$

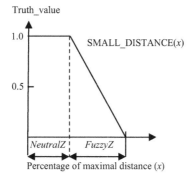

Fig. 2. Schematic definition of the SMALL_DISTANCE linguistic expression.

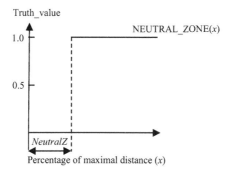

Fig. 3. Schematic definition of the linguistic pattern P2(2) regarding neutral zone.

The truth for this expression is defined in Fig. 3.

In the described situation, pattern P1(1) serves as the criterion for determining the *welfare* of the agents. To calculate the level of this *welfare*, one must evaluate this expression for each agent in a given configuration. This can be achieved by using the formula for computing the truth of an implication proposed by Łukasiewicz [5–7]. If we denote the degree of truth of the left and right sides of the implication as $t(l)$ and $t(r)$, respectively, then:

$$\text{Truth\_of \_P1 (or Truth\_of\_P2)} = \text{minimum}[(1 - t(l) + t(r)] \tag{3}$$

Formula (3) is a generalization of the classical array of truth values for the implication and Truth_of_P1 takes values from the interval [0, 1]. If, for a given agent (e.g., A1), the value of formula (3) in its relationship with another agent (e.g., A2) is less than one, A1 will try to improve its situation by moving towards A2. The rate of this movement is determined by the Truth_value deficit parameter, which is defined as the vector of attracting virtual force between agents VF(A1, A2). The vector VF lies on the line connecting agents A1 and A2 and has a length equal to the Truth_value deficit, that is, VF(A1, A2) = 1 – Truth_of_P1(A1, A2). The agent's movement in the direction of the attraction force in one step of the algorithm involves taking a move proportional to the value of VF. The specific, physical length of this step is specified by the parameter *s*, which depends on the context of the task and is expressed as a percentage of the length of the maximum side of the plane.

In our computer implementation of the model, agents are represented graphically as numbered crosses or squares of arbitrary size. The analysis area is defined as a rectangle of arbitrary size in arbitrary units and distances within the area are defined as parts of the length of the longer side of the area. Interface elements can be easily imagined as the agents in this model. A positive attitude in this context, simply refers to the relationship when interface components are functionally related or occur in operator action sequences, while distance can be identified with the physical size of each element (for more details refer to [8]). The ability to use natural language-like expressions allows LPs to be flexibly applied to optimization tasks that use imprecise knowledge, such as subjective expert opinions about a designed user interface.

3 Analysis of the Wandering Agents Approach for Cases with Known Optimal Solutions

To demonstrate the impact of wandering agents that represent interface elements, we examined standard examples where the optimal layout of the entire system is already known.

3.1 A Simple Layout of Elements Handled Sequentially

Figure 4 shows our application dialogue window with a layout of nine elements to be arranged in sequence. The relationships between the objects are represented by lines connecting consecutive squares, with link unit values displayed.

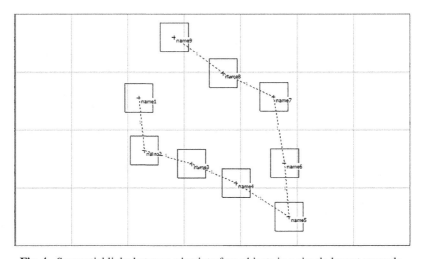

Fig. 4. Sequential links between nine interface objects in a simple layout example.

Agents representing interface components were arranged on a grid with squares measuring 10% of the available area. Their behavior was simulated by defining the linguistic pattern P1 with the Neutral Zone (*NeutralZ*) corresponding to the size of the object and creating negative virtual forces between unrelated objects. Using *NeutralZ* = 5%, *FuzzyZ* = 5%, and step *s* = 1%, we generated a scatter plot (Fig. 5) that fully conforms to pattern P1 (1). In ten trials, all layouts fully conformed to pattern P1 – with a mean truth value of 1. Although the shape of each generated structure was unique, the direct neighborhood of related elements was maintained in each case.

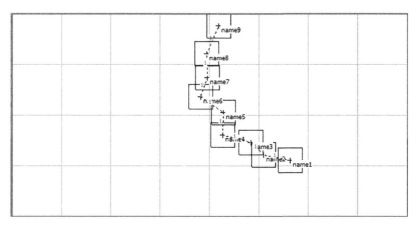

Fig. 5. One of the resulting scattered plots for the simple example with sequential relationships.

As observed, the scatter plot obtained does not resemble a direct design solution, but its structure can greatly assist the designer in making decisions.

3.2 An Example of Complex Interface with Strongly Related and Dimensionally Differentiated Components

A more complex problem in layout design involves analyzing of systems composed of objects with different dimensions and sizes. In the following experiments we simulated such situations. We applied concepts from classical facility layout optimization studies that employed modular rectangular grids models. We used unit-size modules to represent objects of varying sizes. By setting the right relationship values between unit-sized modules that form larger objects, each module can be considered individually. This approach enables the utilization of algorithms like metaheuristic without creating further restrictions. In our experiment, we examined the feasibility of analyzing the arrangement of interface elements that differ in dimension and are composed of strongly connected individual modules.

Figure 6 illustrates the interrelationships between the objects in the studied example. The operation of the interface is performed sequentially, beginning with the START object and ending at the END item. The operations are performed in the order designated by the elements' numbers. Objects are differentiated by size, which is approximately represented by the number of squares with the same number. The mutual relationships between the component agents and the distinguished (central) one for each compound object are twice as big as with the next object in the sequence. This ensures common wandering of component agents.

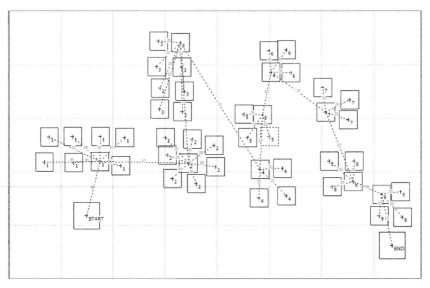

Fig. 6. Relationships between singular components forming compound objects in the example involving the complex interface.

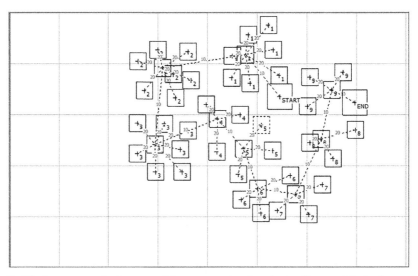

Fig. 7. The best scatter plot in terms of the mean truth value obtained in ten trials for the example from Fig. 6.

The best scatter plot in terms of the mean truth value, obtained in ten trials with the parameters set as in the first example, is shown in Fig. 7.

The truth value of the pattern P1(1) for this solution is 0.98, which demonstrates that the system preserves appropriate neighborhoods for the assumed process sequence. The corresponding neighborhoods of the agents/elements forming the compound objects are also conserved. By repeating the simulations with slightly altered object sizes, that is, for *NeutralZ* = 3% and *FuzzyZ* = 7%, we obtained the result shown in Fig. 8.

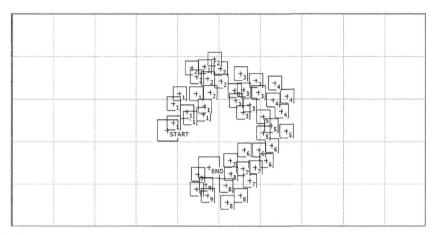

Fig. 8. The simulation result for the complex example with compound objects from Fig. 6 with parameters *NeutralZ* = 3% and *FuzzyZ* = 7%.

The solution has a truth value of 1, which makes the suggestion of a circle-like structure seem plausible. In each of the ten simulations, we obtained similar structures and a pattern truth value of 1.

4   Analysis of the Actual Interface Design

In their work [11], Lin and Wu developed a methodology for optimizing the interface in which typical interactions involve the operating buttons and the keyboard. The optimization is based on an analysis of the difficulty of performing target movements taking into account Fitts' law. The authors empirically verified the optimized interface layout of a boiling water reactor, as shown in Fig. 9.

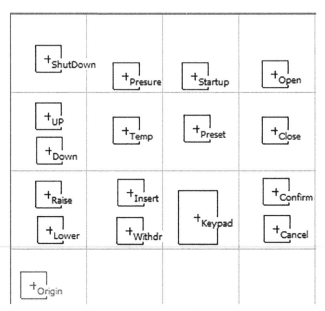

Fig. 9. Relative locations of boiling water reactor components studied in the work [11] and reproduced in our software.

The relationships between the components used in the analysis of this example are put together in the table in Fig. 10.

LINKS	Insert	Withdr	Raise	Lower	Presure	Temp	Startup	Preset	Open	Close	Keypad	Confirm	Cancel	ShutDown	UP	Down	Origin
Insert	0.0	0.0	0.0	0.0	0.0	0.0	0.0	0.0	0.0	0.0	20.0	0.0	0.0	0.0	0.0	0.0	0.0
Withdr	50.0	0.0	0.0	0.0	0.0	0.0	0.0	0.0	0.0	0.0	0.0	0.0	0.0	0.0	0.0	0.0	0.0
Raise	0.0	0.0	0.0	50.0	0.0	0.0	0.0	0.0	0.0	0.0	0.0	0.0	0.0	0.0	0.0	0.0	35.0
Lower	0.0	0.0	20.0	0.0	0.0	0.0	0.0	0.0	0.0	0.0	0.0	0.0	0.0	0.0	0.0	0.0	0.0
Presure	0.0	0.0	0.0	0.0	0.0	60.0	0.0	0.0	0.0	0.0	0.0	0.0	0.0	0.0	0.0	0.0	0.0
Temp	0.0	0.0	0.0	0.0	0.0	0.0	0.0	0.0	0.0	0.0	10.0	0.0	0.0	0.0	0.0	0.0	0.0
Startup	0.0	0.0	0.0	0.0	0.0	0.0	0.0	50.0	0.0	0.0	0.0	0.0	0.0	0.0	0.0	0.0	2.0
Preset	0.0	0.0	0.0	0.0	0.0	0.0	0.0	0.0	0.0	0.0	10.0	0.0	0.0	0.0	0.0	0.0	0.0
Open	0.0	0.0	0.0	0.0	0.0	0.0	0.0	0.0	0.0	50.0	0.0	4.0	0.0	0.0	0.0	0.0	0.0
Close	0.0	0.0	0.0	0.0	0.0	0.0	0.0	0.0	0.0	0.0	0.0	0.0	0.0	0.0	0.0	0.0	0.0
Keypad	0.0	0.0	0.0	0.0	0.0	0.0	0.0	0.0	0.0	0.0	0.0	0.0	40.0	0.0	0.0	0.0	0.0
Confirm	0.0	0.0	0.0	0.0	0.0	0.0	0.0	0.0	0.0	0.0	0.0	0.0	50.0	0.0	0.0	0.0	45.0
Cancel	0.0	0.0	0.0	0.0	0.0	0.0	0.0	0.0	0.0	0.0	0.0	0.0	0.0	0.0	0.0	0.0	4.0
ShutDown	0.0	0.0	0.0	0.0	0.0	0.0	0.0	0.0	0.0	0.0	0.0	1.0	0.0	0.0	0.0	0.0	0.0
UP	0.0	0.0	0.0	0.0	0.0	0.0	0.0	0.0	0.0	0.0	0.0	0.0	0.0	0.0	0.0	50.0	15.0
Down	0.0	0.0	0.0	0.0	0.0	0.0	0.0	0.0	0.0	0.0	0.0	0.0	0.0	0.0	0.0	0.0	0.0
Origin	20.0	0.0	35.0	0.0	10.0	0.0	0.0	10.0	4.0	0.0	0.0	0.0	4.0	1.0	15.0	0.0	0.0

Fig. 10. Relationships between objects for the analysis of boiling water reactor interface objects performed in work [11].

An additional optimization assumption was that the entire interface was placed to the right of the operator. Origin object's relationship to other items is illustrated by the frequency of target movements from the neutral position of the operator's hand where the Origin object is placed. The best result of 10 simulations had Truth value of 1, using the same model parameters as in the first experiment. This scattered plot is shown in Fig. 11.

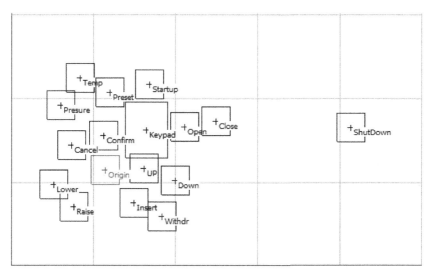

Fig. 11. The best scatter plot out of ten simulations with mean truth equal 1 for the boiling water reactor interface example.

Obtaining a concentration of objects in the lower left part of the screen was possible due to the introduction in our application of the ability to block individual agents in a specific location. We placed the Origin object in this location. As a result, the other agents adjusted their wandering behavior. By comparing the solution obtained from the scattered plot with the original one, it is easy to see the high degree of correspondence between the two. Treating the obtained layout as a hint that suggests the structure of mutual neighbors of objects, one can now use a mouse to modify the objects' arrangement, taking into account the physical limitations of the panel layout (see Fig. 12).

The proposed layout differs slightly from the optimal one shown in Fig. 9, but both designs have identical Truth_of_P1 values of 0.85.

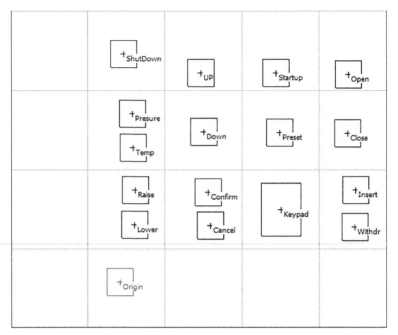

Fig. 12. The interface panel for the boiling water reactor example after manual rearrangement of objects. It takes into account the neighborhoods from Fig. 11 and the actual layout in Fig. 9.

5   Summary

The presented in this work examples of the use of scattered plots demonstrate the potential of the proposed approach in the field of graphical interface design. The diversity of proposals obtained from the agents' wanderings appears to be a particularly advantageous aspect of this early stage interface building analysis. Formulating parameters and design criteria in a manner similar to natural language enables the flexible and wide use of expert knowledge in the design process. Although the obtained plots are not the final, optimal solution for any task, they can provide important clues in finding such solutions by considering the proposed arrangements in the formulation of the final interface layout.

Interestingly, manual correction of obtained scattered plots, which is possible in our application, provides the designer with the freedom to create different variants of good solutions. In particular, the designer can consider interaction usability aspects that are not covered by formal evaluation, such as aesthetic preferences. This area, can also be significantly extended in future research. For example, by incorporating aesthetic quality indicators of the interface as shown in the works of Seckler et al. [17] and Deng & Wang [4] into our scatter plots and further support the decision-making process regarding the final interface layout.

Expanding the possibilities of formulating design criteria is undoubtedly an encouraging direction for future research and the development of our methodology. It is especially important since the design of visual communication is a multi-criteria process by nature. It is easy to see that the similar character of the tasks of designing the arrangement of objects in production systems, particularly in logistics, provides an interesting area for further investigations and analyses. Therefore, applying the proposed framework to solve widely understood management problems is certainly a promising perspective.

Acknowledgement. The research was partially financially supported by the Polish National Science Centre grant no. 2019/35/B/HS4/02892: *Intelligent approaches for facility layout problems in management, production, and logistics.*

References

1. Adamic, P., Kakiashvili, T., Koczkodaj, W.W., Babiy, V., Janicki, R., Tadeusiewicz, R.: Pairwise comparisons and visual perceptions of equal area polygons. Percept. Mot. Skills **108**, 37–42 (2009). https://doi.org/10.2466/PMS.108.1.37-42
2. Bevan, N., Carter, J., Harker, S.: Iso 9241-11 revised: what have we learnt about usability since 1998? In: Kurosu, M. (ed.) HCI 2015. LNCS, vol. 9169, pp. 143–151. Springer, Cham (2015). https://doi.org/10.1007/978-3-319-20901-2_13
3. Bonney, M.C., Williams, R.W.: CAPABLE. A computer program to layout controls and panels. Ergonomics **20**, 297–316 (1977). https://doi.org/10.1080/00140137708931629
4. Deng, L., Wang, G.: Quantitative evaluation of visual aesthetics of human-machine interaction interface layout. Comput. Intell. Neurosci. **2020** (2020).https://doi.org/10.1155/2020/9815937
5. Grobelny, J.: The fuzzy approach to facilities layout problems. Fuzzy Sets Syst. **23**, 175–190 (1987). https://doi.org/10.1016/0165-0114(87)90057-1
6. Grobelny, J.: Fuzzy-based linguistic patterns as a tool for the flexible assessment of a priority vector obtained by pairwise comparisons. Fuzzy Sets Syst. **296**, 1–20 (2016). https://doi.org/10.1016/J.FSS.2015.05.012
7. Grobelny, J., Karwowski, W., Zurada, J.: Applications of fuzzy-based linguistic patterns for the assessment of computer screen design quality. Int. J. Hum. Comput. Interact. **7**, 193–212 (2009). https://doi.org/10.1080/10447319509526121
8. Grobelny, J., Michalski, R.: Linguistic patterns as a framework for an expert knowledge representation in agent movement simulation. Knowl. Based Syst. **243**, 108497 (2022). https://doi.org/10.1016/J.KNOSYS.2022.108497
9. Hosseini-Nasab, H., Fereidouni, S., Fatemi Ghomi, S.M.T., Fakhrzad, M.B.: Classification of facility layout problems: a review study. Int. J. Adv. Manuf. Technol. **94**(1–4), 957–977 (2017). https://doi.org/10.1007/s00170-017-0895-8
10. Kusiak, A., Heragu, S.S.: The facility layout problem. Eur. J. Oper. Res. **29**, 229–251 (1987). https://doi.org/10.1016/0377-2217(87)90238-4
11. Lin, C.J., Wu, C.: Improved link analysis method for user interface design – modified link table and optimisation-based algorithm. Behav. Inf. Technol. **29**, 199–216 (2009). https://doi.org/10.1080/01449290903233892
12. McCormick, E.J.: Human Factors in Engineering and Design, 4th edn. McGraw-Hill Education, New York (1976)
13. Moshagen, M., Musch, J., Göritz, A.S.: A blessing, not a curse: experimental evidence for beneficial effects of visual aesthetics on performance. Ergonomics **52**, 1311–1320 (2009). https://doi.org/10.1080/00140130903061717
14. Pérez-Gosende, P., Mula, J., Díaz-Madroñero, M.: Facility layout planning. an extended literature review. Int. J. Prod. Res. **59**, 3777–3816 (2021). https://doi.org/10.1080/00207543.2021.1897176

15. Saaty, T.L.: A scaling method for priorities in hierarchical structures. J. Math. Psychol. **15**, 234–281 (1977). https://doi.org/10.1016/0022-2496(77)90033-5

16. Sargent, T.A., Kay, M.G., Sargent, R.G.: A methodology for optimally designing console panels for use by a single operator. Hum. Factors **39**, 389–409 (1997). https://doi.org/10. 1518/001872097778827052

17. Seckler, M., Opwis, K., Tuch, A.N.: Linking objective design factors with subjective aesthetics: an experimental study on how structure and color of websites affect the facets of users' visual aesthetic perception. Comput. Hum. Behav. **49**, 375–389 (2015). https://doi.org/10. 1016/J.CHB.2015.02.056

18. Singh, S.P., Sharma, R.R.K.: A review of different approaches to the facility layout problems. Int. J. Adv. Manuf. Technol. **30**, 425–433 (2006). https://doi.org/10.1007/S00170-005-0087- 9/METRICS

19. Sonderegger, A., Sauer, J.: The influence of design aesthetics in usability testing: effects on user performance and perceived usability. Appl. Ergon. **41**, 403–410 (2010). https://doi.org/ 10.1016/J.APERGO.2009.09.002

20. Wang, S., Xu, C., Xiao, L., Ding, A.S.: The implicit aesthetic preference for mobile marketing interface layout—an ERP study. Front. Hum. Neurosci. **15**, 550 (2021). https://doi.org/10. 3389/FNHUM.2021.728895/BIBTEX

Approaching AI: A Practical Guide to Understanding and Using AI for HCI

Maria Karam[1]([⊠]) and Michael Luck[2]

[1] The Inventors Nest, Toronto, Canada
`maria@theinventorsnest.com`
[2] Department of Informatics, King's College London, London, UK
`michael.luck@kcl.ac.uk`

Abstract. Artificial intelligence (AI), is an important evolution in computer science that is only beginning to take hold within the HCI communities. But while the science of AI was twice pronounced dead, it continues to evolve, so do the number of definitions, concepts, applications, and theories that are included in the study of AI. Understanding the definitions and concepts, the functions, terms and relationships associated with this sub-discipline of computer science can be challenging. Today, HCI researchers have an opportunity to begin to apply AI concepts to designing interactions and interfaces that will represent an evolution to the way humans use computers. However, because of the complexities and seemingly disconnected research efforts, HCI researchers must develop a clear and practical understanding of AI — the discipline, concepts, technologies, and terminology — to effectively develop the safe and trusted AI applications of the future. Towards this goal, this paper presents a high-level overview of AI, its history, and the key components, terms, and technologies that currently represent the constantly evolving science. Our goal is to motivate and support the adoption of AI as a safe and trusted layer of computer interactions towards the development of a new paradigm for HCI research.

Keywords: artificial intelligence · AI · human-computer interactions

1 Introduction

Artificial intelligence (AI) is a term that has many connotations, implications, identities, and applications, and with as many misconceptions, myths, and misguided notions about what it is, what it does, how it works and how it can impact our world [27,39]. Although AI as a branch of computer science has been in development for over 50 years, there is a great diversity of approaches between the many disciplines that contribute to the study of AI, its systems, methodologies, visions, and potential interactions. This is apparent when we examine some of the definitions used to describe AI. For example, when first coined by John McCarthy at the Dartmouth College summer workshop of 1956 [31], artificial intelligence was defined as:

> "... the science and engineering of making intelligent machines, especially intelligent computer programs. It is related to the similar task of using computers to understand human intelligence, but AI does not have to confine itself to methods that are biologically observable."

© The Author(s), under exclusive license to Springer Nature Switzerland AG 2023
H. Degen and S. Ntoa (Eds.): HCII 2023, LNAI 14050, pp. 519–532, 2023.
https://doi.org/10.1007/978-3-031-35891-3_32

From the Oxford English Dictionary (OED) [37], AI is described as:

> "The capacity of computers or other machines to exhibit or simulate intelligent behaviour; the field of study concerned with this. Abbreviated AI."

The landing page for IBM's AI portal states that [22]:

> "Artificial intelligence leverages computers and machines to mimic the problem-solving and decision-making capabilities of the human mind."

And Russell and Norvig's very popular classic textbook, *Artificial Intelligence: A Modern Approach* [41] defines AI as:

> "The designing and building of intelligent agents that receive percepts from the environment and take actions that affect that environment."

In addition to inconsistencies (or what some might call *richness*) in the definitions of AI, elements of the discipline, including intelligent agents, machine learning, natural language processing, neural networks, knowledge graphs, and so on, are so complex that it is often unclear how they fit together within the wider AI field. For many, there is a sentiment that there is no coherence to AI as a discipline. One approach to developing a paradigm for linking the different research strands of AI is to create a strong human computer interaction (HCI) program, and to understand AI from that perspective. Similar to the discipline of HCI, AI is deeply rooted in the study of human cognition and computer science, linguistics, psychology, mathematics, and philosophy.

While HCI researchers continue to inspire and contribute to the development of novel forms of computer interactions, AI represents a significant opportunity to support a long awaited move away from the desktop computing paradigm, towards the original vision of ubiquitous computing (ubicomp) that Mark Weiser, CTO of Xerox Park described in the 1980s [46]. Weiser's vision was to make the computer invisible, while continuing to provide services that can help humans achieve our goals by understanding our needs and desires within the context of computer-enabled interactions and systems. Although we have seen many new technologies develop over the years, including pervasive, mobile, tangible, ambient, and contextually aware systems, we continue to develop interfaces that are tied to the desktop paradigm, rather than interactions that can help us evolve towards a new era of computing [2].

In an attempt to motivate HCI researchers to adopt AI as a new and important tool that can potentially support the contextual awareness and autonomous interactions required to develop new and useful interaction models, this paper provides an overview of AI, its history, and the key concepts and technologies that contribute to its study. Our goal is to provide enough information to motivate and empower HCI researchers to adopt AI as an important concept that can help improve our lives, while providing exciting new opportunities to develop novel approaches to improving computer interactions, and augmenting human intelligence.

2   A Little History

While AI is fundamentally rooted in computer science [15,22,34,41], the concepts that have inspired and guided the development of computational intelligence are based on human intelligence and cognition, linguistics, and behaviour [20]. As with any multi-disciplinary efforts, there are also as many perspectives to consider when discussing AI, stemming from philosophy, linguistics, psychology, cognitive science, ethics, and social science. While it is important to understand the views on AI from the many disciplines that have contributed to its development, in this paper we focus primarily on the perspective of AI as a sub-discipline of computer science.

In this respect, AI is a technical field that has incorporated many of the theoretical concepts on which it was founded, including human cognition and human intelligence, while struggling to progress amid the early development stages of computers. As with most new technologies, AI (and its goal of making machines that "think") has also been the centre of many social fears and dystopian visions, even before it was ever developed as a semi-mature science. This provides an even more compelling reason to ensure that there is a clear understanding of the technology and approaches behind AI, to help us avoid some of the potential problems about which we — society — have been forewarned in literature and popular culture [33].

2.1 The Birth of AI

Although the exploration of the concepts surrounding thought and intelligence that extend beyond the human brain has been of interest throughout human history [20], the term *artificial intelligence* was not coined until 1956 at Dartmouth College, New Hampshire, when a group of scientists gathered for a workshop to consider the possibility of developing computers that could think [31]. Even before the now famous *Dartmouth Workshop*, scientists had already developed computer programs that could play chess [15] and solve mathematical problems [34]. Yet since computers were still novel in the 1950s AI was an extremely challenging goal then, and one which continues to pose great challenges for computer science today.

In the early days of AI, formal reasoning and logic represented some of the main techniques that were used [31]. Separately, research in neuroscience from as early as the 1930s suggested that the brain was essentially using electrical signals to process thought, which led to the notion that the brain was effectively a digital system [26] and motivated the continued interest in the field. Research into AI continued to develop throughout the 1970s in both of these approaches, despite facing many challenges in maintaining funding, and in developing the science in general.

2.2 The Death of AI

The first 'winter' of AI occurred from 1974 to 1980, when governments and organisations that had supported AI since Dartmouth lost confidence and stopped funding AI projects. This was likely due to the slow development of the discipline, partially caused by the limitations in the speed, memory capacity, and power of computers, as well as the limited understanding of cognition and how one could approach developing computational implementations of intelligence [31].

Despite the loss of funding, research continued and, by the mid 1980s new approaches to AI were emerging. These included the development and deployment of expert systems, machine learning, and more powerful computers. Nevertheless, AI entered its second winter in 1987 when personal computers started to become popular, causing some of the expensive specialised supercomputers used in AI to become obsolete. At the same time, the study of robotics and cybernetics started to gain popularity as a potentially new approach to developing systems intelligence, with a focus on the use of sensory perception as a bottom-up approach to developing intelligence, rather than the symbolism-based representation previously prevalent [7, 8].

By the 2000s the increased availability of computational power, combined with new systems like Deep Blue, capable of exhibiting intelligence through its mastery of the game of chess [23], saw AI once again gain popularity. In addition, the emergence of what became known as intelligent or autonomous agents, demonstrated an ability to combine decision theory and rationality in a distinctive approach to AI [18]. Greater maturity in the discipline saw an increased formality and rigour through the use of mathematics, logic probability, and decision theory, providing more effective approaches to simulating intelligence.

2.3   AI: The Rebirth and Today

Since the early 2010s AI has experienced a great resurgence with new developments, including deep learning, big data, and other computing technologies that contributed to some major advances in performance and processing capability. In particular, advances in the areas of natural language processing (NLP), image processing, and recommender systems contributed new AI-based applications and systems that are capable of performing many tasks that some regard as effectively exhibiting key traits of intelligence.

In particular, commercial organizations (including IBM [22], Google [13] and OpenAI [35] to name just a few) have taken a lead in continuing to fund and develop AI to a stage where systems can now compose music [12], hold conversations [44], create unique images from text [29, 36], autopilot commercial aircraft [40], and support autonomous vehicles [40]. Even small businesses are using and developing AI systems for customer service and analysis tasks using services such as Google's cloud [13], and open source development tools like PyTorch's machine learning framework [38] and Open AI's suite of tools and applications [35].

3   Artificial Intelligence: A Selective Perspective

Given the resurgence of AI, one important question to consider is how HCI researchers can incorporate the technology in moving towards innovating in user interfaces and interactions, while avoiding the potential dangers of these powerful techniques [10]. Ongoing and relevant concerns include privacy, safety, and trust, since many AI programs are currently capable of accessing information about online users, their habits and behaviours, interests and connections to others, and allowing those organizations that are collecting user data to leverage user information to develop, for example, marketing campaigns aimed at manipulating people in relation to business and politics [10, 19, 42].

For the HCI researcher, these issues must be understood, to help ensure that AI can develop as a transparent, accountable and fair addition to computer science, as well as to society. In addition, maintaining a human-in-the-loop philosophy could reduce the potential of harm that AI can cause when its methods are not clearly described or understood. A move towards exploiting AI is well within the scope of existing methodologies and practices of HCI, which is founded on the notion of understanding and supporting humans and their interactions with computers. In addition to evaluating software, and informing the design of specific applications, HCI as a discipline can help further support the development and acceptance of AI both for applications used by people and as an underpinning research tool for the support of research and development in other disciplines.

Against this background, the rest of this paper describes some of the main features of AI, providing an overview of the field, and suggesting new perspectives that can support HCI researchers and practitioners in adopting AI to drive the next evolution of computer interactions and systems.

3.1 Defining AI

While AI can be understood in many ways, as we have discussed above, it is essentially concerned with development of machines that exhibit intelligent behaviour (however that is defined). By analogy to humans, we can view computer hardware as the physical component of intelligence — rather like the brain — with AI representing the functional components of intelligence that operate on that hardware (or the perception or reasoning the brain supports). This is, to some extent, an interesting perspective on Descartes's mind-body problem, providing a philosophical stance on AI [43]. However, one way to see AI is as the identification and implementation of human intelligence in machines, still an important and significant challenge.

Yet, as mentioned above, definitions of AI are as varied as the perspectives that contribute to the discipline, and are still contentious. For example, the following view was expressed at the Dartmouth workshop [31]:

"...to proceed on the basis of the conjecture that every aspect of learning or any other feature of intelligence can in principle be so precisely described that a machine can be made to simulate it".

This encapsulation is very broad, and suggests that AI should aim to replicate all of the processes associated with human intelligence. However, since the Dartmouth workshop, concepts of AI have shifted between the notion of simulating human intelligence and developing actual reasoning machines. Indeed, as a complex and relatively new area, we can anticipate that AI will continue to evolve in response to new developments in neuroscience, cognitive science and computer science, and as novel approaches to implementing intelligence are developed. For example, other, more recent perspectives take AI to be the study of intelligent rational agents, rather than the effort to simulate human intelligence using machines [41]. This agent-based approach avoids some of the philosophical or even psychological questions surrounding AI, focusing instead on autonomous decision-making, independent of the verisimilitude to humans.

3.2   Machine Intelligence and Simulating Human Cognition

While the ultimate goal of AI is to develop machines that can exhibit intelligence, AI is only possible through the development of creative approaches to translating the concepts of thought into computational terms. In 1950, Alan Turing provided an early definition of the concept of AI based on "whether or not it is possible for machinery to show intelligent behaviour" rather than asking if machines can actually think [43], which helped to better frame the problem in machine terms. At that time, much less was understood about cognition or intelligence, but some aspects that were identified included the concepts of attention, consciousness, decision making, emotions, learning, language, memory, perception, reasoning, and social cognition, which helped to narrow down the problem space to a handful of functions.

Today, after almost 70 years of research on AI, many of the identified targeted traits of *human* intelligence have effectively been implemented computationally, even if only in simulation, and are briefly described in the following list:

- Attention: achievable using digital sensors, notification systems, and schedules that can detect changes and monitor the environment.
- Consciousness: it is not clear what this would look like in computational terms, although there have been efforts to simulate consciousness (and claims of encountering it!) [14, 47].
- Decision-making: achievable using heuristics, machine learning and predictive functions.
- Emotions: achievable using simulation in virtual agents, chatbots, and other systems that interact with humans — the key question is whether these systems have utility.
- Language: natural language processing has enabled almost flawless language capabilities in AI.
- Learning: supported by machine learning techniques (such as neural networks, reinforcement learning and many more) learning is very effective in many different domains, given sufficient and adequate data.
- Memory: with much increased capability, storage is generally no longer a problem as it once was.
- Perception: visual and auditory information is already digitized, and haptics and tactile interfaces are also gaining competence in computer perception, with the potential for extra sensory perception through a variety of environmental sensing devices.
- Social cognition: important for the development of conversation models and other applications where knowledge about human interactions will improve the operation of AI that is human-centred.

With the current technology available to support intelligent behaviours, HCI researchers have an incredibly rich set of tools and concepts to exploit in the design of new applications that leverage AI, as well as novel approaches to using AI to solve problems and interact with computers. However, as the science of AI is still relatively young, there is a great deal of change that we should expect over the next few years, including the development of new interactions that will potentially create as big an impact in the world as did the Internet, mobile phones, and personal computers over the past 40 years.

3.3 Physical Embodiment

AI has always maintained a strong relationship with robotics and remote teleoperation applications [32], allowing robots to process and understand the world, and supporting real time interactions with objects in the physical world through sensors. Computer vision, audio and tacile devices are supported by AI models that can allow a robot to recognize objects, and to interact with them. HCI research has an important role to play here, in providing the insight and foresight that can help to ensure that robots are developed with the safety and benefit of humans as paramount [6].

3.4 Intelligent Agents

Intelligent agents can be understood as independent computer systems that can interact with their environment using sensors to perceive their surroundings in order to achieve certain goals or to perform tasks. For many, their primary function is to act autonomously (in the sense that they are designed to operate without requiring explicit instructions from an external source), sometimes on behalf of another entity (human or machine). Following Russel and Norvig [41], agents can be classified according to their primary capability, as described below.

- Simple reflex agents: devices like smart thermometers, which are limited by specific sets of instructions that allow them to change the temperature, or turn on or off, based on schedules and other hard-coded information.
- Model-based reflex agents: reflex agents that can store state information to allow them to act based on a previous state, adding an additional layer of capability and flexibility.
- Goal-based agents: achieve a goal that is determined by a particular task or state that they are designed to satisfy.
- Utility agents: more processing power allows them to compare states, and to determine optimal approaches to reaching their goals, based on changes in the data they perceive and store.
- Learning agents: maintain state information and internal models, and are capable of assessing behaviours and updating their models to improve performance based on feedback and new data.

Some perspectives on intelligent agents suggest that, in combination with AI, we could produce a form of intelligence that surpasses that of a human, realised using autonomous agents capable of achieving super-human unsupervised learning. However, despite the fears of some, it remains important to ensure that the potential dangers can be mitigated by maintaining a level of human control over our interactions with computational agents and AI systems [27,39].

4 Data and Machine Learning: Some Key Concepts

4.1 Data

As we will see below, machine learning refers to a subset of AI techniques focused on improving performance over time, or adapting to new circumstances. Of course, data forms the basis of any machine learning system. This ranges from numerical data to image data, to vast sets of human-centred data stored in databases that serve up the information and knowledge models necessary to articulate information in a format that can be computationally processed. For example, to successfully compete in the game show, Jeopardy, IBM's Watson downloaded the entire contents of Wikipedia, and complete data from other encyclopedias and dictionaries, which had to be tagged and organized in a way to allow Watson to make rational decisions that could connect the questions to the correct responses found within the data [23].

At that time, there were few sources of data large enough to support the amount of information required to develop effective machine learning models that could reason across specific domains of knowledge. Yet as the Internet started to grow, so did the sources of data that became available, providing new areas of knowledge to which machine learning could be applied. It was the combination of the vast amounts of data and the massive computing resources that eventually transformed machine learning techniques (and deep learning in particular) into the powerful techniques we have today. In addition to the original datasets provided by Wikipedia and the CIA World Factbook [48], datasets continued to be developed, often contributed by researchers interested in applying machine learning to their specific areas of knowledge. However, for any new domain of knowledge to be included in machine learning or AI applications, it is necessary to collect, organize, and annotate the data in a format that can support the kind of reasoning and structure required by current machine learning technologies.

4.2   Machine Learning

As indicated above, machine learning is a sub-discipline of AI that supports computers in making decisions, predictions, and solving problems based on their ability to perform reasoning across large data sets, without having to be specifically programmed. Machine learning uses different algorithms that can apply formal logic, statistical methods and other mathematical functions to make connections, descriptions, predictions or suggestions about the data. Machine learning can be supervised, which requires labelled datasets, unsupervised, which looks for patterns within unlabelled data, or use reinforcement techniques where the system learns by trial and error [11,24,41]. Perhaps most famously, the kind of machine learning that has been used in many image and speech processing systems uses artificial neural networks and is often referred to as deep learning.

Artificial neural networks are loosely modeled on the human brain, with potentially millions of individual nodes, each assigned to different weights that represent a value that incoming data must meet before that node is activated, and which in turn send that data to another node or layer of nodes for further processing [21]. Neural networks use a technique known as *backpropagation* to support the process of learning from incorrect responses, based on sending data that is output from the network back into the network to improve their models and continually update the weights assigned to the nodes to learn from the error, and attempt to improve results on subsequent iterations [25].

Deep learning uses multiple layers of neural networks so that data can be processed on multiple dimensions [25,41] and generate very effective results. Deep learning architectures are used in speech recognition, image processing, drug design, and other areas that require complex problem solving approaches, where *deep* refers to the multiple levels of machine learning processes performed on each data point.

Training is a process in machine learning system that uses large sets of data as samples of the information that is being presented to the machine. The datasets are conceivably organized as database tables where columns represent an attribute or variable, and rows represent the individual instances of each variable or a chunk of knowledge included in the domain of interest [5, 16]. In a supervised learning approach, data must be annotated before it can be used, so that the features of the contents of each cell can be described. For example, image and video data requires certain features of the image to be highlighted, segmented, annotated, and marked up with with keywords that describe the details of each feature. Then, images that contain faces are marked up to identify features including the nose, eyes, ears, eyebrows, and any other detail that is deemed important to understanding that image.

Once annotated, the data can be loaded into the machine learning algorithm for training. During the training phase, the system can learn to identify each of the specific features that has been annotated, and use mathematical approaches to model that information so that it can identify similar features in new images. A validation phase is then used to allow the system to alter the model when incorrect identifications or classifications of an image are made.

Some new approaches to support unsupervised learning are emerging, including *zero-shot*, *one-shot*, or *few-shot* learning, which attempt to build machine learning models that are trained using a few, or no training samples. Although these techniques are still being developed, they are often used in image recognition applications where there are limited numbers of examples, as in medical imaging applications [3, 21].

4.3   Natural Language Processing

Machine learning systems have been effectively combined with natural language processing (NLP) to create the very successful speech generation and recognition applications that are currently available for everyday use. OpenAI has developed a set of language processing models that has had great success in demonstrating language abilities in AI [9] and is currently being used to support many companies who are turning to natural language as a means of supporting computer interactions for their platforms. OpenAI [35] continues to develop their GPT-N models (generative pre-trained transformer) that include more effective language capabilities, which are now being implemented in Microsoft's new Edge and Bing browsers [28] to provide natural language style interactions with search engines.

Natural language processing originates in the field of linguistics [9, 41], and represents a great example of how one area of knowledge can be translated into a format that can be implemented by AI. However, while language models are capable of producing and detecting speech, new domains of knowledge still require datasets to be developed and processed. This is so that the specific nuances and content of that area are available for the AI system to understand and make sense of when producing speech applications for specific contexts or new domains [45].

4.4   Image Processing

Computer vision and graphics have long been a research focus in computer science that has contributed significantly to the development of image processing systems in AI. Applications that can identify faces, objects in nature, animals, and other visual content are now available for anyone to use. These include Midjourney [29] and OpenAI's Dall-E-2 [36], which are capable of generating and modifying images based on text descriptions that can be input to the system by users. This is a great example of the combination of computer vision and NLP to implement a novel application that is both useful and fun.

An interesting side-effect of successful image processing in AI applications is the development of *deepfakes*, which are real images that have been modified into different contexts or formats that are very effective in the art of deception [30]. While it is sometimes possible to detect images and videos that have been faked, the algorithms are quickly improving to a point where they will be very difficult to detect in the near future. These are certainly associated with deepfakes, which is an challenging problem to address, especially as more applications of this deceptive application of AI continues to impact peoples lives [4, 19].

5   Challenges for AI

It is critical to ensure that new and existing AI applications that use people's personal information are safe, respectful of privacy, and ethical in handling and storing the information. Over the past decade, companies like Meta, TikTok, Amazon, and Google [19] have been profiting from user data through selling information to marketing companies and political organizations that use the information to identify political opinions [42], for example. There are also additional challenges including a need to maintain transparency in the sense that many AI techniques (when using neural networks or similar) are considered black box approaches and cannot readily be understood by users (and sometimes developers). In response, explainable AI aims to make these opaque machine learning models more explicit and clear, by providing information that can explain how an answer was derived [17]. Similarly, there is great concern over the potential for bias in machine learning, especially when the data used in training is derived from unreliable sources such as social media or simply when the underlying data reflects historical bias or prejudice.

Other issues to consider may arise once we allow AI systems to gain access to our devices, vehicles, smart home appliances, email, credit card info, media services, and other personal information that link to the physical world. In essence, this unification of AI with the physical world may be the root of the concerns that have been illustrated in films over the last century [33]. Even if AI was generally harmless (a very moot point), many more potential problems arise once large corporations, greedy villains, or malevolent agents control the AI systems that have access to our physical world and resources. To address some of the more obvious dangers in these types of AI system, there are mitigation techniques that can help us avoid the dystopian vision that many adversaries of AI have been warning us about. Indeed, HCI researchers may be in a good position to consider the development of methods to detect dangers in upcoming AI projects, or to devise rules, like Asimov did with his robots, to apply to future implementations [1]. The table below lists some literature and films from the last 200 years, and suggests some approaches we can take to avoid the potential disastrous situations that fictional AI can cause.

Year	Film/Book Title	Setting	AI Type	Dangers	Prevention	Other considerations
1818	Frankenstein	1700s	Reanimated brain – Organic Robot	Super strong humanoid AI robots	Regulate robotics that are humanoid	Don't reanimate dead people
1929	Metropolis	2027	Centralised Machine running a cities infrastructure	single source of control of infrastructure	Decentralise infrastructure control, Keep humans in the loop Don't let giant corporations run your infrastructure	Don't allow a single machine or corporation to control all resources
1929	Metropolis	2027	Robot	Super strong humanoid AI robots	Regulate robotics that are humanoid, Ensure there is an easily accessible off switch, Don't let robots have the ability to generate their own power without an override, Avoid evil scientists	Watch out for deepfake robots who impersonate actual humans
1973	Westworld	1983	Robot	Super strong humanoid AI robots	Regulate robotics that are humanoid, Don't abuse your robots, they may have feelings too Ensure there is an easy way to shut off power, Design robots so they are distinguishable from humans.	Don't build robots that are stronger than people, Ensure there is an off switch
1982	Blade Runner	2019	Robot	Super strong humanoid AI robots	Regulate humanoid robots	Don't enslave robots, Don't abuse robots.
1984	The Terminator	2029/1984	Centralised Machine running a urban infrastructure	Super strong humanoid AI robots	Don't give AI systems access to their own power source without an off switch	Don't allow a single machine or corporation to monopolise resources
1992	The Lawnmower Man	20th century	Centralised Machine running urban infrastructure	Single source controlling infrastructure	Decentralisation of control, Keep human in the loop	Ensure there is an off switch for the agents
1999	The Matrix	2199	Centralised Machine running urban infrastructure	Single source of control of infrastructure	Don't give AI systems control oi their own power	Ensure robots and AI system don't have full control of your devices, resources and infrastructure

6   AI and the Future: An HCI Perspective

Similarly to the 1980's when HCI was beginning to develop into its own discipline, AI is introducing a new set of techniques and methodologies into computer science, and this has now developed to the stage where it can be effectively used to inspire new and innovative computer interactions. It is important to note that the HCI community was fundamental to the development of user centred design, user experience, and other aspects of computer interactions that put the user first and helped to develop systems that were intuitive and effective to humans. Now that AI is emerging as the next paradigm in computer interactions, HCI can leverage the knowledge and methodologies of interaction research from the past 30 years in support of designing and developing new approaches to AI that put the safety and well being of humans at the centre of AI applications that interact with humans. In addition, there is a great opportunity to begin to consider the development of interactions rather than just interfaces that use AI, to create a more empirical approach to developing HCI for AI [2].

In general (though not exclusively), AI systems have primarily been developed to perform very specific tasks, with available applications today tending to focus on only a few domains, such as image processing and generation [29, 36], speech and natural language processing [44], expert systems and game playing machines [23], autonomous robot and vehicle navigation [32, 40]. As AI continues to expand into new territory, HCI can continue to influence and innovate through envisioning and designing new ways to apply machine intelligence to helping humans make their way through this world. Indeed, given the growing number of tools and resources available to support new AI applications, HCI researchers have an opportunity to start developing new interaction models and scenarios that leverage the available tools to support early design, prototyping, and envisioning work [13, 22, 35, 38].

AI is a relatively new domain for many HCI researchers to explore, yet this is the right time to start to adopt AI into our computer interaction work as an inspiring new paradigm for designing the interactions of the future, or for supporting and implementing some existing paradigms that have yet come to light [46].

References

1. Asimov, I., Robot, I.: Doubleday science fiction, Doubleday, Garden City, NY (1950)
2. Beaudouin-Lafon, M.: Designing interaction, not interfaces. In: Proceedings of the Working Conference on Advanced Visual Interfaces, pp. 15–22. AVI 2004, Association for Computing Machinery, New York, NY, USA (2004)
3. Bengio, Y., Lecun, Y., Hinton, G.: Deep learning for AI. Commun. ACM **64**(7), 58–65 (2021)
4. Black, E., et al.: Reasoning and interaction for social artificial intelligence. AI Commun. **35**(4), 309–325 (2022)
5. Blum, A.L., Langley, P.: Selection of relevant features and examples in machine learning. Artif. Intell. **97**(1), 245–271 (1997)
6. Brandão, M., Mansouri, M., Magnusson, M.: Editorial: responsible robotics. Front. Robot. AI **9**, 937612 (2022). https://doi.org/10.3389/frobt.2022.937612
7. Brooks, R.A.: Elephants don't play chess. Robot. Auton. Syst. **6**(1), 3–15 (1990). https://doi.org/10.1016/S0921-8890(05)80025-9. https://www.sciencedirect.com/science/article/pii/S0921889005800259. Designing Autonomous Agents
8. Brooks, R.A.: Intelligence without representation. Artif. Intell. **47**(1), 139–159 (1991). https://doi.org/10.1016/0004-3702(91)90053-M. https://www.sciencedirect.com/science/article/pii/000437029190053M
9. Cambria, E., White, B.: Jumping NLP curves: a review of natural language processing research. IEEE Comput. Intell. Mag. **9**(2), 48–57 (2014). https://doi.org/10.1109/MCI.2014.2307227

10. Cheng, X., Lin, X., Shen, X., Zarifis, A., Mou, J.: The dark sides of AI. Electron. Mark. **32**, 11–15 (2022)
11. Cimiano, P., Paulheim, H.: Knowledge graph refinement: a survey of approaches and evaluation methods. Semantic Web **8**(3), 489–508 (2017)
12. Civit, M., Civit-Masot, J., Cuadrado, F., Escalona, M.J.: A systematic review of artificial intelligence-based music generation: scope, applications, and future trends. Exp. Syst. Appl. **209**, 118190 (2022). https://doi.org/10.1016/j.eswa.2022.118190. https://www.sciencedirect.com/science/article/pii/S0957417422013537
13. Google Cloud. https://console.cloud.google.com/getting-started
14. Collings, E., Ghahramani, Z.: LaMDA: our breakthrough conversation technology (2021). https://blog.google/technology/ai/lamda/
15. Computer History Museum. https://www.computerhistory.org/chess/first-tests/
16. Craven, M., et al.: Learning to construct knowledge bases from the world wide web. Artif. Intell. **118**(1), 69–113 (2000)
17. Ehsan, U., Liao, Q.V., Muller, M., Riedl, M.O., Weisz, J.D.: Expanding explainability: towards social transparency in AI systems. In: Proceedings of the 2021 CHI Conference on Human Factors in Computing Systems. CHI 2021, Association for Computing Machinery, New York, NY, USA (2021)
18. Endriss, U., et al.: Autonomous agents and multiagent systems: perspectives on 20 years of AAMAS. AI Matt. **7**(3), 29–37 (2022)
19. Grandinetti, J.: Examining embedded apparatuses of AI in Facebook and Tiktok. AI and Society, pp. 1–14 (2021)
20. Haenlein, M., Kaplan, A.: A brief history of artificial intelligence: on the past, present, and future of artificial intelligence. California Manag. Rev. **61**(4), 5–14 (2019). https://doi.org/10.1177/0008125619864925. http://journals.sagepub.com/doi/10.1177/0008125619864925
21. Hinton, G.: The next generation of neural networks. In: Proceedings of the 43rd International ACM SIGIR Conference on Research and Development in Information Retrieval, p. 1. SIGIR 2020, Association for Computing Machinery, New York, NY, USA (2020)
22. IBM: What is artificial intelligence (AI)? https://www.ibm.com/topics/artificial-intelligence. Accessed 10 Feb 2023
23. IBM: (2012). http://www-03.ibm.com/ibm/history/ibm100/us/en/icons/deepblue/
24. Ji, S., Pan, S., Cambria, E., Marttinen, P., Yu, P.S.: A survey on knowledge graphs: representation, acquisition, and applications. IEEE Trans. Neural Netw. Learn. Syst. **33**(2), 494–514 (2022)
25. LeCun, Y., Bengio, Y., Hinton, G.: Deep learning. Nature **521**(7553), 436–444 (2015)
26. Macpherson, T., et al.: Natural and artificial intelligence: a brief introduction to the interplay between AI and neuroscience research. Neural Netw. Off. J. Int. Neural Netw. Soc. **144**, 603–613 (2021)
27. McLean, S., Read, G.J.M., Thompson, J., Baber, C., Stanton, N.A., Salmon, P.M.: The risks associated with artificial general intelligence: a systematic review. J. Exper. Theoret. Artif. Intell. 35(4), 1–15 (2021). https://doi.org/10.1080/0952813X.2021.1964003
28. Mehdi, Y.: Reinventing search with a new AI-powered Microsoft Bing and Edge, your copilot for the web. https://blogs.microsoft.com/blog/2023/02/07/reinventing-search-with-a-new-ai-powered-microsoft-bing-and-edge-your-copilot-for-the-web/ (2023)
29. Midjourney. https://www.midjourney.com/home/
30. Mirsky, Y., Lee, W.: The creation and detection of deepfakes: a survey. ACM Comput. Surv. 54(1), 1–41 (2021)
31. Moor, J.: The Dartmouth college artificial intelligence conference: the next fifty years. AI Mag. **27**(4), 87 (2006)
32. Murphy, R.R.: Introduction to AI Robotics, second edition. MIT Press (2019)

33. Nader, K., Toprac, P., Scott, S., Baker, S.: Public understanding of artificial intelligence through entertainment media. AI 'I&' Society (2022)

34. Newell, A., Simon, H.: The logic theory machine-a complex information processing system. IRE Trans. Inf. Theory **2**(3), 61–79 (1956)

35. OpenAI. https://openai.com/

36. OpenAI. https://openai.com/dall-e-2/

37. Oxford English Dictionary. https://www.oed.com/view/Entry/271625?

38. PyTorch. https://pytorch.org

39. Radanliev, P., De Roure, D., Maple, C., Ani, U.: Super-forecasting the 'technological singularity' risks from artificial intelligence. Evol. Syst. **13**, 747–757 (2022)

40. Read, G.J., O'Brien, A., Stanton, N.A., Salmon, P.M.: Learning lessons for automated vehicle design: Using systems thinking to analyse and compare automation-related accidents across transport domains. Saf. Sci. **153**, 105822 (2022)

41. Russell, S., Norvig, P.: Artificial intelligence: a modern approach. Prentice Hall, 3 edn. (2010)

42. Shipman, F.M., Marshall, C.C.: Ownership, privacy, and control in the wake of cambridge analytica: the relationship between attitudes and awareness. In: Proceedings of the 2020 CHI Conference on Human Factors in Computing Systems, pp. 1–12. CHI 2020, Association for Computing Machinery, New York, NY, USA (2020)

43. Thagard, P.: Parallel computation and the mind-body problem. Cogn. Sci. **10**(3), 301–318 (1986)

44. Trummer, I.: From BERT to GPT-3 codex: harnessing the potential of very large language models for data management. Proc. VLDB Endow. **15**(12), 3770–3773 (2022). https://doi.org/10.14778/3554821.3554896

45. Vinyals, O., Le, Q.V.: A neural conversational model. CoRR abs/1506.05869 (2015)

46. Weiser, M.: The computer for the 21st century. Sci. Am. **265**(3), 94–104 (1991)

47. Wertheimer, T.: Blake Lemoine: Google fires engineer who said AI tech has feelings. BBC News (2022). https://www.bbc.com/news/technology-62275326

48. Wikipedia. https://en.wikipedia.org/w/index.php?title=List_of_datasets_for_machine-learning_research&oldid=1135282041 (2023). Page Version ID: 1135282041

Fuzzy Vector Representation of Project Metrics' Target and Actual Values and Its Application to Project Management

Dorota Kuchta[✉] [iD] and Oksana Yakivets

Faculty of Management, Wroclaw University of Technology, Wybrzeze Wyspianskiego 27,
50-370 Wroclaw, Poland
{dorota.kuchta,oksana.yakivets}@pwr.edu.pl

Abstract. Metrics based project management is seen today as a highly effective and efficient approach to project management, mainly thanks to the personalized visualization possibilities of metrics' values, given by modern technologies. That is why it is important to search for new visualization possibilities of project metrics. In this paper, both the target and actual values of project metrics will take on fuzzy or interval values (a feature that often occurs, e.g., in research projects) and a vector-based representation will be used to represent both graphically, in order to help decision makers to assess the situation in the project. A real-world research project will be used as an illustration.

Keywords: fuzzy number · project dashboard · optimism bias

1 Introduction

Projects today are more and more often "blurry": often, neither their goals nor even their actual outcomes can be represented as crisp numbers. This is a consequence of the fact that project objectives and success criteria become more and more subjective and less quantizable, at least directly, and project resources' consumption is less and less restricted to simply measurable cases, such as consumption of resources and the payroll data. Research work, human assets measured as intellectual and creative potentials: these are the key resources in numerous projects, and these resources attain "modern" goals, which can be described as "creating value" – with "value" far from being limited to financial or other quantitative magnitudes. The blurriness is also caused by human features, such as various type of biases that occur in project planning and control, or political influence, strategic misinterpretation, lack of honesty, etc.

The "blurriness" of projects requires new methods of planning and control. Among others, graphical representations of hardly measurable values, attractive and adapted to individual needs, is required. Therefore, the aim of the paper is to propose a graphical representation of non-exactly known target and actual values occurring in projects, and their relationship. This will facilitate the evaluation of project performance for "blurry" projects.

The structure of the paper is as follows: first we discuss uncertainty in projects and the biases of experts as an additional source of blurriness, then we present basic information about fuzzy numbers and about the role of metrics and dashboards in project management. Finally, we explain the proposed approach, where both the target and the actual values can be presented as fuzzy numbers and both they and their relation are shown graphically using the form of a speedometer. Finally, a real-world research project is used as illustration of the approach. The paper finishes with some conclusions.

2   Materials and Methods

2.1   Uncertainty in Project Management

Uncertainty is defined in many different ways, also in the context of project management [1]. Independently of the definition, it is omnipresent in projects, especially in innovative ones, research projects included. Here we adopt the following definition: "Uncertainty is the state of being uncertain; something you cannot be sure about [2]". Uncertainty is due to numerous reasons: incomplete knowledge, natural variability, unambiguity, human nature, etc.

Uncertainty in this sense means that all project plans are biased and cannot be considered as a stable basis for any decision. Among others, target values, e.g. the targeted project cost or deadlines, should not be presented as crisp, fixed values, because they are hardly ever such. What is more, today project goals often referring not to numbers, but to non-quantitative "values" that certainly have to be measured but their measurement is not unequivocal. The selection of fixed values (a consequence of habits or software, or templates used, e.g. in project calls) for target values leads to misinterpretations of the results, to conclusions about exceeding or not attaining a value that in fact never constituted a reliable target [3].

In relation with the discussion in the previous paragraph, it is important to underline that we will use the term "value" in two different meanings:

- as a "traditional" value, a number;
- a more general, not necessarily easily quantifiable "value" that project stakeholders expect nowadays from their projects (e.g., increased self-esteem of project team members)

In innovation projects, quite often even the actual values are not exactly known, either. For example, the cost of the research work cannot be measures in terms of crisp values, as the time devoted by the researchers to the research work is not easily measurable. In such project it is thus not only the target values that should not be presented as crips numbers, but the actual values, either.

One of the reasons why we are uncertain about the values used in project planning are the frequent biases of experts. We distinguish between optimistic, pessimistic, volatility, and other biases. Here we concentrate on the most important or "dangerous" one that is the reason for numerous project failures: the optimistic bias. The biases may occur both in target and actual values.

2.2 Optimism Bias in Project Management

Optimism bias has been discussed in many contexts in the literature of project management. A good systematic literature review regarding optimism bias can be found in [4].

Optimism bias and strategic misrepresentation can be listed among top ten behavioural biases in project management [5]. Optimism bias can also be considered as a barrier that prevents detecting early warning signs in projects [6], which is a threat in project execution. In [7] the authors show that optimism bias can be observed in both planning phase and execution phase of a project. As far as optimism bias in the context of risk management is concerned, the authors of [8] show that typically opportunities are underestimated, and threats are overestimated. Optimism bias refers to the tendency of people to believe that they are less likely to experience negative events and more likely to experience positive events than other people. These conclusion support the findings from [9] and [10] that optimism arises during the planning of a project and specifically in the estimation activities.

In project planning and management, an optimistic cost or schedule estimate will be low, leading to cost and schedule overruns. An optimistic benefit estimate will be high, leading to benefit shortfalls. Such correlation leads to another conclusion: optimism produces a systematic bias in project outcomes [5].

It is common that strategic project planners and managers sometimes underestimate cost and overestimate benefit to achieve approval for their projects. Optimistic planners and managers also do this, although unintentionally. The result is the same, however, namely cost overruns and benefit shortfalls. Thus, optimism bias and strategic misrepresentation reinforce each other, when both are present in a project [5].

To conclude, it is worth to mention that the projects that look best on paper are the projects with the largest cost underestimates and benefit overestimates, other things being equal. But, the larger the cost underestimate on paper, the greater the cost overrun in reality. And, the larger the overestimate of benefits, the greater the benefit shortfall. Therefore, the projects that have been made to look best on paper become the worst, or unfitted projects in reality [5].

The optimism bias of a person or group can be determined on the basic of historical records, by comparing the values given by the person or group in question in the estimation phase with the actuals [3].

2.3 Fuzzy Numbers

Fuzzy numbers [11] are often used to represent uncertainty. Their simplest form, triangular fuzzy numbers, are defined by three values $\underline{p}, \hat{p}, \overline{p}$, such that $\underline{p} \leq \hat{p} \leq \overline{p}$ and denoted as $\tilde{P} = \left(\underline{p}, \hat{p}, \overline{p} \right)$. They are associated with a so-called membership function μ_P (1), defined on the set $\Re$ of real numbers and representing the possibility or acceptance degrees of the respective real numbers.

$$\mu_P(x) = \begin{cases} 0 \text{ for } x \leq \underline{p} \text{ or } x \geq \overline{p} \\ \frac{x-\underline{p}}{\hat{p}-\underline{p}} \text{ for } x \in \left(\underline{p}, \hat{p}\right) \\ \frac{\overline{p}-x}{\overline{p}-\hat{p}} \text{ for } x \in \left[\hat{p}, \overline{p}\right) \end{cases} \tag{1}$$

If $\tilde{P}$ represents a target value in a situation of uncertainty, when this value cannot realistically be set as a fixed value, the meaning of (1) may be twofold:

- if value $\hat{p}$ is attained, the satisfaction of the decision makers would be full (equal to 1), and it descends in both direction away from $\hat{p}$ down to 0;
- the possibility degree of attaining $\hat{p}$ is the highest, the other values are less possible to be attained – the further from $\hat{p}$, the smaller – down to 0.

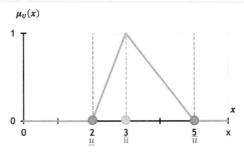

Fig. 1. Representation of the triangular fuzzy number (2, 3, 5) by means of the membership function.

Fuzzy numbers can be added, subtracted, multiplied, divided or compared by and with each other. The result of such operations performed on triangular fuzzy numbers is not always a triangular fuzzy number, but we always get as a result a membership function representing the possibility or satisfaction degree of the product (Fig. 1).

Formula (1) is usually presented as a triangle. In this paper, however, we will propose another graphical representation of (1), in line with the following section that presents the idea of project metrics. First of all, however, let us consider two selected possibilities of aggregating the information conveyed by two triangular fuzzy numbers $\tilde{P} = \left(\underline{p}, \hat{p}, \overline{p}\right)$ and $\tilde{T} = \left(\underline{t}, \hat{t}, \overline{t}\right)$.

- Let us assume that $\tilde{P}$ represents an estimated target value, e.g., project cost, and $\tilde{T}$ the percentage of the estimated target value that should be accepted in the official project plan. For example, if optimism bias is present, this percentage will be smaller or equal to 1. Then we would define the official target value through the function

$$\mu_S(x) = min(\mu_P(x), \mu_T(x)) \tag{2}$$

Formula (2) represent the target value in the case of the impossibility to determine it exactly, reinforced by the presence of a bias;

- Let us assume that $\tilde{P}$ represents the estimated target value, e.g., project cost, from the official project plan, and $\tilde{T}$ the actual value. The attainment degree of the target value can be represented as the fuzzy number $\tilde{W}$, defined as

$$\tilde{W} = \left(\underline{p} - \overline{t}, \hat{p} - \hat{t}, \overline{p} - \underline{t} \right) \tag{3}$$

The fuzzy number (3) should be presented in relation to the crisp number 0: the more it exceeds 0, the better.

The problem of aggregating several fuzzy numbers is complex. First, the aggregation depends on the information conveyed by the fuzzy numbers, secondly, even for the same information content, several aggregation possibilities exist and the final choice has to be made with the participation of the decision maker for whom the aggregation is prepared.

2.4 Project Metrics and Dashboards

As recent project management literature recommends [12], today's project management should be based on metrics, understood as categories of quantifiable data relevant to project performance. Metrics should be embedded in project dashboards, adapted to the perception and needs of individual project stakeholders. The dashboards should use recent findings in visualisation [13], so that the information is conveyed in the most effective and personalised way.

The metrics can be presented in many graphical forms: line and bar graphs, gauges, geographic maps, progress bars, color-coded alerts.

Often dashboard use the speedometer form, as one to which the decision makers are used as car drivers. We propose to present fuzzy numbers in the form of fuzzy vectors embedded in the form of speedometers, and to apply this approach to project metrics, and more exactly, to target and actual values.

3 Proposal

We propose to represent both the target values set in the project planning stage and the actual values as fuzzy numbers. This will concern the project cost, duration, as well as other quantities following from project goals; in modern project management it will be above all the value expected from the project-by-project stakeholders. It is true that in most cases actual values will be known as crisp numbers, but in the most innovative project the usage of intellectual resources, the time devoted to the work and, above all, the value delivered to the recipient will not be easily measurable. Let us emphasize that a crisp value or an interval are special cases of triangular fuzzy numbers, thus the case of actual values being represented as individual numbers or intervals are covered by our approach.

The proposed procedure is as follows:

- In the planning stage of the project:

- identify all the project objectives and the criteria of their fulfillment

– identify the respective numerical values, possibly in the fuzzy form, asking experts for the possibility of attaining individual values, as well as for satisfaction degrees
– identify the uncertainty linked to each value
– identify the estimation biases shown by the experts in the past
– adjust the target values
– agree with each decision maker on the content of the dashboard, as well as on the form (e.g., the colors used).

• In the execution stage of the project:

– collect actual values of the targets, making sure not to reduce their "blurriness" (if it is not known exactly, use an interval or a fuzzy number to represent it)
– identify the biases and adjust the representation of the actual values accordingly
– use selected aggregation methods to juxtapose and compare the actual and target values and present the result in the dashboards.

• The dashboards have to be updated on a regular basic till the very end of the project.

Instead of a triangle, we propose to present triangular fuzzy numbers in the form of a fuzzy vector, resembling a speedometer, as shown in Fig. 2. The higher the value of the membership function, the stronger the colour.

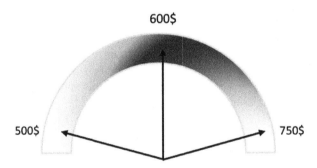

Fig. 2. Representation of the triangular fuzzy number (500$, 600$, 750$) in the form of a speedometer.

For example, Fig. 2 may represent the target value of project cost. The most possible or the most satisfactory values are indicated by means of the most intensive colour. The least intensive colour shows the least possibility/satisfaction degrees. Other examples will be given later on.

4   Example of Application

Let us consider a real world research project, whose aim was to elaborate a tailor made costing system for a university. For several reasons, the project did not fully succeed. It is worth stating that optimism bias appeared during the planning of the project, specifically in the estimation activities: the project plan, its purpose and importance was optimistic due to the specific features of the academic community, which was not prepared for such fundamental changes that could occur during the implementation of the project and afterwards. The optimistic bias tendency also concerned the conditions for obtaining data for the implementation of the project. Let us analyse an example target values from the project:

An analysis of the features of the group (the historical records) that estimated the target cost showed the estimation bias (100%, 120%, 150%) (Fig. 3), which means that most frequently the actual values constituted about 120% of the original estimation, and value close to 150% were also possible. This fact was not taken into account during project implementation.

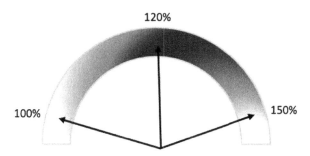

Fig. 3. Target cost estimation bias in the project example.

The target cost was estimated as 500$ (a crisp number can be considered to be a special case of a triangular fuzzy number). If the optimistic bias from Fig. 3 was taken into account then, instead of a single target value 500$, the fuzzy target value from Fig. 2 would have been considered, in line with formula (2). Thus, not simply 500$ would be expected as the desirable project cost, but rather values around 600$, with less, but still possible values close to 750$. The original crips target value 500$ is simply unrealistic.

Suppose the project has finished and the actual cost should in theory be known. However, as the time of the research work cannot be determined exactly, it was only known to be between 400$ and 550$, with the possibility degree attaining its maximum for 550$ (another special case of triangular fuzzy number). Figure 4 presents then, in the form of a dashboard, the attainment degree of the target value from Fig. 2, according to formula (3), at the background of the reference value 0. The number in Fig. 4 is considerably shifted to the right form 0, thus the attainment degree is high, which is clear from the graphical presentation.

The decision maker can easily, at one glance, evaluate the place of the actual values at the background of the target value. Further differences in the intensity of colours can be also considered.

In the project in question there were several important target values. Most of them were estimated in the planning phase too optimistically and, on top of that, the existence of various scenarios was simple ignored. Also, the actual values were collected always in the form of a crisp estimate, even if it was known that it was just an estimate of an immeasurable quantity. E.g., the researchers were paid the salary planned in the project

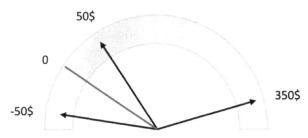

Fig. 4. Attainment degree of the target value from Fig. 2 in the project example.

definition phase, but in certain periods they worked much more on the project, without even measuring their working time. University resources (officially, not attributed to the project) were used to make up for the needs arising from uncertainty and the resulting frequents changes. For that reason, the control of the project, performed in a traditional way, using crisp values was not efficient. But additionally, the complete lack of graphical representation of the project course made this control difficult, as it required the analysis of traditional tables – that contained traditional, biased or disformed values. The usage od's an approach as the one proposed here would have not prevented the project from the partial failure, but would have weakened this failure, making earlier reaction possible.

5   Conclusions

The approach proposed here allows us to represent in graphical way, in the form of a dashboard, fuzzy target values for projects, where the fuzziness may be caused by the bias of the human estimators, the nature of the project, its resources, or other factors. The approach allows to represent non-crisp actual values too, as well as the (non-crisp) attainment degree of the target values. Thus, our approach contributes to the modern needs and approaches to project management, indispensable to face modern project management challenges.

The approach is based on graphics, which in turn suits the perception of modern generations. Traditional reports or tables are no longer attractive or even acceptable, information not about current numbers, but about general tendencies is expected. The relevant information should be carefully selected for each recipient and presented in such a way that an efficient decision-making process is possible. Our proposal constitutes an attempt to address these needs. Other visualisation methods should be considered too [14, 15].

The approach should be tested in real world projects. Project types have to be taken into account here [16]: the approach will be adequate for those with more uncertainty involved, but for some project types of the relation between the advantages and cost would be far too low. It seems, however, that it should be more appealing to non-mathematicians than the classical, triangle-or interval-based representation of fuzzy numbers. It should be, nevertheless, adapted to individual needs and perception of individual decision makers. It should be underlined, however, that the preparation of the graphics is possible with basic software, used by all organisations, thus it does not require any investment.

An important limitation of the proposed approach is the identification of the uncertainty and its mathematical representation. Usually, the expert knowledge is used here [3], but the existence of the biases can distort the information obtained in this way. That is why it is important to keep track of the estimates and the actuals, assigned to various experts, and process them accordingly [17], and, at the same time, undertake steps to limit the optimism bias [18].

References

1. Perminova, O., Gustafsson, M., Wikström, K.: Defining uncertainty in projects – a new perspective. Int. J. Proj. Manag. **26**(1), 73–79 (2008)
2. Oxford Dictionary of Current English (2005)
3. Hulett, D.: Integrated Cost-Schedule Risk Analysis. Taylor & Francis (2016)
4. Prater, J., Kirytopoulos, K., Tony, M.: Optimism bias within the project management context: a systematic quantitative literature review. Int. J. Manag. Proj. Bus. **10**, 370–385 (2017)
5. Flyvbjerg, B.: Top ten behavioral biases in project management: an overview. Proj. Manag. J. **52**(6), 531–546 (2021)
6. Hajikazemi, S., Andersen, B., Klakegg, O.: Barriers against effective responses to early warning signs in projects. Int. J. Proj. Manag. **33**, 1068–1083 (2015)
7. Kutsch, E., Maylor, H., Weyer, B., Lupson, J.: Performers, trackers, lemmings and the lost: sustained false optimism in forecasting project outcomes — evidence from a quasi-experiment. Int. J. Proj. Manag. **29**, 1070–1081 (2011)
8. Farooq, M.U., Thaheem, M.J., Arshad, H.: Improving the risk quantification under behavioural tendencies: a tale of construction projects. Int. J. Proj. Manag. **36**(3), 414–428 (2018)
9. Tyebjee, T.T.: Behavioral biases in new product forecasting. Int. J. Forecast. **3**(3), 393–404 (1987)
10. Flyvbjerg, B.: Public planning of mega-projects: overestimation of demand and underestimation of costs in decision-making on mega-projects: cost-benefit analysis. Planning and Innovation, 120–144, (2008)
11. Zadeh, L.A.: Fuzzy sets. Inf. Control **8**(3), 338–353 (1965)
12. Kerzner, H.R.: Project Management Metrics, KPIs, and Dashboards. John Wiley & Sons Inc, New York (2013)
13. Eckerson, W.W.: Performance Dashboards: Measuring, Monitoring, and Managing your Business, 2nd edn. Wiley, Hoboken, N.J (2011)
14. Dikmen, I., Hartmann, T.: Seeing the risk picture: visualization of project risk information. In: Proceedings of the EG-ICE 2020 Workshop on Intelligent Computing in Engineering (2020)
15. Killen, C.P., Geraldi, J., Kock, A.: The role of decision makers' use of visualizations in project portfolio decision making. Int. J. Proj. Manag. **38**(5), 267–277 (2020)
16. Lehmann, O.F.: An introduction to a typology of projects. PM World J. **5**(12) (2016)
17. Marchwicka, E.D., Kuchta, D.: Critical path for projects with activity durations modelled as Z-fuzzy numbers. J. Multiple-Valued Logic and Soft Comput. **9**, 539–559 (2022)
18. Flyvbjerg, B.: Curbing optimism bias and strategic misrepresentation in planning: reference class forecasting in practice. Eur. Plan. Stud. **16**, 3–21 (2008)

Perception of the Fuzzy Number Indeterminacy Change in Vector and Triangle Representations – Implications for Graphical User Interface Design

Dorota Kuchta⬤, Jerzy Grobelny⬤, Rafał Michalski$^{(\boxtimes)}$ ⬤, and Jan Schneider⬤

Faculty of Management, Wroclaw University of Science and Technology,
27 Wybrzeże Wyspiańskiego Street, 50-370 Wrocław, Poland
{dorota.kuchta,jerzy.grobelny,rafal.michalski,
jan.schneider}@pwr.edu.pl

Abstract. The purpose of the study is to learn about and analyze people's preferences regarding two visual representations of the uncertainty of parameter estimates for decision makers. The research is related to the perception of fuzzy numbers represented classically by triangles and, more recently, in the form of specifically constructed vectors. In a series of pairwise comparisons, the participants were to determine which representation of the change in the selected parameter is clearer. The obtained results are then analyzed and formally statistically verified. The presented investigation findings extend the knowledge about subjective assessments of different graphical ways of presenting parameter uncertainty. From a practical point of view, the obtained results provide recommendations for the design of graphical user interfaces in which fuzzy data are presented to users.

Keywords: Fuzzy number visualization · Fuzzy number vector representation · Visual processing · Project uncertainty · Usability

1 Introduction

There are many areas where decision-making takes place in a highly uncertain environment. Thus, it is not surprising that the use of fuzzy numbers and other artificial intelligence-based concepts are seen as possibly beneficial in achieving goals on various nature. In complex situations numerous parameters have to be monitored and/or controlled, thus strong software support seems to be highly desirable. Therefore, designers of graphical user interfaces of such applications should have appropriate knowledge, based a on scientific examination that would allow them to present uncertain data in an optimal way.

A prominent example of such a field is project management. It is widely accepted that projects are endeavours with a usually high level of uncertainty [9]. Uncertainty with respect to the values of various project parameters present during planning, but

© The Author(s), under exclusive license to Springer Nature Switzerland AG 2023
H. Degen and S. Ntoa (Eds.): HCII 2023, LNAI 14050, pp. 542–554, 2023.
https://doi.org/10.1007/978-3-031-35891-3_34

persisting almost to the project end, results from such factors as errors, natural variability, inability to retrieve full knowledge, or just existing ambiguities. Therefore, project management based solely on crisp (not fuzzy, real) numbers often contributes to project failures [4]. On the other hand, in general, formally defined fuzzy numbers can be troublesome for people without appropriate mathematical background. However, the idea of their simplest triangular-like form could be relatively easy understood and used by practitioners in various fields. To fully specify a parameter represented by a triangular fuzzy number, it is only necessary to provide three assessments, that is, the optimistic, most possible, and pessimistic values. Such a perspective seems to be intuitional for any expert in the given field. In the context of project or production management (as well as in others areas) these values facilitate making effective decisions regarding project execution, meeting production costs, and assessing time requirements.

Experts usually update their initial estimates on the regular basis taking advantage of new information incoming over time. Changes in these assessments may have a considerable impact on the final success of the endeavour so it is necessary to systematically monitor and analyse them and react accordingly. The importance of paying such a close attention to the variability of a number of parameters even seems to be an important part of critical success factors. For instance, in study [18], the *Agile techniques and change management* dimension was identified by exploratory factor analysis as one of the four crucial dimensions of project management success in IT service area.

To support the decision-makers in handling the changes in dedicated software, one can take advantage of graphical user interfaces designed in the form resembling a dashboard (see, e.g., [6]). They, naturally, should be constructed in such a way the ensures the highest possible level of usability. Thus, there is a question what is the best way of graphically presenting the changes in the triangular fuzzy numbers representing the given uncertain parameter. The answer to this question is especially important in light of the studies showing that adequate visualisation techniques facilitate communication in project uncertainty management [16].

The typical way of visualizing triangular fuzzy numbers is using triangles that show the shape of the membership function. However, in our previous study [8, 15] we suggested the use of vectors for graphical representation of triangular fuzzy numbers. The results of simple experiments with users showed that vector capability to convey information about parameter uncertainty is comparable with triangles.

Currently, we continue research in this direction. In particular, we investigate what is the perception of changes in triangular fuzzy number indeterminacy both in their triangular and vector representations. Participants' subjective opinions on this issue investigated in this study refer to the satisfaction component of the uncertainty representation usability.

The rest of the paper is organized as follows: in Sect. 2, we present basic information about the triangular and vector representations of triangular fuzzy numbers. In Sect. 3 we describe the experiment and analyse the results. The paper ends with a discussion and conclusion section.

2 Triangles and Vectors as Two Uncertainty Visualization Approaches

In this section, we briefly present two different ways of representing typical triangular fuzzy numbers. Usually, they are presented on the graph that visualizes their membership function. Given the specific definition of the triangular fuzzy number, a part of the graph resembles a classical triangle. Let us assume that an imprecise parameter has been assessed by a human by providing three values $\underline{u}, \hat{u}, \overline{u}$. We may refer to them as the least possible, most possible and greatest possible values, respectively. The triangular fuzzy number corresponding to these evaluations can be expressed as $\tilde{U} = \left(\underline{u}, \hat{u}, \overline{u} \right)$. Its membership function μ_U (x) is defined on the set $\Re$ of real numbers and specifies the possibility degrees of given real numbers. A sample membership function of a triangular fuzzy number $\tilde{U}(2, 3, 5)$ is given in Fig. 1.

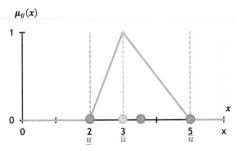

Fig. 1. Membership function based visualisation of parameter U determined by numbers 2, 3, 5.

Triangular fuzzy number can also be uniquely represented by a specifically constructed vector. Such a visualisation proposal was put forward in [8, 15]. In Fig. 2, we show how the same triangular fuzzy number $\tilde{U}(2, 3, 5)$ from Fig. 1 looks in a vector graphical form.

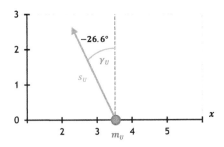

Fig. 2. Vector visualisation of parameter U determined by numbers 2, 3, 5.

The vector representation of the triangular fuzzy number $\overrightarrow{U}\left(\underline{u}, \hat{u}, \overline{u} \right)$ is defined by three values $\{m_U, s_U, \gamma_U\}$ where:

- $(m_U, 0)$ is a starting point of the vector and m_U is computed as $\left(\overline{u} + \underline{u} \right)/2$;

- s_U specifies vector's length and can be calculated as $\overline{u} - \underline{u}$;
- γ_U is the angle between the vector and line $x = m_U$ and amounts to $tan^{-1}(\hat{u} - m_U)$; positive angles denote the inclination to the right and negative ones – to the left.

For further discussion one should notice that the angle γ_U is equal zero when the most possible value $\hat{u}$ is the same as the average value m_U of the pessimistic and optimistic values $\overline{u}$ and $\underline{u}$. The above described representations of triangular fuzzy numbers were subject to experimental research concerned with the perception of fuzzy number indeterminacy change presented visually to subjects. The details of the examination are provided in the following sections.

3 Method

3.1 Participants

Overall 69 subjects took part in the survey. They were mainly volunteer students from Wroclaw University of Science and Technology in Poland between 18 and 45 years old. The mean age amounted to 23.48 years with the standard deviation of 3.47 whereas median equaled 23 years. Among participants the majority constituted women – 49 which accounted for 71%. They all gave their informed consent to take part in the study.

3.2 Experimental Task and Variables

The experimental design included effects that would provide some more insight into the perception of the fuzzy number uncertainty changes both in the triangular and vector graphical representations. The experimental task was to give subjective evaluation of different variants of these representations in terms of their saliency of change in fuzzy number uncertainty. In particular, the following factors were investigated.

Independent Variables. Two graphical representations of triangular fuzzy numbers were studied: classically visualized as triangles and in the form of vectors. They constituted the first factor investigated in the present study and their mathematical foundations were briefly described in Sect. 2. In this research, we focused specifically on the perception of change in one feature related with fuzzy numbers, that is, the information about the indeterminacy of the given imprecise parameter. Graphically, this property is related either to the length of the triangle support or the vector length.

Three different levels of the parameter indeterminacy value change were examined, namely, (1) the change by one unit from value two to three, (2) the change by two units from value two to four, and (3) the change by one unit from value three to four. The investigated factors and their levels are graphically shown in Fig. 3.

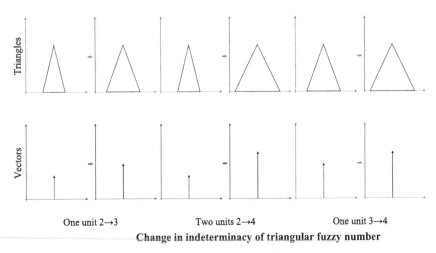

One unit 2→3   Two units 2→4   One unit 3→4

Change in indeterminacy of triangular fuzzy number

Fig. 3. Factors and their levels examined in the current study: graphical representation (vectors, triangles) and the indeterminacy value change (IC: One unit 2 → 3, Two units 2 → 4, One unit 3 → 4).

Dependent Measures. We employed two different dependent variables for examining subjective opinions of respondents. The preferences were measured by relative weights obtained from the pairwise comparisons of all experimental conditions. According to [7], pairwise comparisons improves accuracy of assessments a have been successfully applied in many studies for obtaining subjective hierarchies (see, e.g., [2, 3, 10–12]). Here, for retrieving stimuli preferences, we also use this approach within the Analytic Hierarchy Process methodology (AHP) [13, 14]. The same technique allowed us to compute the consistency ratios for every subject.

The participants were asked to respond to the question: *Which figure shows a more salient increase in fuzzy number indeterminacy?* They gave their responses on a 5-point two-directional, linguistic scale recommended in the AHP approach, that is *Equally salient, Somewhat more salient, More salient, Considerably more salient, Decisively more salient.* One of the comparisons presented by the supporting software is shown in Fig. 4.

Który rysunek pokazuje wyraźniejszy wzrost niepewności?

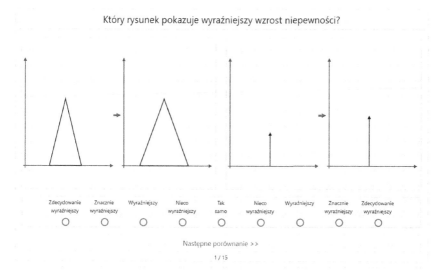

| Zdecydowanie wyraźniejszy | Znacznie wyraźniejszy | Wyraźniejszy | Nieco wyraźniejszy | Tak samo | Nieco wyraźniejszy | Wyraźniejszy | Znacznie wyraźniejszy | Zdecydowanie wyraźniejszy |

Następne porównanie >>

1 / 15

Fig. 4. A view of a sample pairwise comparison of experimental conditions from the study software. Participants evaluated on a 5-point two-directional, linguistic scale which figure shows a more salient increase in fuzzy number indeterminacy.

3.3 Experimental Design

A mixture of the two examined factors' levels allowed us to specify six experimental conditions. There were two types of graphical representations of triangular fuzzy numbers and three indeterminacy level changes (see Fig. 3). We employed the within-subject design, that is every subject tested all six experimental conditions.

3.4 Procedure

The data gathering procedure was carried out exclusively via the internet. The subjects received the general information about the study along with the hyperlink directing them to a slideshow with the voice recorded detailed description of the research. The last slide included hyperlink to the React.js-based experimental application. After the mouse click, it opened in the default local web browser. On the first page of the software, participants were asked to read and accept the informed consent for participating in the study. They also provided their gender and age. Then, the application, one by one presented the subjects with all necessary pairwise comparisons of the examined experimental conditions. They appeared in a random order. The data first were gathered first locally in the web browser internal variables and, after completing the whole procedure, sent to the remote server.

4 Results

The collected experimental data were aggregated and imported to the TIBCO Statistica version 13.3 software [17]. The conducted analysis concerned both consistency ratios and relative weights and involved basic descriptive statistics and analysis of variance. The results are presented in the next subsections.

4.1 Descriptive Statistics

Consistency Ratios. The average value of consistency ratios for all examined participants amounted to 0.15 with a mean standard error of 0.012. The distribution was somewhat positively skewed as the median (0.13) was a little bit lower than the mean value. The lowest value of this parameter was as low as 0.0011 whereas the highest equaled 0.518.

Relative Weights. Main descriptive statistics regarding the calculated relative weights for all presented stimuli are put together and presented in Table 1.

Table 1. Basic descriptive statistics of relative weights for all experimental conditions.

Graphical Representation	Indeterminacy Change	Mean	Median	Minimum	Maximum	Std Deviation	Mean Std Error
Triangle	IC_2 → 3	0.110	0.102	0.028	0.288	0.053	0.0064
	IC_2 → 4	0.335	0.345	0.049	0.563	0.131	0.0158
	IC_3 → 4	0.111	0.085	0.027	0.457	0.081	0.0097
Vector	IC_2 → 3	0.080	0.067	0.026	0.251	0.048	0.0057
	IC_2 → 4	0.277	0.287	0.041	0.512	0.125	0.0151
	IC_3 → 4	0.087	0.082	0.023	0.209	0.049	0.0059
All		0.167	0.111	0.023	0.563	0.134	0.0066

The higher values of the relative weights correspond to the higher saliency perception of the fuzzy number indeterminacy change for a given experimental condition. One can observe the biggest scores in terms of average values and medians for the figures presenting the change by two units. Similar results appeared both for triangle and vector representations. For these experimental conditions one can also notice the biggest values of variability parameters, that is standard deviations and mean standard errors. These data are graphically illustrated in Fig. 5.

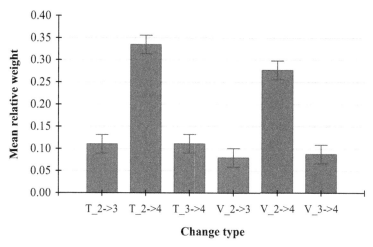

Fig. 5. Mean relative weights for all experimental conditions. Vertical bars denote 0.95 confidence intervals [$F(5, 492) = 75.6, p<0.0001$].

4.2 Analysis of Variance

Consistency Ratios. A one-way analysis of variance was used to check if there were any discrepancies in consistency ratio values for men and women. The results showed that there were no statistically significant differences between mean consistency ratios computed for males and females [$F(1, 67) = 0.321, p = 0.573$].

Relative Weights. In order to verify if, and to what extent the differences in average relative weight values for the examined effects are statistically meaningful, we conducted a two-way analysis of variance analysis of variance *Change Magnitude × Graphical representation*. The obtained results are summarized in Table 2.

Table 2. Main results of the three-way analysis of variance *Change Magnitude × Graphical representation*.

Effect	SS	df	MSS	F	p
Indeterminacy Change (IC)	4.01	2	2.01	257	<0.0001[*]
Graphical Representation (GR)	0.143	1	0.143	18.4	<0.0001[*]
IC × GR	0.022	2	0.011	1.40	0.248
Error	3.19	408	0.0078		

[*]$\alpha<0.0001$

The analysis revealed that both investigated factors, that is *Graphical Representation* and *Indeterminacy Change* were statistically significant: $F(2, 408) = 257, p < 0.0001$, and $F(2, 408) = 257, p < 0.0001$, respectively. The interaction between them occurred to be statistically irrelevant $F(2, 408) = 1.4, p = 0.248$.

The graphical illustration of the average relative weight values for the *Indeterminacy Change* factor is given in Fig. 6. It shows that participants overall perceived the biggest saliency of the change in the level of indeterminacy for two-unit changes (IC_2->4). The discrepancy between one-unit changes IC_2->3 versus IC_3->4 seems to be considerably less distinct.

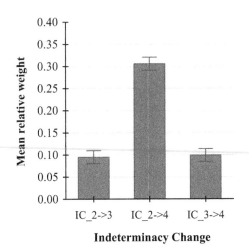

Indeterminacy Change

Fig. 6. Mean relative weights for the *Indeterminacy Change* effect. Vertical bars denote 0.95 confidence intervals $[F(2, 408) = 257, p < 0.0001]$.

To further examine the differences between the Indeterminacy Change factor levels, a series of pairwise LSD post-hoc tests were performed. The outcomes of these analyses are provided in Table 3 and they show that the only insignificant difference is between two levels involving one-unit changes in the fuzzy number indeterminacy.

Table 3. Pairwise LSD post-hoc analysis results for the *Indeterminacy Change* effect $[F(2, 408) = 257, p < 0.0001]$.

Indeterminacy Change	IC_2→3	IC_2→4
IC_2→3	×	
IC_2→4	<0.0001	×
IC_3→4	0.69	<0.0001

Mean relative weights for the *Graphical Representation* factor levels are demonstrated in Fig. 7. The results confirm the initial graphical data presented in the section with basic descriptive statistics. The subjects clearly perceived changes in indeterminacy of fuzzy numbers presented as triangles as more salient than those shown in the form of vectors.

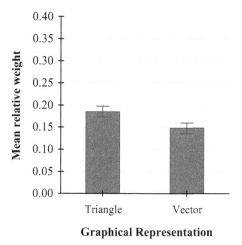

Fig. 7. Mean relative weights for the *Graphical Representation* effect. Vertical bars denote 0.95 confidence intervals [$F(1, 408) = 18.4, p < 0.0001$].

Although the interaction the *Indeterminacy Change* × *Graphical Representation* interaction effect was insignificant as a whole, we decided to verify if there were any statistically significant discrepancies between the examined factor levels. The graphical illustration of this interaction result is provided in Fig. 8.

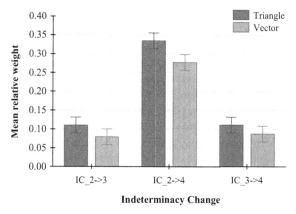

Fig. 8. Mean relative weights for the *Indeterminacy Change* × *Graphical Representation* interaction effect. Vertical bars denote 0.95 confidence intervals [$F(2, 408) = 1.40, p = 0.248$].

A relatively clear-cut pattern can be observed: the use of triangles to visualize the indeterminacy changes of the fuzzy number occurred to be better perceived than applying the vector representation. The detailed pairwise LSD post-hoc tests of these differences are presented in Table 4. The results show that for all indeterminacy change types the difference in mean relative weights between the vector and triangular representation was statistically significant.

Table 4. Pairwise LSD post-hoc analysis results for the *Indeterminacy Change × Graphical Representation* interaction effect $[F(2, 406) = 1.4, p = 0.248]$.

Indeterminacy Change	Graphical Representation	IC_2→3 Triangle	IC_2→4 Vector	IC_3→4 Triangle	IC_2→3 Vector	IC_2→4 Triangle
IC_2→3	Triangle	×				
IC_2→3	Vector	0.0417^*	×		×	
IC_2→4	Triangle	$<0.0001^{**}$	$<0.0001^{**}$	×		
IC_2→4	Vector	$<0.0001^{**}$	$<0.0001^{**}$	0.0002^*	×	
IC_3→4	Triangle	0.965	0.0375^*	$<0.0001^{**}$	$<0.0001^{**}$	×
IC_3→4	Vector	0.128	0.605	$<0.0001^{**}$	$<0.0001^{**}$	0.117

5 Discussion and Conclusion

In this empirical research, we focused on extending our knowledge on the users' perception of changes in one of the features of the triangular fuzzy numbers. We examined two different graphical representations of these fuzzy numbers and manipulated their levels of indeterminacy. Graphically, the changes were expressed by different lengths of vectors or bases of triangles depending on the type of representation.

We employed pairwise comparisons and AHP methodology to retrieve participants' subjective opinions in the form of relative weights regarding the perceived change in indeterminacy saliencies. The thorough formal statistical analysis, both descriptive and inferential, revealed considerable differences in mean relative scores for the two investigated factors. The triangular graphical representation of the fuzzy number was rated as significantly better in showing indeterminacy changes than its vector counterpart. Moreover, this effect held consistently irrespective of the second factor related with the magnitude and type of the fuzzy number indeterminacy. This was a surprising finding as our previous research results suggested that both representations are comparable in terms of efficiency and effectiveness.

There are several reasons that may explain the observed inconsistency between these studies. First, in the present research, we investigated only one aspect of the uncertainty which is represented by a triangular fuzzy number. In our previous research, apart from the indeterminacy we also involved most possible values. Therefore, a possible future study could include changes in both of those features simultaneously to resolve the conflicting results. Another reason can be associated with relatively small magnitude of the indeterminacy level changes. Extending the experiment by adding a variety of additional levels of this factor could shed some more light on this phenomenon. Also, the position of the segment representing the indeterminacy (a horizontal one in triangles, rotating one in vectors) may have some influence, which should be the object of further studies. Furthermore, since our previous results indicated that there can be differences between women and men, the prospective study should more balanced in terms of gender. This would allow for including this factor into the analysis of variance and perform more comprehensive data exploration.

From the methodological point of view, to better understand subjects' perception of both representations in the future experiments, we will consider using group ranking based on [5] and different monitoring of consistency in pairwise comparisons based on [1].

Despite somewhat unexpected results, the presented experiment outcomes extend the body of knowledge on the subjective perception of triangular fuzzy number graphical representation. Thanks to rapid development in artificial intelligence methods and techniques, the processing of fuzzy, imperfect, or imprecise data for various purposes is becoming more and more common in different areas. Therefore, it is necessary to develop appropriate recommendations for graphical user interfaces in software supporting such activities. The results presented in this study, which sheds some more light on how people perceive examined aspects of uncertainty visualisation, can be considered as a next step in this direction.

Acknowledgement. The work of Jerzy Grobelny and Rafał Michalski was partially financially supported by the Polish National Science Centre grant no. 2019/35/B/HS4/02892: *Intelligent approaches for facility layout problems in management, production, and logistics.*

References

1. Bozóki, S., Fülöp, J., Koczkodaj, W.W.: An LP-based inconsistency monitoring of pairwise comparison matrices. Math Comput. Model **54**, 789–793 (2011). https://doi.org/10.1016/J.MCM.2011.03.026
2. Grobelny, J., Michalski, R.: Various approaches to a human preference analysis in a digital signage display design. Human Factors and Ergonomics in Manuf. Service Ind. **21**, 529–542 (2011). https://doi.org/10.1002/HFM.20295
3. Grobelny, J., Michalski, R.: The role of background color, interletter spacing, and font size on preferences in the digital presentation of a product. Comput. Human Behav. **43**, 85–100 (2015). https://doi.org/10.1016/J.CHB.2014.10.036
4. Hulett, D.T.: Integrated Cost-Schedule Risk Analysis, 1st edn. Routledge, London (2011)
5. Janicki, R., Koczkodaj, W.W.: A weak order approach to group ranking. Comput. Math. Appl. **32**, 51–59 (1996). https://doi.org/10.1016/0898-1221(96)00102-2
6. Kerzner, H.R.: Project Management Metrics, KPIs, and Dashboards : A Guide to Measuring and Monitoring Project Performance, 3rd edn. Wiley, New York (2017)
7. Koczkodaj, W.W.: Statistically accurate evidence of improved error rate by pairwise comparisons. Percept Mot Skills **82**, 43–48 (1996). https://doi.org/10.2466/pms.1996.82.1.43
8. Kuchta, D., Grobelny, J., Michalski, R., Schneider, J.: Vector and triangular representations of project estimation uncertainty: effect of gender on usability. In: Paszynski, M., Kranzlmüller, D., Krzhizhanovskaya, V.V., Dongarra, J.J., Sloot, P.M.A. (eds.) ICCS 2021. LNCS, vol. 12747, pp. 473–485. Springer, Cham (2021). https://doi.org/10.1007/978-3-030-77980-1_36
9. Larson, E.W., Gray, C.F.: Project Management: The Managerial Process. 7th ed. McGraw-Hill Education (2017)
10. Michalski, R.: Examining users' preferences towards vertical graphical toolbars in simple search and point tasks. Comput. Human Behav. **27**, 2308–2321 (2011). https://doi.org/10.1016/j.chb.2011.07.010
11. Michalski, R.: The influence of color grouping on users' visual search behavior and preferences. Displays **35** (2014). https://doi.org/10.1016/j.displa.2014.05.007

12. Płonka, M., Grobelny, J., Michalski, R.: Conjoint analysis models of digital packaging information features in customer decision-making. Int. J. Inf. Technol. Decis. Mak. (2022). https://doi.org/10.1142/S0219622022500766
13. Saaty, T.L.: A scaling method for priorities in hierarchical structures. J Math Psychol **15**, 234–281 (1977). https://doi.org/10.1016/0022-2496(77)90033-5
14. Saaty, T.L.: The Analytic Hierarchy Process. McGraw Hill, New York (1980)
15. Schneider, J., Kuchta, D., Michalski, R.: A vector visualization of uncertainty complementing the traditional fuzzy approach with applications in project management. Appl. Soft Comput. (2023)
16. Streeb, D., El-Assady, M., Keim, D.A., Chen, M.: Why visualize? untangling a large network of arguments. IEEE Trans. Vis Comput. Graph **27**, 2220–2236 (2021). https://doi.org/10.1109/TVCG.2019.2940026
17. TIBCO Software Inc. (2017) TIBCO Statistica, version 13.3
18. Zaleski, S., Michalski, R.: Success factors in sustainable management of IT service projects: exploratory factor analysis. Sustainability **13**, 4457 (2021). https://doi.org/10.3390/SU13084457

Volition Learning: What Would You Prefer to Prefer?

Mohamed Lechiakh$^{(\boxtimes)}$ (ID) and Alexandre Maurer

UM6P School of Computer Science, Mohammed VI Polytechnic University,
Benguerir, Morocco
{mohamed.lechiakh,alexandre.maurer}@um6p.ma

Abstract. When queried, humans do not always give their utmost attention to provide their best possible answer. In particular, they may give different answers to the same question, depending on their level of concentration and interest. This raises a challenge for ethical preference learning. Arguably, we would prefer to learn what humans answer after thoughtful considerations, rather than what they answer when they are tired and lack focus. To distinguish it from instinctive unreflexive preferences, the former is sometimes called a *volition*. In this paper, we propose a basic machine learning approach to learn volitions rather than preferences. To do so, we developed a pairwise comparison model that learns from comparison ratings of pairs of items based on selected quality features. We considered the time spent in producing these ratings as an important contextual metadata: we assume that it effectively contributes to describe volitional behavior, rather than noisy preference-based behavior. Then, we designed an evaluation methodology based on a volition prediction method, that we defined using the learned parameters of our model. We run extensive simulations using synthetic data, as well as a real-world dataset, to validate our claims about users' volitional behaviors. The experimental results proved the efficiency of our model to provide concrete measurements of important volition-dependent parameters, which can be used primarily to assess the reliability and the importance of users' decisions, as well as their level of confidence and knowledge. In general, our model can serve as a foundation for further theoretical and empirical investigations in this topic. It may further incentivize research interest towards friendly and beneficial human-AI interactive systems (e.g., recommender systems) using the theory of volition.

Keywords: volition · preference · recommender systems

1 Introduction

Nowadays, humans are frequently exposed to many AI-based systems in different areas of their life (transportation, shopping, public services, academic learning, ...). Interestingly, online services make an increasing use of AI, in order to provide personalized quality services while maintaining high user satisfaction and engagement rate. For instance, recommender systems (RS) are often used in an interactive and conversational way to perfectly model users' preferences

© The Author(s), under exclusive license to Springer Nature Switzerland AG 2023
H. Degen and S. Ntoa (Eds.): HCII 2023, LNAI 14050, pp. 555–574, 2023.
https://doi.org/10.1007/978-3-031-35891-3_35

and understand their behavior. To do this, RS use different preference learning methods to implicitly infer user tastes and choices, which will be used to filter content and recommend relevant items. Such personalization attempts, however, may result in expensive information hiding and actions, which are at odds with user preferences and goals, due to the difficulty of modeling user preferences, as well as the inefficiency of the automated inference of most systems [1]. Thus, human-AI interaction systems that generally involve user behavior modeling applications (e.g., RS) are a challenging topic for the human-computer interaction (HCI) community [2].

Designing friendly and beneficial preference learning-based AI systems implies that they have human-favorable values, which requires comprehensive insights into human goals and preferences. However, constructing these insights is very difficult, because of the ambiguity of defining and modeling user preferences. This ambiguity comes from the dynamic nature of user preferences, which are only partially known, inconsistent, incoherent, and highly context-dependent [3].

In the context of recommendation platforms, which are a popular application of preference learning-based AI systems, recommendation algorithms use different techniques and theories to effectively recommend to users their most likely favorite items [30]. This is mainly based on how users' preferences are represented and tracked within these systems. Definitely, the construction of user preferences depends on various psychological factors [4], which highly influence user behavior and preferences. Then, these preferences are practically approximated by capturing explicit user feedback (clicks, likes, ratings, comments, dwell time,) and implicit feedback (user navigation data, information of item-specific chats). Moreover, the contextual meta-data and the user's personal information are also considered, to define and optimize user engagement and satisfaction metrics. Other solutions based on *preference elicitation* methods [5] are proposed to better represent user preferences, by first collecting them through decision-support choice mechanisms. We argue that this behavioral and expressed preference data may be used to create particularly empowering recommendation experiences. However, they typically predict immediate user decisions that reflect what users actually do, and not what they really wanted. Thus, they leave serious doubts regarding whether or not they accurately reflect users' "true preferences", and are in line with their values and long-term goals [6,7].

In HCI research, the question of how to close the gap between what users actually do and what they "truly want" to accomplish has a reasonably long history. In spite of the reasonable intuitive definitions that have been produced, this question is often treated in an unsatisfactory and superficial way, due to its philosophical and theoretical complexity [8]. To generally address this question, we should design well-aligned AI systems that use powerful preference elicitation techniques, eliciting correct preference information from the user. In such techniques, it is frequently assumed that humans make optimal decisions, with deviations from this assumption reflecting "random noise" in their choices (i.e., original preferences) [9]. Arguably, human decision-making will definitely deviate from this optimality because of the psychological aspects of preference construction, such as preference visibility and choice overload, and other aspects such as time, personality, emotions, and cognitive biases [4].

More precisely, we describe optimal human decisions, i.e., the actions they took when they had more information and more time to deliberate. This is crucially related to human volition rather than simple "noisy" preference. In other words, volition is what you would *prefer to prefer* if you had more trust and consciousness about your true preferences. In this context, Yudkowsky [10] proposed using Coherent Extrapolated Volition (CEV) as the optimal thing to do in order to align preference-based AI systems. Yudkowsky poetically defines CEV as "our wish if we knew more, thought faster, were more the people we wished we were, had grown up farther together; where the extrapolation converges rather than diverges, where our wishes cohere rather than interfere; extrapolated as we wish that extrapolated, interpreted as we wish that interpreted". Thus, extrapolated volition is related to an extrapolated decision-making process where human psychology demonstrates a high level of stability, focus, self-knowledge and self-control to correctly consider all facts and arguments, while manifesting preferences and choices.

A lot of previous research tackled *preference* learning. In this paper, we propose to go further, and to tackle *volition* learning. We know that human will is easily reshaped and diverted by internal personality traits, cognitive styles, body and brain state, and outside environmental effects. We even believe that the external factors are necessary to understand the psycho-physiology of humans, through investigating ambiguous patterns of their thoughts and behavior. More generally, humans' original thoughts frequently do not match up with their concrete actions. In this work, we are interested in this link between thought and action that lies at the heart of volition, which we try to quantitatively measure using contextual metadata. We believe that volition learning would be more effective for presenting a comprehensive picture about human preferences and choices, which would definitely improve the quality of human preference-based systems. It is noteworthy that it is very challenging to concretely define volition and to set a unified reference modeling. Yet, we have been able to provide a first machine learning-based model to learn volition through a theoretical and experimental approach, rather than a purely philosophical or qualitative study, as it is commonly done in this research area. Therefore, we summarize our main contributions as follows:

- We proposed a pairwise-comparison volitional model by considering that a preference is typically a volition corrupted by an additive noise. We considered the time spent for submitting these comparison ratings as an important contextual meta-data, that strongly depends on this noise. We used the Bradley-Terry model, levaraging users' confidence level inputs to better learn the parameters of our volitional model.

– We proposed a volition prediction method, which we use to design the evaluation methodology of our model, and experimentally validate its performance through extensive simulations.
– We performed simulations with synthetic data that demonstrates the accuracy of our model' trained parameters, in comparison with the ground truth values. The findings support our assumption that longer durations are more likely to be associated with volitional behaviors.
– We performed simulations with a real dataset that perfectly fits to our model's inputs and structure. These experiments validate our results obtained with synthetic data, and they helped to present more explainability about users' behavior and volitional decisions. In general, contrary to what is frequently regarded as wholly internally generated [15], we demonstrated that this volitional behavior may be significantly influenced by the environmental context variables, in the case of preference-based pairwise comparison systems.
– We provided the source code for this research work, and made it publicly accessible to the community.

2 Literature Review

2.1 Volition

A considerable number of preference learning-based systems (e.g., RS) rely on predictive modeling: they predict user behavior using algorithmic feedback interaction metrics (ratings, clicks,). These systems are often blamed for not providing enough information about the mental processes mediating that behavior. In general, people do not always behave according to their beliefs, expectations, values, or intentions. This has sparked intense interest in the theories of volition and action to understand transitions from cognitive aspects of human psychology to substantial related actions. The research question of understanding and modeling the human volition has a relatively long history. However, due to the lack of experimental methods to study volition, it has often been neglected by contemporary philosophy and experimental psychology, which has led to very few empirical studies of volitional behavior [16–18]. In this context, a majority of prior works have been concentrated on the definition of volition, and addressing the gap between the theories of volition and action from many psychological perspectives [15]. This involved the study of important aspects of the "will psychology", namely, motivation and intention, since volition is often considered as the "act of will" [19–21]: we know what we want (goals or intentions) based on a motivation construct, and when we act on what we want through some volitional process, we do so by making a conscious decision. Thus, volitional factors affect the transition from goals or intentions to action, which in turn affects both performance and subsequent motivation.

A large number of recent research works have studied volition through (educational) learning environments [22, 25, 26]. These works have primarily analyzed how volitional processes affect intention creation, intrinsic goal orientation, self-efficacy on cognitive engagement and motivation, based on psychological theories. It is noteworthy that the process of learning presents a perfect framework to exploit important volitional aspects (e.g., motivation, self-control and self-regulation), which enable to measure and model volition with experimental crowd studies, using simplified behavioral and mathematical models. Within this frame of work, [23,24] proposed empirical studies using the framework of the integrative theory of Motivation, Volition, and Performance (MVP) to develop and statistically evaluate a mathematical MVP model for evaluating students' learning experiences in digital learning environments. Their results show how student's cognitive capabilities, motivation and volitional processes could be positive or negative predictors of student's satisfaction.

In addition, we found that certain writings touch on some behaviorism and thought-action issues that are closely related to volition without even mentioning the term *volition*. In this context, Warren Teitelman [14] announced his DWIM's theory (Do What I Mean) in 1960, which promotes the development of more user-values aligned systems, which tend to interpret users' true intentions and push them to make correct actions. This was some of the initial works that implicitly approached the problem of volition from a philosophical system design perspective, which has been critiqued for inducing a lot of system bias.

2.2 User Modeling in Human-AI Interactive Systems

The user modeling techniques could be potentially useful to improve the collaborative nature of HCI systems, which generally aim to allow the development of systems that are easy, user-friendly and pleasant to use [28]. These models can be defined as the representations that systems have of users, which may represent personal characteristics (e.g., traits, personality), cognitive styles, resources and processing, knowledge of tasks, or psycho-physical aspects [29]. When psychological theories are applied to HCI, the system's pleasurability and ease can be operationalized in terms of user preferences and behavior, through their interactions with the system. This system's performance could be further enhanced with the benefits of AI based models [31].

Basically, research in HCI aims to build useful and usable systems which can predict user behavior accurately across a wide range of configurations and use cases, or improve usability through enhanced interaction. In a different perspective, AI research generally aims to build models that enable the recreation of human intelligence in systems by displaying intelligent behaviors [29]. Until recently, the potential for using this intelligence to create useful and usable systems has not reached general acceptance or even recognition from the HCI research community. As a result, this has led to address user modeling with different goals and scopes in each discipline, which has drastically limited its efficiency and beneficial impact. However, the significant advancements in AI over the past few years, particularly in knowledge representation and machine learning techniques, have helped to build intelligent and user-friendly systems which, when combined with HCI theory and human-centered AI approaches [32], can lead to new applications for AI, that have not yet been imagined [27]. In this context, a lot of research has been done to improve user modeling techniques as a key tool for supporting human-AI interaction systems such as conversational agents [35,36], intelligent assistants [37,38], information retrieval systems [39], recommendation and preference elicitation systems [5,33,34], to name a few.

While human-AI interaction may be very helpful to provide more personalized content that aligns with users' preferences, the automated filtering and optimization of this content in the background may lead to expensive information hiding, which is at odds with user expectations and goals. Thus, the automated inference based on user models (as well as other system models) are typically performed under uncertainty, which may demonstrate irrelevant actions and unpredictable behaviors. To mitigate such effects, a large body of works exists and continues to grow around how to increase the transparency and the explainability of AI systems [40,44] alongside with the HCI community, which has proposed principles and guidelines [1] for designing user interfaces and interaction for AI-based applications.

In this context, Gruas et al. [41] showed that adopting a more theoretical perspective (based on psychological models) would efficiently help to identify the root cause behind users' behaviors, which may thereby benefit personalization opportunities for data-driven personalization systems like RS. These psychological models are related to user traits (e.g., personality, cognitive styles and susceptibility to persuasive strategies), which are difficult to measure and capture from interaction behaviors. However, despite the increasing research interest in this direction, the work is still mostly limited to empirical studies using statistical approaches for better behavior interpretations and preference learning. A limited number of researchers focused on the preference nature structure and its construction mechanism. For instance, Liu et al. [42] considered that users' interest are affected by intent factors that represent users' current needs, and preference factors that are relatively stable and learned continuously over time. They proposed a mechanism to separately learn these features that have often been mixed up by existing works. The same principle is adopted by [43], that supposed an hierarchical discrimination between user intentions and user preferences to build a key-array memory network for next-item recommendation.

As previously stated, intention (or intent) is the initial state of mind when we consider doing something. Once it begins the implementation into action, it is called volition (act of mind), which, under certain noise conditions, develops into preference. Thus, volition is more significant to characterize user willpower and judge their decision and action, than the intention (which remains a thought under refinement). In this paper, we propose a machine learning-based approach to learn this volition. We use contextual metadata about the time spent in pairwise comparison of items to characterize thoughtful behaviors.

3   Pairwise Comparison Volitional Model

In this section, we first present the preference learning problem, based on the Bradley-Terry model [11]. Then, we propose a very simple model to learn volition.

3.1   Preference Learning

In many preference learning models, it is common to model a user's preference by a vector $\theta \in \mathbb{R}^d$. Given a set $\mathcal{D}$ of data collected by querying the preferences, a loss function $\mathcal{L}$ can usually be written as

$$\mathcal{L}(\theta, \mathcal{D}) = \sum_{k \in \mathcal{D}} \ell(\theta, x_k) + \mathcal{R}(\theta), \tag{1}$$

where ℓ is a function that depends on user inputs of the user, and $\mathcal{R}$ is a regularization function.

In Bayesian models, ℓ is typically the negative log-likelihood of data point x_k given preferences θ, while $\mathcal{R}$ is the negative log-prior on θ, so that the loss now becomes equal to the negative log-posterior given dataset $\mathcal{D}$, up to a constant independent from θ. Minimizing the loss function is then equivalent to computing a maximum-a-posteriori.

For instance, in the Bradley-Terry model [11], x is a comparison between two alternatives i and j, whose feature representations are vectors $r_i, r_j \in \mathbb{R}^d$. We then have $\ell(\theta, i \succ j) = -\log \mathbb{P}\left[i \succ j \mid \theta\right] = -\log \sigma\left(\theta^T(r_i - r_j)\right)$, where $\sigma : \mathbb{R} \to \mathbb{R}$ is the sigmoid function $\sigma(t) = 1/(1 + e^{-t})$.

3.2   Volition Learning

In this paper, we propose a volition learning model, which considers that, when queried, the user's preference θ used in the query may differ from their volition ν. Here, we have $\theta, \nu \in \mathbb{R}^d$, where d is the space dimension of feature representation of human preference (or volition). In our case, d represents the number of quality features of items in our pairwise comparison model. We consider a set $\mathcal{U}_N$ of N users, and $\mathcal{I}_M$ is the set of M items. Let the query $x_{k,u} = \{(x_{k,u}^{(i)}, x_{k,u}^{(j)}) |\, `i \succ j'\}$ represents the $k^{th}$ comparison (denoted as $`i \succ j'$) by user u of item i being preferred to item j, based on her rating vectors $x_{k,u}^{(i)}$ and $x_{k,u}^{(j)}$ respectively, where $i, j \in \mathcal{I}_M$. In this work, we consider that user preferences and volition sequentially change over time, depending on users' comparison behavior. We denote by $\xi_{k,u} = \theta_{k,u} - \nu_{k,u}$ the discrepancy, and we assume that such noises $\xi_{k,u}$ are independent and identically distributed.

Moreover, we consider that each data point associated to the query $x_{k,u}$ comes with a contextual metadata $y_{k,u}$. In other words, we now consider the dataset $\mathcal{D}_u = \{(x_{k,u}, y_{k,u})_k\}$, belonging to user u. We assume that the probability of observing the contextual metadata $y_{k,u}$ depends on the value of $\xi_{k,u}$.

To account for this, we then consider the loss function

$$\mathcal{L}(\nu_u, \mathcal{D}_u) = \sum_{k \in [\mathcal{D}_u]} \left(-\log \mathbb{P}\left[\xi_{k,u} \mid \nu_{k,u}\right] - \log \mathbb{P}\left[y_{k,u} \mid \nu_{k,u}, \xi_{k,u}\right] + \ell(\nu_{k,u} + \xi_{k,u}, x_{k,u}) \right)$$
$$+ \mathcal{R}(\nu_u).$$
(2)

where l is the Bradley-Terry loss function, $\mathcal{R}(.)$ is a convex regularization, and ν_u is the vector of $\nu_{k,u}$.

We now assume that the discrepancy $\xi_{k,u}$ does not depend on $\nu_{k,u}$, and that $y_{k,u}$ depends only on $\xi_{k,u}$. We then have:

$$\mathcal{L}(\nu_u, \mathcal{D}_u) = \sum_{k \in [\mathcal{D}_u]} \left(-\log \mathbb{P}\left[\xi_{k,u}\right] - \log \mathbb{P}\left[y_{k,u} \mid \xi_{k,u}\right] + \ell(\nu_{k,u} + \xi_{k,u}, x_{k,u}) \right)$$
$$+ \mathcal{R}(\nu_u).$$
(3)

Moreover, we may assume that the noise $\xi_{k,u}$ follows a Gaussian distribution $\mathcal{N}(\bar{\xi}, \sigma_\xi^2 I)$, which now makes the loss function depend on these additional parameters, i.e.:

$$\mathcal{L}(\nu_u, \bar{\xi}, \sigma_\xi, \mathcal{D}_u) = \sum_{k \in [\mathcal{D}_u]} \left(\frac{(\xi_{k,u} - \bar{\xi})^2}{2\sigma_\xi^2} - \log \mathbb{P}\left[y_{k,u} \mid \xi_{k,u}\right] + \ell(\nu_{k,u} + \xi_{k,u}, x_{k,u}) \right)$$
$$+ \mathcal{R}(\nu_u).$$
(4)

Finally, we still have to determine how $\xi_{k,u}$ impacts the observed contextual metadata $y_{k,u}$. Then, we should adapt our model to the collected contextual metadata.

3.3   Context-Dependent Effects

In this section, we discuss some important contextual meta-data that could be captured from the user evaluation session of the pairwise comparisons of items. Basically, we build our analysis on this intuition: volitional behaviors (which are associated to small values of $\xi_{k,u} \sim \mathcal{N}(\bar{\xi}, \sigma_\xi^2 I)$) are produced by more thoughtful decisions and reasonable actions. Then, we consider a threshold ψ such that the condition $\|\xi_{k,u}\|_2 / d \le \psi$ characterizes more volitional behaviors, as claimed by our intuition. Then, based on this property, we consider the following features:

- **Contextual meta-data:** For simplicity, we consider the metadata $y_{k,u}$: "total duration time of the comparisons for all rating features related to query $x_{k,u}$ of user u". We suppose that $y_{k,u}$ follows an exponential distribution of parameter $\|\bar{\xi}\|_2$.

– **Confidence level:** Typically, We assume that the user confidence level c, which may be given to assess the trustworthiness of her response, gets greater values when $\|\xi_{k,u}\|_2/d \leq \psi$. We use the random utility model (RUM), also known as Thurstone's model [12]. This model considers the utility of an item i as a random variable U_i defined by $U_i = s_i + \epsilon_i$, where s_i is the expected score (inherent quality), and the error ϵ_i is a random noise reflecting unobservable effects within the user response. We extend this model to account for the user confidence information using the parameter c as a scaling factor to control the noise. We then have, $U_i = s_i + \frac{\epsilon_i}{c}$.

Loss Function of the Pair-Comparison Model. For a given query $x_{k,u}$, we have $\mathbb{P}[i \succ j \mid s_i, s_j, c] = \mathbb{P}[\epsilon_j - \epsilon_i \leq c(s_i - s_j)] = F(c(s_i - s_j))$, where F is the CDF (Cumulative Distribution Function) of $\epsilon = \epsilon_j - \epsilon_i$, and ϵ_i and ϵ_j are two i.i.d. random variables. It is clear that, the larger c is, the more accurate the user is. Then, we consider $s_i = f(\theta, x_{k,u})$ such that f is a function defined on user preferences and item features. In our case, we set f to be linear, and ϵ follows a Gumbel distribution with mean 0 and scale parameter 1. In addition, s_i and s_j scores represent the ratings' representations vectors $x_{k,u}^{(i)}$ and $x_{k,u}^{(j)}$, respectively. We use $r_{k,u}^{(ij)} = x_{k,u}^{(i)} - x_{k,u}^{(j)}$ to model the comparison result of items i and j based on the quality features. Then, for a user u, we describe the Bradley-Terry loss function as

$$
\begin{aligned}
\ell(\nu_{k,u} + \xi_{k,u}; i \succ j) &= -\log \mathbb{P}[i \succ j \mid \nu_{k,u}, \xi_{k,u}] \\
&= -\log \sigma\left((\nu_{k,u} + \xi_{k,u})^T (c_{k,u} \times (x_{k,u}^{(i)} - x_{k,u}^{(j)}))\right),
\end{aligned} \tag{5}
$$

where $c_{k,u}$ is the confidence vector given for the query $x_{k,u}$, and σ is the sigmoid function. We note that $c_{k,u}$ represents the confidence level vector of ratings given by user u, based on the evaluated quality features (of number d). For our model, we considered five confidence levels: "skip", "unsure", "sure", "confident" and "extremely confident". Then, we translated these levels into the respective confidence values in the following set: $C_w = \{0, 0.5, 1, 1.3, 1.5\}$. Now, the user dataset $\mathcal{D}_u$ becomes $\mathcal{D}_u = \{(x_k, y_{k,u}, c_{k,u})_k\}$. Then, the loss function of user u is given by

$$
\mathcal{L}(\nu_u, \bar{\xi}, \sigma_\xi, \mathcal{D}_u) = \sum_{k \in [\mathcal{D}_u]} \left(\frac{(\xi_{k,u} - \bar{\xi})^2}{2\sigma_\xi^2} + y_{k,u}\|\bar{\xi}\|_2 - \ell(\nu_{k,u} + \xi_{k,u}; i \succ j)\right) \\
+ \lambda \alpha_u \|\nu_u\|_2^2, \tag{6}
$$

where ℓ is the loss function given by the Eq. 5, $\alpha_u = \sum_{k \in \mathcal{D}_u} \frac{2c_{k,u}}{C + c_{k,u}}$ models the confidence level vector, and $\lambda > 0$ is a tuning parameter. Intuitively, when a user specifies confidence levels for all rating features using high values, we will have $c_{k,u} \longrightarrow C$, then α_k converges to k. But if she gave few confidence information with low values, then $c_{k,u} \longrightarrow 0$, which means that α_k converges to 0. Typically, we set $C = d * max\{c, c \in C_w\}$. Thus, we get $C = 1.5 \times d$.

3.4 Multi-user Model

It is important to consider multiple users to better estimate the parameters like $\bar{\xi}$ or σ_ξ. The loss function is then simply obtained by adding up all user losses:

$$\mathcal{L}(\boldsymbol{\nu}, \bar{\xi}, \sigma_\xi, \mathcal{D}) = \sum_{u \in \mathcal{U}_N} \sum_{k \in [\mathcal{D}_u]} \left(\frac{(\xi_{k,u} - \bar{\xi})^2}{2\sigma_\xi^2} + y_{k,u} \left\| \bar{\xi} \right\|_2 - \ell(\nu_{k,u} + \xi_{k,u}; i \succ j) \right)$$
$$+ \lambda \sum_{u \in \mathcal{U}_N} \alpha_u \left\| \nu_u \right\|_2^2,$$

$$(7)$$

where $\mathcal{D} = [\mathcal{D}_u]_{u \in \mathcal{U}_N}$ and $\boldsymbol{\nu} = [\nu_u]_{u \in \mathcal{U}_N}$.

4 Experiments

To evaluate the performance of our model, we first proceed by experimental simulations using synthetic (fake) data generation. Then, we perform offline simulations using a real dataset.

4.1 Description of the Experiments

In our simulations, each user is presented with a series of pairs of items (randomly generated in the case of synthetic data, or taken from her consumption history in the case of the real dataset) and asked to compare them using a set of quality features. Our model is implemented in Python using PyTorch's deep learning framework[1].

We first start by simulations with synthetic data in which we ran extensive experiments to understand the model's outputs and fine-tune its hyperparameters. We used the Adam optimization algorithm, which has shown to have better convergence results. Then, we performed simulations with the real dataset of Tournesol [13], which we used to validate our results and to further optimize upon the model hyper-parameters. In both simulation approaches, the model learns the estimated mean vector $\tilde{\bar{\xi}}$ and the covariance matrix $\tilde{\sigma}_\xi$ of the noise $\xi_{k,u}$ as global parameters of the system. In addition, it learns for each user the estimated volition vector $\tilde{\nu}_u$, which models the pure unbiased preference that this user has developed by comparing the pairs of items (supposedly time-ordered) as they appear in her history (input data).

4.2 Evaluation Methodology

During the test phase, we generally assess our model's accuracy for predicting the users' ratings by optimizing the best associated (noisy) preference $p_{k,u} = \tilde{\nu}_{k,u} + n_s$, whose volition $\tilde{\nu}_{k,u}$ is already learned by our model, and where n_s is a

---

[1] Our project code is available on Github: https://github.com/MLechiakh/Volition_learning.

noise fixed accordingly. More precisely, we sample a set N_s of probably delivered noises following $\mathcal{N}(\bar{\xi}, \tilde{\sigma}_\xi)$. Each one will be added to her learned volition $\tilde{\nu}_{k,u}$ to build a set of noisy preferences: $\mathcal{P}_{k,u} = \{p_{k,u} | p_{k,u} = \tilde{\nu}_{k,u} + n_s, n_s \in N_s\}$. Then, we use the contextual metadata $y_{k,u}$ and the given weight vector to calculate the following predicted preference probability:

$$P(i \succ j | p_{k,u}, D_u) = \sigma(\mathbb{P}\left[i \succ j \,\middle|\, p_{k,u}, r_{k,u}^{(ij)}, c_{k,u}\right] \times pdf_\mathcal{E}(y_{k,u} | n_s)) \qquad (8)$$

where $pdf_\mathcal{E}(y_k | n_s)$ is the probability density function of $y_{k,u}$ conditioned on the random preference noise $n_s \sim \mathcal{N}(\bar{\xi}, \tilde{\sigma}_\xi)$ that is associated with its query $x_{k,u}$, $y_{k,u} \sim \mathcal{E}(\|n_s\|_2)$ and

$$\mathbb{P}\left[i \succ j \,\middle|\, p_{k,u}, r_{k,u}^{(ij)}, c_{k,u}\right] = \sigma\left(c_{k,u} \times p_{k,u}^T r_{k,u}^{(ij)}\right)$$

such that $r_{k,u}^{(ij)} \in \mathbb{R}^d$ and $y_{k,u}, c_{k,u} \in D_u$. Then, we extract the optimal volition noise associated with the query $x_{k,u}$, using the equation:

$$\tilde{\xi}_{k,u}^* = \left(\arg\max_{p_{k,u} \in \mathcal{P}_{k,u}} P(i \succ j | p_{k,u}, D_u)\right) - \tilde{\nu}_{k,u} \qquad (9)$$

In the rest of this paper, we simply refer to $\tilde{\xi}_{k,u}^*$ by $\xi_{k,u}$. We use a threshold ψ to decide if a rating is considered as produced by a volition of the user, when $\|\xi_{k,u}\|_2 / d \le \psi$. Basically, the lower the value of ψ is, the more volitional behavior is generated.

4.3 Empirical Evaluation: Simulation with Synthetic Data

With this simulation, we aim to validate the following questions:

- **Q1:** Does the model succeeds to approach the ground truth values of the volition noise parameters (i.e. $\tilde{\bar{\xi}} \approx \bar{\xi}$ and $\tilde{\sigma}_\xi \approx \sigma_\xi$)?
- **Q2:** What is the model's accuracy in predicting the user preference modes (volition, or simple preference, as fixed by the ground truth of the test set) given her rating information $r_{k,u}^{(ij)}$?
- **Q3:** How does the volition noise impact the user's behavior?

Experimental Settings. In the following, we describe the experimental settings used in this simulation:

Ground truth (GT): We consider a system of $M = 100000$ videos and $N = 1000$ users. We generate a user's data point $(x_{k,u}, y_{k,u}, c_{k,u} | \nu_{k,u}, \theta_{k,u}, \xi_{k,u})$ related to the comparison of i and j by initially assuming that $\nu_{k,u}$ and θ_k follow a Gaussian distribution $\mathcal{N}(0, 1)$. We have $\xi_{k,u} = \theta_{k,u} - \nu_{k,u}$, such that ξ_k follows $\mathcal{N}(\bar{\xi}, \sigma_\xi)$. We set $\bar{\xi} = 0$ and $\sigma_\xi = 2$. Then, we define a probability density function based on the

Bradley-Terry model, which we use to generate random ratings $r_{k,u}^{(ij)}$ for the comparisons '$i \succ j$', according to d quality features. Thereafter, we generate random comparison durations $y_{k,u}$ following $\mathcal{E}(\|\xi_{k,u}\|_2)$, and we choose random values of $c_{k,u}$ among $\{0, 0.5, 1, 1.3, 1.5\}$. We consider that each user rates 10 distinct items, each along d criteria, which produces a total of 25 pair comparisons data points which constitute the user dataset D_u. Using this configuration, we obtained a final generated dataset of 25000 data points for 1000 users. In this simulation, we split this dataset into a training set (80%) and a test set (20%). Note that small setting values are chosen, due to computational resource constraints.

Training: The model's hyper-parameters, namely, the global learning rate lr_g (adjusted for learning the Gaussian parameters of $\xi_{k,u}$) and the local learning rate lr_c (adjusted for learning the users' volition vector) are manually tuned with extensive testing configuration cases. The final optimized values of these parameters, that are used for training our model, are $lr_g = 0.001$, $lr_c = 0.2$ and $\lambda = 0.5$.

Testing: We consider $\psi = 0.5$ for both the GT and our testing methodology to ensure fair judgements when evaluating the proportion of volitional queries using Eq. 9, under the condition $\|\xi_{k,u}\|_2 \leq \psi$. Typically, ψ is set slightly higher, in order to maintain a large number of volitional ratings (queries judged to be volitional) for testing purposes. Then, the final results are calculated and averaged over 3 reproducible experiments for $d = 1, 2, 3, 5, 7, 9$.

Evaluation Metrics. We use distance evaluation metrics to assess the performance of our learned volitional model by approximating the GT pre-set parameter values, where $d_1(\bar{\xi}, \tilde{\bar{\xi}}) = euclidean(\bar{\xi}, \tilde{\bar{\xi}})$, $d_2(\sigma_\xi - \tilde{\sigma}_\xi) = euclidean(\sigma_\xi, \tilde{\sigma}_\xi)$ and $d_3(\nu_{k,u}, \tilde{\nu}_u) = \frac{1}{N} \sum_{u=1}^{u=N} euclidean(\nu_u, \tilde{\nu}_u)$, where $\tilde{\nu}_u = [\tilde{\nu}_1, ..., \tilde{\nu}_k]_u$ (with $\tilde{\nu}_k \in \mathbb{R}^d$) is the user volition vector that has been optimized till the last data point in D_u; and $euclidean(.,.)$ is the euclidean distance. In addition, the accuracy and F1-score measure the performance of our model for predicting volitional user queries, in which $\|\xi_{k,u}\|_2 / d < \psi$.

Analysis and Discussion of the Results. First, according to the results shown in Table 1, We initially assessed our model's training efficiency in terms of approximating the GT's values in the experimentation with the training set. Then, we address **Q1** by calculating the distances d_1 and d_2 between the GT parameter values of the Gaussian variable $\xi_{k,u}$ with their values learned by our volitional model. In addition, we calculate the average sum of euclidean distances between the volition vectors ν_u used in the GT's queries and their corresponding values $\tilde{\nu}_u$ learned by our model for all users. In general, the values of d_1, d_2 and d_3 demonstrate good performance of our model training (with its fine-tuned hyper-parameters values) in approaching the GT's values. These results show low values for these distances, which grow marginally as the dimension of features representation space (i.e., the number of quality features) d increases.

Table 1. The evaluation of the performance of our model for different quality features $d = 1, 2, 3, 5, 7, 9$ through (1) comparing our learned model's parameter values with the GT settings of the training set by measuring distances d_1, d_2 and d_3, and (2) evaluating the accuracy and F1-score of predicting volitional queries based on GT of the test set for $\psi = 0.5$.

	d=1	d=2	d=3	d=5	d=7	d=9
$d_1(\bar{\xi}, \tilde{\bar{\xi}})$	0.02	0.02	0.03	0.04	0.04	0.06
$d_2(\sigma_\xi, \tilde{\sigma}_\xi)$	0.36	0.52	0.68	0.87	1.06	1.18
$d_3(\nu_u, \tilde{\nu}_u)$	4.37	6.28	7.68	9.99	11.8	13.39
Accuracy %	69.48	68.36	24.64	32.6	48	66.64
F1-score %	17	18	35	48	63	79

In addition, the performance results in the test set indicate good accuracy values for dimensions $d = 1$ and $d = 2$, but it unexpectedly declines for $d = 3$. From $d = 3$ to $d = 9$, the F1-scores and accuracy values increased significantly, indicating that high precision and recall values were reached.

Overall, the results of d_3 distance prove that our model performs well in reconstructing the volition vector behind each query of the GT while ensuring satisfying accuracy performance, which answers the question **Q2**. Thus, we can conclude that the more quality rating features the user evaluates through her pairwise comparison queries, the more information the model can infer about her preferences, which allows it to accurately forecast her volitional queries, as clearly shown for $d = 7$ and $d = 9$. Second, Fig. 1 shows how the contextual metadata $y_{k,u}$ (i.e., the comparison duration of pairs of items) could impact the volitional behavior of users, which addresses the question **Q3**. Thus, we found that higher values of $y_{k,u}$ are associated with lower values of $\|\xi_k\|_2$, confirming our intuition (stated in Sect. 3.3) that spending more time in evaluating the pair of items will probably lead to more thoughtful (volitional) decisions. As a result, our hypothesis introduced in Sect. 3.3 concerning the distribution of $y_{k,u}$ is confirmed.

4.4 Empirical Evaluation: Simulation with Real Data

In this section, we perform simulations using a real world dataset to experimentally prove some important findings about user behavior and psychology. We aim to validate the results of our simulations with synthetic data, and present more behavioral explanations of human interaction and judgements. In the case of simulations with real data, it is not possible to tackle the questions **Q1** and **Q2**, because no ground truth GT could be established. However, we will try to address the question **Q3** by showing the different relationships that the learned noise (given by Eq. 9) has with some aspects of human behaviors. In this context, we will provide insightful results to support our claims in the assumptions mentioned in Sect. 3.3.

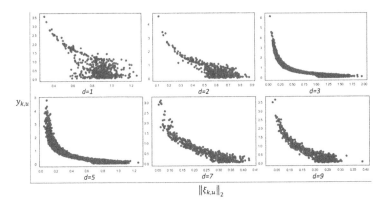

$y_{k,u}$

$\|\xi_{k,u}\|_2$

Fig. 1. Visualization of the relationship between the contextual metadata $y_{k,u}$ and the normalized noise values $\|\xi_{k,u}\|_2$, that are determined by our evaluation methodology (using Eq. 9) for increased values of the number of quality features d.

Dataset. We use a real dataset provided by the open source project *Tournesol*[2], a decision-making collaborative platform based on pairwise comparisons of *Youtube*'s videos. We find that *Tournesol*'s dataset [13] perfectly fits our model inputs, since it provides comparisons based on specified quality features with confidence levels (weights). Most importantly, this dataset included the time spent while making each pairwise comparison, which is a key factor of the effectiveness of our approach (see Table 2 for some statistics about the dataset). For better results, we only keep users with more than one comparison queries. Furthermore, we make the assumption that a user can submit her comparison ratings based on the nine quality features in a reasonable amount of time, which is less than 15 min. Then, we remove incomplete queries with missing entries of $y_{k,u}$, and queries whose values of $y_{k,u}$ are beyond the duration of 15 min. At the end, we got a clean dataset with 316 users, 7900 comparison queries and 2765 videos.

Table 2. Tournesol dataset statistics.

#Users	#Videos	#Comparisons	Avg-duration	Weights	Quality features	Rating range
414	2925	8217	60s	[0, 0.5, 1, 1.3, 1.5]	"reliability", "importance', "engaging", "pedagogy', "layman friendly", "diversity inclusion", "backfire risk", "better habits", "entertaining"	[0, 100]

Analysis of the Results. *Q3.1*: *How is the time spent rating pairwise comparisons $y_{k,u}$ related to the volitional noise $\xi \sim \mathcal{N}(\tilde{\xi}, \tilde{\sigma}_\xi)$?* In Fig. 2, the histograms

2 https://tournesol.app/.

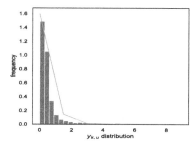

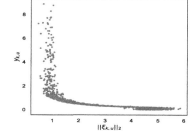

Fig. 2. Histograms of the probability distribution of the query's duration values $y_{k,u}$ (from the training set) with the exponential *pdf* curve of $\mathcal{E}(\tilde{\lambda})$ where $\tilde{\lambda} = 1.59$ is analytically calculated.

Fig. 3. The variations of the query's duration values $y_{k,u}$ from the test set with their associated normalized values of noise $\|\xi_{k,u}\|_2$ learned by our model.

model the probability distribution of the query's duration values contained in the training set, which show that $y_{k,u}$ follows an exponential distribution of an unknown parameter $\tilde{\lambda}$. Analytically, we proved this result using the Maximum Likelihood Estimation principle to approximate the value of $\tilde{\lambda}$ that maximizes its likelihood. Using this mathematical technique, we get $\tilde{\lambda} \approx K / \sum_{k=1}^{K} y_{k,u}$, where K is the number of $y_{k,u}$ entries. Thus, we calculated this value for the training set, and we found $\tilde{\lambda} = 1.59$. The curve of the exponential distribution function *pdf* using this value is depicted in the same figure, which show that 1.59 is indeed a good approximation of the parameter of this distribution.

In our work, we have supposed that $y_{k,u}$ follows an exponential distribution of parameter $\|\bar{\xi}\|_2$ (see Sect. 3.3). After training our model, we got an estimated value $\left\|\tilde{\bar{\xi}}\right\|_2 = 1.6$, which almost equal to the analytical value $\tilde{\lambda} = 1.59$. Thus, we can say that our model successfully approximates the parameter of the exponential distribution of $y_{k,u}$, which has been proven to equal $\left\|\tilde{\bar{\xi}}\right\|_2$, as supposed by our approach.

In addition, Fig. 3 shows that high values of $y_{k,u}$ correspond to small values of the queries' noises (i.e., more volitional queries). This means that users take more time to deliver more volitional decisions about their comparison decisions of pairs of items. Therefore, these results validate our findings with simulations using synthetic data, which confirm our intuition about long durations of $y_{k,u}$, that likely correspond to more volitional behaviors.

Q3.2*: How could our approach be used to interpret user confidence levels when making their pairwise comparison decisions?* Given our intuition that small values of query's noises are responsible of effective volitional behavior (as we proved by the analysis of question **Q3.1**), we consider that $\psi = 0.23$, for describing volitional queries based on the condition $\|\xi_{k,u}\|_2 / d \le \psi$. This is represented in Fig. 3 by the threshold $\|\xi_{k,u}\|_2 \approx 2$, below which the corresponding values of $y_{k,u}$ slightly decline under 0.5 min, whereas $\|\xi_{k,u}\|_2$ increases considerably.

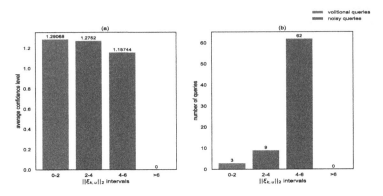

Fig. 4. Visualization of the queries' average confidence weights (left-side figure (a)) and the total number of queries in which users did not indicate their confidence levels (right-side figure (b)), classified by volitional and noisy queries (distinguished by $\psi = 0.23$)

Figure 4:(a) presents the average confidence weights for users' queries whose values of $\|\xi_{k,u}\|_2$ fall inside the 2-sized defined intervals. We can clearly see that volitional queries (which correspond to the volitional interval $[0, \psi \times d] = [0, 2]$) result in the higher value of the average confidence weights associated with these queries. Noisy queries show yet decreasing values of this average across the subdivided intervals. These results indicate that a user exhibits less confidence regarding her rating behavior when she experiences more noise on her volition. In the same context, Fig. 4:(b) shows that the number of queries where users omitted to express their confidence level (i.e., $c_{k,u} = 0$) goes dramatically higher with noisy queries. Then, users show more willingness to express their confidence levels and to be more confident about their judgments when they behave according to their volition rather than their simple (noisy) preferences.

Similarly, Fig. 5:(c) presents the average confidence weights of queries according to their durations $y_{k,u}$, based on their volitional or noisy nature. In this case, volitional queries correspond to $y_{k,u} > 0.49$ and the noisy ones are for $y_{k,u} \leq 0.49$. Here, the value 0.49 is calculated using the threshold $\psi = 0.23$ and the result of Fig. 3. The results of Fig. 5:(c) show that volitional queries that are associated to longer comparison durations (i.e., $context_{k,u} > 0.49$) achieve the best average confidence weights (≈ 1.3) compared to noisy queries (≈ 1.2). In addition, based on Fig. 5:(d), we found only 3 volitional queries in which users did not give their confidence level feedback, while this number equals 71 for noisy queries. We can therefore draw the conclusion that users' lengthy decision-making processes for pairwise video comparisons are more likely to be driven by volitional attitude, which instills more confidence and trust in their behavior in general.

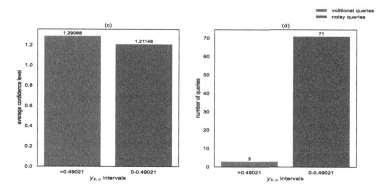

Fig. 5. Visualization of the queries' average confidence levels (left figure (c)) and the total number of queries made by users that skip mentioning their confidence levels (right figure (d)) in relation with interval values of $y_{k,u}$. These intervals are determined based on volitional and noisy queries when the threshold $\psi = 0.23$.

5   Conclusion and Future Works

In this paper, we investigated the problem of volition learning by putting forth a pairwise comparison machine learning model, taking into account the fact that a preference is essentially a pure volition that has been tainted by unexpected noise. We take advantage of the influence of the time spent performing comparisons on pairs of items (based on selected quality features) for better learning our model's volition and noise parameters. The choice of this time contextual metadata is justified by the importance of the flow of time in explaining natural phenomena and human beings' behaviors. In our work, it concerns the comparison results of pairs of items, which can be affected by individual cognitive capabilities and personal traits. These psychological features could help improve user modeling from a volitional perspective, which would lead to a better understanding of individual preferences and behaviors. Thus, we build our model based on the assumption that the distribution of this time metadata exponentially depends on the volition noise (supposed Gaussian), which parameters are learnt by the model. Our results using simulations with synthetic data and real world dataset lead to confirm interesting user behaviors. First, the considered relation between preference and volition (with the additive Gaussian noise) presents a good mathematical approach to model volition of users' queries using the proposed pairwise comparison model. As a result, the smaller the values of this noise, the more volitional user queries we have. Moreover, we highlight the crucial role of the rating duration contextual information for the good performance of our model. Second, volitional users' queries involve high confidence levels regarding the submitted decisions, while noisy queries involve doubtful feedback, in which users even refrain from expressing their confidence. Third, longer comparison periods are most probably related to more volitional behavior. Thus, such rating duration analysis may provide useful insight to measure the trustworthiness of users' feedback, as well as their knowledge and expertise.

More generally, any user preference-dependent activity (e.g., recommendation ratings, item rankings, choice voting,) can be seriously timed to construct useful metadata, which could be later exploited to develop efficient volition learning models. In this context, we highly recommend to address more interest in developing volition-based systems that benefit from the power of volition to create efficient human value-aligned and human-AI interactive systems. Despite the challenges that such systems may face, due to the complexity of approaching human volition, we emphasize the importance of capturing relevant contextual metadata to be used for delivering satisfying results. In particular, our proposed volitional model represent a first attempt for the design of preference-based ranking systems (e.g., recommendation platforms) that optimize their recommendation services based on user' volition rather than (noisy) preferences. Furthermore, it could be exploited to build explainable active learning recommender systems that ethically assist and correct user choices, which would help to provide beneficial, personalized and friendly services.

References

1. Amershi, S., et al.: Guidelines for Human-AI Interaction. Association for Computing Machinery (2019). https://doi.org/10.1145/3290605.3300233
2. Calero Valdez, A., Ziefle, M., Verbert, K.: HCI for Recommender Systems: the Past, the Present and the Future. Proceedings Of The 10th ACM Conference On Recommender Systems, pp. 123–126 (2016). https://doi.org/10.1145/2959100.2959158
3. Tarleton, N.: Coherent extrapolated volition: a meta-level approach to machine ethics. Machine Intelligence Research Institute (2010)
4. Atas, M., Felfernig, A., Polat-Erdeniz, S., Popescu, A., Tran, T.N.T., Uta, M.: Towards psychology-aware preference construction in recommender systems: overview and research issues. J. Intell. Inf. Syst. **57**(3), 467–489 (2021). https://doi.org/10.1007/s10844-021-00674-5
5. Sepliarskaia, A., Kiseleva, J., Radlinski, F., Rijke, M.: Preference Elicitation as an Optimization Problem. In: Proceedings Of The 12th ACM Conference On Recommender Systems, pp. 172–180 (2018). https://doi.org/10.1145/3240323.3240352
6. Ekstrand, M., Willemsen, M.: Behaviorism is not enough: better recommendations through listening to users. In: Proceedings Of The 10th ACM Conference On Recommender Systems, pp. 221–224 (2016). https://doi.org/10.1145/2959100.2959179
7. Liang, Y.: Recommender system for developing new preferences and goals. In: Proceedings of the 13th ACM Conference on Recommender Systems, pp. 611–615 (2019). https://doi.org/10.1145/3298689.3347054
8. Lyngs, U., Binns, R., Van Kleek, M., Shadbolt, N.: "So, Tell Me What Users Want, What They Really, Really Want!". Extended Abstracts Of The 2018 CHI Conference on Human Factors in Computing Systems, pp. 1–10 (2018). https://doi.org/10.1145/3170427.3188397
9. Evans, O., Stuhlmüller, A., Goodman, N.: Learning the preferences of ignorant, inconsistent agents. In: Proceedings Of The Thirtieth AAAI Conference On Artificial Intelligence, pp. 323–329 (2016)

10. Yudkowsky, E.: Coherent extrapolated volition. Singularity Institute For Artificial Intelligence (2004)
11. Bradley, R., Terry, M.: Rank analysis of incomplete block designs: I. The method of paired comparisons. Biometrika. **39**, 324–345 (1952)
12. Thurstone, L.: A law of comparative judgment. Scaling, pp. 81–92 (2017)
13. Hoang, L., et al.: Tournesol: A quest for a large, secure and trustworthy database of reliable human judgments. ArXiv. abs/2107.07334 (2021)
14. Teitelman, W.: Pilot: a step towards man-computer symbiosis. Massachusetts Institute of Technology (1966)
15. Frith, C.: The psychology of volition. Exp. Brain Res. **229**, 289–299 (2013)
16. O'Neil, W.: The experimental investigation of volition. Austral. J. Psychol. Philos. **11**, 300–307 (1933)
17. Nielsen, T.: Volition: a new experimental approach. Scand. J. Psychol. **4**, 225–230 (1963)
18. Zhu, J.: Understanding volition. Philos. Psychol. **17**, 247–273 (2004)
19. Halisch, F., Kuhl, J.: Motivation, intention, and volition. Springer Science & Business Media (2012). https://doi.org/10.1007/978-3-642-70967-8
20. Achtziger, A., Gollwitzer, P.: Motivation and volition in the course of action. Motivation and Action, pp. 485–527 (2018)
21. Ghoshal, S., Bruch, H.: Going beyond motivation to the power of volition. MIT Sloan Manag. Rev. **44**, 51–57 (2003)
22. Garcia, T., McCann, E., Turner, J., Roska, L.: Modeling the mediating role of volition in the learning process. Contemp. Educ. Psychol. **23**, 392–418 (1998)
23. Novak, E.: Toward a mathematical model of motivation, volition, and performance. Comput. Educ. **74**, 73–80 (2014). https://www.sciencedirect.com/science/article/pii/S0360131514000190
24. Novak, E., Daday, J., McDaniel, K.: Using a mathematical model of motivation, volition, and performance to examine students'e-text learning experiences. Educ. Technol. Res. Develop. **66**, 1189–1209 (2018)
25. Elstad, E.: Heidelberg. Encyclopedia Of The Sciences Of Learning, pp. 3429–3433 (2012). https://doi.org/10.1007/978-1-4419-1428-6_102
26. Keller, J., Ucar, H., Kumtepe, A.: Development and validation of a scale to measure volition for learning. Open Praxis. **12**, 161–174 (2020)
27. Yang, Q., Steinfeld, A., Rosé, C., Zimmerman, J.: Re-examining whether, why, and how human-AI interaction is uniquely difficult to design. Association for Computing Machinery (2020). https://doi.org/10.1145/3313831.3376301
28. Fischer, G.: User modeling in human-computer interaction. User Model. User-adapt. Interact. **11**, 65–86 (2001)
29. Johnson, H.: Relationship between user models in HCI and AI. IEE Proceed.-Comput. Digital Techniques. **141**, 99–103 (1994)
30. Shah, K., Salunke, A., Dongare, S., Antala, K.: Recommender systems: an overview of different approaches to recommendations. In: 2017 International Conference On Innovations In Information, Embedded And Communication Systems (ICIIECS), pp. 1–4 (2017)
31. Li, Y., Kumar, R., Lasecki, W., Hilliges, O.: Artificial intelligence for HCI: a modern approach. In: Extended Abstracts Of The 2020 CHI Conference On Human Factors In Computing Systems, pp. 1–8 (2020). https://doi.org/10.1145/3334480.3375147
32. Xu, W., Dainoff, M., Ge, L., Gao, Z.: Transitioning to human interaction with AI systems: new challenges and opportunities for HCI professionals to enable human-centered AI. Int. J. Hum. -Comput. Interact. pp. 1–25 (2022). https://doi.org/10.1080/10447318.2022.2041900

33. Motamedi, E. User-Centric Item Characteristics for Modeling Users and Improving Recommendations. Association for Computing Machinery (2021). https://doi.org/10.1145/3450613.3459659

34. Cella, L.: MoDelling user behaviors with evolving users and catalogs of evolving items. Adjunct Publication Of The 25th Conference On User Modeling, Adaptation And Personalization, pp. 115–116 (2017). https://doi.org/10.1145/3099023.3102251

35. Ferland, L., Koutstaal, W.: How's Your Day Look? The (Un)Expected Sociolinguistic Effects of User Modeling in a Conversational Agent. Association for Computing Machinery (2020). https://doi.org/10.1145/3334480.3375227

36. Musto, C., Narducci, F., Polignano, M., Gemmis, M., Lops, P., Semeraro, G.: Towards queryable user profiles: introducing conversational agents in a platform for holistic user modeling. Association for Computing Machinery (2020). https://doi.org/10.1145/3386392.3399298

37. Kiseleva, J., Williams, K., Hassan Awadallah, A., Crook, A., Zitouni, I., Anastasakos, T.: Predicting User Satisfaction with Intelligent Assistants. Association for Computing Machinery (2016). https://doi.org/10.1145/2911451.2911521

38. Guha, R., Gupta, V., Raghunathan, V., Srikant, R.: User Modeling for a Personal Assistant. Association for Computing Machinery (2015). https://doi.org/10.1145/2684822.2685309

39. Zhuang, M.: Modelling user behaviour based on process. In: Proceedings Of The 25th Conference On User Modeling, Adaptation And Personalization, pp. 343–346 (2017). https://doi.org/10.1145/3079628.3079705

40. Kulesza, T., Burnett, M., Wong, W., Stumpf, S.: Principles of Explanatory Debugging to Personalize Interactive Machine Learning. In: Proceedings Of The 20th International Conference On Intelligent User Interfaces, pp. 126–137 (2015). https://doi.org/10.1145/2678025.2701399

41. Graus, M., Ferwerda, B.: Theory-grounded user modeling for personalized HCI. Personalized Human-computer Interaction (2019)

42. Liu, Z., et al.: Intent preference decoupling for user representation on online recommender system. In: Proceedings Of The Twenty-Ninth International Joint Conference On Artificial Intelligence (2021)

43. Zhu, N., Cao, J., Liu, Y., Yang, Y., Ying, H., Xiong, H.: Sequential modeling of hierarchical user intention and preference for next-item recommendation. In: Proceedings Of The 13th International Conference On Web Search And Data Mining, pp. 807–815 (2020). https://doi.org/10.1145/3336191.3371840

44. Rader, E., Cotter, K., Cho, J.: Explanations as mechanisms for supporting algorithmic transparency. In: Proceedings Of The 2018 CHI Conference On Human Factors In Computing Systems, pp. 1–13 (2018). https://doi.org/10.1145/3173574.3173677

The Feasibility Study of AI Image Generator as Shape Convergent Thinking Tool

Yu-Hsu Lee[ORCID] and Tzu-Hsun Lin[✉][ORCID]

National Yunlin University of Science and Technology, Yunlin 64002, Taiwan R.O.C.
jameslee@yuntech.edu.tw, jc.tony.29@gmail.com

Abstract. This study aims to (1) investigate the feasibility of AI generation as a tool for shape convergent thinking, (2) compare the differences in computing style and user experience between the two software programs Midjourney (MJ) and Dall-E2 (D2), and (3) analyze and optimize the impact of the adjectives given to the AI on the generated results.

In the experiment, six people (three male and three female) with design experience were recruited to use an expert-designed word list to describe six different types of household items and to input them into the MJ and D2 software to generate product shapes. The results were compared with the original images and scored for similarity, acceptability on the System Usability Scale (SUS) and one-to-one semi-structured interviews. According to the analysis of the results, the average similarity between the AI-generated images and the original product was 48.3%, with an average similarity of 47.7% in (MJ) and 48.8% in (D2) for both software. The results show that AI performs better on simple structured shapes, as the Pantone chair scores 81.67% similarity in (MJ) compared to 36.67% for the Red and Blue chair, and the Bialetti Moka Express scores 80% similarity in (D2) compared to 31.67% for the Alessi espresso maker 9090 scored 31.67%. According to the participant interviews, (MJ) is more suitable for brainstorming as it has more variation in form and its generative style is more artistic, while (D2) produces results that are too often partial and less thought-provoking, but has an advantage over (MJ) as a shape convergent tool because of the way details are presented.

Keywords: Ai Text to Image Generator · Midjourney · Dall-E2 · Product Shape

1 Research Background

In recent years, with the rapid development of AI-generated technologies, AI-generated art tools have proliferated, and in late August 2022, an artwork designed by the AI-generated software Midjourney won the fine art competition at the Colorado State Fair in the United States, winning the digital art category. This has led to a public outcry, both positive and negative. The AI generation software requires only the input of simple words in natural language to drive the algorithm and generate a series of word-based creations in seconds. The AI-powered generation tool enables creative ideas to be developed more quickly and with fewer resources, offering designers a range of different design

© The Author(s), under exclusive license to Springer Nature Switzerland AG 2023
H. Degen and S. Ntoa (Eds.): HCII 2023, LNAI 14050, pp. 575–589, 2023.
https://doi.org/10.1007/978-3-031-35891-3_36

possibilities (Epstein et al., 2020). Artificial Intelligence will be a new way of thinking and implementing design (Jaruga-Rozdolska, 2022). By harnessing the power of AI generation, designers can more quickly identify the best design path. By giving AI generation a clear stylistic direction and shape description, multiple design concepts can be generated quickly, helping users to speed up the design process.

1.1 Motivation

Whether or not AI generation can replace designers in their creative work is a question that has been debated and researched by many. Apart from whether the generation of a large number of images can help users to think outside the box (Karras et al., 2020), it is also worth exploring whether the user can give the AI precise descriptions to allow the 'intelligent generation' to collect data and think about it instead, thereby replacing the designer in the creation process. On the other hand, the question of whether the images calculated by the AI through text are close to the original expectations of the user is a topic that the research hopes to explore. In this study, the AI-generated software (MJ) and (D2) were used as tools for the experiment. Six existing classic products' pictures were described in terms of shape and style and entered into the two AI-generated software for calculation. The similarity between the AI-generated images and the existing products was compared across subjects to explore the feasibility of AI generation as a tool for shape convergent thinking. This study treats AI mapping as a design aid that needs to understand how to communicate with the designer before it can help develop ideas, and how well the designer can represent the image in his or her mind in words. In order to evaluate if the AI calculates whether the result is close to the designer's original idea.

2 Literature Review

2.1 AI Generation

Josh Vermillion (2022) in his research discusses about how to teach artificial intelligence to move from random sampling to images, and points out that AI mapping is different from the way we have designed in the past, and that using language to visualize our ideas is a new design experience for designers. While designers and illustrators are perfectly capable of generating their own graphics to design and communicate ideas, AI generation offers two different value propositions: the first is speed, with each image taking only 30–90 s to complete. Secondly, randomness and non-deterministic factors from machine training, AI generation can produce many different ways of interpreting ideas (Marcus et al. 2022, Moral-Andrés et al., 2022), resulting in unexpected results that can further help designers in the early stages of conceptualization and imagination. This study aims to test the accuracy of AI generated results using a word list designed in collaboration with design experts as a reference.

The AI generation software Midjourney entered public beta on 12 July 2022, and the software was launched via the Discord server, which released version 4 on 10 November 2022. Midjourney is currently only available through its official Dis-cord bot on Discord, by sending messages directly to the bot, or by inviting the bot to access third-party servers.

The user must use the imagine command and enter a prompt to generate an image. Jason M. Allen's digital art work 'Théâtre D'opéra Spatial', created by Midjourney, won the 'Digital Art/Digital Alteration of Photographs' category at the Colorado State Fair, giving the world a glimpse of the power of AI in drawing and creation. With this software, we hope to test whether AI generation can fully represent the ideas in the user's mind and thus help us in our creative work. DALL-E 2 was originally released by OpenAI (https:// OpenAI.com) on 5 January 2021 as the first generation of DALL-E. A new version of DALL-E 2 was released in April 2022, along with an editor that allows simple modifications to the output, but the program is still in the research phase and access is limited to a small number of beta users. Dall-E 2 is available as a website and is generated by direct text input, with a generation log on the right hand side for preview and playback. OpenAI claims that the new version of DALL-E 2 can generate photorealistic images from text descriptions. This study aims to test whether AI generation can come close to realistic products by looking at existing products and the results generated. The two software packages mentioned above are among the most mature and easy-to-use AI generation soft-ware in the field, and Midjourney version 4 and Dall-E2 (without the editor) were used as the tools for this experiment.

2.2 AI-Generated Correlation Research

Borji (2022) used open source image data from the COCO dataset for 'person', 'man', 'woman', 'men', 'women', 'child', 'child', 'face', 'girl', 'boy', etc. The three AI mapping tools were used to generate portrait images, in addition to collecting real faces from the same database and pair comparison them two by two using the computer. Real human faces were also collected from the same database and the Frechet Inception Distance (FID) score was calculated by randomly comparing them to investigate the difference between Stable Diffusion (SD), Midjourney (MJ) and DALL-E 2 (DE 2). The results of the study showed that SD was more effective than the other two tools and MJ was more surrealistic and anime style. This study takes into account the fact that SD requires more parameters to be entered and is more complex to learn and use than the other two tools. The study also focuses on the participants' subjective perception of the stylistic features of the product, so MJ and DE, which do not require much configuration, are used as comparators.

Conwell and Ullman (2022) use DALL-E 2 to explore the ability of AI to compute relationships between objects, such as the physical relationships of in, on, under, covering, near, covered by, hanging over, and tied to, and the agentic relation-ships of push, pull, touch, hit, kick, help, and hinder. Seventy-five sentences were formed with object-object associations, such as 'a spoon in a cup', 'a cup on a spoon', 'a teacup under a cylinder', etc. Participants were asked to select the pictures that matched the sentences. After 1350 pictures had been calculated by DE 2, 169 participants were asked to select the pictures that matched the descriptions of the sentences from the 18 pictures displayed, and the results were scored ac-cording to participants' subjective feeling. The results of the experiment showed that participants found DE 2 to be less consistent with the sentences in terms of calculating object relationships, with only about 22% agreement so far. In this study, the product style descriptions were also pre-designed with a fixed sentence pattern. Participants selected adjectives and completed similar structured sentences, which were then subjectively rated by the participants on a 1–10 Likert scale.

2.3 Product Shape and Adjective Description

The use of adjectives to describe the appearance of products has been established in design research for many years (Hung et al., 2014. Wang et al., 2022), Nagamachi (1995) proposes three applications of Kansei Engineering, the first of which is to categorize the components of a product, analyze the shape elements corresponding to the image of the product, and have the target users rate the appearance of the product using adjectives (Wang, 2012). The correlation coefficient of the adjectives can then be used to design the corresponding product appearance. Tanoue et al. (1997) used a Kansei Engineering approach to translate roomy and oppressive perceptions into numerical values for the interior spaces of cars as an important reference for interior design. Kansei Engineering can be described as a method of numerically describing human subjective feelings in words prior to the development of AI algorithms. Subsequent research has included applications of other theories, such as neural-like networks (Chuang and Chen, 2004) Training the system to improve accuracy is similar to the process of training AI to convert text to images today. In this study, the adjectives chosen by different participants for classic product shapes were used as stimuli to understand the similarity between the words described and the images generated by different AI tools, and also to explore the features observed by different participants for the same product shape.

3 Experiment

3.1 Experimental Steps

In this study, the similarity between the results generated by (MJ) and (D2) soft-ware and the actual samples was evaluated with reference to the experimental methods of Ali Borji (2022) and Conwell and Ullman (2022). The participants were six design students (3 male and 3 female, aged 22–25) with design experience. They were asked to describe three classic chairs and three classic teapots using a list of adjectives selected by experts to describe the products as they saw fit. The adjectives were then put into a fixed sentence format by the researchers, and the sentences were fed into two AI-generating software programs to calculate. The results were rated by the subjects for similarity to the original product, and a sys-tem usability scale was completed. At the end of the experiment, a semi-structured interview was conducted to summarize the differences between the two software products, their acceptability and the effectiveness of the design in augmenting thinking.

3.2 Experimental Reference Products

In this study, three designers' classic chairs and teapots (Figs. 1 and 2) were selected by the expert assessment method, which was used to test the accuracy of AI-generated products in constructing specific shapes. Three products with different characteristics were deliberately chosen to test whether the AI generation was particularly accurate in constructing the shape of a particular shape. The classic chairs are the Panton Chair, the Red and Blue Chair and the Swan Chair, where the Panton Chair is a single curved surface and streamlined form, the Red and Blue Chair is made up of several geometric blocks with a simple linearity, and the Swan Chair is a curved block with a rounded form. The Bialetti Moka Express, the Alessi 9090 espresso machine and the Alessi AAM33 Moka Pot are three examples of coffeepot, the Bialetti Moka Express with its variation of diamond and cylindrical shapes, the Alessi 9090 espresso machine with its cylindrical shape and the Alessi AAM33 Moka Pot espresso machine with its gently curved shape.

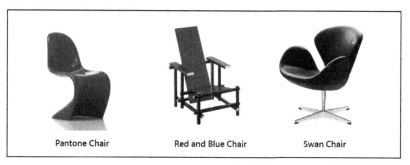

Fig. 1. Three classic chairs. Image source. Pantone Chair: https://reurl.cc/MXroR3. Red and Blue Chair: https://reurl.cc/MXro83. Swan Chair: https://reurl.cc/WqjoG7

Fig. 2. Three classic chairs. Image source. Bialetti Moka Express: https://reurl.cc/EXkv1a. Alessi Espresso Maker 9090: https://reurl.cc/ym2aYy. Alessi AAM33 Moka Pot: https://reurl.cc/deRoL2

3.3   Experimental Software and Word Planning

In this study, two AI generators, Midjourney and DALL-E 2, were used to conduct experimental tests. Firstly, Midjourney generates four images at a time and has two functions, U and V. U generates a more detailed version of a selected image and V generates four additional subtle variations of a selected image. Dall-E 2 generates four images at a time and has a generation record on the right-hand side for preview and playback. These two software packages are the most mature and easy-to-use AI generation software in the field, so they were chosen as the experimental tools for this study. In order to enable participants to describe the shape of the product more accurately, a list of words was developed in collaboration with design experts to create four different categories of words: style, shape, material and color (Fig. 3) (the two categories that had a greater impact on the results were style and shape, which are used as illustrations in the text). The adjectives chosen by the participants were then filled in with a fixed sentence pat-tern (Fig. 4) and entered into two AI tools. The AI-generated image and the original product image were then presented on the computer screen for evaluation and participants were asked to rate the results.

(Style)				
(Succinct)	(Complicated)	(Geometric)	(organic)	(Conservative)
(Strong)	(dull)	(simple)	(Fragile)	(science fiction)
(gentle)	(Unique)	(Traditional)	(General)	(sharp)
(stationary)	(generic)	(sensual)	(Personalized)	(rounded)
(Dynamic)	(formal)	(Rational)	(Technology)	(Avant Garde)
(heavy)	(Casual)	(Soft)	(flexible)	(conflicting)
(Lightweight)	(fancy)	(rigid)	(Streamlined)	(Solid)
(Modern)	(plain)	(Rough)	(Fashionable)	(elegant)
(Classical)	(vulgar)	(Delicate)	(interesting)	(Lively)
(Shape)				
(Mesh)	(Semi-circular)	(Angle cone)	(vertical)	(surface shaping)
(Tubular)	(Irregular)	(Cylinder)	(Non vertical)	(Bend Pipe)
(Columnar)	(organic)	(Egg)	(Curve shaping)	(Organic linear)
(Spherical)	(Three Legged)	(Square)	(Composite shape)	(conical)
(Block)	(Four Legs)	(Round)	(Rectangle)	(Linear arrangement)
(Sheet)	(One piece molding)	(One support point)	(Oval shape)	

Fig. 3. Illustration of an example word list.

Sentence examples :

The shape of a chair is _____ , the style is _____ , the material is _____ , the color is _____ , product view

The shape of a Moka Pot is _____ , the style is _____ , the material is _____ , the color is _____ , product view

After input :

The shape of a chair is Irregular surface shaping and curve shaping, the style is soft and streamilned and elegant , the material is smooth polished and shiny , the color is high chroma red and reflective, product view

The shape of a Moka Pot is angle cone and block and sheet, the style is succinct and geometric and sharp, the material is shiny aluminum alloy and matte , the colour are silver low chroma and high color value, product view

Fig. 4. Illustration of a sentence example.

3.4 Experimental Procedure

Since the AI generation software does not have a fixed length of time to generate. In order to make the experimental process smooth, this study adopted a pre-questionnaire survey in which the participants first checked the adjectives of the six experimental materials through a questionnaire. Then the researcher entered the sentences into the AI generation software for pre-computation. There were 5 computations for each product, 10 for both software, and 4 images were generated for each computation (Fig. 5) (40 images for one product and two software). For each product, participants were asked to select the most similar image from the AI mapping results and then rate the similarity (on a scale of 1–10) by cross-tabulating with a questionnaire. The procedure for this study is as follows:

a Before the experiment, participants were asked to choose 1 to 3 adjectives from each category in the word list to complete the sample sentence pattern (Fig. 4).
b The completed sentences were entered by the researchers into the MJ and D2 software to generate.
c The participant selects the closest image to the original product from the generated results (e.g. Fig. 5).
d The selected images were scored for similarity and two software programs were tested.
e The system usability scale is completed by the participant at the end of the experiment and a semi-structured interview is conducted.

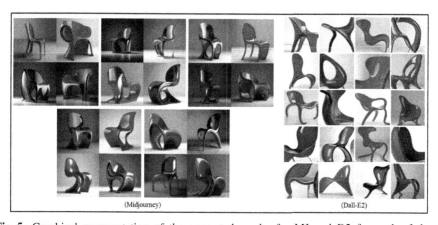

(Midjourney)   (Dall-E2)

Fig. 5. Graphical representation of the generated results for MJ and D2 for each of the 5 calculations.

3.5 Evaluation of the Results Obtained

After completing the AI image generation, the participants were asked to select one image from each of the two software generated that was the most similar to the original product, and to compare it with the original product based on details such as shape, colour and material, and to give a similarity score (using a scale of 1 to 10) as shown in (Fig. 6). To further understand the contribution of AI generation to design convergence, a semi-structured interview was conducted after the experiment. The outline of the interview was divided into three main parts: the first part focused on the reasons why the subjects chose similar drawings and why they chose to use these terms for their products; the second part focused on the differences between the two AI generation software and the future possibilities of AI generation; and the third part focused on the impact of AI generation on the design process and design thinking.

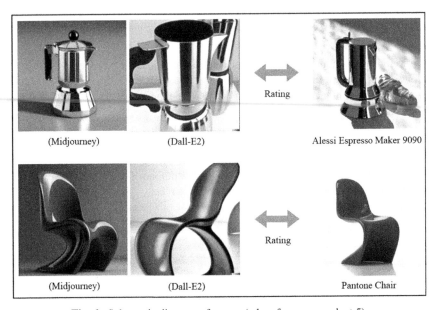

Fig. 6. Schematic diagram of scores (taken from respondent 5).

4   Research Results

4.1 Experimental Results

Due to the large number of images generated, the results generated for a participant (female, aged 23) are displayed as an example (Figs. 7 and 8), with the red circled image being the final choice of the participant. This experiment was con-ducted to analyze the results generated and the final choice of the participant. From the first generation of chairs, it can be seen that Midjourney performs better than Dall-E2 in the calculation of chairs and expresses the characteristics of the original product. On the other hand, Dall-E2 produced a number of strange viewing angles and some images were difficult to identify as chairs, but participants commented that Dall-E2 produced visuals and materials that were closer to reality.

The initial results for the teapot show that the two software programs have similar performance comparing with to generate the classic chairs. The Midjourney has a more

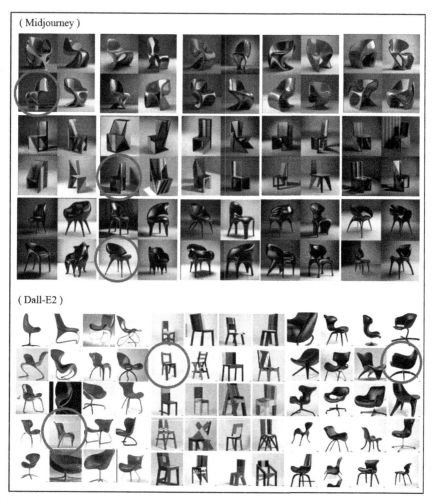

Fig. 7. Results of three chairs generated 5 times each by Midjourney and DALL-E 2 using the same text description.

distinctive appearance, but in the color section there are many colors that are not present in the original product, and the shape is also more different from the original product, and during interviews some participants suggested that the Midjourney is more of an abstract art style. The results generated by the Dall-E2 for all three teapots were too similar so that participants felt it was difficult to select one different result; it was initially found that the input product name had a greater influence on the result on Dall-E2. In general, the AI generation is not yet mature enough for the complex shape of a coffeepot. It demands more precise descriptions of the body, spout, handles, etc. In this study, the results obtained from the coffee maker and moka pot from AI calculation were completely different.

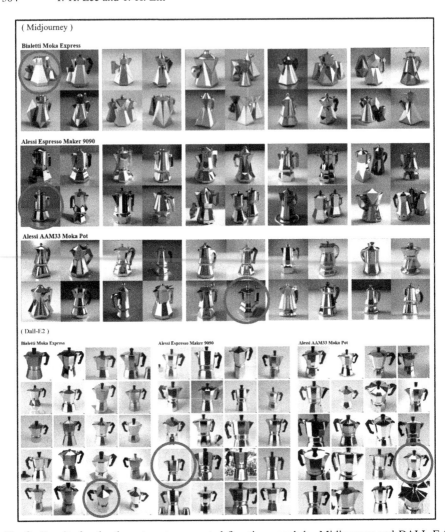

Fig. 8. Results for the three teapots generated five times each by Midjourney and DALL-E 2 using the same text description.

4.2 Analysis of AI-Generated Experimental Results

The average similarity between the AI-generated images and the original product was found to be 48.3% after an experiment using AI-generated images to compare existing products; the average similarity between the two software models is 47.7% for Midjourney and 48.8% for Dall-E2, which is still below the expected similarity of 60% or more. All six respondents gave positive feedback on the ability of AI generation to help present ideas in the mind, saying that it would be useful for those with weak sketching and presentation skills to communicate with professional designers, but that AI generation as a tool for astringent thinking was only 60% to 70% complete, and that it was still necessary to sort the data manually.

Fig. 9. Results selected by the six participants (Midjourney).

This study used AI-generated images to score the similarity of six existing products and produced several results. In terms of similarity, the Pantone chair has the highest average similarity rating of 81.67% among the six products generated by Midjourney. The Red and Blue Chair was the lowest at 36.67% (Fig. 9); the Bialetti Moka Express had the highest average similarity of 80% in the Dall-E2 generated similarity ratings while Alessi 9090 was the lowest at 31.67% (see Fig. 10). The results of the interviews show that for the Pantone chair without legs, both the curved shape and the one-piece shapes were fully expressed in the results generated by Midjourney (surface shape and one-piece shape were the terms chosen more frequently by the participants). Especially in the case of the Pantone chair without legs, where the overall difference lies in the curved detail and the height of the back, while the rest of the chair is well represented. In the case of the Red and Blue Chair, apart from the color and material of the chair, the other components of the Midjourney, such as the thickness to size ratio, the structure of the bars and the shape of the armrests, where the significant difference from the original product were not performed as expected.

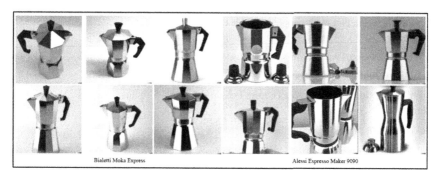

Fig. 10. Results selected by the six participants (Dall-E2).

The Bialetti Moka Express is similar in shape to the original in the Dall-E2 results for both the curve and the handle, and the overall proportions are well expressed, with the exception of a few differences in the detailing of the handle and the gloss of the material itself, which are quite similar to the original. The Alessi 9090 is generated in the Dall-E2 and the result is a shape with many corners that differ significantly from the roundness of the original; the lid is also inconsistent with the original. Although the handle is similar with the original such as the material and position are expressed, but the overall resemblance is slightly lacking.

4.3 AI Generated Software Ease of Use Evaluation

The system usability scale was applied to Midjourney and Dall-E2 by means of a questionnaire at the end of the experiment to explore the acceptability of the two tools by the participants. The results showed that Midjourney scored an average of 63.3 points and Dall-E2 scored 72 points (Table 1). The Dall-E2 is generally considered to have a simple and easy to read interface, and the website format can be used anywhere with a mobile phone, making it easier for first time users to get used to AI generation. Midjourney can only be activated via the Discord server and requires additional commands to generate, making the process too complex to use, but has more features to give users more control over AI generation.

Table 1. Midjourney and Dall-E2 Usability Scale.

System Usability Scale (SUS)	Midjourney	Dall-E2
1. I think that I would like to use this system frequently	3.67	3
2. I found the system unnecessarily complex	2	1.5
3. I thought the system was easy to use	3.67	4.33
4. I think that I would need the support of a technical person to be able to use this system	3.5	2.5
5. I found the various functions in this system were well integrated	3.83	3.83
6. I thought there was too much inconsistency in this system	2.17	3
7. I would imagine that most people would learn to use this system very quickly	2.83	4.33
8. I found the system very cumbersome to use	2.17	1.67
9. I felt very confident using the system	3.67	4.17
10. I needed to learn a lot of things before I could get going with this system	2.5	2.17
Total number of points	35.01	30.5
Total SUS score	63.3	72

5 Conclusion

5.1 The Feasibility of AI Generation as a Tool for Astringent Thinking

The preliminary conclusion from the results of the experiment and the retrospective interviews with the six participants is that the participants generally agreed that AI generation is feasible as a tool for designing astringent thinking, but that it cannot completely replace manual work. Due to the random nature of AI generation, which still requires manual review after the first generation, only 60 to 70% of ideas can be expressed, which may help those who cannot generate ideas quickly to come up with ideas in their heads, but for users with design skills this method can still only be used as an aid for the time being.

It was found that Dall-E2 to be clearer and more efficient. For example, participants also mentioned that Dall-E2's interface is easier to use and more intuitive, particularly the history bar on the right-hand side, which allows users to navigate through past records generated better than Midjourney.

5.2 The Differences in Computing Style and User Experience Between the Two Software Packages

The results of the SUS technology acceptability subjective preference scale, completed by six respondents, showed that Midjourney scored an average of 63.3 on the software usability scale, while Dall-E2 scored an average of 72 (Table 1). In subsequent semi-structured interviews, the participants generally found Midjourney to be computationally demanding in terms of typing commands and cumbersome in terms of finding past results. This makes it more difficult to organize the data when you need to think about it in a convergent way, and the learning threshold is higher than with Dall-E2, where you can just open a web page and type directly. The Pantone Chair had an average similarity of 81.67% in the Midjourney calculation, the highest of the six products, while the Bialetti Moka Express had an average similarity of 80% in the Dall-E2 calculation, the second highest of the six products. Initially, it is judged that products consisting of a single large area or block, such as the Pantone Chair, are easier to calculate in Midjourney, while products with more stylistic detail, such as the Bialetti Moka Express, are better suited for Dall-E2 calculations when performing style crunching.

5.3 Provide the Impact of AI Adjectives on the Generated Results

In this experiment we found that the AI generation engine was still rather vague in its understanding of the meaning of the word. For example, in the case of the Bialetti moka pot, inputting the word (moka pot) into both types of software produced results similar to Fig. 11, with an overall square, sharp shape and a relatively short spout, whereas inputting (coffee pot) produced results similar to Fig. 12, with a more rounded overall shape and many images with elongated spouts. From the results of this experiment, it was found that the definition of the product words had a greater impact on the generated results for product shapes composed of composite shapes. Changing only the product name for the same sentence can affect the whole result, while changing other words such as style and shape for the same product name can cause only minor changes.

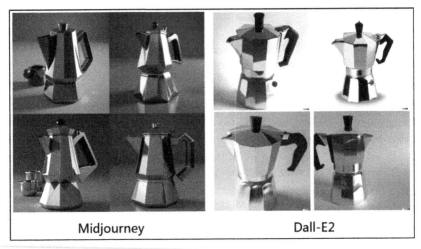

Fig. 11. Input results from the two AI generation software for Moka Pot.

Fig. 12. Input results from the two AI generation software for Coffee Pot.

The results generated showed a similarity of over 80% between the Pantone Chair and the Bialetti Moka Express, as well as feedback from the six participants that the expertly designed shapes did not present any difficulties in terms of terminology selection; instead, the product name had a greater impact on the results, followed by the description of the style and shape. A subsequent refinement of the experiment will be used to generate appropriate product names for the three coffee pots, hopefully further improving the similarity of results.

5.4 Future Recommendations

In this study, the choice of product name was found to have a significant effect on the results, as this experiment did not have a suitable product name for each product in advance, resulting in too many similar results for the teapots. Further-more, in order to speed up the experimental process, this study used a method of pre-generating picture results and then presenting them to the subjects for selection. This reduced subject engagement and also made it impossible to make timely changes to the input words during the experiment. Improvements will be made in subsequent experiments to address these issues, in the hope that the generated results will be more similar to the expected results.

References

Borji, A.: Generated Faces in the Wild: Quantitative Comparison of Stable Diffusion, Midjourney and Dall-e 2. arXiv preprint arXiv:2210.00586 (2022)

Conwell, C., Ullman, T.: Testing Relational Understanding in Text-Guided Image Generation. arXiv preprint arXiv:2208.00005 (2022)

Chuang, M.C., Chen, C.: Exploring the relationship between the product form features and feature composition and user's Kansei evaluation. J. Design **9**(3), 43–58 (2004). https://doi.org/10.6381/JD.200409.0043

Epstein, Z., Levine, S., Rand, D.G., Rahwan, I.: Who gets credit for ai-generated art? Iscience **23**(9), 101515 (2020)

Hung, Y.C., Lin, Y.H., Lin, C.C., Liu, C.T.: The application of kansei engineering and morphological analysis in product form design. Int. J. Systematic Innov. **3**(1) (2014)

Jaruga-Rozdolska, A.: Artificial intelligence as part of future practices in the architect's work: MidJourney generative tool as part of a process of creating an architectural form. Architectus (2022)

Karras, T., Laine, S., Aittala, M., Hellsten, J., Lehtinen, J., Aila, T.: Analyzing and improving the image quality of stylegan. In: Proceedings of the IEEE/CVF conference on computer vision and pattern recognition, pp. 8110–8119 (2020)

Marcus, G., Davis, E., Aaronson, S.: A Very Preliminary Analysis of Dall-e 2. arXiv preprint arXiv:2204.13807 (2022)

Moral-Andrés, F., Merino-Gómez, E., Reviriego, P., Lombardi, F.: Can Artificial Intelligence Reconstruct Ancient Mosaics? arXiv preprint arXiv:2210.06145 (2022)

Nagamachi, M.: Kansei engineering: a new ergonomic consumer-oriented technology for product development. Int. J. Ind. Ergonomics **15**(1), 3–11 (1995)

Tanoue, C., Ishizaka, K., Nagamachi, M.: Kansei engineering: a study on perception of vehicle interior image. Int. J. Ind. Ergonomics **19**(2), 115–128 (1997)

Vermillion, J.: Iterating the Design Process Using AI Diffusion Models (2022)

Wang, K.-C.: Exploring the affective design feature of an AR product by using the kansei engineering scheme. National Digital Library of Theses and Dissertations in Taiwan (2012). https://hdl.handle.net/11296/5egbnk

Wang, Y., et al.: Perceptual quantitative decision making and evaluation of product stylable topology design. Processes **10**(9), 1819 (2022)

Application Potential of Stable Diffusion in Different Stages of Industrial Design

Miao Liu(ID) and Yifei Hu(✉)

East China University of Science and Technology, Shanghai, China
Ether_star@outlook.com

Abstract. The Stable diffusion [1] is a system composed of three parts – text encoder, latent diffusion model and autoencoder decoder. With the open source of Stable diffusion, more and more users begin to use stable diffusion to generate digital art, modify images and explore more applications. However, the application potential of stable diffusion in the different stages of industrial design is not yet clear. We divide the process of industrial design into four stages and focus on exploring its application in the sketching stage and rendering stage.

We discussed whether the Stable-diffusion model can well express the concepts related to industrial design (product category, shape, color, material), explored the composability of the different finetune ways, and enabled Stable diffusion model to effectively transform the text prompt and image prompt into high-quality design scheme. It shows that finetuned stable diffusion model can help designers to build intent map and push structure deduction work. Also, with simple image hints and text prompt, finetuned stable diffusion model which trained from a specific product can do attribute, background and illumination modifications to the renderings.

Keywords: Stable Diffusion · Industrial design · Rendering

1 Introduction

1.1 Definitions

Industrial Design. Industrial design involves a wide range of categories, which can be divided into many categories according to different research emphases. WDO (or World Design Organization) defined it as a strategic problem-solving process that drives innovation, builds business success, and leads to a better quality of life through innovative products, systems, services, and experiences [17]. In the narrow sense, systematic design is based on product design, and the core idea is that products and users have a good affinity and matching. The industrial design discussed in this paper is the latter one.

Stable Diffusion (and Its Development). Diffusion models [2] are inspired by non-equilibrium thermodynamics. They define a Markov chain of diffusion steps to slowly add random noise to data and then learn to reverse the diffusion process to construct desired

H. Degen and S. Ntoa (Eds.): HCII 2023, LNAI 14050, pp. 590–609, 2023.
https://doi.org/10.1007/978-3-031-35891-3_37

data samples from the noise. Several diffusion-based generative models have been proposed with similar ideas underneath, including diffusion probabilistic models [3], noise-conditioned score network [4], and denoising diffusion probabilistic models [5].

Latent diffusion model [1] runs the diffusion process in the latent space of (4,64,64) instead of pixel space, making training cost lower and inference speed faster. It is motivated by the observation that most bits of an image contribute to perceptual details and the semantic and conceptual composition still remains after aggressive compression. LDM loosely decomposes the perceptual compression and semantic compression with generative modeling learning by first trimming off pixel-level redundancy with autoencoder and then manipulate/generate semantic concepts with diffusion process on learned latent [2].

Thanks for StabilityAI and other contributors' work, Stable diffusion was open source and publicly available which was developed based on Latent diffusion model. To generate images, Stable Diffusion uses CLIP [8] to project a text prompt into a joint text-image embedding space, and select a rough, noisy image that is semantically close to the input prompt. This image is then subject to a denoising method based on the latent diffusion model to produce the final image. In addition to a text prompt, the Text-to-Image generation script within Stable Diffusion allows users to input various parameters such as sampling type, output image dimensions, and seed value.

1.2 Motivation

Researches of Stable Diffusion in Different Field
Face Generation. Ali Borji et al. [16] compare Stable Diffusion, Midjourney, and DALL-E 2 in their ability to generate photorealistic faces in the wild. They find that Stable Diffusion generates better faces than the other systems, according to the FID score. We also introduce a dataset of generated faces in the wild dubbed GFW, including a total of 15,076 faces.

Art Education. Using a sample of 72,980 Stable Diffusion prompts, Nassim Dehouche et al. [6] propose a formalization of this new medium of art creation and assess its potential for teaching the history of art, aesthetics, and technique. Their findings indicate that text-to-Image AI has the potential to revolutionize the way art is taught, offering new, cost-effective possibilities for experimentation and expression.

Application of AI in Industrial Design
Tendency: In recent years, the combination of artificial intelligence and other cutting-edge technologies with industrial design has created a new thinking of industrial design, set off a huge wave of industrial design reform, and triggered the public's deep thinking on the development bottleneck of traditional industrial design and future development.

Limitations: The lack of samples in a particular industrial field makes it difficult for AI technology to be applied in industrial design industry quickly, which is one of the key factors restricting intelligence in industrial field.

Pros and Cons of Stable Diffusion
Pros: Tractability and flexibility are two conflicting objectives in generative modeling.

Tractable models can be analytically evaluated and cheaply fit data, but they cannot easily describe the structure in rich datasets. Flexible models can fit arbitrary structures in data, but evaluating, training, or sampling from these models is usually expensive. Diffusion models are both analytically tractable and flexible [2]. Also, more and more ways to finetune (or personalize) stable diffusion have been developed which will be introduced in Part 2.

Cons: Diffusion models rely on a long Markov chain of diffusion steps to generate samples, so it can be quite expensive in terms of time and compute. Pre-training weight of stable diffusion was opened source which means a lot of time and compute was saved.

2 Methods

2.1 Different Personalized Training Concepts of Stable Diffusion

Textual Inversion
In the text-encoding stage of most text-to-image models, the first stage involves converting the prompt into a numerical representation. This is typically done by converting the words into tokens, each equivalent to an entry in the model's dictionary. These entries are then converted into an "embedding" - a continuous vector representation for the specific token. These embeddings are usually learned as part of the training process. In our work, we find new embeddings that represent specific, user-provided visual concepts. These embeddings are then linked to new pseudo-words, which can be incorporated into new sentences like any other word. In a sense, we are performing inversion into the text-embedding space of the frozen model. This process was named as 'Textual Inversion' [18].

Dreambooth
Firstly we use the prompt containing special characters and classes (example: "a [identifier] [class noun]" [14], where identifier represents a rare character. The reason for selecting a rare character is that the model does not have a prior knowledge of the character, otherwise the character is likely to be confused between the model prior and the new injection concept; Class noun is a description of the rough semantics of the subject. By binding rare characters and class, the model can bind the priori and identifier of the class to fine-tune the low-resolution text-to-image model. Among them, fine-tuning the model on a small number of data is easy to cause the problem of overriding and language drift. For this reason, the author proposes a class-specific prior reservation loss. This is also the main innovation of this paper. The output result of prompt (A [class noun]) before the model fine-tune is used to be regular with the output result of the current model in prompt (a [identifier] [class noun]), so as to ensure the priori of the class. Secondly, fine-tune the super-resolution model, mainly to produce high-fidelity images.

Dreambooth method was raised on Imagen model which is not open source. Thanks for Huggingface's work [19], dreambooth method has been transformed into stable diffusion. Dreambooth method can generate photos which keeps most of semantics of the trained object, while other attribute like background is editable.

Dreambooth LoRA
It's a developed version of dreambooth [19]. The final results of dreambooth(fully fined-tuned model) is very large. LoRA instead attempts to fine-tune the 'residual' of the model instead of the entire model: i.e., train the ΔW instead of W.

$$W' = W + \Delta W$$

where we can further decompose ΔW into low-rank matrices: $\Delta W = AB^T$, where $A \in \mathbb{R}^{n \times d}$, $B \in \mathbb{R}^{m \times d}$, $d \ll n$. This is the key idea of LoRA. We can then fine-tune A and B instead of W. In the end, you get an insanely small model as A and B are much smaller than W.

Native Train
Unlike dreambooth [9], Native Training uses dataset for training directly and does not require Class images. All images will be used for training. However, you need to prepare an Instance Prompt for each image.

2.2 Industrial Design Stages and Man-Machine Cooperation Methods

There are many phased methods in industrial design. We choose to phase the industrial design process into four stages (Fig. 1).

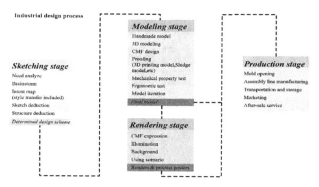

Fig. 1. Four stages of industrial design.

The tasks faced by each stage are shown in the figure below. The final output of each stage will be used as input to next stage. In order to explore man-machine cooperation methods, specifically Designer-StableDiffusion cooperation methods, we have comprehensively considered the form of stable diffusion input-output and input-output in different stages. The input forms that can be used for stable diffusion are text prompt and image prompt, and the output is image. The sketching stage input is fuzzy design requirements, and the output is the determined design scheme (image form). The modeling stage inputs images and outputs 3d models. In the rendering stage, the input is a 3D model, which needs a lot of fine-tuning, and the output is an image. Production stage is to synthesize the output of the above stages and conduct actual production and sales. For the reason of output form matching, we choose the sketching stage and rendering stage as the entry point.

3   Experiments

We designed the experiment, and used the fine-tuning method introduced in Part 2 to test the application of the stable diffusion model in the sketching stage and the rendering stage.

3.1   Sketching Stage

In sketching stage, designers need to understand pain points, analyze needs, build intention map, and brainstorm firstly. Then they do sketch deduction, carry out 3D structure deduction and basically determine the design scheme. We designed some experiments to test how stable diffusion can help designers in intention map, Sketch deduction and 3D structure deduction. Whether the expression effect of table diffusion in the field of industrial design is excellent needs to be tested by experiments.

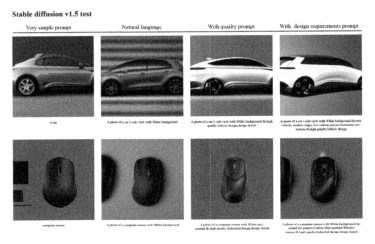

Fig. 2. Building intent map with stable diffusion v1.5.

Intent Map
While maintaining other generation parameters, we directly add more prompts to basic items (cars and computer mouse) to test whether stable diffusion can directly generate the intent map according to the design requirements. We found that the addition of design

requirements prompts can indeed modify the shape of products in the generated results (Fig. 2). The changing of the generated results due to the addition of new concepts may inspire designers to explore product improvement or find innovative points. For example, 'electric vehicle, modern shape, low carbon and environment protection' is added in the changes from Fig. 3 to Fig. 4 in line 1. As a result, this car has changed from a sports car to a hatchback. In reality, the average carbon emission of hatchback is also less than that of sports cars. Although this is the result of the new token coded by the text encoder to the u-net, the diffusion model cannot understand what environmental protection is from human logic, but it can express the probability of environmental protection from the pre-training parameters, which is an advantage brought by the huge training set and the use of the CLIP text encoder with a vocabulary of up to 60 million.

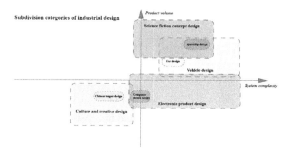

Fig. 3. Venn diagram of four design segments.

Possible defects exists in intent map creation using stable diffusion v1.5. First of all, the dataset of this model is very large. With a dataset of 2.1 billion, its weight is relatively average, and there is no special optimization in the field of industrial design. Stable diffusion initial weight has been frozen four months ago, but the design trends are changing.The good news is that we have many ways to fine-tune the stable diffusion model to achieve special optimization in the field of industrial design. Therefore, we used the pre-training parameters of stable diffusion v1.5 as the basis to conduct specialized training for a specific design category in four industrial design subdivisions. These four subdivisions do not represent all industrial design fields. We used the volume of products and the complexity of the design system as two dimensions to sort out the four industrial design subdivisions and the specific design category inside (Fig. 3). The four specific design categories finally selected are spaceship design, car design, computer mouse design and Chinese teapot design.

Dataset and Train. Our data set comes from the public image data on Pinterest, and is manually collected. Photos that do not conform to the semantics are removed from the dataset. The total number of images of these our specific design categories on Pinterest varies greatly, so we do not control the number of datasets to be equal, but the number of these datasets does not differ in order of magnitude. We use BLIP to mark each image, and use the native train method to train 40 epochs. The training results are as follows. When generating, we maintain the same generation parameters except prompt words. Each specialized model has a better representation of the images generated in the field of its training set (Images on the diagonal show that.) (Fig. 4) than stable diffusion v1.5.

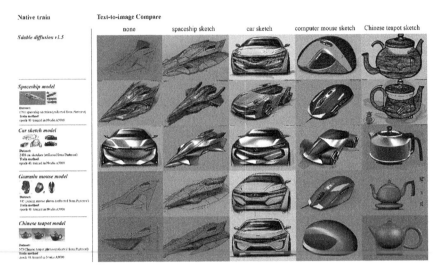

Fig. 4. Dataset and effects of native train.

At the same time, these four trained models have not lost the generalization ability, and have a good expression of the semantics that have not been strengthened. These four models have been uploaded to the hugging face [10–13]. We test these four models to test their ability in the direction of style transfer.

Style Transfer. (Fig. 5) Style transfer is a common method applied in the sketching stage. There are many types of style transfer. It is common to transfer the design style of one product to another. Streamline design is one of the most popular design styles in the United States in the 1930s and 1940s. It was developed from decorative art and took the sleek and smooth streamline body as the main form. It was initially mainly used in the design of transportation vehicles, and transfered to various other product design fields.At present, there are many comcepts like visual attribute transfer through deep image analogy [7] that can do style transfer. We also tried stable diffusion v1.5 and the four trained models of the above.

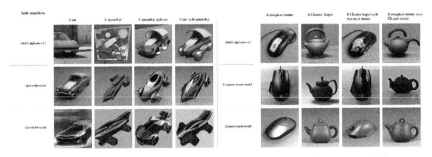

Fig. 5. Style transfer between cars and spaceship (left). Style transfer between Chinese teapot and computer models (right).

First of all, we try the style transfer between spaceship and car, and generate objects separately and crosswise in four columns. We first noticed that the stable diffusion model generates a hand-painted work of a spaceship rather than a design component. This may be due to the fact that the images with the concept of spaceship in stable diffusion dataset are more hand-painted work but not design sketch. We can observe that these two models through native train maintain good generalization ability, the generation of a single concept such as 'A car', 'A spaceship' is not contaminated. At the same time, in the style transfer image, the semantics of the subject can be preserved. 'A spaceship style car' can retain the semantics of the car in both trained models, and 'A car style space ship' is also similar. The attribute (style) can also be expressed. Especially when we keep the seeds same in each line, this phenomenon can be more obvious. The column 3 and 4 are all like the fusion products of column 1 and 2. In column 3 their semantic is more inclined to car, while in column 4 their semantic is more inclined to spaceship.

In the right half, the generalization ability of the two native trained models is also good, but the result of style transfer is not perfect. 'A computer mouse style Chinese teapot' seems to retain only the semantics of 'Chinese tea pot', while 'A Chinese tea pot style computer mouse' is inconsistent in the two models' results. Some Chinese characters are generated in the computer mouse model's result, but in the Chinese teapot model's result, a computer mouse with pottery texture is generated.

The success of style transfer between cars and spaceships may be due to their similar design subdivision areas, or the similarity of the token vector transformed by CLIP. The imperfect style transfer between the computer mouse and the Chinese teapot may be the opposite reason.

Sketch Deduction and Structure Deduction
We use image-to image to test the ability of Stage diffusion in Sketch deduction and Structure deduction. Image to images does not break away from the basic structure of stable diffusion, but replaces the random initial noise with the input image plus a certain amount of Gaussian noise. The design sketch we selected is one of a series of design drawings drawn by one author (Hu), aiming at designing a unique mini mouse. This form and outline of computer mouse is not common. Its spatial structure is still in a relatively vague state for the author, and the uncertainty of the sketch makes it possible to have a great change space. Based on the above reasons, we choose this sketch as the test input to test the deduction ability of the stable diffusion model for an unknown form. We tested four stages of sketches, line draw stage, simple color stage, simple light and shadow stage, finished stage. The x-axis is the increase of denoising (0.6–0.9, interval 0.05). For each input image, we tested it with both stable dispersion v1.5 and gaming mouse model (one of the four models trained above).

(Fig. 6) First of all, we find that whether the input initial image has light and shadow largely determines the stereoscopic sense of the generated image. Under different denoising intensities, the stereoscopic sense of the generated image of line draw and simple color sketch is significantly weaker than the latter two. When the denoising intensity reaches 0.8 or more, the degree of compliance with the original contour will decrease a lot, in other words, the difference between the outputs and inputs will be large. The details and stereoscopic sense generated by the Gaming mouse model are better than that of the stable diffusion v1.5. In the results obtained from these four input images,

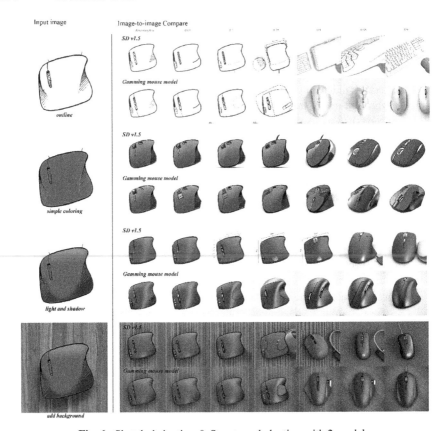

Fig. 6. Sketch deduction & Structure deduction with 2 models.

many details that are not in the original sketch are generated, such as the segmentation of materials, the segmentation of small surfaces on the edge of the original surface, and the addition of led lights. These are all good directions for structure.

The light and shadow of the product in the sketch is imagined (or a speculation of 3D structure based on the designer's learning and experience) by the designer. The accuracy of the light, shadow and spatial structure in the hand-drawn sketch is related to the spatial imagination and experience of the designer. However, by sending sketches to image-to-image and changing the generate seed in stable diffusion, a large number of different, detailed, intuitive spatial structures can be generated, which brings a lot of inspiration for the designer's sketch deduction and structure deduction. Compared with the input sketches, these output images are closer to the quality of the product renderings or photos and shows more reasonable 3D structure to the designer. It may play a certain role in the designer's subsequent modeling and surface construction.

3.2 Rendering Stage

CMF (or color, material and finishing) expression is an important part in rendering stage. In the promotion of industrial design project, especially in rendering stage, designers often face a large number of attribute modifications tasks, such as material replacement or color adjustment, which will consume a lot of time and computing resource. Also, designers often need to rendered images of user interaction with products, and product images in different using scenarios. Sometimes designers use different background images in rendering software for background changing. More often, designers need to build scenes, adjust illumination in rendering software and even re-compose images through Photoshop.

The different training methods of stable diffusion such as dreambooth and dreambooth LoRA bring possibility to improve these pain points. We tested two methods (introduced in part two) in attribute modification of rendering object and background and illumination modification.

Dreambooth Train and Attribute Modifications

Dreambooth method can modify the attributes of the main body without changing its semantics [14], so we designed 4 basic experiments to modify one attribute while preserving its semantics, respectively testing and modifying the color, material, interaction, and use environment. Then we designed a comprehensive experiment to modify 2 and more attributes while preserving its semantics.

Dataset and Train. (Fig. 7) Chair design is a subdivision of office furniture design under industrial design. In order to judge the training effect and obtain a consistent data set, we choose to use an office chair designed by one author (Hu). The form and structure features of this chair are as follows: the crossed backrest structure, the connection between armrest and base, a small grip under the armrest, the special neck pillow and cushion.

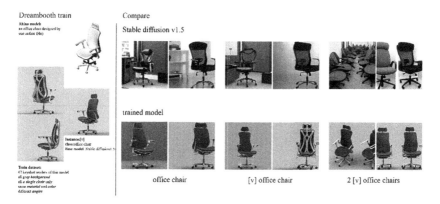

Fig. 7. Dataset is renderings of an office chair. Comparison effect before and after training.

In keyshot, we set up camera rotation and rendered 31 diagrams in both horizontal and vertical directions, resulting in 62 rendering diagrams as a training set. The resolution of these renderings is 512×512. Their background is grey. The chair material and color in renderings is consistent. We used stable diffusion v1.5 as the base model for fine tuning and using dreambooth training method to train 40 epochs at 512 resolution and batch size 2. The trained model with train dataset has been uploaded to huggingface [5].

The benchmark comparison between the trained model and the original model is shown in the figure. The comparison is made between using only class prompt, using identifier ([v]) and class prompt, and testing its plural form. As you can see, whether or not we use the marker [v], the results are sufficiently similar to the dataset chair, but using the identifier [v] can more accurately express the styling and structural characteristics of the chair, such as the grip under the armrest.

Color Modification: (Fig. 8) The way to change the color attribute is to use identifier ([v]) and class noun, followed by a prompt that defines the color of the material. Because the pre-experiment shows that if only one color prompt is used, the background color may be changed. Interestingly, in the generated image, the color changes only occur on the backrest, seat cushion and neck pillow. It should be noted that these parts in dataset only appear black. The colors of other parts of the generated image are consistent with those in dataset. What is more surprising is that while changing the color of the chair surface, the generated image also shows that the diffuse reflection mode of the chair surface is well preserved, which means it does not change the type of material.

We have listed the standard color values of color prompt under each picture for comparison. First, we tested RGB and yellow. The overall hue is consistent with prompt, but grayer. Then we tested some common non-pure colors, which can also be effectively expressed. Finally, we tested some colors whose names are not very common, such as paleturquoise (some kind of light blue) and lemonchiffon (some kind of gray yellow). Surprisingly, these uncommon colors have good expression. This provides the possibility to modify the color of the prod the color of Product surface in rendered image.

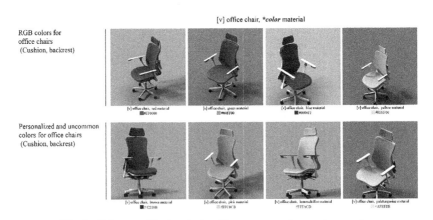

Fig. 8. Color modification tests with common colors and rare colors.

Material Modification: (Fig. 9)The way to change the material attribute is to use identifier ([v]) and class, followed by a prompt that defines the material. This will have a slight difference from the result of using identifier ([v]) material class noun, but will not affect the composition of the overall picture. First of all, we tested the common materials used to manufacture office chairs (cushions, backrests, and neck pillows part), including mesh cloth, leather, sponge rubber, and fabric. We can clearly observe the difference of diffuse reflection on the surface of these four materials. At the same time,

[v] office chair, *material*

Common materials for
office chairs
(Cushion, backrest)

Uncommon materials for
office chairs
(Cushion, backrest)

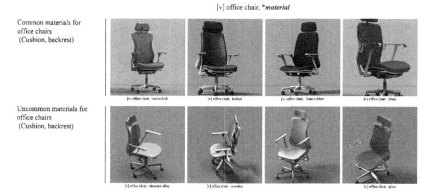

Fig. 9. Material modification tests with common materials and uncommon materials.

mesh cloth can even express the sense of translucency. However, there is something that does not conform to the spatial logic: the back structure cannot be generated through mesh cloth. Similar to the experiment of changing the color, the material changes only occurred on the backrest, cushion and neck pillow.Then we tested some materials that are not commonly used to make office chairs, such as titanium alloy, wood, gold and glass. Now the material change extends to the handrail and base.

Background Modification. (Fig. 10) Same as the previous method, we put the attribute describing the environment behind. First, we tested some natural and artificial environments commonly used in renderings, including indoor and outdoor. All images in dataset are gray backgrounds. The background modification method we used can well preserve the semantics of the chair while changing the background. For the evaluation of the image quality of these chairs with scenes, we found that there is a certain probability that the images (city, sea) generated without complex description have a depth of field. In rendering software or Photography, we need to increase the aperture or lens focal length to achieve this. The quality of some scenarios (forest) is imperfect, but on the whole, they still have certain usability.

Then we tested the color of the background. We also added color value labels under each image. We note that even if color is only used to describe the environment, the main body of the chair still has a small probability of presenting this color. What's surprising is that environment color prompt motivation will make the lighting, diffuse reflection and shadow details of the chair surface change in line with it, so that the chair will not have a sudden feeling. At present, it seems that the neural network filter provided by Adobe in Photoshop can also achieve the effect of changing the main lighting while changing the background. At the same time, using the fuzzy description like 'rainbow' or 'mixed color' can also produce a background with gradient color or multiple color blocks.

Interaction Modification: (Fig. 11)We try to use the natural language prompt to describe the interaction between users and products, so as to generate. We found that the probability of generating low-quality pictures increased after adding the interaction between products and people. Using scene images are an important part of the design effect presentation, and always be applied in design posters. Many design teams choose

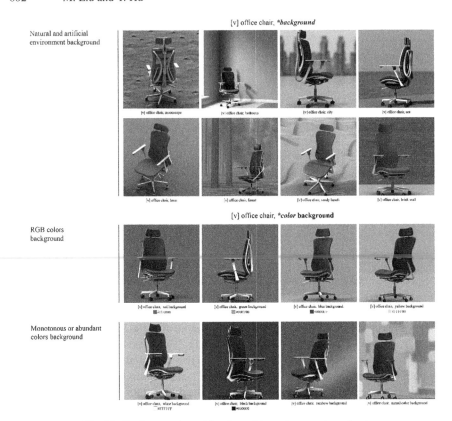

Fig. 10. Background modification with environments and colors.

to use real models for shooting or use real human pictures for Photoshop processing. Using trained stable diffusion models to generate using senses can composite image more efficiently. Any person, pet, and other subjects can be used as prompt to generate images that interact with the trained products, making the using scene images more free to express. However, the disadvantage is that the rationality of this interaction cannot be guaranteed. For example, in this experiment, most of the characters' feet are suspended which is reasonable.

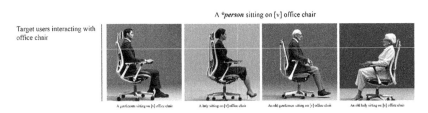

Fig. 11. Interaction modification with different people.

Comprehensive Modification. (Fig. 12) We tested the modification of two and three attributes. In the experiment of changing two attributes, we first tested two color attributes. In some cases (black and orange), a color segmentation on surface will be generated, which doesn't exist in dataset. In industrial design, the segmentation of color on the same surface is a common method to increase the contrast and bring a sense of rhythm. Although this method of color segmentation cannot be accurately controlled. In other cases, two color attributes will be assigned to different parts of the chair, which is also cannot be accurately controlled. Then we try to use two material attributes. The same as the above, the two materials can exist on the product at the same time, but the position cannot be accurately controlled.

In the experiment of three attributes, we describe 'a person sitting on the attribute 1 [v] chair, (in the scene of) attribute 2' as prompt. First of all, we used two color attributes, and the person attribute. An interesting phenomenon of color exchange has occurred here. The color describing the chair has been transferred to the background. The reason for this phenomenon may be the sequence problem after the text encoder converts sentence into token, which needs to be verified later. Another possible reason is that both the chair and the background can be described by the color attribute. If using the attribute that can only limit the chair such as 'leather' (limiting the material) and welded (expressing the connection method), it may improve this situation. Finally, we tested the modification of a material attribute, a environmental attribute and a person attribute. The image content is basically correct, but the overall quality is not as perfect as the image that only changes one attribute, and the semantic expression of the trained chair is not completely accurate.

Experiments of Dreambooth LoRA Train and Illumination Modification

Dataset and Train. (Fig. 13) We use a computer mouse designed by one author (Hu) as the dataset for the same reason as the previous experiment. It is easy to obtain the dataset and judge the training effect. The shape of this mouse is special. It is designed for users to control the left button with thumb, and the right button with little finger. There are two sensors at the front of the mouse, and there is a wheel near the left button. The function of the mouse is not expanded here, but there is no similar product now. We used 45 renderings of it which have have different material colors, shoot angles and background. With dreambooth LoRA method we trained the model for 40 epochs. Same as dreambooth train, we defined an identifier noun ([v]) and use class noun (computer mouse).

The result of dreambooth LoRA is matrix interpolation which occupies smaller storage space than a finetuned stable diffusion model. But when generating photos, it has to combined with original model to apply the changed weights. Here is simple comparison. Whether we use identifier noun or not, the results have a good consistence with train dataset.

Simple Attribute Modification. (Fig. 14) Like the previous experiment, we first test the generalization ability of this training method by changing a single attribute. The changed attribute is the color, material, use environment and interaction. It performs well in color modification and material modification, and can effectively retain the semantics of the trained mouse. Although the environment in prompt is successfully generated in the environment modification, the product itself also has a large deformation. When we

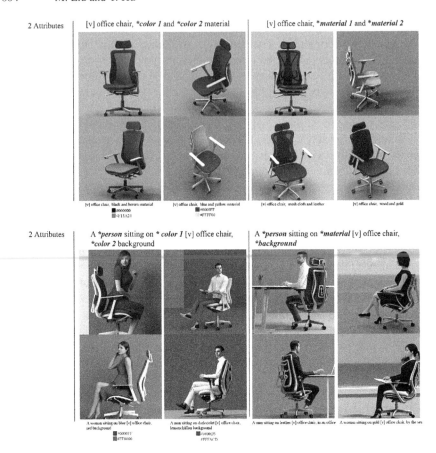

Fig. 12. Comprehensive modification with 2 attributes and 3 attributes.

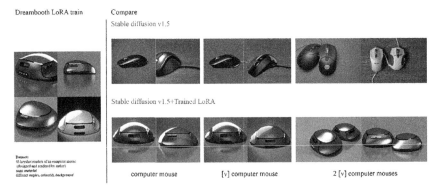

Fig. 13. Dataset is renderings of a mouse. Comparison effect before and after training.

[v] computer mouse, *color material

[v] computer mouse, *material

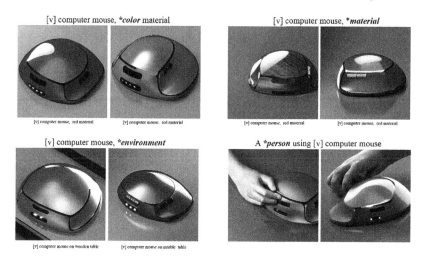

[v] computer mouse, *environment

A *person using [v] computer mouse

Fig. 14. Single attribute modifications.

want to generate the use scene graph, we find it difficult to directly generate the correct interaction between hand and computer mouse through text prompt.

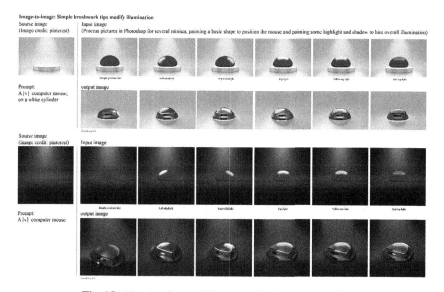

Fig. 15. Illumination modification with simple image hints.

Illumination Modification with Simple Image-to-Image Hints. (Fig. 15) We designed an experiment to test the illumination modification using simple input images which have illumination information and text prompts without illumination information. Our input images are simple expressions of light and shadow with very simple strokes painted on the drawing software, which is quite easy for a design beginner or even a non-practitioner.

The variables we tested mainly include the presence of illumination, the change of light position (left, top, right), and the change of light color at the same position. The text prompt and other generation parameters are consistent. First of all, if there is no light on the prompt image, the resulting image is darker than those with light prompt. Secondly, it is suggested that the change of light position on the image has a significant impact on the result image, and it can indeed control the light position on the product surface. However, we found that when using the prompt image that only changes the light color, the generated image may not reflect the Modification of light color, and may even lead to the change of the material color of the product surface. Therefore, we further test and consider using both image prompt and text prompt containing light information.

Complex Illumination Modification with Image-to-Image Hints. (Fig. 16) We draw some simple images (line1) to represent complex light sources often used in product renderings. Some are of the same color (two blue point lights), and some are of different colors (red light sources left and blue light source right). Use these as input images to test both simple text prompts and prompts containing light information. We found that only using simple text prompts (line2) cannot effectively express the color of the light source. The prompt words containing light source information (line3) can express the color of the light source, but the position is not particularly accurate. In general, the effect of Illumination is better in the image produced by the latter (line3). The sixth column is a special lighting scene (all edge lights), and the expression is very consistent regardless of whether the light source prompt word is added.

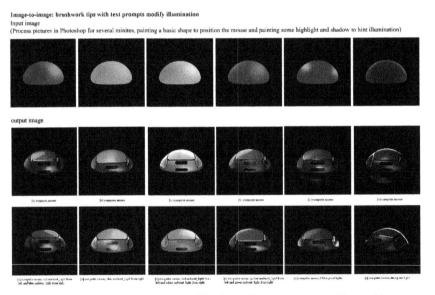

Fig. 16. Complex illumination modification with text prompts and image hints.

4 Conclusion

4.1 Contributions

Our contribution is to design experiments to test the stable diffusion model and its different training methods applied to the Sketching stage and rendering stage of industrial design.

In sketching stage, through qualitative analysis we have determined that stable diffusion v1.5 can provide visual images in the form of superposition of design concepts when building the intent map. We used native train to train the models of four product categories and successfully conducted the style transfer between different products. Finally, we use one of the four models and stable diffusion v1.5 to perform a sketch deduction and structural deduction using image-to-image, which proves that they can create a richer and more specific product structure and provide an intuitive image for the determination of product form and structure.

In rendering stage, we used two different branch methods of dreambooth training in two products to prove that the trained model can completely restore the shape and details of the trained product renderings. In the attribute modification project, the modification of color and material can very well change the attributes without damaging the semantics of the product. The outputs is almost equivalent to those renderings changing the color and material in the rendering software. For the modification of the background and use scenario, the flexibility is very high, but for the contact position of the interaction and the interaction method cannot be accurately controlled, which may be lack of priori of the interaction form of the certain product. For illumination modification, using simple image prompts can effectively change the lighting position of the product, but it has no effect on lighting color (above denoising 0.7). To optimize the adjustment of lighting color, more text prompts of illumination need to be added.

4.2 Limitations

Instability In several experimental projects, the experimental results show that the stable diffusion model also has some instability. For example, the control of the specific position of highlight in illumination modification. In the actual rendering work, the adjustment of illumination is very detailed. Some design departments even have the position of renderers who focus on adjusting renderings. The image obtained by the stable diffusion model using illumination modification method we tested cannot fully meet the application in high-resolution scenes (such as advertising curtain wall).

Lack of Quantitative Analysis Our research lacks quantitative analysis. If want to quantitatively evaluate the application of stable diffusion in industrial design with some existing analytical tools, such as analytic hierarchy process, we will face the problem of requiring a large number of testers and a considerable number of design sketches and products which actually put into the market. This will involve intellectual property issues, which may need to be carried out in the design department of a large enterprise. At the same time, the evaluation of design is quite subjective, especially when using the same framework to evaluate different design categories, how to quantify the impact of subjective feelings also needs further study.

4.3 Discussions

Photo or Model? Although the image is intuitive, its usability in industrial design is not as good as 3D model data or image data containing depth map. The result of stable diffusion v1.5 is image data without depth map. Recently, StablilyAI has also released Stable diffusion v2.0 to support the editing of depth map of image. The initial work of our team was carried out on stable diffusion v1.0 and v1.5. At first, we did not render the depth map when making datasets (which is supported by many rendering software like keyshot), so we choose not to transfer our research to Stable diffusion v2.0. In future work we may test stable diffusion v2.0 which supports depth map to achieve better 3D effects by training dataset with matching depth map data. What is more gratifying is that dream fusion [15] has carried out a lot of work on text-to-model diffusion models, which may help industrial design in the modeling stage in the future.

Data Security and Intellectual Property Inevitably, industrial design is a kind of modern service industry, which is closely related to the manufacturing industry and to some extent aims at obtaining commercial benefits. The use of AI to assist industrial design will inevitably involve the data source of training sets, and further, the protection of intellectual property rights. And the issues related to industrial design, such as enterprise secrets, appearance patent and invention patents, are bound to trigger more discussions.

Part of the image data used in Part 3 of this article comes from Pinterest. At present, Pinterest does not prohibit users from using its data for AI deep learning [20]. The other part images we used is some non-commercial design projects (curriculum design) carried out by one author(Hu). In order to avoid disputes over intellectual property rights, our team canceled the original plan of applying the test stability diffusion model to commercial projects.

Integration of Whole Workflow Between Designers and Stable Diffusion In many cases, design renderings are a tool and a medium for communication between teams in the process of promoting design projects. Learning the characteristics of products using the stable diffusion model will increase the cost (it will not cost a lot, 3000steps for just half an hour in Nvidia 3070ti) of training small personalized models, but it can be more simple and fast in adjusting the color, surface material, lighting direction, and background environment of products. Moreover, the use of rendering software does not conflict with the use of stable diffusion model to generate product images, but can become a complementary relationship. The rendering software provides dataset for the stable diffusion model. The relatively excellent images generated by the stable diffusion model can be used as a reference for the next rendering of ultra- high resolution images. The designer can re-improve the various attributes of the product and render the environment according to the image prompts provided by the stable diffusion model.

We only discussed the application of several stages in the narrow industrial design process, but in fact, the training methods extracted with various visual semantics of stable diffusion rely on only simple image data, and the total number of data sets is very flexible. Even with small data sets, good training results can be obtained, which depends entirely on the needs of the design team. In the future, it may even be applied in product gene extraction, corporate image unification, and industry fashion trend exploration.

References

1. Rombach, R., Blattmann, A., Lorenz, D., et al.: High-resolution image synthesis with Latent Diffusion Models. In: arXiv.org. https://arxiv.org/abs/2112.10752 (2022)
2. Weng, Lilian. (2021). What are Diffusion Models? Lil'Log. https://lilianweng.github.io/posts/2021-07-11-diffusion-models/
3. Sohl-Dickstein, J., Weiss, E.A., Maheswaranathan, N., Ganguli, S.: Deep Unsupervised Learning Using Nonequilibrium Thermodynamics. In: arXiv.org. https://arxiv.org/abs/1503.03585 (2015)
4. Song, Y., Ermon, S.: Generative Modeling by Estimating Gradients of the Data Distribution. In: arXiv.org. https://arxiv.org/abs/1907.05600 (2020)
5. Ho, J., Jain, A., Abbeel, P.: Denoising Diffusion Probabilistic Models (2020). In: arXiv.org. https://arxiv.org/abs/2006.11239. Accessed 9 Feb 2023
6. Dehouche, N., Dehouche, K.: What is in a Text-to-Image Prompt: The Potential of Stable Diffusion in Visual Arts Education (2023). In: arXiv.org. https://arxiv.org/abs/2301.01902. Accessed 9 Feb 2023
7. Liao, J., Yao, Y., Yuan, L., et al.: Visual Attribute Transfer Through Deep Image Analogy. arXiv preprint arXiv: 1705. 01088 (2017)
8. Openai Openai/CLIP: Contrastive Language-image Pretraining. In: GitHub. https://github.com/openai/CLIP. Accessed 9 Feb 2023
9. Team SDB. Dreambooth. In: AiDraw (2022). https://stable-diffusion-book.vercel.app/en/train/DreamBooth/#native-training_1. Accessed 9 Feb 2023
10. Alicefir/car-sketch-V1 · hugging face. In: AliceFir/Car-sketch-V1 · Hugging Face. https://huggingface.co/AliceFir/Car-sketch-V1. Accessed 8 Feb 2023
11. Alicefir/Chinese-teapot-v1 · hugging face. In: AliceFir/Chinese-teapot-V1 · Hugging Face. https://huggingface.co/AliceFir/Chinese-teapot-V1. Accessed 8 Feb 2023
12. Alicefir/mouse-design-v1 · hugging face. In: AliceFir/Mouse-design-V1 · Hugging Face. https://huggingface.co/AliceFir/Mouse-design-V1. Accessed 8 Feb 2023
13. Alicefir/spaceship-design-V1 at main. In: AliceFir/Spaceship-Design-V1 at main. https://huggingface.co/AliceFir/Spaceship-Design-V1/tree/main. Accessed 8 Feb 2023
14. Ruiz, N., Li, Y., Jampani, V., et al.: DreamBooth: Fine Tuning Text-to-Image Diffusion Models for Subject-Driven Generation (2022). In: arXiv.org. https://arxiv.org/abs/2208.12242. Accessed 8 Feb 2023
15. Poole, B., Jain, A., Barron, J.T., Mildenhall, B.: Dreamfusion: Text-to-3d using 2D Diffusion (2022). In: arXiv.org. https://arxiv.org/abs/2209.14988. Accessed 9 Feb 2023
16. Borji, A.: Generated Faces in the Wild: Quantitative Comparison of Stable Diffusion, Midjourney and dall-e 2 (2022). In: arXiv.org. https://arxiv.org/abs/2210.00586. Accessed 9 Feb 2023
17. Definition of industrial design. In: WDO. https://wdo.org/about/definition/
18. Gal, R., Alaluf, Y., Atzmon, Y., et al.: An Image is Worth One Word: Personalizing Text-to-Image generation Using Textual Inversion (2022). In: arXiv.org. https://arxiv.org/abs/2208.01618. Accessed 9 Feb 2023
19. Cloneofsimo Cloneofsimo/Lora: Using Low-Rank Adaptation to Quickly Fine-tune Diffusion Models. In: GitHub. https://github.com/cloneofsimo/lora. Accessed 9 Feb 2023
20. In: Pinterest Policy. https://policy.pinterest.com/zh-hans/community-guidelines. Accessed 10 Feb 2023

Design Intelligence – AI and Design Process Modules to Foster Collaboration Between Design, Data (Science) and Business Experts

Jennifer Moosbrugger[✉]

Bauhaus Universität Weimar, Geschwister-Scholl-Straße 8/15, 99423 Weimar, Germany
`jennifer.moosbrugger@uni-weimar.de`

Abstract. Artificial Intelligence (AI), Machine Learning (ML) and Deep Learning (DL) are perceived as a new design material. Lack of user engagement and trust in these systems due to failure or other bad user experience is one results that comes with this issue. The age of AI therefore seeks for new, processes, methods and tools for Design, User Experience (UX) and Human-Computer Interaction (HCI) practitioners. This paper presents findings and insights from various case study research in the industrial AI domain. Collaboration between designers and data scientists is perceived as crucial asset in that regard. For the fruitful development of AI and ML infused systems, their processes and terminology need to be aligned to foster co-operative creativity. This is where the proposed solution of this paper contributes with a process framework of 7 modules with their related activities, their flow and dependencies.

Keywords: design · industrial AI · ML · UX · HCI · process · methods · tools

1 Introduction

Artificial Intelligence, Machine Learning and Deep Learning are perceived as a new design material [1, 2]. A few publications in the design, UX and HCI research community, as well as in the area of AI and ML touch upon this issue [3, 4]. These statements are outlined in more detail in Sect. 1.1 Related Work in this paper. However, more insights deriving from real world use cases can still add value to the overall discussion, especially from the industrial AI domain. This is why the solution this paper proposes is based on case study research which described in detail in Sect. 2. Case Study Research. This very broad view of the pitfalls and challenges when developing AI infused systems is furthermore expanded in Sect. 3. Expert Interviews. The insights and findings from those different sources clearly reveal that the age of AI asks for new processes, methods and tools for Design, User Experience and Human-Computer Interaction practitioners. Collaboration between designers, data scientists, as well as business domain experts is perceived as one crucial requirement. The proposed solution offered by this paper makes this precise contribution in Sect. 4. Process Framework of seven modules and their related activities their flows and dependencies.

H. Degen and S. Ntoa (Eds.): HCII 2023, LNAI 14050, pp. 610–628, 2023.
https://doi.org/10.1007/978-3-031-35891-3_38

1.1 Related Work

The information and challenges for design, UX and HCI practitioners in the age of AI and ML were revealed through a systematic review of AI/ML publications concerned with Human-Centered-Design (HCD). This review followed the SPIDER framework [5] to define eligibility criteria for the systematic review of qualitative research publications. The final list of publications was then filtered through a PRISMA flow diagram [6, 7]. This list was enhanced with information and input found in books [8, 9].

1.2 Structured Literature Review Analysis

SPIDER framework eligibility criteria:

(S)ample: Designers (HCD/UX/HCI) of AI/ML-based systems, products, and solutions (in the context of industrial AI)
(P)henomenon of (I)nterest: Research that examines the development for AI/ML-based technology by designers (HCD/UX/HCI) and their resulting challenges
Study (D)esign: All types of research designs
(E)valuation: Research that presents insights and findings from the experience and perspective of designers (HCD/UX/HCI) in the area of AI/ML
(R)esearch Type: Peer reviewed research in English, German

Information sources: Google scholar, Researchgate, SAGE, conference proceedings (e.g., AAAI, CHI, HCII).

Search Strategy:

Domain/context (e.g. Industry, 'real world', best practice, art, design)
AND human-centered design (e.g. Design Thinking, UX, HCD, HCI, HAI)
AND AI/ML related terms (e.g. intelligent agent, AI, ML, deep learning, neural nets, predictions)

List of included content from PRISMA flow diagram: n = 16 [1–4 & 10–21].

1.3 Insights and Findings

The papers included from the systematic literature review revealed the reasons and problems that were relevant and occurred during the development of AI/ML infused projects from a UX design perspective. A lot of the literature from scientific sources was not written by design practitioners themself but is based on qualitative interviews with them. Overall, the systematic review supported the hypothesis that AI/ML is a new design material. Broadly speaking - because AI/ML systems are very complex [20], and design outcomes are non-deterministic and therefore dynamic [10, 19]. To enable designers to work with this new material the gaps that need to be filled and missing items added were identified. Designers lack, a) AI/ML expertise [1, 2, 16, 17]. They are not familiar with statistical data sets, often based on telemetry, sensor and quantitative data. They understand AI/ML capabilities broadly, but not specifically. On the other hand, there is a lack of AI/ML training targeted towards design, UX and HCI practitioners [12, 13]. Furthermore, b) current design tools do not serve the needs of AI/ML development [11, 14, 18]. They needed either to be adapted, for example, user journeys and workflows, prototyping and testing possibilities [8], as well as new ones created, such as, AI/ML systems monitoring, as well as integration and response to feedback loops [9]. Further, a lack of c) AI/ML exemplars and abstractions/best practice sharing [18] and, d) collaboration with AI/ML experts [15] is needed to partly overcome these challenges.

2   Case Study Research

To further elaborate on the pitfalls and challenges relevant to the intersection of design, UX, HCI and AI/ML further case study research within the domain of industrial AI was conducted. As the researcher is an UX designer and an active member of the development team, this research adds a new perspective to the academic discourse. The purpose of this exploratory sequential research was first, a qualitative exploration of a small sample to determine if the qualitative findings could be generalized to a larger sample. The first phase of the research was a qualitative case study about developing of an ML solution within an industrial setting through conducting semi-structured 1to1 interviews with the development team and involved stakeholders of a huge German-based corporation producing hardware and software components for the factory automation market. The initial qualitative semi-structured 1to1 interviews with the eight (P1–P8) team members aimed to get a clearer understanding of key issues from their points of view, from a design, data, and business perspective. The initial qualitative findings were used to develop assessment measures that could be administered to a large sample. The cross-case validation phase collected data from two other case studies from companies producing similar hardware components for the factory automation market. All three cases investigated used the same ML technology - time series predictions for their factory planning processes - which means they can be compared. The cross-case approach enabled the initial findings to be validated and explore any additional issues that might emerge.

2.1   Research Design Meta-sample

In the following pages 'Meta-Sample' refers to the initial case study used to identify the first relevant themes during the development process to assess the missing Human-Centered-Design focus hypothesis was an issue for pitfalls and/or challenges amongst other issues. 'Beta-Sample(s)' refers to the cross-case validation studies, making sure the initial findings are transferable to other, similar cases and checking no additional, emerging themes have been missed.

2.2   Data Collection

This case study research used various data collection principles:

1. Multiple sources of information - interviews, observations, project results (such as presentations, dashboards, software), literature review;

2. Storage of information in a case study database with anonymous data, transcripts, interview guides and field reports;
3. Maintenance of an audit trail.

The educational background of the researcher of this work, was a valuable source of knowledge for data collection and analysis. Being equipped with qualitative data approaches from ethnographic field work methods and tools helped to define the initial steps for gathering case study data. Data collection for the Meta-Sample was done by direct participation and observation at the early stages of the development process. The qualitative semi-structured 1to1 interviews with all the team members, involved stakeholders and management were conducted close to the final implementation phase of the development process. In addition, there was direct observation of and with the users before the implementation of the time series prediction forecast and afterwards.

The interview guide had three different sections: a) overall project set up related questions, b) process related questions, and c) HCD/UX related questions. In total eight 1:1 interviews with the team members and relevant stakeholders were conducted (P1–P8). The chosen respondents represented a variety of opinions, hence qualitative data input, but also appeared to be the right level of input to reveal shared concerns by all the participants, indicating validity and reliability of the first part of the case study research as the basis of informed and data driven decisions for the next steps. All the interviews were transcribed. Impressions from the contextual inquiry/participant observations were used to support the sensemaking and data interpretation, as well as the project results available and accessible to the researcher.

2.3   Data Analysis and Synthesis

This case study research used these methods of data analysis:

1. Immersion in the data;
2. Inductive and deductive data analysis tagging/(open) coding (descriptive and thematic [22]);
3. Theme/Framework development;
4. Evaluation of the findings;
5. Narrative and storyline.

The first part of the data analysis followed an inductive approach, appropriate to the qualitative data gathered from the interviews, not associated with any theoretical framework. First, the transcribed interviews were read to find meaningful sections. Second, these sections were analyzed to find patterns and codes, especially any challenges or barriers which occurred during the development of the AI system, which were then examined. The data was organized into topics and codes attached. Third, these codes were systematically grouped into larger categories concerned with similar issues - the same code could appear with more than one category. This was an iterative process, going back and forth through the data, refining, and renaming the codes and patterns and identifying how they were related to each other. The next step involved grouping the categories again to establish a comprehensive set of themes. The data analysis produced 59 codes, 4 groups and 15 themes. Fourth, it was necessary to evaluate whether the data gathered contained enough evidence to support the themes by making clusters of a) the codes that have been expected, b) codes that were a surprise, and c) codes that were unusual, then comparing these to the overall AI challenges from other domains and the external sources mentioned in section related work of this paper. This illustrates the deductive approach of the research. Fifth and finally, naming themes a short, representative phrase representing the essence of each and adding a short description to make the concept underlying each theme obvious, clear to reflect the meanings embedded in the data collected.

2.4 Insights and Findings

The interview participants described the overall process in very different steps, so the team encountered unforeseen problems and had to tackle a lot of challenges. The project took longer than initially planned. Some participants left the team, new ones joined. The acceptance and adoption level by the users of the time series prediction were low. Most of the team members that developed the solution were aware of those issues. Nevertheless, they were mostly pleased with their work and the overall outcome, but also pointed out that they could have done their job better.

The research with and for the Meta-Sample was meant to reveal all the pitfalls and challenges, as well as shed light on positive aspects and drivers to gain a better picture and overview without any focus on particular areas at the start. This means the list of codes and categories is extensive. However, most of the findings were then sorted and grouped into themes due to their similar character or how they were expressed.

The established themes were grouped by their relation and relevance a) to AI projects and development in general (1–4), b) to the given use cases (5–12), and c) to HCD/UX/HCI expertise (13–15). Some themes relate to more than one group, boundaries being fluent. The participant shortcut indicates which interviewees mentioned a particular issue, making ranking by importance also possible. A sample quote together with a short description was added to support each finding.

01. Missing AI/ML-Expertise (All)
P7: "We learned a lot about what AI can and cannot do, what the limitations are."

The initial part of the interview asked all participants about their AI expertise. It was interesting that the AI experts compared themselves to other experts in the field and therefore never reached the highest score. The non-experts rated themselves more highly compared to the experts. They compared themselves not with experts in the field, but to their own knowledge at the beginning of the project and again towards the end. There was no agreement by the interview participants about the level of AI expertise needed, but all agreed that a basic knowledge of AI/ML capabilities would be useful for the overall development process.

02. Wrong Expectations Management (All)
P5: "… it is necessary to communicate that the part of data preparation and consolidation takes a lot of time and effort, …".

One of the major issues mentioned by all interview participants was the expectation of the technology - either wrong or too high. This goes hand in hand with the first insight concerning AI expertise. Whereas the experts understood the limitations and basic conditions necessary for projects based on AI/ML technology to succeed, this was not clear to the business domain experts. Since the current hype of the AI/ML technology plays an important role in business domain, AI/ML is perceived to be the solution to every problem open to digital enablement.

03. Trust in the Output (P1, P2, P3, P4, P6, P7)

P6: "We were able to prove that our forecast was better than the planning data. Nevertheless, the planners did not trust the AI forecast, …".

Related to a lack of knowledge and unrealistic expectations, lack of trust on the user's side in the output of the algorithms was mentioned by most of the interview participants. There was also the potential of losing their jobs which increased the trust issues. It took time, a lot of conversations and testing phases until users had gained trust in the system's output. It was also necessary for the developers to admit that not all products could be predicted with a high degree of accuracy by an algorithm. Both sides had to agree to any compromises.

04. Culture and Mindset (Change Management) (P2, P3, P7)

P3: "What we also did in parallel to the development of the technological solution was in the whole area of change management."

Most of the interview participants were aware of the pitfalls and challenges. A couple realized that a lot of the issues came from the business culture and the mindsets of the people involved. In their view, management change activities should be integrated into this kind of project. This is also the case for other projects in digitalization. Fear of job loss, new ways of working and change in habits and attitudes go hand in hand with any necessary structural transformations.

05. Gap Between ML and the Business Domain (P4, P5, P6, P7, P8).

P5: "… They somehow have a very clear idea of what the problem is, but the translation into a data analytics solution or decision support is definitely a mismatch."

A couple of the interview participants perceived a gap between the AI/ML and business domains. They described it as different languages used and different goals to reach. They also mentioned the matter of AI/ML expertise and the business domain not really knowing if their problem they identified was a good fit for an AI/ML solution. Also, the AI/ML expert could equally not be familiar with the business domain data, its meaning and potential predispositions, or data quality issues. Also, the definition of what constitutes a useful initial data set for training and testing algorithms is impossible without AI/ML and business experts closely collaborating with each other.

06. KPI's (Definition of Done) (P1, P2, P3, P4, P5)

P1: "What was really difficult there was to judge whether or not it was a good prediction."

The team mentioned a couple of times when it had been very hard to decide and agree on how to judge the algorithm's performance. While the AI/ML experts were more into error and accuracy measures, the business domain experts were more interested in economic values and comparison with the manual planning process. This led to a lot of discussions, shifting requirements and priorities, making it hard to judge whether the initial goal of the project had been finally reached.

07. Analysis Status Quo (Current Process)/involvement of the Factory Planners (All)

P8: "It would have been very helpful in my opinion to watch the planners do their job. Learning on the job for 2, 3 days. We would have cut down a lot of discussions."

All the interview participants named the current manual planning process as the source for the recurrent problems. Each planner did their manual product planning slightly differently, which was related to the nature of their products (labels: high-/low runner, exotic, sparse). It was therefore very hard for outsiders to fully understand it. In addition, due to the lack of the involvement and availability of the factory planners during the project, any attempt to make changes was unfeasible, making it impossible to fit the algorithmic figures into that process. It was clear that it would have been helpful to adapt the process to the AI/ML technology, but this was never the scope of the project and therefore was not touched upon by the team.

08. Iterative Working Mode (All)

P5: "To keep the sprints (set period of time to develop and completed items and being. Ready for review) and present results on a regular basis was key for the success of this project."

The nature of AI/ML projects is their uncertainty and volatility. A lot depends on the quality of the data and access to it, but also on the know-how and human concepts and expectations initially stated. All the interview participants agreed that an iterative working model with predefined sprints and regular touch points was a fundamental requirement to give the team the flexibility to react to unforeseen challenges and situations, as well as keep everybody in the loop. In the best-case scenario, this means not wasting too much time with a backlog of items, either unnecessary or error prone.

09. (Project) Starting Point/Goal (P4, P7, P8)

P8: "My initial task was to rationalize the planner's jobs. So, I can totally understand that they did not want to support our project."

The initial goal of this project was to improve the factory plan based on ML, because the manual plan had a very low accuracy rate compared to the actual product orders. The initial idea of higher management was to replace humans in that equation. The factory planners were aware of this goal. They were unwilling and not open to improving their planning proposals through AI/ML technology. For them, it was an insult to their expertise, know-how and skills. This set the stage for their motivation and willingness to collaborate to reach that goal, which was obviously not very high. This shows how important and relevant human-focus in technological endeavors has to be. The set up can change a lot, for good or bad.

10. Feedback Structure, Structured Feedback - Feedback Loop (P1, P3, P4, P7)

P3: "Feedback... Timely, from all, because of course, it's also an incredible amount of data, you also have to talk, to get the feedback and what s/he does with the feedback when someone says it fits or doesn't fit... Everyone decides this from a completely different perspective."

The team collected user feedback from the factory planners. This was a very unstructured process and most of the time, the team had no idea how to incorporate the feedback, or decided not to incorporate it at all. Therefore, collecting feedback was not a loop. From the UX perspective, this was a very negative experience for the factory planners. They provided the team with feedback, but most of the time, could not see their input reflected in the results. This could become an even gibber issue when the AI/ML predictions need to be retrained. Not using user feedback is counterintuitive to AI/ML potential, whose' key value is the ability to learn and improve over time.

11. Data Quality and Consistency (P3, P6, P7)
P7: "We have a lot of data, but the quality is not always good."

During the project, it became apparent that the data sources used had a kind of 'bias'. Since the development team received the data on customer orders from different areas of the company, it was only after some poor results from the neural networks that it became clear that something was wrong with it. The reason was that in the different data-supplying departments, canceled orders were represented differently. This resulted in various revisions of the models and additional efforts to clean the data.

12. Way of Communication/Biased Presentations (P2, P4, P6)
P2: "We tend to present our forecasts too positively."

Three interview participants mentioned that they had the impression that sometimes they did not do a good job in communicating their results. They often focused their presentation on the positive outcome, to please the management, but at the same time, offending the work and expertise of the factory planners, and fueling unrealistic expectations by the management side while increasing pressure on the factory planners.

13. HCD/UX/HCI Value and Usefulness (P1, P2, P3, P4, P5, P7) vs. (P6, P8)
P1: "If design is only adding additional requirements... that is tricky, if it helps to focus and decide whether or not to develop a certain feature or setting, then it is valuable."

Most participants agreed that HCD/UX can add value to the development of AI/ML infused systems. Orienting, managing, prioritizing, eliminating and human focus were mentioned as positive aspects of HCD/UX activities. However, it was difficult to fully incorporate the insights gained from user research into the further development of the AI solution. Not all were able to be transferred 1:1 into a statistical based model, showing the gap between human and data-centered approaches. On top, it also became clear that for a couple of participants, HCD/UX activities were not perceived as a crucial part of overall AI/ML development. They mentioned HCD/UX related issues, without really making any connection to the practice.

14. HCD/UX/HCI Timing (P4, P6, P7)
P4: "I think the shitty thing was we got the interview done after we had set some requirements." (P4).

HCD/UX activities are sensitive to the right timing. If they come too late in the process, they cannot influence the direction at that point and are perceived as a burden instead of a valuable activity.

15. Definition of HCD/UX/HCI and Awareness (P1, P3)

P3: "I think a lot of people associate it with making applications look nice."

In Germany, design has a very special connotation and limited meaning. It therefore makes sense to stick to the terminology of HCD, UX and HCI.

2.5 Summary

Some of the issues discovered were not surprising, since they can be found in secondary research and the general literature about AI/ML [23]. The interviews worked as a reality check and set those findings in context of a real project. However, some of the themes revealed new insights into best practice approaches of combining insights from design, data and business domains, adding to the current research and knowledge base. Not all of the issues that emerged are relevant or should be tackled by the HCD/UX/HCI practitioner but are related to other roles and experts. However, it became quite clear how important a systematic approach is. AI expertise, expectation management and gaps in the collaboration of the different domain experts were mentioned by all the respondents. A huge issue was the understanding of the current manual planning processes and the involvement of their users, supporting the initial hypothesis that lack of human-focus is a big issue (amongst others). To be more specific, the Meta-Sample case study showed the involvement of the user throughout the design and development phases could not be ensured. The solution consequently did not meet the users' expectations and they were not able to integrate it into their daily work routine. In addition, they did not have control over any of the system's features, so in case of error or a missing data point, they had no opportunity to chance of changing the systems behavior or understand what caused the malfunction [24]. These initial Meta-Sample findings served as a basis for further investigations with the Beta-Sample studies.

2.6 Case Study 02 and 03 (Beta-Samples) Cross-Case Validation

The research design, data collection, analysis and synthesis followed the same approach as the Meta-Sample. In total, seven additional 1to1 interviews with the (P9–P14 including E1 from an external agency) were conducted in the Beta-Samples.

2.7 Insights and Findings

All the use cases followed a very different development process and starting point. Beta-Sample 01 hired an external agency to develop the AI/ML solution, due to a lack of skills in their own team. Beta-Sample 02 hired a data scientist before starting the project and trained him as a factory planner. In this way, AI expertise, as well as domain knowledge were combined in one person. The goal of the project was not to replace the factory planners, but to increase the numbers of employees with a different skill set.

This was very helpful during the development of the AI/ML solution. However, when scaling the concept to other factories, they faced very similar issues to the other teams. This additional research mainly supported the initial findings from the Meta-Sample use case. However, another theme was added: 16. External vs. internal software. Two of the three case studies developed their own software solution and infrastructure for the final product, whereas the 01 Beta-Sample team used a 3rd party solution. This had a huge impact on the time taken for the final deployment phase of the project.

16. External vs. Internal Software

P9: "That's a standard tool, but we do not have that in the company world, so that's a third-party provider, but it's a standard tool. One with a solution from a consulting company."

One of the Beta-Samples used a 3rd party software solution to implement their AI/ML system. Both approaches – internal and external - have their pros and cons, which are important considerations while designing AI systems and so was added to the list of themes. The team, from a technical point of view was faster in their implementation, because they were able to use a given, readymade infrastructure as there was no need for them to spend time setting it up in the first place. However, one disadvantage is that their lack flexibility regarding the restricted choices and use of limited to certain ML models. This is especially an issue with products that were difficult to predict, as well as new product releases. On top of this, if any new product needs to be integrated into the system solution, the team would need the expertise of the external consultancy again.

2.8 Conclusion

This case study research (Meta- and Beta-Samples) identified the overall pitfalls and challenges when designing smart algorithms in the industrial AI domain. It showed that a lack of a human-focus and missing information and understanding of the workflow of the users was a big concern. It also became clear that a lack of Human-Centered-Design is not the only problem encountered during the development. This initial collection of issues revealed clearly that the hypothesis of a lack of Human-Centered-Design is supported, and other potential research areas and subject matters revealed. The two Beta-Samples also confirmed these initial findings, also showing that the development process differed greatly among all projects. These findings were shared with the research community in two research papers during the HCI International 2020 and 2021 [25, 26]. The logical next step was to further explore the designer's role within the overall research area, by mapping these themes identified with additional research informed by expert interviews. The expert perspective could sharpen the industrial AI/ML perspective, as well as bring the knowledge from different case studies and allow more comparison.

3   Expert Interviews

This section aims to match the data collected and gathered from the Meta- and Beta-Samples with insights from experts and projects from different areas, not only to validate the findings, but also check for unexposed issues. In total, 4 expert interviews were conducted.

3.1   Research Design

The interview guide for the expert interviews was different from to the case study interviews. They were more structured and not targeted on a specific project, but an overall comparison of different projects, to evaluate the initial case study findings. The interviewed experts have a lot of experience of many different industrial, as well as more commercial AI/ML development projects. Data analysis was done in a similar manner to the case study interviews, but additional codes and patterns emerged. In addition to the already described cluster of issues, a section about lessons learned and strategic decisions and proposed offerings were revealed.

3.2   Insights and Findings

The expert interviews contained a lot of additional insights from the AI/ML field in general, as well as specifically HCD/UX/HCI focused ones. They revealed in what way some of the case study (Meta and Beta-Samples) themes are also specifically HCD/UX/HCI related.

01b. HCD/UX Professionals Lack AI/ML-Expertise (E4, E5)

A lack of AI/ML expertise also occurred HCD/UX domain. Most designers are not experts in the field of AI/ML, so can also have unrealistic expectations of the technology, and so they cannot judge or evaluate how the technology can be a valuable addition to help to find solutions.

05B. Gap Between ML and Design Domain (E2, E4)

HCD/UX experts often have no direct access to a data scientist or ML engineer, either because there is no data scientist in the team, or professions work in different departments. In addition, their procedures and ways of working are not aligned, which makes collaboration very hard. Furthermore, they also have different focus areas; while AI/ML is focused on data, HCD/UX approaches heavily have a human-centric focus. Both approaches are highly valuable for the development of AI/ML solutions, it is a matter of aligning these worlds.

14b. HCD/UX Timing (E4, E5)

A lot of UX professionals join in the process late and are not involved in the development stages. This point had been made before but received additional attention from both experts in the field.

15b. HCD/UX Value & Awareness (E5)

Most HCD/UX designers are not aware of the AI/ML demand for new processes, methods, and tools. They do not think that they can add value to such a technically driven process and domain. This means that enabling designers to contribute to the field it is also partly a matter of building awareness amongst them that AI/ML need their inputs and points of view, as well as being a tool for guiding them on how and where to start.

3.3 Summary and Conclusion

Sections 01 to 03 described the approaches and resources use for deriving insights and findings from the intersection of HCD/UX/HCI practitioners and the AI/ML domain. The literature revealed that designers lack a) AI/ML expertise, b) current design tools do not serve the demands for AI/ML development, c) AI/ML exemplars & abstractions/best practice sharing is lacking, as is d) collaboration with AI/ML experts. These findings indicate that AI and ML are a new design material. Case study research from three samples in the industrial AI domain with participants from the design, data and business domains identified 16 themes, which were grouped by their relationship and relevance a) for AI projects and development in general (1–4), b) to the given use cases (5–12 + 16), and c) to the HCD/UX/HCI expertise (13–15). Lack of Human-Centered-Design was identified as a main reason for pitfalls and challenges, among others. Finally, expert interviews revealed how the rich spectrum of themes from the case study research were even HCD/UX/HCI specific. These findings open the door for Human-Centered-Design activities in the age of AI, which in turn affect the decisions and practice of designers, and requiring new methods and tools, which the following section contributes to.

4   Process Framework

This section presents the transfer of the insights and findings from the presented research into practical applications for designers - integrating AI/ML into design practice. As well as the aspects mentioned above, it should provide a starting point for designers and practitioners beginning to work with AI infused systems. During a lot of conversations with designers, students, as well as businesspeople, it became clear that information about AI appears overwhelming, and they had no idea at what point a designer could potentially add value during the development process. Non experts have a hard time finding an entry point. The material is either too generic or too specialized and tech heavy. The same applies to the Human-Centered-AI principles [27–29]; without a context it is difficult to follow the prompts. Overall, any attempt to support the design community to get their heads around AI/ML needs to provide a systematic approach, with a starting point and from there the different paths to follow, depending on their know- how, skillset and level of involvement.

4.1   Focus on Aligned Processes and Tools for Human-Centered and Data-Centered Approaches (+Business Expertise)

The case study research revealed some pitfalls and challenges when designing AI/ML systems in the industrial domain. A lack of HCD/UX expertise was one factor amongst others. 2 out of the 3 cases had no dedicated HCD/UX practitioner in their development team. This picture was also reflected in literature review. HCD/UX are not necessarily perceived as crucial factors in every use case. However, in the teams with that expertise it was perceived to be an important part of the overall process. It is also very important to find the right time for the related HCD/UX activities input.

The industrial AI domain is very technology and data driven. It is therefore necessary to align the proposed solution for designers towards this factor. A collaboration between data scientists, business experts and HCD/UX designers seemed to be a valuable asset in that regard. Therefore, the idea of integrating these perspectives in the final solution crucial. Trying to map the ideal AI/ML development process where all the professions could contribute their valuable know-how is therefore the baseline for the practical part of this paper. Using methods and tools from the related fields, the outcome needs to reflect a shared workflow, common terminology, and language, as well as boundary objects, such as templates, that help the professions involved in the collaboration.

Step 01 - AI & Design Process Mapping

The initial idea was to gain an overview and starting point of relevant AI/ML aspects by mapping project development steps to highlight where designers can make the biggest contribution. This mapping was based on several real-world scenarios and use cases directly tied to the development process. Combining methods and tools with a process and concrete instructions regarding the required steps and actions seems to be a promising combination to enable designers in the age of AI to embrace this new design material. Additionally, the notational form of a map suits the visual thinking styles and approaches of designers, which is currently missing in the overall discourse, but it can also provide business and data experts with a common ground that is not only based on common terminology, but visually represents the different activities where collaborative working is needed. From this initial process mapping, 7 process modules could be derived.

Step 02 – AI & Design Process Modules

Overall, the modules have different layers. At the highest level, each square represents one module, while its size is a code for the importance of the design and its impact. The next layer is the module notation, 1. Set Up, 2. Understand & Define, 3. Input, 4. Modeling, 5. Output, 6. Deployment, 7. Post Processing. Finally, the related activities (each activity is related to concrete actions and tools, both 'new' and 'old', but these are not included in this paper, due to word limitations) and their flow and dependencies are visually presented (see Fig. 1). The whole representation is 'modular', meaning it is possible to combine some of the modules and leave others out. This is why it is possible to produce different kinds of project patterns as shown in the following figures (see Figs. 2 and 3).

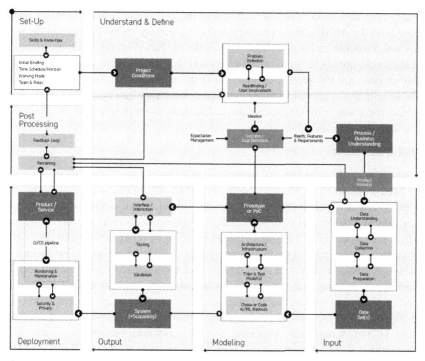

Fig. 1. An overview of the design and AI process modules, consisting of 7 modules; Set Up, Understand & Define, Input, Modeling, Output, Deployment, Post Processing and the related activities, milestones, and their dependencies for each module.

Fig. 2. Project pattern that runs through module 1–7 (this is a very theoretical project pattern; due to the highly iterative nature of ML projects this linear approach is very unusual).

Fig. 3. Initial exploratory data or PoC/Prototyping phase before project set up with iterative development cycles (this is a very typical project pattern).

4.2 Detailed Module Descriptions

Module Set Up

This activity represents the starting point of a project. It can be a rough idea, vision, problem, concept, PoC, MVP, data set, finished product that needs to be redefined. The initial assumption is that it can somehow be solved by an AI/ML infused solution. It is also very helpful to gain an initial overview of the given data to judge if the quality and amount meet the AI/ML data set requirements. Agreement on the duration of the project - start and desirable end point - need to be defined. Based on the briefing, timing, and working mode, the choice of team members and their roles can be made. The outcomes of this module are the project conditions. If the necessary skills and experts are not available within the team, hiring an external consultancy can be the solution. Adding new team members or making the strategic decisions to get the relevant people on board can be an alternative solution.

Module Understand & Define

The activities in this module are strongly inter-related and dependent on each other. They need to go hand in hand. A clear understanding and definition of problem and user engagement are the requirements to start ideation and define what is necessary for success and define (sub)goals. HCD/UX designers can facilitate the conversation and lead the needfinding activities. The integration of other team members is highly recommended to offer them firsthand experience. Research has shown that success/goal definition is crucial action item relevant for other modules as well. When not following the whole process map, but using modules individually, it is still helpful to clarify this procedure. The outcomes of this module are a process & business understanding and it is heavily driven by human-centered activities informing the data-driven aspects. In this module, HCD/UX designers' expertise is at its maximum, serving to generate deeper understanding of the business domain knowledge and user workflow. If this is not clear, it is necessary to start over again and repeat this module.

Product Vision (validation item)

Formulating a shared product vision(s) should be possible after accomplishing module 1 and 2. This step is the transition from problem space into solution space. The focus is on human desirability, before jumping into technical feasibility and business viability. In this activity HCD/UX designers can contribute their imaginative potential and visualization skills. They should include the other team members in the process and encourage them to think outside the technological feasibility and business viability.

Module Input

The steps of this module heavily depend on and influence each other. Sometimes the borders are blurred, and activities cannot be divided as easily as suggested. However, it is crucial to understand that AI/ML algorithms heavily depend on the input data and that this module is therefore very important overall. Designers can contribute with their human-centered perspective and data visualization skills, but it is also important to understand statistical data sets and be familiar with data preparation activities. The designer's level of knowledge is central for the involvement of their expertise in this module. The data scientists and ML engineers must also work closely together to make sure the data and AI/ML methods are aligned. Close collaboration with the business domain experts is crucial since they are familiar with the data. The outcome of this module is a single or multiple data set. This module takes up a lot of time and resources, more than 50% of AI/ML projects are data work. Well-defined problem statements, clear understanding of the process and business domain and a shared product vision make it easier to focus on the data necessary to respond to the challenges. If something concerning the data is not clear at the end of this module, it is necessary repeat the process from the start.

Module Modeling

The steps of this module heavily depend on and influence each other. Sometimes the boundaries are blurred, and activities cannot be as easily separated as stated. The designer's level of knowledge and expertise being appropriate is vital for their contribution in this module. Coding skills would help but are not essential. AutoML solutions provide a framework that can also be used by designers. However, prototyping in a low fidelity and fail fast manner is hardly possible. Model behavior and performance need to be measured with real data. This module requires high level ML engineer expertise. The outcome of this module is a (high fidelity) Prototype/Proof of Concept (PoC) or Minimum Viable Product (MVP), to prove, or in later iterations, make sure that whether the data input creates a meaningful model performance, so that the AI/ML approach is the best way forward. However, a bad model performance can be for various reasons. One could be the wrong choice of AI/ML method, in which case, it is necessary to start the module over again. It is also possible that the problem lies within the data input. Going through the input module is the path to follow, in this case. It can also be helpful to have second thoughts on the success and goals aimed for. A check on whether the error metric or level of accuracy were too optimistic might be necessary. If the model's performance is bad, it is necessary to start over again - or if it is not going anywhere, this marks the exit point for the given development project.

Module Output

This module implies a lot of actions related to HCD/UX design tasks. Close collaboration with data scientists and ML engineers to predict system behavior and potential functionality in a positive, as well as negative spectrum need to be considered and made visible and clear for the user(s). The turn from static interfaces to smart and dynamic interactions represents a new design material. Potential outcomes and outputs are too complex to be planned in very detail. Failure and malfunction are inevitable and need to be incorporated as a design feature. If the outcome of this module results in an AI/ML solution which produces a stable and accurate output, on small, as well as larger data sets, and the user interface supports the user to reach his/her goal and trust in the system's output, and the business domain experts perceive it as a value addition from either a time or cost efficient perspective, then the transfer from a PoC towards a productive system can be made. Scalability refers to the notion that an implemented system, in a best-case scenario, could be transferred to use in similar cases or other business units with similar problems as well. If the AI/ML system is very error prone and transparency and explainability are hard to achieve, it is necessary to start again with the modeling module, which might lead back to the input module. If testing results show bad user experience, it is necessary to begin again with the module and redesign the interface/interaction.

Input, modeling and output modules are strongly interdependent, and a few iterations are necessary to reach the status of an AI/ML system that is accurate, usable and time and cost efficient (combining business viability, technological feasibility and user desirability).

Module Deployment

The final deployment of the system requires a few other things to be well-handled. Decisions about the architecture and infrastructure from the modeling module play an important role, as does the connection to the data sources from the input module. A lot of the data handling, such as preprocessing and cleaning, or running the AI/ML model on that data will have been performed manually up to this module. For a productive system, those tasks need to be automated, taking data security and privacy into account, as well as managing access rights and ongoing activities such as monitoring and maintenance (DevOps). The outcome of this module is a product/service (productive). This module turns the output from the former modules into a productive environment. This is a rather low area of activity for HCD/UX design. An IT department or related service could take over from here. The best-case scenario is to integrate them as early in the development as possible.

Module Post Processing

There are tasks such as updating and retraining models to incorporate new data points from feedback that go further than regular monitoring and maintenance (CI/CD) activities. Strategies and concepts on how to deal with those items is helpful and is partly the responsibility of the development team. Strategic decisions can be supported by the HCD/UX as well as data science and ML engineers together with business domain experts and the IT department. The final implementation of such strategies and concepts might be made by the IT department. This module might result in a completely new project when, over time, the product or service shows that a new problem has occurred or developing a new solution would be beneficial for the user and the business. Also, new data points might make it necessary to go back to the input module, or a new AI/ML method might support going back to the modeling module.

4.3   Conclusion

This paper has proposed a strong collaborative approach between designers, data scientists and business domain experts. The research results suggest 7 process modules and their related activities, flow, and dependencies. Each activity is related to concrete actions and tools from the three related domains (design, data, business). The process modules incorporate the research findings from the structured literature review, case study research and expert interviews. The proposed process modules are flexible in their use and can be combined in different ways. They include activities that relate to multiple points to consider regarding AI and ML as a new design material - lack of AI expertise, missing methods, and tools - as well as the need to bridge the gap between design, data, and business driven approaches, by offering an AI and design system approach, instead of separate solutions. The version presented in this paper has already been tested and evaluated with practitioners in the field and through additional case studies, also outside the industrial AI domain. Therefore, the process modules offer a solid approach that can be transferred to other domains, set ups, and use cases, hoping to help the HCD/UC/HCI community to become familiar with and use this new material.

5   Outlook

The research area of design for AI is immature and exists on current ideas and concepts that will evolve over time, as well as their use in practice. The described process modules should serve as initial guidance but going further might need the addition of more modules or iterate the given ones. Collecting more case studies and using the process modules to visualize their development journey is a possible next step. This would also contribute to the missing best practice sharing in the design and AI area. Based on this idea, a workshop was organized at the HCI International 2021 conference: 'Use Cases of Designing AI-enabled Interactive Systems' and an initial framework to collect and document AI infused project exemplars was developed [30]. Both solutions complement each other, but additional value will be created when they are being used in practice by practitioners in various roles, areas, and in different settings.

References

1. Dove, G., et al.: UX design innovation: challenges for working with machine learning as a design material. In: CHI Proceedings, pp. 278–288 (2017)
2. Yang, Q.: MachineLearning as a UX design material: how can we imagine beyond automation, recommenders, and reminders? In: The 2018 AAAI Spring Symposium Series, pp. 467–472 (2018)
3. Yang, Q.: The role of design in creating machine-learning-enhanced user experience. In: The AAAI 2017 Spring Symposium on Designing the User Experience of Machine Learning Systems, pp. 406–411 (2017)
4. Wu, Q., Zhang, C.J.: A paradigm shift in design driven by AI. In: Degen, H., Reinerman-Jones, L. (eds.) HCII 2020. LNCS, vol. 12217, pp. 167–176. Springer, Cham (2020). https://doi.org/10.1007/978-3-030-50334-5_11
5. Cooke, A., et al.: Beyond PICO: the SPIDER tool for qualitative evidence synthesis. Qual. Health Res. **22**(10), 1435–1443 (2012)
6. Page, M., et al.: The PRISMA 2020 statement: an updated guideline for reporting systematic reviews. BMJ Res. Methods Report. **372**(71) (2021)
7. PRISMA statement. https://prisma-statement.org. Accessed 21 Jan 2023
8. Shneiderman, B.: Human-Centered AI. Oxford University Press, Oxford (2022)
9. Maeda, J.: How to Speak Machine - Computational Thinking for the Rest of Us. Penguin Random House LLC (2019)
10. van Allen, P.: Reimagining the goals and methods of UX for ML/AI. In: The AAAI 2017 Spring Symposium on Designing the User Experience of Machine Learning Systems, pp. 431–434 (2017)
11. van Allen, P.: Prototyping: ways of prototyping. Interactions **25**(6), 46–51 (2018)
12. Bergström, E., Wärnestål, P.: Exploring the design context of AI-powered services: a qualitative investigation of designers' experiences with machine learning. In: Degen, H., Ntoa, S. (eds.) HCII 2022. LNCS, vol. 13336, pp. 3–21. Springer, Cham (2022). https://doi.org/10.1007/978-3-031-05643-7_1

13. Fiebrink, R., Gillies, M.: Introduction on the special issue of human centered machine learning. ACM Trans. Interact. Intell. Syst. **8**(2), 1–7 (2018). Article no. 7
14. Fiebrink, R.: Machine learning education for artists, musicians, and other creative practitioners. ACM Trans. Comput. Educ. **19**(4), 1–32 (2019)
15. Girardin, F., Lathia, N.: When user experience designers partner with data scientists. In: The AAAI 2017 Spring Symposium on Designing the User Experience of Machine Learning Systems, pp. 376–381 (2017)
16. Kun, P., et al.: Design enquiry through data: appropriating a data science workflow for the design process. In: Proceedings of British HCI 2018, Belfast, UK, pp. 1–12 (2018)
17. Kun, P., et al.: Creative data work in the design process. In: ACM Creativity and Cognition 2019, San Diego, US, pp. 346–358 (2019)
18. Wallach, D.P., Flohr, L.A., Kaltenhauser, A.: Beyond the buzzwords: on the perspective of AI in UX and vice versa. In: Degen, H., Reinerman-Jones, L. (eds.) HCII 2020. LNCS, vol. 12217, pp. 146–166. Springer, Cham (2020). https://doi.org/10.1007/978-3-030-50334-5_10
19. Yang, Q., et al.: Investigating how experienced UX designers effectively work with machine learning. In: Conference on Designing Interactive Systems, pp. 585–596 (2018)
20. Yang, Q., et al.: Re-examining whether, why, and how human-AI interaction is uniquely difficult to design. In: CHI 2020: Proceedings of the 2020 CHI Conference on Human Factors in Computing Systems, pp. 1–13 (2020)
21. Zdanowska, S., Taylor, A.S.: A study of UX practitioners' roles in designing real-world, enterprise ML systems. In: CHI 2022, ACM Conference on Human Factors in Computing Systems, pp. 1–15 (2022)
22. Braun, V., Clarke, V.: Using thematic analysis in psychology. Qual. Res. Psychol. **3**(2), 77–101 (2006)
23. Chui, M., et al.: McKinsey Global Institute: Notes from the AI Frontier, discussion paper (2018). https://www.mckinsey.com/*/media/mckinsey/featured%20insights/artificial%20intelligence/notes%20from%20the%20ai%20frontier%20applications%20and%20value%20of%20deep%20learning/mgi_notes-from-ai-frontier_discussion-paper.ashx. Accessed 21 Jan 2023
24. ISO 9241-210:2019-07, Ergonomics of human-system interaction - Part 210: Human-centred design for interactive systems (ISO 13407:1999-06). Accessed 21 Jan 2023
25. Heier, J., Willmann, J., Wendland, K.: Design intelligence - pitfalls and challenges when designing AI algorithms in B2B factory automation. In: Degen, H., Reinerman-Jones, L. (eds.) HCII 2020. LNCS, vol. 12217, pp. 288–297. Springer, Cham (2020). https://doi.org/10.1007/978-3-030-50334-5_19
26. Heier, J.: Design intelligence - taking further steps towards new methods and tools for designing in the age of AI. In: Degen, H., Ntoa, S. (eds.) HCII 2021. LNCS (LNAI), vol. 12797, pp. 202–215. Springer, Cham (2021). https://doi.org/10.1007/978-3-030-77772-2_13
27. Amershi, S., et al.: Guidelines-for-human-AI-interaction. In: CHI 2019, Glasgow, Scotland, UK, pp. 1–13 (2019)
28. Google: People AI Guidebook. https://pair.withgoogle.com. Accessed 21 Jan 2023
29. IBM: Design for AI. https://www.ibm.com/design/ai. Accessed 21 Jan 2023
30. Moosbrugger, J., Ntoa, S.: A unified framework to collect and document AI-infused project exemplars. In: Chen, J.Y.C., Fragomeni, G., Degen, H., Ntoa, S. (eds.) HCII 2022. LNCS, vol. 13518, pp. 407–420. Springer, Cham (2022). https://doi.org/10.1007/978-3-031-21707-4_29

Interaction Design for Hybrid Intelligence: The Case of Work Place Risk Assessment

Martin Westhoven[1][(✉)] [iD] and Thomas Herrmann[2] [iD]

[1] Federal Institute for Occupational Safety and Health, Friedrich-Henkel-Weg 1-25,
44149 Dortmund, Germany
westhoven.martin@baua.bund.de
[2] Ruhr-University Bochum, Universitätsstraße 150, 44801 Bochum, Germany

Abstract. Occupational safety relies on systematic and reliable work place risk assessments. It is estimated, though that for high percentages of work places, no risk assessment is ever done. Since meanwhile technological progress and a far-spread lack of specialized personnel complicate matters, our idea is to use AI techniques to support work place risk assessment and thus to ultimately lower the requirements to get started. For such a tool to be accepted in the target context though, it needs to be usable, which requires a thoughtful interaction design. In this work we present the use case of work place risk assessment by providing an overview over the general process, underlying data, appropriate algorithms, and user requirements. We then proceed to match this use case against inter-action design guidelines targeting human AI-interaction, especially those which understand human-AI interaction as interaction with a socio-technical system. By considering multiple guidelines, we further outline how the different guidelines come together in an actual use case.

Keywords: Occupational Safety · Risk Assessment · Artificial Intelligence · Interaction Design

1 Introduction

Work place risk assessment plays a pivotal role in occupational safety. In Germany for example, law mandates employers to per-form a risk assessment. It is estimated, though that for up to 50% of work places, no risk assessment has ever been done (Arbeits-schutzkonferenz 2014). In many cases, it seems either that these requirements are easily dismissed as being unnecessary or that they require too much effort to be met in detail.

At the same time, innovative technologies increase the complexity of work environments (Barth et al. 2017), while a far-spread lack of specialized personnel further aggravates the problem (IFA 2021).

With AI advances in recent years, especially in methods to handle complex and heterogeneous data, using AI approaches to support work place risk assessments is now more viable than ever before. In Germany, the most promising areas for AI support in occupational safety appear to be improving hazard awareness and accessibility to risk

H. Degen and S. Ntoa (Eds.): HCII 2023, LNAI 14050, pp. 629–639, 2023.
https://doi.org/10.1007/978-3-031-35891-3_39

assessments and their results (Arbeitsschutzkonferenz 2014). Our goal is thus to provide an AI-application taking work place parameters as input to generate prioritized lists of risks and possible measures to mitigate them, as outlined in Westhoven and Adolph (2022). The key to make AI-based risk assessment feasible is a proper interaction design, which needs to be tailored to the usage of the complex data to be considered. In this paper, we ask which approaches could fit the task of AI-based risk assessment for the workplace, and how Human-AI interaction should be designed for this task, based on a thorough understanding of the systems' operational context. To this end, we provide an overview over the general process of work place risk assessment, over underlying data sources, over relevant algorithms, and over user requirements.

To understand which data is available and has to be handled in this context, Westhoven (2022) performed expert interviews to elicit process information and requirements. As most available data is in text form, Natural Language Processing (NLP, see e.g. Chowdhary (2020)) needs to be considered, e.g. as outlined by Westhoven and Jadid (In Press), but also integrated handling of high-dimensional data (Mirza et al. 2019) and few-shot learning (Wang et al. 2020) are promising.

The interviews clearly indicate the necessity to keep important decisions in the hand of humans. A promising approach for designing AI in this regard is to aim for a hybrid intelligence (Kamar 2016). Hybrid intelligence combines human and artificial intelligence to collectively achieve superior performance and to allow for continuous reciprocal learning.

This work systematically explores the case of AI-supported work place risk analysis to explicate the practical implications of an integrated human-AI interaction design trying to meet the elicited requirements by combining the aforementioned approach of hybrid intelligence with surrounding work on the specialty of interacting with AI (Yang et al. 2020), on general guidelines for interaction with AI (Amershi et al. 2019), and on further socio-technical aspects (Herrmann 2022; Kurvinen et al. 2008).

2   Use Case: AI Support for Workplace Risk Assessment

In this section, we provide a short introduction into the general process of workplace risk assessment, the underlying data of this process, feasible algorithms, and finally some insights regarding requirements.

2.1   General Process

Occupational safety hinges on identifying and assessing hazards and risks at workplaces. Based on these, measures can be taken to mitigate or eliminate risks in an objective and efficient manner. As shown in Fig. 1 these basic steps are repeated until the remaining risk is deemed acceptable.

Our idea is to make the introductory steps of identifying and assessing hazards more accessible by employing an artificial intelligence decision support system. Until this day, safety practitioners typically perform both of these steps in person with little technical support. They thus have to process all the available data on a specific workplace to then decide if a hazard is present, which risk it poses, and if and how it can be mitigated.

Fig. 1. Generic occupational safety process of identifying and assessing risks and then possibly taking measures to mitigate them.

2.2 Underlying Data

Westhoven (2022) performed expert interviews, one of the most effective forms of requirements elicitation (Davis et al. 2006), to gather requirements and conditions of supporting occupational safety risk analysis. As Westhoven (2022) gathered, much of the data is available as more or less structured, and more or less digitalized text. Sometimes, the textual data is further processed into risk scores, e.g. by using the Key Indicator Method (Steinberg 2012). For most workplaces, environmental data is gathered only by means of the natural senses of the safety practitioner, the employee and her or his superior. The much higher effort of gathering technical sensor data is typically reserved for high-risk workplaces. Figure 2 gives an (incomplete) overview over the typical data sources for identifying and assessing workplace hazards.

Textual data comes in different forms. Workplace descriptions can provide a broad informational base regarding hazards and risks. However, especially for standard workplaces, e.g. offices, they are often very generic, if they do exist at all. For most machine learning approaches, the small numbers of fitting descriptions are insufficient.

A larger corpus of text data is to be expected for technical data sheets regarding machinery and dangerous substances. These are non-standardized and can vary greatly in quality. Especially automated translations for product data sheets from abroad can cause a large human effort in understanding intention and correcting errors. Thresholds and Measures regarding substances can also be found in technical guidelines, norms and standards.

The most common tool covering nearly every imaginable workplace are checklists for hazard identification and risk assessment, which provide relatively well structured text. They are provided by many different institutions and for various use cases and work contexts, resulting in sometimes significantly overlapping items. The US OSHA publishes the Small Business Safety and Health Handbook (OSHA 2022), providing an overview over checklists for the different areas to be covered.

Another source of unstructured text is accident data, which at its core typically contains a textual description supplemented by keywords and meta data. For example, the US OSHA again provides a public domain database of roughly 25.000 fatal work

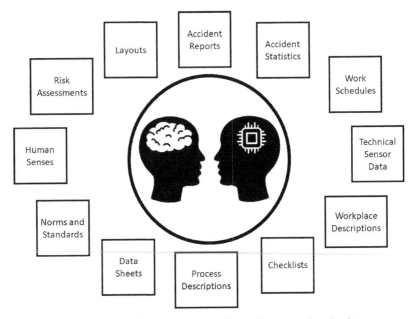

Fig. 2. Data sources and data processing entities in the occupational safety process.

accidents including keywords (https://www.osha.gov/ords/imis/accidentsearch.search). Similar databases also exist in Germany, both compiled by the Federal Institute for Occupational Safety and Health and by the accident insurances. These databases, however, are not public domain, requiring more effort to access.

Finally, institutions such as OSHA or employer's liability insurance associations provide hints at safety and measures for controlling risks.

Apart from textual data and human or machine sensing, there are several other types of data, which can be of use for risk assessments. For example, layout plans or digital models are often available, although sometimes not up-to-date. They can be used to assess distances and spaces at the work place. Other types of data containing risk information are work schedules, statistics, both company- or branch-specific, and accident data. The concept outlined in Westhoven and Adolph (2022) focuses on physiological risk factors since they are the main cause for severe accidents. Psychological factors are much more difficult to assess and thus omitted for our case, even though in general, AI could possibly handle them as well.

2.3 Algorithms and Labels

The available data determines the choice of applicable AI methods. Due to the prevalence of textual data, Natural Language Processing (NLP) is a central research field to be considered. It covers a wide range of particular problems such as machine translation, speech recognition, information retrieval, language modelling and information summarization (Chowdhary 2020), and recently made quick advances by using deep learning techniques (Otter et al. 2020). The availability of large amounts of data is central to recent advances in NLP. Sometimes, the need for such large amounts of data for a specific application field can be circumvented by using transfer learning from an adjacent field, but success is not guaranteed.

The integration of numerical or categorical data requires a combination with other methods, though. It is an open question, if such an amount of widely differing dimensions can be handled in an integrated way, or if ensembles of specialized sub-systems are needed. The integrated handling of high-dimensional data is a recurring problem in biomedicine and biostatistics, providing a starting point in this regard (Mirza et al. 2019).

Labels for supervised learning can be extracted from existing occupational safety risk assessments, accident models, or from other events, where no persons were injured. However, due to the complexity of risk management data and labels are often only sparsely available (Clemen and Winkler 1999). So called few-shot learning can potentially compensate for this lack of training data by integrating a priori knowledge (Wang et al. 2020). It aims to deliver comparable results to deep learning with only a fraction of the data requirements.

2.4 Expert Requirements

Westhoven (2022) compiled requirements regarding a possible digital or AI system elicited from occupational safety practitioners. The desired core functionality should be the identification of hazards, risk analysis, prioritized lists of possible control measures, and hints regarding further associated risks. A support system should also be able to translate regulatory requirements into concrete measures, which assure compliance.

An important aspect is human control of final decisions. The decision which measure to take, including the final say in documentation tasks, is to remain under human control. A four-eyes principle needs to be implemented to avoid errors and blind spots. To keep safety professionals in contact with the work context, also personal in situ assessments, and meetings and talks with helpers, such as e.g. safety advisors, need to be retained.

Transparency was named a priority to understand and trust proposed measures and also why alternative measures were not chosen. Trust was believed to be increased, when input data is known to be reliable and safe, e.g. by way of coming from an institution with certified quality management. The interviewees mentioned several possibilities to increase the comprehensibility of the system's output, namely by providing a comparable real-world sample case, applicable technical rules or visual highlighting of relevant input data.

3 Integrated Human-AI Interaction Design

In this section, we first look into the AI specific aspects, which seemingly make interaction design for human-AI interaction so hard. We then follow up by taking a more detailed look into interaction design when AI is understood as a socio-technical system and highlight how the design guidelines can be implemented for our use case.

3.1 Human-AI UX Challenges

When talking about human-AI interaction, it is helpful to remind oneself as to why designing human-AI interaction is much more challenging than other HCI. Yang et al. (2020) provide a systematic overview of reported UX challenges when designing for interaction with AI systems. For our case of workplace risk assessment, the challenges of prototyping for AI, setting up user expectations, and the collaboration between the stakeholders are especially relevant. There seems to be no consensus, however, as to what the underlying root-causes are (Yang et al. 2020). In addition to the overview on AI UX Challenges, Yang et al. (2020) propose two central attributes, which make designing AI-interaction especially difficult: Capability uncertainty, including a lack of knowledge on system performance and errors, and output complexity. According to the authors, handling capability uncertainty condenses down to anticipating "situated, user-encountered capability" and is typically caused by uncertainty of how data, algorithm, and user will perform together (Yang et al. 2020). Explaining what a system can do and how well it performs is also reflected in the AI interaction design guidelines compiled by Amershi et al. (2019). These guidelines target the initialization phase of a systems lifecycle to reduce capability uncertainty beforehand. Output complexity then again is a problem encountered for very large system output spaces and is absent in small output spaces, where designers can accommodate for every possible type of error. Yang et al. (2020) finally propose four levels of AI systems' design complexity along the dimensions of both capability uncertainty and output complexity. Level one is a system with fixed capabilities and a small output set, which can be handled with established HCI methods. When systems produce broader sets of possible outputs or continue to learn after deployment, design becomes more difficult.

Looking at our case of risk assessment of workplaces again, an AI decision support system would be of level four design complexity, as it would ideally both deliver a broad range of possible control measures and continue to learn from various data sources after deployment as well. This implicates that our interaction design will need to consider the user-system co-evolution as well as user and/or context adaption. Both of these can be supported by implementing the guidelines on interaction context by Amershi et al. (2019), which target both the context-sensitive timing of interaction possibilities and the display of context-relevant information. Adaption to user and context should be performed only cautiously (Amershi et al. 2019).

3.2 AI, the Socio-technical System

The need to consider the user-system co-evolution together with the requirements of keeping the human in control over important decisions and to support an adequate build-up of trust require to look at the problem from a socio-technical perspective.

Studying interaction design, Kurvinen et al. (2008) argue for the use of experience prototypes, meaning prototypes enabling all stakeholders to experience the interaction for themselves in contrast to e.g. just seeing a demonstrator. A prototype is then understood as a pair of a piece of technology and a set of people using it in social situations, where social situations are defined as interactions between people that are mediated or influenced by the technology (Kurvinen et al. 2008). While their focus on everyday use of technology is not an exact match to our use case, the paradigm explicitly addresses the need to study the evolution of interaction over time, which we will need for continuous learning as well. According to Kurvinen et al. (2008), some conceptual framework is needed to guide observations and conceptual work when studying social interactions. They themselves based their work on symbolic interactionism and ethnomethodology, but any inductive theory would be fitting.

Creating prototypes and studying their use in this way, a more detailed description and understanding of the social factors of the socio-technical system can be gained. This provides a starting point for studying the interaction design for our use case of AI-supported workplace risk assessment.

For the actual design of interaction specifics, Dellermann et al. (2019) propose a fitting framework for so-called hybrid intelligence (see e.g. Kamar (2016)). Hybrid intelligence combines human and machine intelligence for superior collective performance and the capability of continuous reciprocal learning. As AI can yield impressive results in specific areas, but still struggles when faced with many tasks, such as applying expertise to decision making (Kamar 2016), this combination is necessary to fully exploit the potential of AI support. The reciprocal learning aspect is furthermore of special importance for our use case, as trust, and everything more than a superficial feeling of control, will require a relatively deep understanding of the system.

Dellermann et al. (2021) compiled a taxonomy of design knowledge along the four meta-dimensions of task characteristics, learning paradigm, AI-human interaction and human-AI interaction. While the first two subsume mostly descriptive aspects, Dellermann et al. (2021) provide several insights on interaction design for the interaction meta-dimensions.

On the human-AI interaction meta-dimension, we can identify several specialties of our case of workplace risk assessment. First, machine teaching is spread along different teaching modes, namely demonstration, troubleshooting and verification. Then, also expertise requirements are spread between domain experts and end users, since we will need multiple user groups of differing expertise in the final system. Regarding the amount of human input, a potential issue becomes apparent: While collective human input would be desirable to reduce bias and increase comparability, the number of involved domain experts in a deployed system could be too small, or even down to one expert, and thus require falling back to using individual input. If a sufficient number of expert users are available, the aggregation of their inputs would be task- and not human-dependent, since an elimination of human bias is desirable for safety tasks. Mitigating social bias is also a guideline by Amershi et al. (2019), where it covers the social aspects of interaction together with the guideline of matching the social norms of the target context. Last, we will need to keep in mind that the users typically require some form of incentive to use the system. While the employer could mandate the use of the system, strengthening the ability to draw intrinsic rewards such as learning new things or achieving fulfilling work results seems to be a more promising vector to ensure the intended long-term interaction with the AI system.

Looking into the meta-dimension of AI-human interaction, our use case again spreads along different modes. The querying strategy will typically be offline, but also active learning can be employed. Especially when connected to databases which are automatically updated, an active learning query strategy could be helpful, e.g. if inconsistencies are discovered by the AI. Machine feedback is planned to be recommendations or at least predictions. Optimization of human plans could be a viable line for future research, though. As stated above, interpretability is an important requirement in the light of our use case's safety critical context. Since the underlying model will probably be a very complex one, rendering global interpretability a very hard target, it makes sense to aim for local prediction interpretability, which means the ability to make sense of a single prediction or recommendation. Algorithm transparency is desirable from a regulation point of view, but will not be useful for normal operations due to a lack of machine learning expertise at the user base.

Retaining and improving human competencies must not be neglected if human experts are to competently control the AI system. Herrmann (2022) identified interaction modes with AI systems with potential to support competency development for not only the domain itself, but also regarding context and the machine learning technology itself. Thus, over time, the user-related requirements could shift and consequently enable complex forms of interaction, e.g. regarding algorithm transparency.

As one of the most central aspects in understanding AI systems, explanations and possibilities for exploration form an interaction mode that is crucial to develop competencies regarding the AI system itself, but also regarding the underlying domain knowledge. According to Herrmann (2022), a social component should be included to connect the users among each other for support. For our use case, explanations are necessary to make the decision process transparent and to verify the correctness of recommendations. Especially for error states, explanations are helpful to gain insights into the systems inner workings (Amershi et al. 2019). Being able to explore the system is also desirable, not only for furthering human understanding of the AI system, but also since it would be akin to a simulation of the domain, wherein the user could add hypothetical values or even safety measures and get a prediction of its effects on the overall situation. To ideally support the development of competencies, consideration of and adjustment to the user mental model should be included.

A related mode is testing, where the user can test the system in its target context regarding accuracy and AI error sources. This could be integrated with the simulation functions for exploration in our use case. In addition, the mode of re-training could be attached to such functions, as its function for competency development is the assessment of the effect of re-training and possibly reverting the training if the results are somehow undesirable. The interaction mode of switching underlying data sets or even the analytical methods goes one step further and provides the ability to circumvent data- or method-specific AI errors. When combined with the capability to process overwriting human rules, it strengthens correctability, which is a relevant feature for AI in safety critical contexts. Furthermore, the interaction mode of refinement, that is the purposeful alteration of case-wise data to assess the influence of a cases condition onto its solution, can be added to the modes calling for some kind of simulation environment. Refinement could well be combined with the guideline by Amershi et al. (2019) of providing a scoping of services when the AI is in doubt, resulting in suggestions for further refinement.

The domain of workplace risk assessment almost forces us to have the mode of flexible input sequencing and filtering, which stimulates self-reflection about the task. As especially incident reports are often very heterogeneous and incomplete, any AI system would need to be able to compensate for missing data and as such could also offer to the user to only fill in some data fields in a sequence chosen by the user. Another domain-driven interaction mode is the identification and comparison of similar cases, as this is a typical approach to find a practical solution to safety problems. Herrmann (2022) argues that this mode ties in with explainability, as presenting a similar case can also help understanding and error checking why the AI chose some measure. The interaction mode of Vetoing, the rejection or ignoring of an AI proposal, can also be counted among the modes that are basically set for the domain of workplace risk assessment. Due to the safety critical nature of the task and the user's responsibility for the results, Vetoing is simply a necessity. It is furthermore also one of the efficiency guidelines compiled by Amershi et al. (2019), which state that invocation, dismissal and correction of AI services need to be usable in an efficient way.

Intervention describes a mode of intervening in the running AI process if needed. It is actually not needed for the case of workplace risk assessment, as the AI process will typically be active only by request. Only when some kind of AI component for real-time monitoring of safety comes into play, it would need to be addressed. The opposite mode, critiquing, observes the user and provides feedback if anomalies or errors are detected. For our case, this could be a check if a solution diverges too strongly from those of similar cases. As such, it would improve safety by double-checking the human performance.

It should be noted that Herrmann and Pfeiffer (2022) further add to the socio-technical perspective by considering also organizational practices supporting HCAI. While this is certainly an important aspect for our case of workplace risk assessment, we will currently ignore organizational aspects due to the system not leaving experimental status in the near future.

4   Conclusion and Outlook

We introduced the use case of AI-supported workplace risk assessment by providing a brief overview over the general process, underlying data sources, possible algorithms, and expert requirements. We then proceeded to investigate literature on human-AI interaction design to connect their points to our case and thereby outline the scope of an interaction concept. We located the use case in this literature and showed, where and partially how the different aspects can be integrated.

Central components for the use case of workplace risk assessment are identified to be an explanation engine as well as a flexible simulation environment. The latter could offer a variety of possibilities to explore the system itself, but also single cases. Both are relevant for addressing the problems of capability uncertainty and also of output complexity.

In future work, we will report the results of actually implementing the interaction concept and thereby providing feedback regarding an integrated framework for human-AI interaction design encompassing at its base the sources we drew upon in this paper.

There are many more aspects of human-AI interaction, which are studied in detail in other work, such as supporting organizational aspects (Herrmann and Pfeiffer 2022) or the thoughts on balancing automation and control by Shneiderman (2020), which we didn't cover in this paper. Integrating such further relevant aspects could add to the benefit of showing how all this partially overlapping interaction design knowledge comes together in an actual implementation.

References

Amershi, S., et al.: Guidelines for human-AI interaction. Paper presented at the Proceedings of the 2019 CHI Conference on Human Factors in Computing Systems (2019)

Arbeitsschutzkonferenz: Grundauswertung der Beschäftigtenbefragung 2015 und 2011 - beschäftigtenproportional gewichtet (2014)

Barth, C., Eickholt, C., Hamacher, W., Schmauder, M.: Bedarf an Fachkräften für Arbeitssicherheit in Deutschland, Dortmund (2017)

Chowdhary, K.: Natural language processing. Fundam. Artif. Intell., 603–649 (2020)

Clemen, R.T., Winkler, R.L.: Combining probability distributions from experts in risk analysis. Risk Anal. **19**(2), 187–203 (1999)

Davis, A., Dieste, O., Hickey, A., Juristo, N., Moreno, A.M.: Effectiveness of requirements elicitation techniques: Empirical results derived from a systematic review. Paper presented at the 14th IEEE International Requirements Engineering Conference (RE 2006) (2006)

Dellermann, D., Calma, A., Lipusch, N., Weber, T., Weigel, S., Ebel, P.: The future of human-AI collaboration: a taxonomy of design knowledge for hybrid intelligence systems. arXiv preprint arXiv:2105.03354 (2021)

Dellermann, D., Ebel, P., Söllner, M., Leimeister, J.M.: Hybrid intelligence. Bus. Inf. Syst. Eng. **61**(5), 637–643 (2019)

Herrmann, T.: Promoting human competences by appropriate modes of interaction for human-centered-AI. Paper presented at the International Conference on Human-Computer Interaction (2022)

Herrmann, T., Pfeiffer, S.: Keeping the organization in the loop: a socio-technical extension of human-centered artificial intelligence. AI Soc., 1–20 (2022)

IFA: Arbeitswelten. Menschenwelten. Prioritäten für den Arbeitsschutz von morgen, Berlin (2021)

Kamar, E.: Directions in hybrid intelligence: complementing AI systems with human intelligence. Paper presented at the IJCAI (2016)

Kurvinen, E., Koskinen, I., Battarbee, K.: Prototyping social interaction. Des. Issues **24**(3), 46–57 (2008)

Mirza, B., Wang, W., Wang, J., Choi, H., Chung, N.C., Ping, P.: Machine learning and integrative analysis of biomedical big data. Genes **10**(2), 87 (2019)

OSHA, U.: Small Business Safety and Health Handbook (2022)

Otter, D.W., Medina, J.R., Kalita, J.K.: A survey of the usages of deep learning for natural language processing. IEEE Trans. Neural Netw. Learn. Syst. **32**(2), 604–624 (2020)

Shneiderman, B.: Human-centered artificial intelligence: reliable, safe & trustworthy. Int. J. Hum. Comput. Interact. **36**(6), 495–504 (2020)

Steinberg, U.: New tools in Germany: development and appliance of the first two KIM ("lifting, holding and carrying" and "pulling and pushing") and practical use of these methods. Work **41**(Suppl. 1), 3990–3996 (2012)

Wang, Y., Yao, Q., Kwok, J.T., Ni, L.M.: Generalizing from a few examples: a survey on few-shot learning. ACM Comput. Surv. (CSUR) **53**(3), 1–34 (2020)

Westhoven, M.: Requirements for AI support in occupational safety risk analysis. In: Proceedings of Mensch und Computer 2022, pp. 561–565 (2022)

Westhoven, M., Adolph, L.: Concept for Supporting Occupational Safety Risk Analysis with a Machine Learning Tool. In: Stephanidis, C., Antona, M., Ntoa, S. (eds.) HCI International 2022 Posters. HCII 2022. Communications in Computer and Information Science, vol 1580. Springer, Cham (2022). https://doi.org/10.1007/978-3-031-06417-3_63

Westhoven, M., Jadid, A.: Supporting work place risk assessments by means of natural language processing. Paper presented at the 69th GfA Frühjahrskongress, Hannover, Germany (in Press)

Yang, Q., Steinfeld, A., Rosé, C., Zimmerman, J.: Re-examining whether, why, and how human-AI interaction is uniquely difficult to design. Paper presented at the Proceedings of the 2020 CHI Conference on Human Factors in Computing Systems (2020)

Illustration of the Usable AI Paradigm in Production-Engineering Implementation Settings

Hajo Wiemer[1], Felix Conrad[1(✉)], Valentin Lang[1], Eugen Boos[1], Mauritz Mälzer[1], Kim Feldhoff[1], Lucas Drowatzky[1], Dorothea Schneider[1], and Steffen Ihlenfeldt[1,2]

[1] Faculty of Mechanical Engineering, Institute of Mechatronic Engineering, Technische Universität Dresden, Helmholtzstr. 7a, 01069 Dresden, Germany
felix.conrad@tu-dresden.de

[2] Fraunhofer-Institut für Werkzeugmaschinen und Umformtechnik IWU, Reichenhainer Str. 88, 09126 Chemnitz, Germany

Abstract. Data-driven methods, machine learning and artificial intelligence methods are not yet exploited to their intended potential in solving the technical-technological challenges, especially in industrial applications, despite versatile development progress. This is mainly justified by the insufficient practicality of AI solutions. To exploit the potential of AI methods, technical practitioners often rely on interdisciplinary collaboration with data science specialists or consultants. In any development and application of AI methods, a plethora of methods must be mastered for solution-oriented acquisition, pre-processing and quality assurance of required data, as well as for the selection of suitable algorithms and their adaptation. Coping with this complexity usually requires a great deal of effort, both for the individual domain expert and for the data engineers and data analysts. Complexity and intransparency of AI methods therefore hinder the effectiveness and efficiency of AI deployment. Focusing on user-friendly delivery of AI-based applications, the paradigm of Usable AI (UAI) has been defined. This paper first summarizes the UAI paradigm. Finally, some application examples from the field of production engineering illustrate how UAI can improve the practical applicability of AI methods for domain experts.

Keywords: Usable AI · Explainable AI · Applicable AI · Domain-specific AI · Human-Computer Interaction

1 Introduction

The authors work in an interdisciplinary research group located in the "Chair of Machine Tool Development and Adaptive Controls" at the Technische Universität Dresden, which has its roots in the development and analysis of machine tools and processes running on them. The research group works on solutions for the use of data in engineering applications, especially in production engineering. The research projects focus mainly on the following key areas: a) condition monitoring for predictive maintenance and for quality prediction, b) root cause analysis for detecting the causes of damage to machine elements and for quality defects, c) optimization of process parameters in individual processes and in production process chains, d) support for the commissioning of machines and production processes.

Characteristic for our work is that we select and test the appropriate algorithms for the above mentioned application tasks. Last but not least, an essential part of our work is dedicated to the adaptation and integration of the algorithms for their deployment in the production work processes, so that the users from production can work efficiently and effectively with the AI-based applications. The users of our solutions are usually experts from production and have no or only weak expertise on the data-driven approach or AI. Therefore, the practicable provision of data-based applications on the hall floor is the focus of our work.

In line with the understanding of the various roles of data scientists, we see ourselves, among other things, as "mediators" or "translators" between the AI experts and the individual specialist departments in production. We need to understand and support their activities. A lack of understanding and consideration of the practical needs from the application activities leads in implementation to AI-based applications that are not accepted by the user. This is confirmed by surveys in the companies.

13 surveys were evaluated in Wiemer et al. to understand the challenges and barriers to implementing and working with AI-based systems in manufacturing practice [1]. A total of 4,696 industrial companies were surveyed about existing barriers to digitization and the use of AI. The surveys were conducted by various associations and institutes such as acatech (German Academy of Science and Engineering) [2], bitkom (industry association of the German information and telecommunications sector) [3, 4], Stiftung Arbeit und Umwelt der IG BCE [5], BDI [6], Verband der TÜV e. V. [7], and the German Federal Ministry for Economic Affairs and Energy (BMWi) [8, 9]. From the feedback of these surveys, four possible areas of action to improve the situation could be classified: 1) strategy and management, 2) technology and R&D, 3) functionality and applicability, and 4) regulators and legislation. As a conclusion of this meta-study, it was elaborated that one of the main reasons for the reluctance to use AI-based applications can be attributed to the lack of usability of the applications. This means that users are not supported well enough, not comprehensibly enough. In order to increase the willingness and the prospects of success in the introduction of AI applications, it is therefore necessary to improve the usability of AI in practice in a broader sense, especially with regard to solution transparency and user competence. It is apparent that previous approaches to increasing the transparency of black-box-like AI algorithms are not yet sufficient to close the gap between Data Science and its users in certain domains. There is still a need to provide engineers and practitioners in the field with sufficient support for AI applications.

Both aspects outlined above, the experiences and requirements of daily project work as well as the analysis of the industry situation, have motivated the development of the Usable AI (UAI) Paradigm. In Sect. 2 of this paper, the UAI Concept is summarized. In Sect. 3, examples from various development projects are outlined to illustrate the need and usefulness of each feature of UAI. In addition, the examples illustrate measures that can be used to improve the practical applicability (i.e., usability) of AI solutions.

2 Usable AI (UAI) in a Nutshell

The paradigm of Usable AI (UAI) has been justified in detail by Wiemer et al. [1]. Briefly, the idea and motivation is based on the lack of consideration of the aspect of usability in the widely used classical definitions of the term "artificial intelligence" e.g. Rich [10] or Ertel [11]. In this understanding, the focus is on emulating human intelligence in machine-processable algorithms.

The Independent High-Level Expert Group on Artificial Intelligence of the European Commission developed the following definition: "Artificial intelligence (AI) systems are software (and possibly also hardware) systems designed by humans that, given a complex goal, act in the physical or digital dimension by perceiving their environment through data acquisition, interpreting the collected structured or unstructured data, reasoning on the knowledge, or processing the information, derived from this data and deciding the best action(s) to take to achieve the given goal. AI systems can either use symbolic rules or learn a numeric model, and they can also adapt their behaviour by analysing how the environment is affected by their previous actions." [12].

With this enhanced view that AI systems are a special kind of software, the conclusion was obvious to apply to AI the criteria for user-friendliness of software (usability). The international standard ISO 9241-11 "Ergonomics of human-system interaction - Usability - Definitions and concepts" states that "Usability refers to the outcome of interaction with a system, product or service", not as a property of a product, but as "a broader concept than what is commonly understood by "user-friendliness" or "ease of use"" [13]. In computer science in particular, the term usability in the narrower sense describes a user-friendly, ergonomic design. Nielsen describes this specific understanding of the term in terms of the defining attributes of learnability, efficiency, memorability, error, and satisfaction [14].

The elements of the UAI paradigm are shown in Fig. 1 and serve as a blueprint for considering all user needs. The sub-attributes must be considered to achieve usability of an AI application. Consequently, it is critical to consider all attributes when determining user requirements for a given use case and to tailor solution approaches to the user role, goal, and domain context in each of these categories.

To meet these criteria in the application of AI-based applications, it is appropriate to introduce a supporting layer of UAI between the AI model itself and the users from the domain (see Fig. 2). The UAI paradigm places an interactive communicative layer between the user-centric bottom-up view (user provides data and makes request to AI application) and the model-based top-down view (AI application provides requests or results to user). The concept aims to ensure that this communicative layer is proactively addressed by both sides. The UAI level should provide structure, comprehensible methodological knowledge, and guidance tailored to each user. The methods provided must take into account the needs of the user roles involved and provide the means to the extent necessary for application. In particular, the communicative UAI layer also provides a common basis for making domain-specific requirements visible.

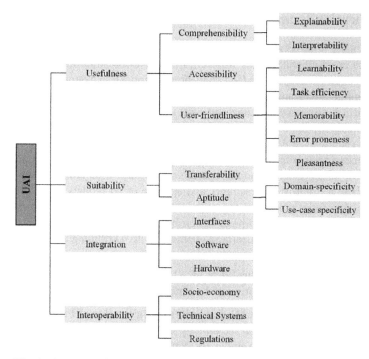

Fig. 1. Anatomy of the Usable Artificial Intelligence (UAI) Paradigm [1].

By providing domain context for method developers, supporting target communication in the domain context, and making data science insights understandable to users, UAI creates a great leap in the applicability of AI methods. Figure 2 illustrates the interaction of the 3 layers associated by emphasized application examples elaborated next.

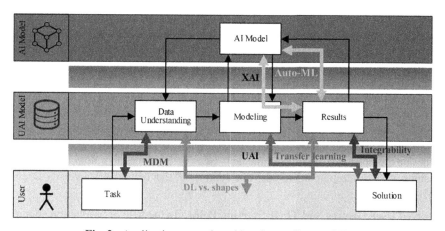

Fig. 2. Application examples addressing attributes of UAI.

3 Application Examples

Different interactions between the user and the AI application are illustrated with examples, which are deliberately very different in order to illustrate the scope of the UAI concept. In accordance with the UAI concept, the application examples can be assigned to the AI application framework shown in Fig. 2.

Section 3.1 discusses explainability and integrability of AI for engineers in data mining-suitable digitization of production systems. Section 3.2 covers the interoperability of data required for AI applications in materials development (MDM). Section 3.3 presents emerging approaches to the comprehensibility and aptitude of condition monitoring of time-series data for machine operators. Section 3.4 elaborates on how Auto-ML can contribute to improve accessibility and aptitude of AI models, exemplified by the prediction of material properties for materials researchers. Section 3.5 covers how the transferability of AI-based computer vision between different application domains is enabled by means of Transfer Learning approaches in 3D printing applications.

3.1 Explainability and Integrability of AI for SME Engineers in Data Mining-Suitable Digitization of Production Systems

The Need for Support in Data Mining Suitable Digitization of Production Systems. The current trend in production technology is towards the collection and evaluation of machine sensor data, for example for condition monitoring, predictive quality or predictive maintenance applications [15]. The majority of companies have recognised the technical and economic potential of such data-driven solutions and would like to develope their own [16]. While large companies already offer their own solutions, SMEs encounter almost insurmountable hurdles when developing their own solutions due to the often limited human resources and lack of experience in data mining [17]. Various process models, such as RAMI 4.0 [18], CRISP-DM [19], DMME [20] or the ISO standard 17359 [21], already exist to support development. However, these are often too abstract and therefore only of limited help [17].

In the context of the use case "digitization of production systems for data mining" [22], a process model was extended with adapted design and development methods that enables engineers in production technology to independently upgrade and prepare machines for data mining. The essential goal here is to design and deploy a data acquisition system to create a documented data basis meeting the requirements for a reliable data analysis in a way that a data scientist is capable of building data models.

The method supported process model was developed and successfully deployed in data mining projects with SMEs in domains ranging from manufacturing to concrete mixers. To illustrate the properties Explainability and Integrability of the UAI paradigm, the process model is applied to an AI based condition monitoring use case for linear guides on the machine "smart machine bed" (see Fig. 3) in the laboratory of the chair of machine tools development and adaptive controls of the Technical University Dresden [23].

Involved User Groups and Their Starting Point. In the field of production engineering, data mining projects involve at least engineers and data scientists. Both groups have

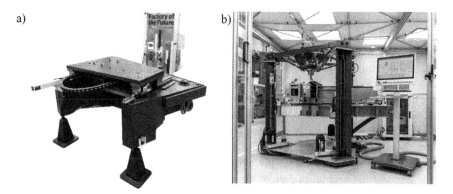

Fig. 3. a) Smart machine bed as part of a 5 axis CNC for research in the field of AI based condition monitoring and predictive maintenance of linear guides and b) 3-axis Cartesian serial kinematic in lightweight construction MAX.

different tasks in such a project. The data scientist is supposed to prepare data sets and apply algorithms for analysis, but does not know the given production system and the effects to be searched for in the data set sufficiently. He depends on reliable data sets in terms of contained information and data quality and needs documentation on variables contained and states to be analyzed, which he expects from an engineer. The engineer is able to make data from the machine available and can define analysis targets. However, he is not sufficiently aware of the data scientists requirements on data and documentation. To ensure the success of the project, there is a need for support for the engineer in accomplishing his task. This is where the Explainability property of the UAI paradigm becomes important. The requirements of the data scientist must be translated for the engineer into precise instructions with applicable methods (see Fig. 4). Furthermore, the engineer wants a data acquisition solution that is technically easy to integrate into his machine. This is aimed at the property of Integrability.

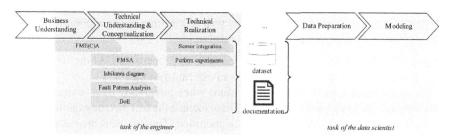

Fig. 4. Exchange between engineer and data scientist in a data mining project according to the DMME.

Explainability. The engineer obtains initial support in defining economic and technical objectives by first identifying frequently occurring problems, for example in the area of manufacturing quality or availability of his machine. Using the failure mode effect analysis (FMEA) commonly used in engineering, he prioritizes these based on criteria such as cost, frequency of occurrence and severity and makes a selection for the project. In the next step, suitable physical measurands are to be found for the analysis targets in order to make the symptoms of the anomalies measurable. For this purpose, the failure mode and symptoms analysis (FMSA) method is used, which is also familiar in engineering. Since there are often interactions between machine and process, these influencing factors must be identified by applying Ishikawa analysis, otherwise regular changes in normal operation can lead to a falsely detected anomaly. To derive the technical requirements for sensors that can measure the identified effects, a fault pattern analysis is proposed in the next step. In this process, the anomaly symptoms are quantified, for example, on the basis of the geometric data of the machine component. Based on the quantified requirements, suitable sensors can be selected by comparison with their data sheets. Finally, a test plan must be developed by means of DoE, using the influencing factors determined by the Ishikawa analysis as experimental parameters and simply defining the corresponding parameter ranges.

In the linear guide use case, for example, maintenance and wear problems such as insufficient lubrication or pitting were considered as analysis targets. In this case, pitting was given the highest priority using the FMEA, and the aim was to detect it.

By applying FMSA, vibration, for example on the carriage, could be determined as a measurable symptom of pitting. The Ishikawa analysis identified, for example, varying movement speeds of the feed axis as an influencing variable. In the fault pattern analysis, the maximum permissible speeds and rolling element diameters were used to determine the characteristic vibration frequencies of the linear bearing. A maximum bandwidth of 500 Hz was calculated and a maximum vibration amplitude of $\pm 4g$ was estimated. The experimental design includes both pitting and normal conditions and different velocity levels from 5 to 40 m/min as experimental parameters. A direct comparison of the experimental data (see Fig. 5) shows that there are distinguishable vibration characteristics (in the time and frequency domain) between the two states and thus a good data basis for the analysis. The engineer was able to create a reliable basis for the data scientist with tools and methods that are common to him. Again, for the data scientist there is a well understandable documentation about the contained information in the data set (anomaly classes, influence parameters) as well as a symptom description to select an optimal feature engineering or analysis algorithm.

Integrability. Integrability (for technical systems) as property of UAI means to allow a smooth interaction of the with embedded and external systems.

There are often restrictions and constraints when integrating data acquisition solutions, for example in the case of a retrofit. These include the fact that the existing machine structure or control technology must not be modified. Thus, sensor integration is often only possible in a minimal invasive way. In the application described, linear guides exist with integrated vibration sensors that can measure directly at the point of origin. However, one constraint was that the guides must not be replaced. In addition, no changes were allowed to be made to the machine control system.

Therefore, a retrofit of mobile vibration sensors was chosen, which, however, meet the requirements for data acquisition and transmit the acquired data via WLAN to a post-fitted edge computer.

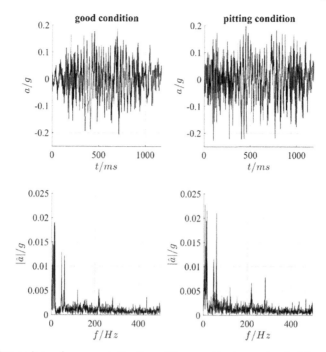

Fig. 5. Comparison of measured vibration of linear guides in good and pitting condition.

3.2 Interoperability of Data Required for AI Applications in Materials Design

Motivation. The availability of data in materials design strongly influences the performance of the applied AI models [24, 25]. Therefore, data management is of particular importance for the usability of AI models. In order to consider and analyze cross-process linkages, a global view on the data set in analyzable form is necessary. This requires well-documented data which can be combined to global data sets. The transformation of data such that the data is in analyzable form is a part of the data pre-processing step in the data analysis chain/life cycle.

Challenges. Data documentation is often not done or documentations are not stored in a structured way. Different notations are used, such that documentations are not comprehensible and/or not complete.

Due to the interdisciplinary nature of collaborative projects, it is often a collaborative effort involving researchers from different fields [26]. Collaborative projects in engineering usually consist of research partners from different fields. Research topics are viewed from many different perspectives, including numerical experiments, imaging test methods, time-dependent simulations. Different research partners/laboratories work together in collaborative projects, each of them having their own technical language, their own organizational rules, and their own work instructions. Researchers from different disciplines work on the same research topics. However, as they come from different domains, they usually employ different notations for the same issues, have different development goals, and use different methods and data. A common, rather simple example for such inconsistencies across laboratory boundaries is the usage of names for physical quantities and units (e.g., elastic modulus, E modulus, Young's modulus, modulus of elasticity etc.). As many collaborative projects are not only interdisciplinary, but also multicultural, researchers come from different cultures, thus speak different languages (e.g., English, German) with different dialects. This reinforces inconsistencies in the data documentation.

Similar challenges arise when labelling test specimens and components. Each laboratory uses its own local labelling system, thus, the same component has different laboratory local identifiers.

Requirements. A good research data management (RDM) has to fulfil many requirements like data completeness, high data quality, good comprehensibility, common working culture, high efficiency and acceptance, protection/security, practicability, sustainability, or high availability [27]. The FAIR principles (findability, accessibility, interoperability, reusability) are the core of the RDM requirements. As the main goal is to provide datasets that can be used as input for the application of AI based methods, the data has to be firstly available in an analyzable form. Thus, in the following, we focus on the data interoperability requirement. Analyzing relations between process variables across process boundaries requires that process local data sets can be combined/merged to a global data set. An analyzable data set of high data quality depends mainly on the following:

- A systematic documentation of the data using a uniform naming of the technical terms used. For a comprehensible documentation of experiments, it is necessary that processes, machines and materials are completely described. The schemes for the documentations should be compatible with existing documentation schemes from other disciplines so that they can be reused and combined.
- A systematic identity management for marking components beyond laboratory boundaries, which has to be in line with the laboratory-specific working methods in order to be able to clearly identify components and track them across laboratory boundaries. For a global view of data across project partner borders, a global identity management of test samples is required, which is in line with the project partner's local ID management. Thus, a proper ID management is required to combine data from different processes and to trace samples along process chains.

Solution Approach. The solution approach to meet the data interoperability requirement is based on a systematic metadata management [28]. The workflow is shown in Fig. 6. Based on a domain-specific ontology, metadata is generated that is used in process-specific metadata schemas to document the research data. The metadata schemas have different chapters (e.g., administrative and technical metadata) and contain key-value pairs in each chapter. The key names are terms from the ontology, the value names are the corresponding possible forms (e.g., value ranges for numeric properties).

Using a domain-specific dictionary of synonyms (thesaurus), which lists technical terms that have the same meaning or are similar to technical terms, it is ensured that the individual researcher can keep to his or her familiar terminology even in an interdisciplinary environment. Constant readjustment to new research partners is not necessary. Nevertheless, it is ensured that the data remains comprehensible and therefore usable for other researchers internally and externally.

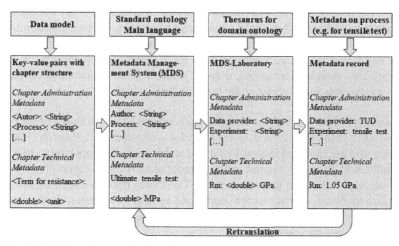

Fig. 6. Workflow for ensuring data interoperability in collaborative research projects.

Implementation and Results. The design and implementation of data management systems, taking into account the data interoperability requirement, was carried out in several interdisciplinary research projects, including the following collaborative projects:

- *Collaborative project AMTwin:* Scientists from different research institutions are collaboratively investigating the linkages between the manufacturing process, material and the final component properties using an experimental-numerical approach. The project aims at simulation methods for the design of additive manufacturing processes and components manufactured with them. Test methods are developed that are required for process monitoring, microstructure characterization, quality testing and validation of the simulations [29]. The implementation in AMTwin is based on MS SharePoint which serves as the web frontend for the management of the data documentations. Forms in SharePoint are used to document research data. Forms are connected to a taxonomy derived from a domain-specific ontology such that only technical terms are available in the ontology can be chosen, leading to a high-quality data documentation. A thesaurus is connected to the used taxonomy. As a result, a merged data set has been obtained containing data from different processes which can be analysed using AI applications [30].
- *Collaborative project GRK2250:* Scientists from multiple research institutions are jointly investigating design concepts for strengthening existing buildings with textile-reinforced concrete. This research aims to significantly improve the impact resistance

of existing buildings by attaching thin layers of strengthening material. Therefore, the behavior of textile-reinforced concrete and its influence on existing concrete structures, especially in high dynamic loading conditions, is being studied with experimental, simulative and data-based investigations [31]. The data management in GRK2250 is implemented with the commercial software "Detact", which is being further developed for this research project for the purpose of research data management. Metadata documentation is standardized through the binding use of metadata templates. The corresponding entries in these templates are synchronized via a thesaurus. This results in a database with complete metadata and completely consistent terminology. For the user-friendliness of the database, there is a web frontend with which the data can be uploaded and from which all implemented functionalities can be controlled. This includes various functions for searching the metadata and various tools for visualization and analysis of the research data.

Conclusions. The solution presented offers advantages for the usability of the existing database. It is ensured that the data are recorded comprehensibly through clear documentation and are thus understood by all researchers. The interoperability of the data across laboratory boundaries is ensured by a proper identity management of components, processes, machines across these boundaries. This makes the data usable for subsequent data-driven analyses even across laboratory and process boundaries. Furthermore, the results generated based on the research data are reproducible on a qualitatively level due to the detailed data documentation.

3.3 Comprehensibility and Aptitude of Condition Monitoring on Time Series Data for Machine Operators

Time series are of considerable importance for technical applications, especially in the domain of machine tools. Tool wear monitoring and chatter detection, for example, are topics with persisting relevance in milling machines [32]. Machine Learning has come to widespread application for these tasks, yet it results in increasingly abstract models, that can be highly performant and at the same time cumbersome to use [33].

For clarification, tool wear monitoring refers to the task of correctly predicting the quality status of the milling tool or its remaining useful life respectively. The main challenge is posed by the nonlinear behavior, showing sudden deterioration potential. Chatter detection refers to the task of identifying an unstable process condition. It causes unwanted effects, e.g., lower surface quality of the product or higher tool wear.

Each of the two tasks (tool wear monitoring and chatter detection) has a long-standing field of research in which a number of solutions have been called for. Historically, a variety of solutions has shown to (partially) solve early detection of chatter and classification of the machining state. Initially, by the use of rule-based approaches in the time and frequency domain [34]. Later on, by the use of elaborate feature engineering as well as sampling based methods [35]. With the advent of computing power that is sufficient for the training of large neural networks, deep learning techniques are used more and more often. Critical to model development is the accuracy of its predictive capability. With deep learning in particular, an increase in predictive power is realized at the expense of understandability, explainability and usability [36].

Next to various ideas on explaining the prediction process of deep learning models for higher transparency, an means to increased usability of the model is to refine the AI task. A change of the output format (and/or the processing pipeline) is promising with respect to the UAI paradigm. An approach based on shapes is discussed for two use cases at LWM.. A comparison of "end-to-end" deep learning methods and shape based approaches is used for the illustration of the property *Comprehensibility* of the UAI paradigm.

MAX Environment. The environment for the comparison is test bed "MAX" (Fig. 3b). It is used for research on thermal behavior of machine tools. "MAX" contains a 3-axis Cartesian serial kinematic in lightweight construction (X, Y, Z), which enables targeted error correction in all 6 degrees of freedom using the parallel drives in Y and Z. The sensory framework of the testbed records numerous sensor data to analyze highly dynamic three-axes-milling processes [37]. The use cases in consideration are the prediction of component temperatures based on machine data and the detection of anomalous behavior in the motion profile.

Deep Learning. Regarding the prediction of component temperatures, Boos et al. have shown that a Temporal Fusion Transformer (TFT) model can be trained to successfully predict component temperatures taking into account only axis positions, velocities and motor currents of 5 engines [37]. A sample prediction is shown in Fig. 7.

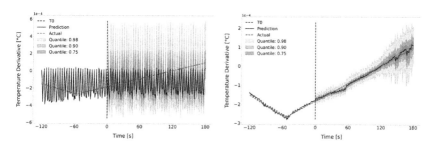

Fig. 7. Time series of the temperature recorded [37].

Shape Analysis. For the detection of anomalous behavior in the motion profile, Piece-wise Aggregate Approximation (PAA) and shapelet extraction are combined to assist in monitoring and anomaly detection for the motion profile. Zhang argue that shape-lets are well-suited for anomaly detection because anomalies can often only be detected on the basis of a short period of time within the time series can be detected [38]. With respect to subsequence matching, other authors have considered the comparison of the entire time series as more accurate [39]. The algorithm chosen for extracting the shapelets is the Random Shapelet Transform [40]. First, a composite dataset is formed by concatenation of the PAA-transformed time series. A distance matrix is calculated, which contains distances between each combination of two time series of the dataset. A first, qualitative assessment of the transformation is contained in the distance profile. Second, motifs and discords are extracted and clustered, resulting already in interpretable references for healthy or unhealthy machine conditions, shown in Fig. 8. The result is a suitable solution that seems to be a promising candidate for a usability-centered approach.

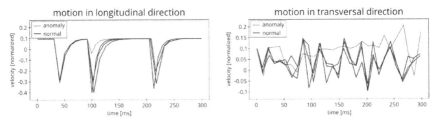

Fig. 8. Anomaly detection for healthy or unhealthy machine conditions through shape analysis.

Comprehensibility. According to the UAI paradigm, comprehensibility refers to explainability on the one hand, and interpretability on the other. The former is defined by the possibility to make the functionality of the solution communicable. The other is defined as the possibility to understand the results of the approach. In both respects, the DL approach is problematic. Especially for the user role of the machine operator, elementary questions about the reasoning of the prediction result remain unanswered. While the prediction of temperature values can be used to operate the machine, the relationship between machine data and prediction is completely opaque and difficult to access (if at all), even for user roles more accustomed with AI.

Shapelets, on the contrary, allow for explanation and interpretation through a greater parallelism to human intuitive reasoning. A direct link between sequences that are meaningful in the source domain and the classification comprises a less convoluted flow of information. In addition, as the linking method is based on a distance metric it contains a familiar logic having equivalents in everyday life.

3.4 Accessibility and Aptitude of AI Models for Materials Researchers in Materials Property Prediction

The usage of AI is rising in materials design and applied for materials property analysis, material discovery and quantum chemistry [41]. This has led to enormous progress, which is why broader applicability of AI is being pursued through the UAI concept. Solutions for accessibility and aptitude of AI in this domain are presented in this illustration.

There are already several methodologies for applying AI in engineering, e.g., CRISP-DM [42] and DMME [20]. However, these methodologies do not answer which of the numerous AI methods should be used under which circumstances. Moreover, the step 'model building' is not further supported with a guideline on when to apply which models. Looking closer into the task of 'model building' reveals an enormous number of possibilities that a non-AI expert cannot assess. The work towards UAI presented in this illustration provides guidance on which models to use, how much data is needed and how to validate the model's performance reliably. This is done in the domain of materials design for materials property prediction. Thereby, the following attributes of UAI have been addressed:

Accessibility. The application of ML is still a time-consuming procedure. Moreover, the constant development of new ML models makes it difficult to keep up with the latest developments. Automated machine learning (AutoML) could solve these problems and simplify the ML modeling process. The tedious pre-processing of data, feature engineering, model creation, and optimization are automated and therefore do not have to be performed by the user. As a result, AutoML provides the opportunity to make ML accessible to non-experts, improve ML efficiency, and accelerate ML research.

Suitability (Aptitude). While the reduction in effort is immediately apparent, it remains unclear how well models obtained using AutoML perform to predict materials properties compared to models created manually by the researchers. Therefore, in the framework presented in [24], the predictive quality of ML models obtained with AutoML was benchmarked with the results manually created and published by researchers. For this objective, 13 data sets from the literature that were publicly available and had at least one publication providing a manual data-mining analysis were investigated. Some data sets provided the information for several material properties with the respective analysis, so that a total of 20 prediction tasks could be compared. The datasets were utilized exactly as in the original publications to complete the same prediction tasks with four different AutoML tools. The results were then compared with each other to create a benchmark. Therefore a relative score was created, for which a relative score of 1 means the same performance as the manual reference (black line in Fig. 9) and above 1 means better performance. More details on the implementation settings can be found in [24].

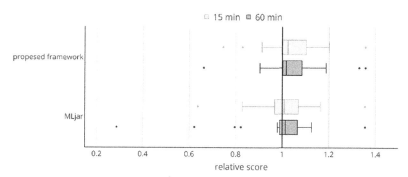

Fig. 9. The relative results of our proposed framework and the AutoML tool MLjar per training time for predicting material properties compared to the manual results of the literature. The literature results are normalized to 1. A higher relative score means a better prediction quality than the reference literature.

AutoML has been shown to provide models with a higher prediction than manual modeling by researchers. In comparing 20 prediction tasks to the published manual results, AutoML found a better model for 16 predictions with 60 min of training time and 15 predictions with 15 min of training. The results are displayed in Fig. 9. So, for this use-case, the question of which model has the highest performance can be best answered by AutoML. Researchers in the domain of materials design can profit from the improved performance by using AutoML.

This study also investigated how the amount of available data affects the performance of the ML models for the prediction of materials properties, which is shown in Fig. 10. The found relationship follows the findings from Zhang et al. [25]. However, it could be defined more precisely by integrating the feature size. The scaled error (mean absolute error divided by the value range) shows a higher correlation with the dataset size divided by the number of features. As in Zhang et al. [5], the power law was used for the approximation. The R^2 value between scaled error and dataset size is 0.30 and could be increased with the integration of the feature size to $R^2 = 0.54$, cf. Figure 10.

In this framework, nested cross-validation (NCV) was implemented. In [43], it could be shown that for the typical small data sets in material design (>1000 data points), the performance can be overestimated with typical state-of-the-art model evaluation methods (hold-out, cross-validation). Therefore a nested CV is highly recommended for such datasets, as the performance can be estimated more reliably.

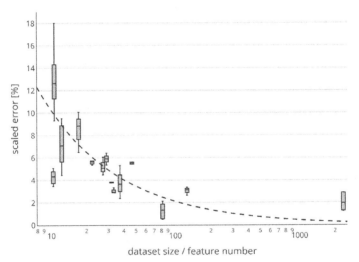

Fig. 10. The scaled error of the investigated tasks after 60 min training time, with respect to the shape of the data set. The blue dashed line shows the fitted curve of scaled error $= 0.51 \times$ (dataset size/feature number)$^{-0.690}$ with $R^2 = 0.54$. (Color figure online)

Interfaces. The implementation for the application of AutoML has been made available on GitHub in addition to the paper. Thus, the entire framework consisting of 4 different AutoML tools can be controlled with only one command from the command line. Furthermore, using Mljar-Studio [44], the individual AutoML Tool MLjar can also be operated via a graphical user interface. This increases usability even more. However, if only this tool is used, the performance decreases slightly, but it is still much better than manual modeling, see Fig. 9.

Integrability. The parallel use of the 4 Auto-ML tools comes with various integrability problems. Not all tools run on all operating systems. In addition, the dependencies of the AutoML tools are mutually exclusive, so they cannot be used together in one environment. This problem was solved using docker containers, so only docker installation is necessary to use all AutoML tools. Docker is available for Windows, Linux and mac OS.

3.5   Transferability of AI Based Computer Vision in 3D-Print Applications

Motivation. This use case addresses the development of a real-time control system for a fused deposition modeling (FDM) additive manufacturing process, in particular material extrusion problems in the FDM process for monitoring via datasets from external sources combined with data generated experimentally with different extrusion factors (Fig. 11). To solve the problem of small dataset, data augmentation methods are applied to increase the dataset size, and a migration learning approach is adopted to ensure the generalization capability of this deep learning framework. Several popular deep learning frameworks are evaluated for their accuracy in this scenario and the selection is evaluated. FDM printers work by depositing layer by layer temporarily melted plastic materials onto a moving platform building up geometry of a final product. The complexity of the parameters and the invisibility of the print interior can cause the printer to create mistakes and cause unexpected defects. This can result in a product that does not offer of the required quality. Insufficient fluid flow can lead to clogging of the print head, which further threatens the printer itself. Therefore exists a need to alert extrusion defects during the printing process to provide for the quality of the product and the safety of the printer. The aim is to enable a detection system that detects extrusion defects, based on a deep learning network for classification. An executable program is designed in python to take live images from a camera, feed them into a trained model for classification, and warn when defects are detected.

Figure 11d shows the classes or labels and in addition one image of the corresponding class. The class Over Extrusion has 12268 images, Okay Extrusion 13228 and in Under Extrusion 14726 images, while the class Empty Area has 3179 images.

Challenges. In order to avoid overfitting, many methods have been proposed, such as dropout, regularisation, model pre-processing, and data augmentation. Data augmentation refers to the techniques that synthetically expand a data set by applying transformations to the existing examples, thus augmenting the amount of available training data. Although the new data points are not independent and identically distributed, data augmentation implicitly regularizes the models and improves generalization, as established by statistical learning theory [45]. The larger the sample dataset, the better the generalization ability of the model after training. This appears to be hint that the value of hyperparameters of weight decay and dropout largely depend on the architecture and any modification requires the fine-tuning of the regularization parameters. That is not the case with data augmentation, which again seems to easily adapt to the new architectures because its potential depends mostly on the type of training data. In contrast to the

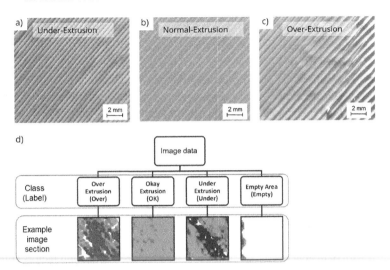

Fig. 11. a–c) Images of surface appearances on FDM-printed parts in case of a) Under-Extrusion, b) Normal-Extrusion, and c) Over-Extrusion, and d) applied class assignment in data processing.

techniques mentioned above, Data Augmentation approaches overfitting from the root of the problem, the training dataset [46].

Traditional machine learning methods extract features manually and have complex work in analyzing features and building feature extraction frameworks, which also means that traditional machine learning methods are not advantageous when dealing with complex scenarios and large amounts of data containing complex features. Unlike traditional machine learning, deep learning frameworks are currently very complex with millions of parameters to obtain accurate features, for example, a deep CNN structure with only 5 convolutional and 3 fully connected layers plus a Softmax classifier already contains over 60 million parameters. A large number of parameters poses the following two main problems for CNNs [47]:

- Model requires large amounts of labeled data to train,
- Hardware requires powerful GPUs to help to compute.

Solution. In applications where large amounts of training data or computational power are lacking, direct use of a deep network can suffer from severe overfitting and ultimately poor generalization of the model [47]. Research has shown that cross-domain learning can be used to potentially improve results for target learners as long as the two domains are related, since the training data and target data, although existing in different sub-domains, are connected by a high-level common domain [48]. This provides an idea for migration learning. If a proven model is first trained and developed for a task, and then the similarities between the data, task, and model are exploited to apply the trained model to a new task, this is the essence of transfer learning. For example, a model trained on a base dataset (ImageNet), VGG, now trains part of its neural network with a new application tailored dataset, thus learning the features of the new task, rather than learning everything from scratch [49]. Applications of the transfer learning solution have been successfully applied to include text sentiment classification, image classification, human activity classification, software defect classification, and multilingual text classification [48].

The experiment was carried out by selecting an IDS uEye 1240, which is connected to a Beckhoff Industrial PC via a USB 2.0 interface. The camera is fixed to the z-axis and remains stationary relative to the print head in the x- and y-direction. The distance of the camera from the FDM print head is in the coordinates $(-20, +80)$ and this difference is written into the layer code that controls the captured image in the print. After matching the software modeling environment to the printer used for this experiment, a print-shoot cycle execution process was designed to obtain data for both under- and normal extrusion. The data was to be augmented to reduce overfitting problems caused by the inadequate quantity of the data set. Finally, a program was written to automatically split the training and test sets in an 8:2 ratio and to obtain labels that could be easily read into the model using the dataload function of PyTorch. The second step was to write training and testing functions in python, customizing parameters such as epoch, batch size, loss function, and optimization function. The parameters obtained after training on the ImageNet are frozen except for the last layer, and the last layer is rewritten for custom classification.

Migration learning is employed offering advantages like solving the problem of overfitting due to insufficient datasets, reducing the burden of training on hardware. There are several well-established frameworks for image classification, of which the VGG and ResNet families are very popular, with different input and output and neural network structures. These frameworks have been maturely integrated into deep learning frameworks and support calls that can be modified afterward or used directly for task training. By the use of migration learning on the commonly used image classification model ResNet series and VGG series the training of a dataset captured on an FDM printer is completed. In particular, the deep learning framework VGG16, VGG19, ResNet50 and ResNet101 are imported in PyTorch. As all previous neural layers remain freeze, the last fully connected layer is modified to classification. The model with the best predictions is determined based on evaluation of its performance, including accuracy, recall, precision, F1 score and confusion matrix.

Finally, the performance of these deep learning frameworks was evaluated using confusion matrices and visualization of the result graphs (see Fig. 12).

It can be recognized that structured surfaces (OK-Extrusion, Over-Extrusion, Empty-Extrusion) are well detected, but the model can only insufficiently distinguish between structured surfaces and empty areas (Empty Area). Table 1 shows typical metrics for the model according to classes. The Accuracy of the model with original dataset is 72%. Except for the Empty class, the model has a high precision value but a low recall value. The Accuracy of the model with augmented dataset is 79%. As augmentation shows weak contribution to the models accuracy, further internally or externally acquired image data must be additionally incorporated to improve the accuracy of the models and to train a model for 3D printing applications.

Transferability. Developments in deep learning, e.g., artificial neural networks, transfer learning, and combined approaches to feature engineering, offer extended opportunities to transfer model functionalities to adjacent domains. For example, image-based process

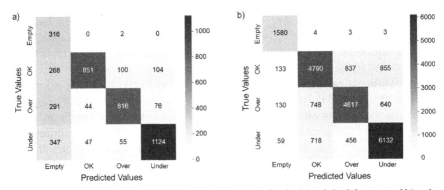

Fig. 12. Confusion matrices of VGG16 based model a) trained with original dataset and b) trained with augmented dataset.

Table 1. Performance metrices of the models.

	VGG16				VGG16 with augmented data			
	Empty	OK	Over	Under	Empty	OK	Over	Under
Precision	0.28	0.90	0.84	0.86	0.83	.77	0.78	0.80
Recall	0.99	0.64	0.67	0.76	.99	.72	0.75	0.83
F1 Score	0.44	0.67	0.76	0.81	.90	.74	0.77	0.82
Accuracy	0.72				0.79			

monitoring can use artificial neural networks whose layers are largely pre-trained and where only a few layers are trained on a specific new use case. The transfer learning strategy not only reduces the training effort for the particular production application, but also improves the functionality of the AI model, as the pre-trained layers lead to better generalizability of the AI solution.

4 Conclusion

AI has shown great potential in learning complex patterns and making predictions about yet unknown data domains, as long as the problem is clearly defined and describable with adequate codifiable information. User-oriented application examples were presented in the AI application framework in line with the UAI concept. The explainability and integrability of AI for engineers in data mining-suitable digitization of production systems was elaborated. Interoperability of data required for AI applications in materials development (MDM) was covered. Novel approaches to make condition monitoring of time series data comprehensible and apt for machine operators were presented. The example of predicting material properties for materials researchers was used to explain how Auto-ML can help improve accessibility and aptitude of AI models. Transfer learning approaches in 3D printing applications were discussed to facilitate the transferability of AI-based computer vision between multiple application domains.

Further research will need to contribute to improving Learnability, Task Efficiency, and Error Proneness of AI in order to substantially assist in improving user-friendliness of AI. In addition, interoperability will become a major development priority for AI usability, which will be driven not only by technical considerations, but also by socio-economics and regulations.

References

1. Wiemer, H., et al.: Need for UAI – anatomy of the paradigm of usable artificial intelligence for domain-specific AI applicability. Multimodal Technol. Interact. (2023)
2. acatech: Künstliche Intelligenz in der Industrie (2020)
3. Berg, A.: Industrie 4.0 – jetzt mit KI. Gehalten auf der bitkom Hannover April 1 (2019)
4. Rohleder, B.: Industrie 4.0 – so digital sind Deutschlands Fabriken. Gehalten auf der bitkom Hannover April 7 (2021)
5. Hutapea, L., Malanowski, N.: Potenziale und Hindernisse bei der Einführung digitaler Technik in der kunststoffverarbeitenden Industrie. Stiftung Arbeit und Umwelt der IG BCE
6. Röhl, K.-H., Bolwin, L., Hüttl, P.: Datenwirtschaft in Deutschland. BDI Bundesverbands der Deutschen Industrie e.V (2021)
7. Bühler, J., Fliehe, M., Shahd, M.: Künstliche Intelligenz in Unternehmen. Verband der TÜV e. V
8. Seifert, I., et al.: Potenziale der Künstlichen Intelligenz im produzierenden Gewerbe in Deutschland. iit-Institut für Innovation und Technik in der VDI/VDE Innovation + Technik GmbH (2018)
9. Weber, K., Bertschek, I., Ohnemus, J., Ebert, M.: Monitoring-Report Wirtschaft DIGITAL 2018. Bundesministerium für Wirtschaft und Energie (BMWi) (2018)
10. Rich, E., Knight, K.: Artificial Intelligence. McGraw–Hill, New York (1991)
11. Ertel, W.: Grundkurs Künstliche Intelligenz: Eine praxisorientierte Einführung. Springer, Wiesbaden (2021)
12. Smuha, N.: A definition of AI: Main capabilities and scientific disciplines. Eur. Comm. **9** (2018)
13. International Standard ISO 9241-11 Second edition 2018-03
14. Nielsen, J.: Usability Engineering. Academic Press, Boston (1993)
15. Zimmermann, V.: Artificial intelligence: high growth potential but low penetration in SMEs. KFW (2021)
16. Schröder, C.: The Challenges of Industry 4.0 for Small and Medium-sized Enterprises. Friedrich-Ebert-Stiftung, Bonn (2016)
17. Baptista, L.F., Barata, J.: Piloting industry 4.0 in SMEs with RAMI 4.0: an enterprise architecture approach. Procedia Comput. Sci. **192**, 2826–2835 (2021). https://doi.org/10.1016/j.procs.2021.09.053
18. Deutsches Institut für Normung: DIN SPEC 91345 Referenzarchitekturmodell Industrie 4.0 (RAMI4.0) (2016)
19. Wirth, R., Hipp, J.: CRISP-DM: towards a standard process model for data mining. In: Proceedings of the 4th International Conference on the Practical Applications of Knowledge Discovery and Data Mining. Springer, London (2000)
20. Huber, S., Wiemer, H., Schneider, D., Ihlenfeldt, S.: DMME: data mining methodology for engineering applications – a holistic extension to the CRISP-DM model. Procedia CIRP **79**, 403–408 (2019). https://doi.org/10.1016/j.procir.2019.02.106
21. Deutsches Institut für Normung: DIN ISO 17359 Zustandsüberwachung und -diagnostik von Maschinen - Allgemeine Anleitungen (2018)

22. Drowatzky, L., Wiemer, H., Ihlenfeldt, S.: Data mining suitable digitization of production systems – a methodological extension to the DMME. In: Liewald, M., Verl, A., Bauernhansl, T., Möhring, HC. (eds) WGP 2022. LNPE, pp. 524–534. Springer, Cham (2023). https://doi.org/10.1007/978-3-031-18318-8_53

23. Schwarzenberger, M., Drowatzky, L., Wiemer, H., Ihlenfeldt, S.: Transferable condition monitoring for linear guidance systems using anomaly detection. In: Behrens, B.-A., Brosius, A., Drossel, W.-G., Hintze, W., Ihlenfeldt, S., Nyhuis, P. (eds.) WGP 2021. LNPE, pp. 497–505. Springer, Cham (2022). https://doi.org/10.1007/978-3-030-78424-9_55

24. Conrad, F., Mälzer, M., Schwarzenberger, M., Wiemer, H., Ihlenfeldt, S.: Benchmarking AutoML for regression tasks on small tabular data in materials design. Sci. Rep. **12**, 19350 (2022). https://doi.org/10.1038/s41598-022-23327-1

25. Zhang, Y., Ling, C.: A strategy to apply machine learning to small datasets in materials science. npj Comput. Mater. **4**, 1–8 (2018). https://doi.org/10.1038/s41524-018-0081-z

26. Morillo, F., Bordons, M., Gómez, I.: Interdisciplinarity in science: a tentative typology of disciplines and research areas. J. Am. Soc. Inform. Sci. Technol. **54**, 1237–1249 (2003). https://doi.org/10.1002/asi.10326

27. Feldhoff, K., Wiemer, H.: Praktikables, Ontologie-basiertes Forschungsdatenmanagement in der Additiven Fertigung. In:: Brockmann, S., Krupp, U. (Hrsg.) Werkstoffprüfung 2021 - Werkstoffe und Bauteile auf dem Prüfstand (2021)

28. Wiemer, H., Feldhoff, K., Ihlenfeldt, S.: FDM als Service für ein typisches Verbundprojekt in den Ingenieurwissenschaften auf Basis einer ontologie-basierten Verschlagwortung. Gehalten auf der November 22 (2021)

29. Raßloff, A., Wiemer, H., Zimmermann, W., Kästner, M.: Datengetriebene Prozess-, Werkstoff- und Strukturanalyse für die Additive Fertigung (AMTwin). DVM Workshop' Grundlagen und Beispiele zur Digitalisierung für die Materialforschung und -prüfung, Berlin (2020)

30. Feldhoff, K., Wiemer, H.: AI-based prediction of the quality of additively manufactured components. In: Materials Science and Engineering Congress (MSE 2022) (2022)

31. Signorini, C., Mechtcherine, V.: Mineral-bonded composites for enhanced structural impact safety: the vision of the DFG GRK 2250. In: Beiträge zum 61. Forschungskolloquium mit 9. Jahrestagung des DAfStb, pp. 13–18. TU Dresden (2022)

32. Serin, G., Sener, B., Ozbayoglu, A.M., Unver, H.O.: Review of tool condition monitoring in machining and opportunities for deep learning. Int. J. Adv. Manuf. Technol. **109**(3–4), 953–974 (2020). https://doi.org/10.1007/s00170-020-05449-w

33. Kaluarachchi, T., Reis, A., Nanayakkara, S.: A review of recent deep learning approaches in human-centered machine learning. Sensors **21**, 2514 (2021)

34. Delio, T., Tlusty, J., Smith, S.: Use of audio signals for chatter detection and control (1992)

35. Navarro-Devia, J.H., Chen, Y., Dao, D.V., Li, H.: Chatter detection in milling processes—a review on signal processing and condition classification. Int. J. Adv. Manuf. Technol., 1–38 (2023)

36. Yang, G., Ye, Q., Xia, J.: Unbox the black-box for the medical explainable AI via multi-modal and multi-centre data fusion: a mini-review, two showcases and beyond. Inf. Fus. **77** (2021). https://doi.org/10.1016/j.inffus.2021.07.016

37. Boos, E., Thiem, X., Wiemer, H., Ihlenfeldt, S.: Improving a deep learning temperature-forecasting model of a 3-axis precision machine with domain randomized thermal simulation data. In: Liewald, M., Verl, A., Bauernhansl, T., Möhring, HC. (eds.) WGP 2022. LNPE, pp. 574–584. Springer, Cham (2023). https://doi.org/10.1007/978-3-031-18318-8_58

38. Zhang, L.: Shape-based time series mining for process monitoring and anomaly detection (2021)

39. Bagnall, A., Lines, J., Bostrom, A., Large, J., Keogh, E.: The great time series classification bake off: a review and experimental evaluation of recent algorithmic advances. Data Min. Knowl. Disc. **31**(3), 606–660 (2016). https://doi.org/10.1007/s10618-016-0483-9
40. Bostrom, A., Bagnall, A.: Binary shapelet transform for multiclass time series classification. In: Transactions on Large-Scale Data-and Knowledge-Centered Systems XXXII: Special Issue on Big Data Analytics and Knowledge Discovery, pp. 24–46 (2017)
41. Wei, J., et al.: Machine learning in materials science (2019)
42. Wirth, R., Hipp, J.: CRISP-DM: towards a standard process model for data mining. In: Proceedings of the 4th International Conference on the Practical Applications of Knowledge Discovery and Data Mining, p. 11 (2000)
43. Conrad, F., Boos, E., Mälzer, M., Wiemer, H., Ihlenfeldt, S.: Impact of data sampling on performance and robustness of machine learning models in production engineering. In: Liewald, M., Verl, A., Bauernhansl, T., Möhring, HC. (eds.) WGP 2022. LNPE, pp. 463–472. Springer, Cham (2023). https://doi.org/10.1007/978-3-031-18318-8_47
44. Płońska, A., Płoński, P.: MLJAR: State-of-the-art Automated Machine Learning Framework for Tabular Data. Version 0.10.3 (2021). https://github.com/mljar/mljar-supervised
45. Hernández-García, A., König, P.: Further advantages of data augmentation on convolutional neural networks. Gehalten auf der (2018)
46. Shorten, C., Khoshgoftaar, T.M.: A survey on image data augmentation for deep learning. J. Big Data **6**(1), 1–48 (2019). https://doi.org/10.1186/s40537-019-0197-0
47. Han, D., Liu, Q., Fan, W.: A new image classification method using CNN transfer learning and web data augmentation. Expert Syst. Appl. **95**, 43–56 (2018). https://doi.org/10.1016/j.eswa.2017.11.028
48. Weiss, K., Khoshgoftaar, T.M., Wang, D.: A survey of transfer learning. J. Big Data **3**(1), 1–40 (2016). https://doi.org/10.1186/s40537-016-0043-6
49. Hussain, M., Bird, J.J., Faria, D.R.: A study on CNN transfer learning for image classification. In: Lotfi, A., Bouchachia, H., Gegov, A., Langensiepen, C., McGinnity, M. (eds.) UKCI 2018. AISC, vol. 840, pp. 191–202. Springer, Cham (2019). https://doi.org/10.1007/978-3-319-97982-3_16

Author Index

Printed in the United States
by Baker & Taylor Publisher Services